THE SITUATION OF THE STORY

Short Fiction in Contemporary Perspective

edited by
Diana Young

Bedford Books *of* St. Martin's Press

BOSTON

For Bedford Books
Publisher: Charles H. Christensen
Associate Publisher/General Manager: Joan E. Feinberg
Managing Editor: Elizabeth M. Schaaf
Developmental Editor: Jane Betz
Production Editor: Tara L. Masih
Copyeditor: Kathryn Blatt
Text Design: Melinda Grosser for *silk*
Cover Design: Steve Snider

Library of Congress Catalog Card Number: 92–52521

Manufactured in the United States of America.

6 5 4 3 2
f e d c b a

For information, write: St. Martin's Press, Inc.
175 Fifth Avenue, New York, NY 10010

Editorial Offices: Bedford Books *of* St. Martin's Press
29 Winchester Street, Boston, MA 02116

ISBN: 0–312–04473–9

Acknowledgments

Lee K. Abbott, "The End of Grief." From *Strangers in Paradise* by Lee K. Abbott. Reprinted by permission of The Putnam Publishing Group. Copyright © 1987 by Lee K. Abbott.

Conrad Aiken, "Strange Moonlight." From *The Collected Stories of Conrad Aiken* by Conrad Aiken. Copyright © 1962 by Conrad Aiken. Reprinted by permission of Schocken Books, published by Pantheon Books, a division of Random House, Inc.

Toni Cade Bambara, "Maggie of the Green Bottles." From *Gorilla, My Love* by Toni Cade Bambara. Copyright © 1968 by Toni Cade Bambara. Reprinted by permission of Random House, Inc.

Allen Barnett, "The *Times* As It Knows Us." From *The Body and Its Dangers and Other Stories.* Copyright © 1990 by Allen Barnett. Reprinted by permission of St. Martin's Press Inc., New York.

Ann Beattie, "It's Just Another Day in Big Bear City, California." From *Distortions.* Copyright © 1974, 1975, 1976 by Ann Beattie. Used with permission from International Creative Management, Inc.

Acknowledgments and copyrights are continued at the back of the book on pages 790–791, which constitute an extension of the copyright page.

PREFACE
To the Instructor

The Situation of the Story was born from my frustration with the sameness of college anthologies and from my sense that there must be overlooked stories by heavily anthologized writers as well as stories of comparable merit by lesser-known authors. I set out to gather other stories, ignored for too long, that might be taught just as successfully as those that had grown so familiar, often moving through the entire corpus of a writer's work, not infrequently discovering a stunning text buried by the dust of routine. I consulted informally with professors and writers (but mostly with writers who are also professors), asking them to identify their favorite seldom—or never—reprinted story or stories, or those that prompted the most engaged responses from their students. In a few cases, though, when a familiar story defined one of my chapter themes, I respected its claim to inclusion here. I was also interested in presenting both women and contemporary writers, whose work so often expands the possibilities for imagining and developing new traditions.

Just as the desire to bring together fresh stories defines this anthology, so too does its arrangement, which situates them within groupings that are suggestive of contemporary critical and theoretical ideas. Simply because so few of these stories are anthologized routinely, they have not yet been cemented into a traditional context or eclipsed by past associations, but rather are more open to unfettered discussion and original interpretation. As I read and reread these stories, they began to generate ideas for and actually to shape the chapters in this anthology. The result: some chapters focus on theme, others on form, and others on style, but all reflect current theories and debates and all allow you to place the short story within an unexplored and vigorous critical context.

By design, the editorial apparatus is minimal. Each chapter opens with a short introduction that explains its focus and then positions the stories within that framework. Each story is accompanied by a brief biographical footnote on its writer.

The Editor's Notes that accompany *The Situation of the Story* discuss and offer questions for each story as well as present questions that compare the stories within the anthology. Further, the Notes suggest writing assignments and critical, theoretical, and literary sources that students might turn to in their research. Again, since little is written about many of these stories, the Notes may give you a starting point for your discussion.

ACKNOWLEDGMENTS I received much help from many people as I col-lected these stories. First I want to thank Nancy Huddleston Packer, who not only taught me the history of the short story at Stanford University, but also offered her substantial help from beginning to end. I want to thank George Garrett, who sent me in fruitful new directions. Both of these writers who are also readers were most generous with their shrewd readings and vast reading list, and their influence pervades this collection.

Thanks to writer Ann Packer, who shared the stories she most admires. Thanks to all the members of the dinner party at Paul and Kathryn Hunter's, who quickly reached consensus that Truman Capote's "Children on Their Birthdays" was their favorite underprinted story. Gail Perez shared her infinite reading list with me and helped devise evocative chapter titles.

Other thanks are owed to Peter Sattler, Christopher Looby, William Veeder, C. Michael Curtis, Ruthie Battestin, and Jay Flegelman as well as to all those who discussed their favorite story candidates with me.

Thanks to Beth Castrodale and to copyeditor Kathryn Blatt, who has a great eye. Thanks to Tara Masih, for making those production deadlines sinuous. Thank you, Jane Betz, for your support throughout this project—and for making the entire process so enjoyable.

Thank you, Chuck Christensen and Joan Feinberg.

And thank you, Bill Brown.

CONTENTS

THREE
Refashioning the Story of the Self 173

FOUR
Stories of Speech, Stories of Silence 299

EIGHT
The Fabulous 673

ONE

The Form
of American Laughter

It used to be thought that only highly serious language could address serious subjects, only solemnity could address love or death or the divine. But, as this group of stories shows, the American comic tradition braves it all, often by means of a reversal in fortune: the high are brought low, the outsider becomes the insider, the end is the beginning. In Flannery O'Connor's "The Comforts of Home," Thomas, a widow's pompous and exasperated son, is outraged by the reversal that happens in his respectable household when his mother takes in a young girl from jail. Ann Beattie's "It's Just Another Day in Big Bear City, California" invests the Martians with the prosaic bureaucratic requirements of corporate employees, creating comic effect by exaggerating not difference, but sameness: she gives her spacemen a taste for L. L. Bean and Scrabble. In Mark Twain's "The $30,000 Bequest," a woman, after being told she's due to inherit money from a distant relative of her husband's, makes herself into a multimillionaire—but the actual riches always elude her grasp.

Sometimes characters, though not high and mighty, are so self-absorbed and self-important that we long to laugh at them. Eudora Welty's very title, "Why I Live at the P.O.," suggests these traits: what kind of a character issues such an explanation? The story details the minutiae of a family fight, in which we are addressed directly, in first-person narration, as though we too were members of Sister's family, as though we understood every colloquialism, even as though we could see her directly. "'This is the way she looks,' I says, and I looked like this," says Sister, reproducing the face she's making at her mother in the story. Sister's self-absorption is so complete that she assumes we can see her, just the way a toddler thinks his parents feel what he feels.

Like Sister's little world of China Grove, the tiny doings of the Paradisers, a women's Fife and Drum Corps, take up center stage in William Goyen's "Tapioca Surprise." In this story we can see how the comic subverts authority, how humor can even work toward subverting death—the final authority. "Tapioca Surprise" renders the impending deaths so hilarious and improbable that the terror is tamed, replaced by the telling detail that, during the emergency, the town's richest lady wore her genuine Japanese kimona. And just as the high and the low are reversed, so does death become rebirth, so that the head Paradiser is delivered back to her special dessert after all.

Although the comic can undermine the authority of social forms, within the comic itself everything can be transformed. Ironically, in Stephen Crane's "The Bride Comes to Yellow Sky," the violent pattern of an outlaw is itself a social form, against which the townspeople take their usual measures. But only the sheriff's new marriage can subvert the outlaw's ambush and, in the face of this new estate, the lawless becomes lawful.

The comic works by means of the unexpected, foils us by turning our expectations inside out. And these stories offer us a cast of characters to relish, quirky, surprising, rapt in the tales of their own lives. Through them we get a glimpse into the heart of the comic, where even the Martians join us in our search for redemption.

FLANNERY O'CONNOR

The Comforts of Home

Thomas withdrew to the side of the window and with his head between the wall and the curtain he looked down on the driveway where the car had stopped. His mother and the little slut were getting out of it. His mother emerged slowly, stolid and awkward, and then the little slut's long slightly bowed legs slid out, the dress pulled above the knees. With a shriek of laughter she ran to meet the dog, who bounded, overjoyed, shaking with pleasure, to welcome her. Rage gathered throughout Thomas's large frame with a silent ominous intensity, like a mob assembling.

It was now up to him to pack a suitcase, go to the hotel, and stay there until the house should be cleared.

He did not know where a suitcase was, he disliked to pack, he needed his books, his typewriter was not portable, he was used to an electric blanket, he could not bear to eat in restaurants. His mother, with her daredevil charity, was about to wreck the peace of the house.

The back door slammed and the girl's laugh shot up from the kitchen, through the back hall, up the stairwell and into his room, making for him like a bolt of electricity. He jumped to the side and stood

From her birth in Savannah in 1925 to her modest life in the town of Milledgeville, Flannery O'Connor was in one way or another always connected to her native state of Georgia. This life in the Deep South and the author's own intensely felt Catholicism intertwined in such bizarre and caustically humorous novels as *Wise Blood* (1952) and short story collections as *A Good Man Is Hard to Find* (1955). Suffering during the last decade of her life from lupus erythematosus, O'Connor raised peafowl on her mother's Georgia farm and eventually died from her illness in 1964. She was thirty-nine years old.

glaring about him. His words of the morning had been unequivocal: "If you bring that girl back into this house, I leave. You can choose—her or me."

She had made her choice. An intense pain gripped his throat. It was the first time in his thirty-five years . . . He felt a sudden burning moisture behind his eyes. Then he steadied himself, overcome by rage. On the contrary: she had not made any choice. She was counting on his attachment to his electric blanket. She would have to be shown.

The girl's laughter rang upward a second time and Thomas winced. He saw again her look of the night before. She had invaded his room. He had waked to find his door open and her in it. There was enough light from the hall to make her visible as she turned toward him. The face was like a comedienne's in a musical comedy—a pointed chin, wide apple cheeks, and feline empty eyes. He had sprung out of his bed and snatched a straight chair and then he had backed out the door, holding the chair in front of him like an animal trainer driving out a dangerous cat. He had driven her silently down the hall, pausing when he reached it to beat on his mother's door. The girl, with a gasp, turned and fled into the guest room.

In a moment his mother had opened her door and peered out apprehensively. Her face, greasy with whatever she put on it at night, was framed in pink rubber curlers. She looked down the hall where the girl had disappeared. Thomas stood before her, the chair still lifted in front of him as if he were about to quell another beast. "She tried to get in my room," he hissed, pushing in. "I woke up and she was trying to get in my room." He closed the door behind him and his voice rose in outrage. "I won't put up with this! I won't put up with it another day!"

His mother, backed by him to her bed, sat down on the edge of it. She had a heavy body on which sat a thin, mysteriously gaunt and incongruous head.

"I'm telling you for the last time," Thomas said, "I won't put up with this another day." There was an observable tendency in all of her actions. This was, with the best intentions in the world, to make a mockery of virtue, to pursue it with such a mindless intensity that everyone involved was made a fool of and virtue itself became ridiculous. "Not another day," he repeated.

His mother shook her head emphatically, her eyes still on the door.

Thomas put the chair on the floor in front of her and sat down on it. He leaned forward as if he were about to explain something to a defective child.

"That's just another way she's unfortunate," his mother said. "So awful, so awful. She told me the name of it but I forget what it is but it's something she can't help. Something she was born with. Thomas," she said and put her hand to her jaw, "suppose it were you?"

Exasperation blocked his windpipe. "Can't I make you see," he croaked, "that if she can't help herself you can't help her?"

His mother's eyes, intimate but untouchable, were the blue of great distances after sunset. "Nimpermaniac," she murmured.

"Nymphomaniac," he said fiercely. "She doesn't need to supply you with any fancy names. She's a moral moron. That's all you need to know. Born without the moral faculty—like somebody else would be born without a kidney or a leg. Do you understand?"

"I keep thinking it might be you," she said, her hand still on her jaw. "If it were you, how do you think I'd feel if nobody took you in? What if you were a nimpermaniac and not a brilliant smart person and you did what you couldn't help and . . ."

Thomas felt a deep unbearable loathing for himself as if he were turning slowly into the girl.

"What did she have on?" she asked abruptly, her eyes narrowing.

"Nothing!" he roared. "Now will you get her out of here!"

"How can I turn her out in the cold?" she said. "This morning she was threatening to kill herself again."

"Send her back to jail," Thomas said.

"I would not send *you* back to jail, Thomas," she said.

He got up and snatched the chair and fled the room while he was still able to control himself.

Thomas loved his mother. He loved her because it was his nature to do so, but there were times when he could not endure her love for him. There were times when it became nothing but pure idiot mystery and he sensed about him forces, invisible currents entirely out of his control. She proceeded always from the tritest of considerations—it was the *nice thing to do*—into the most foolhardy engagements with the devil, whom, of course, she never recognized.

The devil for Thomas was only a manner of speaking, but it was a manner appropriate to the situations his mother got into. Had she been in any degree intellectual, he could have proved to her from early Christian history that no excess of virtue is justified, that a moderation of good produces likewise a moderation in evil, that if Antony of Egypt had stayed at home and attended to his sister, no devils would have plagued him.

Thomas was not cynical and so far from being opposed to virtue, he saw it as the principle of order and the only thing that makes life bearable. His own life was made bearable by the fruits of his mother's saner virtues—by the well-regulated house she kept and the excellent meals she served. But when virtue got out of hand with her, as now, a sense of devils grew upon him, and these were not mental quirks in himself or the old lady, they were denizens with personalities, present though not visible, who might any moment be expected to shriek or rattle a pot.

The girl had landed in the county jail a month ago on a bad check charge and his mother had seen her picture in the paper. At the breakfast table she had gazed at it for a long time and then had passed it over the coffee pot to him. "Imagine," she said, "only nineteen years old and in that filthy jail. And she doesn't look like a bad girl."

Thomas glanced at the picture. It showed the face of a shrewd ragamuffin. He observed that the average age for criminality was steadily lowering.

"She looks like a wholesome girl," his mother said.

"Wholesome people don't pass bad checks," Thomas said.

"You don't know what you'd do in a pinch."

"I wouldn't pass a bad check," Thomas said.

"I think," his mother said, "I'll take her a little box of candy."

If then and there he had put his foot down, nothing else would have happened. His father, had he been living, would have put his foot down at that point. Taking a box of candy was her favorite nice thing to do. When anyone within her social station moved to town, she called and took a box of candy; when any of her friend's children had babies or won a scholarship, she called and took a box of candy; when an old person broke his hip, she was at his bedside with a box of candy. He had been amused at the idea of her taking a box of candy to the jail.

He stood now in his room with the girl's laugh rocketing away in his head and cursed his amusement.

When his mother returned from the visit to the jail, she had burst into his study without knocking and had collapsed full-length on his couch, lifting her small swollen feet up on the arm of it. After a moment, she recovered herself enough to sit up and put a newspaper under them. Then she fell back again. "We don't know how the other half lives," she said.

Thomas knew that though her conversation moved from cliché to cliché there were real experiences behind them. He was less sorry for the girl's being in jail than for his mother having to see her there. He would have spared her all unpleasant sights. "Well," he said and put away his journal, "you had better forget it now. The girl has ample reason to be in jail."

"You can't imagine what all she's been through," she said, sitting up again, "listen." The poor girl, Star, had been brought up by a stepmother with three children of her own, one an almost grown boy who had taken advantage of her in such dreadful ways that she had been forced to run away and find her real mother. Once found, her real mother had sent her to various boarding schools to get rid of her. At each of these she had been forced to run away by the presence of perverts and sadists so monstrous that their acts defied description. Thomas could tell that his mother had not been spared the details that she was sparing him. Now and again when she spoke vaguely, her voice shook and he could tell that she was remembering some horror that had been put to her graphically. He had hoped that in a few days the memory of all this would wear off, but it did not. The next day she returned to the jail with Kleenex and cold-cream and a few days later, she announced that she had consulted a lawyer.

It was at these times that Thomas truly mourned the death of his father though he had not been able to endure him in life. The old man would have had none of this foolishness. Untouched by useless compassion, he would (behind her back) have pulled the necessary strings with his crony, the sheriff, and the girl would have been packed off to the state penitentiary to serve her time. He had always been engaged in some enraged action until one morning when (with an angry glance at his wife as if she alone were responsible) he had dropped dead at the breakfast table. Thomas had inherited his father's reason without his ruthlessness and his mother's love of good without her tendency to pursue it. His plan for all practical action was to wait and see what developed.

The lawyer found that the story of the repeated atrocities was for the most part untrue, but when he explained to her that the girl was a psychopathic personality, not insane enough for the asylum, not criminal enough for the jail, not stable enough for society, Thomas's mother was more deeply affected than ever. The girl readily admitted that her story was untrue on account of her being a congenital liar; she lied, she said, because she was insecure. She had passed through the hands of several psychiatrists who had put the finishing touches to her education. She knew there was no hope for her. In the presence of such an affliction as this, his mother seemed bowed down by some painful mystery that nothing would make endurable but a redoubling of effort. To his annoyance, she appeared to look on *him* with compassion, as if her hazy charity no longer made distinctions.

A few days later she burst in and said that the lawyer had got the girl paroled—to her.

Thomas rose from his Morris chair, dropping the review he had been reading. His large bland face contracted in anticipated pain. "You are not," he said, "going to bring that girl here!"

"No, no," she said, "calm yourself, Thomas." She had managed with difficulty to get the girl a job in a pet shop in town and a place to board with a crotchety old lady of her acquaintance. People were not kind. They did not put themselves in the place of someone like Star who had everything against her.

Thomas sat down again and retrieved his review. He seemed just to have escaped some danger which he did not care to make clear to himself. "Nobody can tell you anything," he said, "but in a few days that girl will have left town, having got what she could out of you. You'll never hear from her again."

Two nights later he came home and opened the parlor door and was speared by a shrill depthless laugh. His mother and the girl sat close to the fireplace where the gas logs were lit. The girl gave the immediate impression of being physically crooked. Her hair was cut like a dog's or an elf's and she was dressed in the latest fashion. She was training on him a long familiar sparking stare that turned after a second into an intimate grin.

"Thomas!" his mother said, her voice firm with the injunction not to bolt, "this is Star you've heard so much about. Star is going to have supper with us."

The girl called herself Star Drake. The lawyer had found that her real name was Sarah Ham.

Thomas neither moved nor spoke but hung in the door in what seemed a savage perplexity. Finally he said, "How do you do, Sarah," in a tone of such loathing that he was shocked at the sound of it. He reddened, feeling it beneath him to show contempt for any creature so pathetic. He advanced into the room, determined at least on a decent politeness and sat down heavily in a straight chair.

"Thomas writes history," his mother said with a threatening look at him. "He's president of the local Historical Society this year."

The girl leaned forward and gave Thomas an even more pointed attention. "Fabulous!" she said in a throaty voice.

"Right now Thomas is writing about the first settlers in this county," his mother said.

"Fabulous!" the girl repeated.

Thomas by an effort of will managed to look as if he were alone in the room.

"Say, you know who he looks like?" Star asked, her head on one side, taking him in at an angle.

"Oh, someone very distinguished!" his mother said archly.

"This cop I saw in the movie I went to last night," Star said.

"Star," his mother said, "I think you ought to see only the best ones. I don't think crime stories would be good for you."

"Oh this was a crime-does-not-pay," Star said, "and I swear this cop looked exactly like him. They were always putting something over on the guy. He would look like he couldn't stand it a minute longer or he would blow up. He was a riot. And not bad looking," she added with an appreciative leer at Thomas.

"Star," his mother said, "I think it would be grand if you developed a taste for music."

Thomas sighed. His mother rattled on and the girl, paying no attention to her, let her eyes play over him. The quality of her look was such that it might have been her hands, resting now on his knees, now on his neck. Her eyes had a mocking glitter and he knew that she was well aware he could not stand the sight of her. He needed nothing to tell him he was in the presence of the very stuff of corruption, but blameless corruption because there was no responsible faculty behind it. He was looking at the most unendurable form of innocence. Absently he asked himself what the attitude of God was to this, meaning if possible to adopt it.

His mother's behavior throughout the meal was so idiotic that he could barely stand to look at her and since he could less stand to look at Sarah Ham, he fixed on the sideboard across the room a continuous gaze of disapproval and disgust. Every remark of the girl's his mother met as if it deserved serious attention. She advanced several plans for the wholesome use of Sarah's spare time. Sarah Ham paid no more attention to this advice than if it came from a parrot. Once when Thomas inadvertently looked in her direction, she winked. As soon as he had swallowed the last spoonful of dessert, he rose and muttered, "I have to go, I have a meeting."

"Thomas," his mother said, "I want you to take Sarah home on your way. I don't want her riding in taxis by herself at night."

For a moment Thomas remained furiously silent. Then he turned and left the room. Presently he came back with a look of obscure determination on his face. The girl was ready, meekly waiting at the parlor door. She cast up at him a great look of admiration and confidence. Thomas did not offer his arm but she took it anyway and moved out of the house and down the steps, attached to what might have been a miraculously moving monument.

"Be good!" his mother called.

Sarah Ham snickered and poked him in the ribs.

While getting his coat he had decided that this would be his opportunity to tell the girl that unless she ceased to be a parasite on his mother, he would see to it, personally, that she was returned to jail. He would let her know that he understood what she was up to, that he was not an innocent and that there were certain things he would not put up with. At his desk, pen in hand, none was more articulate than Thomas. As soon as he found himself shut into the car with Sarah Ham, terror seized his tongue.

She curled her feet up under her and said, "Alone at last," and giggled.

Thomas swerved the car away from the house and drove fast toward the gate. Once on the highway, he shot forward as if he were being pursued.

"Jesus!" Sarah Ham said, swinging her feet off the seat, "where's the fire?"

Thomas did not answer. In a few seconds he could feel her edging closer. She stretched, eased nearer, and finally hung her hand limply over his shoulder. "Tomsee doesn't like me," she said, "but I think he's fabulously cute."

Thomas covered the three and a half miles into town in a little over four minutes. The light at the first intersection was red but he ignored it. The old woman lived three blocks beyond. When the car screeched to a halt at the place, he jumped out and ran around to the girl's door and opened it. She did not move from the car and Thomas was obliged to wait. After a moment one leg emerged, then her small white crooked face appeared and stared up at him. There was something about the look of it that suggested blindness but it was the blindness of those who don't know that they cannot see. Thomas was curiously sickened. The empty eyes moved over him. "Nobody likes me," she said in a sullen tone. "What if you were me and I couldn't stand to ride you three miles?"

"My mother likes you," he muttered.

"Her!" the girl said. "She's just about seventy-five years behind the times!"

Breathlessly Thomas said, "If I find you bothering her again, I'll have you put back in jail." There was a dull force behind his voice though it came out barely above a whisper.

"You and who else?" she said and drew back in the car as if now she did not intend to get out at all. Thomas reached into it, blindly grasped the front of her coat, pulled her out by it and released her. Then he lunged back to the car and sped off. The other door was still hanging open and her laugh, bodiless but real, bounded up the street as if it were about to jump in the open side of the car and ride away with him. He reached over and slammed the door and then drove toward home, too angry to attend his meeting. He intended to make his mother well-aware of his displeasure. He intended to leave no doubt in her mind. The voice of his father rasped in his head.

Numbskull, the old man said, put your foot down now. Show her who's boss before she shows you.

But when Thomas reached home, his mother, wisely, had gone to bed.

The next morning he appeared at the breakfast table, his brow lowered and the thrust of his jaw indicating that he was in a dangerous humor. When he intended to be determined, Thomas began like a bull that, before charging, backs with his head lowered and paws the ground. "All right now listen," he began, yanking out his chair and sitting down, "I have something to say to you about that girl and I don't intend to say it but once." He drew breath. "She's nothing but a little slut. She makes fun of you behind your back. She means to get everything she can out of you and you are nothing to her."

His mother looked as if she too had spent a restless night. She did not dress in the morning but wore her bathrobe and a gray turban around her head, which gave her face a disconcerting omniscient look. He might have been breakfasting with a sibyl.

"You'll have to use canned cream this morning," she said, pouring his coffee. "I forgot the other."

"All right, did you hear me?" Thomas growled.

"I'm not deaf," his mother said and put the pot back on the trivet. "I know I'm nothing but an old bag of wind to her."

"Then why do you persist in this foolhardy . . ."

"Thomas," she said, and put her hand to the side of her face, "it might be . . ."

"It is not me!" Thomas said, grasping the table leg at his knee.

She continued to hold her face, shaking her head slightly. "Think of all you have," she began. "All the comforts of home. And morals, Thomas. No bad inclinations, nothing bad you were born with."

Thomas began to breathe like someone who feels the onset of asthma. "You are not logical," he said in a limp voice. "*He* would have put his foot down."

The old lady stiffened. "You," she said, "are not like him."

Thomas opened his mouth silently.

"However," his mother said, in a tone of such subtle accusation that she might have been taking back the compliment, "I won't invite her back again since you're so dead set against her."

"I am not set against her," Thomas said. "I am set against your making a fool of yourself."

As soon as he left the table and closed the door of his study on himself, his father took up a squatting position in his mind. The old man had had the countryman's ability to converse squatting, though he was no countryman but had been born and brought up in the city and only moved to a smaller place later to exploit his talents. With steady skill he had made them think him one of them. In the midst of a conversation on the courthouse lawn, he would squat and his two or three companions would squat with him with no break in the surface of the talk. By gesture he had lived his lie; he had never deigned to tell one.

Let her run over you, he said. You ain't like me. Not enough to be a man.

Thomas began vigorously to read and presently the image faded. The girl had caused a disturbance in the depths of his being, somewhere out of the reach of his power of analysis. He felt as if he had seen a tornado pass a hundred yards away and had an intimation that it would turn again and head directly for him. He did not get his mind firmly on his work until mid-morning.

Two nights later, his mother and he were sitting in the den after their supper, each reading a section of the evening paper, when the telephone began to ring with the brassy intensity of a fire alarm. Thomas reached for it. As soon as the receiver was in his hand, a shrill female voice screamed into the room, "Come get this girl! Come get her! Drunk! Drunk in my parlor and I won't have it! Lost her job and come back here drunk! I won't have it!"

His mother leapt up and snatched the receiver.

The ghost of Thomas's father rose before him. Call the sheriff, the old man prompted. "Call the sheriff," Thomas said in a loud voice. "Call the sheriff to go there and pick her up."

"We'll be right there," his mother was saying. "We'll come and get her right away. Tell her to get her things together."

"She ain't in no condition to get nothing together," the voice screamed. "You shouldn't have put something like her off on me! My house is respectable!"

"Tell her to call the sheriff," Thomas shouted.

His mother put the receiver down and looked at him. "I wouldn't turn a dog over to that man," she said.

Thomas sat in the chair with his arms folded and looked fixedly at the wall.

"Think of the poor girl, Thomas," his mother said, "with nothing. Nothing. And we have everything."

When they arrived, Sarah Ham was slumped spraddle-legged against the banister on the boarding house front-steps. Her tam was down on her forehead where the old woman had slammed it and her clothes were bulging out of her suitcase where the old woman had thrown them in. She was carrying on a drunken conversation with herself in a low personal tone. A streak of lipstick ran up one side of her face. She allowed herself to be guided by his mother to the car and put in the back seat without seeming to know who the rescuer was. "Nothing to talk to all day but a pack of goddamned parakeets," she said in a furious whisper.

Thomas, who had not got out of the car at all, or looked at her after the first revolted glance, said, "I'm telling you, once and for all, the place to take her is the jail."

His mother, sitting on the back seat, holding the girl's hand, did not answer.

"All right, take her to the hotel," he said.

"I cannot take a drunk girl to a hotel, Thomas," she said. "You know that."

"Then take her to a hospital."

"She doesn't need a jail or a hotel or a hospital," his mother said, "she needs a home."

"She does not need mine," Thomas said.

"Only for tonight, Thomas," the old lady sighed. "Only for tonight."

Since then eight days had passed. The little slut was established in the guest room. Every day his mother set out to find her a job and a place to board, and failed, for the old woman had broadcast a warning. Thomas kept to his room or the den. His home was to him home, workshop, church, as personal as the shell of a turtle and as necessary. He could not believe that it could be violated in this way. His flushed face had a constant look of stunned outrage.

As soon as the girl was up in the morning, her voice throbbed out in a blues song that would rise and waver, then plunge low with insinuations of passion about to be satisfied and Thomas, at his desk, would lunge up and begin frantically stuffing his ears with Kleenex. Each time he started from one room to another, one floor to another, she would be certain to appear. Each time he was halfway up or down the stairs, she would either meet him and pass, cringing coyly, or go up or down behind him, breathing small tragic spearmint-flavored sighs. She appeared to adore Thomas's repugnance to her and to draw it out of him every chance she got as if it added delectably to her martyrdom.

The old man—small, wasp-like, in his yellowed panama hat, his seersucker suit, his pink carefully soiled shirt, his small string tie— appeared to have taken up his station in Thomas's mind and from there, usually squatting, he shot out the same rasping suggestion every time the boy paused from his forced studies. Put your foot down. Go to see the sheriff.

The sheriff was another edition of Thomas's father except that he wore a checkered shirt and a Texas type hat and was ten years younger. He was as easily dishonest, and he had genuinely admired the old man. Thomas, like his mother, would have gone far out of his way to avoid his glassy pale blue gaze. He kept hoping for another solution, for a miracle.

With Sarah Ham in the house, meals were unbearable.

"Tomsee doesn't like me," she said the third or fourth night at the supper table and cast her pouting gaze across at the large rigid figure of Thomas, whose face was set with the look of a man trapped by insufferable odors. "He doesn't want me here. Nobody wants me anywhere."

"Thomas's name is Thomas," his mother interrupted. "Not Tomsee."

"I made Tomsee up," she said. "I think it's cute. He hates me."

"Thomas does not hate you," his mother said. "We are not the kind of people who hate," she added, as if this were an imperfection that had been bred out of them generations ago.

"Oh, I know when I'm not wanted," Sarah Ham continued. "They didn't even want me in jail. If I killed myself I wonder would God want me?"

"Try it and see," Thomas muttered.

The girl screamed with laughter. Then she stopped abruptly, her face puckered and she began to shake. "The best thing to do," she said, her teeth clattering, "is to kill myself. Then I'll be out of everybody's way. I'll go to hell and be out of God's way. And even the devil won't want me. He'll kick me out of hell, not even in hell . . ." she wailed.

Thomas rose, picked up his plate and knife and fork and carried them to the den to finish his supper. After that, he had not eaten another meal at the table but had had his mother serve him at his desk. At these meals, the old man was intensely present to him. He appeared to be tipping backwards in his chair, his thumbs beneath his galluses, while he said such things as, She never ran me away from my own table.

A few nights later, Sarah Ham slashed her wrists with a paring knife and had hysterics. From the den where he was closeted after supper, Thomas heard a shriek, then a series of screams, then his mother's scurrying footsteps through the house. He did not move. His first instant of hope that the girl had cut her throat faded as he realized she could not have done it and continue to scream the way she was doing. He returned to his journal and presently the screams subsided. In a moment his mother burst in with his coat and hat. "We have to take her to the hospital," she said. "She tried to do away with herself. I have a tourniquet on her arm. Oh Lord, Thomas," she said, "imagine being so low you'd do a thing like that!"

Thomas rose woodenly and put on his hat and coat. "We will take her to the hospital," he said, "and we will leave her there."

"And drive her to despair again?" the old lady cried. "Thomas!"

Standing in the center of his room now, realizing that he had reached the point where action was inevitable, that he must pack, that he must leave, that he must go, Thomas remained immovable.

His fury was directed not at the little slut but at his mother. Even though the doctor had found that she had barely damaged herself and had raised the girl's wrath by laughing at the tourniquet and putting only a streak of iodine on the cut, his mother could not get over the incident. Some new weight of sorrow seemed to have been thrown across her shoulders, and not only Thomas, but Sarah Ham was infuriated by this, for it appeared to be a general sorrow that would have found another object no matter what good fortune came to either of them. The experience of Sarah Ham had plunged the old lady into mourning for the world.

The morning after the attempted suicide, she had gone through the house and collected all the knives and scissors and locked them in a drawer. She emptied a bottle of rat poison down the toilet and took up the roach tablets from the kitchen floor. Then she came to Thomas's study and said in a whisper, "Where is that gun of his? I want you to lock it up."

"The gun is in my drawer," Thomas roared, "and I will not lock it up. If she shoots herself, so much the better!"

"Thomas," his mother said, "she'll hear you!"

"Let her hear me!" Thomas yelled. "Don't you know her kind never kill themselves? Don't you . . . ."

His mother slipped out the door and closed it to silence him and

Sarah Ham's laugh, quite close in the hall, came rattling into his room. "Tomsee'll find out. I'll kill myself and then he'll be sorry he wasn't nice to me. I'll use his own lil gun, his own lil ol' pearl-handled revollervuh!" she shouted and let out a loud tormented-sounding laugh in imitation of a movie monster.

Thomas ground his teeth. He pulled out his desk drawer and felt for the pistol. It was an inheritance from the old man, whose opinion it had been that every house should contain a loaded gun. He had discharged two bullets one night into the side of a prowler, but Thomas had never shot anything. He had no fear that the girl would use the gun on herself and he closed the drawer. Her kind clung tenaciously to life and were able to wrest some histrionic advantage from every moment.

Several ideas for getting rid of her had entered his head but each of these had been suggestions whose moral tone indicated that they had come from a mind akin to his father's, and Thomas had rejected them. He could not get the girl locked up again until she did something illegal. The old man would have been able with no qualms at all to get her drunk and send her out on the highway in his car, meanwhile notifying the highway patrol of her presence on the road, but Thomas considered this below his moral stature. Suggestions continued to come to him, each more outrageous than the last.

He had not the vaguest hope that the girl would get the gun and shoot herself, but that afternoon when he looked in the drawer, the gun was gone. His study locked from the inside, not the out. He cared nothing about the gun, but the thought of Sarah Ham's hands sliding among his papers infuriated him. Now even his study was contaminated. The only place left untouched by her was his bedroom.

That night she entered it.

In the morning at breakfast, he did not eat and did not sit down. He stood beside his chair and delivered his ultimatum while his mother sipped her coffee as if she were both alone in the room and in great pain. "I have stood this," he said, "for as long as I am able. Since I see plainly that you care nothing about me, about my peace or comfort or working conditions, I am about to take the only step open to me. I will give you one more day. If you bring the girl back into this house this afternoon, I leave. You can choose—her or me." He had more to say but at that point his voice cracked and he left.

At ten o'clock his mother and Sarah Ham left the house.

At four he heard the car wheels on the gravel and rushed to the window. As the car stopped, the dog stood up, alert, shaking.

He seemed unable to take the first step that would set him walking to the closet in the hall to look for the suitcase. He was like a man handed a knife and told to operate on himself if he wished to live. His huge hands clenched helplessly. His expression was a turmoil of indecision and outrage. His pale blue eyes seemed to sweat in his broiling face. He closed them for a moment and on the back of his lids, his father's image leered at him. Idiot! the old man hissed, idiot! The criminal slut stole your gun! See the sheriff! See the sheriff!

It was a moment before Thomas opened his eyes. He seemed newly stunned. He stood where he was for at least three minutes, then he turned slowly like a large vessel reversing its direction and faced to door. He stood there a moment longer, then he left, his face set to see the ordeal through.

He did not know where he would find the sheriff. The man made his own rules and kept his own hours. Thomas stopped first at the jail where his office was, but he was not in it. He went to the courthouse and was told by a clerk that the sheriff had gone to the barber shop across the street. "Yonder's the deppity," the clerk said and pointed out the window to the large figure of a man in a checkered shirt, who was leaning against the side of a police car, looking into space.

"It has to be the sheriff," Thomas said and left for the barber shop. As little as he wanted anything to do with the sheriff, he realized that the man was at least intelligent and not simply a mound of sweating flesh.

The barber said the sheriff had just left. Thomas started back to the courthouse and as he stepped on to the sidewalk from the street, he saw the lean, slightly stooped figure gesticulating angrily at the deputy.

Thomas approached with an aggressiveness brought on by nervous agitation. He stopped abruptly three feet away and said in an over-loud voice, "Can I have a word with you?" without adding the sheriff's name, which was Farebrother.

Farebrother turned his sharp creased face just enough to take Thomas in, and the deputy did likewise, but neither spoke. The sheriff removed a very small piece of cigarette from his lip and dropped it at his feet. "I told you what to do," he said to the deputy. Then he moved off with a slight nod that indicated Thomas could follow him if he wanted to see him. The deputy slunk around the front of the police car and got inside.

Farebrother, with Thomas following, headed across the courthouse square and stopped beneath a tree that shaded a quarter of the front lawn. He waited, leaning slightly forward, and lit another cigarette.

Thomas began to blurt out his business. As he had not had time to prepare his words, he was barely coherent. By repeating the same thing over several times, he managed at length to get out what he wanted to say. When he finished, the sheriff was still leaning slightly forward, at an angle to him, his eyes on nothing in particular. He remained that way without speaking.

Thomas began again, slower and in a lamer voice, and Farebrother let him continue for some time before he said, "We had her oncet." He then allowed himself a slow, creased, all-knowing, quarter smile.

"I had nothing to do with that," Thomas said. "That was my mother."

Farebrother squatted.

"She was trying to help the girl," Thomas said. "She didn't know she couldn't be helped."

"Bit off more than she could chew, I reckon," the voice below him mused.

"She has nothing to do with this," Thomas said. "She doesn't know I'm here. The girl is dangerous with that gun."

"*He*," the sheriff said, "never let anything grow under his feet. Particularly nothing a woman planted."

"She might kill somebody with that gun," Thomas said weakly, looking down at the round top of the Texas type hat.

There was a long time of silence.

"Where's she got it?" Farebrother asked.

"I don't know. She sleeps in the guest room. It must be in there, in her suitcase probably," Thomas said.

Farebrother lapsed into silence again.

"You could come search the guest room," Thomas said in a strained voice. "I can go home and leave the latch off the front door and you can come in quietly and go upstairs and search her room."

Farebrother turned his head so that his eyes looked boldly at Thomas's knees. "You seem to know how it ought to be done," he said. "Want to swap jobs?"

Thomas said nothing because he could not think of anything to say, but he waited doggedly. Farebrother removed the cigarette butt from his lips and dropped it on the grass. Beyond him on the courthouse porch a group of loiterers who had been leaning at the left of the door moved over to the right where a patch of sunlight had settled. From one of the upper windows a crumpled piece of paper blew out and drifted down.

"I'll come along about six," Farebrother said. "Leave the latch off the door and keep out of my way—yourself and them two women too."

Thomas let out a rasping sound of relief meant to be "Thanks," and struck off across the grass like someone released. The phrase, "them two women," stuck like a burr in his brain—the subtlety of the insult to his mother hurting him more than any of Farebrother's references to his own incompetence. As he got into his car, his face suddenly flushed. Had he delivered his mother over to the sheriff—to be a butt for the man's tongue? Was he betraying her to get rid of the little slut? He saw at once that this was not the case. He was doing what he was doing for her own good, to rid her of a parasite that would ruin their peace. He started his car and drove quickly home but once he had turned in the driveway, he decided it would be better to park some distance from the house and go quietly in by the back door. He parked on the grass and on the grass walked in a circle toward the rear of the house. The sky was lined with mustard-colored streaks. The dog was asleep on the back doormat. At the approach of his master's step, he opened one yellow eye, took him in, and closed it again.

Thomas let himself into the kitchen. It was empty and the house was quiet enough for him to be aware of the loud ticking of the kitchen clock. It was a quarter to six. He tiptoed hurriedly through the hall to the front door and took the latch off it. Then he stood for a moment listening. From behind the closed parlor door, he heard his mother snoring softly and presumed that she had gone to sleep while reading. On the other side of the hall, not three feet from his study, the little slut's black coat and red pocketbook were slung on a chair. He heard water running upstairs and decided she was taking a bath.

He went into his study and sat down at his desk to wait, noting with distaste that every few moments a tremor ran through him. He sat for a minute or two doing nothing. Then he picked up a pen and began to draw squares on the back of an envelope that lay before him. He looked at his watch. It was eleven minutes to six. After a moment he idly drew the center drawer of the desk out over his lap. For a moment he stared at the gun without recognition. Then he gave a yelp and leaped up. She had put it back!

Idiot! his father hissed, idiot! Go plant it in her pocketbook. Don't just stand there. Go plant it in her pocketbook!

Thomas stood staring at the drawer.

Moron! the old man fumed. Quick while there's time! Go plant it in her pocketbook.

Thomas did not move.

Imbecile! his father cried.

Thomas picked up the gun.

Make haste, the old man ordered.

Thomas started forward, holding the gun away from him. He opened the door and looked at the chair. The black coat and red pocketbook were lying on it almost within reach.

Hurry up, you fool, his father said.

From behind the parlor door the almost inaudible snores of his mother rose and fell. They seemed to mark an order of time that had nothing to do with the instants left to Thomas. There was no other sound.

Quick, you imbecile, before she wakes up, the old man said.

The snores stopped and Thomas heard the sofa springs groan. He grabbed the red pocketbook. It had a skin-like feel to his touch and as it opened, he caught an unmistakable odor of the girl. Wincing, he thrust in the gun and then drew back. His face burned an ugly dull red.

"What is Tomsee putting in my purse?" she called and her pleased laugh bounced down the staircase. Thomas whirled.

She was at the top of the stair, coming down in the manner of a fashion model, one bare leg and then the other thrusting out the front of her kimona in a definite rhythm. "Tomsee is being naughty," she said in a throaty voice. She reached the bottom and cast a possessive leer at Thomas whose face was now more gray than red. She reached out, pulled the bag open with her finger and peered at the gun.

His mother opened the parlor door and looked out.

"Tomsee put his pistol in my bag!" the girl shrieked.

"Ridiculous," his mother said, yawning. "What would Thomas want to put his pistol in your bag for?"

Thomas stood slightly hunched, his hands hanging helplessly at the wrists as if he had just pulled them up out of a pool of blood.

"I don't know what for," the girl said, "but he sure did it," and she proceeded to walk around Thomas, her hands on her hips, her neck thrust forward and her intimate grin fixed on him fiercely. All at once her expression seemed to open as the purse had opened when Thomas reached it. She stood with her head cocked on one side in an attitude of disbelief. "Oh boy," she said slowly, "is he a case."

At that instant Thomas damned not only the girl but the entire order of the universe that made her possible.

"Thomas wouldn't put a gun in your bag," his mother said. "Thomas is a gentleman."

The girl made a chortling noise. "You can see it in there," she said and pointed to the open purse.

You *found* it in her bag, you dimwit! the old man hissed.

"I found it in her bag!" Thomas shouted. "The dirty criminal slut stole my gun!"

His mother gasped at the sound of the other presence in his voice. The old lady's sybil-like face turned pale.

"Found it my eye!" Sarah Ham shrieked and started for the pocketbook, but Thomas, as if his arm were guided by his father, caught it first and snatched the gun. The girl in a frenzy lunged at Thomas's throat and would actually have caught him around the neck had not his mother thrown herself forward to protect her.

Fire! the old man yelled.

Thomas fired. The blast was like a sound meant to bring an end to evil in the world. Thomas heard it as a sound that would shatter the laughter of sluts until all shrieks were stilled and nothing was left to disturb the peace of perfect order.

The echo died away in waves. Before the last one had faded, Farebrother opened the door and put his head inside the hall. His nose wrinkled. His expression for some few seconds was that of a man unwilling to admit surprise. His eyes were clear as glass, reflecting the scene. The old lady lay on the floor between the girl and Thomas.

The sheriff's brain worked instantly like a calculating machine. He saw the facts as if they were already in print: the fellow had intended all along to kill his mother and pin it on the girl. But Farebrother had been too quick for him. They were not yet aware of his head in the door. As he scrutinized the scene, further insights were flashed to him. Over her body, the killer and the slut were about to collapse into each other's arms. The sheriff knew a nasty bit when he saw it. He was accustomed to enter upon scenes that were not as bad as he had hoped to find them, but this one met his expectations.

1946

ANN BEATTIE

It's Just Another Day in Big Bear City, California

Spaceship, flying saucer, an hallucination . . . they don't know yet. They don't even notice it until it is almost over their car. Estelle, who has recently gone back to college, is studying Mortuary Science. Her husband, Alvin William "Big Bear" Benton, is so drunk from the party they have just left that he wouldn't notice if it were Estelle, risen from the passenger seat, up in the sky. Maybe that's where she'd like to be— floating in the sky. Or in the morgue with bodies. Big Bear Benton thinks she is completely nuts, and people who are nuts can do anything. *Will* do anything. Will go back to school after ten years and study Mortuary Science. It's enough to make him get drunk at parties. They used to ask his wife about the children at these parties, but now they ask, subtly, about the bodies. They are more interested in dead bodies than his two children. So is Estelle. He is not interested in anything, according to his wife, except going to parties and getting drunk.

Spaceship, flying saucer, an hallucination . . . Big Bear concentrates on the object and tells himself that he is just hallucinating. There is a pinpoint of light, actually a spot of light about the size of a tennis ball, dropping through space. Then it is the size of a football . . . he is trying to think it is a real object, no matter what it is doing up there . . . but maybe it's a flying saucer. Or a spaceship. He looks at Estelle, who is also drunk. She is staring at her hands, neatly folded on her lap. Those hands roam around in dead bodies the way coyotes roam around the desert—just for something to do. This is the first time he has ever been glad to concentrate on Mortuary Science. Like reading the stock pages in the bathroom.

Ann Beattie was born in Washington, D.C., in 1947, a year that positions her squarely in the baby-boom generation. This affiliation is reflected in much of her work, and for many readers, Beattie has become a chronicler of the cohort that came of age in the 1960s (Beattie graduated from American University in 1969). Her 1976 novel, *Chilly Scenes of Winter*, traces the loss and disaffection that many of these people experienced in the following decades. Beattie currently lives in Charlottesville, Virginia.

"What is that?" Big Bear says, fighting to stay calm.

"Well, you know what it looks like," Estelle says. "It looks like a spaceship."

"Yeah, I know. But what is it really?"

Now that Estelle is becoming educated and urbane, he has become more childish. He is always asking questions.

"I don't know. It's a spaceship come to take us to Mars."

Big Bear begins to worry about the car being blown over. The car is a 1965 Peugeot, a real piece of crap that Big Bear would have gotten rid of long ago if it had not belonged to his wife's brother, who died in Viet Nam. His wife won't hear of getting rid of the car. She has some of her brother's underwear that she won't take out of the drawer. It's in Big Bear's drawer, in fact—not hers—and her reason for that is that it's men's underwear. But her brother's car is done for now, because the wind is going to blow it over and mash the roof.

"What's going on?" Big Bear yells to Estelle. It comes out a whisper. It occurs to Big Bear that this is some kind of joke. He would discuss with Estelle the possibility of the people at the party pulling a joke on them, but it's too noisy to converse. Through the windstorm he hears, "Earthlings! We are visitors from a friendly planet" and wets his pants.

Big Bear hears Estelle in the kitchen, memorizing: "The heart is a hollow muscular pump surrounded by the pericardium. . . ." Just by the tone of her voice, he understands that there is no hope for the human body. His two children, Sammy and David, stand around the kitchen eating cookies and listening to their mother. They like it better than talking to Big Bear, which makes him brood. His children are interested in intestines, the liver, bones, tissue, the optic nerve. It makes Big Bear sick just to think about it. If he could think of an excuse to stop giving Sammy and David an allowance, he would.

Big Bear tilts back his La-Z-Boy reclining chair and examines his feet, which block his view of the television.

Big Bear gives his wife a valentine, shyly. He thinks that the saleswoman might have been making a fool of him when she told him that the huge card with the quilted taffeta heart and embossed cupids would get across his message best. The card cost two dollars and fifty cents. The woman was young and had aviator glasses and an ironic smile. He prides himself in knowing women, but lately he doesn't trust any of them. Imagine Estelle enrolling in college, signing up for Mortuary Science. "Oh, this is lovely," she said when Big Bear gave her the valentine. He didn't want to mess it up in case there was something she could do with the card, so he just wrote his name on a little piece of paper and tucked it in the card. It falls out when Estelle opens it. He is standing right in front of her—she knows who its from—why did he even put the piece of paper in? She picks it up. "Love, Bear," it says. "Oh, this is lovely," she says. Valentine's Day is not one of Big Bear's favorite occasions. He always feels like a fool. His wife did not give him a valentine. She forgot, she says. But she doesn't forget about the pericardium that surrounds that hollow muscular pump that no longer beats with love for him.

"Roll up your window," Big Bear says. Estelle is rolling down her window. She is rolling it down to throw her cigarette away. A spaceship has landed in front of their Peugeot and she is rolling down her window.

"Earthlings! Like you, we have ears, but they are very sensitive. We can hear what you are saying and do not want you to be afraid."

Big Bear stares. A round dome that seems to be made of something soft—foam rubber?—bobs slightly in front of them. The thing covers the whole road.

"We also read minds. There are three of us, and two of us speak English."

"Oh, holy shit!" Big Bear says. "Estelle?"

She has rolled the window down and is letting the smoke from another cigarette she just lit blow out of the car.

"We will leave our spaceship, Bill and Estelle. Please do not worry."

"God almighty," Big Bear says. "Roll it up, Estelle."

"What does it matter?" Estelle says. Big Bear reaches across her lap and rolls up the window. The car is still running, his foot is still on the brake. He thinks about trying to get around the spaceship. There is no way to get around it without driving into a marsh. Big Bear throws the car into reverse and starts backward, but when he does that a wind stops the car and slowly pulls it forward again.

"Please get out of your car," the voice says.

There is a man standing in the road. He has on a shirt and a pair of slacks. His face is red. He waves.

"Come on," Estelle says.

"Stay in the car, Estelle."

"We need pictures of both of you," the voice says.

Big Bear's pants are wet. He cringes. Estelle has left the car and is walking toward the red-faced man. He thinks about stepping on the gas and crushing her, running into her from behind, not letting her have her way.

"Estelle?" he says to the empty seat.

"Please get out," the voice says.

"I'm not getting out," Big Bear says.

"We must have pictures. There are twenty exposures on the roll."

"What do you need pictures for?"

"To take back, Bill. They sent us for pictures."

"What are they going to do with the pictures?"

"I don't know. I just take the pictures."

Big Bear rubs his hand over his face. "I will never drink again," he says. "Estelle?" he says.

"This is a random landing. We'll never see you again. We need twenty pictures, and we would like to be your friends before we leave. Please get out of the car."

Estelle is talking to the man. He rolls down his window and puts his head out. It smells damp. There is a lot of fog. The lights have been turned out on the spaceship, and it is hard to tell just how large it is. It looked huge in the sky over the car, but it doesn't look that big now. Just big enough to block to road. Big Bear puts the car in reverse again. Just as before, a stream of air draws him forward.

"We found you by accident. You'll do fine for the pictures, though. If you'll please get out."

Big Bear wants to go home and go to sleep. Big Bear wants to go home and throw away all his liquor. He wants his children. His children!

"What are you going to do to me?" he asks again.

"Take your picture," the man says.

Disgusted, Big Bear opens the door and gets out. He walks forward. The man shakes his hand and introduces himself as Bobby. Estelle smiles at him.

"You're drunk," Big Bear says to Estelle.

"That's okay," the man says. "If you two could stand by your car?"

Big Bear doesn't want to turn his back on the man.

"The other ones?" Big Bear asks.

"Donald is playing a game inside. He's tired of coming to Earth."

"What game?" Big Bear asks suspiciously, not sure why he's suspicious.

"Scrabble. He was worried about using the word 'toque.' That's a foreign word, isn't it?"

"Toe?"

"Toque."

"I'm drunk as a skunk," Big Bear says.

"Bear, you'll never make it."

"We'll make it."

"Why should you even try to make it?" Laura says. Laura is the wife of the man whose party Big Bear and Estelle have attended.

"Big Bear can make it!" Big Bear yells.

"You're a big oaf," Laura says, and walks away. That leaves her husband to get their coats.

"If we don't make it, I'll end up the same place I'd be working tomorrow anyway," Estelle says. Estelle is more drunk than Big Bear, and Big Bear is focusing on his feet to stay alert.

"What are you ashamed of?" Estelle asks Big Bear.

"Nothing. What are you talking about?" He fears that another one of her honesty sessions is coming on—a talk about how she wishes she had never married him or had children.

"You're staring at the floor, Bear. What's the matter with you?"

"He's drunk," their host says good-naturedly. Big Bear and Paul, their host, were in the service together. It was Paul's idea to keep calling him Big Bear when they got back to America. In Japan, a geisha came up with the name. Laura will have no part of it. She calls him Alvin. Big Bear holds Estelle's coat, happy to get away from the party.

The Peugeot is parked in Paul's driveway. Death. Death everywhere. Japan, Viet Nam, Mortuary Science.

"What's the matter with you, Bear?" Estelle asks. "You're not really too drunk to drive, are you?"

"Daddy! Did you know that there was a Big Bear City in California?"

"No."

"I found out in geography. My teacher said to ask if it was named for you."

"I've never met your teacher. How did she know I was called Big Bear?"

"I told her."

"Well, stop telling everybody. That's just a joke, you know."

"But that's what everybody calls you."

"Go watch TV or something."

"What are you two talking about?" Estelle calls from the kitchen.

"Geography," Big Bear answers.

"Mom, there's a place called Big Bear City in California."

"I don't want to hear any more about it," Big Bear says.

"What are you so grumpy about?" Estelle asks, standing in the kitchen doorway. "You're as grumpy as a bear."

"Oh, come off it. You two leave me alone."

"Why is that always what you want? Why can't anybody talk to you?" Estelle says.

"Leave me alone," Big Bear says, and tilts himself out of view in his La-Z-Boy reclining chair.

"I thought jumping rope with the intestine was a joke," Estelle says. "That's not what you're doing, is it? It's not really an intestine?"

"No, there are no cows on Mars, so we consider your milk a delicacy. We have alcohol. Juniper berries grow in profusion. It's really very pretty, all the bushes, in addition to the gin it produces."

"Are they coming out?" Big Bear asks, nodding toward the spaceship.

"We've been on so many missions that they just don't care any more."

"What do they come for, then?"

"There has to be a certain number aboard."

"What for?"

"I never asked. We keep busy, though."

"What do you do?"

"Well, Donald likes to play games. He got some jigsaw puzzles the last time we were here, and he never tires of that, particularly a round puzzle that's a pizza."

"He just plays games?"

"They drink milk if we stop for it. We have to stop in the woods, of course, and there usually aren't any stores. They loved Maine. There were stores in the middle of nowhere."

"We love Maine," Estelle says.

"It's awfully nice," the spaceman says.

"Are you going to take more pictures?" Big Bear asks.

"I'm just trying to think . . . where would be a good spot?"

"Can't we just stand by the car?"

"I think they'll want variety."

Estelle smiles. "Would you like me to take off my clothes?" she asks.

"She's kidding," Big Bear says.

"I thought we'd take those later," the spaceman says.

"We're not taking our clothes off," Big Bear says.

"I'll put you under a spell, Bill," the spaceman says.

"You can't put me under any spell."

"Please try not to be hostile. I personally have no interest in taking nude photographs."

"Then let's leave that crap out."

"I can't leave it out. They said to get some."

"Tell them it was foggy and it didn't turn out."

"I'll undress," Estelle says.

"Don't you think it's a little cold for nude posing?" Big Bear says.

"Yes," the spaceman says. "Maybe we should go to your place."

Sleep soundly, sweet ones. Don't wake up and want water, or you might see the spacemen in the kitchen. You don't like it when·your brother plays with your special toys . . . how would you like it if a spaceman was tapping pegs through holes and squares through squares? You wouldn't like it. It's good you're a sound sleeper. One of the spacemen is in the bathroom. Imagine walking into the bathroom and seeing a spaceman urinating.

"I said I'm not too drunk to drive, and I'm not."

"You're no judge. Laura is probably right."

"Side with me. I'm your husband."

"In effect I am siding with you. If you had an accident . . ."

"Big Bear doesn't have accidents."

"Like John Wayne?"

"What are you taunting me for? You want to get home or don't you?"

"It might be better if I drove."

"It might be better, but you're not going to do it."

"All right. But drive slowly. There's so much fog."

"This piece of crap car isn't helping us any. The thing's so light, a wind would blow it over. When are you going to give up and let me turn it in for another one?"

"I thought flashy cars didn't matter to you."

"What did I say about flash? I just said a car—a decent car."

"This is a decent car. It was driven by my brother before he died in that horrible war."

"Where did you get his underwear from in the first place?"

"I don't want to talk about my brother."

"I don't want that underwear in my drawer. Where the hell did you get your brother's underwear?"

"Where do you think? From his drawer."

"Well, why did you take that, if it isn't prying?"

"It's not as though I just took that."

"What else did you take?"

"I took his things. I don't want to talk about my brother, Bear."

"What things? Tell me or I'm not going to pull out of the driveway, and Laura can wave and scowl all night."

"I took shirts and sweaters. Satisfied?"

The car pulls out of the driveway. Big Bear despises the car.

"Why haven't I ever seen them?"

"I put them away for the boys."

"They don't want your brother's stuff. By the time it fits them they wouldn't wear anything that unfashionable."

"I am not aware of radical style changes in men's sweaters."

"I want the underwear to go! You keep the shirts. I'll throw out the underwear."

"You keep your hands off my brother's things."

"You put it in my drawer and order me not to touch it. Why didn't you put it in your own damn drawer?"

"It makes me sad."

"Then get rid of it."

"Can't we please talk about something else? I thought you liked my brother."

"I didn't have anything against your brother, but I don't want his underwear in my drawer."

"If you keep driving this fast, you'll die before it can be removed."

"Don't change the subject. The subject is underwear. You can keep it under your pillow if you want, but get it out of my drawer."

"Yes, sir."

"I don't feel guilty," Big Bear says. "Nobody would put up with that."

In front of their car something hovers in the sky, but it's too close to be a plane. It's shapeless, which is funny, because it's close enough to figure out a shape. A mound. A mound?

"What's that?" Big Bear asks.

"Maybe we should get the uncomfortable pictures over with, and then we could take a few more by the car, or over there."

"Oh, cut it out," Big Bear says. "No nudie shots."

"I'm a family man, too, Bill. I'd like to just simplify matters and get home to my family. Could you drop your pants?"

"No."

Estelle is unbuttoning her coat.

"No," Big Bear says to her, and grabs her hand. She tries to get it away from him.

Estelle is shrugging her dress down, smiling at the spaceman.

The camera clicks.

"How old are your children?" she asks.

"That's enough!" Big Bear says. "Can we go home?"

"I'd like the others, and then you can go on your way."

"It's too God damn cold," Big Bear says.

"Let's take them to our place, Bear. We could give them milk and they could take the other pictures."

"That would be fine," the spaceman says.

"You're not invited," Big Bear says.

"I was just invited." The spaceman smiles politely. "I'll get the others."

"I thought they had to stay with the ship."

"I'm doing you a favor, Bill. Would you rather stay here longer?"

Big Bear shivers. What if Sammy and David drank the last of the milk.

The other spacemen are named Donald and Fred. There is something wrong with Fred; his wrists are bent funny, and his mouth wrinkles when he tries to smile, which is all of the time. "He's retarded," Donald says. Good God, Big Bear thinks. Won't Fred hear Donald?

"We've been stuck with him on the last seven missions," Donald says.

They are walking up Big Bear's front walk. They are inside the house. The babysitter has gone to sleep in the spare bedroom. She turned off all the lights. Big Bear can't see. Donald has a flashlight. He turns it on.

"Thanks," Big Bear says.

He heads for the light switch. Fred, it seems, is not only retarded, but violent. He struggles with Donald and wins. Fred has the flashlight. He pokes it into his mouth. His cheeks light up. No one tries to take the flashlight away from Fred. "I've had it up to here with him," Donald says, but no one tries to get the flashlight. Big Bear has located the light switch, so it's okay. Sort of okay. Fred's cheeks are orange.

"Did you know that this was called mooning in the sixties? College kids did it."

The spaceman snaps away. Estelle is making a fool of herself.

"What are you going to bring me, Daddy?" the spaceman's son asks.

"You're greedy."

"What are you going to bring me?"

"What do you want?"

"More goldfish."

"The damn things die. I bring them all the way back and they're dead in a week."

"I told you. That's because I need a real aquarium with a pump and a filter."

"It's too much trouble to bring the things back. Isn't there something else I could bring you?"

"No, I want that."

"I'll do it if I have time. You just can't buy goldfish everywhere."

"Go where you can get them."

"This is my mission, kid. Okay?"

"When are you going to take me with you?"

"When you grow up."

"I *am* grown up."

"Grownups don't want goldfish."

"How did it go in the morgue, Estelle?"

"Fine," Estelle says.

"Did you cut up dead bodies?"

Estelle comes into the living room. She can hardly wait to see if Big Bear is drunk. Estelle stares at Big Bear, who is reclining in his La-Z-Boy reclining chair. She sees that he is reclining because he is drunk.

"I thought you were going to Pete's party tonight."

"We were *both* going."

"That's what I said," Estelle says.

"But now we're *not* both going," Big Bear grins. "We're not going anywhere."

"I know!" Estelle cries. She doubles over, as though somebody just passed her a football.

"Jesus Christ," Big Bear says. "I didn't know you wanted to go to Pete's. I'm not so drunk we can't go. Stand up, for Christ's sake. What's the matter with you, Estelle?"

"I hate not to be the perfect host," Big Bear says to the spacemen. "But tomorrow is another day and . . ."

They seem not to have understood. If they smoked, Big Bear could empty the ashtrays.

"To be honest with you," Big Bear says, although none of the spacemen seem interested, "we've had a big night and it's about time for you to go."

"The disgusting thing," Donald says. "Blowing bubbles in his milk."

"We're all out of milk, now, Bobby. It's about time for you to go," Big Bear says.

"I hope he falls over and we can just leave him," Donald says.

Fred has thrown a glass of milk against the wall. The glass was soft plastic, so it just bounced. The sound wasn't loud enough to awaken Sammy and David. Estelle finds herself looking on the bright side of the spaceman's little *faux pas*.

At a gas station in Big Bear City, California, a little boy gets out of his mother's car to buy a soft drink.

Laura takes Big Bear's coat. She turns to look at Big Bear as he walks away. I hope he picks the hors d'oeuvres that have liver hidden inside them, she thinks.

"Mommy!" the little boy says. "I put the money in and nothing happened."

"Push the coin release."

"What's that?"

"Can I help?" the service attendant asks.

"That's all right," the little boy's mother says. "I'll take care of it." She goes to the machine and pushes the coin-release lever. Nothing happens.

Lying in a field in Viet Nam, in the second before he dies, Estelle's brother wonders what will happen to his Peugeot. He wonders why he's thinking of his Peugeot instead of Estelle or his mother or father. Rather, he starts to wonder, but dies before the thought is fully formulated.

"Maybe I could get a picture of the two of you by the door. Could you get together and pretend that you're going grocery shopping?"

"We don't have to pretend we're going grocery shopping. We'll just stand by the door, as if we're going out."

"Pretend you're going grocery shopping," the spaceman says.

"We look the same way whether we're going to the PTA meeting, or going to get groceries, or to visit her parents."

"Then, just stand by the door as though you were doing one of those things, please Bill."

"Wake up, Estelle," Big Bear says. "Wake up. Come on, Estelle." Big Bear says. "This is the last picture. Are you going to wake up?"

"The machine doesn't work," the little boy's mother says to the service-station attendant. Just one more problem on grocery day in Big Bear City, California.

"You had quite a night," the babysitter says cheerfully. The babysitter and Sammy are awake. David is still sleeping. Big Bear envies David.

"I didn't know I left the milk bottle out," the babysitter says apologetically.

"Actually, we came home a while ago and some friends had milk."

The babysitter looks at the milk glasses. She also sees that one that has been thrown against the dining-room wall.

"Good-night," Big Bear says, and climbs the stairs. Since they did not smoke, Estelle will have no ashtrays to empty and will join him soon. Not that he really cares. He is so tired he'd sleep with the spacemen. Except Fred . . . Jesus, it sure is good they loaded him out of the house, Big Bear thinks. If I had irritated them, they might have left him. Big Bear is glad that he only has Sammy and David. If they had tried for a girl, like Estelle wanted, it might have been retarded.

Big Bear falls into bed, with visions of Fred. It rhymes: bed, Fred. Big Bear falls asleep.

There has been a spaceship sighting in Reno, Nevada, and that's where Estelle wants to go.

"Estelle, you heard them say that there are a lot of other spacemen. Any of them could have flown over Reno, Nevada."

"We haven't taken a trip in years. The boys should see some of the country."

"Aren't you going to summer school? What happened to your plans?"

"I don't want to talk about it."

"I paid a year's tuition. I'd like to have a talk about why you're quitting."

"Something disgusting happened."

"What?"

"I want to go to Reno," Estelle says. "Will you take me or won't you?"

"The spaceship won't still be there."

"There have been sightings all around Reno."

"We're going to take the boys to Reno and sit in a motel waiting to hear rumors of spaceships?"

"It's my birthday," Estelle says. "You have to please me on my birthday, and I want to take a trip."

"What do you mean, I have to please you on your birthday?"

"I suppose you don't have to be nice to me if you don't want to, Bear. Excuse my presumption."

"I already am nice to you. That night with the spacemen I let you act like a jackass. Anybody else would have straightened you out."

"How gallant of you not to criticize me in front of my friends."

"Friends? You met them once."

"Of course no one would want to be my friend," Estelle says. "Excuse me."

"I didn't say they weren't your friends. I did say that. I don't know. Let's forget this, okay?"

"Let's go to Reno, Nevada."

"Oh, leave me alone," Big Bear says.

Big Bear meant to avoid this card shop, but it's so convenient, and he doesn't have the time to look all around for another place to get Estelle's birthday card. The woman will probably not be there anyway.

The woman is there. She finds Big Bear as he stands browsing through the Relative Birthday group of cards. She asks if she can help him.

"No, thanks," Big Bear says.

"This is a nice one," the saleswoman says, taking a big pink card down.

Big Bear looks. There is a plastic window, in the shape of a heart, through which a blond lady is visible. "My Darling" it says across the top of the card.

"I don't like that one," Big Bear says.

"Then look at this one." She hands Big Bear a blue card with bluer velvet bluebirds on it. The bluebirds trail a ribbon that spells "Happy Birthday, Darling" as it unrolls.

"Okay," Big Bear says. "Fine."

The card costs one dollar and fifty cents. For a card! It takes the woman a long time to slip it carefully into the bag. It takes her a long time to count out his change. He is never going to come to this card shop again.

"Thank you, sir," the saleswoman says, with her usual ironic smile.

Big Bear holds the bag tightly and makes the mistake of crushing the velvet bird.

"You're wrecked. You going to work like that?"

"I couldn't work there if I wasn't wrecked."

"You should avoid getting wrecked sometime and try it."

"I don't want a job."

"Then that means I have to have one. So don't criticize me for getting wrecked."

"You're wrecked." The saleswoman's boyfriend laughs. He is also wrecked.

"Look at this one, look at this," Bobby says.

His friend's face turns red. "Put the things away," his friend says.

"Look, look, this one was Estelle's idea."

"I'm sure."

"No, I swear. She said this was a craze on campus in the sixties."

"*This* was something they did at college?"

"And look at this one. This is Bill pretending he's going to work. Look at it!"

"I've seen these things a dozen times already. Put those disgusting things away," his friend says.

"I'll put them away, but you've got to see the expression on her face in this one."

"I'm not likely to see her face in this series."

The spaceman's friend has just made a witty remark. Bobby appreciates it and starts laughing uncontrollably. He'd be doing that even if his friend weren't there, though. These pictures really kill him.

"Now the Air Force is even admitting that it's tied up with them," Big Bear says from his La-Z-Boy reclining chair.

"What do they say?"

"I just told you. All those sightings over Nebraska. The Air Force is coming out and admitting it."

"What do they *say*, Bear?"

"You love this subject, don't you? You love to talk about the spacemen."

"Who brought it up?" Estelle says.

"I did. I know you love the subject," Big Bear says.

"These bluebirds sing a happy tune. They say that you are mine . . ."

She is convulsed with laughter, that crazy, wiped-out laughter with no tears accompanying it. The eyes get wider and wider—wide enough to pour tears, but the laughter is all that comes.

"Why don't you stop memorizing the cards? Just take your shoes off and relax."

"It had bluebirds on the front with a ribbon and a blue background, and it said 'These bluebirds sing . . .'"

"You're going to lose your job the first time you do a wiped-out thing like this with a customer."

"The bluebirds! The fucking bluebirds!"

"What the hell was that?"

"Probably hit ducks again. Remember the time we took off through a whole flock of them?" Bobby says.

"Disgusting," Donald says, but he is looking at Fred and not thinking about possible dead ducks.

"What are you mad at me for?" the little boy asks. "What did I do?"

"You didn't do anything. You got your soft drink. Drink it."

"You couldn't make the machine work either," the little boy says.

"It was broken," his mother says.

"Then what are you mad about?"

"I'm mad because you just add to the confusion. I want to get the groceries and go home and put them away. All right? Sit back and finish your drink."

It is just another day in Big Bear City, California.

1974

MARK TWAIN

The $30,000 Bequest

Lakeside was a pleasant little town of five or six thousand inhabitants, and a rather pretty one, too, as towns go in the Far West. It had church accommodations for thirty-five thousand, which is the way of the Far West and the South, where everybody is religious, and where each of the Protestant sects is represented and has a plant of its own. Rank was unknown in Lakeside — unconfessed, anyway; everybody knew everybody and his dog, and a sociable friendliness was the prevailing atmosphere.

Saladin Foster was book-keeper in the principal store, and the only high-salaried man of his profession in Lakeside. He was thirty-five years old, now; he had served that store for fourteen years; he had begun in his marriage-week at four hundred dollars a year, and had climbed steadily up, a hundred dollars a year, for four years; from that time forth his wage had remained eight hundred — a handsome figure indeed, and everybody conceded that he was worth it.

His wife, Electra, was a capable helpmeet, although — like himself — a dreamer of dreams and a private dabbler in romance. The first thing she did, after her marriage — child as she was, aged only nineteen — was to buy an acre of ground on the edge of the town, and pay down the cash for it — twenty-five dollars, all her fortune. Saladin had less, by fifteen. She instituted a vegetable garden there, got it farmed on shares by the nearest neighbor, and made it pay her a hundred per cent a year. Out of Saladin's first year's wage she put thirty dollars in the savings-bank, sixty out of his second, a hundred out of his third, a hundred and fifty out of his fourth. His wage went to eight hundred a year, then, and

Mark Twain was born Samuel Langhorne Clemens in 1835. His early experiences were centered around the river life of Hannibal, Missouri, where his family moved when he was four. After an excursion to the East Coast, Twain returned to the Mississippi, where he became a steamboat pilot and found his pen name: mark twain is the two-fathom mark on a rope that gauges the water's depth. Twain, whose first writings were published in local newspapers, slowly gained a national reputation as a humorist and lecturer. His trenchant wit, good-natured nostalgia, and knowledge of Midwest custom and dialect combine in such works as *Life on the Mississippi* (1883) and *The Adventures of Huckleberry Finn* (1884). In his later years, Twain's cynicism about the state of human affairs grew while his financial situation worsened. He died in 1910 in Redding, Connecticut, not yet finished with the drafts of his final work, *The Mysterious Stranger* (1916).

meantime two children had arrived and increased the expenses, but she banked two hundred a year from the salary, nevertheless, thenceforth. When she had been married seven years she built and furnished a pretty and comfortable two-thousand-dollar house in the midst of her garden-acre, paid half of the money down and moved her family in. Seven years later she was out of debt and had several hundred dollars out earning its living.

Earning it by the rise in landed estate; for she had long ago bought another acre or two and sold the most of it at a profit to pleasant people who were willing to build, and would be good neighbors and furnish a general comradeship for herself and her growing family. She had an independent income from safe investments of about a hundred dollars a year; her children were growing in years and grace; and she was a pleased and happy woman. Happy in her husband, happy in her children, and the husband and the children were happy in her. It is at this point that this history begins.

The youngest girl, Clytemnestra—called Clytie for short—was eleven; her sister, Gwendolen—called Gwen for short—was thirteen; nice girls, and comely. The names betray the latent romance-tinge in the parental blood, the parents' names indicate that the tinge was an inheritance. It was an affectionate family, hence all four of its members had pet names. Saladin's was a curious and unsexing one—Sally; and so was Electra's—Aleck. All day long Sally was a good and diligent book-keeper and salesman; all day long Aleck was a good and faithful mother and housewife, and thoughtful and calculating business woman; but in the cozy living-room at night they put the plodding world away, and lived in another and a fairer, reading romances to each other, dreaming dreams, comrading with kings and princes and stately lords and ladies in the flash and stir and splendor of noble palaces and grim and ancient castles.

2

Now came great news! Stunning news—joyous news, in fact. It came from a neighboring state, where the family's only surviving relative lived. It was Sally's relative—a sort of vague and indefinite uncle or second or third cousin by the name of Tilbury Foster, seventy and a bachelor, reputed well off and correspondingly sour and crusty. Sally had tried to make up to him once, by letter, in a bygone time, and had not made that mistake again. Tilbury now wrote to Sally, saying he should shortly die, and should leave him thirty thousand dollars, cash;

not for love, but because money had given him most of his troubles and exasperations, and he wished to place it where there was good hope that it would continue its malignant work. The bequest would be found in his will, and would be paid over. *Provided*, that Sally should be able to prove to the executors that he had *taken no notice of the gift by spoken word or letter, had made no inquiries concerning the moribund's progress toward the everlasting tropics, and had not attended the funeral.*

As soon as Aleck had partially recovered from the tremendous emotions created by the letter, she sent to the relative's habitat and subscribed for the local paper.

Man and wife entered into a solemn compact, now, to never mention the great news to any one while the relative lived, lest some ignorant person carry the fact to the death-bed and distort it and make it appear that they were disobediently thankful for the bequest, and just the same as confessing it and publishing it, right in the face of the prohibition.

For the rest of the day Sally made havoc and confusion with his books, and Aleck could not keep her mind on her affairs, nor even take up a flower-pot or book or a stick of wood without forgetting what she had intended to do with it. For both were dreaming.

"Thir-ty thousand dollars!"

All day long the music of those inspiring words sang through those people's heads.

From her marriage-day forth, Aleck's grip had been upon the purse, and Sally had seldom known what it was to be privileged to squander a dime on non-necessities.

"Thir-ty thousand dollars!" the song went on and on. A vast sum, an unthinkable sum!

All day long Aleck was absorbed in planning how to invest it, Sally in planning how to spend it.

There was no romance-reading that night. The children took themselves away early, for the parents were silent, distraught, and strangely unentertaining. The good-night kisses might as well have been impressed upon vacancy, for all the response they got; the parents were not aware of the kisses, and the children had been gone an hour before their absence was noticed. Two pencils had been busy during that hour —note-making; in the way of plans. It was Sally who broke the stillness at last. He said, without exultation:

"Ah, it'll be grand, Aleck! Out of the first thousand we'll have a horse and a buggy for summer, and a cutter and a skin lap-robe for winter."

Aleck responded with decision and composure—

"Out of the *capital?* Nothing of the kind. Not if it was a million!"

Sally was deeply disappointed; the glow went out of his face.

"Oh, Aleck!" he said, reproachfully. "We've always worked so hard and been so scrimped; and now that we are rich, it does seem—"

He did not finish, for he saw her eye soften; his supplication had touched her. She said, with gentle persuasiveness:

"We must not spend the capital, dear, it would not be wise. Out of the income from it—"

"That will answer, that will answer, Aleck! How dear and good you are! There will be a noble income, and if we can spend that—"

"Not *all* of it, dear, not all of it, but you can spend a part of it. That is, a reasonable part. But the whole of the capital—every penny of it—must be put right to work, and kept at it. You see the reasonableness of that, don't you?"

"Why, ye-s. Yes, of course. But we'll have to wait so long. Six months before the first interest falls due."

"Yes—maybe longer."

"Longer, Aleck? Why? Don't they pay half-yearly?"

"*That* kind of an investment—yes; but I sha'n't invest in that way."

"What way, then?"

"For big returns."

"Big. That's good. Go on, Aleck. What is it?"

"Coal. The new mines. Cannel. I mean to put in ten thousand. Ground floor. When we organize, we'll get three shares for one."

"By George, but it sounds good, Aleck! Then the shares will be worth—how much? And when?"

"About a year. They'll pay ten per cent half-yearly, and be worth thirty thousand. I know all about it; the advertisement is in the Cincinnati paper here."

"Land, thirty thousand for ten—in a year! Let's jam in the whole capital and pull out ninety! I'll write and subscribe right now—tomorrow it may be too late."

He was flying to the writing-desk, but Aleck stopped him and put him back in his chair. She said:

"Don't lose your head so. We mustn't subscribe till we've got the money; don't you know that?"

Sally's excitement went down a degree or two, but he was not wholly appeased.

"Why, Aleck, we'll *have* it, you know—and so soon, too. He's probably out of his troubles before this; it's a hundred to nothing he's selecting his brimstone-shovel this very minute. Now, I think—"

Aleck shuddered, and said:

"How *can* you, Sally! Don't talk in that way, it is perfectly scandalous."

"Oh well, make it a halo, if you like, *I* don't care for his outfit, I was only just talking. Can't you let a person talk?"

"But why should you *want* to talk in that dreadful way? How would you like to have people talk so about *you*, and you not cold yet?"

"Not likely to be, for *one* while, I reckon, if my last act was giving away money for the sake of doing somebody a harm with it. But never mind about Tilbury, Aleck, let's talk about something worldly. It does seem to me that that mine is the place for the whole thirty. What's the objection?"

"All the eggs in one basket—that's the objection."

"All right, if you say so. What about the other twenty? What do you mean to do with that?"

"There is no hurry; I am going to look around before I do anything with it."

"All right, if your mind's made up," sighed Sally. He was deep in thought awhile, then he said:

"There'll be twenty thousand profit coming from the ten a year from now. We can spend that, can't we, Aleck?"

Aleck shook her head.

"No, dear," she said, "it won't sell high till we've had the first semi-annual dividend. You can spend part of that."

"Shucks, only *that*—and a whole year to wait! Confound it, I—"

"Oh, do be patient! It might even be declared in three months—it's quite within the possibilities."

"Oh, jolly! oh, thanks!" and Sally jumped up and kissed his wife in gratitude. "It'll be three thousand—three whole thousand! how much of it can we spend, Aleck? Make it liberal—do, dear, that's a good fellow."

Aleck was pleased; so pleased that she yielded to the pressure and conceded a sum which her judgment told her was a foolish extravagance —a thousand dollars. Sally kissed her half a dozen times and even in that way could not express all his joy and thankfulness. This new access of gratitude and affection carried Aleck quite beyond the bounds of prudence, and before she could restrain herself she had made her darling another grant—a couple of thousand out of the fifty or sixty which she meant to clear within a year out of the twenty which still remained of the bequest. The happy tears sprang to Sally's eyes, and he said:

"Oh, I want to hug you!" And he did it. Then he got his notes and sat down and began to check off, for first purchase, the luxuries which he should earliest wish to secure. "Horse — buggy — cutter —

lap-robe — patent-leathers — dog — plug-hat — church-pew — stem-winder—new teeth—*say,* Aleck!"

"Well?"

"Ciphering away, aren't you? That's right. Have you got the twenty thousand invested yet?"

"No, there's no hurry about that; I must look around first, and think."

"But you are ciphering; what's it about?"

"Why, I have to work for the thirty thousand that comes out of the coal, haven't I?"

"Scott, what a head! I never thought of that. How are you getting along? Where have you arrived?"

"Not very far—two years or three. I've turned it over twice; once in oil and once in wheat."

"Why, Aleck, it's splendid! How does it aggregate?"

"I think—well, to be on the safe side, about a hundred and eighty thousand clear, though it will probably be more."

"My! isn't it wonderful? By gracious! luck has come our way at last, after all the hard sledding. Aleck!"

"Well?"

"I'm going to cash in a whole three hundred on the missionaries— what real right have we to care for expenses!"

"You couldn't do a nobler thing, dear; and it's just like your generous nature, you unselfish boy."

The praise made Sally poignantly happy, but he was fair and just enough to say it was rightfully due to Aleck rather than to himself, since but for her he should never have had the money.

Then they went up to bed, and in their delirium of bliss they forgot and left the candle burning in the parlor. They did not remember until they were undressed; then Sally was for letting it burn; he said they could afford it, if it was a thousand. But Aleck went down and put it out.

A good job, too; for on her way back she hit on a scheme that would turn the hundred and eighty thousand into half a million before it had had time to get cold.

3

The little newspaper which Aleck had subscribed for was a Thursday sheet; it would make the trip of five hundred miles from Tilbury's village and arrive on Saturday. Tilbury's letter had started on Friday, more than a day too late for the benefactor to die and get into that week's issue, but in plenty of time to make connection for the next output. Thus the Fosters had to wait almost a complete week to find out whether anything of a satisfactory nature had happened to him or not. It was a long, long week, and the strain was a heavy one. The pair could hardly have borne it if their minds had not had the relief of wholesome diversion. We have seen that they had that. The woman was piling up fortunes right along, the man was spending them—spending all his wife would give him a chance at, at any rate.

At last the Saturday came, and the *Weekly Sagamore* arrived. Mrs. Eversly Bennett was present. She was the Presbyterian parson's wife, and was working the Fosters for a charity. Talk now died a sudden death—on the Foster side. Mrs. Bennett presently discovered that her hosts were not hearing a word she was saying; so she got up, wondering and indignant, and went away. The moment she was out of the house, Aleck eagerly tore the wrapper from the paper, and her eyes and Sally's swept the columns for the death-notices. Disappointment! Tilbury was not anywhere mentioned. Aleck was a Christian from the cradle, and duty and the force of habit required her to go through the motions. She pulled herself together and said, with a pious two-per-cent trade joyousness:

"Let us be humbly thankful that he has been spared; and—"

"Damn his treacherous hide, I wish—"

"Sally! For shame!"

"I don't care!" retorted the angry man. "It's the way *you* feel, and if you weren't so immorally pious you'd be honest and say so."

Aleck said, with wounded dignity:

"I do not see how you can say such unkind and unjust things. There is no such thing as immoral piety."

Sally felt a pang, but tried to conceal it under a shuffling attempt to save his case by changing the form of it—as if changing the form while retaining the juice could deceive the expert he was trying to placate. He said:

"I didn't mean so bad as that, Aleck; I didn't really mean immoral piety, I only meant—well, conventional piety, you know; er—shop piety; the—the — why, *you* know what I mean. Aleck—the—well, where you put up the plated article and play it for solid, you know, without intending anything improper, but just out of trade habit, ancient policy, petrified custom, loyalty to —to—hang it, I can't find the right words, but *you* know what I mean, Aleck, and that there isn't any harm in it. I'll try again. You see, it's this way. If a person—"

"You have said quite enough," said Aleck, coldly; "let the subject be dropped."

"*I'm* willing," fervently responded Sally, wiping the sweat from his forehead and looking the thankfulness he had no words for. Then, musingly, he apologized to himself. "I certainly held threes—I *know* it —but I drew and didn't fill. That's where I'm so often weak in the game. If I had stood pat—but I didn't. I never do. I don't know enough."

Confessedly defeated, he was properly tame now and subdued. Aleck forgave him with her eyes.

The grand interest, the supreme interest, came instantly to the front again; nothing could keep it in the background many minutes on a stretch. The couple took up the puzzle of the absence of Tilbury's death-notice. They discussed it every which way, more or less hopefully, but they had to finish where they began, and concede that the only really sane explanation of the absence of the notice must be—and without doubt was—that Tilbury was not dead. There was something sad about it, something even a little unfair, maybe, but there it was, and had to be put up with. They were agreed as to that. To Sally it seemed a strangely inscrutable dispensation; more inscrutable than usual, he thought; one of the most unnecessarily inscrutable he could call to mind, in fact—and said so, with some feeling; but if he was hoping to draw Aleck he failed; she reserved her opinion, if she had one; she had not the habit of taking injudicious risks in any market, worldly or other.

The pair must wait for next week's paper—Tilbury had evidently postponed. That was their thought and their decision. So they put the subject away, and went about their affairs again with as good heart as they could.

Now, if they had but known it, they had been wronging Tilbury all the time. Tilbury had kept faith, kept it to the letter; he was dead, he had died to schedule. He was dead more than four days now and used to it; entirely dead, perfectly dead, as dead as any other new person in the cemetery; dead in abundant time to get into that week's *Sagamore*, too, and only shut out by an accident; an accident which could not happen to a metropolitan journal, but which happens easily to a poor little village rag like the *Sagamore*. On this occasion, just as the editorial page was being locked up, a gratis quart of strawberry water-ice arrived from Hosteter's Ladies' and Gents' Ice-Cream Parlors, and the stickful of rather chilly regret over Tilbury's translation got crowded out to make room for the editor's frantic gratitude.

On its way to the standing-galley Tilbury's notice got pied. Otherwise it would have gone into some future edition, for *Weekly Sagamores* do not waste "live" matter, and in their galleys "live" matter is immortal, unless a pi accident intervenes. But a thing that gets pied is dead, and for such there is no resurrection; its chance of seeing print is gone, forever and ever. And so, let Tilbury like it or not, let him rave in his grave to his fill, no matter—no mention of his death would ever see the light in the *Weekly Sagamore.*

4

Five weeks drifted tediously along. The *Sagamore* arrived regularly on the Saturdays, but never once contained a mention of Tilbury Foster. Sally's patience broke down at this point, and he said, resentfully:

"Damn his livers, he's immortal!"

Aleck gave him a very severe rebuke, and added, with icy solemnity:

"How would you feel if you were suddenly cut off just after such an awful remark had escaped out of you?"

Without sufficient reflection Sally responded:

"I'd feel I was lucky I hadn't got caught with it *in* me."

Pride had forced him to say something, and as he could not think of any rational thing to say he flung that out. Then he stole a base—as he called it—that is, slipped from the presence, to keep from getting brayed in his wife's discussion-mortar.

Six months came and went. The *Sagamore* was still silent about Tilbury. Meantime, Sally had several times thrown out a feeler—that is, a hint that he would like to know. Aleck had ignored the hints. Sally now resolved to brace up and risk a frontal attack. So he squarely proposed to disguise himself and go to Tilbury's village and surreptitiously find out as to the prospects. Aleck put her foot on the dangerous project with energy and decision. She said:

"What can you be thinking of? You do keep my hands full! You have to be watched all the time, like a little child, to keep you from walking into the fire. You'll stay right where you are!"

"Why, Aleck, I could do it and not be found out—I'm certain of it."

"Sally Foster, don't you know you would have to inquire around?"

"Of course, but what of it? Nobody would suspect who I was."

"Oh, listen to the man! Some day you've got to prove to the executors that you never inquired. What then?"

He had forgotten that detail. He didn't reply; there wasn't anything to say. Aleck added:

"Now then, drop that notion out of your mind, and don't ever meddle with it again. Tilbury set that trap for you. Don't you know it's a trap? He is on the watch, and fully expecting you to blunder into it.

Well, he is going to be disappointed—at least while I am on deck. Sally!"

"Well?"

"As long as you live, if it's a hundred years, don't you ever make an inquiry. Promise!"

"All right," with a sigh and reluctantly.

Then Aleck softened and said:

"Don't be impatient. We are prospering; we can wait; there is no hurry. Our small dead-certain income increases all the time; and as to futures, I have not made a mistake yet—they are piling up by the thousands and the tens of thousands. There is not another family in the state with such prospects as ours. Already we are beginning to roll in eventual wealth. You know that, don't you?"

"Yes, Aleck, it's certainly so."

"Then be grateful for what God is doing for us, and stop worrying. You do not believe we could have achieved these prodigious results without His special help and guidance, do you?"

Hesitatingly, "N-no, I suppose not." Then, with feeling and admiration, "And yet, when it comes to judiciousness in watering a stock or putting up a hand to skin Wall Street I don't give in that *you* need any outside amateur help, if I do wish I—"

"Oh, *do* shut up! I know you do not mean any harm or any irreverence, poor boy, but you can't seem to open your mouth without letting out things to make a person shudder. You keep me in constant dread. For you and for all of us. Once I had no fear of the thunder, but now when I hear it I—"

Her voice broke, and she began to cry, and could not finish. The sight of this smote Sally to the heart, and he took her in his arms and petted her and comforted her and promised better conduct, and upbraided himself and remorsefully pleaded for forgiveness. And he was in earnest, and sorry for what he had done and ready for any sacrifice that could make up for it.

And so, in privacy, he thought long and deeply over the matter, resolving to do what should seem best. It was easy to *promise* reform; indeed he had already promised it. But would that do any real good, any permanent good? No, it would be but temporary—he knew his weakness, and confessed it to himself with sorrow—he could not keep the promise. Something surer and better must be devised; and he devised it. At cost of precious money which he had long been saving up, shilling by shilling, he put a lightning-rod on the house.

At a subsequent time he relapsed.

What miracles habit can do! and how quickly and how easily habits are acquired—both trifling habits and habits which profoundly change us. If by accident we wake at two in the morning a couple of nights in succession, we have need to be uneasy, for another repetition can turn the accident into a habit; and a month's dallying with whisky—but we all know these commonplace facts.

The castle-building habit, the day-dreaming habit—how it grows! what a luxury it becomes; how we fly to its enchantments at every idle moment, how we revel in them, steep our souls in them, intoxicate ourselves with their beguiling fantasies—oh yes, and how soon and how easily our dream life and our material life become so intermingled and so fused together that we can't quite tell which is which, any more.

By and by Aleck subscribed for a Chicago daily and for the *Wall Street Pointer.* With an eye single to finance she studied these as diligently all the week as she studied her Bible Sundays. Sally was lost in admiration, to note with what swift and sure strides her genius and judgment developed and expanded in the forecasting and handling of the securities of both the material and spiritual markets. He was proud of her nerve and daring in exploiting worldly stocks, and just as proud of her conservative caution in working her spiritual deals. He noted that she never lost her head in either case; that with a splendid courage she often went short on worldly futures, but heedfully drew the line there—she was always long on the others. Her policy was quite sane and simple, as she explained it to him: what she put into earthly futures was for speculation, what she put into spiritual futures was for investment; she was willing to go into the one on a margin, and take chances, but in the case of the other, "margin her no margins"—she wanted to cash in a hundred cents per dollar's worth, and have the stock transferred on the books.

It took but a very few months to educate Aleck's imagination and Sally's. Each day's training added something to the spread and effectiveness of the two machines. As a consequence, Aleck made imaginary money much faster than at first she had dreamed of making it, and Sally's competence in spending the overflow of it kept pace with the strain put upon it, right along. In the beginning, Aleck had given the coal speculation a twelvemonth in which to materialize, and had been loath to grant that this term might possibly be shortened by nine months. But that was the feeble work, the nursery work, of a financial fancy that had had no teaching, no experience, no practice. These aids soon came, then that nine months vanished, and the imaginary ten-thousand-dollar investment came marching home with three hundred per cent profit on its back!

It was a great day for the pair of Fosters. They were speechless for joy. Also speechless for another reason: after much watching of the market, Aleck had lately, with fear and trembling, made her first flyer on a "margin," using the remaining twenty thousand of the bequest in this risk. In her mind's eye she had seen it climb, point by point— always with a chance that the market would break—until at last her anxieties were too great for further endurance—she being new to the margin business and unhardened, as yet—and she gave her imaginary broker an imaginary order by imaginary telegraph to sell. She said forty thousand dollars' profit was enough. The sale was made on the very day that the coal venture had returned with its rich freight. As I have said, the couple were speechless. They sat dazed and blissful that night, trying to realize the immense fact, the overwhelming fact, that they were actually worth a hundred thousand dollars in clean, imaginary cash. Yet so it was.

It was the last time that ever Aleck was afraid of a margin; at least afraid enough to let it break her sleep and pale her cheek to the extent that this first experience in that line had done.

Indeed it was a memorable night. Gradually the realization that they were rich sank securely home into the souls of the pair, then they began to place the money. If we could have looked out through the eyes of these dreamers, we should have seen their tidy little wooden house disappear, and a two-story brick with a cast-iron fence in front of it take its place; we should have seen a three-globed gas-chandelier grow down from the parlor ceiling; we should have seen the homely rag carpet turn to noble Brussels, a dollar and a half a yard; we should have seen the plebeian fireplace vanish away and a recherché, big base-burner with isinglass windows take position and spread awe around. And we should have seen other things, too; among them the buggy, the lap-robe, the stove-pipe hat, and so on.

From that time forth, although the daughters and the neighbors saw only the same old wooden house there, it was a two-story brick to Aleck and Sally; and not a night went by that Aleck did not worry about the imaginary gas-bills, and get for all comfort Sally's reckless retort: "What of it? We can afford it."

Before the couple went to bed, that first night that they were rich, they had decided that they must celebrate. They must give a party— that was the idea. But how to explain it—to the daughters and the neighbors? They could not expose the fact that they were rich. Sally was willing, even anxious, to do it; but Aleck kept her head and would not allow it. She said that although the money was as good as in, it would be as well to wait until it was actually in. On that policy she took her stand, and would not budge. The great secret must be kept, she said —kept from the daughters and everybody else.

The pair were puzzled. They must celebrate, they were determined to celebrate, but since the secret must be kept, what could they celebrate? No birthdays were due for three months. Tilbury wasn't available, evidently he was going to live forever; what the nation *could* they celebrate? That was Sally's way of putting it; and he was getting impatient, too, and harassed. But at last he hit it—just by sheer inspiration, as it seemed to him—and all their troubles were gone in a moment; they would celebrate the Discovery of America. A splendid idea!

Aleck was almost too proud of Sally for words—she said *she* never would have thought of it. But Sally, although he was bursting with delight in the compliment and with wonder at himself, tried not to let on, and said it wasn't really anything, anybody could have done it. Whereat Aleck, with a prideful toss of her happy head, said:

"Oh, certainly! Anybody could—oh, anybody! Hosannah Dilkins, for instance! Or maybe Adelbert Peanut—oh, *dear*—yes! Well, I'd like to see them try it, that's all. Dear-me-suz, if they could think of the discovery of a forty-acre island it's more than *I* believe they could; and as for a whole continent, why, Sally Foster, you know perfectly well it would strain the livers and lights out of them and *then* they couldn't!"

The dear woman, she knew he had talent; and if affection made her over-estimate the size of it a little, surely it was a sweet and gentle crime, and forgivable for its source's sake.

5

The celebration went off well. The friends were all present, both the young and the old. Among the young were Flossie and Gracie Peanut and their brother Adelbert, who was a rising young journeyman tinner, also Hosannah Dilkins, Jr., journeyman plasterer, just out of his apprenticeship. For many months Adelbert and Hosannah had been showing interest in Gwendolen and Clytemnestra Foster, and the parents of the girls had noticed this with private satisfaction. But they suddenly realized now that that feeling had passed. They recognized that the changed financial conditions had raised up a social bar between their daughters and the young mechanics. The daughters could now look higher—and must. Yes, must. They need marry nothing below the grade of lawyer or merchant; poppa and momma would take care of this; there must be no mésalliances.

However, these thinkings and projects and theirs were private, and did not show on the surface, and therefore threw no shadow upon the celebration. What showed upon the surface was a serene and lofty contentment and a dignity of carriage and gravity of deportment which compelled the admiration and likewise the wonder of the company. All noticed it, all commented upon it, but none was able to divine the secret of it. It was a marvel and a mystery. There several persons remarked, without suspecting what clever shots they were making:

"It's as if they'd come into property."

That was just it, indeed.

Most mothers would have taken hold of the matrimonial matter in the old regulation way; they would have given the girls a talking to, of a solemn sort and untactful—a lecture calculated to defeat its own purpose, by producing tears and secret rebellion; and the said mothers would have further damaged the business by requesting the young mechanics to discontinue their attentions. But this mother was different. She was practical. She said nothing to any of the young people concerned, nor to any one else except Sally. He listened to her and understood; understood and admired. He said:

"I get the idea. Instead of finding fault with the samples on view, thus hurting feelings and obstructing trade without occasion, you merely offer a higher class of goods for the money, and leave nature to take her course. It's wisdom, Aleck, solid wisdom, and sound as a nut. Who's your fish? Have you nominated him yet?"

No, she hadn't. They must look the market over—which they did. To start with, they considered and discussed Bradish, rising young lawyer, and Fulton, rising young dentist. Sally must invite them to dinner. But not right away; there was no hurry, Aleck said. Keep an eye on the pair, and wait; nothing would be lost by going slowly in so important a matter.

It turned out that this was wisdom, too; for inside of three weeks Aleck made a wonderful strike which swelled her imaginary hundred thousand to four hundred thousand of the same quality. She and Sally were in the clouds that evening. For the first time they introduced champagne at dinner. Not real champagne, but plenty real enough for the amount of imagination expended on it. It was Sally that did it, and Aleck weakly submitted. At bottom both were troubled and ashamed, for he was a high-up Son of Temperance, and at funerals wore an apron which no dog could look upon and retain his reason and his opinion; and she was a W.C.T.U., with all that that implies of boiler-iron virtue and unendurable holiness. But there it was; the pride of riches was beginning its disintegrating work. They had lived to prove, once more, a sad truth which had been proven many times before in the world: that whereas principle is a great and noble protection against showy and degrading vanities and vices, poverty is worth six of it. More than four hundred thousand dollars to the good! They took up the matrimonial matter again. Neither the dentist nor the lawyer was mentioned; there was no occasion, they were out of the running. Disqualified. They discussed the son of the pork-packer and the son of the village banker. But finally, as in the previous case, they concluded to wait and think, and go cautiously and sure.

Luck came their way again. Aleck, ever watchful, saw a great and risky chance, and took a daring flyer. A time of trembling, of doubt, of awful uneasiness followed, for non-success meant absolute ruin and nothing short of it. Then came the result, and Aleck, faint with joy, could hardly control her voice when she said:

"The suspense is over, Sally—and we are worth a cold million!"

Sally wept for gratitude, and said:

"Oh, Electra, jewel of women, darling of my heart, we are free at last, we roll in wealth, we need never scrimp again. It's a case for Veuve Cliquot!" and he got out a pint of spruce-beer and made sacrifice, he saying "Damn the expense," and she rebuking him gently with reproachful but humid and happy eyes.

They shelved the pork-packer's son and the banker's son, and sat down to consider the Governor's son and the son of the Congressman.

6

It were a weariness to follow in detail the leaps and bounds the Foster fictitious finances took from this time forth. It was marvelous, it was dizzying, it was dazzling. Everything Aleck touched turned to fairy gold, and heaped itself glittering toward the firmament. Millions upon millions poured in, and still the mighty stream flowed thundering along, still its vast volume increased. Five millions—ten millions—twenty—thirty—was there never to be an end?

Two years swept by in a splendid delirium, the intoxicated Fosters scarcely noticing the flight of time. They were now worth three hundred million dollars; they were in every board of directors of every prodigious combine in the country; and still, as time drifted along, the millions went on piling up, five at a time, ten at a time, as fast as they could tally them off, almost. The three hundred doubled itself—then doubled again—and yet again—and yet once more.

Twenty-four hundred millions!

The business was getting a little confused. It was necessary to take an account of stock, and straighten it out. The Fosters knew it, they felt it, they realized that it was imperative; but they also knew that to do it properly and perfectly the task must be carried to a finish without a break when once it was begun. A ten-hours' job; and where could *they* find ten leisure hours in a bunch? Sally was selling pins and sugar and calico all day and every day; Aleck was cooking and washing dishes and sweeping and making beds all day and every day, with none to help, for the daughters were being saved up for high society. The Fosters knew there was one way to get the ten hours, and only one. Both were ashamed to name it; each waited for the other to do it. Finally Sally said:

"Somebody's got to give in. It's up to me. Consider that I've named it—never mind pronouncing it out aloud."

Aleck colored, but was grateful. Without further remark, they fell. Fell, and—broke the Sabbath. For that was their only free ten-hour stretch. It was but another step in the downward path. Others would follow. Vast wealth has temptations which fatally and surely undermine the moral structure of persons not habituated to its possession.

They pulled down the shades and broke the Sabbath. With hard and patient labor they overhauled their holdings and listed them. And a long-drawn procession of formidable names it was! Starting with the Railway Systems, Steamer Lines, Standard Oil, Ocean Cables, Diluted Telegraph, and all the rest, and winding up with Klondike, De Beers, Tammany Graft, and Shady Privileges in the Post-office Department.

Twenty-four hundred millions, and all safely planted in Good Things, gilt-edged and interest-bearing. Income, $120,000,000 a year. Aleck fetched a long purr of soft delight, and said:

"Is it enough?"

"It is, Aleck."

"What shall we do?"

"Stand pat."

"Retire from business?"

"That's it."

"I am agreed. The good work is finished; we will take a long rest and enjoy the money."

"Good! Aleck!"

"Yes, dear?"

"How much of the income can we spend?"

"The whole of it."

It seemed to her husband that a ton of chains fell from his limbs. He did not say a word; he was happy beyond the power of speech.

After that, they broke the Sabbaths right along, as fast as they turned up. It is the first wrong steps that count. Every Sunday they put in the whole day, after morning service, on inventions—inventions of ways to spend the money. They got to continuing this delicious dissipation until past midnight; and at every séance Aleck lavished millions upon great charities and religious enterprises, and Sally lavished like sums upon matters to which (at first) he gave definite names. Only at first. Later the names gradually lost sharpness of outline, and eventually faded into "sundries," thus becoming entirely—but safely—undescriptive. For Sally was crumbling. The placing of these millions added seriously and most uncomfortably to the family expenses—in tallow candles. For a while Aleck was worried. Then, after a little, she ceased to worry, for the occasion of it was gone. She was pained, she was grieved, she was ashamed; but she said nothing, and so became an accessory. Sally was taking candles; he was robbing the store. It is ever thus. Vast wealth, to the person unaccustomed to it, is a bane; it eats into the flesh and bone of his morals. When the Fosters were poor, they could have been trusted with untold candles. But now they—but let us not dwell upon it. From candles to apples is but a step: Sally got to taking apples; then soap; then maple-sugar; then canned goods; then crockery. How easy it is to go from bad to worse, when once we have started upon a downward course!

Meantime, other effects had been milestoning the course of the Fosters' splendid financial march. The fictitious brick dwelling had given place to an imaginary granite one with a checker-board mansard roof; in time this one disappeared and gave place to a still grander home— and so on and so on. Mansion after mansion, made of air, rose, higher, broader, finer, and each in its turn vanished away; until now in these latter great days, our dreamers were in fancy housed, in a distant region, in a sumptuous vast palace which looked out from a leafy summit upon a noble prospect of vale and river and receding hills steeped in tinted mists—and all private, all the property of the dreamers; a palace swarming with liveried servants, and populous with guests of fame and power, hailing from all the world's capitals, foreign and domestic.

This palace was far, far away toward the rising sun, immeasurably remote, astronomically remote, in Newport, Rhode Island, Holy Land of High Society, ineffable Domain of the American Aristocracy. As a rule they spent a part of every Sabbath—after morning service—in this sumptuous home, the rest of it they spent in Europe, or in dawdling around in their private yacht. Six days of sordid and plodding fact life at home on the ragged edge of Lakeside and straitened means, the seventh in Fairyland—such had become their program and their habit.

In their sternly restricted fact life they remained as of old—plodding, diligent, careful, practical, economical. They stuck loyally to the little Presbyterian Church, and labored faithfully in its interests and stood by its high and tough doctrines with all their mental and spiritual energies. But in their dream life they obeyed the invitations of their fancies, whatever they might be, and howsoever the fancies might change. Aleck's fancies were not very capricious, and not frequent, but Sally's scattered a good deal. Aleck, in her dream life, went over to the Episcopal camp, on acount of its large official titles; next she became High-church on account of the candles and shows; and next she naturally changed to Rome, where there were cardinals and more candles. But these excursions were a nothing to Sally's. His dream life was a glowing and continuous and persistent excitement, and he kept every part of it fresh and sparkling by frequent changes, the religious part along with the rest. He worked his religions hard, and changed them with his shirt.

The liberal spendings of the Fosters upon their fancies began early in their prosperities, and grew in prodigality step by step with their advancing fortunes. In time they became truly enormous. Aleck built a university or two per Sunday; also a hospital or two; also a Rowton hotel or so; also a batch of churches; now and then a cathedral; and once, with untimely and ill-chosen playfulness, Sally said, "It was a cold day when she didn't ship a cargo of missionaries to persuade unreflecting Chinamen to trade off twenty-four carat Confucianism for counterfeit Christianity."

This rude and unfeeling language hurt Aleck to the heart, and she went from the presence crying. That spectacle went to his own heart, and in his pain and shame he would have given worlds to have those unkind words back. She had uttered no syllable of reproach—and that cut him. Not one suggestion that he look at his own record—and she could have made, oh, so many, and such blistering ones! Her generous silence brought a swift revenge, for it turned his thoughts upon himself, it summoned before him a spectral procession, a moving vision of his life as he had been leading it these past few years of limitless prosperity, and as he sat there reviewing it his cheeks burned and his soul was steeped in humiliation. Look at her life—how fair it was, and tending ever upward; and look at his own—how frivolous, how charged with mean vanities, how selfish, how empty, how ignoble! And its trend—never upward, but downward, ever downward!

He instituted comparisons between her record and his own. He had found fault with her—so he mused—*he!* And what could he say for himself? When she built her first church what was he doing? Gathering other blasé multimillionaires into a Poker Club; defiling his own palace with it; losing hundreds of thousands to it at every sitting, and sillily vain of the admiring notoriety it made for him. When she was building her first university, what was he doing? Polluting himself with a gay and dissipated secret life in the company of other fast bloods, multimillionaires in money and paupers in character. When she was building her first foundling asylum, what was he doing? Alas! When she was projecting her noble Society for the Purifying of the Sex, what was he doing? Ah, what, indeed! When she and the W.C.T.U. and the Woman with the Hatchet, moving with resistless march, were sweeping the fatal bottle from the land, what was he doing? Getting drunk three times a day. When she, builder of a hundred cathedrals, was being gratefully welcomed and blest in papal Rome and decorated with the Golden Rose which she had so honorably earned, what was he doing? Breaking the bank at Monte Carlo.

He stopped. He could go no further; he could not bear the rest. He rose up, with a great resolution upon his lips: this secret life should be revealed, and confessed; no longer would he live it clandestinely; he would go and tell her All.

And that is what he did. He told her All; and wept upon her bosom; wept, and moaned, and begged for her forgiveness. It was a profound shock, and she staggered under the blow, but he was her own, the core of her heart, the blessing of her eyes, her all in all, she could deny him nothing, and she forgave him. She felt that he could never again be quite to her what he had been before; she knew that he could only repent, and not reform; yet all morally defaced and decayed as he was, was he not her own, her very own, the idol of her deathless worship? She said she was his serf, his slave, and she opened her yearning heart and took him in.

7

One Sunday afternoon some time after this they were sailing the summer seas in their dream yacht, and reclining in lazy luxury under the awning of the after-deck. There was silence, for each was busy with his own thoughts. These seasons of silence had insensibly been growing more and more frequent of late; the old nearness and cordiality were waning. Sally's terrible revelation had done its work; Aleck had tried hard to drive the memory of it out of her mind, but it would not go, and the shame and bitterness of it were poisoning her gracious dream life. She could see now (on Sundays) that her husband was become a bloated and repulsive Thing. She could not close her eyes to this, and in these days she no longer looked at him, Sundays, when she could help it.

But she—was she herself without blemish? Alas, she knew she was not. She was keeping a secret from him, she was acting dishonorably toward him, and many a pang it was costing her. *She was breaking the compact, and concealing it from him.* Under strong temptation she had gone into business again; she had risked their whole fortune in a purchase of all the railway systems and coal and steel companies in the country on a margin, and she was now trembling, every Sabbath hour, lest through some chance word of hers he find it out. In her misery and remorse for this treachery she could not keep her heart from going out to him in pity; she was filled with compunctions to see him lying there, drunk and content, and never suspecting. Never suspecting—trusting her with a perfect and pathetic trust, and she holding over him by a thread a possible calamity of so devastating a—

"*Say*—Aleck?"

The interrupting words brought her suddenly to herself. She was grateful to have that persecuting subject from her thoughts, and she answered, with much of the old-time tenderness in her tone:

"Yes, dear."

"Do you know, Aleck, I think we are making a mistake—that is, you are. I mean about the marriage business." He sat up, fat and groggy and benevolent, like a bronze Buddha, and grew earnest. "Consider— it's more than five years. You've continued the same policy from the start: with every rise, always holding on for five points higher. Always when I think we are going to have some weddings, you see a bigger thing ahead, and I undergo another disappointment. *I* think you are too hard to please. Some day we'll get left. First, we turn down the dentist and the lawyer. That was all right—it was sound. Next, we turned down the banker's son and the pork-butcher's heir—right again, and sound. Next, we turned down the Congressman's son and the Governor's— right as a trivet, I confess it. Next the Senator's son and the son of the Vice-President of the United States—perfectly right, there's no permanency about those little distinctions. Then you went for the aristocracy; and I thought we had struck oil at last—yes. We would make a plunge at the Four Hundred, and pull in some ancient lineage, venerable, holy, ineffable, mellow with the antiquity of a hundred and fifty years, disinfected of the ancestral odors of salt-cod and pelts all of a century ago, and unsmirched by a day's work since; and then! why, then the marriages, of course. But no, along comes a pair of real aristocrats from Europe, and straightway you throw over the half-breeds. It was awfully discouraging, Aleck! Since then, what a procession! You turned down the baronets for a pair of barons; you turned down the barons for a pair of viscounts; the viscounts for a pair of earls; the earls for a pair of marquises; the marquises for a brace of dukes. *Now*, Aleck, cash in!— you've played the limit. You've got a job lot of four dukes under the hammer; of four nationalities; all sound in wind and limb and pedigree, all bankrupt and in debt up to the ears. They come high, but we can afford it. Come, Aleck, don't delay any longer, don't keep up the suspense: take the whole lay-out, and leave the girls to choose!"

Aleck had been smiling blandly and contentedly all through this arraignment of her marriage policy; a pleasant light, as of triumph with perhaps a nice surprise peeping out through it, rose in her eyes, and she said, as calmly as she could:

"Sally, what would you say to—*royalty?*"

Prodigious! Poor man, it knocked him silly, and he fell over the garboard strake and barked his shin on the catheads. He was dizzy for a moment, then he gathered himself up and limped over and sat down by his wife and beamed his old-time admiration and affection upon her in floods, out of his bleary eyes.

"By George!" he said, fervently, "Aleck, you *are* great—the greatest woman in the whole earth! I can't ever learn the whole size of you. I can't ever learn the immeasurable deeps of you. Here I've been considering myself qualified to criticize your game. *I!* Why, if I had stopped to think, I'd have known you had a lone hand up your sleeve. Now, dear, heart, I'm all red-hot impatience—tell me about it!"

The flattered and happy woman put her lips to his ear and whispered a princely name. It made him catch his breath, it lit his face with exultation.

"Land!" he said, "it's a stunning catch! He's got a gambling-hell, and a graveyard, and a bishop, and a cathedral—all his very own. And all gilt-edged five-hundred-per-cent stock, every detail of it; the tidiest little property in Europe. And that graveyard—it's the selectest in the world: none but suicides admitted; *yes*, sir, and the free-list suspended, too, *all* the time. There isn't much land in the principality, but there's enough: eight hundred acres in the graveyard and forty-two outside. It's a *sovereignty*—that's the main thing; *land's* nothing. There's plenty land, Sahara's drugged with it."

Aleck glowed; she was profoundly happy. She said:

"Think of it, Sally—it is a family that has never married outside the Royal and Imperial Houses of Europe; our grandchildren will sit upon thrones!"

"True as you live, Aleck—and bear scepters, too; and handle them as naturally and nonchalantly as I handle a yardstick. It's a grand catch, Aleck. He's corralled, is he? Can't get away? You didn't take him on a margin?"

"No. Trust me for that. He's not a liability, he's an asset. So is the other one."

"Who is it, Aleck?"

"His Royal Highness Sigismund-Siegfried-Lauenfeld-Dinkelspiel-Schwartzenberg Blutwurst, Hereditary Grand Duke of Katzenyammer."

"No! You can't mean it!"

"It's as true as I'm sitting here, I give you my word," she answered.

His cup was full, and he hugged her to his heart with rapture, saying:

"How wonderful it all seems, and how beautiful! It's one of the oldest and noblest of the three hundred and sixty-four ancient German principalities, and one of the few that was allowed to retain its royal estate when Bismarck got done trimming them. I know that farm, I've been there. It's got a rope-walk and a candle-factory and an army. Standing army. Infantry and cavalry. Three soldiers and a horse. Aleck, it's been a long wait, and full of heartbreak and hope deferred, but God knows I am happy now. Happy, and grateful to you, my own, who have done it all. When is it to be?"

"Next Sunday."

"Good. And we'll want to do these weddings up in the very regalest style that's going. It's properly due to the royal quality of the parties of the first part. Now as I understand it, there is only one kind of marriage that is sacred to royalty, exclusive to royalty: it's the morganatic."

"What do they call it that for, Sally?"

"I don't know; but anyway it's royal, and royal only."

"Then we will insist upon it. More—I will compel it. It is morganatic marriage or none."

"That settles it!" said Sally, rubbing his hands with delight. "And it will be the very first in America. Aleck, it will make Newport sick."

Then they fell silent, and drifted away upon their dream wings to the far regions of the earth to invite all the crowned heads and their families and provide gratis transportation for them.

8

During three days the couple walked upon air, with their heads in the clouds. They were but vaguely conscious of their surroundings; they saw all things dimly, as through a veil; they were steeped in dreams, often they did not hear when they were spoken to; they often did not understand when they heard; they answered confusedly or at random; Sally sold molasses by weight, sugar by the yard, and furnished soap when asked for candles, and Aleck put the cat in the wash and fed milk to the soiled linen. Everybody was stunned and amazed, and went about muttering, "What *can* be the matter with the Fosters?"

Three days. Then came events! Things had taken a happy turn, and for forty-eight hours Aleck's imaginary corner had been booming. Up —up—still up! Cost point was passed. Still up—and up—and up! Five points above cost—then ten—fifteen—twenty! Twenty points cold profit on the vast venture, now, and Aleck's imaginary brokers were shouting frantically by imaginary long-distance, "Sell! sell! for Heaven's sake sell!"

She broke the splendid news to Sally, and he, too, said, "Sell! sell —oh, don't make a blunder, now, you own the earth!—sell, sell!" But she set her iron will and lashed it amidships, and said she would hold on for five points more if she died for it.

It was a fatal resolve. The very next day came the historic crash, the record crash, the devastating crash, when the bottom fell out of Wall Street, and the whole body of gilt-edged stocks dropped ninety-five points in five hours, and the multi-millionaire was seen begging his bread in the Bowery. Aleck sternly held her grip and "put up" as long as she could, but at last there came a call which she was powerless to meet, and her imaginary brokers sold her out. Then, and not till then, the man in her was vanished, and the woman in her resumed sway. She put her arms about her husband's neck and wept, saying:

"I am to blame, do not forgive me, I cannot bear it. We are paupers! Paupers, and I am so miserable. The weddings will never come off; all that is past; we could not even buy the dentist, now."

A bitter reproach was on Sally's tongue: "I *begged* you to sell, but you—" He did not say it; he had not the heart to add a hurt to that broken and repentant spirit. A nobler thought came to him and he said:

"Bear up, my Aleck, all is not lost! You really never invested a penny of my uncle's bequest, but only its unmaterialized future; what we have lost was only the increment harvested from that future by your incomparable financial judgment and sagacity. Cheer up, banish these griefs; we still have the thirty thousand untouched; and with the experience which you have acquired, think what you will be able to do with it in a couple of years! The marriages are not off, they are only postponed."

These were blessed words. Aleck saw how true they were, and their influence was electric; her tears ceased to flow, and her great spirit rose to its full stature again. With flashing eye and grateful heart, and with hand uplifted in pledge and prophecy, she said:

"Now and here I proclaim—"

But she was interrupted by a visitor. It was the editor and proprietor of the *Sagamore*. He had happened into Lakeside to pay a duty-call upon an obscure grandmother of his who was nearing the end of her pilgrimage, and with the idea of combining business with grief he had looked up the Fosters, who had been so absorbed in other things for the past four years that they had neglected to pay up their subscription. Six dollars due. No visitor could have been more welcome. He would know all about Uncle Tilbury and what his chances might be getting to be, cemeterywards. They could, of course, ask no questions, for that would squelch the bequest, but they could nibble around on the edge of the subject and hope for results. The scheme did not work. The obtuse editor did not know he was being nibbled at; but at last, chance accomplished what art had failed in. In illustration of something under discussion which required the help of metaphor, the editor said:

"Land, it's as tough as Tilbury Foster!—as *we* say."

It was sudden, and it made the Fosters jump. The editor noticed it, and said, apologetically:

"No harm intended, I assure you. It's just a saying; just a joke, you know—nothing in it. Relation of yours?"

Sally crowded his burning eagerness down, and answered with all the indifference he could assume:

"I—well, not that I know of, but we've heard of him." The editor was thankful, and resumed his composure. Sally added: "Is he—is he —well?"

"Is he *well?* Why, bless you he's in Sheol these five years!"

The Fosters were trembling with grief, though it felt like joy. Sally said, non-committally—and tentatively:

"Ah, well, such is life, and none can escape—not even the rich are spared."

The editor laughed.

"If you are including Tilbury," he said, "it don't apply. *He* hadn't a cent; the town had to bury him."

The Fosters sat petrified for two minutes; petrified and cold. Then, white-faced and weak-voiced, Sally asked:

"Is it true? Do you *know* it to be true?"

"Well, I should say! I was one of the executors. He hadn't anything to leave but a wheelbarrow, and he left that to me. It hadn't any wheel, and wasn't any good. Still, it was something, and so, to square up, I scribbled off a sort of a little obituarial send-off for him, but it got crowded out."

The Fosters were not listening—their cup was full, it could contain no more. They sat with bowed heads, dead to all things but the ache at their hearts.

An hour later. Still they sat there, bowed, motionless, silent, the visitor long ago gone, they unaware.

Then they stirred, and lifted their heads wearily, and gazed at each other wistfully, dreamily, dazed; then presently began to twaddle to each other in a wandering and childish way. At intervals they lapsed into silences, leaving a sentence unfinished, seemingly either unaware of it or losing their way. Sometimes, when they woke out of these silences they had a dim and transient consciousness that something had happened to their minds; then with a dumb and yearning solicitude they would softly caress each other's hands in mutual compassion and support, as if they would say: "I am near you, I will not forsake you, we will bear it together; somewhere there is release and forgetfulness, somewhere there is a grave and peace; be patient, it will not be long."

They lived yet two years, in mental night, always brooding, steeped in vague regrets and melancholy dreams, never speaking; then release came to both on the same day.

Toward the end the darkness lifted from Sally's ruined mind for a moment, and he said:

"Vast wealth, acquired by sudden and unwholesome means, is a snare. It did us no good, transient were its feverish pleasures; yet for its sake we threw away our sweet and simple and happy life—let others take warning by us."

He lay silent awhile, with closed eyes; then as the chill of death crept upward toward his heart, and consciousness was facing from his brain, he muttered:

"Money had brought him misery, and he took his revenge upon us, who had done him no harm. He had his desire: with base and cunning calculation he left us but thirty thousand, knowing we would try to increase it, and ruin our life and break our hearts. Without added expense he could have left us far above desire of increase, far above the temptation to speculate, and a kinder soul would have done it; but in him was no generous spirit, no pity, no—"

1904

EUDORA WELTY

Why I Live at the P.O.

I was getting along fine with Mama, Papa-Daddy, and Uncle Rondo until my sister Stella-Rondo just separated from her husband and came back home again. Mr. Whitaker! Of course I went with Mr. Whitaker first, when he first appeared here in China Grove, taking "Pose Yourself" photos, and Stella-Rondo broke us up. Told him I was one-sided. Bigger on one side than the other, which is a deliberate, calculated falsehood: I'm the same. Stella-Rondo is exactly twelve months to the day younger than I am and for that reason she's spoiled.

She's always had anything in the world she wanted and then she'd throw it away. Papa-Daddy give her this gorgeous Add-a-Pearl necklace when she was eight years old and she threw it away playing baseball when she was nine, with only two pearls.

So as soon as she got married and moved away from home the first thing she did was separate! From Mr. Whitaker! This photographer with the popeyes she said she trusted. Came home from one of those towns up in Illinois and to our complete surprise brought this child of two.

Mama said she like to make her drop dead for a second. "Here you had this marvelous blonde child and never so much as wrote your mother a word about it," says Mama. "I'm thoroughly ashamed of you." But of course she wasn't.

Stella-Rondo just calmly takes off this *hat*, I wish you could see it. She says, "Why, Mama, Shirley-T.'s adopted, I can prove it."

"How?" says Mama, but all I says was, "H'm!" There I was over the hot stove, trying to stretch two chickens over five people and a completely unexpected child into the bargain without one moment's notice.

Novelist and short-story writer Eudora Welty is best known for her poignant and detailed accounts of the regional manners and customs of the Mississippi Delta and the town of Jackson, where she was born in 1909. After attending Mississippi State College for Women, Welty started her writing career at both a local newspaper and a radio station, even acting as a publicity agent for the Works Progress Administration (WPA). The readership for her short stories grew, however, with the publication of such works as the collection *A Curtain of Green* (1941) and the 1946 novel *Delta Wedding*. She won the O. Henry Award in both 1942 and 1943 for her sketches of southern life. Welty continues to live and write in Mississippi.

"What do you mean—'H'm'?" says Stella-Rondo, and Mama says, "I heard that, Sister."

I said that oh, I didn't mean a thing, only that whoever Shirley-T. was, she was the spit-image of Papa-Daddy if he'd cut off his beard, which of course he'd never do in the world. Papa-Daddy's Mama's papa and sulks.

Stella-Rondo got furious! She said, "Sister, I don't need to tell you you got a lot of nerve and always did have and I'll thank you to make no future reference to my adopted child whatsoever."

"Very well," I said. "Very well, very well. Of course I noticed at once she looks like Mr. Whitaker's side too. That frown. She looks like a cross between Mr. Whitaker and Papa-Daddy."

"Well, all I can say is she isn't."

"She looks exactly like Shirley Temple to me," says Mama, but Shirley-T. just ran away from her.

So the first thing Stella-Rondo did at the table was turn Papa-Daddy against me.

"Papa-Daddy," she says. He was trying to cut up his meat. "Papa-Daddy!" I was taken completely by surprise. Papa-Daddy is about a million years old and's got this long-long beard. "Papa-Daddy, Sister says she fails to understand why you don't cut off your beard."

So Papa-Daddy l-a-y-s down his knife and fork! He's real rich. Mama says he is, he says he isn't. So he says, "Have I heard correctly? You don't understand why I don't cut off my beard?"

"Why," I says, "Papa-Daddy, of course I understand, I did not say any such a thing, the idea!"

He says, "Hussy!"

I says, "Papa-Daddy, you know I wouldn't any more want you to cut off your beard than the man in the moon. It was the farthest thing from my mind! Stella-Rondo sat there and made that up while she was eating breast of chicken."

But he says, "So the postmistress fails to understand why I don't cut off my beard. Which job I got you through my influence with the government. 'Bird's nest'—is that what you call it?"

Not that it isn't the next to smallest P.O. in the entire state of Mississippi.

I says, "Oh, Papa-Daddy," I says, "I didn't say any such a thing, I never dreamed it was a bird's nest, I have always been grateful though this is the next to smallest P.O. in the state of Mississippi, and I do not enjoy being referred to as a hussy by my own grandfather."

But Stella-Rondo says, "Yes, you did say it too. Anybody in the world could of heard you, that had ears."

"Stop right there," says Mama, looking at *me*.

So I pulled my napkin straight back through the napkin ring and left the table.

As soon as I was out of the room Mama says, "Call her back, or she'll starve to death," but Papa-Daddy says, "This is the beard I started growing on the Coast when I was fifteen years old." He would of gone on till nightfall if Shirley-T. hadn't lost the Milky Way she ate in Cairo.

So Papa-Daddy says, "I am going out and lie in the hammock, and you can all sit here and remember my words: I'll never cut off my beard as long as I live, even one inch, and I don't appreciate it in you at all." Passed right by me in the hall and went straight out and got in the hammock.

It would be a holiday. It wasn't five minutes before Uncle Rondo suddenly appeared in the hall in one of Stella-Rondo's flesh-colored kimonos, all cut on the bias, like something Mr. Whitaker probably thought was gorgeous.

"Uncle Rondo!" I says. "I didn't know who that was! Where are you going?"

"Sister," he says, "get out of my way, I'm poisoned."

"If you're poisoned stay away from Papa-Daddy," I says. "Keep out of the hammock. Papa-Daddy will certainly beat you on the head if you come within forty miles of him. He thinks I deliberately said he ought to cut off his beard after he got me the P.O., and I've told him and told him and told him, and he acts like he just don't hear me. Papa-Daddy must of gone stone deaf."

"He picked a fine day to do it then," says Uncle Rondo, and before you could say "Jack Robinson" flew out in the yard.

What he'd really done, he'd drunk another bottle of that prescription. He does it every single Fourth of July as sure as shooting, and it's horribly expensive. Then he falls over in the hammock and snores. So he insisted on zigzagging right on out to the hammock, looking like a half-wit.

Papa-Daddy woke up with this horrible yell and right there without moving an inch he tried to turn Uncle Rondo against me. I heard every word he said. Oh, he told Uncle Rondo I didn't learn to read till I was eight years old and he didn't see how in the world I ever got the mail put up at the P.O., much less read it all, and he said if Uncle Rondo could only fathom the lengths he had gone to get me that job! And he said on the other hand he thought Stella-Rondo had a brilliant mind and deserved credit for getting out of town. All the time he was just lying there swinging as pretty as you please and looping out his beard, and poor Uncle Rondo was *pleading* with him to slow down the hammock, it was making him as dizzy as a witch to watch it. But that's what Papa-Daddy likes about a hammock. So Uncle Rondo was too dizzy to get turned against me for the time being. He's Mama's only brother and is a good case of a one-track mind. Ask anybody. A certified pharmacist.

Just then I heard Stella-Rondo raising the upstairs window. While she was married she got this peculiar idea that it's cooler with the windows shut and locked. So she has to raise the window before she can make a soul hear her outdoors.

So she raises the window and says, "*Oh!*" You would have thought she was mortally wounded.

Uncle Rondo and Papa-Daddy didn't even look up, but kept right on with what they were doing. I had to laugh.

I flew up the stairs and threw the door open! I says, "What in the wide world's the matter, Stella-Rondo? You mortally wounded?"

"No," she says, "I am not mortally wounded but I wish you would do me the favor of looking out that window there and telling me what you see."

So I shade my eyes and look out the window.

"I see the front yard," I says.

"Don't you see any human beings?"

"I see Uncle Rondo trying to run Papa-Daddy out of the hammock," I says. "Nothing more. Naturally, it's so suffocating-hot in the house, with all the windows shut and locked, everybody who cares to stay in their right mind will have to go out and get in the hammock before the Fourth of July is over."

"Don't you notice anything different about Uncle Rondo?" asks Stella-Rondo.

"Why, no, except he's got on some terrible-looking flesh-colored contraption I wouldn't be found dead in, is all I can see," I says.

"Never mind, you won't be found dead in it, because it happens to be part of my trousseau, and Mr. Whitaker took several dozen photographs of me in it," says Stella-Rondo. "What on earth could Uncle Rondo *mean* by wearing part of my trousseau out in the broad open daylight without saying so much as 'Kiss my foot,' *knowing* I only got home this morning after my separation and hung my negligee up on the bathroom door, just as nervous as I could be?"

"I'm sure I don't know, and what do you expect me to do about it?" I says. "Jump out the window?"

"No, I expect nothing of the kind. I simply declare that Uncle Rondo looks like a fool in it, that's all," she says. "It makes me sick to my stomach."

"Well, he looks as good as he can," I says. "As good as anybody in reason could." I stood up for Uncle Rondo, please remember. And I said to Stella-Rondo, "I think I would do well not to criticize so freely if I were you and came home with a two-year-old child I had never said a word about, and no explanation whatever about my separation."

"I asked you the instant I entered this house not to refer one more time to my adopted child, and you gave me your word of honor you would not," was all Stella-Rondo would say, and started pulling out every one of her eyebrows with some cheap Kress tweezers.

So I merely slammed the door behind me and went down and made some green-tomato pickle. Somebody had to do it. Of course Mama had turned both the niggers loose; she always said no earthly power could hold one anyway on the Fourth of July, so she wouldn't even try. It turned out that Jaypan fell in the lake and came within a very narrow limit of drowning.

So Mama trots in. Lifts up the lid and says, "H'm! Not very good for your Uncle Rondo in his precarious condition, I must say. Or poor little adopted Shirley-T. Shame on you!"

That made me tired. I says, "Well, Stella-Rondo had better thank her lucky stars it was her instead of me came trotting in with that very peculiar-looking child. Now if it had been me that trotted in from Illinois and brought a peculiar-looking child or two, I shudder to think of the reception I'd of got, much less controlled the diet of an entire family."

"But you must remember, Sister, that you were never married to Mr. Whitaker in the first place and didn't go up to Illinois to live," says Mama, shaking a spoon in my face. "If you had I would of been just as overjoyed to see you and your little adopted girl as I was to see Stella-Rondo, when you wound up with your separation and came on back home."

"You would not," I says.

"Don't contradict me, I would," says Mama.

But I said she couldn't convince me though she talked till she was blue in the face. Then I said, "Besides, you know as well as I do that that child is not adopted."

"She most certainly is adopted," says Mama, stiff as a poker.

I says, "Why, Mama, Stella-Rondo had her just as sure as anything in this world, and just too stuck up to admit it."

"Why, Sister," said Mama. "Here I thought we were going to have a pleasant Fourth of July, and you start right out not believing a word your own baby sister tells you!"

"Just like Cousin Annie Flo. Went to her grave denying the facts of life," I remind Mama.

"I told you if you ever mentioned Annie Flo's name I'd slap your face," says Mama, and slaps my face.

"All right, you wait and see," I says.

"I," says Mama, "*I* prefer to take my children's word for anything when it's humanly possible." You ought to see Mama, she weighs two hundred pounds and has real tiny feet.

Just then something perfectly horrible occurred to me.

"Mama," I says, "can that child talk?" I simply had to whisper! "Mama, I wonder if that child can be—you know—in any way? Do you realize?" I says, "that she hasn't spoken one single, solitary word to a human being up to this minute? This is the way she looks," I says, and I looked like this.

Well, Mama and I just stood there and stared at each other. It was horrible!

"I remember well that Joe Whitaker frequently drank like a fish," says Mama. "I believed to my soul he drank *chemicals.*" And without another word she marches to the foot of the stairs and calls Stella-Rondo.

"Stella-Rondo? O-o-o-o-o! Stella-Rondo!"

"What?" says Stella-Rondo from upstairs. Not even the grace to get up off the bed.

"Can that child of yours talk?" asks Mama.

Stella-Rondo says, "Can she what?"

"Talk! Talk!" says Mama. "Burdyburdyburdyburdy!"

So Stella-Rondo yells back, "Who says she can't talk?"

"Sister says so," says Mama.

"You didn't have to tell me, I know whose word of honor don't mean a thing in this house," says Stella-Rondo.

And in a minute the loudest Yankee voice I ever heard in my life yells out, "OE'm Pop-OE the Sailor-r-r Ma-a-an!" and then somebody jumps up and down in the upstairs hall. In another second the house would of fallen down.

"Not only talks, she can tap-dance!" calls Stella-Rondo. "Which is more than some people I won't name can do."

"Why, the little precious darling thing!" Mama says, so surprised. "Just as smart as she can be!" Starts talking baby talk right there. Then she turns on me. "Sister, you ought to be thoroughly ashamed! Run upstairs this instant and apologize to Stella-Rondo and Shirley-T."

"Apologize for what?" I says. "I merely wondered if the child was normal, that's all. Now that she's proved she is, why, I have nothing further to say."

But Mama just turned on her heel and flew out, furious. She ran right upstairs and hugged the baby. She believed it was adopted. Stella-Rondo hadn't done a thing but turn her against me from upstairs while I stood there helpless over the hot stove. So that made Mama, Papa-Daddy, and the baby all on Stella-Rondo's side.

Next, Uncle Rondo.

I must say that Uncle Rondo has been marvelous to me at various times in the past and I was completely unprepared to be made to jump out of my skin, the way it turned out. Once Stella-Rondo did something perfectly horrible to him—broke a chain letter from Flanders Field—and he took the radio back he had given her and gave it to me. Stella-Rondo was furious! For six months we all had to call her Stella instead of Stella-Rondo, or she wouldn't answer. I always thought Uncle Rondo had all the brains of the entire family. Another time he sent me to Mammoth Cave with all expenses paid.

But this would be the day he was drinking that prescription, the Fourth of July.

So at supper Stella-Rondo speaks up and says she thinks Uncle Rondo ought to try to eat a little something. So finally Uncle Rondo said he would try a little cold biscuits and ketchup, but that was all. So *she* brought it to him.

"Do you think it wise to disport with ketchup in Stella-Rondo's flesh-colored kimono?" I says. Trying to be considerate! If Stella-Rondo couldn't watch out for her trousseau, somebody had to.

"Any objections?" asks Uncle Rondo, just about to pour out all of the ketchup.

"Don't mind what she says, Uncle Rondo," says Stella-Rondo. "Sister has been devoting this solid afternoon to sneering out my bedroom window at the way you look."

"What's that?" says Uncle Rondo. Uncle Rondo has got the most terrible temper in the world. Anything is liable to make him tear the house down if it comes at the wrong time.

So Stella-Rondo says, "Sister says, 'Uncle Rondo certainly does look like a fool in that pink kimono!'"

Do you remember who it was really said that?

Uncle Rondo spills out all the ketchup and jumps out of his chair and tears off the kimono and throws it down on the dirty floor and puts his foot on it. It had to be sent all the way to Jackson to the cleaners and repleated.

"So that's your opinion of your Uncle Rondo, is it?" he says. "I look like a fool, do I? Well, that's the last straw. A whole day in this house with nothing to do, and then to hear you come out with a remark like that behind my back!"

"I didn't say any such a thing, Uncle Rondo," I says, "and I'm not saying who did, either. Why, I think you look all right. Just try to take care of yourself and not talk and eat at the same time," I says. "I think you better go lie down."

"Lie down my foot," says Uncle Rondo. I ought to of known by that he was fixing to do something perfectly horrible.

So he didn't do anything that night in the precarious state he was in—just played Casino with Mama and Stella-Rondo and Shirley-T. and gave Shirley-T. a nickel with a head on both sides. It tickled her nearly to death, and she called him "Papa." But at 6:30 A.M. the next morning, he threw a whole five-cent package of some unsold one-inch firecrackers from the store as hard as he could into my bedroom and they every one went off. Not one bad one in the string. Anybody else, there'd be one that wouldn't go off.

Well, I'm just terrible susceptible to noise of any kind, the doctor has always told me I was the most sensitive person he had ever seen in his whole life, and I was simply prostrated. I couldn't eat! People tell me they heard it as far as the cemetery, and old Aunt Jep Patterson, that had been holding her own so good, thought it was Judgment Day and she was going to meet her whole family. It's usually so quiet here.

And I'll tell you it didn't take me any longer than a minute to make up my mind what to do. There I was with the whole entire house on Stella-Rondo's side and turned against me. If I have anything at all I have pride.

So I just decided I'd go straight down to the P.O. There's plenty of room there in the back, I says to myself.

Well! I made no bones about letting the family catch on to what I was up to. I didn't try to conceal it.

The first thing they knew, I marched in where they were all playing Old Maid and pulled the electric oscillating fan out by the plug, and everything got real hot. Next I snatched the pillow I'd done the needlepoint on right off the davenport from behind Papa-Daddy. He went "Ugh!" I beat Stella-Rondo up the stairs and finally found my charm bracelet in her bureau drawer under a picture of Nelson Eddy.

"So that's the way the land lies," says Uncle Rondo. There he was, piecing on the ham. "Well, Sister, I'll be glad to donate my army cot if you got any place to set it up, providing you'll leave right this minute and let me get some peace." Uncle Rondo was in France.

"Thank you kindly for the cot and 'peace' is hardly the word I would select if I had to resort to firecrackers at 6:30 A.M. in a young girl's bedroom," I says to him. "And as to where I intend to go, you seem to forget my position as postmistress of China Grove, Mississippi," I says. "I've always got the P.O."

Well, that made them all sit up and take notice.

I went out front and started digging up some four-o'clocks to plant around the P.O.

"Ah-ah-ah!" says Mama, raising the window. "Those happen to be my four-o'clocks. Everything planted in that star is mine. I've never known you to make anything grow in your life."

"Very well," I says. "But I take the fern. Even you, Mama, can't stand there and deny that I'm the one watered that fern. And I happen to know where I can send in a box top and get a packet of one thousand mixed seeds, no two the same kind, free."

"Oh, where?" Mama wants to know.

But I says, "Too late. You 'tend to your house, and I'll 'tend to mine. You hear things like that all the time if you know how to listen to the radio. Perfectly marvelous offers. Get anything you want free."

So I hope to tell you I marched in and got that radio, and they could of all bit a nail in two, especially Stella-Rondo, that it used to belong to, and she well knew she couldn't get it back, I'd sue for it like a shot. And I very politely took the sewing-machine motor I helped pay the most on to give Mama for Christmas back in 1929, and a good big calendar, with the first-aid remedies on it. The thermometer and the Hawaiian ukulele certainly were rightfully mine, and I stood on the step-ladder and got all my watermelon-rind preserves and every fruit and vegetable I'd put up, every jar. Then I began to pull the tacks out of the bluebird wall vases on the archway to the dining room.

"Who told you you could have those, Miss Priss?" says Mama, fanning as hard as she could.

"I bought 'em and I'll keep track of 'em," I says. "I'll tack 'em up one on each side of the post-office window, and you can see 'em when you come to ask me for your mail, if you're so dead to see 'em."

"Not I! I'll never darken the door to that post office again if I live to be a hundred," Mama says. "Ungrateful child! After all the money we spent on you at the Normal."

"Me either," says Stella-Rondo. "You can just let my mail lie there and *rot*, for all I care. I'll never come and relieve you of a single, solitary piece."

"I should worry," I says. "And who you think's going to sit down and write you all those big fat letters and postcards, by the way? Mr. Whitaker? Just because he was the only man ever dropped down in China Grove and you got him—unfairly—is he going to sit down and write you a lengthy correspondence after you come home giving no rhyme nor reason whatsoever for your separation and no explanation for the presence of that child? I may not have your brilliant mind, but I fail to see it."

So Mama says, "Sister, I've told you a thousand times that Stella-Rondo simply got homesick, and this child is far too big to be hers," and she says, "Now, why don't you just sit down and play Casino?"

Then Shirley-T. sticks out her tongue at me in this perfectly horrible way. She has no more manners than the man in the moon. I told her she was going to cross her eyes like that some day and they'd stick.

"It's too late to stop me now," I says. "You should have tried that yesterday. I'm going to the P.O. and the only way you can possibly see me is to visit me there."

So Papa-Daddy says, "You'll never catch me setting foot in that post office, even if I should take a notion into my head to write a letter some place." He says, "I won't have you reachin' out of that little old window with a pair of shears and cuttin' off any beard of mine. I'm too smart for you!"

"We all are," says Stella-Rondo.

But I said, "If you're so smart, where's Mr. Whitaker?"

So then Uncle Rondo says, "I'll thank you from now on to stop reading all the orders I get on postcards and telling everybody in China Grove what you think is the matter with them," but I says, "I draw my own conclusions and will continue in the future to draw them." I says, "If people want to write their innermost secrets on penny postcards, there's nothing in the wide world you can do about it, Uncle Rondo."

"And if you think we'll ever *write* another postcard you're sadly mistaken," says Mama.

"Cutting off your nose to spite your face then," I says. "But if you're all determined to have no more to do with the U.S. mail, think of this: What will Stella-Rondo do now, if she wants to tell Mr. Whitaker to come after her?"

"Wah!" says Stella-Rondo. I knew she'd cry. She had a conniption fit right there in the kitchen.

"It will be interesting to see how long she holds out," I says. "And now—I am leaving."

"Good-bye," says Uncle Rondo.

"Oh, I declare," says Mama, "to think that a family of mine should quarrel on the Fourth of July, or the day after, over Stella-Rondo leaving old Mr. Whitaker and having the sweetest little adopted child! It looks like we'd all be glad!"

"Wah!" says Stella-Rondo, and has a fresh conniption fit.

"*He* left *her*—you mark my words," I says. "That's Mr. Whitaker. I know Mr. Whitaker. After all, I knew him first. I said from the beginning he'd up and leave her. I foretold every single thing that's happened."

"Where did he go?" asks Mama.

"Probably to the North Pole, if he knows what's good for him," I says.

But Stella-Rondo just bawled and wouldn't say another word. She flew to her room and slammed the door.

"Now look what you've gone and done, Sister," says Mama. "You go apologize."

"I haven't the time, I'm leaving," I says.

"Well, what are you waiting around for?" asks Uncle Rondo.

So I just picked up the kitchen clock and marched off, without saying "Kiss my foot," or anything, and never did tell Stella-Rondo good-bye.

There was a nigger girl going along on a little wagon right in front.

"Nigger girl," I says, "come help me haul these things down the hill, I'm going to live in the post office."

Took her nine trips in her express wagon. Uncle Rondo came out on the porch and threw her a nickel.

And that's the last I've laid eyes on any of my family or my family laid eyes on me for five solid days and nights. Stella-Rondo may be telling the most horrible tales in the world about Mr. Whitaker, but I haven't heard them. As I tell everybody, I draw my own conclusions.

But oh, I like it here. It's ideal, as I've been saying. You see, I've got everything cater-cornered, the way I like it. Hear the radio? All the war news. Radio, sewing machine, book ends, ironing board and that great big piano lamp—peace, that's what I like. Butter-bean vines planted all along the front where the strings are.

Of course, there's not much mail. My family are naturally the main people in China Grove, and if they prefer to vanish from the face of the earth, for all the mail they get or the mail they write, why, I'm not going to open my mouth. Some of the folks here in town are taking up for me and some turned against me. I know which is which. There are always people who will quit buying stamps just to get on the right side of Papa-Daddy.

But here I am, and here I'll stay. I want the world to know I'm happy.

And if Stella-Rondo should come to me this minute, on bended knees, and attempt to explain the incidents of her life with Mr. Whitaker, I'd simply put my fingers in both my ears and refuse to listen.

1941

WILLIAM GOYEN

Tapioca Surprise

Before the rainstorm broke on the little town that unusual autumn afternoon, the whole world seemed to turn apple green, as if it were sick, and not a thing stirred, no leaf or limb or anything. And then, in the green stillness that was like the sick town holding its breath, there descended upon the telephone wires in front of Opal Ducharm's house a flock of blackbirds to sit all in a quiet row there. "Blackbirds at even', misery and grievin'," Mrs. Ducharm recited at her window, where she happened to be to watch Mrs. Sangley across the street. Rentha Sangley had just appeared on her porch with her head and face swaddled in an ostentatious bandage, so that she looked like some nun, and she was sweeping the leaves in the still moment before the storm would break. The whole town seemed to be waiting, except Rentha Sangley, who was showing off her bandage to the neighborhood to try to get sympathy.

And then it turned very dark and a little wind started and Mrs. Ducharm saw Rentha Sangley go in her house. The blackbirds flurried and broke their pattern, and they left the telephone wire swinging. The leaves, some of them big and tough as hides, began rolling and flying; and one leaf rushed in through the door Mrs. Opal Ducharm opened, and lay still on her rug. She slammed the door and stared at the leaf and recited, sensitive to omens, "Leaf on the floor, trouble galore . . ." and picked up the leaf.

Now big raindrops slapped on the sidewalks, and right away there was a steady colorless pour. This meant, without one doubt, that the Paradisers—of which Opal Ducharm was President—could not meet on the high school football field to practice their special number. And that they would have to miss another time of practicing for when the Grand Paradiser, Hester Shrift, would come next week to review the performance of their Fife and Drum Corps that was so renowned

Novelist and short-story writer, playwright and critical essayist, William Goyen was born in 1915 in Trinity, Texas. It was in this state that he set the action of his psychologically charged first novel, *House of Breath* (1950). During the 1960s, Goyen frequently associated with the playwrights' unit of the Actors Studio, sometimes writing original works and other times helping to adapt his own prose fiction for the stage. He is probably best remembered, though, for his short stories, which merited the O. Henry Award in 1976. Goyen died of leukemia in Los Angeles in 1983.

throughout the very state . . . and because of her, since she had organized and trained Paradisers all over the country. "You blackbirds, you leaf. This is what you were telling me, and maybe even more," Opal Ducharm said, going right to her phone. She did have a feeling of everything all wrong and ominous, the way she sometimes did.

She tried her phone again. No, it still would not work! But thank goodness Maudie Rickett had called in time—she was the last to get through before the phone had gone deaf on the other end, when the sky had first begun to gather and threaten. "Maudie," Opal had said, "We'll all come on, in spite of if it rains, to my house and see what we can drum up—socially. It's necessary to the morale of the organization to *assemble*—in *some* way—despite *natural* interferences. You call your list and tell it of the change." And then she had started calling her list —for even the President had a list—when of all things this deafness smote the other end of her phone. She couldn't get a person to answer, no one said a thing. Now how could that be? Then she tried, hung up and tried again, but she could never get anyone, not even Central.

Of all times to have this unusual thing happen to the phone! She would just have to run across to Rentha Sangley's and use her phone. This would also be an excellent chance to find out the meaning of her big bandage, what kind of accident or trouble had beset her *this* time. She ran through rain and flying leaves and knocked on Rentha Sangley's door, using not her knuckles but the special knocker that was a woodpecker carved by Mr. Sangley before he passed.

Rentha Sangley appeared. It seemed her eyes were the only unbandaged thing left upon her face. "I saw your bandage from my window, and *what* happened to you, your poor thing?" But before Mrs. Sangley could get a word out edgewise through the wrappings, Opal Ducharm put first things first and said, "Rentha, honey, could I use your phone in an emergency?"

"It was a little cyst," Rentha said, showing Opal the phone. "I could have had bloodpoison or a cancer, and lucky to have neither." She walked painfully but proudly under the burden of the bandage, almost as if she were wearing a new big hat. "Dr. Post cut it out yesterday, using a little chloroform on me."

But Opal Ducharm already had Central on the phone and she was explaining the crazy condition of her phone—which was more serious than any cyst cut out. "I'll run right home, honey," she said to the telephone operator, whom she knew personally. "I'm across the street at Rentha Sangley's and you try ringing me at home. This is an emergency."

"I do hope you'll be healed up soon, Rentha," Opal commiserated, and went for the door. "I have to hurry now to my phone."

"Oh I'll be all right," she said, weakly and with a pained face. And then she bellowed towards the kitchen, "Grandma Sangley you stay out of my hard sauce!"

"How is Grandma Sangley?" Opal Ducharm asked, opening the door.

"Into everything. And me encumbered like this . . ."

But Opal was already running down the steps and out into the rain. I just hope all the ladies will know not to go to the football field but to come to my house, she said to herself, running.

As she opened her door she heard the thrilling sound of her phone ringing. This must be the operator. She ran and answered, but there was nothing. Opal Ducharm said hello again. Still no response from the other end. Yet there was the feeling of somebody there, like somebody hiding in a house and not answering your call. What a kind of a phone to have! she declared. And today of all days. Then she said into the phone:

"Now honey, don't you say a word because I can't hear you, you'll be just wasting your sweet breath. You may be that little operator I just talked to over at Rentha Sangley's phone but I can't tell, I mean how could I?; and you may be a Paradiser and if you are, then this phone is broken on your end, I don't know why, but just listen to me, this is for *you*. This is Opal Ducharm, President of the Paradisers, Unit No. 22, as you know, and since it's just pouring down bullfrogs, as you *know*, we cannot practice for our special performance for the Grand Paradiser Hester Shrift at the high school football field but will convene at my house for a get-together instead. Don't talk, don't talk! I can hear your little clicking but don't try to talk, honey, because I can't hear you. Just listen to me. We have to *postpone* because of this downpour. Just come on straight to my house instead of to the football field. *And call your list.* do you hear? *Call your list* and tell it of the change." She waited, but there was not a sound, not even the little clicking, and so she banged down the receiver and was so unnerved she wanted to cry. But the phone rang again, and again there was no sound. She went through her speech again. This happened over and over, and each time she told again the story of the meeting at her house until she was hoarse. I just hope some word has got through to the Paradisers, she said.

To calm herself and to forget her anxiety, she stood at the door and called Sister, her sweet cat. Sister arrived miraculously, the way she always did, out of silence and nowhere, tail high in the air, and brushing against everything, dawdling to torment Opal. She seized her and squeezed her harder than she meant, until Sister's claws came out of her; and then she kissed Sister's purple ears. She sat down with her and felt a claw in her thigh. "Why sweet Sister," she said, "you act like you despise me." And then she spoke a long whispered confidence to her and felt the claw loosen. Opal was hungry. But she would wait for the Tapioca. Still, at this moment, she did not know which she loved more: Tapioca or Sister.

And then it was four o'clock and time for the meeting—and rain rain rain.

But the usually expert machinery of the list-calling did not work so smoothly and everyone was confused. There was some women at the football field, drenched in the rain, and some no place at all, so far as the callers could make out, for no one answered any place that was called. The result was only a fragment of Paradisers at Opal Ducharm's house, twelve women out of twenty-eight . . . two lonely squads. "We'll just have a little social," Opal Ducharm said, trying to make the most of a bad situation—which was one of the tenets of the Paradisers—for they had a whole philosophy of life; they did not just blow fife and beat drum. "Anyway I *feel* like a relaxin' social," Opal said. "But one word," she added. "Be sure to get your dresses in shape. We will all, of course, wear our white formals. With white corsages. This must, as you know, be perfect for the Grand Paradiser."

The ladies all sat around talking about their troubles and afflictions, the way they loved to do. Opal Ducharm went to her kitchen and started preparing refreshments, which was this time Tapioca. She could hear Moselle Lessups telling about her dentist, Dr. Gore, who was all the scandal in the town because he had been discovered practicing without a license. "He *knows* his profession," she was declaring, "and I don't care *what* they say about his certificate, whether it's forged or not. He can tell you what every tooth in your head is up to. And in a fascinatin' way. And holds a little mirror up so you can see his work in progress. Some people don't like to see, just want to close their eyes till it's all over. But if you *know,* it helps, *I* think.

"'You see, Mrs. Lessups,' Dr. Gore showed me in the little tooth mirror, 'a big molar is pushin some little ones away from it. It found the vacancy left by the tooth you had pulled out and it has tried to lean over into this vacant place. Do you understand?' he says. 'Yes,' I said . . . 'but . . .' 'We can't have that big old molar doin this to all those other little teeth,' he says, 'can we?', with such a tenderness and real interest and affection for the teeth. 'But what will we do?' I says. 'Pull it right out,' he says. 'It's no good to you,' he says, just as though he suddenly despised my big molar. 'It's crowdin all those other smaller ones and jammin them all together in too little a space.' 'Well,' I says, 'Dr. Gore, I don't want all my good teeth pushed to the front like old Boney Vinson's down at the Station!' I says and laughed. 'But use deadening because you know how nervous I am.'"

The ladies listened and wagged their heads.

Then Paradiser Clover Sugrew gave one of her imitations that quietened the room down for a few minutes until Mrs. Mack McCutcheon burst up from her chair over everybody and went off into one of her exaggerations that nobody could stop—you just had to let her go on through with it to the end, like a rock that suddenly, for no good reason, started falling down a hill. It was about her Napropath for her nervous headaches.

"It is caused by one little nerve!" she cried, before anybody hardly knew what the score was, "made like a . . . oh, we all have it, you have it and I have it, this little nerve . . . let's see, what's its name, never *can* remember it, ought to, it's the cause of all my misery, ought to know it better'n my own name—aw shoot, can't think of its name now . . . but *any*way, this little ever-what-it-is nerve just stops working—on my Junction Board . . . which is situated right back here at the bottom of my neck and right between my shoulders. Don't look so *morbid,* you all, you all have one too, we all have, all have a Junction Board so don't look so morbid. Anyway . . . imagine your Junction Board as like a switchboard—this is what the Napropath tells me—all the nerves are there, they are all there, switchin on, switchin off, pluggin in calls to the brain. Well, when *it* stops workin—'why, please tell me,' I asked my Napropath; and he shrugged his shoulders to say, 'That's the mystery, Mrs. McCutcheon; now drop your chin;' when *it* stops, then (wouldn't you know), two *other* nerves—the, let's see—oh don't know their names either. *Any*way—we've all got these, too—these two nerves running down your chest on either side—*then* the headache starts. But the most *peculiar* thing is that I have a *tramp nerve.* It just wanders around, can never tell where it'll be next—aren't our bodies a miracle? The good Lord made such a masterpiece when he made these bodies, works of art, a mystery for all to behold . . . . . ."

Mrs. Mack McCutcheon stopped abruptly and what came in over her dead silence was Mrs. Randall's voice saying, "all I said was 'I never in my life!' and turned and walked right out of Neiman-Marcuses with me a new hat on."

As Mrs. Randall was the one who had money and drove to Dallas to buy all her clothes, the subject of her exclamation was urgently important to the other ladies. They listened to her. She was telling about the little male milliner in Neiman-Marcuses. "I tell you I never in my life heard anybody be able to talk about a hat the way he does. He said, 'This is *your* hat, Mrs. Randall, I knew it the moment I put it on your head. This hat is a nice statement on your head. Not saying too much, just enough. Just the right kind of a statement for you to make goin down the street—not a shriek, not a sigh, but a good-size, sure and strong positive yes!, Mrs. Randall.' How he can talk about a hat, that Lucien Silvero, brought in by Nieman-Marcuses from New York!"

Opal Ducharm was whipping her cream for the Tapioca Surprise and listening when she could to all the stories that were like a stitching party in her living room. Then she put her bowl of firm cream on the table and turned to the bowls of Tapioca looking very special, ready for the cream.

A noise was behind her and she turned around to find Sister the cat upon the table over her cream. She could not clap her hands fast enough, however, to stop Sister from dragging her tongue across the top. Then she cried, softly so the ladies could not hear, "Shoo, you Sister!" and Sister sprang away and ran to sit by the door, where she casually began cleaning her face and whiskers. "You hateful Sister!" Opal whispered as she smoothed over the little rut left by the cat's tongue. "Now you go outdoors!"—and she opened the door for the cat.

Opal Ducharm put the cream on the Tapioca, it looked so delicious, and then she stood at her kitchen door with the tray and said with real charm, "Surprise, Paradisers!"; and all the conversation stopped. The ladies loved the surprise refreshments at the meetings, and all tried to be original.

The surprise was passed round and admired, and all the Paradisers crooned with delight. And then they all started in on it.

When Opal Ducharm went to the kitchen to get her bowl, she spied through her window what looked like a sprawled cat in the driveway. She ran out to Sister and found her truly dead and not sleeping or playing possum. Sister was lying over on her side, drawn long and limp; and her paws were thrust out from her as if she had died trying to hold away whatever kind of death had taken her. Round her black lips were speckles of whipcream and some still hanging on her whiskers. And then Opal saw the whole picture in a flash. "Poisoned by the cream!" she gasped. Just like those fifty-four people that got bacteria in the banana cream pie at the Houston cafeteria. She rushed up the steps through the door and as she ran she was beholding the image of twelve Paradisers lying flung down like the cat, poisoned dead: Ora Stevens, Moselle Lessups, Clover Sugrew, and all the others, drawn out and limp on her living room floor, all the fifes and drums stilled forever. She flew to the living room, flung out her hands and cried, "Stop the Surprise!

Stop! Stop! It is deadly poison and has just killed the cat!" and knocked flying to the floor a spoonful that Esther Borglund was just about to devour. And then she told the bewildered Paradisers about her discovery of the cat, dead in the driveway with the cream on her whiskers and how earlier she had caught Sister with her tongue in the bowl of cream. The ladies were stunned, but Opal shouted, "Get your purses and we'll all run to Victory Hospital just around the corner, that's the quickest thing;" and to Myrtle Dubuque who was already on the phone she yelled "Myrtle that phone's dead, too, dead as Sister and dead as we'll all be if we don't hurry hurry. . . ."; and they all rushed out. By grace, the Paradiser Lieutenant was there—it was Johnny Sue Redundo—and with her whistle, which she blew at once and, as if by magic, organized rout into loose squads which lurched without their usual and State-renowned precision, but as valiantly as they could, towards Victory Hospital.

At Victory Hospital the Head Registered Nurse, Viola Privins, was doing all she knew to keep the ladies calm until Dr. Sam Berry could help them—applying cold towels, taking pulses, giving antidotes. Mrs. Cairns had a thermometer in her mouth and many of the ladies had hypos for shock. Cots were put up in the hall by the Emergency Room like the time of the Flu epidemic, but most of the ladies were just too sick to lie down. In fact, the ladies were getting sicker and sicker; some thought they were ready to have a convulsion; and Mrs. Randall, the sickest of all, kept seeing her face writhing and going purple in her mirror. (She had just gobbled up most of her dish of Tapioca, she loved it so.) One Paradiser fainted, and the fattest—it was Ora Starnes—had to be laid out her full length and weight in the Emergency Room, where she was brought to with a cold cloth and ammonia. But when she opened her eyes upon a nurse helping in a stabbed and bleeding derelict, she snuffed out again quick as a candle and hogged the only emergency table.
     There was the question as to who should go in to the stomach pump first, since there was only one pump. Some said the officers should go, others suggested alphabetical order, Mrs. Lessups insisted that those who ate the most should go, and Leta Cratz said the sanest thing of all when she shouted, "The sickest should be first—Mrs. Randall is nearly dyin'!"
     In the midst of all this pandemonium, Myrtle Dubuque, the secretary of the Paradisers and elected that because she was so calm all the time, was moving up and down among the Paradisers, patting them and saying "Honey, be calm!" She was as steady as if she were taking down the minutes of a rowdy business meeting.

Finally Opal Ducharm, the President, took hold of the situation and reminded all that the motto of the Paradisers was Charity, Unselfishness and Service—and went in first to the pump, which had just arrived with Dr. Berry, with exemplary dignity even in pain. This inspired others to self-effacement except Sarah Galt (who was only a probationary member anyway) who said she was not going to wait any longer and was going to call her personal family physician.

The ladies started going in to Dr. Berry, one by one, and he was efficient and sweet with each patient. But you can imagine what confusion little Victory Hospital was in. It was just the time for the patients' supper but not a one got it. Everything was delayed, compresses, pulses, pills and bedpans; and red lights begged from most every room. But there was no nurse to answer. "This would be the worst tragedy in the town since the time the grandstand collapsed at the May Fete," a little student nurse, Lucy Bird, said. Mrs. Laura Vance, the richest woman in the town and in Victory Hospital for one of her rest cures, put on her Japanese Kimona (from her actual trip to Japan) and came out to assist. But by this time half the town was there. "What is it?" somebody asked Lew Tully who was in, again, for a drying out. "Beats me, but from what I can tell, somebody tried to poison and then rape twelve Paradisers."

"Why'd he want to poison 'em?"

"Why'd he want to rape 'em?" answered Lew.

Paradisers came running in who, in spite of the expert machinery of the list-calling, could not be reached when there was important official information about the organization to be relayed, but had immediately heard, without the slightest difficulty of being reached, of the tragedy of the Tapioca. But most of them were of no help at all, they just got in the way; and Myra Pugh got a hypo she didn't merit, in the scramble. Volunteers came from all over, even Jack the Ant Killer was there—why, nobody knew, but he thought he could help; and Mack Sims of the Valley Gold Dairy was there because he had sold the cream and was afraid the Paradisers might get out an injunction against him for poisoning them, especially if anybody died. Some husbands came, but not Jock Ducharm, this was his day in Bewley, selling his product; and anyway those who did come just got in the way, except Mr. Cairns, a real businessman with sense, who immediately called Honey Grove Hospital, twenty miles away, for their stomach pump, and it was coming by ambulance immediately. A reporter from *The Bee* came in and Opal Ducharm appointed Grace Kunsy to act as temporary publicity chairman since the regular one, Ora Starnes, was just too sick to say one word for the papers.

By the time several of the ladies had survived the ordeal of the stomach pump and were standing around or lying on the cots, feeling saved and relieved, if languorous, the panic began to subside a little, and it appeared that the women would all come through. Opal Ducharm was complaining that there should be more stomach pumps in a hospital this size and that the Paradisers should have a Bazaar to raise funds for these. She put it on the agenda for the next meeting.

So no one died, and with the help of the volunteers, it was finally over, every stomach was purged, and about nine o'clock that night Dr. Sam Berry pronounced them all out of danger. The women were told to rest for a while, but not a one would stay at Victory Hospital. Mrs. Delancy, the smoker of the group, had another cigarette, and they all went home.

Poor Opal Ducharm, of course, felt the sting of the near-tragedy most severely, for it seemed her fault, and yet it couldn't be. She got home weak and exhausted.

"It just makes me sick, I declare to my soul," she was saying to herself as she opened the door, when there was Jock, her husband. "And where in the name of the Savior have you been?" she yelled, knowing perfectly well that it was his day in Bewley.

"I just got in about twenty minutes ago, Opal. You know today was my day to go to Bewley."

And when Opal saw that Jock was not going to be sympathetic, this was going to be too much. But then he never did care anything about the Paradisers, wouldn't even become an Auxiliary, and wear the special tie-clasp, like the other husbands, but bowled instead. "If they want me in the Auxiliary let 'em meet another night besides Tuesdays. That's my bowling night," he said. This was a source of great hurt and shame to Opal who, after all, *was* the President.

"Well you shouldn't have gone to Bewley today! You missed something near-fatal. You could have helped, which you never do, so never mind."

"Helped what?"

"I had to have my stomach pumped, that's all. But never mind."

"You know I sell my product in Bewley on Tuesdays, Opal. And what did you swallow, for Christ's sakes?"

"Something poisoned. But never mind."

"Well Opal, we'll get back to the poison in a minute, but what I'm trying to tell you is that Sister is dead."

"Oh don't remind me of that because she was poisoned too!"

"Poisoned? Well I don't know about you, Opal, but that damned cat wasn't poisoned. What I'm trying to tell you is that Ruta Tanner just left here. She came to tell you that when she drove in the driveway during your meeting she believes she hit a cat. She felt a thud and saw something lying on its side in the driveway. Now how much closer can you get to the fact that she ran over Sister and killed her?"

"Oh to my Savior!" Opal wailed. "But why didn't Ruta come in here and tell me? It would have saved us all from so much suffering!"

"She said she was too upset to come in and disturb the meeting with such bad news. And especially seeing as how, since she's on probation for drilling drunk under the influence of martinis at the Thanksgiving Special March, she felt too humiliated to come in on a meeting. If you ask me, she's been hitting the gin like a bat outta hell since you all expelled her—or whatever the hell you did. She said to tell you that she tried to call you from Pig Stand No. 2 but your 'phone wouldn't work. Anyways, I called her a dumb hit-and-run-driver and said I was going to sue her and that lounge-lizard husband of hers with the beer-belly. I don't want to get mixed up in it, lemme alone. I've been in Bewley all day tryin to sell my product to a bunch of numb-skulls."

"Oh where is poor Sister now?" Opal shrieked and tore at the divan which Sister's claws had already shredded in places.

"I just put her in an A&P shopping bag and will bury her directly. What else can I do, for God's sake? If you don't get hold of yourself you're going to have to have more than your stomach pumped. Your brains, for Christsakes. Anyway," he said, under his breath as he went to the refrigerator to get a beer, "there'll be less cat hair all over every-thing in the house . . . . *including* my blue suit which by now *looks* like Sister. I was about ready to give it to her."

Opal Ducharm could have been humiliated by this comment, but she was now going through such various feelings that she didn't know which to settle for. At first she felt elated because nobody was poisoned, and then she thought of Sister killed and was heart-broken. She started to call the poor exhausted women all pumped half to death for nothing, but she remembered her dead phone and felt rage. Then she really got just plain fed-up with the whole thing and in a second decided to eliminate every feeling but one, her appetite, and started for the kitchen.

"Well," she said. "I know what *I'm* going right to the icebox and do. That's eat me a good big helping of that Tapioca. There's an awful lot left and I didn't even get to taste of it."

And from the refrigerator she drew out a finger wrapped with whipcream and smacked it up with a brave tongue in a kind of toast to the killed cat and to the whole affair, and, bringing a mound of the good Tapioca, came in and sat down by Jock.

"When I've quieted down and can stand to recall it, I'll tell you the whole terrible thing," she advised Jock.

"Whenever you're ready," Jock said. "Shall I wait—or bury the cat?"

1974

STEPHEN CRANE

The Bride Comes to Yellow Sky

I

The great Pullman was whirling onward with such dignity of motion that a glance from the window seemed simply to prove that the plains of Texas were pouring eastward. Vast flats of green grass, dull-hued spaces of mesquit and cactus, little groups of frame houses, woods of light and tender trees, all were sweeping into the east, sweeping over the horizon, a precipice.

A newly married pair had boarded this coach at San Antonio. The man's face was reddened from many days in the wind and sun, and a direct result of his new black clothes was that his brick-colored hands were constantly performing in a most conscious fashion. From time to time he looked down respectfully at his attire. He sat with a hand on

Born in 1871 in Newark, New Jersey, Stephen Crane was the fourteenth child of Dr. Jonathan Crane—a Methodist minister who preached and published against the evils of such popular entertainments as dancing, the theater, and the novel. Crane rebelled against his father's dogma, eventually entering into a literary career with the private publication of *Maggie: A Girl of the Streets* (1893), a gritty account of life in the ethnic enclaves of New York's inner city. Works such as *Maggie* and *The Red Badge of Courage* (1895) earned Crane a variety of stylistic descriptions: realist, impressionist, naturalist, symbolist. Crane spent many years as a war correspondent, until ill health and financial hardship finally forced him back to his home in London. He died of tuberculosis in a German sanitarium in 1900 at the age of twenty-eight.

each knee, like a man waiting in a barber's shop. The glances he devoted to other passengers were furtive and shy.

The bride was not pretty, nor was she very young. She wore a dress of blue cashmere, with small reservations of velvet here and there, and with steel buttons abounding. She continually twisted her head to regard her puff sleeves, very stiff, straight, and high. They embarrassed her. It was quite apparent that she had cooked, and that she expected to cook, dutifully. The blushes caused by the careless scrutiny of some passengers as she had entered the car were strange to see upon this plain, under-class countenance, which was drawn in placid, almost emotionless lines.

They were evidently very happy. "Ever been in a parlor-car before?" he asked, smiling with delight.

"No," she answered; "I never was. It's fine, ain't it?"

"Great! And then after a while we'll go forward to the diner, and get a big lay-out. Finest meal in the world. Charge a dollar."

"Oh, do they?" cried the bride. "Charge a dollar? Why, that's too much—for us—ain't it, Jack?"

"Not this trip, anyhow," he answered bravely. "We're going to go the whole thing."

Later he explained to her about the trains. "You see, it's a thousand miles from one end of Texas to the other; and this train runs right across it, and never stops but four times." He had the pride of an owner. He pointed out to her the dazzling fittings of the coach; and in truth her eyes opened wider as she contemplated the sea-green figured velvet, the shining brass, silver, and glass, the wood that gleamed as darkly brilliant as the surface of a pool of oil. At one end a bronze figure sturdily held a support for a separated chamber, and at convenient places on the ceiling were frescoes in olive and silver.

To the minds of the pair, their surroundings reflected the glory of their marriage that morning in San Antonio; this was the environment of their new estate; and the man's face in particular beamed with an elation that made him appear ridiculous to the negro porter. This individual at times surveyed them from afar with an amused and superior grin. On other occasions he bullied them with skill in ways that did not make it exactly plain to them that they were being bullied. He subtly used all the manners of the most unconquerable kind of snobbery. He oppressed them; but of this oppression they had small knowledge, and they speedily forgot that infrequently a number of travellers covered them with stares of derisive enjoyment. Historically there was supposed to be something infinitely humorous in their situation.

"We are due in Yellow Sky at 3:42," he said, looking tenderly into her eyes.

"Oh, we are?" she said, as if she had not been aware of it. To evince surprise at her husband's statement was part of her wifely amiability. She took from a pocket a little silver watch; and as she held it before her, and stared at it with a frown of attention, the new husband's face shone.

"I bought it in San Anton' from a friend of mine," he told her gleefully.

"It's seventeen minutes past twelve," she said, looking up at him with a kind of shy and clumsy coquetry. A passenger, noting this play, grew excessively sardonic, and winked at himself in one of the numerous mirrors.

At last they went to the dining-car. Two rows of negro waiters, in glowing white suits, surveyed their entrance with the interest, and also the equanimity, of men who had been forewarned. The pair fell to the lot of a waiter who happened to feel pleasure in steering them through their meal. He viewed them with the manner of a fatherly pilot, his countenance radiant with benevolence. The patronage, entwined with the ordinary deference, was not plain to them. And yet, as they returned to their coach, they showed in their faces a sense of escape.

To the left, miles down a long purple slope, was a little ribbon of mist where moved the keening Rio Grande. The train was approaching it at an angle, and the apex was Yellow Sky. Presently it was apparent that, as the distance from Yellow Sky grew shorter, the husband became commensurately restless. His brick-red hands were more insistent in their prominence. Occasionally he was even rather absent-minded and far-away when the bride leaned forward and addressed him.

As a matter of truth, Jack Potter was beginning to find the shadow of a deed weigh upon him like a leaden slab. He, the town marshal of Yellow Sky, a man known, liked, and feared in his corner, a prominent person, had gone to San Antonio to meet a girl he believed he loved, and there, after the usual prayers, had actually induced her to marry him, without consulting Yellow Sky for any part of the transaction. He was now bringing his bride before an innocent and unsuspecting community.

Of course people in Yellow Sky married as it pleased them in accordance with a general custom; but such was Potter's thought of his duty to his friends, or of their idea of his duty, or of an unspoken form which does not control men in these matters, that he felt he was heinous. He had committed an extraordinary crime. Face to face with this girl in San Antonio, and spurred by his sharp impulse, he had gone headlong over all the social hedges. At San Antonio he was like a man hidden in the dark. A knife to sever any friendly duty, any form, was easy to his hand in that remote city. But the hour of Yellow Sky—the hour of daylight—was approaching.

He knew full well that his marriage was an important thing to his town. It could only be exceeded by the burning of the new hotel. His friends could not forgive him. Frequently he had reflected on the advisability of telling them by telegraph, but a new cowardice had been upon him. He feared to do it. And now the train was hurrying him toward a scene of amazement, glee, and reproach. He glanced out of the window at the line of haze swinging slowly in toward the train.

Yellow Sky had a kind of brass band, which played painfully, to the delight of the populace. He laughed without heart as he thought of it. If the citizens could dream of his prospective arrival with his bride, they would parade the band at the station and escort them, amid cheers and laughing congratulations, to his adobe home.

He resolved that he would use all the devices of speed and plainscraft in making the journey from the station to his house. Once within the safe citadel, he could issue some sort of vocal bulletin, and then not go among the citizens until they had time to wear off a little of their enthusiasm.

The bride looked anxiously at him. "What's worrying you, Jack?"

He laughed again. "I'm not worrying, girl; I'm only thinking of Yellow Sky."

She flushed in comprehension.

A sense of mutual guilt invaded their minds and developed a finer tenderness. They looked at each other with eyes softly aglow. But Potter often laughed the same nervous laugh; the flush upon the bride's face seemed quite permanent.

The traitor to the feelings of Yellow Sky narrowly watched the speeding landscape. "We're nearly there," he said.

Presently the porter came and announced the proximity of Potter's home. He held a brush in his hand, and, with all his airy superiority gone, he brushed Potter's new clothes as the latter slowly turned this way and that way. Potter fumbled out a coin and gave it to the porter, as he had seen others do. It was a heavy and muscle-bound business, as that of a man shoeing his first horse.

The porter took their bag, and as the train began to slow they moved forward to the hooded platform of the car. Presently the two engines and their long string of coaches rushed into the station of Yellow Sky.

"They have to take water here," said Potter, from a constricted throat and in mournful cadence, as one announcing death. Before the train stopped his eye had swept the length of the platform, and he was glad and astonished to see there was none upon it but the station-agent, who, with a slightly hurried and anxious air, was walking toward the water-tanks. When the train had halted, the porter alighted first, and placed in position a little temporary step.

"Come on, girl," said Potter, hoarsely. As he helped her down they each laughed on a false note. He took the bag from the negro, and bade his wife cling to his arm. As they slunk rapidly away, his hang-dog glance perceived that they were unloading the two trunks, and also that the station-agent, far ahead near the baggage-car, had turned and was running toward him, making gestures. He laughed, and groaned as he laughed, when he noted the first effect of his marital bliss upon Yellow Sky. He gripped his wife's arm firmly to his side, and they fled. Behind them the porter stood, chuckling fatuously.

II

The California express on the Southern Railway was due at Yellow Sky in twenty-one minutes. There were six men at the bar of the Weary Gentleman saloon. One was a drummer who talked a great deal and rapidly; three were Texans who did not care to talk at that time; and two were Mexican sheep-herders, who did not talk as a general practice in the Weary Gentleman saloon. The barkeeper's dog lay on the board walk that crossed in front of the door. His head was on his paws, and he glanced drowsily here and there with the constant vigilance of a dog that is kicked on occasion. Across the sandy street were some vivid green grass-plots, so wonderful in appearance, amid the sands that burned near them in a blazing sun, that they caused a doubt in the mind. They exactly resembled the grass mats used to represent lawns on the stage. At the cooler end of the railway station, a man without a coat sat in a tilted chair and smoked his pipe. The fresh-cut bank of the Rio Grande circled near the town, and there could be seen beyond it a great plum-colored plain of mesquit.

Save for the busy drummer and his companions in the saloon, Yellow Sky was dozing. The new-comer leaned gracefully upon the bar, and recited many tales with the confidence of a bard who has come upon a new field.

"—and at that moment that the old man fell downstairs with the bureau in his arms, the old woman was coming up with two scuttles of coal, and of course—"

The drummer's tale was interrupted by a young man who suddenly appeared in the open door. He cried: "Scratchy Wilson's drunk, and has turned loose with both hands." The two Mexicans at once set down their glasses and faded out of the rear entrance of the saloon.

The drummer, innocent and jocular, answered: "All right, old man. S'pose he has? Come in and have a drink, anyhow."

But the information had made such an obvious cleft in every skull in the room that the drummer was obliged to see its importance. All had become instantly solemn. "Say," said he, mystified, "What is this?" His three companions made the introductory gesture of eloquent speech; but the young man at the door forestalled them.

"It means, my friend," he answered, as he came into the saloon, "that for the next two hours this town won't be a health resort."

The barkeeper went to the door, and locked and barred it; reaching out of the window, he pulled the heavy wooden shutters, and barred them. Immediately a solemn, chapel-like gloom was upon the place. The drummer was looking from one to another.

"But, say," he cried, "what is this, anyhow? You don't mean there is going to be a gun-fight?"

"Don't know whether there'll be a fight or not," answered one man, grimly; "but there'll be some shootin'—some good shootin'."

The young man who had warned them waved his hand. "Oh, there'll be a fight fast enough, if any one wants it. Anybody can get a fight out there in the street. There's a fight just waiting."

The drummer seemed to be swayed between the interest of a foreigner and a perception of personal danger.

"What did you say his name was?" he asked.

"Scratchy Wilson," they answered in chorus.

"And will he kill anybody? What are you going to do? Does this happen often? Does he rampage around like this once a week or so? Can he break in that door?"

"No; he can't break down that door," replied the barkeeper. "He's tried it three times. But when he comes you'd better lay down on the floor, stranger. He's dead sure to shoot at it, and a bullet may come through."

Thereafter the drummer kept a strict eye upon the door. The time had not yet called for him to hug the floor, but, as a minor precaution, he sidled near the wall. "Will he kill anybody?" he said again.

The men laughed low and scornfully at the question.

"He's out to shoot, and he's out for trouble. Don't see any good in experimentin' with him."

"But what do you do in a case like this? What do you do?"

A man responded: "Why, he and Jack Potter—"

"But," in chorus the other men interrupted, "Jack Potter's in San Anton'."

"Well, who is he? What's he got to do with it?"

"Oh, he's the town marshal. He goes out and fights Scratchy when he gets on one of these tears."

"Wow!" said the drummer, mopping his brow. "Nice job he's got."

The voices had toned away to mere whisperings. The drummer wished to ask further questions, which were born of an increasing anxiety and bewilderment; but when he attempted them, the men merely looked at him in irritation and motioned him to remain silent. A tense waiting hush was upon them. In the deep shadows of the room their eyes shone as they listened for sounds from the street. One man made three gestures at the barkeeper; and the latter, moving like a ghost, handed him a glass and a bottle. The man poured a full glass of whisky, and set down the bottle noiselessly. He gulped the whisky in a swallow, and turned again toward the door in immovable silence. The drummer saw that the barkeeper, without a sound, had taken a Winchester from beneath the bar. Later he saw this individual beckoning to him, as he tiptoed across the room.

"You better come with me back of the bar."

"No, thanks," said the drummer, perspiring; "I'd rather be where I can make a break for the back door."

Whereupon the man of bottles made a kindly but peremptory gesture. The drummer obeyed it, and, finding himself seated on a box with his head below the level of the bar, balm was laid upon his soul at sight of various zinc and copper fittings that bore a resemblance to armor-plate. The barkeeper took a seat comfortably upon an adjacent box.

"You see," he whispered, "this here Scratchy Wilson is a wonder with a gun—a perfect wonder; and when he goes on the war-trail, we hunt our holes—naturally. He's about the last one of the old gang that used to hang out along the river here. He's a terror when he's drunk. When he's sober he's all right—kind of simple—wouldn't hurt a fly— nicest fellow in town. But when he's drunk—whoo!"

There were periods of stillness. "I wish Jack Potter was back from San Anton'," said the barkeeper. "He shot Wilson up once—in the leg —and he would sail in and pull out the kinks in this thing."

Presently they heard from a distance the sound of a shot, followed by three wild yowls. It instantly removed a bond from the men in the darkened saloon.

There was a shuffling of feet. They looked at each other. "Here he comes," they said.

III

A man in a maroon-colored flannel shirt, which had been purchased for purposes of decoration, and made principally by some Jewish women on the East Side of New York, rounded a corner and walked into the middle of the main street of Yellow Sky. In either hand the man held a long, heavy, blue-black revolver. Often he yelled, and these cries rang through a semblance of a deserted village, shrilly flying over the roofs in a volume that seemed to have no relation to the ordinary vocal strength of a man. It was as if the surrounding stillness formed the arch of a tomb over him. These cries of ferocious challenge rang against walls of silence. And his boots had red tops with gilded imprints, of the kind beloved in winter by little sledding boys on the hillsides of New England.

The man's face flamed in a rage begot of whisky. His eyes, rolling, and yet keen for ambush, hunted the still doorways and windows. He walked with the creeping movement of the midnight cat. As it occurred to him, he roared menacing information. The long revolvers in his hands were as easy as straws; they were removed with an electric swiftness. The little fingers of each hand played sometimes in a musician's way. Plain from the low collar of the shirt, the cords of his neck straightened and sank, straightened and sank, as passion moved him. The only sounds were his terrible invitations. The calm adobes preserved their demeanor at the passing of this small thing in the middle of the street.

There was no offer of fight—no offer of fight. The man called to the sky. There were no attractions. He bellowed and fumed and swayed his revolvers here and everywhere.

The dog of the barkeeper of the Weary Gentleman saloon had not appreciated the advance of events. He yet lay dozing in front of his master's door. At sight of the dog, the man paused and raised his revolver humorously. At sight of the man, the dog sprang up and walked diagonally away, with a sullen head, and growling. The man yelled, and the dog broke into a gallop. As it was about to enter the alley, there was a loud noise, a whistling, and something spat the ground directly before it. The dog screamed, and, wheeling in terror, galloped headlong in a new direction. Again there was a noise, a whistling, and sand was kicked viciously before it. Fear-stricken, the dog turned and flurried like an animal in a pen. The man stood laughing, his weapons at his hips.

Ultimately the man was attracted by the closed door of the Weary Gentleman saloon. He went to it and, hammering with a revolver, demanded drink.

The door remaining imperturbable, he picked a bit of paper from the walk, and nailed it to the framework with a knife. He then turned his back contemptuously upon this popular resort and, walking to the opposite side of the street and spinning there on his heel quickly and lithely, fired at the bit of paper. He missed it by a half inch. He swore at himself, and went away. Later he comfortably fusiladed the windows of his most intimate friend. The man was playing with this town; it was a toy for him.

But still there was no offer of fight. The name of Jack Potter, his ancient antagonist, entered his mind, and he concluded that it would be a glad thing if he should go to Potter's house, and by bombardment induce him to come out and fight. He moved in the direction of his desire, chanting Apache scalp-music.

When he arrived at it, Potter's house presented the same still front as had the other adobes. Taking up a strategic position, the man howled a challenge. But this house regarded him as might a great stone god. It gave no sign. After a decent wait, the man howled further challenges, mingling them with wonderful epithets.

Presently there came the spectacle of a man churning himself into deepest rage over the immobility of a house. He fumed at it as the winter wind attacks a prairie cabin in the north. To the distance there should have gone the sound of a tumult like the fighting of two hundred Mexicans. As necessity bade him, he paused for breath or to reload his revolvers.

IV

Potter and his bride walked sheepishly and with speed. Sometimes they laughed together shamefacedly and low.

"Next corner, dear," he said finally.

They put forth the efforts of a pair walking bowed against a strong wind. Potter was about to raise a finger to point the first appearance of the new home when, as they circled the corner, they came face to face with a man in a maroon-colored shirt, who was feverishly pushing cartridges into a large revolver. Upon the instant the man dropped his revolver to the ground and, like lightning, whipped another from its holster. The second weapon was aimed at the bridegroom's chest.

There was silence. Potter's mouth seemed to be merely a grave for his tongue. He exhibited an instinct to at once loosen his arm from the woman's grip, and he dropped the bag to the sand. As for the bride, her face had gone as yellow as old cloth. She was a slave to hideous rites, gazing at the apparitional snake.

The two men faced each other at a distance of three paces. He of the revolver smiled with a new and quiet ferocity.

"Tried to sneak up on me," he said. "Tried to sneak up on me!" His eyes grew more baleful. As Potter made a slight movement, the man thrust his revolver venomously forward. "No; don't you do it, Jack Potter. Don't you move a finger toward a gun just yet. Don't you move an eyelash. The time has come for me to settle with you and I'm goin' to do it my own way, and loaf along with no interferin'. So if you don't want a gun bent on you, just mind what I tell you."

Potter looked at his enemy. "I ain't got a gun on me, Scratchy," he said. "Honest, I ain't." He was stiffening and steadying, but yet somewhere at the back of his mind a vision of the Pullman floated: the sea-green figured velvet, the shining brass, silver, and glass, the wood that gleamed as darkly brilliant as the surface of a pool of oil—all the glory of marriage, the environment of the new estate. "You know I fight when it comes to fighting, Scratchy Wilson; but I ain't got a gun on me. You'll have to do all the shootin' yourself."

His enemy's face went livid. He stepped forward, and lashed his weapon to and fro before Potter's chest. "Don't you tell me you ain't got no gun on you, you whelp. Don't tell me no lie like that. There ain't a man in Texas ever seen you without no gun. Don't take me for no kid." His eyes blazed with light, and his throat worked like a pump.

"I ain't takin' you for no kid," answered Potter. His heels had not moved an inch backward. "I'm taking' you for a damn fool. I tell you I ain't got a gun, and I ain't. If you're goin' to shoot me up, you better begin now; you'll never get a chance like this again."

So much enforced reasoning had told on Wilson's rage; he was calmer. "If you ain't got a gun, why ain't you got a gun?" he sneered. "Been to Sunday-school?"

"I ain't got a gun because I've just come from San Anton' with my wife. I'm married," said Potter. "And if I'd thought there was going to be any galoots like you prowling around when I brought my wife home, I'd had a gun, and don't you forget it."

"Married?" said Scratchy, not at all comprehending.

"Yes, married. I'm married," said Potter, distinctly.

"Married!" said Scratchy. Seemingly for the first time, he saw the drooping, drowning woman at the other man's side. "No!" he said. He was like a creature allowed a glimpse of another world. He moved a pace backward, and his arm, with the revolver, dropped to his side. "Is this the lady?" he asked.

"Yes; this is the lady," answered Potter.

There was another period of silence.

"Well," said Wilson at last, slowly, "I s'pose it's all off now."

"It's all off if you say so, Scratchy. You know I didn't make the trouble." Potter lifted his valise.

"Well, I 'low it's off, Jack," said Wilson. He was looking at the ground. "Married!" He was not a student of chivalry; it was merely that in the presence of this foreign condition he was a simple child of the earlier plains. He picked up his starboard revolver, and, placing both weapons in their holsters, he went away. His feet made funnel-shaped tracks in the heavy sand.

1898

T W O

The Ends of Childhood

In William Faulkner's "Barn Burning," children inevitably suffer "the terrible handicap of being young, the light weight of [their] few years, just heavy enough to prevent [their] soaring free of the world as it seemed to be ordered but not heavy enough to keep [them] footed solid in it, to resist it and try to change the course of its events." The stories in this group suggest that childhood is understood best in the moment of leaving it, often under duress, at the hands of adults, in pain. Unlike the more leisurely novel, the short story can narrow its focus to a particular moment of change or of realization. And when the protagonist is a child, that moment can mark the movement out of childhood and into a powerful knowledge of the world.

Leaving childhood means leaving the world where the fragility of life has not yet intruded and where the imagination reigns supreme. These stories share a powerful representation of the imagination of the child. In "Strange Moonlight," Conrad Aiken's young protagonist endows a little girl with the power of symbolizing imagination itself, incarnating all its riches and exoticism and strangeness; the realization of the girl's death tears open the boy's insulated bubble. Bill, in Elizabeth Spencer's "Moon Rocket," spends much of his time as the alien Dongoo from the planet Orion, but he discovers his intricately populated constellation is finally unable to support life; he too is indoctrinated into the world of unfairness and threat, and he too discovers he needs human relationships in this world.

A child's imaginary world is isolated and individual; the further away the child moves from it, the greater is the realization that there are contingencies involved in being human, that people are caught in a complicated web of relationships. The eccentric young Miss Bobbit, in "Children on Their Birthdays" (Truman Capote), instills in a teenage boy the more subtle knowledge behind becoming an adult human being. In appreciating her difference, he learns to prize "the queer things in him, like the pecan tree and liking books and caring enough about people to let them hurt him."

In these stories, the boundaries of childhood are outlined by the new kinds of knowledge—including self-knowledge—that the protagonists earn. The checkout clerk in John Updike's "A & P" is just old enough to try to change the course of events, and his stand, taken on principle, ends in his realization that the new character he has become is in for a hard life.

"Miles City, Montana" (Alice Munro) describes another way that childhood can end. Its protagonist, a mother, gains her own final adulthood when she realizes that adults cannot help their godlike power and error. She sees that her children are going to have to forgive her for being an imperfect adult, just as she is going to have to forgive her parents for all their "natural, and particular, mistakes."

All these stories illustrate the bravery children need in order to confront the irruption of the adult world into their own, as well as illustrating the importance of achieving the self-knowledge that will allow them success and worth and citizenship in the human family. But the flight through space, from Orion to Earth, entails a change in atmosphere, as disturbing and threatening as surfacing too quickly from the ocean's floor.

WILLIAM FAULKNER

Barn Burning

The store in which the Justice of the Peace's court was sitting smelled of cheese. The boy, crouched on his nail keg at the back of the crowded room, knew he smelled cheese, and more: from where he sat he could see the ranked shelves close-packed with the solid, squat, dynamic shapes of tin cans whose labels his stomach read, not from the lettering which meant nothing to his mind but from the scarlet devils and the silver curve of fish—this, the cheese which he knew he smelled and the hermetic meat which his intestines believed he smelled coming in intermittent gusts momentary and brief between the other constant one, the smell and sense just a little of fear because mostly of despair and grief, the old fierce pull of blood. He could not see the table where the Justice sat and before which his father and his father's enemy (*our enemy* he thought in that despair; *ourn! mine and hisn both! He's my father!*)

Born in New Albany, Mississippi, in 1897, William Faulkner was raised, educated, and artistically shaped in the nearby city of Oxford—a town that served as the setting for many of Faulkner's novels under the fictional name of Jefferson, the capital of the mythical Yoknapatawpha County. After one year at the University of Mississippi and a number of unsuccessful publications, Faulkner resolved to write for his own pleasure and about his family's history. The result was many of his best-known works: *The Sound and the Fury* (1929), *Sartoris* (1929), and *As I Lay Dying* (1930). Widespread fame for the writer did not materialize, however, until the 1946 publication of the anthology, *The Portable Faulkner,* and the Nobel Prize for literature, which was awarded in 1949. Faulkner died in 1962, just short of his sixty-fifth birthday.

stood, but he could hear them, the two of them that is, because his father had said no word yet:

"But what proof have you, Mr. Harris?"

"I told you. The hog got into my corn. I caught it up and sent it back to him. He had no fence that would hold it. I told him so, warned him. The next time I put the hog in my pen. When he came to get it I gave him enough wire to patch up his pen. The next time I put the hog up and kept it. I rode down to his house and saw the wire I gave him still rolled on to the spool in his yard. I told him he could have the hog when he paid me a dollar pound fee. That evening a nigger came with the dollar and got the hog. He was a strange nigger. He said, 'He say to tell you wood and hay kin burn.' I said, 'What?' 'That whut he say to tell you,' the nigger said. 'Wood and hay kin burn.' That night my barn burned. I got the stock out but I lost the barn."

"Where is the nigger? Have you got him?"

"He was a strange nigger, I tell you. I don't know what became of him."

"But that's not proof. Don't you see that's not proof?"

"Get that boy up here. He knows." For a moment the boy thought too that the man meant his older brother until Harris said, "Not him. The little one. The boy," and, crouching, small for his age, small and wiry like his father, in patched and faded jeans even too small for him, with straight, uncombed, brown hair and eyes gray and wild as storm scud, he saw the men between himself and the table part and become a lane of grim faces, at the end of which he saw the Justice, a shabby, collarless, graying man in spectacles, beckoning him. He felt no floor under his bare feet; he seemed to walk beneath the palpable weight of the grim turning faces. His father, stiff in his black Sunday coat donned not for the trial but for the moving, did not even look at him. *He aims for me to lie,* he thought, again with that frantic grief and despair. *And I will have to do hit.*

"What's your name, boy?" the Justice said.

"Colonel Sartoris Snopes," the boy whispered.

"Hey?" the Justice said. "Talk louder. Colonel Sartoris? I reckon anybody named for Colonel Sartoris in this country can't help but tell the truth, can they?" The boy said nothing. *Enemy! Enemy!* he thought; for a moment he could not even see, could not see that the Justice's face was kindly nor discern that his voice was troubled when he spoke to the man named Harris: "Do you want me to question this boy?" But he could hear, and during those subsequent long seconds while there was absolutely no sound in the crowded little room save that of quiet and intent breathing it was as if he had swung outward at the end of a grape vine, over a ravine, and at the top of the swing had been caught in a prolonged instant of mesmerized gravity, weightless in time.

"No!" Harris said violently, explosively. "Damnation! Send him out of here!" Now time, the fluid world, rushed beneath him again, the voices coming to him again through the smell of cheese and sealed meat, the fear and despair and the old grief of blood:

"This case is closed. I can't find against, you, Snopes, but I can give you advice. Leave this country and don't come back to it."

His father spoke for the first time, his voice cold and harsh, level, without emphasis: "I aim to. I don't figure to stay in a country among people who . . ." he said something unprintable and vile, addressed to no one.

"That'll do," the Justice said. "Take your wagon and get out of this country before dark. Case dismissed."

His father turned, and he followed the stiff black coat, the wiry figure walking a little stiffly from where a Confederate provost's man's musket ball had taken him in the heel on a stolen horse thirty years ago, followed the two backs now, since his older brother had appeared from somewhere in the crowd, no taller than the father but thicker, chewing tobacco steadily, between the two lines of grim-faced men and out of the store and across the worn gallery and down the sagging steps and among the dogs and half-grown boys in the mild May dust, where as he passed a voice hissed:

"Barn burner!"

Again he could not see, whirling; there was a face in a red haze, moonlike, bigger than the full moon, the owner of it half again his size, he leaping in the red haze toward the face, feeling no blow, feeling no shock when his head struck the earth, scrabbling up and leaping again, feeling no blow this time either and tasting no blood, scrabbling up to see the other boy in full flight and himself already leaping into pursuit as his father's hand jerked him back, the harsh, cold voice speaking above him: "Go get in the wagon."

It stood in a grove of locusts and mulberries across the road. His two hulking sisters in their Sunday dresses and his mother and her sister in calico and sunbonnets were already in it, sitting on and among the sorry residue of the dozen and more movings which even the boy could remember—the battered stove, the broken beds and chairs, the clock inlaid with mother-of-pearl, which would not run, stopped at some fourteen minutes past two o'clock of a dead and forgotten day and time, which had been his mother's dowry. She was crying, though when she saw him she drew her sleeve across her face and began to descend from the wagon. "Get back," the father said.

"He's hurt. I got to get some water and wash his . . ."

"Get back in the wagon," his father said. He got in too, over the tail-gate. His father mounted to the seat where the older brother already sat and struck the gaunt mules two savage blows with the peeled willow, but without heat. It was not even sadistic; it was exactly that same quality which in later years would cause his descendants to over-run the engine before putting a motor car into motion, striking and reining back in the same movement. The wagon went on, the store with its quiet crowd of grimly watching men dropped behind; a curve in the road hid it. *Forever* he thought. *Maybe he's done satisfied now, now that he has . . .* stopping himself, not to say it aloud even to himself. His mother's hand touched his shoulder.

"Does hit hurt?" she said.

"Naw," he said. "Hit don't hurt. Lemme be."

"Can't you wipe some of the blood off before hit dries?"

"I'll wash to-night," he said. "Lemme be, I tell you."

The wagon went on. He did not know where they were going. None of them ever did or ever asked, because it was always somewhere, always a house of sorts waiting for them a day or two days or even three days away. Likely his father had already arranged to make a crop on another farm before he . . . Again he had to stop himself. He (the father) always did. There was something about his wolflike independence and even courage when the advantage was at least neutral which impressed strangers, as if they got from his latent ravening ferocity not so much a sense of dependability as a feeling that his ferocious conviction in the rightness of his own actions would be of advantage to all whose interest lay with his.

That night they camped, in a grove of oaks and beeches where a spring ran. The nights were still cool and they had a fire against it, of a rail lifted from a nearby fence and cut into lengths—a small fire, neat, niggard almost, a shrewd fire; such fires were his father's habit and custom always, even in freezing weather. Older, the boy might have remarked this and wondered why not a big one; why should not a man who had not only seen the waste and extravagance of war, but who had in his blood an inherent voracious prodigality with material not his own, have burned everything in sight? Then he might have gone a step farther and thought that that was the reason: that niggard blaze was the living fruit of nights passed during those four years in the woods hiding from all men, blue or gray, with his strings of horses (captured horses, he called them). And older still, he might have divined the true reason: that the element of fire spoke to some deep mainspring of his father's being, as the element of steel or of powder spoke to other men, as the one weapon for the preservation of integrity, else breath were not worth the breathing, and hence to be regarded with respect and used with discretion.

But he did not think this now and he had seen those same niggard blazes all his life. He merely ate his supper beside it and was already half asleep over his iron plate when his father called him, and once more he followed the stiff back, the stiff and ruthless limp, up the slope and on to the starlit road where, turning, he could see his father against the stars but without face or depth—a shape black, flat, and bloodless as though cut from tin in the iron folds of the frockcoat which had not been made for him, the voice harsh like tin and without heat like tin:

"You were fixing to tell them. You would have told him." He didn't answer. His father struck him with the flat of his hand on the side of the head, hard but without heat, exactly as he had struck the two mules at the store, exactly as he would strike either of them with any stick in order to kill a horse fly, his voice still without heat or anger: "You're getting to be a man. You got to learn. You got to learn to stick to your own blood or you ain't going to have any blood to stick to you. Do you think either of them, any man there this morning, would? Don't you know all they wanted was a chance to get at me because they knew I had them beat? Eh?" Later, twenty years later, he was to tell himself, "If I had said they wanted only truth, justice, he would have hit me again." But now he said nothing. He was not crying. He just stood there. "Answer me," his father said.

"Yes," he whispered. His father turned.

"Get on to bed. We'll be there tomorrow."

To-morrow they were there. In the early afternoon the wagon stopped before a paintless two-room house identical almost with the dozen others it had stopped before even in the boy's ten years, and again, as on the other dozen occasions, his mother and aunt got down and began to unload the wagon, although his two sisters and his father and brother had not moved.

"Likely hit ain't fitten for hawgs," one of the sisters said.

"Nevertheless, fit it will and you'll hog it and like it," his father said. "Get out of them chairs and help your Ma unload."

The two sisters got down, big, bovine, in a flutter of cheap ribbons; one of them drew from the jumbled wagon bed a battered lantern, the other a worn broom. His father handed the reins to the older son and began to climb stiffly over the wheel. "When they get unloaded, take the team to the barn and feed them." Then he said, and at first the boy thought he was still speaking to his brother: "Come with me."

"Me?" he said.

"Yes," his father said. "You."

"Abner," his mother said. His father paused and looked back—the harsh level stare beneath the shaggy, graying, irascible brows.

"I reckon I'll have a word with the man that aims to begin tomorrow owning me body and soul for the next eight months."

They went back up the road. A week ago—or before last night, that is—he would have asked where they were going, but not now. His father had struck him before last night but never before had he paused afterward to explain why; it was as if the blow and the following calm, outrageous voice still rang, repercussed, divulging nothing to him save the terrible handicap of being young, the light weight of his few years, just heavy enough to prevent his soaring free of the world as it seemed to be ordered but not heavy enough to keep him footed solid in it, to resist it and try to change the course of its events.

Presently he could see the grove of oaks and cedars and the other flowering trees and shrubs where the house would be, though not the house yet. They walked beside a fence massed with honeysuckle and Cherokee roses and came to a gate swinging open between two brick pillars, and now, beyond a sweep of drive, he saw the house for the first time and at that instant he forgot his father and the terror and despair both, and even when he remembered his father again (who had not stopped) the terror and despair did not return. Because, for all the twelve movings, they had sojourned until now in a poor country, a land of small farms and fields and houses, and he had never seen a house like this before. *Hit's big as a courthouse* he thought quietly, with a surge of peace and joy whose reason he could not have thought into words, being too young for that: *They are safe from him. People whose lives are a part of this peace and dignity are beyond his touch, he no more to them than a buzzing wasp: capable of stinging for a little moment but that's all; the spell of this peace and dignity rendering even the barns and stable and cribs which belong to it impervious to the puny flames he might contrive . . .* this, the peace and joy, ebbing for an instant as he looked again at the stiff black back, the stiff and implacable limp of the figure which was not dwarfed by the house, for the reason that it had never looked big anywhere and which now, against the serene columned backdrop, had more than ever that impervious quality of something cut ruthlessly from tin, depthless, as though, sidewise to the sun, it would cast no shadow. Watching him, the boy remarked the absolutely undeviating course which his father held and saw the stiff foot come squarely down in a pile of fresh droppings where a horse had stood in the drive and which his father could have avoided by a simple change of stride. But it ebbed only for a moment, though he could not have thought this into words either, walking on in the spell of the house, which he could even want but without envy, without sorrow, certainly never with that ravening and jealous rage which unknown to him walked in the ironlike black coat before him: *Maybe he will feel it too. Maybe it will even change him now from what maybe he couldn't help but be.*

They crossed the portico. Now he could hear his father's stiff foot as it came down on the boards with clocklike finality, a sound out of all proportion to the displacement of the body it bore and which was not dwarfed either by the white door before it, as though it had attained to a sort of vicious and ravening minimum not to be dwarfed by anything—the flat, wide, black hat, the formal coat of broadcloth which had once been black but which had now that friction-glazed greenish cast of the bodies of old house flies, the lifted sleeve which was too large, the lifted hand like a curled claw. The door opened so promptly that the boy knew the Negro must have been watching them all the time, an old man with neat grizzled hair, in a linen jacket, who stood barring the door with his body, saying, "Wipe yo foots, white man, fo you come in here. Major ain't home nohow."

"Get out of my way, nigger," his father said, without heat too, flinging the door back and the Negro also and entering, his hat still on his head. And now the boy saw the prints of the stiff foot on the doorjamb and saw them appear on the pale rug behind the machinelike deliberation of the foot which seemed to bear (or transmit) twice the weight which the body compassed. The Negro was shouting "Miss Lula! Miss Lula!" somewhere behind them, then the boy, deluged as though by a warm wave by a suave turn of carpeted stair and a pendant glitter of chandeliers and a mute gleam of gold frames, heard the swift feet and saw her too, a lady—perhaps he had never seen her like before either—in a gray, smooth gown with lace at the throat and an apron tied at the waist and the sleeves turned back, wiping cake or biscuit dough from her hands with a towel as she came up the hall, looking not at his father at all but at the tracks on the blond rug with an expression of incredulous amazement.

"I tried," the Negro cried. "I tole him to . . ."

"Will you please go away?" she said in a shaking voice. "Major de Spain is not at home. Will you please go away?"

His father had not spoken again. He did not speak again. He did not even look at her. He just stood stiff in the center of the rug, in his hat, the shaggy iron-gray brows twitching slightly above the pebble-colored eyes as he appeared to examine the house with brief deliberation. Then with the same deliberation he turned; the boy watched him pivot on the good leg and saw the stiff foot drag round the arc of the turning, leaving a final long and fading smear. His father never looked at it, he never once looked down at the rug. The Negro held the door. It closed behind them, upon the hysteric and indistinguishable woman-wail. His father stopped at the top of the steps and scraped his boot clean on the edge of it. At the gate he stopped again. He stood for a moment, planted stiffly on the stiff foot, looking back at the house. "Pretty and white, ain't it?" he said. "That's sweat. Nigger sweat. Maybe it ain't white enough yet to suit him. Maybe he wants to mix some white sweat with it."

Two hours later the boy was chopping wood behind the house within which his mother and aunt and the two sisters (the mother and aunt, not the two girls, he knew that; even at this distance and muffled by walls the flat loud voices of the two girls emanated an incorrigible idle inertia) were setting up the stove to prepare a meal, when he heard the hooves and saw the linen-clad man on a fine sorrel mare, whom he recognized even before he saw the rolled rug in front of the Negro youth following on a fat bay carriage horse—a suffused, angry face vanishing, still at full gallop, beyond the corner of the house where his father and brother were sitting in the two tilted chairs; and a moment later, almost before he could have put the axe down, he heard the hooves again and watched the sorrel mare go back out of the yard, already galloping again. Then his father began to shout one of the sisters' names, who presently emerged backward from the kitchen door dragging the rolled rug along the ground by one end while the other sister walked behind it.

"If you ain't going to tote, go on and set up the wash pot," the first said.

"You, Sarty!" the second shouted. "Set up the wash pot!" His father appeared at the door, framed against that shabbiness, as he had been against that other bland perfection, impervious to either, the mother's anxious face at his shoulder.

"Go on," the father said. "Pick it up." The two sisters stooped, broad, lethargic; stooping, they presented an incredible expanse of pale cloth and a flutter of tawdry ribbons.

"If I thought enough of a rug to have to git hit all the way from France I wouldn't keep hit where folks coming in would have to tromp on hit," the first said. They raised the rug.

"Abner," the mother said. "Let me do it."

"You go back and git dinner," his father said. "I'll tend to this."

From the woodpile through the rest of the afternoon the boy watched them, the rug spread flat in the dust beside the bubbling wash-pot, the two sisters stooping over it with that profound and lethargic reluctance, while the father stood over them in turn, implacable and grim, driving them though never raising his voice again. He could smell the harsh homemade lye they were using; he saw his mother come to the door once and look toward them with an expression not anxious now but very like despair; he saw his father turn, and he fell to with the axe and saw from the corner of his eye his father raise from the ground a flattish fragment of field stone and examine it and return to the pot, and this time his mother actually spoke: "Abner. Abner. Please don't. Please, Abner."

Then he was done too. It was dusk; the whippoorwills had already begun. He could smell coffee from the room where they would presently eat the cold food remaining from the mid-afternoon meal, though when he entered the house he realized they were having coffee again probably because there was a fire on the hearth, before which the rug now lay spread over the backs of the two chairs. The tracks of his father's foot were gone. Where they had been were now long, water-cloudy scoriations resembling the sporadic course of a lilliputian mowing machine.

It still hung there while they ate the cold food and then went to bed, scattered without order or claim up and down the two rooms, his mother in one bed, where his father would later lie, the older brother in the other, himself, the aunt, and the two sisters on pallets on the floor. But his father was not in bed yet. The last thing the boy remembered was the depthless, harsh silhouette of the hat and coat bending over the rug and it seemed to him that he had not even closed his eyes when the silhouette was standing over him, the fire almost dead behind it, the stiff foot prodding him awake. "Catch up the mule," his father said.

When he returned with the mule his father was standing in the black door, the rolled rug over his shoulder. "Ain't you going to ride?" he said.

"No. Give me your foot."

He bent his knee into his father's hand, the wiry, surprising power flowed smoothly, rising, he rising with it, on to the mule's bare back (they had owned a saddle once; the boy could remember it though not when or where) and with the same effortlessness his father swung the rug up in front of him. Now in the starlight they retraced the afternoon's path, up the dusty road rife with honeysuckle, through the gate and up the black tunnel of the drive to the lightless house, where he sat on the mule and felt the rough warp of the rug drag across his thighs and vanish.

"Don't you want me to help?" he whispered. His father did not answer and now he heard again that stiff foot striking the hollow portico with that wooden and clocklike deliberation, that outrageous overstatement of the weight it carried. The rug, hunched, not flung (the boy could tell that even in the darkness) from his father's shoulder struck the angle of wall and floor with a sound unbelievably loud, thunderous, then the foot again, unhurried and enormous; a light came on in the house and the boy sat, tense, breathing steadily and quietly and just a little fast, though the foot itself did not increase its beat at all, descending the steps now; now the boy could see him.

"Don't you want to ride now?" he whispered. "We kin both ride now," the light within the house altering now, flaring up and sinking. *He's coming down the stairs now,* he thought. He had already ridden the mule up beside the horse block; presently his father was up behind him and he doubled the reins over and slashed the mule across the neck, but before the animal could begin to trot the hard, thin arm came round him, the hard, knotted hand jerking the mule back to a walk.

In the first red rays of the sun they were in the lot, putting plow gear on the mules. This time the sorrel mare was in the lot before he heard it at all, the rider collarless and even bareheaded, trembling, speaking in a shaking voice as the woman in the house had done, his father merely looking up once before stooping again to the hame he was buckling, so that the man on the mare spoke to his stooping back:

"You must realize you have ruined that rug. Wasn't there anybody here, any of your women . . ." he ceased, shaking, the boy watching him, the older brother leaning now in the stable door, chewing, blinking slowly and steadily at nothing apparently. "It cost a hundred dollars. But you never had a hundred dollars. You never will. So I'm going to charge you twenty bushels of corn against your crop. I'll add it in your contract and when you come to the commissary you can sign it. That won't keep Mrs. de Spain quiet but maybe it will teach you to wipe your feet off before you enter her house again."

Then he was gone. The boy looked at his father, who still had not spoken or even looked up again, who was now adjusting the loggerhead in the hame.

"Pap," he said. His father looked at him—the inscrutable face, the shaggy brows beneath which the gray eyes glinted coldly. Suddenly the boy went toward him, fast, stopping as suddenly. "You done the best you could!" he cried. "If he wanted hit done differently why didn't he wait and tell you how? He won't git no twenty bushels! He won't git none! We'll gether hit and hide hit! I kin watch . . ."

"Did you put the cutter back in that straight stock like I told you?"

"No, sir," he said.

"Then go do it."

That was Wednesday. During the rest of that week he worked steadily, at what was within his scope and some which was beyond it, with an industry that did not need to be driven nor even commanded twice; he had this from his mother, with the difference that some at least of what he did he liked to do, such as splitting wood with the half-size axe which his mother and aunt had earned, or saved money somehow, to present him with at Christmas. In company with the two older women (and on one afternoon, even one of the sisters), he built pens for the shoat and the cow which were a part of his father's contract with the landlord, and one afternoon, his father being absent, gone somewhere on one of the mules, he went to the field.

They were running a middle buster now, his brother holding the plow straight while he handled the reins, and walking beside the straining mule, the rich black soil shearing cool and damp against his bare ankles, he thought *Maybe this is the end of it. Maybe even that twenty bushels that seems hard to have to pay for just a rug will be a cheap price for him to stop forever and always from being what he used to be;* thinking, dreaming now, so that his brother had to speak sharply to him to mind the mule: *Maybe he even won't collect the twenty bushels. Maybe it will all add up and balance and vanish—corn, rug, fire; the terror and grief, the being pulled two ways like between two teams of horses—gone, done with for ever and ever.*

Then it was Saturday; he looked up from beneath the mule he was harnessing and saw his father in the black coat and hat. "Not that," his father said. "The wagon gear." And then, two hours later, sitting in the wagon bed behind his father and brother on the seat, the wagon accomplished a final curve, and he saw the weathered paintless store with its tattered tobacco- and patent-medicine posters and the tethered wagons and saddle animals below the gallery. He mounted the gnawed steps behind his father and brother, and there again was the lane of quiet, watching faces for the three of them to walk through. He saw the man in spectacles sitting at the plank table and he did not need to be told this was a Justice of the Peace; he sent one glare of fierce, exultant, partisan defiance at the man in collar and cravat now, whom he had seen but twice before in his life, and that on a galloping horse, who now wore on his face an expression not of rage but of amazed unbelief which the boy could not have known was at the incredible circumstance of being sued by one of his own tenants, and came and stood against his father and cried at the Justice: "He ain't done it! He ain't burnt . . ."

"Go back to the wagon," his father said.

"Burnt?" the Justice said. "Do I understand this rug was burned too?"

"Does anybody here claim it was?" his father said. "Go back to the wagon." But he did not, he merely retreated to the rear of the room, crowded as that other had been, but not to sit down this time, instead, to stand pressing among the motionless bodies, listening to the voices:

"And you claim twenty bushels of corn is too high for the damage you did to the rug?"

"He brought the rug to me and said he wanted the tracks washed out of it. I washed the tracks out and took the rug back to him."

"But you didn't carry the rug back to him in the same condition it was in before you made the tracks on it."

His father did not answer, and now for perhaps half a minute there was no sound at all save that of breathing, the faint, steady suspiration of complete and intent listening.

"You decline to answer that, Mr. Snopes?" Again his father did not answer. "I'm going to find against you, Mr. Snopes. I'm going to find that you were responsible for the injury to Major de Spain's rug and hold you liable for it. But twenty bushels of corn seems a little high for a man in your circumstances to have to pay. Major de Spain claims it cost a hundred dollars. October corn will be worth about fifty cents. I figure that if Major de Spain can stand a ninety-five dollar loss on something he paid cash for, you can stand a five-dollar loss you haven't earned yet. I hold you in damages to Major de Spain to the amount of ten bushels of corn over and above your contract with him, to be paid to him out of your crop at gathering time. Court adjourned."

It had taken no time hardly, the morning was but half begun. He thought they would return home and perhaps back to the field, since they were late, far behind all other farmers. But instead his father passed on behind the wagon, merely indicating with his hand for the older brother to follow with it, and crossed the road toward the blacksmith shop opposite, pressing on after his father, overtaking him, speaking, whispering up at the harsh, calm face beneath the weathered hat: "He won't git no ten bushels neither. He won't git one. We'll . . ." until his father glanced for an instant down at him, the face absolutely calm, the grizzled eyebrows tangled above the cold eyes, the voice almost pleasant, almost gentle:

"You think so? Well, we'll wait till October anyway."

The matter of the wagon—the setting of a spoke or two and the tightening of the tires—did not take long either, the business of the tires accomplished by driving the wagon into the spring branch behind the shop and letting it stand there, the mules nuzzling into the water from time to time, and the boy on the seat with the idle reins, looking up the slope and through the sooty tunnel of the shed where the slow hammer rang and where his father sat on an upended cypress bolt, easily, either talking or listening, still sitting there when the boy brought the dripping wagon up out of the branch and halted it before the door.

"Take them on to the shade and hitch," his father said. He did so and returned. His father and the smith and a third man squatting on his heels inside the door were talking, about crops and animals; the boy, squatting too in the ammoniac dust and hoof-parings and scales of rust, heard his father tell a long and unhurried story out of the time before the birth of the older brother even when he had been a professional horsetrader. And then his father came up beside him where he stood before a tattered last year's circus poster on the other side of the store, gazing rapt and quiet at the scarlet horses, the incredible poisings and convolutions of tulle and tights and the painted leers of comedians, and said, "It's time to eat."

But not at home. Squatting beside his brother against the front wall, he watched his father emerge from the store and produce from a paper sack a segment of cheese and divide it carefully and deliberately into three with his pocket knife and produce crackers from the same sack. They all three squatted on the gallery and ate, slowly, without talking; then in the store again, they drank from a tin dipper tepid water smelling of the cedar bucket and of living beech trees. And still they did not go home. It was a horse lot this time, a tall rail fence upon and along which men stood and sat and out of which one by one horses were led, to be walked and trotted and then cantered back and forth along the road while the slow swapping and buying went on and the sun began to slant westward, they—the three of them—watching and listening, the older brother with his muddy eyes and his steady, inevitable tobacco, the father commenting now and then on certain of the animals, to no one in particular.

It was after sundown when they reached home. They ate supper by lamplight, then, sitting on the doorstep, the boy watched the night fully accomplish, listening to the whippoorwills and the frogs, when he heard his mother's voice: "Abner! No! No! Oh, God. Oh, God. Abner!" and he rose, whirled, and saw the altered light through the door where a candle stub now burned in a bottle neck on the table and his father, still in the hat and coat, at once formal and burlesque as though dressed carefully for some shabby and ceremonial violence, emptying the reservoir of the lamp back into the five-gallon kerosene can from which it had been filled, while the mother tugged at his arm until he shifted the lamp to the other hand and flung her back, not savagely or viciously, just hard, into the wall, her hands flung out against the wall for balance, her mouth open and in her face the same quality of hopeless despair as had been in her voice. Then his father saw him standing in the door.

"Go to the barn and get that can of oil we were oiling the wagon with," he said. The boy did not move. Then he could speak.

"What . . ." he cried. "What are you . . ."

"Go get that oil," his father said. "Go."

Then he was moving, running, outside the house, toward the stable: this the old habit, the old blood which he had not been permitted to choose for himself, which had been bequeathed him willy nilly and which had run for so long (and who knew where, battening on what of outrage and savagery and lust) before it came to him. *I could keep on,* he thought. *I could run on and on and never look back, never need to see his face again. Only I can't. I can't,* the rusted can in his hand now, the liquid sploshing in it as he ran back to the house and into it, into the sound of his mother's weeping in the next room, and handed the can to his father.

"Ain't you going to even send a nigger?" he cried. "At least you sent a nigger before!"

This time his father didn't strike him. The hand came even faster than the blow had, the same hand which had set the can on the table with almost excruciating care flashing from the can toward him too quick for him to follow it, gripping him by the back of his shirt and on to tiptoe before he had seen it quit the can, the face stooping at him in breathless and frozen ferocity, the cold, dead voice speaking over him to the older brother who leaned against the table, chewing with that steady, curious, sidewise motion of cows:

"Empty the can into the big one and go on. I'll catch up with you."

"Better tie him up to the bedpost," the brother said.

"Do like I told you," the father said. Then the boy was moving, his bunched shirt and the hard, bony hand between his shoulder-blades, his toes just touching the floor, across the room and into the other one, past the sisters sitting with spread heavy thighs in the two chairs over the cold hearth, and to where his mother and aunt sat side by side on the bed, the aunt's arms about his mother's shoulders.

"Hold him," the father said. The aunt made a startled movement. "Not you," the father said. "Lennie. Take hold of him. I want to see you do it." His mother took him by the wrist. "You'll hold him better than that. If he gets loose don't you know what he is going to do? He will go up yonder." He jerked his head toward the road. "Maybe I'd better tie him."

"I'll hold him," his mother whispered.

"See you do then." Then his father was gone, the stiff foot heavy and measured upon the boards, ceasing at last.

Then he began to struggle. His mother caught him in both arms, he jerking and wrenching at them. He would be stronger in the end, he knew that. But he had no time to wait for it. "Lemme go!" he cried. "I don't want to have to hit you!"

"Let him go!" the aunt said. "If he don't go, before God, I am going up there myself!"

"Don't you see I can't?" his mother cried. "Sarty! Sarty! No! No! Help me, Lizzie!"

Then he was free. His aunt grasped at him but it was too late. He whirled, running, his mother stumbled forward on to her knees behind him, crying to the nearer sister: "Catch him, Net! Catch him!" But that was too late too, the sister (the sisters were twins, born at the same time, yet either of them now gave the impression of being, encompassing as much living meat and volume and weight as any other two of the family) not yet having begun to rise from the chair, her head, face, alone merely turned, presenting to him in the flying instant an astonishing expanse of young female features untroubled by any surprise even, wearing only an expression of bovine interest. Then he was out of the room, out of the house, in the mild dust of the starlit road and the heavy rifeness of honeysuckle, the pale ribbon unspooling with terrific slowness under his running feet, reaching the gate at last and turning in, running, his heart and lungs drumming, on up the drive toward the lighted house, the lighted door. He did not knock, he burst in, sobbing for breath, incapable for the moment of speech; he saw the astonished face of the Negro in the linen jacket without knowing when the Negro had appeared.

"De Spain!" he cried, panted. "Where's . . ." then he saw the white man too emerging from a white door down the hall. "Barn!" he cried. "Barn!"

"What?" the white man said. "Barn?"

"Yes!" the boy cried. "Barn!"

"Catch him!" the white man shouted.

But it was too late this time too. The Negro grasped his shirt, but the entire sleeve, rotten with washing, carried away, and he was out that door and in the drive again, and had actually never ceased to run even while he was screaming into the white man's face.

Behind him the white man was shouting, "My horse! Fetch my horse!" and he thought for an instant of cutting across the park and climbing the fence into the road, but he did not know the park nor how high the vine-massed fence might be and he dared not risk it. So he ran down the drive, blood and breath roaring; presently he was in the road again though he could not see it. He could not hear either: the galloping mare was almost upon him before he heard her, and even then he held his course, as if the very urgency of his wild grief and need must in a moment more find him wings, waiting until the ultimate instant to hurl himself aside and into the weed-choked roadside ditch as the horse thundered past and on, for an instant in furious silhouette against the stars, the tranquil early summer night sky which, even before the shape of the horse and rider vanished, stained abruptly and violently upward: a long, swirling roar incredible and soundless, blotting the stars, and he springing up and into the road again, running again, knowing it was too late yet still running even after he heard the shot and, an instant later, two shots, pausing now without knowing he had ceased to run, crying, "Pap! Pap!", running again before he knew he had begun to run, stumbling, tripping over something and scrabbling up again without ceasing to run, looking backward over his shoulder at the glare as he got up, running on among the invisible trees, panting, sobbing, "Father! Father!"

At midnight he was sitting on the crest of a hill. He did not know it was midnight and he did not know how far he had come. But there was no glare behind him now and he sat now, his face toward the dark woods which he would enter when breath was strong again, small, shaking steadily in the chill darkness, hugging himself into the remainder of his thin, rotten shirt, the grief and despair now no longer terror and fear but just grief and despair. *Father. My father,* he thought. "He was brave!" he cried suddenly, aloud but not loud, no more than a whisper: "He was! He was in the war! He was in Colonel Sartoris' cav'ry!" not knowing that his father had gone to that war a private in the fine old European sense, wearing no uniform, admitting the authority of and giving fidelity to no man or army or flag, going to war as Malbrouck himself did: for booty—it meant nothing and less than nothing to him if it were enemy booty or his own.

The slow constellations wheeled on. It would be dawn and then sun-up after a while and he would be hungry. But that would be to-morrow and now he was only cold, and walking would cure that. His breathing was easier now and he decided to get up and go on, and then he found that he had been asleep because he knew it was almost dawn, the night almost over. He could tell that from the whippoorwills. They were everywhere now among the dark trees below him, constant and inflectioned and ceaseless, so that, as the instant for giving over to the day birds drew nearer and nearer, there was no interval at all between them. He got up. He was a little stiff, but walking would cure that too as it would the cold, and soon there would be the sun. He went on down the hill, toward the dark woods within which the liquid silver voices of the birds called unceasing—the rapid and urgent beating of the urgent and quiring heart of the late spring night. He did not look back.

1939

CONRAD AIKEN

Strange Moonlight

It had been a tremendous week—colossal. Its reverberations around him hardly yet slept—his slightest motion or thought made a vast symphony of them, like a breeze in a forest of bells. In the first place, he had filched a volume of Poe's tales from his mother's bookcase, and had had in consequence a delirious night in inferno. Down, down he had gone with heavy clangs about him, coiling spouts of fire licking dryly at an iron sky, and a strange companion, of protean shape and size, walking and talking beside him. For the most part, this companion seemed to be nothing but a voice and a wing—an enormous jagged black wing, soft and drooping like a bat's; he had noticed veins in it. As for the voice, it had been singularly gentle. If it was mysterious, that was no doubt because he himself was stupid. Certainly it had sounded placid and reasonable, exactly, in fact, like his father's explaining a

Conrad Aiken was born in 1889 in Savannah, Georgia. His narratives of spiritual terror and self-awareness are greatly influenced by the psychoanalytic theories of Freud, as well as by his own traumatic memory of finding at a young age the dead bodies of his parents (Aiken's father killed his wife and then himself). Aiken graduated from Harvard University, where he was a schoolmate and friend of such writers as T. S. Eliot and e. e. cummings. He is remembered for both his Pulitzer Prize–winning poetry and such prose works as *Blue Voyage* (1927) and the autobiographical *Ushant: An Essay* (1952). Living much of his life in England, Aiken was influential in introducing American poets to the British. He died in the city of his birth in 1973.

problem in mathematics; but, though he had noticed the orderly and logical structure, and felt the inevitable approach toward a vast and beautiful or terrible conclusion, the nature and meaning of the conclusion itself always escaped him. It was as if, always, he had come just too late. When, for example, he had come at last to the black wall that inclosed the infernal city, and seen the arched gate, the voice had certainly said that if he hurried he would see, through the arch, a far, low landscape of extraordinary wonder. He had hurried, but it had been in vain. He had reached the gate, and for the tiniest fraction of an instant he had even glimpsed the wide green of fields and trees, a winding blue ribbon of water, and a gleam of intense light touching to brilliance some far object. But then, before he had time to notice more than that every detail in this fairy landscape seemed to lead toward a single shining solution, a dazzling significance, suddenly the infernal rain, streaked fire and rolling smoke, had swept it away. Then the voice had seemed to become ironic. He had failed, and he felt like crying.

He had still, the next morning, felt that he might, if the opportunity offered, see that vision. It was always just round the corner, just at the head of the stairs, just over the next page. But other adventures had intervened. Prize-day, at school, had come upon him as suddenly as a thunderstorm—the ominous hushed gathering of the entire school into one large room, the tense air of expectancy, the solemn speeches, all had reduced him to a state of acute terror. There was something unintelligible and sinister about it. He had, from first to last, a peculiar physical sensation that something threatened him, and here and there, in the interminable vague speeches, a word seemed to have eyes and to stare at him. His prescience had been correct—abruptly his name had been called, he had walked unsteadily amid applause to the teacher's desk, had received a small black pasteboard box; and then had cowered in his chair again, with the blood in his temples beating like gongs. When it was over, he had literally run away—he didn't stop till he reached the park. There, among the tombstones (the park had once been a graveyard) and trumpet-vines, he sat on the grass and opened the box. He was dazzled. The medal was of gold, and rested on a tiny blue satin cushion. His name was engraved on it—yes, actually cut into the gold; he felt the incisions with his fingernail. It was an experience not wholly to be comprehended. He put the box down in the grass and detached himself from it, lay full length, resting his chin on his wrist, and stared first at a tombstone and then at the small gold object, as if to discover the relation between them. Humming-birds, tombstones, trumpet-vines, and a gold medal. Amazing. He unpinned the medal from its cushion, put the box in his pocket, and walked slowly homeward, carrying the small, live, gleaming thing between fingers and thumb as if it were a bee. This was an experience to be carefully concealed from mother and father. Possibly he would tell Mary and John. . . . Unfortunately, he met his father as he was going in the door, and was thereafter drowned, for a day, in a glory without significance. He felt ashamed, and put the medal away in a drawer, sternly forbidding Mary and John to look at it. Even so, he was horribly conscious of it— its presence there burned him unceasingly. Nothing afforded escape from it, not even sitting under the peach tree and whittling a boat.

II

The oddest thing was the way these and other adventures of the week all seemed to unite, as if they were merely aspects of the same thing. Everywhere lurked that extraordinary hint of the enigma and its shining solution. On Tuesday morning, when it was pouring with rain, and he and Mary and John were conducting gigantic military operations in the back hall, with hundreds of paper soldiers, tents, cannon, battleships, and forts, suddenly through the tall open window, a goldfinch flew in from the rain, beat wildly against a pane of glass, darted several times to and fro above their heads, and finally, finding the open window, flashed out. It flew to the peach tree, rested there for a moment, and then over the outhouse and away. He saw it rising and falling in the rain. This was beautiful—it was like the vision in the infernal city, like the medal in the grass. He found it impossible to go on with the Battle of Gettysburg and abandoned it to Mary and John, who instantly started to quarrel. Escape was necessary, and he went into his own room, shut the door, lay on his bed, and began thinking about Caroline Lee.

John Lee had taken him there to see his new air-gun and a bag of BB shot. The strange house was dim and exciting. A long winding dark staircase went up from near the front door, a clock was striking in a far room, a small beautiful statue of a lady, slightly pinkish, and looking as if it had been dug out of the earth, stood on a table. The wallpaper beside the staircase was rough and hairy. Upstairs, in the playroom, they found Caroline, sitting on the floor with a picture book. She was learning to read, pointing at the words with her finger. He was struck by the fact that, although she was extraordinarily strange and beautiful, John Lee did not seem to be aware of it and treated her as if she were quite an ordinary sort of person. This gave him courage, and after the air-gun had been examined, and the bag of BB shot emptied of its gleaming heavy contents and then luxuriously refilled, he told her some of the words she couldn't make out. "And what's this?" she had said—he could still hear her say it, quite clearly. She was thin, smaller than himself, with dark hair and large pale eyes, and her forehead and hands looked curiously transparent. He particularly noticed her hands when she brought her five-dollar goldpiece to show him, opening a little jewel box which had in it also a necklace of yellow beads from Egypt and a pink shell from Tybee Beach. She gave him the goldpiece to look at, and while he was looking at it put the beads round her neck. "Now, I'm an Egyptian!" she said, and laughed shyly, running her fingers to and fro over the smooth beads. A fearful temptation came upon him. He coveted the goldpiece, and thought that it would be easy to steal it. He shut his hand over it and it was gone. If it had been John's, he might have done so, but, as it was, he opened his hand again and put the goldpiece back in the box. Afterwards, he stayed for a long while, talking with John and Caroline. The house was mysterious and rich, and he hadn't at all wanted to go out of it, or back to his own humdrum existence. Besides, he liked to hear Caroline talking.

But although he had afterwards for many days wanted to go back to that house, to explore further its dim rich mysteriousness, and had thought about it a great deal, John hadn't again suggested a visit, and he himself had felt a curious reluctance about raising the subject. It had been, apparently, a vision that was not to be repeated, an incursion into a world that was so beautiful and strange that one was permitted of it only the briefest of glimpses. He had, almost, to reassure himself that the house was really there, and for that reason he made rather a point of walking home from school with John Lee. Yes, the house was there —he saw John climb the stone steps and open the huge green door. There was never a sign of Caroline, however, nor any mention of her; until one day he heard from another boy that she was ill with scarlet fever, and observed that John had stayed away from school. The news didn't startle or frighten him. On the contrary, it seemed just the sort of romantic privilege in which such fortunate people would indulge. He felt a certain delicacy about approaching the house, however, to see if the red quarantine sign had been affixed by the door, and carefully avoided Gordon Square on his way home from school. Should he write her a letter or send her a present of marbles? For neither action did there seem to be sufficient warrant. But he found it impossible to do nothing, and later in the afternoon, by a very circuitous route which took him past the county jail—where he was thrilled by actually seeing a prisoner looking out between the gray iron bars—he slowly made his way to Gordon Square and from a safe distance, more or less hiding himself behind a palmetto tree, looked for a long while at the wonderful house, and saw, sure enough, the red sign.

Three days later he heard that Caroline Lee was dead. The news stunned him. Surely it could not be possible? He felt stifled, frightened, and incredulous. In a way, it was just what one would expect of Caroline, but none the less he felt outraged. How was it possible for anyone, whom one actually knew, to *die?* Particularly anyone so vividly and beautifully remembered! The indignity, the horror, of death obsessed him. *Had* she actually died? He went again to Gordon Square, not knowing precisely what it was that he expected to find, and saw something white hanging by the green door. But if, as it appeared, it was true that Caroline Lee, somewhere inside the house, lay dead, lay motionless, how did it happen that he, who was so profoundly concerned, had not at all been consulted, had not been invited to come and talk with her, and now found himself so utterly and hopelessly and forever excluded—from the house, as from her? This was a thing which he could not understand. As he walked home, pondering it, he thought of the five-dollar goldpiece. What would become of it? Probably John would get it, and, if so, he would steal it from him. . . . All the same, he was glad he hadn't taken it.

To this reflection he came back many times, as now once more with the Battle of Gettysburg raging in the next room. If he had actually taken it, what a horror it would have been! As it was, the fact that he had resisted the temptation, restored the goldpiece to the box, seemed to have been a tribute to Caroline's beauty and strangeness. Yes, for nobody else would he have made the refusal—nobody on earth. But, for her, it had been quite simple, a momentary pang quickly lost in the pleasure of hearing her voice, watching her pale hands twisting the yellow beads, and helping her with her reading. "And what's this?" she had said, and "Now I'm an Egyptian!" . . . What was death that could put an end to a clear voice saying such things? . . . Mystery was once more about him, the same mystery that had shone in the vision of the infernal city. There was something beautiful which he could not understand. He had felt it while he was lying in the grass among the tombstones, looking at the medal; he had felt it when the goldfinch darted in from the rain and then out again. All these things seemed in some curious way to fit together.

III

The same night, after he had gone to bed, this feeling of enormous and complicated mystery came upon him again with oppressive weight. He lay still, looking from his pillow through the tall window at the moonlight on the white outhouse wall, and again it seemed to him that the explanation for everything was extraordinarily near at hand if he could only find it. The mystery was like the finest of films, like the moonlight on the white wall. Surely, beneath it, there was something solid and simple. He heard someone walk across the yard, with steps that seemed astoundingly far apart and slow. The steps ceased, a door creaked. Then there was a cough. It was old Selena, the Negro cook, going out for wood. He heard the sticks being piled up, then the creak of the door again, and again the slow steps on the hard baked ground of the yard, æons apart. How did the peach tree look in the moonlight? Would its leaves be dark, or shiny? And the chinaberry tree? He thought of the two trees standing there motionless in the moonlight, and at last felt that he must get out of bed and look at them. But when he had reached the hall, he heard his mother's voice from downstairs, and he went and lay on the old sofa in the hall, listening. Could he have heard aright? His mother had just called his father "Boy!" Amazing!

"It's two parties *every* week, and sometimes three or four, that's excessive. You know it is."

"Darling, I *must* have *some* recreation!"

His father laughed in a peculiar angry way that he had never heard before—as strange, indeed, as his mother's tone had been.

"Recreation's all right," he said, "but you're neglecting your family. If it goes on, I'll have another child—that's all."

He got off the sofa and went softly down the stairs to the turn of the railing. He peered over the banisters with infinite caution, and what he saw filled him with horror. His mother was sitting on his father's knee, with her arms about his neck. She was kissing him. How awful! . . . He couldn't look at it. What on earth, he wondered as he climbed back into bed, was it all about? There was something curious in the way they were talking, something not at all like fathers and mothers, but more like children, though he couldn't in the least understand it. At the same time, it was offensive.

He began to make up a conversation with Caroline Lee. She was sitting under the peach tree with him, reading her book. What beautiful hands she had! They were transparent, somehow, like her forehead, and her dark hair and large pale eyes delighted him. Perhaps she *was* an Egyptian!

"It must be nice to live in your house," he said.

"Yes, it's very nice. And you haven't seen half of it, either."

"No, I haven't. I'd like to see it all. I liked the hairy wallpaper and the pink statue of the lady on the table. Are there any others like it?"

"Oh, yes, lots and lots! In the secret room downstairs, where you heard the silver clock striking, there are fifty other statues, all more beautiful than that one, and a collection of clocks of every kind."

"Is your father very rich?"

"Yes, he's richer than anybody. He has a special carved ivory box to keep his collars in."

"What does it feel like to die—were you sorry?"

"Very sorry! But it's really quite easy—you just hold your breath and shut your eyes."

"Oh!"

"And when you're lying there, after you've died, you're really just pretending. You keep very still, and you have your eyes *almost* shut, but really you know everything! You watch the people and listen to them."

"But don't you want to talk to them, or get out of bed, or out of your coffin?"

"Well, yes, at first you do—but it's nicer than being alive."

"Why?"

"Oh, I don't know! You understand everything so easily!"

"How nice that must be!"

"It is."

"But after they've shut you up in a coffin and sung songs over you and carried you to Bonaventure and buried you in the ground, and you're down there in the dark with all that earth above you—isn't that horrible?"

"Oh, no! . . . As soon as nobody is looking, when they've all gone home to tea, you just get up and walk away. You climb out of the earth just as easily as you'd climb out of bed."

"That's how you're here now, I suppose."

"Of course!"

"Well, it's very nice."

"It's lovely. . . . Don't I look just as well as ever?"

"Yes, you do."

There was a pause, and then Caroline said:

"I know you wanted to steal my goldpiece—I was awfully glad when you put it back. If you had asked me for it, I'd have given it to you."

"I like you very much, Caroline. Can I come to Bonaventure and play with you?"

"I'm afraid not. You'd have to come in the dark."

"But I could bring a lantern."

"Yes, you could do that."

. . . It seemed to him that they were no longer sitting under the peach tree, but walking along the white shell-road to Bonaventure. He held the lantern up beside a chinquapin tree, and Caroline reached up with her pale, small hands and picked two chinquapins. Then they crossed the little bridge, walking carefully between the rails on the sleepers. Mossy trees were all about them; the moss, in long festoons, hung lower and lower, and thicker and thicker, and the wind made a soft, seething sound as it sought a way through the gray ancient forest.

IV

It had been his intention to explore, the next morning, the vault under the mulberry tree in the park—his friend Harry had mentioned that it was open, and that one could go down very dusty steps and see, on the dark floor, a few rotted boards and a bone or two. At breakfast he enlisted Mary and John for the expedition; but then there were unexpected developments. His father and mother had abruptly decided that the whole family would spend the day at Tybee Beach. This was festive and magnificent beyond belief. The kitchen became a turmoil. Selena ran to and fro with sugar sandwiches, pots of deviled ham, cookies, hard-boiled eggs, and a hundred other things; piles of beautiful sandwiches were exquisitely folded up in shining, clean napkins, and the wicker basket was elaborately packed. John and Mary decided to take their pails with them, and stamped up and downstairs, banging the pails with the shovels. He himself was a little uncertain what to take. He stood by his desk wondering. He would like to take Poe's tales, but that was out of the question, for he wasn't supposed to have the book at all. Marbles, also, were dismissed as unsuitable. He finally took his gold medal out of its drawer and put it in his pocket. He would keep it a secret, of course.

All the way to the station he was conscious of the medal burning in his pocket. He closed his fingers over it, and again felt it to be a live thing, as if it were buzzing, beating invisible wings. Would his fingers have a waxy smell, as they did after they'd been holding a June bug, or tying a thread to one of its legs? . . . Father carried the basket, Mary and John clanked their pails, everybody was talking and laughing. They climbed into the funny, undignified little train, which almost immediately was lurching over the wide, green marshes, rattling over red-iron bridges enormously complicated with girders and trusses. Great excitement when they passed the gray stone fort, Fort Pulaski. They'd seen it once from the river, when they were on the steamer going to the cotton islands. His father leaned down beside Mary to tell her about Fort Pulaski, just as a cloud shadow, crossing it, made it somber. How nice his father's smile was! He had never noticed it before. It made him feel warm and shy. He looked out at the interminable green marshes, the flying clouds of rice-birds, the channels of red water lined with red mud, and listened intently to the strange complex rhythm of the wheels on the rails and the prolonged melancholy wail of the whistle. How curious it all was! His mother was sitting opposite him, very quiet, her gray eyes turned absently toward the window. She wasn't looking at things—she was thinking. If she had been looking at things, her eyes would have moved to and fro, as Mary's were doing.

"Mother," he said, "did you bring our bathing suits?"

"Yes, dear."

The train was rounding a curve and slowing down. They had suddenly left the marshes and were among low sand dunes covered with tall grass. He saw a man, very red-faced, just staggering over the top of one of the dunes and waving a stick. . . . It was hot. They filed slowly off the train and one by one jumped down into the burning sand. How strange it was to walk in! They laughed and shrieked, feeling themselves helpless, ran and jumped, straddled up the steep root-laced sides of dunes and slid down again in slow, warm avalanches of lazy sand. Mother and father, picking their way between the dunes, walked slowly ahead, carrying the basket between them—his father pointed at something. The sunlight came down heavily like sheets of solid brass and they could feel the heat of the sand on their cheeks. Then at last they came out on the enormous white dazzling beach with its millions of shells, its black-and-white striped lighthouse, and the long, long sea, indolently blue, spreading out slow, soft lines of foam, and making an interminable rushing murmur like trees in a wind.

He felt instantly a desire, in all this space and light, to run for miles and miles. His mother and father sat under a striped parasol. Mary and John, now barefooted, had begun laborious and intense operations in the sand at the water's edge, making occasional sallies into the sliding water. He began walking away along the beach close to the waves, keeping his eye out for any particularly beautiful shell, and taking great care not to step on jellyfish. Suppose a school of flying fish, such as he had seen from the ship, should swim in close to the beach and then, by mistake, fly straight up onto the sand? How delightful that would be! It would be almost as exciting as finding buried treasure, a rotten chest full of goldpieces and seaweed and sand. He had often dreamt of thrusting his hand into such a sea-chest and feeling the small, hard, beautiful coins mixed with sand and weed. Some people said that Captain Kidd had buried treasure on Tybee Beach. Perhaps he'd better walk a little closer to the dunes, where it was certainly more likely that treasure would have been hidden. . . . He climbed a hot dune, taking hold of the feathery grass, scraping his bare legs on the coarse leaves, and filling his shoes with warm sand. The dune was scooped at the top like a volcano, the hollow all ringed with tall, whistling grass, a natural hiding place, snug and secret. He lay down, made excessively smooth a hand's breadth of sand, then took the medal out of his pocket and placed it there. It blazed beautifully. Was it as nice as the five-dollar goldpiece would have been? He liked especially the tiny links of the little gold chains by which the shield hung from the pin-bar. If only Caroline could see it! Perhaps if he stayed here, hidden from the family, and waited till they had gone back home, Caroline would somehow know where he was and come to him as soon as it was dark. He wasn't quite sure what would be the shortest way from Bonaventure, but Caroline would know —certainly. Then they would spend the night here, talking. He would exchange his medal for the five-dollar goldpiece, and perhaps she would bring, folded in a square of silk, the little pink statue. . . . Thus equipped, their house would be perfect. . . . He would tell her about the goldfinch interrupting the Battle of Gettysburg.

V

The chief event of the afternoon was the burial of his father, who had on his bathing suit. He and Mary and John all excitedly labored at this. When they had got one leg covered, the other would suddenly burst hairily out, or an arm would shatter its mold, and his father would laugh uproariously. Finally they had him wholly buried, all except his head, in a beautiful smooth mound. On top of this they put the two pails, a lot of pink shells in a row, like the buttons of a coat, and a collection of seaweeds. Mother, lying under her parasol, laughed lazily, deliciously. For the first time during the day she seemed to be really happy. She began pelting small shells at father, laughing in an odd, delightful, teasing way, as if she was a girl, and father pretended to be furious. How exactly like a new grave he looked! It was singularly as Caroline had described it, for there he was all alive in it, and talking, and able to get up whenever he liked. Mary and John, seeing mother throw shells, and hearing her teasing laughter, and father's comic rage, became suddenly excited. They began throwing things wildly—shells, handfuls of seaweed, and at last sand. At this, father suddenly leapt out of his tomb, terrifying them, scattered his grave clothes in every direction, and galloped gloriously down the beach into the sea. The upturned brown soles of his feet followed him casually into a long, curling green wave, and then his head came up shaking like a dog's and blowing water, and his strong white arms flashed slowly over and over in the sunlight as he swam far out. How magnificent! . . . He would like to be able to do that, to swim out and out and out, with a sea-gull flying close beside him, talking.

Later, when they had changed into their clothes again in the salty-smelling wooden bathhouse, they had supper on the veranda of the huge hotel. A band played, the colored waiters bowed and grinned. The sky turned pink, and began to dim; the sea darkened, making a far sorrowful sound; and twilight deepened slowly, slowly into night. The moon, which had looked like a white thin shell in the afternoon, turned now to the brightest silver, and he thought, as they walked silently toward the train, of which they could see the long row of yellow windows, that the beach and dunes looked more beautiful by moonlight than by sunlight. . . . How mysterious the flooded marshes looked, too, with the cold moon above them! They reminded him of something, he couldn't remember what. . . . Mary and John fell asleep in the train; his father and mother were silent. Someone in the car ahead was playing a concertina, and the plaintive sound mingled curiously with the clacking of the rails, the rattle of bridges, the long, lugubrious cry of the whistle. Hoo-o! Hoo-o! Where was it they were going—was it to anything so simple as home, the familiar house, the two familiar trees, or were they, rather, speeding like a fiery comet toward the world's edge, to plunge out into the unknown and fall down and down forever?

No, certainly it was not to the familiar. . . . Everything was changed and ghostly. The long street, in the moonlight, was like a deep river, at the bottom of which they walked, making scattered, thin sounds on the stones, and listening intently to the whisperings of elms and palmettos. And their house, when at last they stopped before it, how strange it was! The moonlight, falling through the two tall swaying oaks, cast a moving pattern of shadow and light all over its face. Slow swirls and spirals of black and silver, dizzy gallops, quiet pools of light abruptly shattered, all silently followed the swishing of leaves against the moon. It was like a vine of moonlight, which suddenly grew all over the house, smothering everything with its multitudinous swift leaves and tendrils of pale silver, and then as suddenly faded out. He stared up at this while his father fitted the key into the lock, feeling the ghostly vine grow strangely over his face and hands. Was it in this, at last, that he would find the explanation of all that bewildered him? Caroline, no doubt, would understand it; she was a sort of moonlight herself. He went slowly up the stairs. But as he took the medal and a small pink shell out of his pocket, and put them on his desk, he realized at last that Caroline was dead.

1966

ELIZABETH SPENCER

Moon Rocket

A cone of light fell on the open tablet, its page blank except for the formula $x = \frac{\pi}{r^2}$ printed across the top line. Bill looked up from his desk at the white wall before him. An equation, short and simple as this one, had divided the atom. It lifted huge rockets from their launching pads, roaring flame, their noses true upon the zenith, with the great oiled cylinder below, turning, turning, turning, silent in the tremendous certainty of power.

And with him inside!

Just back of the nickel and sapphire plated nose, in a room rife with instruments and gauges, in a chair no larger than this one . . . He trembled, right down through his shoe soles, and had turned back to his equation, when a knock sounded at his door.

Everybody had to knock. If they didn't, he would turn into Dongoo, the flying saucer pilot, and speak nothing but Orion. "That's because you wouldn't knock," he would explain. "It wasn't *me*, Bill," his sister would argue. "It was Mother that didn't knock." "I don't care!" he would say, sometimes in English, sometimes in Orion. Once he had gone everywhere on all fours speaking Orion and, from time to time, barking. He at last explained, getting up after he had driven a splinter into his knee, that he was Zoa, faithful dog of Dongoo, the flying saucer pilot. His father, who had an aunt by marriage named Zoa, said that it was a girl's name and wouldn't do. "Let's not make it any *more* complicated," his mother advised. "Anyway, dogs can't talk," his sister said. She thought she had him there: she was very dumb. "They can on Orion," he hardly took the trouble to reply.

So now they knocked.

Elizabeth Spencer was born in 1921 into a prosperous Mississippi farming family. After graduating from Belhaven College in Jackson, she attended Vanderbilt University, which was at the time the seat of the renaissance of southern literature. There Spencer came to terms with the giants (and rivals) in the field—William Faulkner and Eudora Welty—and adopted for her own style a precise and polished realism. Her first novels were set in her home state. But in 1953 Spencer carried her southern sensibility worldwide, living in both Italy and Quebec and including these places and experiences in such works as *The Light in the Piazza* (1960). Spencer is currently a professor of creative writing at the University of North Carolina, Chapel Hill.

"Come in!" he remembered to say.

The door cracked softly open. It was his mother. "Did you forget about Trick or Treat?" she asked.

"Oh!" He turned around in his chair like a busy executive and rapidly stroked his palm across that part of his head where a forelock would have grown if he had not had a crew cut. It was a sign he was worried.

"They called you twice," she told him. "They waited a long long time."

He remembered now, back through the ages, the centuries, the great wash and wallow of clouds swirling, streaming, foaming, forming—breaking now like the wash of the ocean against rocks, now blown aside to expose the deep naked sky itself, shot into the immense reaches with worlds that turned to lights in green in red in blue in crystal white, as far as thought could reach to them, where meteors like Cadillacs scorched by, and white gleaming stuff fell into his face like snow, and anybody could see the answer to No. 9, though No. 10 looked hard enough to keep him for a while . . . he remembered back to ten minutes or twenty or no time at all ago when the children all came into the living room, as they had promised, to get his sister and him. The breath of cheerful cold in the house had come back all the way to where he was. He was happy they had come. He heard the murmur of their voices answering things his mother and father asked them, and now he would go out and see all the costumes, the masks, and smell up close the chilly excitement.

All the candy!

He jumped up and snatched from the bed where it was laid out for him, his red cloak with the black band at the top that buttoned closely at the throat, like Mandrake the Magician's cape, in the funny books, only not nearly so long. He put on his horrible mask, tying a careful knot to shorten the rubber band. The band prickled as it rolled on his crew cut down the slope of his head at the back. The coarse stiffened paper of the mask cut into the bridge of his nose. But in the mirror, didn't he look awful? He tried to make things worse, sticking out his tongue, making his ears waggle or his hair bristle straight up. He tossed on his black cowboy hat and drew the string up tight under his chin, bringing the brim down so no skin showed between the top of the mask and the hat. The results satisfied him perfectly. He stopped making faces, and thought that now, now was the moment to dash out among them, spin through and around them, admire them and be admired. He loved them. It would help his love along not even to know them in their masks and puffy long sleeves, or witches' skirts, and white ghost draperies. Should he wear his cowboy boots and maybe even take his gun? He didn't know. He took off the cape and laid it carefully on the bed, took off his hat and mask, and went to get the cowboy boots out of his closet. Then he sat down at the desk again and began to finish No. 10, the one he hadn't quite seen the answer to, though it would only take a minute. It had been sometime during this minute that his sister and his mother and his sister again had come and knocked and called and knocked again. "Just a minute," he had said. Hadn't he already foreseen everything that would happen, known already all the admiring and the love? It wasn't time yet to think beyond that.

Now it was too late. They were gone. He was filled with regret, though the solution to the problem stood beautifully, unassailably true on the top line of the new sheet. He sat stroking his hair.

His mother, who had prepared herself for this very thing, told him that all the others would be at Dicky Martin's house right now, for Dicky's mother had asked them to come there first and have some hot chocolate with gingerbread men—goblins and witches and ghosts, all the different shapes—she had heard about it on the telephone. That would make everything all right, wouldn't it? "Yes," he agreed, after considering it. "I believe it would."

When he went out the door, he tried to plant one of his great big smacks on his mother's cheek, but the horrible mask got in the way.

"Is he all squared away?" his father asked, as she came back into the living room.

"I think I broke through the sound barrier," she said. "He'll be O.K. now."

"Do you think he gets any *worse?*" he asked.

"He's just the same as he always was," she said. She kept up an amused tone—perhaps a good thing.

Bill had not gone far toward Dicky Martin's house when he ran into Janey. Janey was a Korean war orphan who had been adopted by some people who didn't have any little girl or little boy either. She had a face like the moon, broad with craters here and there on it: he thought this especially after he had seen the pictures of the far side of the moon, for her hair came down, making a fringe of shadows, and the front side of the moon had a man's face, broad and jolly, if petrified.

"Hey, Janey," he said, "what are you?"

"I'm a goblin," she said. She had a squeaky voice. It turned out that Janey was late because her mother hadn't finished her costume when the others came by. Bill's mother said that Janey was more American than her mother, whose name was plain Mrs. Brown, and who was never on time with a single thing.

"What's your name in Korean, Janey?" he asked her. He had asked her this a lot of times, for he liked to hear her reply, something that sounded like a little mouse telling you *its* name.

"You forgot your Trick or Treat basket," he said. "Everybody has to have one, to put all the candy in. You had one last year, remember?"

"Mother forgot," said Janey. She stopped short. "I'll go back."

"No, you can have mine," he said. "I'll carry it and you tell everybody it's yours."

"Then where are you going to put your candy?" she wondered in falsetto.

"In with yours. We'll divide later."

"O.K."

Walking together, step in step, with long matched strides, they ascended the rising street, but when they reached the corner to turn down to Dicky Martin's house, Bill kept right on going. The Martins' lights were near, just a few houses below, and you could hear giggles and shrieks of laughter. Janey had stopped. Bill turned back to her. "This way," she said, pointing.

"O.K.," he said, "in a minute. I want to go up here just a little way first. Come on. Janey, come on with me."

She hesitated a long time, but in the end she came, without asking any questions either. They had been friends all along, ever since he had brought her home with him from school without asking anybody, and his mother had been in bed sick and had sent Janey home because she couldn't stand noise in the house, any noise at all. Later, his mother had worried for fear Janey would think she had been discriminated against and sent away for being a Korean, so she acted especially nice to Janey after that and had a long talk with Bill to get him to be especially nice to Janey too. He did not pay any attention because none of this had anything to do with him and Janey.

He took Janey with him to the very top of the hill where the street ended. Here there was a barricade of crossed lumber, carelessly knocked together, and flares burned in low black pots, ugly as mines. They made a ghostly light leaping up against the sky now and again, turning the night black, even making the neatly drawn finish of the suburban street look ragged, unprecise, and open to flickering marvels. The children observed this without fear. They had always lived in a suburb, no house of which was more than ten years old: they could remember when the very trees were no taller than they themselves were now. If they had seen a real ghost, they would have thought only that it was one of their friends, dressed up, desiring candy.

Though the barrier and the flares seemed to mark the end of the hill, for the light rendered everything beyond itself a blank, Bill knew that the hill continued, and it became a new sort of terrain, strangely satisfying. He approached the lowest point of the barrier and stepped across. "Come on," he looked back to say.

"I can't," Janey squeaked. "It says Do Not Trespass."

He walked back and took her hand. Like her face, her hand was broad, and warmer than was usual for hands, as though her Oriental skin had a temperature all its own. She came forward slowly, like a blind person might, not mistrusting him, but simply hesitant in herself, though when he stepped over the barrier she came right over too. They stood together past the light and black-smelling smoke of the flares, hand in hand, in their strange garb, facing outward. Soon they could see the night for the first time, a large sky with strong, rapid masses of cloud, and a good many stars. Now, too, the land they stood on opened before them, and presently they could see it all.

It was a bare, dry land, with no trees, nothing growing on it. To the right, sinking down the fall of the hill, stood a row of small square houses, all dark. Some had timbers stacked near them, and large cratelike boxes for mixing cement. Pipes came down the raw sides of one or two, but were not joined to anything. Plank sidewalks had been laid for the workmen who came in the daytime to roll their wheelbarrows along from house to house. All the doors were empty and all the windows were black.

To the left the land was bare even of houses. It fell away more sharply, but large mounds of fresh earth marked it, like dunes, and long fissures scarred it, cracks such as an earthquake might make. Straight ahead of them was a little square house sitting on two large rollers, and towering behind it, a bulldozer and a machine with a long neck for biting the earth up and dumping it elsewhere. Bill knew the names of all the things here and he also knew exactly what was being done here: what they called a new subdivision. In the afternoons when he walked home from school the warm fall sun would be full of the sound of long buzzes and pauses that the machines made. He sometimes climbed up to the barrier and watched their ponderous maneuvers.

Yet now as he took a fresh grip on Janey's hand and drew her forward, he said: "You know where we are? This is the moon!"

"Really?" Janey said.

"Look up there," he said, pointing to the sky. "You don't see any moon up there, do you?"

She examined the sky while the clouds pushed silently on, and agreed.

"That's because we're *on it!*" He was terribly excited. He almost shouted.

He wanted to run forward with Janey in the marvelous floating giant steps of everybody's dreams. Perhaps, from that moment on, he might actually have made this his normal method of motion, to the astonishment of everybody in the whole world; for strange things are happening every day.

But Bill had taken only one or two such steps when he noticed something new at a little distance before them: a wheelbarrow maybe, sitting just back of one of the dunes. Then he saw when it moved, straightening up, that it wasn't a wheelbarrow at all, but somebody, grown up but not a man like their daddies, short but not a child like themselves, and though wearing tight black pants and a sweater of exaggerated weight and size, not to be thought of as in a costume, even on Halloween. Bill had seen boys like him by daylight. They were in the upper grades of schools he was still too young to attend. They grouped talking in front of little hole-in-the-wall cafés in an older part of town where the movie houses were, down below the new shopping center. He was not surprised to find one on the moon.

The boy backed off a step or two, bending almost double at the waist, seeking shadow. "Get away!" he whispered to them and made a shooing motion with his hands. "Get on away from here!"

"Who are you?" Bill asked, right out loud, but the boy continued to whisper, "I'm the night watchman. You little devils are not supposed to be here. Get out!"

"If you're the night watchman," Bill asked, "where is your flash-light?"

At that the boy decided to run at them in earnest. Bill knew now what to do; for all of us when we get to the moon will know exactly how to act. Out there on the distant fields of the heavens, chivalry still lives. Innocent maidens tremble in their little space suits at the approach of the wicked, and it is up to a stalwart rocket man to stand his ground. "Get behind me, Janey," he said, and pulled her back of him until they were standing like two slices of bread in a sandwich. Though he called her Janey, he had already decided that she was Thera the Moon Maiden.

He called out to the boy: "We're just children in Halloween suits, and we don't want to hurt anything."

On the low horizon far beyond the hill, the lights of a city were flashing up upon the clouds. This would be one of the great moon cities, lighted with sun borrowed from the other hemisphere, and surrounded by such high walls that from the earth they looked like barren craters. The boy would be one of those people who had killed somebody or robbed a bank or something in the city and had been condemned to walk out of it. He had been sent out alone while the policemen watched him. He had walked up a ramp to the towering plate glass gates, at a certain point breaking the electric current, so that the gates slid up automatically, and then he took one last bitter look back at the green city full of gardens and swimming pools with water sprays on everybody's lawn, with rainbows in ten colors playing in them, and then he walked out and the gates sank down again. So now he was out here in the dry chilly dark, trying to scare Dongoo and his friend Thera, who only wanted to reach the city.

Since the boy would not listen to the truth, but kept coming on at them, Bill leaned down and picked up a good-sized chunk of moon-hardened earth and threw it at him, to stop him. When the earth struck him, the boy leaned down in turn, saying something ugly, and caught up what looked like a club. He was coming on faster now, and when Dongoo charged at him to catch his arm he hurled the club at them.

The weapon missed Dongoo, but Thera the Moon Maiden gave a little cry and fell down. The next instant, Dongoo had plunged with flailing arms into the criminal from the moon city, who though at first in retreat, taken by surprise, rallied and struck Dongoo such a whack on the side of his head that he went off spinning and turning crazily, and fell down with his head reeling. When he could look up, he had begun to cry without deciding to, because the blow had been ugly and it had hurt. The quality that was so ugly had been the relentlessness— no instant of softening consideration that here was only a little boy in a Halloween suit. Was it only the dizziness or were there really not one bad boy, but lots of them, who had been thronging the shadows just out of sight, and now were running away? He didn't know. "Mean, mean, mean!" he tried to cry out, after them all, and running a few steps now this way, now that, he looked for wherever they might have gone to, and wished for his daddy and Janey's daddy to come and do all the things to them that he was too little to do himself. His mask was knocked to one side, his brave cape was in a sorry tangle about his arm. His broad black hat had fallen in the dust and been stepped on. He picked it up with a sob.

Then he heard a whimpering sound behind him and looked back.

Thera the Moon Maiden was sitting up, right where she had fallen. With her head in her hands, she was making the little sound, over and over. It was the exact sound, though she did not remember it, that she had been making in the debris of a burning Korean village, when a voice had said, "Well, whadayaknow!" and a pair of hands had reached down to her, and lifted her whole and safe without a scratch on her anywhere, out of a building where no two splinters were left together and every stone was blasted as fine as face powder. This sound, it seemed, always had the most marvelous results. When he heard it, Dongoo knew exactly what to do again.

He went to her and helped her up, dusting all the dirt off her space suit and out of her hair and off her cheek. Then he picked up the club the mean boy had thrown (it was an old corn stalk, with roots like bird claws clutching a heavy portion of dried earth). He put it in his Trick or Treat basket, in case he needed it, for defense. Then, once more, they set out together.

When they got to Dicky Martin's house, everybody was gone. Dicky Martin's mother came out on the front steps and admired their costumes. She offered to make them some more hot chocolate, but said that all the gingerbread men were eaten up. "No, thank you," Bill said. She made them promise to go straight home and not to look for the others, because it was Saturday night, after all, and there had been some bad neighborhood gangs of boys wandering around even in this district and she didn't know what the country was coming to.

Down the Martins' sidewalk and later on the street itself, Bill kept walking ahead of Janey with long steps, now circling back and around her, while she moved chunkily along in her orange goblin suit, and once when he circled her he heard her say, in her little voice:

"The night watchman threw a rock at us, but you chased him away."

He did not try to correct her, though he knew that none of it was true, even to the rock. It was what *was* true that kept worrying him, that he was trying to cast off by taking longer and longer steps, furling his cape in the night air, but still he could not feel any better. Back of all his painful new knowledge stood two ideas: one was that children in Halloween suits ought not to be thrown at and knocked down; the other was that Dongoo, the Rocket Man, ought to Win.

When they got to Janey's house, "This is where I live," she said and stopped, but he felt for the first time he could remember that it was necessary to be with somebody rather than to be alone. So he asked Janey to go to the drugstore and get something to eat, a chocolate milk shake maybe. And he continued to worry, all the while, and not to say anything.

Janey wanted a strawberry ice cream soda instead of a milk shake and he ordered one scoop of ice cream in a dish for himself, as he had known all along he would have to, because he just had a quarter. While they were waiting, Janey began telling him a long story about how her daddy caught a cold sitting up without any socks on to watch the late movie. When the soda came, she had to stand up on her knees on the seat to reach the straw.

Watching her, little by little, Bill began to feel O.K. again. He took off his horrible mask to eat the ice cream. At last he said, his eyes narrowing humorously, though he was tinged through with that knowledge which is always a lot like sadness: "You're from the moon."

"I'm not either," she said. "I'm from Green Avenue, just the same as you are."

"Your name is Thera," he pursued.

"It's not either," she said, and finished her ice cream soda with a snort of the straw. "My name is Janey Brown."

Taking up the long spoon, she began to eat the ice cream remaining in the tall glass, bending forward until her broad face hung almost directly over the mouth of the glass, the spoon moving into her mouth with the mysterious quickness of thinking about it. Only the slight motion of her jaw betrayed what pleasure she took in the flavored mixture, juicy with strawberry, tingling with carbonated foam.

1981

TRUMAN CAPOTE

Children on Their Birthdays

Yesterday afternoon the six-o'clock bus ran over Miss Bobbit. I'm not sure what there is to be said about it; after all, she was only ten years old, still I know no one of us in this town will forget her. For one thing, nothing she ever did was ordinary, not from the first time that we saw her, and that was a year ago. Miss Bobbit and her mother, they arrived on that same six-o'clock bus, the one that comes through from Mobile. It happened to be my cousin Billy Bob's birthday, and so most of the children in town were here at our house. We were sprawled on the front porch having tutti-frutti and devil cake when the bus stormed around Deadman's Curve. It was the summer that never rained; rusted dryness coated everything; sometimes when a car passed on the road, raised dust would hang in the still air an hour or more. Aunt El said if they didn't pave the highway soon, she was going to move down to the seacoast; but she'd said that for such a long time. Anyway, we were sitting on the porch, tutti-frutti melting on our plates, when suddenly, just as we were wishing that something would happen, something did; for out of the red road dust appeared Miss Bobbit. A wiry little girl in a starched lemon-colored party dress, she sassed along with a grown-up mince, one hand on her hip, the other supporting a spinsterish umbrella. Her mother, lugging two cardboard valises and a wind-up victrola, trailed in the background. She was a gaunt shaggy woman with silent eyes and a hungry smile.

All the children on the porch had grown so still that when a cone of wasps started humming, the girls did not set up their usual holler. Their attention was too fixed upon the approach of Miss Bobbit and her mother, who had by now reached the gate. "Begging your pardon,"

Truman Capote was born in New Orleans in 1924. After his parents' divorce he spent much of his youth with relatives, living in small towns across the deep South. This landscape was transformed into a surreal, gothic setting for his first, widely acclaimed novel, *Other Voices, Other Rooms* (1948). His subject matter, though, was restricted neither geographically nor generically, with much of his later writing smudging the line between reportage and literature. For example, *In Cold Blood* (1966), his account of a multiple murder in Kansas, was labeled a "nonfiction novel." For most of his life Capote traversed the country gathering material and writing travel sketches and celebrity portraits. He died in Los Angeles in 1984.

called Miss Bobbit in a voice that was at once silky and childlike, like a pretty piece of ribbon, and immaculately exact, like a movie star or a schoolmarm, "but might we speak with the grown-up persons of the house?" This, of course, meant Aunt El; and, at least to some degree, myself. But Billy Bob and all the other boys, no one of whom was over thirteen, followed down to the gate after us. From their faces you would have thought they'd never seen a girl before. Certainly not like Miss Bobbit. As Aunt El said, whoever heard tell of a child wearing make-up? Tangee gave her lips an orange glow, her hair, rather like a costume wig, was a mass of rosy curls, and her eyes had a knowing, penciled tilt; even so, she had a skinny dignity, she was a lady, and, what is more, she looked you in the eye with manlike directness. "I'm Miss Lily Jane Bobbit, Miss Bobbit from Memphis, Tennessee," she said solemnly. The boys looked down at their toes, and, on the porch, Cora McCall, whom Billy Bob was courting at the time, led the girls into a fanfare of giggles. "*Country* children," said Miss Bobbit with an understanding smile, and gave her parasol a saucy whirl. "My mother"—and this homely woman allowed an abrupt nod to acknowledge herself—"my mother and I have taken rooms here. Would you be so kind as to point out the house? It belongs to a Mrs. Sawyer." Why, sure, said Aunt El, that's Mrs. Sawyer's, right there across the street. The only boardinghouse around here, it is an old tall dark place with about two dozen lightning rods scattered on the roof: Mrs. Sawyer is scared to death in a thunderstorm.

Coloring like an apple, Billy Bob said, please ma'am, it being such a hot day and all, wouldn't they rest a spell and have some tutti-frutti? and Aunt El said yes, by all means, but Miss Bobbit shook her head. "Very fattening, tutti-frutti; but *merci* you kindly," and they started across the road, the mother half-dragging her parcels in the dust. Then, and with an earnest expression, Miss Bobbit turned back; the sunflower yellow of her eyes darkened, and she rolled them slightly sideways, as if trying to remember a poem. "My mother has a disorder of the tongue, so it is necessary that I speak for her," she announced rapidly and heaved a sigh. "My mother is a very fine seamstress; she has made dresses for the society of many cities and towns, including Memphis and Tallahassee. No doubt you have noticed and admired the dress I am wearing. Every stitch of it was hand-sewn by my mother. My mother can copy any pattern, and just recently she won a twenty-five-dollar prize from the *Ladies' Home Journal*. My mother can also crochet, knit, and embroider. If you want any kind of sewing done, please come to my mother. Please advise your friends and family. Thank you." And then, with a rustle and a swish, she was gone.

Cora McCall and the girls pulled their hair-ribbons nervously, suspiciously, and looked very put out and prune-faced. I'm *Miss* Bobbit, said Cora, twisting her face into an evil imitation, and I'm Princess Elizabeth, that's who I am, ha, ha, ha. Furthermore, said Cora, that dress was just as tacky as could be; personally, Cora said, all my clothes come from Atlanta; plus a pair of shoes from New York, which is not even to mention my silver turquoise ring all the way from Mexico City, Mexico. Aunt El said they ought not to behave that way about a fellow child, a stranger in the town, but the girls went on like a huddle of witches, and certain boys, the sillier ones that liked to be with the girls, joined in and said things that made Aunt El go red and declare she was going to send them all home and tell their daddies, to boot. But before she could carry forward this threat Miss Bobbit herself intervened by traipsing across the Sawyer porch, costumed in a new and startling manner.

The older boys, like Billy Bob and Preacher Star, who had sat quiet while the girls razzed Miss Bobbit, and who had watched the house into which she'd disappeared with misty, ambitious faces, they now straightened up and ambled down to the gate. Cora McCall sniffed and poked out her lower lip, but the rest of us went and sat on the steps. Miss Bobbit paid us no mind whatever. The Sawyer yard is dark with mulberry trees and it is planted with grass and sweet shrub. Sometimes after a rain you can smell the sweet shrub all the way into our house; and in the center of this yard there is a sundial which Mrs. Sawyer installed in 1912 as a memorial to her Boston bull, Sunny, who died after having lapped up a bucket of paint. Miss Bobbit pranced into the yard toting the victrola, which she put on the sundial; she wound it up, and started a record playing, and it played the Court of Luxemborg. By now it was almost nightfall, a firefly hour, blue as milkglass; and birds like arrows swooped together and swept into the folds of trees. Before storms, leaves and flowers appear to burn with a private light, color, and Miss Bobbit, got up in a little white skirt like a powderpuff and with strips of gold-glittering tinsel ribboning her hair, seemed, set against the darkening all around, to contain this illuminated quality. She held her arms arched over her head, her hands lily-limp, and stood straight up on the tips of her toes. She stood that way for a good long while, and Aunt El said it was right smart of her. Then she began to waltz around and around, and around and around she went until Aunt El said, why, she was plain dizzy from the sight. She stopped only when it was time to rewind the victrola; and when the moon came rolling down the ridge, and the last supper bell had sounded, and all the children had gone home, and the night iris was beginning to bloom, Miss Bobbit was still there in the dark turning like a top.

We did not see her again for some time. Preacher Star came every morning to our house and stayed straight through to supper. Preacher is a rail-thin boy with a butchy shock of red hair; he has eleven brothers and sisters, and even they are afraid of him, for he has a terrible temper, and is famous in these parts for his green-eyed meanness: last Fourth of July he whipped Ollie Overton so bad that Ollie's family had to send him to the hospital in Pensacola; and there was another time he bit off half a mule's ear, chewed it and spit it on the ground. Before Billy Bob got his growth, Preacher played the devil with him, too. He used to drop cockleburrs down his collar, and rub pepper in his eyes, and tear up his homework. But now they are the biggest friends in town: talk alike, walk alike; and occasionally they disappear together for whole days, Lord knows where to. But during these days when Miss Bobbit did not appear they stayed close to the house. They would stand around in the yard trying to slingshot sparrows off telephone poles; or sometimes Billy Bob would play his ukulele, and they would sing so loud Uncle Billy Bob, who is Judge for this county, claimed he could hear them all the way to the courthouse: *send me a letter, send it by mail, send it in care of the Birming-ham jail.* Miss Bobbit did not hear them; at least she never poked her head out the door. Then one day Mrs. Sawyer, coming over to borrow a cup of sugar, rattled on a good deal about her new boarders. You know, she said, squinting her chicken-bright eyes, the husband was a crook, uh huh, the child told me herself. Hasn't an ounce of shame, not a mite. Said her daddy was the dearest daddy and the sweetest singing man in the whole of Tennessee. . . . And I said, honey, where is he? and just as offhand as you please she says, Oh, he's in the penitentiary and we don't hear from him no more. Say, now, does that make your blood run cold? Uh huh, and I been thinking, her mama, I been thinking she's some kinda foreigner: never says a word, and sometimes it looks like she don't understand what nobody says to her. And you know, they eat everything *raw. Raw* eggs, *raw* turnips, carrots —no meat whatsoever. For reasons of health, the child says, but ho! she's been straight out on the bed running a fever since last Tuesday.

That same afternoon, Aunt El went out to water her roses, only to discover them gone. These were special roses, ones she'd planned to send to the flower show in Mobile, and so naturally she got a little hysterical. She rang up the Sheriff, and said, listen here, Sheriff, you come over here right fast. I mean somebody's got off with all my Lady Anne's that I've devoted myself to heart and soul since early spring. When the Sheriff's car pulled up outside our house, all the neighbors along the street came out on their porches, and Mrs. Sawyer, layers of cold cream whitening her face, trotted across the road. Oh shoot, she said, very disappointed to find no one had been murdered, oh shoot, she said, nobody's stole them roses. Your Billy Bob brought them roses over and left them for little Bobbit. Aunt El did not say one word. She just marched over to the peach tree, and cut herself a switch. Ohhh, Billy Bob, she stalked along the street calling his name, and then she found him down at Speedy's garage, where he and Preacher were watching Speedy take a motor apart. She simply lifted him by the hair and, switching blueblazes, towed him home. But she couldn't make him say he was sorry and she couldn't make him cry. And when she was finished with him he ran into the backyard and climbed high into the tower of a pecan tree and swore he wasn't ever going to come down. Then his daddy stood at the window and called to him: Son, we aren't mad with you, so come down and eat your supper. But Billy Bob wouldn't budge. Aunt El went and leaned against the tree. She spoke in a voice soft as the gathering light. I'm sorry, son, she said, I didn't mean whipping you so hard like that. I've fixed a nice supper, son, potato salad and boiled ham and deviled eggs. Go away, said Billy Bob, I don't want no supper, and I hate you like all-fire. His daddy said he ought not to talk like that to his mother, and she began to cry. She stood there under the tree and cried, raising the hem of her skirt to dab at her eyes. I don't hate you, son. . . . If I didn't love you, I wouldn't whip you. The pecan leaves began to rattle; Billy Bob slid slowly to the ground, and Aunt El, rushing her fingers through his hair, pulled him against her. Aw, Ma, he said, Aw, Ma.

After supper Billy Bob came and flung himself on the foot of my bed. He smelled all sour and sweet, the way boys do, and I felt very sorry for him, especially because he looked so worried. His eyes were almost shut with worry. You're s'posed to send sick folks flowers, he said righteously. About this time we heard the victrola, a lilting faraway sound, and a night moth flew through the window, drifting in the air delicate as the music. But it was dark now, and we couldn't tell if Miss Bobbit was dancing. Billy Bob, as though he were in pain, doubled up on the bed like a jackknife; but his face was suddenly clear, his grubby boy-eyes twitching like candles. She's so cute, he whispered, she's the cutest dickens I ever saw, gee, to hell with it, I don't care, I'd pick all the roses in China.

Preacher would have picked all the roses in China, too. He was as crazy about her as Billy Bob. But Miss Bobbit did not notice them. The sole communication we had with her was a note to Aunt El thanking her for the flowers. Day after day she sat on her porch, always dressed to beat the band, and doing a piece of embroidery, or combing curls in her hair, or reading a Webster's dictionary—formal, but friendly enough; if you said good-day to her, she said good-day to you. Even so, the boys never could seem to get up the nerve to go over and talk with her, and most of the time she simply looked through them, even when they tomcatted up and down the street trying to get her eye. They wrestled, played Tarzan, did fool-headed bicycle tricks. It was a sorry business. A great many girls in town strolled by the Sawyer house two and three times within an hour just on the chance of getting a look. Some of the girls who did this were: Cora McCall, Mary Murphy Jones, Janice Ackerman. Miss Bobbit did not show any interest in them either. Cora would not speak to Billy Bob anymore. The same was true with Janice and Preacher. As a matter of fact, Janice wrote Preacher a letter in red ink on lace-trimmed paper in which she told him he was vile beyond all human beings and words, that she considered their engagement broken, that he could have back the stuffed squirrel he'd given her. Preacher, saying he wanted to act nice, stopped her the next time she passed our house, and said, well, hell, she could keep that old squirrel if she wanted to. Afterward, he couldn't understand why Janice ran away bawling the way she did.

Then one day the boys were being crazier than usual; Billy Bob was sagging around in his daddy's World War khakis, and Preacher, stripped to the waist, had a naked woman drawn on his chest with one of Aunt El's old lipsticks. They looked like perfect fools, but Miss Bobbit, reclining in a swing, merely yawned. It was noon, and there was no one passing in the street, except a colored girl, baby-fat and sugarplum-shaped, who hummed along carrying a pail of blackberries. But the boys, teasing at her like gnats, joined hands and wouldn't let her go by, not until she paid a tariff. I ain't studyin' no tariff, she said, what kinda tariff you talkin' about, mister? A party in the barn, said Preacher, between clenched teeth, mighty nice party in the barn. And she, with a sulky shrug, said, huh, she intended studyin' no barn parties. Whereupon Billy Bob capsized her berry pail, and when she, with despairing, piglike shrieks, bent down in futile gestures of rescue, Preacher, who can be mean as the devil, gave her behind a kick which sent her sprawling jellylike among the blackberries and the dust. Miss Bobbit came tearing across the road, her finger wagging like a metronome; like a schoolteacher she clapped her hands, stamped her foot, said: "It is a well-known fact that gentlemen are put on the face of this earth for the protection of ladies. Do you suppose boys behave this way in towns like Memphis, New York, London, Hollywood, or Paris?" The boys hung back and shoved their hands in their pockets. Miss Bobbit helped the colored girl to her feet; she dusted her off, dried her eyes, held out a handkerchief and told her to blow. "A pretty pass," she said, "a fine situation when a lady can't walk safely in the public daylight."

Then the two of them went back and sat on Mrs. Sawyer's porch; and for the next year they were never far apart, Miss Bobbit and this baby elephant, whose name was Rosalba Cat. At first, Mrs. Sawyer raised a fuss about Rosalba being so much at her house. She told Aunt El that it went against the grain to have a nigger lolling smack there in plain sight on her front porch. But Miss Bobbit had a certain magic, whatever she did she did it with completeness, and so directly, so solemnly, that there was nothing to do but accept it. For instance, the tradespeople in town used to snicker when they called her *Miss* Bobbit; but by and by she was Miss Bobbit, and they gave her stiff little bows as she whirled by spinning her parasol. Miss Bobbit told everyone that Rosalba was her sister, which caused a good many jokes; but like most of her ideas, it gradually seemed natural, and when we would overhear them calling each other Sister Rosalba and Sister Bobbit, none of us cracked a smile. But Sister Rosalba and Sister Bobbit did some queer things. There was the business about the dogs. Now there are a great many dogs in this town, rat terriers, bird dogs, bloodhounds; they trail along the forlorn noon-hot streets in sleepy herds of six to a dozen, all waiting only for dark and the moon, when straight through the lonesome hours you can hear them howling: someone is dying, someone is dead. Miss Bobbit complained to the Sheriff; she said that certain of the dogs always planted themselves under her window, and that she was a light sleeper to begin with; what is more, and as Sister Rosalba said, she did not believe they were dogs at all, but some kind of devil. Naturally the Sheriff did nothing; and so she took the matter into her own hands. One morning, after an especially loud night, she was seen stalking through the town with Rosalba at her side, Rosalba carrying a flower basket filled with rocks; whenever they saw a dog they paused while Miss Bobbit scrutinized him. Sometimes she would shake her head, but more often she said, "Yes, that's one of them, Sister Rosalba," and Sister Rosalba, with ferocious aim, would take a rock from her basket and crack the dog between the eyes.

Another thing that happened concerns Mr. Henderson. Mr. Henderson has a back room in the Sawyer house; a tough runt of a man who formerly was a wildcat oil prospector in Oklahoma, he is about seventy years old and, like a lot of old men, obsessed by functions of the body. Also, he is a terrible drunk. One time he had been drunk for two weeks; whenever he heard Miss Bobbit and Sister Rosalba moving around the house, he would charge to the top of the stairs and bellow down to Mrs.

Sawyer that there were midgets in the walls trying to get at his supply of toilet paper. They've already stolen fifteen cents' worth, he said. One evening, when the two girls were sitting under a tree in the yard, Mr. Henderson, sporting nothing more than a nightshirt, stamped out after them. Steal all my toilet paper, will you? he hollered, I'll show you midgets. . . . Somebody come help me, else these midget bitches are liable to make off with every sheet in town. It was Billy Bob and Preacher who caught Mr. Henderson and held him until some grown men arrived and began to tie him up. Miss Bobbit, who had behaved with admirable calm, told the men they did not know how to tie a proper knot, and undertook to do so herself. She did such a good job that all the circulation stopped in Mr. Henderson's hands and feet and it was a month before he could walk again.

It was shortly afterward that Miss Bobbit paid us a call. She came on Sunday and I was there alone, the family having gone to church. "The odors of a church are so offensive," she said, leaning forward and with her hands folded primly before her. "I don't want you to think I'm a heathen, Mr. C.; I've had enough experience to know that there is a God and that there is a Devil. But the way to tame the Devil is not to go down there to church and listen to what a sinful mean fool he is. No, love the Devil like you love Jesus: because he is a powerful man, and will do you a good turn if he knows you trust him. He has frequently done me good turns, like at dancing school in Memphis. . . . I always called in the Devil to help me get the biggest part in our annual show. That is common sense; you see, I knew Jesus wouldn't have any truck with dancing. Now, as a matter of fact, I have called in the Devil just recently. He is the only one who can help me get out of this town. Not that I live here, not exactly. I think always about somewhere else, somewhere else where everything is dancing, like people dancing in the streets, and everything is pretty, like children on their birthdays. My precious papa said I live in the sky, but if he'd lived more in the sky, he'd be rich like he wanted to be. The trouble with my papa was he did not love the Devil, he let the Devil love him. But I am very smart in that respect; I know the next best thing is very often the best. It was the next best thing for us to move to this town; and since I can't pursue my career here, the next best thing for me is to start a little business on the side. Which is what I have done. I am sole subscription agent in this county for an impressive list of magazines, including *Reader's Digest, Popular Mechanics, Dime Detective,* and *Child's Life.* To be sure, Mr. C., I'm not here to sell you anything. But I have a thought in mind. I was thinking those two boys that are always hanging around here, it occurred to me that they are men, after all. Do you suppose they would make a pair of likely assistants?"

Billy Bob and Preacher worked hard for Miss Bobbit, and for Sister Rosalba, too. Sister Rosalba carried a line of cosmetics called Dewdrop, and it was part of the boys' job to deliver purchases to her customers. Billy Bob used to be so tired in the evening he could hardly chew his supper. Aunt El said it was a shame and a pity, and finally one day when Billy Bob came down with a touch of sunstroke she said, all right, that settled it, Billy Bob would just have to quit Miss Bobbit. But Billy Bob cussed her out until his daddy had to lock him in his room; whereupon he said he was going to kill himself. Some cook we'd had told him once that if you ate a mess of collards all slopped over with molasses, it would kill you sure as shooting; and so that is what he did. I'm dying, he said, rolling back and forth on his bed, I'm dying and nobody cares.

Miss Bobbit came over and told him to hush up. "There's nothing wrong with you, boy," she said. "All you've got is a stomachache." Then she did something that shocked Aunt El very much: she stripped the covers off Billy Bob and rubbed him down with alcohol from head to toe. When Aunt El told her she did not think that was a nice thing for a little girl to do, Miss Bobbit replied: "I don't know whether it's nice or not, but it's certainly very refreshing." After which Aunt El did all she could to keep Billy Bob from going back to work for her, but his daddy said to leave him alone, they would have to let the boy lead his own life.

Miss Bobbit was very honest about money. She paid Billy Bob and Preacher their exact commission, and she would never let them treat her, as they often tried to do, at the drugstore or to the picture show. "You'd better save your money," she told them. "That is, if you want to go to college. Because neither one of you has got the brains to win a scholarship, not even a football scholarship." But it was over money that Billy Bob and Preacher had a big falling-out; that was not the real reason, of course: the real reason was that they had grown cross-eyed jealous over Miss Bobbit. So one day, and he had the gall to do this right in front of Billy Bob, Preacher said to Miss Bobbit that she'd better check her accounts carefully because he had more than a suspicion that Billy Bob wasn't turning over to her *all* the money he collected. That's a damned lie, said Billy Bob, and with a clean left hook he knocked Preacher off the Sawyer porch and jumped after him into a bed of nasturtiums. But once Preacher got a hold on him, Billy Bob didn't stand a chance. Preacher even rubbed dirt in his eyes. During all this, Mrs.

Sawyer, leaning out an upper-story window, screamed like an eagle, and Sister Rosalba, fatly cheerful, ambiguously shouted, Kill him! Kill him! Kill him! Only Miss Bobbit seemed to know what she was doing. She plugged in the lawn hose, and gave the boys a close-up, blinding bath. Gasping, Preacher staggered to his feet. Oh, honey, he said, shaking himself like a wet dog, honey, you've got to decide. "Decide *what?*" said Miss Bobbit, right away in a huff. Oh, honey, wheezed Preacher, you don't want us boys killing each other. You got to decide who is your real true sweetheart. "Sweetheart, my eye," said Miss Bobbit. "I should've known better than to get myself involved with a lot of country children. What sort of businessman are you going to make? Now, you listen here, Preacher Star: I don't want a sweetheart, and if I did, it wouldn't be you. As a matter of fact, you don't even get up when a lady enters the room."

Preacher spit on the ground and swaggered over to Billy Bob. Come on, he said, just as though nothing had happened, she's a hard one, she is, she don't want nothing but to make trouble between two good friends. For a moment it looked as if Billy Bob was going to join him in a peaceful togetherness; but suddenly, coming to his senses, he drew back and made a gesture. The boys regarded each other a full minute, all the closeness between them turning an ugly color: you can't hate so much unless you love, too. And Preacher's face showed all of this. But there was nothing for him to do except go away. Oh, yes, Preacher, you looked so lost that day that for the first time I really liked you, so skinny and mean and lost going down the road all by yourself.

They did not make it up, Preacher and Billy Bob; and it was not because they didn't want to, it was only that there did not seem to be any straight way for their friendship to happen again. But they couldn't get rid of this friendship: each was always aware of what the other was up to; and when Preacher found himself a new buddy, Billy Bob moped around for days, picking things up, dropping them again, or doing sudden wild things, like purposely poking his finger in the electric fan. Sometimes in the evenings Preacher would pause by the gate and talk with Aunt El. It was only to torment Billy Bob, I suppose, but he stayed friendly with all of us, and at Christmastime he gave us a huge box of shelled peanuts. He left a present for Billy Bob, too. It turned out to be a book of Sherlock Holmes; and on the flyleaf there was scribbled, "Friends Like Ivy On the Wall Must Fall." That's the corniest thing I ever saw, Billy Bob said. Jesus, what a dope he is! But then, and though it was a cold winter day, he went in the backyard and climbed up into the pecan tree, crouching there all afternoon in the blue December branches.

But most of the time he was happy, because Miss Bobbit was there, and she was always sweet to him now. She and Sister Rosalba treated him like a man; that is to say, they allowed him to do everything for them. On the other hand, they let him win at three-handed bridge, they never questioned his lies, nor discouraged his ambitions. It was a happy while. However, trouble started again when school began. Miss Bobbit refused to go. "It's ridiculous," she said, when one day the principal, Mr. Copland, came around to investigate, "really ridiculous; I can read and write and there are *some* people in this town who have every reason to know that I can count money. No, Mr. Copland, consider for a moment and you will see neither of us has the time nor energy. After all, it would only be a matter of whose spirit broke first, yours or mine. And besides, what is there for you to teach me? Now, if you knew anything about dancing, that would be another matter; but under the circumstances, yes, Mr. Copland, under the circumstances, I suggest we forget the whole thing." Mr. Copland was perfectly willing to. But the rest of the town thought she ought to be whipped. Horace Deasley wrote a piece in the paper which was titled "A Tragic Situation." It was, in his opinion, a tragic situation when a small girl could defy what he, for some reason, termed the Constitution of the United States. The article ended with a question: *Can she get away with it?* She did; and so did Sister Rosalba. Only she was colored, so no one cared. Billy Bob was not as lucky. It was school for him, all right; but he might as well have stayed home for the good it did him. On his first report card he got three F's, a record of some sort. But he is a smart boy. I guess he just couldn't live through those hours without Miss Bobbit; away from her he always seemed half-asleep. He was always in a fight, too; either his eye was black or his lip was split or his walk had a limp. He never talked about these fights, but Miss Bobbit was shrewd enough to guess the reason why. "You are a dear, I know, I know. And I appreciate you, Billy Bob. Only don't fight with people because of me. Of course they say mean things about me. But do you know why that is, Billy Bob? It's a compliment, kind of. Because deep down they think I'm absolutely wonderful."

And she was right: if you are not admired, no one will take the trouble to disapprove. But actually we had no idea of how wonderful she was until there appeared the man known as Manny Fox. This happened late in February. The first news we had of Manny Fox was a series of jovial placards posted up in the stores around town: Manny Fox Presents the Fan Dancer Without the Fan; then, in smaller print: Also, Sensational Amateur Program Featuring Your Own Neighbors— First Prize, A Genuine Hollywood Screen Test. All this was to take place the following Thursday. The tickets were priced at one dollar each, which around here is a lot of money; but it is not often that we get any kind of flesh entertainment, so everybody shelled out their money and made a great to-do over the whole thing. The drugstore cowboys talked dirty all week, mostly about the fan dancer without the fan, who turned out to be Mrs. Manny Fox. They stayed down the highway at the Chucklewood Tourist Camp; but they were in town all day, driving around in an old Packard which had Manny Fox's full name stenciled on all four doors. His wife was a deadpan pimento-tongued redhead with wet lips and moist eyelids; she was quite large actually, but compared to Manny Fox she seemed rather frail, for he was a fat cigar of a man.

They made the pool hall their headquarters, and every afternoon you could find them there, drinking beer and joking with the town loafs. As it developed, Manny Fox's business affairs were not restricted to theatrics. He also ran a kind of employment bureau: slowly he let it be known that for a fee of $150 he could get for any adventurous boys in the country high-class jobs working on fruit ships sailing from New Orleans to South America. The chance of a lifetime, he called it. There are not two boys around here who readily lay their hands on so much as five dollars; nevertheless, a good dozen managed to raise the money. Ada Willingham took all she'd saved to buy an angel tombstone for her husband and gave it to her son, and Acey Trump's papa sold an option on his cotton crop.

But the night of the show! That was a night when all was forgotten: mortgages, and the dishes in the kitchen sink. Aunt El said you'd think we were going to the opera, everybody so dressed up, so pink and sweet-smelling. The Odeon had not been so full since the night they gave away the matched set of sterling silver. Practically everybody had a relative in the show, so there was a lot of nervousness to contend with. Miss Bobbit was the only contestant we knew real well. Billy Bob couldn't sit still; he kept telling us over and over that we mustn't applaud for anybody but Miss Bobbit; Aunt El said that would be very rude, which sent Billy Bob off into a state again; and when his father bought us all bags of popcorn he wouldn't touch his because it would make his hands greasy, and please, another thing, we mustn't be noisy and eat ours while Miss Bobbit was performing. That she was to be a contestant had come as a last-minute surprise. It was logical enough, and there were signs that should've told us; the fact, for instance, that she had not set foot outside the Sawyer house in how many days? And the victrola going half the night, her shadow whirling on the window shade, and the secret, stuffed look on Sister Rosalba's face whenever asked after Sister Bobbit's health. So there was her name on the program, listed second, in fact, though she did not appear for a long while. First came Manny Fox, greased and leering, who told a lot of peculiar jokes, clapping his hands, ha, ha. Aunt El said if he told another joke like that, she was going to walk straight out: he did, and she didn't. Before Miss Bobbit came on, there were eleven contestants, including Eustacia Bernstein, who imitated movie stars so that they all sounded like Eustacia, and there was an extraordinary Mr. Buster Riley, a jug-eared old wool-hat from way in the back country who played "Waltzing Matilda" on a saw. Up to that point, he was the hit of the show; not that there was any marked difference in the various receptions, for everybody applauded generously, everybody, that is, except Preacher Star. He was sitting two rows ahead of us, greeting each act with a donkey-loud boo. Aunt El said she was never going to speak to him again. The only person he ever applauded was Miss Bobbit. No doubt the Devil was on her side, but she deserved it. Out she came, tossing her hips, her curls, rolling her eyes. You could tell right away it wasn't going to be one of her classical numbers. She tapped across the stage, daintily holding up the sides of a cloud-blue skirt. That's the cutest thing I ever saw, said Billy Bob, smacking his thigh, and Aunt El had to agree that Miss Bobbit looked real sweet. When she started to twirl the whole audience broke into spontaneous applause; so she did it all over again, hissing, "Faster, faster," at poor Miss Adelaide, who was at the piano doing her Sunday-school best. "I was born in China, and raised in Jaypan . . ." We had never heard her sing before, and she had a rowdy sandpaper voice. ". . . if you don't like my peaches, stay away from my can, o-ho o-ho!" Aunt El gasped; she gasped again when Miss Bobbit, with a bump, up-ended her skirt to display blue-lace underwear, thereby collecting most of the whistles the boys had been saving for the fan dancer without the fan, which was just as well, as it later turned out, for that lady, to the tune of "An Apple for the Teacher" and cries of gyp gyp, did her routine attired in a bathing suit. But showing off her bottom was not Miss Bobbit's final triumph. Miss Adelaide commenced an ominous thundering in the darker keys, at which point Sister Rosalba, carrying a lighted Roman candle, rushed onstage and handed it to Miss Bobbit, who was in the midst of a full split; she made it, too, and just as she did the Roman candle burst into fiery balls of red, white and blue, and we all had to stand up because she was singing "The Star-Spangled Banner" at the top of her lungs. Aunt El said afterward that it was one of the most gorgeous things she'd ever seen on the American stage.

Well, she surely did deserve a Hollywood screen test and, inasmuch as she won the contest, it looked as though she were going to get it. Manny Fox said she was: honey, he said, you're real star stuff. Only he skipped town the next day, leaving nothing but hearty promises. Watch the mails, my friends, you'll all be hearing from me. That is what he said to the boys whose money he'd taken, and that is what he said to Miss Bobbit. There are three deliveries daily, and this sizable group gathered at the post office for all of them, a jolly crowd growing gradually joyless. How their hands trembled when a letter slid into their mailbox. A terrible hush came over them as the days passed. They all knew what the other was thinking, but no one could bring himself to say it, not even Miss Bobbit. Postmistress Patterson said it plainly, however: the man's a crook, she said, I knew he was a crook to begin with, and if I have to look at your faces one more day I'll shoot myself.

Finally, at the end of two weeks, it was Miss Bobbit who broke the spell. Her eyes had grown more vacant than anyone had ever supposed they might, but one day, after the last mail was up, all her old sizzle came back. "Okay, boys, it's lynch law now," she said, and proceeded to herd the whole troupe home with her. This was the first meeting of the Manny Fox Hangman's Club, an organization which, in a more social form, endures to this day, though Manny Fox has long since been caught and, so to say, hung. Credit for this went quite properly to Miss Bobbit. Within a week she'd written over three hundred descriptions of Manny Fox and dispatched them to Sheriffs throughout the South; she also wrote letters to papers in the larger cities, and these attracted wide attention. As a result, four of the robbed boys were offered good-paying jobs by the United Fruit Company, and late this spring, when Manny Fox was arrested in Uphigh, Arkansas, where he was pulling the same old dodge, Miss Bobbit was presented with a Good Deed Merit award from the Sunbeam Girls of America. For some reason, she made a point of letting the world know that this did not exactly thrill her. "I do not approve of the organization," she said. "All that rowdy bugle blowing. It's neither good-hearted nor truly feminine. And anyway, what is a good deed? Don't let anybody fool you, a good deed is something you do because you want something in return." It would be reassuring to report she was wrong, and that her just reward, when at last it came, was given out of kindness and love. However, this is not the case. About a week ago the boys involved in the swindle all received from Manny Fox checks covering their losses, and Miss Bobbit, with clodhopping determination, stalked into a meeting of the Hangman's Club, which is now an excuse for drinking beer and playing poker every Thursday night. "Look, boys," she said, laying it on the line, "none of you ever thought to see that money again, but now that you have, you ought to invest it in something practical—like me." The proposition was that they should pool their money and finance her trip to Hollywood; in return, they would get ten percent of her life's earnings which, after she was a star, and that would not be very long, would make them all rich men. "At least," as she said, "in this part of the country." Not one of the boys wanted to do it: but when Miss Bobbit looked at you, what was there to say?

Since Monday, it has been raining buoyant summer rain shot through with sun, but dark at night and full of sound, full of dripping leaves, watery chimings, sleepless scuttlings. Billy Bob is wide-awake, dry-eyed, though everything he does is a little frozen and his tongue is as stiff as a bell tongue. It has not been easy for him, Miss Bobbit's going. Because she'd meant more than that. Than what? Than being thirteen years old and crazy in love. She was the queer things in him, like the pecan tree and liking books and caring enough about people to let them hurt him. She was the things he was afraid to show anyone else. And in the dark the music trickled through the rain: won't there be nights when we will hear it just as though it were really there? And afternoons when the shadows will be all at once confused, and she will pass before us, unfurling across the lawn like a pretty piece of ribbon? She laughed to Billy Bob; she held his hand, she even kissed him. "I'm not going to die," she said. "You'll come out there, and we'll climb a mountain, and we'll all live there together, you and me and Sister Rosalba." But Billy Bob knew it would never happen that way, and so when the music came through the dark he would stuff the pillow over his head.

Only there was a strange smile about yesterday, and that was the day she was leaving. Around noon the sun came out, bringing with it into the air all the sweetness of wisteria. Aunt El's yellow Lady Anne's were blooming again, and she did something wonderful, she told Billy Bob he could pick them and give them to Miss Bobbit for good-bye. All afternoon Miss Bobbit sat on the porch surrounded by people who stopped by to wish her well. She looked as though she were going to Communion, dressed in white and with a white parasol. Sister Rosalba had given her a handkerchief, but she had to borrow it back because she couldn't stop blubbering. Another little girl brought a baked chicken, presumably to be eaten on the bus; the only trouble was she'd forgotten to take out the insides before cooking it. Miss Bobbit's mother said that was all right by her, chicken was chicken; which is memorable because it is the single opinion she ever voiced. There was only one sour note. For hours Preacher Star had been hanging around down at the corner, sometimes standing at the curb tossing a coin, and sometimes hiding behind a tree, as if he didn't want anyone to see him. It made everybody nervous. About twenty minutes before bus time he sauntered up and leaned against our gate. Billy Bob was still in the garden picking roses; by now he had enough for a bonfire, and their smell was as heavy as wind. Preacher stared at him until he lifted his head. As they looked at each other the rain began again, falling fine as sea spray and colored by a rainbow. Without a word, Preacher went over and started helping Billy Bob separate the roses into two giant bouquets: together they carried them to the curb. Across the street there were bumblebees of talk, but when Miss Bobbit saw them, two boys whose flower-masked faces were like yellow moons, she rushed down the steps, her arms outstretched. You could see what was going to happen; and we called out, our voices like lightning in the rain, but Miss Bobbit, running toward those moons of roses, did not seem to hear. That is when the six-o'clock bus ran over her.

1949

JOHN UPDIKE

A & P

In walks these three girls in nothing but bathing suits. I'm in the third checkout slot, with my back to the door, so I don't see them until they're over by the bread. The one that caught my eye first was the one in the plaid green two-piece. She was a chunky kid, with a good tan and a

Born in 1932, John Updike was raised in the town of Shillington, Pennsylvania. His mother, who aspired to be a novelist, was the first to encourage her son to write. Updike graduated summa cum laude from Harvard in 1954, and the following year he entered into a literary and editorial association with *The New Yorker* that continues today. In 1960 he published *Rabbit, Run,* the first of four novels about a small-town Pennsylvania car salesman. These novels embody his skill as an exact, yet subtle, anatomist of American middle-class concerns, mores, and manners and also earned him such honors as the National Book Award in 1964 and the Pulitzer Prize for *Rabbit Is Rich* (1981). Updike has lived in Massachusetts since 1957.

sweet broad soft-looking can with those two crescents of white just under it, where the sun never seems to hit, at the top of the backs of her legs. I stood there with my hand on a box of HiHo crackers trying to remember if I rang it up or not. I ring it up again and the customer starts giving me hell. She's one of these cash-register-watchers, a witch about fifty with rouge on her cheekbones and no eyebrows, and I know it made her day to trip me up. She'd been watching cash registers for fifty years and probably never seen a mistake before.

By the time I got her feathers smoothed and her goodies into a bag —she gives me a little snort in passing, if she'd been born at the right time they would have burned her over in Salem—by the time I get her on her way the girls had circled around the bread and were coming back, without a pushcart, back my way along the counters, in the aisle between the checkouts and the Special bins. They didn't even have shoes on. There was this chunky one, with the two-piece—it was bright green and the seams on the bra were still sharp and her belly was still pretty pale so I guessed she just got it (the suit)—there was this one, with one of those chubby berry-faces, the lips all bunched together under her nose, this one, and a tall one, with black hair that hadn't quite frizzed right, and one of these sunburns right across under the eyes, and a chin that was too long—you know, the kind of girl other girls think is very "striking" and "attractive" but never quite makes it, as they very well know, which is why they like her so much—and then the third one, that wasn't quite so tall. She was the queen. She kind of led them, the other two peeking around and making their shoulders round. She didn't look around, not this queen, she just walked straight on slowly, on these long white prima-donna legs. She came down a little hard on her heels, as if she didn't walk in her bare feet that much, putting down her heels and then letting the weight move along to her toes as if she was testing the floor with every step, putting a little deliberate extra action into it. You never know for sure how girls' minds work (do you really think it's a mind in there or just a little buzz like a bee in a glass jar?) but you got the idea she had talked the other two into coming in here with her, and now she was showing them how to do it, walk slow and hold yourself straight.

She had on a kind of dirty pink—beige maybe, I don't know— bathing suit with a little nubble all over it and, what got me, the straps were down. They were off her shoulders looped loose around the cool tops of her arms, and I guess as a result the suit had slipped a little on her, so all around the top of the cloth there was this shining rim. If it hadn't been there you wouldn't have known there could have been anything whiter than those shoulders. With the straps pushed off, there was nothing between the top of the suit and the top of her head except just *her,* this clean bare plane at the top of her chest down from the shoulder bones like a dented sheet of metal tilted in the light. I mean, it was more than pretty.

She had sort of oaky hair that the sun and salt had bleached, done up in a bun that was unraveling, and a kind of prim face. Walking into the A & P with your straps down, I suppose it's the only kind of face you *can* have. She held her head so high her neck, coming up out of those white shoulders, looked kind of stretched, but I didn't mind. The longer her neck was, the more of her there was.

She must have felt in the corner of her eye me and over my shoulder Stokesie in the second slot watching, but she didn't tip. Not this queen. She kept her eyes moving across the racks, and stopped, and turned so slow it made my stomach rub the inside of my apron, and buzzed to the other two, who kind of huddled against her for relief, and then they all three of them went up the cat-and-dog-food-breakfast-cereal-maca-roni-rice-raisins-seasonings-spreads-spaghetti-soft-drinks-crackers-and-cookies aisle. From the third slot I look straight up this aisle to the meat counter, and I watched them all the way. The fat one with the tan sort of fumbled with the cookies, but on second thought she put the package back. The sheep pushing their carts down the aisle—the girls were walking against the usual traffic (not that we have one-way signs or anything)—were pretty hilarious. You could see them, when Queenie's white shoulders dawned on them, kind of jerk, or hop, or hiccup, but their eyes snapped back to their own baskets and on they pushed. I bet you could set off dynamite in an A & P and the people would by and large keep reaching and checking oatmeal off their lists and muttering "Let me see, there was a third thing, began with A, asparagus, no, ah, yes, applesauce!" or whatever it is they do mutter. But there was no doubt, this jiggled them. A few houseslaves in pin curlers even looked around after pushing their carts past to make sure what they had seen was correct.

You know, it's one thing to have a girl in a bathing suit down on the beach, where what with the glare nobody can look at each other much anyway, and another thing in the cool of the A & P, under the fluorescent lights, against all those stacked packages, with her feet paddling along naked over our checkerboard green-and-cream rubber-tile floor.

"Oh Daddy," Stokesie said beside me. "I feel so faint."

"Darling," I said. "Hold me tight." Stokesie's married, with two babies chalked up on his fuselage already, but as far as I can tell that's the only difference. He's twenty-two, and I was nineteen this April.

"Is it done?" he asks, the responsible married man finding his voice. I forgot to say he thinks he's going to be manager some sunny day, maybe in 1990 when it's called the Great Alexandrov and Petrooshki Tea Company or something.

What he meant was, our town is five miles from a beach, with a big summer colony out on the Point, but we're right in the middle of town, and the women generally put on a shirt or shorts or something before they get out of the car into the street. And anyway these are usually women with six children and varicose veins mapping their legs and nobody, including them, could care less. As I say, we're right in the middle of town, and if you stand at our front doors you can see two banks and the Congregational church and the newspaper store and three real-estate offices and about twenty-seven old freeloaders tearing up Central Street because the sewer broke again. It's not as if we're on the Cape, we're north of Boston and there's people in this town haven't seen the ocean for twenty years.

The girls had reached the meat counter and were asking McMahon something. He pointed, they pointed, and they shuffled out of sight behind a pyramid of Diet Delight peaches. All that was left for us to see was old McMahon patting his mouth and looking after them sizing up their joints. Poor kids, I began to feel sorry for them, they couldn't help it.

Now here comes the sad part of the story, at least my family says it's sad, but I don't think it's so sad myself. The store's pretty empty, it being Thursday afternoon, so there was nothing much to do except lean on the register and wait for the girls to show up again. The whole store was like a pinball machine and I didn't know which tunnel they'd come out of. After a while they come around out of the far aisle, around the light bulbs, records at discount of the Caribbean Six or Tony Martin Sings or some such gunk you wonder they waste the wax on, six-packs of candy bars, and plastic toys done up in cellophane that fall apart when a kid looks at them anyway. Around they come, Queenie still leading the way, and holding a little gray jar in her hands. Slots Three through Seven are unmanned and I could see her wondering between Stokes and me, but Stokesie with his usual luck draws an old party in baggy gray pants who stumbles up with four giant cans of pineapple juice (what do these bums *do* with all that pineapple juice? I've often asked myself). So the girls come to me. Queenie puts down the jar and I take it into my fingers icy cold. Kingfish Fancy Herring Snacks in Pure Sour Cream: 49¢. Now her hands are empty, not a ring or a bracelet, bare as God made them, and I wonder where the money's coming from. Still with that prim look she lifts a folded dollar bill out of the hollow at the center of her nubbled pink top. The jar went heavy in my hand. Really, I thought that was so cute.

Then everybody's luck begins to run out. Lengel comes in from haggling with a truck full of cabbages on the lot and is about to scuttle into that door marked MANAGER behind which he hides all day when the girls touch his eye. Lengel's pretty dreary, teaches Sunday school and the rest, but he doesn't miss that much. He comes over and says, "Girls, this isn't the beach."

Queenie blushes, though maybe it's just a brush of sunburn I was noticing for the first time, now that she was so close. "My mother asked me to pick up a jar of herring snacks." Her voice kind of startled me, the way voices do when you see the people first, coming out so flat and dumb yet kind of tony, too, the way it ticked over "pick up" and "snacks." All of a sudden I slid right down her voice into the living room. Her father and the other men were standing around in ice-cream coats and bow ties and the women were in sandals picking up herring snacks on toothpicks off a big glass plate and they were all holding drinks the color of water with olives and sprigs of mint in them. When my parents have somebody over they get lemonade and if it's a real racy affair Schlitz in tall glasses with "They'll Do It Every Time" cartoons stenciled on.

"That's all right," Lengel said. "But this isn't the beach." His repeating this struck me as funny, as if it had just occurred to him, and he had been thinking all these years the A & P was a great big dune and he was the head lifeguard. He didn't like my smiling—as I say he doesn't miss much—but he concentrates on giving the girls that sad Sunday-school-superintendent stare.

Queenie's blush is no sunburn now, and the plump one in plaid, that I liked better from the back—a really sweet can—pipes up, "We weren't doing any shopping. We just came in for the one thing."

"That makes no difference," Lengel tells her, and I could see from the way his eyes went that he hadn't noticed she was wearing a two-piece before. "We want you decently dressed when you come in here."

"We *are* decent," Queenie says suddenly, her lower lip pushing, getting sore now that she remembers her place, a place from which the crowd that runs the A & P must look pretty crummy. Fancy Herring Snacks flashed in her very blue eyes.

"Girls, I don't want to argue with you. After this come in here with your shoulders covered. It's our policy." He turns his back. That's policy for you. Policy is what the kingpins want. What the others want is juvenile delinquency.

All this while, the customers had been showing up with their carts but, you know, sheep, seeing a scene, they had all bunched up on Stokesie, who shook open a paper bag as gently as peeling a peach, not wanting to miss a word. I could feel in the silence everybody getting nervous, most of all Lengel, who asks me, "Sammy, have you rung up their purchase?"

I thought and said "No" but it wasn't about that I was thinking. I go through the punches, 4, 9, GROC. TOT—it's more complicated than you think, and after you do it often enough, it begins to make a little song, that you hear words to, in my case, "Hello (*bing*) there, you (*gung*) hap-py *pee*-pul (*splat*)!"—the *splat* being the drawer flying out. I uncrease the bill, tenderly as you may imagine, it just having come from between the two smoothest scoops of vanilla I had ever known were there, and pass a half and a penny into her narrow pink palm, and nestle the herrings in a bag and twist its neck and hand it over, all the time thinking.

The girls, and who'd blame them, are in a hurry to get out, so I say "I quit" to Lengel quick enough for them to hear, hoping they'll stop and watch me, their unsuspected hero. They keep right on going, into the electric eye; the door flies open and they flicker across the lot to their car. Queenie and Plaid and Big Tall Goony Goony (not that as raw material she was so bad), leaving me with Lengel and a kink in his eyebrow.

"Did you say something, Sammy?"

"I said I quit."

"I thought you did."

"You didn't have to embarrass them."

"It was they who were embarrassing us."

I started to say something that came out "Fiddle-de-doo." It's a saying of my grandmother's, and I know she would have been pleased.

"I don't think you know what you're saying," Lengel said.

"I know you don't," I said. "But I do." I pull the bow at the back of my apron and start shrugging it off my shoulders. A couple customers that had been heading for my slot begin to knock against each other, like scared pigs in a chute.

Lengel sighs and begins to look very patient and old and gray. He's been a friend of my parents for years. "Sammy, you don't want to do this to your mom and dad," he tells me. It's true, I don't. But it seems to me that once you begin a gesture it's fatal not to go through with it. I fold the apron, "Sammy" stitched in red on the pocket, and put it on the counter, and drop the bow tie on top of it. The bow tie is theirs, if you've ever wondered. "You'll feel this for the rest of your life," Lengel says, and I know that's true, too, but remembering how he made the

pretty girl blush makes me so scrunchy inside I punch the No Sale tab
and the machine whirs "pee-pul" and the drawer splats out. One advantage to this scene taking place in summer, I can follow this up with
a clean exit, there's no fumbling around getting your coat and galoshes.
I just saunter into the electric eye in my white shirt that my mother
ironed the night before, and the door heaves itself open, and outside
the sunshine is skating around on the asphalt.

I look around for my girls, but they're gone, of course. There wasn't
anybody but some young married screaming with her children about
some candy they didn't get by the door of a powder-blue Falcon station
wagon. Looking back in the big windows, over the bags of peat moss
and aluminum lawn furniture stacked on the pavement, I could see
Lengel in my place in the slot, checking the sheep through. His face was
dark gray and his back stiff, as if he'd just had an injection of iron, and
my stomach kind of fell as I felt how hard the world was going to be
to me hereafter.

1961

ALICE MUNRO

Miles City, Montana

My father came across the field carrying the body of the boy who had been drowned. There were several men together, returning from the search, but he was the one carrying the body. The men were muddy and exhausted, and walked with their heads down, as if they were ashamed. Even the dogs were dispirited, dripping from the cold river. When they all set out, hours before, the dogs were nervy and yelping, the men tense and determined, and there was a constrained, unspeakable excitement about the whole scene. It was understood that they might find something horrible.

The boy's name was Steve Gauley. He was eight years old. His hair and clothes were mud-colored now and carried some bits of dead leaves, twigs, and grass. He was like a heap of refuse that had been left out all winter. His face was turned in to my father's chest, but I could see a nostril, an ear, plugged up with greenish mud.

I don't think so. I don't think I really saw all this. Perhaps I saw my father carrying him, and the other men following along, and the dogs, but I would not have been allowed to get close enough to see something like mud in his nostril. I must have heard someone talking about that and imagined that I saw it. I see his face unaltered except for the mud—Steve Gauley's familiar, sharp-honed, sneaky-looking face—and it wouldn't have been like that; it would have been bloated and changed and perhaps muddied all over after so many hours in the water.

To have to bring back such news, such evidence, to a waiting family, particularly a mother, would have made searchers move heavily, but

Finding common ground with many of this century's greatest practitioners of the short story, Alice Munro has referred to herself as a "regional writer." The majority of her work revolves both geographically and psychologically around the insular agricultural communities of southwestern Ontario. Wingham, where Munro was born on July 10, 1931, into a Canadian farming family, reappears as the quiet town of Jubilee in her collections *Dance of the Happy Shades* (1968) and *Something I've Been Meaning to Tell You* (1974). A three-time recipient of the Governor General's Literary Award (most recently for her 1986 collection *The Progress of Love*), Munro received a B.A. from the University of Western Ontario and lives in the village of Clinton, just twenty miles from her birthplace.

what was happening here was worse. It seemed a worse shame (to hear people talk) that there was no mother, no woman at all—no grand-mother or aunt, or even a sister—to receive Steve Gauley and give him his due of grief. His father was a hired man, a drinker but not a drunk, an erratic man without being entertaining, not friendly but not exactly a troublemaker. His fatherhood seemed accidental, and the fact that the child had been left with him when the mother went away, and that they continued living together, seemed accidental. They lived in a steep-roofed, gray-shingled hillbilly sort of house that was just a bit better than a shack—the father fixed the roof and put supports under the porch, just enough and just in time—and their life was held together in a similar manner; that is, just well enough to keep the Children's Aid at bay. They didn't eat meals together or cook for each other, but there was food. Sometimes the father would give Steve money to buy food at the store, and Steve was seen to buy quite sensible things, such as pancake mix and macaroni dinner.

I had known Steve Gauley fairly well. I had not liked him more often than I had liked him. He was two years older than I was. He would hang around our place on Saturdays, scornful of whatever I was doing but unable to leave me alone. I couldn't be on the swing without him wanting to try it, and if I wouldn't give it up he came and pushed me so that I went crooked. He teased the dog. He got me into trouble—deliberately and maliciously, it seemed to me afterward—by daring me to do things I wouldn't have thought of on my own: digging up the potatoes to see how big they were when they were still only the size of marbles, and pushing over the stacked firewood to make a pile we could jump off. At school, we never spoke to each other. He was solitary, though not tormented. But on Saturday mornings, when I saw his thin, self-possessed figure sliding through the cedar hedge, I knew I was in for something and he would decide what. Sometimes it was all right. We pretended we were cowboys who had to tame wild horses. We played in the pasture by the river, not far from the place where Steve drowned. We were horses and riders both, screaming and neighing and bucking and waving whips of tree branches beside a little nameless river that flows into the Saugeen in southern Ontario.

The funeral was held in our house. There was not enough room at Steve's father's place for the large crowd that was expected because of the circumstances. I have a memory of the crowded room but no picture of Steve in his coffin, or of the minister, or of wreaths of flowers. I remember that I was holding one flower, a white narcissus, which must have come from a pot somebody forced indoors, because it was too early for even the forsythia bush or the trilliums and marsh marigolds in the woods. I stood in a row of children, each of us holding a narcissus. We sang a children's hymn, which somebody played on our piano: "When He Cometh, When He Cometh, to Make Up His Jewels." I was wearing white ribbed stockings, which were disgustingly itchy, and wrinkled at the knees and ankles. The feeling of these stockings on my legs is mixed up with another feeling in my memory. It is hard to describe. It had to do with my parents. Adults in general but my parents in particular. My father, who had carried Steve's body from the river, and my mother, who must have done most of the arranging of this funeral. My father in his dark-blue suit and my mother in her brown velvet dress with the creamy satin collar. They stood side by side opening and closing their mouths for the hymn, and I stood removed from them, in the row of children, watching. I felt a furious and sickening disgust. Children sometimes have an excess of disgust concerning adults. The size, the lumpy shapes, the bloated power. The breath, the coarseness, the hairiness, the horrid secretions. But this was more. And the accompanying anger had nothing sharp and self-respecting about it. There was no release, as when I would finally bend and pick up a stone and throw it at Steve Gauley. It could not be understood or expressed, though it died down after a while into a heaviness, then just a taste, an occasional taste —a thin, familiar misgiving.

Twenty years or so later, in 1961, my husband, Andrew, and I got a brand-new car, our first—that is, our first brand-new. It was a Morris Oxford, oyster-colored (the dealer had some fancier name for the color) —a big small car, with plenty of room for us and our two children. Cynthia was six and Meg three and a half.

Andrew took a picture of me standing beside the car. I was wearing white pants, a black turtleneck, and sunglasses. I lounged against the car door, canting my hips to make myself look slim.

"Wonderful," Andrew said. "Great. You look like Jackie Kennedy." All over this continent probably, dark-haired, reasonably slender young women were told, when they were stylishly dressed or getting their pictures taken, that they looked like Jackie Kennedy.

Andrew took a lot of pictures of me, and of the children, our house, our garden, our excursions and possessions. He got copies made, labelled them carefully, and sent them back to his mother and his aunt and uncle in Ontario. He got copies for me to send to my father, who also lived in Ontario, and I did so, but less regularly than he sent his. When he saw pictures he thought I had already sent lying around the house, Andrew was perplexed and annoyed. He liked to have this record go forth.

That summer, we were presenting ourselves, not pictures. We were driving back from Vancouver, where we lived, to Ontario, which we still called "home," in our new car. Five days to get there, ten days there, five days back. For the first time, Andrew had three weeks' holiday. He worked in the legal department at B. C. Hydro.

On a Saturday morning, we loaded suitcases, two thermos bottles —one filled with coffee and one with lemonade—some fruit and sandwiches, picture books and coloring books, crayons, drawing pads, insect repellent, sweaters (in case it got cold in the mountains), and our two children into the car. Andrew locked the house, and Cynthia said ceremoniously, "Goodbye, house."

Meg said, "Goodbye, house." Then she said, "Where will we live now?"

"It's not goodbye forever," said Cynthia. "We're coming back. Mother! Meg thought we weren't ever coming back!"

"I did not," said Meg, kicking the back of my seat.

Andrew and I put on our sunglasses, and we drove away, over the Lions Gate Bridge and through the main part of Vancouver. We shed our house, the neighborhood, the city, and—at the crossing point between Washington and British Columbia—our country. We were driving east across the United States, taking the most northerly route, and would cross into Canada again at Sarnia, Ontario. I don't know if we chose this route because the Trans-Canada Highway was not completely finished at the time or if we just wanted the feeling of driving through a foreign, a very slightly foreign, country—that extra bit of interest and adventure.

We were both in high spirits. Andrew congratulated the car several times. He said he felt so much better driving it than our old car, a 1951 Austin that slowed down dismally on the hills and had a fussy-old-lady image. So Andrew said now.

"What kind of image does this one have?" said Cynthia. She listened to us carefully and liked to try out new words such as "image." Usually she got them right.

"Lively," I said. "Slightly sporty. It's not show-off."

"It's sensible, but it has class," Andrew said. "Like my image."

Cynthia thought that over and said with a cautious pride, "That means like you think you want to be, Daddy?"

As for me, I was happy because of the shedding. I loved taking off. In my own house, I seemed to be often looking for a place to hide— sometimes from the children but more often from the jobs to be done and the phone ringing and the sociability of the neighborhood. I wanted to hide so that I could get busy at my real work, which was a sort of wooing of distant parts of myself. I lived in a state of siege, always losing just what I wanted to hold on to. But on trips there was no difficulty. I could be talking to Andrew, talking to the children and looking at whatever they wanted me to look at—a pig on a sign, a pony in a field, a Volkswagen on a revolving stand—and pouring lemonade into plastic cups, and all the time those bits and pieces would be flying together inside me. The essential composition would be achieved. This made me hopeful and lighthearted. It was being a watcher that did it. A watcher, not a keeper.

We turned east at Everett and climbed into the Cascades. I showed Cynthia our route on the map. First I showed her the map of the whole United States, which showed also the bottom part of Canada. Then I turned to the separate maps of each of the states we were going to pass through. Washington, Idaho, Montana, North Dakota, Minnesota, Wisconsin. I showed her the dotted line across Lake Michigan, which was the route of the ferry we would take. Then we would drive across Michigan to the bridge that linked the United States and Canada at Sarnia, Ontario. Home.

Meg wanted to see, too.

"You won't understand," said Cynthia. But she took the road atlas into the back seat.

"Sit back," she said to Meg. "Sit still. I'll show you."

I could hear her tracing the route for Meg, very accurately, just as I had done it for her. She looked up all the states' maps, knowing how to find them in alphabetical order.

"You know what that line is?" she said. "It's the road. That line is the road we're driving on. We're going right along this line."

Meg did not say anything.

"Mother, show me where we are right this minute," said Cynthia.

I took the atlas and pointed out the road through the mountains, and she took it back and showed it to Meg. "See where the road is all wiggly?" she said. "It's wiggly because there are so many turns in it. The wiggles are the turns." She flipped some pages and waited a moment. "Now," she said, "show me where we are." Then she called to me, "Mother, she understands! She pointed to it! Meg understands maps!"

It seems to me now that we invented characters for our children. We had them firmly set to play their parts. Cynthia was bright and diligent, sensitive, courteous, watchful. Sometimes we teased her for being too conscientious, too eager to be what we in fact depended on her to be. Any reproach or failure, any rebuff, went terribly deep with her. She was fair-haired, fair-skinned, easily showing the effects of the sun, raw winds, pride, or humiliation. Meg was more solidly built, more reticent—not rebellious but stubborn sometimes, mysterious. Her silences seemed to us to show her strength of character, and her negatives were taken as signs of an imperturbable independence. Her hair was brown, and we cut it in straight bangs. Her eyes were a light hazel, clear and dazzling.

We were entirely pleased with these characters, enjoying the contradictions as well as the confirmations of them. We disliked the heavy, the uninventive, approach to being parents. I had a dread of turning into a certain kind of mother—the kind whose body sagged, who moved in a woolly-smelling, milky-smelling fog, solemn with trivial burdens. I believed that all the attention these mothers paid, their need to be burdened, was the cause of colic, bed-wetting, asthma. I favored another approach—the mock desperation, the inflated irony of the professional mothers who wrote for magazines. In those magazine pieces, the children were splendidly self-willed, hard-edged, perverse, indomitable. So were the mothers, through their wit, indomitable. The real-life mothers I warmed to were the sort who would phone up and say, "Is my embryo Hitler by any chance over at your house?" They cackled clear above the milky fog.

We saw a dead deer strapped across the front of a pickup truck.

"Somebody shot it," Cynthia said. "Hunters shoot the deer."

"It's not hunting season yet," Andrew said. "They may have hit it on the road. See the sign for deer crossing?"

"I would cry if we hit one," Cynthia said sternly.

I had made peanut-butter-and-marmalade sandwiches for the children and salmon-and-mayonnaise for us. But I had not put any lettuce in, and Andrew was disappointed.

"I didn't have any," I said.

"Couldn't you have got some?"

"I'd have had to buy a whole head of lettuce just to get enough for sandwiches, and I decided it wasn't worth it."

This was a lie. I had forgotten.

"They're a lot better with lettuce."

"I didn't think it made that much difference." After a silence, I said, "Don't be mad."

"I'm not mad. I like lettuce on sandwiches."

"I just didn't think it mattered that much."

"How would it be if I didn't bother to fill up the gas tank?"

"That's not the same thing."

"Sing a song," said Cynthia. She started to sing:

"Five little ducks went out one day,
Over the hills and far away.
One little duck went
'Quack-quack-quack.'
Four little ducks came swimming back."

Andrew squeezed my hand and said, "Let's not fight."

"You're right. I should have got lettuce."

"It doesn't matter that much."

I wished that I could get my feelings about Andrew to come together into a serviceable and dependable feeling. I had even tried writing two lists, one of things I liked about him, one of things I disliked—in the cauldron of intimate life, things I loved and things I hated—as if I hoped by this to prove something, to come to a conclusion one way or the other. But I gave it up when I saw that all it proved was what I already knew—that I had violent contradictions. Sometimes the very sound of his footsteps seemed to me tyrannical, the set of his mouth smug and mean, his hard, straight body a barrier interposed—quite consciously, even dutifully, and with a nasty pleasure in its masculine authority— between me and whatever joy or lightness I could get in life. Then, with not much warning, he became my good friend and most essential companion. I felt the sweetness of his light bones and serious ideas, the vulnerability of his love, which I imagined to be much purer and more straightforward than my own. I could be greatly moved by an inflexibility, a harsh propriety, that at other times I scorned. I would think how humble he was, really, taking on such a ready-made role of husband, father, breadwinner, and how I myself in comparison was really a secret monster of egotism. Not so secret, either—not from him.

At the bottom of our fights, we served up what we thought were the ugliest truths. "I know there is something basically selfish and basically untrustworthy about you," Andrew once said. "I've always known it. I also know that that is why I fell in love with you."

"Yes," I said, feeling sorrowful but complacent.

"I know that I'd be better off without you."

"Yes. You would."

"You'd be happier without me."

"Yes."

And finally—finally—racked and purged, we clasped hands and laughed, laughed at those two benighted people, ourselves. Their grudges, their grievances, their self-justification. We leap-frogged over them. We declared them liars. We would have wine with dinner, or decide to give a party.

I haven't seen Andrew for years, don't know if he is still thin, has gone completely gray, insists on lettuce, tells the truth, or is hearty and disappointed.

We stayed the night in Wenatchee, Washington, where it hadn't rained for weeks. We ate dinner in a restaurant built about a tree—not a sapling in a tub but a tall, sturdy cottonwood. In the early-morning light, we climbed out of the irrigated valley, up dry, rocky, very steep hillsides that would seem to lead to more hills, and there on the top was a wide plateau, cut by the great Spokane and Columbia rivers. Grainland and grassland, mile after mile. There were straight roads here, and little farming towns with grain elevators. In fact, there was a sign announcing that this county we were going through, Douglas County, had the second-highest wheat yield of any county in the United States. The towns had planted shade trees. At least, I thought they had been planted, because there were no such big trees in the countryside.

All this was marvellously welcome to me. "Why do I love it so much?" I said to Andrew. "Is it because it isn't scenery?"

"It reminds you of home," said Andrew. "A bout of severe nostalgia." But he said this kindly.

When we said "home" and meant Ontario, we had very different places in mind. My home was a turkey farm, where my father lived as a widower, and though it was the same house my mother had lived in, had papered, painted, cleaned, furnished, it showed the effects now of neglect and of some wild sociability. A life went on in it that my mother could not have predicted or condoned. There were parties for the turkey crew, the gutters and pluckers, and sometimes one or two of the young men would be living there temporarily, inviting their own friends and having their own impromptu parties. This life, I thought, was better for my father than being lonely, and I did not disapprove, had certainly no right to disapprove. Andrew did not like to go there, naturally enough, because he was not the sort who could sit around the kitchen table with the turkey crew, telling jokes. They were intimidated by him and contemptuous of him, and it seemed to me that my father, when they were around, had to be on their side. And it wasn't only Andrew who had trouble. I could manage those jokes, but it was an effort.

I wished for the days when I was little, before we had the turkeys. We had cows, and sold the milk to the cheese factory. A turkey farm is nothing like as pretty as a dairy farm or a sheep farm. You can see that the turkeys are on a straight path to becoming frozen carcasses and table meat. They don't have the pretense of a life of their own, a browsing idyll, that cattle have, or pigs in the dappled orchard. Turkey barns are long, efficient buildings—tin sheds. No beams or hay or warm stables. Even the smell of guano seems thinner and more offensive than the usual smell of stable manure. No hints there of hay coils and rail fences and songbirds and the flowering hawthorn. The turkeys were all let out into one long field, which they picked clean. They didn't look like great birds there but like fluttering laundry.

Once, shortly after my mother died, and after I was married—in fact, I was packing to join Andrew in Vancouver—I was at home alone for a couple of days with my father. There was a freakishly heavy rain all night. In the early light, we saw that the turkey field was flooded. At least, the low-lying parts of it were flooded—it was like a lake with many islands. The turkeys were huddled on these islands. Turkeys are very stupid. (My father would say, "You know a chicken? You know how stupid a chicken is? Well, a chicken is an Einstein compared with a turkey.") But they had managed to crowd to higher ground and avoid drowning. Now they might push each other off, suffocate each other, get cold and die. We couldn't wait for the water to go down. We went out in an old rowboat we had. I rowed and my father pulled the heavy, wet turkeys into the boat and we took them to the barn. It was still raining a little. The job was difficult and absurd and very uncomfortable. We were laughing. I was happy to be working with my father. I felt close to all hard, repetitive, appalling work, in which the body is finally worn out, the mind sunk (though sometimes the spirit can stay marvellously light), and I was homesick in advance for this life and this place. I thought that if Andrew could see me there in the rain, red-handed, muddy, trying to hold on to turkey legs and row the boat at the same time, he would only want to get me out of there and make me forget about it. This raw life angered him. My attachment to it angered him. I thought that I shouldn't have married him. But who else? One of the turkey crew?

And I didn't want to stay there. I might feel bad about leaving, but I would feel worse if somebody made me stay.

Andrew's mother lived in Toronto, in an apartment building looking out on Muir Park. When Andrew and his sister were both at home, his mother slept in the living room. Her husband, a doctor, had died when the children were still too young to go to school. She took a secretarial course and sold her house at Depression prices, moved to this apartment, managed to raise her children, with some help from relatives—her sister Caroline, her brother-in-law Roger. Andrew and his sister went to private schools and to camp in the summer.

"I suppose that was courtesy of the Fresh Air fund?" I said once, scornful of his claim that he had been poor. To my mind, Andrew's urban life had been sheltered and fussy. His mother came home with a headache from working all day in the noise, the harsh light of a department-store office, but it did not occur to me that hers was a hard or admirable life. I don't think she herself believed that she was admirable —only unlucky. She worried about her work in the office, her clothes, her cooking, her children. She worried most of all about what Roger and Caroline would think.

Caroline and Roger lived on the east side of the park, in a handsome stone house. Roger was a tall man with a bald, freckled head, a fat, firm stomach. Some operation on his throat had deprived him of his voice —he spoke in a rough whisper. But everybody paid attention. At dinner once in the stone house—where all the dining-room furniture was enormous, darkly glowing, palatial—I asked him a question. I think it had to do with Whittaker Chambers, whose story was then appearing in the *Saturday Evening Post.* The question was mild in tone, but he guessed its subversive intent and took to calling me Mrs. Gromyko, referring to what he alleged to be my "sympathies." Perhaps he really craved an adversary, and could not find one. At that dinner, I saw Andrew's hand tremble as he lit his mother's cigarette. His Uncle Roger had paid for Andrew's education, and was on the board of directors of several companies.

"He is just an opinionated old man," Andrew said to me later. "What is the point of arguing with him?"

Before we left Vancouver, Andrew's mother had written, "Roger seems quite intrigued by the idea of your buying a small car!" Her exclamation mark showed apprehension. At that time, particularly in Ontario, the choice of a small European car over a large American car could be seen as some sort of declaration—a declaration of tendencies Roger had been sniffing after all long.

"It isn't that small a car," said Andrew huffily.

"That's not the point," I said. "The point is, it isn't any of his business!"

We spent the second night in Missoula. We had been told in Spokane, at a gas station, that there was a lot of repair work going on along Highway 2, and that we were in for a very hot, dusty drive, with long waits, so we turned onto the interstate and drove through Coeur d'Alene and Kellogg into Montana. After Missoula, we turned south toward Butte, but detoured to see Helena, the state capital. In the car, we played Who Am I?

Cynthia was somebody dead, and an American, and a girl. Possibly a lady. She was not in a story. She had not been seen on television.

Cynthia had not read about her in a book. She was not anybody who had come to the kindergarten, or a relative of any of Cynthia's friends.

"Is she human?" said Andrew, with a sudden shrewdness.

"No! That's what you forgot to ask!"

"An animal," I said reflectively.

"Is that a question? Sixteen questions!"

"No, it is not a question. I'm thinking. A dead animal."

"It's the deer," said Meg, who hadn't been playing.

"That's not fair!" said Cynthia. "She's not playing!"

"What deer?" said Andrew.

I said, "Yesterday."

"The day before," said Cynthia. "Meg wasn't playing. Nobody got it."

"The deer on the truck," said Andrew.

"It was a lady deer, because it didn't have antlers, and it was an American and it was dead," Cynthia said.

Andrew said, "I think it's kind of morbid, being a dead deer."

"I got it," said Meg.

Cynthia said, "I think I know what morbid is. It's depressing."

Helena, an old silver-mining town, looked forlorn to us even in the morning sunlight. Then Bozeman and Billings, not forlorn in the slight-est—energetic, strung-out towns, with miles of blinding tinsel fluttering over used-car lots. We got too tired and hot even to play Who Am I? These busy, prosaic cities reminded me of similar places in Ontario, and I thought about what was really waiting there—the great tombstone furniture of Roger and Caroline's dining room, the dinners for which I must iron the children's dresses and warn them about forks, and then the other table a hundred miles away, the jokes of my father's crew. The pleasures I had been thinking of—looking at the countryside or drinking a Coke in an old-fashioned drugstore with fans and a high, pressed-tin ceiling—would have to be snatched in between.

"Meg's asleep," Cynthia said. "She's so hot. She makes me hot in the same seat with her."

"I hope she isn't feverish," I said, not turning around.

What are we doing this for, I thought, and the answer came—to show off. To give Andrew's mother and my father the pleasure of seeing their grandchildren. That was our duty. But beyond that we wanted to show them something. What strenuous children we were, Andrew and I, what relentless seekers of approbation. It was as if at some point we had received an unforgettable, indigestible message—that we were far from satisfactory, and that the most commonplace success in life was probably beyond us. Roger dealt out such messages, of course—that was his style—but Andrew's mother, my own mother and father couldn't have meant to do so. All they meant to tell us was "Watch out. Get along." My father, when I was in high school, teased me that I was getting to think I was so smart I would never find a boyfriend. He would have forgotten that in a week. I never forgot it. Andrew and I didn't forget things. We took umbrage.

"I wish there was a beach," said Cynthia.

"There probably is one," Andrew said. "Right around the next curve."

"There isn't any curve," she said, sounding insulted.

"That's what I mean."

"I wish there was some more lemonade."

"I will just wave my magic wand and produce some," I said. "Okay, Cynthia? Would you rather have grape juice? Will I do a beach while I'm at it?"

She was silent, and soon I felt repentant. "Maybe in the next town there might be a pool," I said. I looked at the map. "In Miles City. Anyway, there'll be something cool to drink."

"How far is it?" Andrew said.

"Not so far," I said. "Thirty miles, about."

"In Miles City," said Cynthia, in the tones of an incantation, "there is a beautiful blue swimming pool for children, and a park with lovely trees."

Andrew said to me, "You could have started something."

But there was a pool. There was a park, too, though not quite the oasis of Cynthia's fantasy. Prairie trees with thin leaves—cottonwoods and poplars—worn grass, and a high wire fence around the pool. Within this fence, a wall, not yet completed, of cement blocks. There were no shouts or splashes; over the entrance I saw a sign that said the pool was closed every day from noon until two o'clock. It was then twenty-five after twelve.

Nevertheless I called out, "Is anybody there?" I thought somebody must be around, because there was a small truck parked near the entrance. On the side of the truck were these words: "We have Brains, to fix your Drains. (We have Roto-Rooter too.)"

A girl came out, wearing a red lifeguard's shirt over her bathing suit. "Sorry, we're closed."

"We were just driving through," I said.

"We close every day from twelve until two. It's on the sign." She was eating a sandwich.

"I saw the sign," I said. "But this is the first water we've seen for so long, and the children are awfully hot, and I wondered if they could just dip in and out—just five minutes. We'd watch them."

A boy came into sight behind her. He was wearing jeans and a T-shirt with the words "Roto-Rooter" on it.

I was going to say that we were driving from British Columbia to Ontario, but I remembered that Canadian place names usually meant nothing to Americans. "We're driving right across the country," I said. "We haven't time to wait for the pool to open. We were just hoping the children could get cooled off."

Cynthia came running up barefoot behind me. "Mother. Mother, where is my bathing suit?" Then she stopped, sensing the serious adult negotiations. Meg was climbing out of the car—just wakened, with her top pulled up and her shorts pulled down, showing her pink stomach.

"Is it just those two?" the girl said.

"Just the two. We'll watch them."

"I can't let any adults in. If it's just the two, I guess I could watch them. I'm having my lunch." She said to Cynthia, "Do you want to come in the pool?"

"Yes, please," said Cynthia firmly.

Meg looked at the ground.

"Just a short time, because the pool is really closed," I said. "We appreciate this very much," I said to the girl.

"Well, I can eat my lunch out there, if it's just the two of them." She looked toward the car as if she thought I might try to spring some more children on her.

When I found Cynthia's bathing suit, she took it into the changing room. She would not permit anybody, even Meg, to see her naked. I changed Meg, who stood on the front seat of the car. She had a pink cotton bathing suit with straps that crossed and buttoned. There were ruffles across the bottom.

"She *is* hot," I said. "But I don't think she's feverish."

I loved helping Meg to dress or undress, because her body still had the solid unself-consciousness, the sweet indifference, something of the milky smell, of a baby's body. Cynthia's body had long ago been pared down, shaped and altered, into Cynthia. We all liked to hug Meg, press and nuzzle her. Sometimes she would scowl and beat us off, and this forthright independence, this ferocious bashfulness, simply made her more appealing, more apt to be tormented and tickled in the way of family love.

Andrew and I sat in the car with the windows open. I could hear a radio playing, and thought it must belong to the girl or her boyfriend. I was thirsty, and got out of the car to look for a concession stand, or perhaps a soft-drink machine, somewhere in the park. I was wearing shorts, and the backs of my legs were slick with sweat. I saw a drinking fountain at the other side of the park and was walking toward it in a roundabout way, keeping to the shade of the trees. No place became real till you got out of the car. Dazed with the heat, with the sun on the blistered houses, the pavement, the burned grass, I walked slowly. I paid attention to a squashed leaf, ground a Popsicle stick under the heel of my sandal, squinted at a trash can strapped to a tree. This is the way you look at the poorest details of the world resurfaced, after you've been driving for a long time—you feel the singleness and precise location and the forlorn coincidence of your being there to see them.

Where are the children?

I turned around and moved quickly, not quite running, to a part of the fence beyond which the cement wall was not completed. I could see some of the pool. I saw Cynthia, standing about waist-deep in the water, fluttering her hands on the surface and discreetly watching something at the end of the pool, which I could not see. I thought by her pose, her discretion, the look on her face, that she must be watching some byplay between the lifeguard and her boyfriend. I couldn't see Meg. But I thought she must be playing in the shallow water—both the shallow and deep ends of the pool were out of my sight.

"Cynthia!" I had to call twice before she knew where my voice was coming from. "Cynthia! Where's Meg?"

It always seems to me, when I recall this scene, that Cynthia turns very gracefully toward me, then turns all around in the water—making me think of a ballerina on point—and spreads her arms in a gesture of the stage. "Dis-ap-peared!"

Cynthia was naturally graceful, and she did take dancing lessons, so these movements may have been as I have described. She did say "Disappeared" after looking all around the pool, but the strangely artificial style of speech and gesture, the lack of urgency, is more likely my invention. The fear I felt instantly when I couldn't see Meg—even while I was telling myself she must be in the shallow water—must have made Cynthia's movements seem unbearably slow and inappropriate to me, and the tone in which she could say "Disappeared" before the implications struck her (or was she covering, at once, some ever-ready guilt?) was heard by me as quite exquisitely, monstrously self-possessed.

I cried out for Andrew, and the lifeguard came into view. She was pointing toward the deep end of the pool, saying, "What's that?"

There, just within my view, a cluster of pink ruffles appeared, a bouquet, beneath the surface of the water. Why would a lifeguard stop and point, why would she ask what that was, why didn't she just dive into the water and swim to it? She didn't swim; she ran all the way around the edge of the pool. But by that time Andrew was over the fence. So many things seemed not quite plausible—Cynthia's behavior, then the lifeguard's—and now I had the impression that Andrew jumped with one bound over this fence, which seemed about seven feet high. He must have climbed it very quickly, getting a grip on the wire.

I could not jump or climb it, so I ran to the entrance, where there was a sort of lattice gate, locked. It was not very high, and I did pull myself over it. I ran through the cement corridors, through the disinfectant pool for your feet, and came out on the edge of the pool.

The drama was over.

Andrew had got to Meg first, and had pulled her out of the water. He just had to reach over and grab her, because she was swimming somehow, with her head underwater—she was moving toward the edge of the pool. He was carrying her now, and the lifeguard was trotting along behind. Cynthia had climbed out of the water and was running to meet them. The only person aloof from the situation was the boyfriend, who had stayed on the bench at the shallow end, drinking a milkshake. He smiled at me, and I thought that unfeeling of him, even though the danger was past. He may have meant it kindly. I noticed that he had not turned the radio off, just down.

Meg had not swallowed any water. She hadn't even scared herself. Her hair was plastered to her head and her eyes were wide open, golden with amazement.

"I was getting the comb," she said. "I didn't know it was deep."

Andrew said, "She was swimming! She was swimming by herself. I saw her bathing suit in the water and then I saw her swimming."

"She nearly drowned," Cynthia said. "Didn't she? Meg nearly drowned."

"I don't know how it could have happened," said the lifeguard. "One moment she was there, and the next she wasn't."

What had happened was that Meg had climbed out of the water at the shallow end and run along the edge of the pool toward the deep end. She saw a comb that somebody had dropped lying on the bottom. She crouched down and reached in to pick it up, quite deceived about the depth of the water. She went over the edge and slipped into the pool, making such a light splash that nobody heard—not the lifeguard, who was kissing her boyfriend, or Cynthia, who was watching them. That must have been the moment under the trees when I thought, Where are the children? It must have been the same moment. At that moment, Meg was slipping, surprised, into the treacherously clear blue water.

"It's okay," I said to the lifeguard, who was nearly crying. "She can move pretty fast." (Though that wasn't what we usually said about Meg at all. We said she thought everything over and took her time.)

"You swam, Meg," said Cynthia, in a congratulatory way. (She told us about the kissing later.)

"I didn't know it was deep," Meg said. "I didn't drown."

We had lunch at a take-out place, eating hamburgers and fries at a picnic table not far from the highway. In my excitement, I forgot to get Meg a plain hamburger, and had to scrape off the relish and mustard with plastic spoons, then wipe the meat with a paper napkin, before she would eat it. I took advantage of the trash can there to clean out the car. Then we resumed driving east, with the car windows open in front. Cynthia and Meg fell asleep in the back seat.

Andrew and I talked quietly about what had happened. Suppose I hadn't had the impulse just at that moment to check on the children? Suppose we had gone uptown to get drinks, as we had thought of doing? How had Andrew got over the fence? Did he jump or climb? (He couldn't remember.) How had he reached Meg so quickly? And think of the lifeguard not watching. And Cynthia, taken up with the kissing. Not seeing anything else. Not seeing Meg drop over the edge.

Disappeared.

But she swam. She held her breath and came up swimming.

What a chain of lucky links.

That was all we spoke about—luck. But I was compelled to picture the opposite. At this moment, we could have been filling out forms. Meg removed from us, Meg's body being prepared for shipment. To Vancouver—where we had never noticed such a thing as a graveyard —or to Ontario? The scribbled drawings she had made this morning would still be in the back seat of the car. How could this be borne all at once, how did people bear it? The plump, sweet shoulders and hands and feet, the fine brown hair, the rather satisfied, secretive expression —all exactly the same as when she had been alive. The most ordinary tragedy. A child drowned in a swimming pool at noon on a sunny day. Things tidied up quickly. The pool opens as usual at two o'clock. The lifeguard is a bit shaken up and gets the afternoon off. She drives away with her boyfriend in the Roto-Rooter truck. The body sealed away in some kind of shipping coffin. Sedatives, phone calls, arrangements. Such a sudden vacancy, a blind sinking and shifting. Waking up groggy from the pills, thinking for a moment it wasn't true. Thinking if only we hadn't stopped, if only we hadn't taken this route, if only they hadn't let us use the pool. Probably no one would ever have known about the comb.

There's something trashy about this kind of imagining, isn't there? Something shameful. Laying your finger on the wire to get the safe shock, feeling a bit of what it's like, then pulling back. I believed that Andrew was more scrupulous than I about such things, and at this moment he was really trying to think about something else.

When I stood apart from my parents at Steve Gauley's funeral and watched them, and had this new, unpleasant feeling about them, I thought that I was understanding something about them for the first time. It was a deadly serious thing. I was understanding that they were implicated. Their big, stiff, dressed-up bodies did not stand between me and sudden death, or any kind of death. They gave consent. So it seemed. They gave consent to the death of children and to my death not by anything they said or thought but by the very fact that they had made children—they had made me. They had made me, and for that reason my death—however grieved they were, however they carried on—would seem to them anything but impossible or unnatural. This was a fact, and even then I knew they were not to blame.

But I did blame them. I charged them with effrontery, hypocrisy. On Steve Gauley's behalf, and on behalf of all children, who knew that by rights they should have sprung up free, to live a new, superior kind of life, not to be caught in the snares of vanquished grownups, with their sex and funerals.

Steve Gauley drowned, people said, because he was next thing to an orphan and was let run free. If he had been warned enough and given chores to do and kept in check, he wouldn't have fallen from an untrustworthy tree branch into a spring pond, a full gravel pit near the river—he wouldn't have drowned. He was neglected, he was free, so he drowned. And his father took it as an accident, such as might happen to a dog. He didn't have a good suit for the funeral, and he didn't bow his head for the prayers. But he was the only grownup that I let off the hook. He was the only one I didn't see giving consent. He couldn't prevent anything, but he wasn't implicated in anything, either—not like the others, saying the Lord's Prayer in their unnaturally weighted voices, oozing religion and dishonor.

At Glendive, not far from the North Dakota border, we had a choice—either to continue on the interstate or head northeast, toward Williston, taking Route 16, then some secondary roads that would get us back to Highway 2.

We agreed that the interstate would be faster, and that it was important for us not to spend too much time—that is, money—on the road. Nevertheless we decided to cut back to Highway 2.

"I just like the idea of it better," I said.

Andrew said, "That's because it's what we planned to do in the beginning."

"We missed seeing Kalispell and Havre. And Wolf Point. I like the name."

"We'll see them on the way back."

Andrew's saying "on the way back" was a surprising pleasure to me. Of course, I had believed that we would be coming back, with our car and our lives and our family intact, having covered all that distance, having dealt somehow with those loyalties and problems, held ourselves up for inspection in such a foolhardy way. But it was a relief to hear him say it.

"What I can't get over," said Andrew, "is how you got the signal. It's got to be some kind of extra sense that mothers have."

Partly I wanted to believe that, to bask in my extra sense. Partly I wanted to warn him—to warn everybody—never to count on it.

"What I can't understand," I said, "is how you got over the fence."

"Neither can I."

So we went on, with the two in the back seat trusting us, because of no choice, and we ourselves trusting to be forgiven, in time, for everything that had first to be seen and condemned by those children: whatever was flippant, arbitrary, careless, callous—all our natural, and particular, mistakes.

1986

THREE

Refashioning the Story of the Self

The protagonists of these stories live according to a fixed script—until they find themselves occupying another story, the story that we read. Inevitably this new story brings new knowledge of themselves and the world, and by the end, these characters match their new understanding with a truer self, conjuring up an identity that brings them into balance with the world.

The writers of these stories tell us that the chances of reading oneself accurately is slight. Sometimes a clear reading can only be achieved by first erasing the version someone else has written. Scooter Baker, in Lee K. Abbott's "The End of Grief," has to separate himself from his father's version of himself; to his dad, lost in grief for his brother, who died on the Bataan Death March, Scooter becomes that dead uncle, reborn. Sometimes the act of revising one's own narrative leads to triumph. In Ernest Hemingway's "A Day's Wait," the son battles against his own fear, a fight that allows his father to realize his character. After waiting all day to die, the nine-year-old gives poignant and irrefutable evidence of his own bravery. The protagonist in "Wind and Birds and Human Voices" (Ellen Wilbur) finds the enemy in himself, a discovery that sets him free from madness. Creating a self is often achieved against the outline of something else, or in reaction to the hard edges of the world.

The characters in these stories reach toward a coherent identity, grasp for that other ego, search for an authentic self. Modifying—or even inventing—one's identity is not new, but with the burgeoning interest in self-scrutiny, it is a particularly twentieth-century subject. Sometimes it seems that characters self-consciously invent their own lives. Marya, in "Theft" (Joyce Carol Oates), makes fictions of her background, offers half-truths of her life. In Bharati Mukherjee's "The Tenant," Maya—lost in "the confused world of the immigrant," between continents, countries, apartments, mates—inhabits personae like a tenant does an apartment, only for a while, before moving on to find her true life.

Out of these battles the recomposed self emerges, with its new tale to tell. Waverly Jong, in "Rules of the Game" (Amy Tan), falls in love with the powerful secrets and strategies of chess—Throwing Stones on the Drowning Man, Sand in the Eyes of Advancing Forces, A Double Killing Without Blood—using them, finally, to negotiate the steps of the difficult match between mother and daughter. Lipsha Morrissey, in "Love Medicine" (Louise Erdrich), discovers a totem for his new character: like a dandelion head, he's "a globe of frail seeds that's indestructible." Refashioning the self's story produces new metaphors that are, ultimately, the new means of self-recognition.

LEE K. ABBOTT

The End of Grief

The worst thing, in many ways the only thing, I heard about when I was growing up in the late fifties and early sixties concerned the horrible death of my father's brother, my Uncle Gideon, on the Bataan Death March in April of 1942, an event that for those of you who, like me, were absorbed by the pictures and news reports of the Vietnam War must now seem as peculiarly dated as the times of knights errant and fire-breathing dragons.

"Remember this," my father would say when I was small. "We human beings are capable of some real nasty behavior."

Every family has its own history of heartache, its private record of betrayal or misfortune; but when I was a youngster—and probably because we live so far out of the way, in Deming, New Mexico, in a desert white and scorched and flat as one hell I've heard described—I believed, stupidly, that this infamy, a march of 78,000 native and American troops on a no-account Philippine peninsula, had touched everyone in our own safe world. From my mother, before she became a drunkard who would be carried off one day to live quietly and ever after in a private hospital in Roswell, and before she and Daddy divorced, I had learned about the other tragedies we Bakers and Hopcrafts (her people) had suffered: bankruptcies, disasters associated with weather or automobiles, paper fortunes that blew away like leaves, a drowning, a stillbirth, a black sheep or two. Yet if my mother could look backward for centuries, to the first of my ancestors who settled in the American Southwest in the early 1800s, my father, smart too, and just as familiar with our personal lore, could see only from the beginning of the Second World War to what was its mortal end for the young man I am said to be the spitting image of—my uncle.

Though Lee K. Abbott was born in the Panama Canal Zone in 1947, he staged the action of his short stories repeatedly and insistently within the United States, namely, the small towns of New Mexico where he completed much of his undergraduate and graduate work. Infused with characteristic wit and wordplay, his work has been recognized by a number of awards, such as the Pushcart Prize (for "X") and the Columbia University Graduate School of Journalism's National Magazine Award (for "Time and Fear and Somehow Love"). Abbott has taught English at Case Western Reserve University in Cleveland, Ohio, since 1977.

Now, at thirty-seven, I remember clearly how Daddy, in his odd fashion, used to wish me good night with stories from a past that was no more important to me personally than money is to a rock. When I was in the third grade, he'd tell me—sitting at the foot of my bed, smoking a Pall Mall, an ashtray balanced on his knee—about the diseases the men in II Corps, and my uncle, suffered: dysentery, beriberi, night blindness, hookworm, diarrhea, mysterious swellings. When I was in the fourth grade, a time when I thought only about Little League baseball or swimming meets at the Mimbres Valley Country Club, he was taking me into his office, the newest outbuilding on our ranch, to show me his Department of Army maps and geological surveys.

"They marched from here," he'd say, pointing to a crosshatching of lines identified as Balanga, "on the East Road to Lubao on Route Seven." His finger would trace the route, sometimes a path of gravel and packed dirt. "They would go from Capas by train and walk the next nine miles to Camp O'Donnell."

Yes, these were the names I heard through grammar school and into junior high: Bagac and Orion, the Marvilles Mountains, and island of Luzon, Manila Bay. In the year of my first kiss (with Jane Templeton at an FFA fair in our National Guard armory), he forced me to memorize the titles and honors of the Japanese commander, Lieutenant General Masaharu Homma, and several of his officers, including Colonel Nakayama and Colonel Takatsu. While my friends Dub Spedding and Bobby Hover were collecting memorabilia about Ted Williams and Hammering Hank Aaron, I was reading *Back from the Living Dead*, by Major Bert Bank. My father had sent to Alabama for it, had read it so thoroughly that the pages became creased and soiled and clotted with his notes, and by God I was going to read it, too, just as I would read, when he was finished, books like *Zone of Emptiness*, by Hiroshio Noma, and the documents published by the Allied Translator and Interpretor Section (ATIS), General Headquarters, Southwest Pacific Area. Once, when I was a sophomore at Deming High School, brainy enough to be on the debate team and beefy enough to play varsity Wildcat football, he even gave me a quiz.

"Before the surrender itself," he began, "what were our soldiers eating?"

We sat in his office, its many shelves laden with charts and papers and file folders, his desk a clutter of books and writing materials. On one wall hung a pair of khaki trousers and an Imperial Army battle sword; on another, a partial order of battle.

"Who surrendered, by the way?"

"General King," I answered, a name I knew as well as my own. "On April ninth, approximately fourteen hundred hours."

The room was full of smoke already, and, owing to the glare from the floor lamp behind him, he seemed not so much my father as an old, sly stranger—a wizard, I thought, or an Indian medicine man—whose tests I had to pass in order to live as an adult.

"The food, son," he said, "the meat first."

I recited the list: carabao, pack mule, lizard, dog and monkey, even the meat and eggs from pythons.

"How much did black-market cigarettes cost?"

"Five dollars," I said. "Regularly they were five cents a pack."

He shook his head. "It kept changing," he told me. "Remember the situation: one day a certain price, the next day another. This is vital."

On it went. Name the military hospitals and the officers in charge. How close was Corregidor? Why wouldn't Major General Jones take off his sunglasses? Who was the commander of the 65th Brigade of the Japanese Fourteenth Army? What American college had he attended? Describe the symptoms of malaria. What is Article 3, Chapter 1 of the Japanese Army regulations for handling prisoners of war? Translate *Bushido. Rikutatsu.*

At eleven I stopped him. We'd been at it for two hours. "I got to study," I said. "Physics."

He was shuffling documents, and I wanted to be elsewhere. In my room, I thought. In dreamland. Anywhere.

"Okay," he said. "Tomorrow we'll try something else."

I was at the door when he called me back.

"One more question," he said. "Why wasn't I in the war?"

A wind had come up, from the south and warm as breath. Tomorrow, while we classified soldiers according to sector and probable cause of death, we would have rain.

"Married," I told him.

He was rubbing his forehead, looking into space. "What else?"

"Medical deferment," I said. "Punctured eardrum, flat feet, pulmonary stenosis."

This sort of exchange worsened as I grew older and, in his mind at least, came to resemble more clearly his brother. We had the same forehead, he'd insist, pitching me yet another curled, yellowed photograph he filed in his fireproof cabinets. We had the same hair, too, coarse as thread and more brown than blond. The same watery hazel eyes. Our cheek structures were virtually identical, high and pointed. We even had, my father claimed, comparable habits of mind. We liked puzzles.

Within reason, we took risks: embraced speed, high places, darkness. We hated bullies, dishonesty in our friends. We were nimble, alert, sensitive to climate changes. Gideon had traveled—Palm Springs and Chicago—and so would I. He preferred tall women, so mine, inevitably, would be tall. We were readers but not sissies. When I graduated, Daddy took me out to his office, made me sit, and told me to open the box on his desk.

"It's a present," he said. "You'll like it."

It was a gold Longines, a wristwatch I wear still, and I realized immediately that Daddy had wrapped it himself, maybe a dozen times before he was satisfied.

"Look at the inscription." He leaned across his desk, pointed.

Still in my cap and gown, the tassel tickling my neck, I could hear my mother calling us to the dinner table. The ceremony had been over for an hour.

"Read it," my father told me.

Engraved on the back in small Gothic letters was this: "Gideon Alan Baker. Graduation: 16 June 1940. From his loving brother, Lyman."

"Gideon left it here before he enlisted," Daddy said. "He thought somebody might steal it."

I said thanks and stood to shake hands as I had been taught, firmly and with the palm full.

"You take care of that," he said, coming around his desk; and then I understood, more in my bones than in my brain, that he was smiling as he had smiled in 1940. To his mind, the hand he was holding, long-fingered and too soft, was less mine than his brother's; for him this was an instant of joy he had rescued, as boldly as if it were a person, from a past black and permanent as death itself.

"Gid liked expensive jewelry," Daddy said. "You will, too."

We would break eventually, my father and I, but for three years, while I was at the University of New Mexico, we continued our strange collaboration/review of Bataan, and torture, and my uncle. Within the week of my arrival, even before freshman orientation concluded, my father began writing me, filling his letters with facts I was to confirm in Zimmerman Library. "Find out," he'd scrawl, "who was responsible for the massacre of the 91st Filipino Division." A month later, he asked me to see if a Major Pedro L. Felix had been at Fort Benning, Georgia, on or about 12 October 1941. "What for?" I wrote back. By return mail I had an answer: "Gid mentions him twice. Maybe they met in the National Rice and Corn Corporation warehouse. I'm trying to establish a connection. This man survived four bayonet wounds, including a gash in the intestine."

Even when he admitted himself to Providence Memorial Hospital, in El Paso, to have his gall bladder removed, Daddy wrote—and I imagine now that he did so between visits from his nurses and doctors or after my mother had fallen asleep in her chair. "I need a complete list of General Parker's II Corps headquarters staff," he said once. "Maybe you could try the War College people for me. They stopped acknowledging my inquiries last August." Those letters, his penmanship bunched and tinier than you'd expect from a large man, were wrinkled and stained, as if he'd kept them in his pocket like Kleenex, or under his mattress; and rare was the note that would say, as one did, "Disregard previous request, found info elsewhere. Now have names of stationmaster and Lubao political officer."

Near Christmas that year I told him I wouldn't do any more research. "I'm done with this," I wrote. "You can't expect this of me anymore. It's not fair."

Never had I challenged him on any issue—not what vegetables to eat, nor how a young man treats a lady, nothing—so I spent a week waiting to see him pull up in front of my dormitory in his pickup, his face alive with the rage of betrayal. Instead I got another note, this one typed and arranged as if for business: "All's fine here (except Mother, who wants nothing more to do with me). I hope you're getting out some. The big project with me is to find somebody who knew Gid over there. Do your homework. I am proud of you. Love, your Dad."

As it happened—because of the co-op program I entered (I'm an oil engineer now) and because being away from home seemed to have given me license to explore the large world far from here—I didn't get home much. When I did, it was only for a weekend—hardly long enough, I see now, to note the effect this obsession (if that's all it was) had on my mother. She drank, but everybody I knew drank—Dr. Weems, my father's golfing partners at the club, our trust officer, the cowhands working for us. Alcohol was as much a part of home life as laundry or breakfast; and alcoholics, after all, were other, less fortunate people: the poor, the lonely, the ignorant—not one's own mother. If I had been smarter, I might have seen the effect during my senior spring break, when I came down to tell them I was planning to marry Deborah, now my wife, but for years what I most remembered about those two days was the food my dad ate and the five-thousand-dollar check he forced on me.

"Do you know what your father's favorite flower is?" my mother asked that last afternoon. "The bachelor button. You wouldn't expect that, would you?"

If she was drunk, I did not know it. My thoughts concerned getting back to Albuquerque before dark, and the O-Chem midterm I had to take.

"His favorite composer is Mr. Bobby Worth," she said. "You know, 'Tonight We Love.' But he likes Ray Austin too."

In a housecoat, her hair flyaway and dry-looking, Mother was cleaning the silver, the candelabra and serving dishes, even my baby cup; most of her days were like this, I think, hours that she hoped to fill but never could. Hours that, finally, had shape and color and density. Then she got up, went to the kitchen and returned with an Army messkit, metal and cleverly self-contained. It held a scoop of something like papier-mâché.

"Take this out to your father."

He was eating, I would discover, less than six ounces of overboiled rice once a day, the diet my uncle had survived on for two weeks before the surrender.

"It's an experiment," Daddy told me. "Don't worry, I'm not crazy."

The office was as I remembered, jammed floor to ceiling with documents, and I watched, fascinated, as he arranged himself cross-legged on the floor like a Buddha, the metal messkit under his chin as he ate with his fingers.

"No couches in the bush," he said. "Here, you try it."

He held out, balanced on his fingertips, a lump like wallpaper paste, and without thinking I let him put it in my mouth.

"The strong had to feed the weak," he said. "Carry them, too. Sometimes they carried dead men."

The stuff was gummy, as tasteless as sand, less food than pulp.

"They'd drink from shell craters, once in a while from a stream. A couple pesos got you milk, maybe a turnip."

The rice sat in my mouth like paper. Like ash.

"You want some more?" he asked.

I didn't move, just watched him eat and listened to him describe events nearly twenty-five years old. The violence wasn't all of it, he said. The heat, heavy as wool and thick, contributed, along with the terrain —blackened tree stumps, wallows, rice paddies, dust: a jungle that had become the moon. There was humidity like saddlecloth, and foot sores. Some men ate cane bark. You saw corpses everywhere. In the towns— Lamao, Lubao—the civilians might sneak you a mango. You marched eighteen hours; maybe you got salt, maybe you didn't. Some of the Nips had bikes; you had to run double time to keep up. You went crazy, entered mirages. You died. In the boxcars, narrow gauge and so low you had to stoop, you were packed so tight that the sweat ran down your legs and left your shoes soggy. If you had shoes.

"I can only eat this mush for about three days," Daddy said. "Then I get the runs."

Had my father experimented in other ways to put himself in my uncle's place? Without either a hat or a shirt, had he taken several long hikes in the desert, trying to recreate the exhaustion and pain Gideon must have felt? Had he emptied the tack box in our horse barn to spend a day inside it, cramped and sweaty and alone? I didn't know, didn't want to know. On the afternoon I am writing about, I was frightened —my heart in my ears, my breath ragged and hot, for it was easy to believe, though he kept telling me otherwise, that he had lost his mind, that he did not know this was 1967, or that he lived in America, or that he was a cattle rancher, not a prisoner of war. It was possible to believe that he, like those victims of religious rapture we read about in the papers, had slipped free of himself by a truly black magic. I thought that here, in the familiar quarters of his office, he heard voices, the wet groans and shouts and nightmare whimpers of men dying around him. Here, I thought, between one window that opened toward the Mimbres Mountains and another that faced the blank, shimmering horizon that was Mexico, he saw captains and sergeants without heads or arms, or privates and majors bloated black and left to rot.

"What's your position on this Vietnam thing?" he asked.

On the floor sat his tin messkit, clean as if our dog, Raleigh, had eaten there, and it struck me that I had no position on anything, nothing at all.

"I have a position," Daddy said, "and my position is that you steer clear of it, you understand?"

His eyes remained on me as they had when he began telling me about Gideon—about our skinny-boy thighs, our dumb respect for mechanical contraptions, our rail-stiff spines—but now his eyes were saying, as eyes can, that enough was enough. A brother had died, a son would not.

"They change your classification," he was saying, "you let me know. File for CO, take drugs—I don't care—but you tell them no deal, you hear?"

I heard; yes, I did.

"From now on, you're a Communist," he said. "You're a Russian, a Chinese, anything."

Years later I learned that he had gone to my draft board the day before, in his belt the Colt pistol he took as protection when he strung barbed wire at our section line. As I heard it, Daddy told Mr. Phinizy Spalding, a lifelong friend and the board's part-time director, that Scooter Baker was not going to die in some cesspool half a world away, that Lyman Baker, Sr., himself would see to it that Scooter showed up in panties and bra if it came to that. "I tell you, Phinzy," Daddy is supposed to have hollered in our post office, "you come after my boy, and I'll shoot his goddam foot off myself. You know I will." What I heard is that my father, his hand on the pistol grip, stood for several minutes, trembling with anger, not two paces from Mr. Spalding, muttering again and again, as if he would for a year, the one word that seemed to make the most sense in the world he knew: no, no, no.

But he was standing in front of me now, calm as the day itself, and I wanted to say that I was twenty-one. I was in love with a brunette economics major from Grants. I wasn't a registered voter yet. I was a kid, I was stupid.

"You listen to me," he said. "I'm going to give you some money—a lot of money, buddy—and when the time comes, if it does, you get out, you hear me?"

He was speaking to me, I realized, as he wished he had spoken to Gideon—big brother to little, wise man to dumb.

"You go to Sweden," he told me, his voice full of iron and the working life he loved, "go to Canada, Africa—makes no difference. You just go, you understand?"

We looked at each other, seriously and carefully. He was my father, he expected something of me, and there was a part of me that should know it. From his bent-forward shoulders and his narrowed eyes and the quiver in his cheek, I understood that all this Bataan stuff, the horror stories and the painstaking attention to detail and the grainy, timeworn photographs, had been an expression, unmistakable as slaughter itself, of nothing so much as love and memory and death and my relation among them.

As it turned out, I received a high lottery number when I graduated, so I missed the chance, as my father saw it, to define myself morally, to say what sort of son he'd raised. And in time, I admit, I tried to forget most of this. Deborah and I married, I took a job with Sinclair Oil in Texas for a time, and then, in 1976, just about the month our son Brian was born (he, yes, looks enough like me to look like my uncle, too), I came back here, to Deming, to work for a wildcat gas outfit named Mimbres Drilling, and to help Daddy with the ranch. Though my mother's drinking had led to her removal to Roswell, almost 250 miles away, these were good times: Deborah and I bought the split-level brick house we have, joined the club in our own right, made friends again with those I had grown up with. In the years after he stuffed his check into my shirt pocket and gave me a breath-defeating hug, I tried to believe that my father kept his Bataan studies to himself, more or less. I assumed he still pestered the Defense Department and the Records Division of the National Archives in Washington; but I also assumed— at least until a few years later when he called to tell me to drive out to the ranch to meet somebody—that his studies were no longer so dire, nor so mad. He was a man with a hobby, I had told Deborah, like coin or stamp collecting, or knowing the Latin names of desert plants.

"I want an hour of your time," he told me that night. "Just a little unfinished business."

He was crazy, I thought. He was lonely.

"Please, son. Don't fight me on this."

I have said that we had broken, my father and I, but the break was clean, not spite-filled, and could be fixed to the moment I took his money and left. We had parted, I thought. He had gone one way— backward, toward the past, toward grief—and I had gone another; and we had agreed silently, I thought, that there was an era, begun and ended in violence, that we neither would nor could talk about again.

"You found somebody, didn't you?" I said. "Somebody who knew Gid."

"Yeah," he told me. "An officer."

"After this no more," I told him. I felt slumped inside, as if all there was of link and snap and hook had crashed loose and lay ruined at the pit of me. "I mean it, Daddy."

"Sure," he said. "Just tonight."

The man Daddy wanted me to meet was Colonel Redmon A. Walters, U.S. Army, Ret., who, before serving in Honduras and in the Republic of South Korea, had been in the Philippines. On the march from the West Road to San Fernando he had befriended a twenty-year-old PFC named Baker, Gideon Alan.

"They were in the same regiment," Daddy said, "the Thirty-first Infantry. Both knew Brady."

I guess Daddy already realized that Colonel Walters—"Call me Red," he said, "I'm a civilian now"—had in fact not known any uncle; or, rather, he had known my uncle in the same way you and I know the dead whose ages we are or whose places we see. Yet Red Walters was no liar; he was only a man—like my father—who had felt and heard too much, and to whom truth wasn't a thing of records and graphs and testimony. Truth was the simple elements: light and nerve, fear and hope.

"What kind of a guy was Gid?" Daddy was saying.

Red Walters sat where I usually did, so I leaned against a file cabinet and looked out the window to the part of our toolshed I could see.

"He was tough," Colonel Walters said. "Lots of guys weren't—they caved in right away—but not your brother. He was a son-of-a-bitch, is what he was."

I was hearing them, Red and Daddy, describe an old world they regarded from opposite ends of experience, and I felt nothing. Air was air, earth earth, and way off—in time if not in place—I stood, as alien to this as I would be to affairs on Mars.

"Where exactly did you meet him?" Daddy said.

Over his shoulder I could see a copy of General Homma's personal notes, which had come from the Office of Military History in Tokyo. Near it was the volume General Wainright had submitted to the War Department in 1946, *Report of the USAFFE and USFIP in the Philippine Islands, 1941–1942*. I had read them in another life, it seemed. In another world. With other eyes. With another brain.

"It was in Balanga," Red was saying. "Gid was part of that group in the field beyond the jail."

"Here?" Daddy had pointed to a spot the size of a fingernail. It represented twelve unfenced acres in which thousands of men had been bivouacked during the march.

"Even the Japs didn't know what was up," Red said. "It was pretty confusing."

"I heard it was crazy."

"Filthy," Red Walters said. "No medical facilities, guys dying, flies everywhere. There was a kind of cloud over the place. At night it was incredibly cold."

"He looked pretty bad, I bet."

"We all did," Colonel Walters told us. "Thin like scarecrows, and stupid-looking. Some guys couldn't remember their names. Their units. You just wanted to lie down mostly."

"What about the brutality?"

"You got used to it," he said. "You didn't complain. You shut up."

At this point I realized that Colonel Walters had not met my uncle —the odds against it, and my father's hopes, were too great—but the realization reached me slowly and without real shock, the way bad news must come to the chronically unlucky. It was old news, really. Maybe it was the news God sees, our human story told so often that it has lost its capacity to amaze or to instruct.

"He looked like me, right?" I asked.

At that moment Colonel Walters, gray-haired and now too fleshy at the neck, came alive for me. I could imagine him as he'd once been, hollow-eyed and feeble and broken.

"Hard to tell," he said. "He could've been big once, like you."

"He had my face, though?"

"It's been a long time," he said, "I don't remember faces much anymore."

He was talking about all of them, I think. Clifford Bluemel, Alf Weinstein, Lieutenant Henry G. Lee, Reynaldo Perez, Lieutenant Colonel William E. Chandler, the living and the dead—he was saying that he had known these and more, including the uncle I look like. Gideon was that boy there from Springfield, Missouri, and that one there from Pittsburgh, and that one way over there from Los Angeles; he was the staff sergeant hiding in the thicket, the noncom collapsed at the Blue Moon Dance Hall in San Fernando, the captain weeping in Orani, the one sore or dehydrated or sleeping forever. And so, after I understood this, I had a glass of whiskey with Colonel Walters and my father, and tried to be very quiet. They discussed horror and time; they discussed suffering and where the mind goes during battle and what a creature man is. They used words like "delirium" and "ruthless" and "hunger" —a vocabulary that seemed more appropriate to certain melodramatic books—and then, when the Johnnie Walker was gone, my daddy asked me to see Mr. Walters to his car.

"Hope I've been some help," the man said. His hand was meaty, his grip firm like a gentleman's.

"Yes," Daddy told him. "Invaluable. Thank you very much."

Beside his Ford station wagon, our night black as the cape a witch wears, I asked Colonel Red Walters how my father had gotten in touch with him.

"At William Beaumont," he said, "in Fort Bliss." Twice a year Colonel Walters was driving down from Carlsbad for checkups by the Army doctors. "There was a note on a bulletin board," he told me. "From your dad. Said he wanted to talk to Bataan survivors who'd known his brother. The name rang a bell, so I came up."

As I watched Red Walters drive down our two-mile dirt road toward the highway, I thought about Dr. Hammond Ellis, our Episcopalian minister, and what he says about burdens—a word, as he uses it, that describes what we carry or put aside in time. We can be this or that, he preaches. Good or bad. Generous or stingy like Scrooge. Upright or craven. In any case, we have the option, gotten from our Creator (or from your own self, if that's what you believe), to change. We can be a drinker one day, a teetotaler the next. We can go from dumb to wise, wrathful to peaceful; we can believe or not, trust or not, succeed or not. But always we have that choice. So, standing beside my old empty and dark house, I wondered about my father. He could be crazy now, I thought, or not. Sad, or not.

"Lyman Baker, Junior," I said to myself, "you go in there right now."

I must have sat across from him, in my customary chair, for an hour, watching him—betrayed by the lights in his eyes, and by the way he stubbed out his smokes or tugged at his earlobe—take up his life, piece by piece, his examination of himself as patient and thorough as those given to the livestock that have made him rich. I saw him, I tell you, lift up the burdens Dr. Ellis preaches about, take their measure again, and then, one by one, lay them aside. It was slow, I saw, but it was not painful; and in time he had put aside his boxer's temper and his banker's concern for numbers. He was a man with a plan now, I thought. A before B. Work and play. Then he got up, stretched, rubbed his hands, and a dozen free breaths came back to me.

"I think I'll cut down on the booze," he said. "That would be a good thing, wouldn't it?"

I thought it was and told him so.

"Maybe I'll visit your mother," he said. "It's been a long time."

That was true, too.

"I'm hungry," he said. "Let's go into town, get us a steak."

He was moving now, putting on the leather jacket Deborah had given him for his sixtieth birthday, so I asked him, "What about this?"

I pointed to the books, the charts, the records, the maps—the millions of words and thousands of pictures he knew by heart. I wanted him to sweep them away, I suppose, set the whole mess aflame.

"What about it?" he said. "Just leave it."

I had my hand on a folder, one of thousands that were covered with his notes, and a thought, swift as love, came to me. So this is the end of grief, I thought. Of all his burdens, grief had gone first.

"We'll burn it tomorrow, okay?"

"Sure," he said. "Turn out the light, will you?"

1986

ERNEST HEMINGWAY

A Day's Wait

He came into the room to shut the windows while we were still in bed and I saw he looked ill. He was shivering, his face was white, and he walked slowly as though it ached to move.

"What's the matter, Schatz?"

"I've got a headache."

"You better go back to bed."

"No. I'm all right."

"You go to bed. I'll see you when I'm dressed."

But when I came downstairs he was dressed, sitting by the fire, looking a very sick and miserable boy of nine years. When I put my hand on his forehead I knew he had a fever.

"You go up to bed," I said, "you're sick."

"I'm all right," he said.

When the doctor came he took the boy's temperature.

"What is it?" I asked him.

"One hundred and two."

Downstairs, the doctor left three different medicines in different colored capsules with instructions for giving them. One was to bring down the fever, another a purgative, the third to overcome an acid condition. The germs of influenza can only exist in an acid condition, he explained. He seemed to know all about influenza and said there was nothing to worry about if the fever did not go above one hundred and four degrees. This was a light epidemic of flu and there was no danger if you avoided pneumonia.

World traveler and Nobel Prize–winning author Ernest Hemingway was born in the quiet Chicago suburb of Oak Park in 1899. Hemingway eschewed the conventions of his birthplace, however, and after his graduation from high school took an assignment as a reporter at the Kansas City *Star*, a position that helped to shape his characteristically terse style. He was wounded in World War I while serving as an ambulance driver, an event that found its way into a number of his works, from *The Sun Also Rises* (1926) to *A Farewell to Arms* (1929). Perennially fascinated by the atmosphere of wartime, he served as a correspondent in both the Spanish Civil War and World War II. Often living in Cuba, Hemingway cultivated his celebrity as writer, soldier, and big game hunter until he took his own life in 1961.

Back in the room I wrote the boy's temperature down and made a note of the time to give the various capsules.

"Do you want me to read to you?"

"All right. If you want to," said the boy. His face was very white and there were dark areas under his eyes. He lay still in the bed and seemed very detached from what was going on.

I read aloud from Howard Pyle's *Book of Pirates;* but I could see he was not following what I was reading.

"How do you feel, Schatz?" I asked him.

"Just the same, so far," he said.

I sat at the foot of the bed and read to myself while I waited for it to be time to give another capsule. It would have been natural for him to go to sleep, but when I looked up he was looking at the foot of the bed, looking very strangely.

"Why don't you try to go to sleep? I'll wake you up for the medicine."

"I'd rather stay awake."

After a while he said to me, "You don't have to stay in here with me, Papa, if it bothers you."

"It doesn't bother me."

"No, I mean you don't have to stay if it's going to bother you."

I thought perhaps he was a little lightheaded and after giving him the prescribed capsules at eleven o'clock I went out for a while.

It was a bright, cold day, the ground covered with a sleet that had frozen so that it seemed as if all the bare trees, the bushes, the cut brush, and all the grass and the bare ground had been varnished with ice. I took the young Irish setter for a little walk up the road and along a frozen creek, but it was difficult to stand or walk on the glassy surface and the red dog slipped and slithered and I fell twice, hard, once dropping my gun and having it slide away over the ice.

We flushed a covey of quail under a high clay bank with overhanging brush and I killed two as they went out of sight over the top of the bank. Some of the covey lit in trees, but most of them scattered into brush piles and it was necessary to jump on the ice-coated mounds of brush several times before they would flush. Coming out while you were poised unsteadily on the icy, springy brush they made difficult shooting and I killed two, missed five, and started back pleased to have found a covey close to the house and happy there were so many left to find on another day.

At the house they said the boy had refused to let any one come into the room.

"You can't come in," he said. "You mustn't get what I have."

I went up to him and found him in exactly the position I had left him, white-faced, but with the tops of his cheeks flushed by the fever, staring still, as he had stared, at the foot of the bed.

I took his temperature.

"What is it?"

"Something like a hundred," I said. It was one hundred and two and four tenths.

"It was a hundred and two," he said.

"Who said so?"

"The doctor."

"Your temperature is all right," I said. "It's nothing to worry about."

"I don't worry," he said, "but I can't keep from thinking."

"Don't think," I said. "Just take it easy."

"I'm taking it easy," he said and looked straight ahead. He was evidently holding tight onto himself about something.

"Take this with water."

"Do you think it will do any good?"

"Of course it will."

I sat down and opened the *Pirate* book and commenced to read, but I could see he was not following, so I stopped.

"About what time do you think I'm going to die?" he asked.

"What?"

"About how long will it be before I die?"

"You aren't going to die. What's the matter with you?"

"Oh, yes, I am. I heard him say a hundred and two."

"People don't die with a fever of one hundred and two. That's a silly way to talk."

"I know they do. At school in France the boys told me you can't live with forty-four degrees. I've got a hundred and two."

He had been waiting to die all day, ever since nine o'clock in the morning.

"You poor Schatz," I said. "Poor old Schatz. It's like miles and kilometers. You aren't going to die. That's a different thermometer. On that thermometer thirty-seven is normal. On this kind it's ninety-eight."

"Are you sure?"

"Absolutely," I said. "It's like miles and kilometers. You know, like how many kilometers we make when we do seventy miles in the car?"

"Oh," he said.

But his gaze at the foot of the bed relaxed slowly. The hold over himself relaxed too, finally, and the next day it was very slack and he cried very easily at little things that were of no importance.

1938

ELLEN WILBUR

Wind and Birds and Human Voices

I

Henry Baron has been at the hospital for more than thirty years, like me. But I never set eyes on him till last New Year's Eve when they brought him onto this ward. I pitied him at first. His face is bandaged up. He hasn't much of a face. One bullet got him in the larynx, too. He hasn't spoken since the war. He can't walk either. His legs are no good. He is able to wheel himself in his chair, but often I push him on our daily walks when we go long distances or up hills. He's very frail, a small man like me, but terribly thin. They ought to give him therapy, some exercises to build him up, his strength. But they don't. Till he met me he stayed in bed most of the day. They bathed him and they fed him. They changed his bandages. Beyond that they ignored him. Of course they've given up on all of us "chronics" on this psychiatric ward.

I noticed that Henry (or "the Baron," as I sometimes call him) had no mail or any visitors. He appeared to be completely abandoned. For this also I pitied him. My mother, my brother Bill and sister Kathleen came to see me when they could. My father was never able to visit me. It was too painful for him. But while he was alive I saw him off and on when I felt up to going home for certain holidays.

I was drawn to Henry from the start. I'd pass his room and see him lying there alone and still hour after hour. More often than not he was weeping silently, the tears streaming down across the bandaged face, with no one there to comfort him. The sight of him was disturbing. You don't see tears on our ward. You may see rage or violence, but you don't

Born in 1943 in Montclair, New Jersey, Ellen Wilbur grew up in Massachusetts, New Mexico, Italy, Texas, and Connecticut before settling ten years ago in Cambridge, Massachusetts. She attended Bennington College for two years and Wesleyan University for one year before she quit without a degree, something "that no one would do now," she says. She counts Thomas Mann, Flannery O'Connor, and Katherine Anne Porter among those who influenced her writing. George Garrett, reading one of her first stories written when she was in high school, insisted she send it to the *Transatlantic Review;* the magazine published it. "Writing is discovery," Wilbur says. "Each time I write a story I feel that I unwittingly pose a question; the hard part is finding an answer that I didn't know before I started." Her collection *Wind and Birds and Human Voices* is populated by people who have known loss or tragedy and who have found a way not only to survive, but to prevail.

see tears. The men passed that point years ago. But the Baron's grief seemed sharp and fresh, as if he'd had some recent loss or shock. Sometimes he appeared to weep for days, and the sight of his loneliness and suffering was so forlorn, it made me sick at heart. The nurses hardly seemed to notice him. They drank their coffee, laughed, and gossiped at their station. You could see they didn't give a damn.

I began to visit him. I'd sit in the chair beside his bed and I'd talk to him. He wouldn't make a sound, but I'd know that he was listening. How I knew this, I can't say. He lay completely still and didn't give a single sign, but I knew he heard me. I began to visit him every day, and when I was with him, I noticed that his tears stopped. After about a week he began to squeeze my hand or nod his head to show he understood. This excited me a great deal. In fact I felt triumphant. The more he responded the more I felt compelled to stay with him. Sometimes I'd spend the entire day beside his bed talking. I told him everything about myself. Often I wondered how there could be so much to tell of such an empty repetitious life. But always there was more to add. At first it hardly seemed to matter what I said. Henry listened to it all, his head tipped back so I could see the shapeless hollow of his profile where his cheek was blown away. He drank in every word as if he had a thirst and all my hours of rambling talk were a shower that rained down on him and revived him. A few times I gave the Baron pencil and paper to see how he would answer certain questions. He had great trouble writing. One day it took him five minutes to print the word "yes." I could hardly read his handwriting, it was so bad. But I knew he understood me, every word I said, even if he couldn't put his own thoughts into words. I could tell by the way he shook with laughter at the jokes I told him. (I told him every joke I knew one day.) Or the way he'd sigh or smile, depending on the story, always in tune with what I said.

Our ward is an open ward, which means that the patients are free to leave the building so long as they fill out the sign-out sheet with the time, the destination, and the hour of return. I was the one who got Henry out of bed and took him out-of-doors. It was the first time he'd been outside in years. I could see that he was delighted. It wasn't long before he wanted to go out every day regardless of the weather.

The hospital grounds are enormous. They are gorgeously planted and meticulously gardened. Never have you seen such giant, spreading elms that look like great explosions in the air, or such luxurious lawns of grass so darkly green and thick. There are so many paths, long lanes planted with rows and rows of flowers, all of them perfect. You never see a dead one. "Think of the expense," I've said to Henry. "And who is it for?" Most of the patients never leave the buildings. When we take our daily walks, we rarely see a soul. I push the Baron ahead of me in his chair. His eyes are as good as mine. There is nothing wrong with his hearing or his sense of smell. He enjoys the view the same as I do.

A change came over me as I began to spend my time with Henry Baron. I no longer played cards with the day nurse, Mrs. Cooley. Nor did I shoot the breeze with the attendant, Arthur Little, who'd used to walk the corridors with me and smoke, discussing tennis tournaments and football scores nights when I couldn't sleep. I stopped talking to everyone but Henry. When I was asked a question, I didn't answer it. Mrs. Cooley kept after me at first, and Arthur made it difficult, too. "What's the matter, Paul?" they'd say. "Are you angry? Are you depressed?" But after a while they let me be.

It was a relief to talk to no one but the Baron. It was such a relief that I wrote a letter to my family and I asked them not to visit me for a while. I knew my brother Bill would be happy to receive this news. He'd just been made the president of his company. The more successful he's become, the harder it's been for him to visit me. In his three-piece suit and his white Buick he arrives, his hair still thick and tousled, but now grey, his face a mask of shame when I ask about his work, his pretty wife Melina, who sends me cards for every holiday, and their three children, one of whom is named for me. Bill thinks I must be envious of him. My mother, frail and in her seventies, would be spared the hour of strain in the hospital, a nightmare world through which she's always walked with carefully averted eyes. Behind her cheerful, powdered face I've always felt the misery of her love escape and float across to me as strong as her perfume. My sister, Kathleen, who lives nearby, two towns away, is a social worker, recently divorced from her husband Michael after twenty years. They were never able to have children, which is the disappointment of Kathleen's life. She's overworked and haggard looking now. Her face is colorless and deeply lined. No matter how fond she's always been of me, I knew she too would feel released when I told her I wasn't up to having visitors.

I hadn't known him long before I sensed that Henry and I were kindred creatures with a surprising amount in common. Not just two mental patients bound by our afflictions. I believed that he had been and continued to be a man of sophistication and intelligence. It is intriguing how much you can learn about a man without his ever uttering a word. I sat beside his bed. The sun shone on the white spread, the stiff sheets, and on his hands which lay at his sides with the palms turned up as if to catch the light. The Baron's hands always surprised me. They seemed so large for a man his size. The fingers were long and tapering, delicate and white, the hands of a philosopher or an artist. While I spoke, he listened, staring at the ceiling. Sometimes when he turned to look at me there was such sympathy in his eyes, I felt I could see the whole expression of his face beneath the bandages. Our friendship had changed him too. He no longer wept. Some nights, sensing he was awake, I slipped down the hall to check on him. Often I found him gazing out the window at the moonlit sky. But he seemed completely calm and I felt as proud as if his mood were my accomplishment. In fact I saw a vast improvement in him, a rising of his spirits, and an exuberance that seemed to build, as if he were coming more to life each day. He looked forward to our walks with an eagerness that touched me. Out of doors on a particularly pretty afternoon or evening when the air was pulsing with bird cries or drifting with the fragrance of pine or flowers or fresh mown grass, he would sometimes stop the chair, throw up his hands and hold them up or out in front of him as if he couldn't contain his enthusiasm and would have liked to embrace the whole view for all the beauty he saw in it. Whenever he did this, I felt a peculiar stab of pain, as if the memory of joy, of fearless and ecstatic praise were more than I could bear; I, who always expected the worst.

I saw that Henry was a passionate man. He reminded me of myself, the person I'd used to be so long ago that I could hardly call it myself any longer. I was certain that his rapture would not last, that the novelty of my company and the out-of-doors would wear out. Then, having tasted happiness, I was sure he would like all men be hungry for more. But how much could the Baron hope for? What kind of a life? I expected that eventually, any day now, he would fall into a cavernous depression. I told myself I'd regret that I'd ever spoken with him. But I continued to see him every day.

In the spring we started to play chess. In the morning we'd have a game, usually in Henry's room. He never liked to sit in the dayroom. The sight of the other patients pacing or babbling to themselves or staring off in space depressed him. I was surprised he hadn't gotten used to it. Also the television which is always on. The sound of it got on his nerves. And the bad air. Even in summer with the windows open there is a strong smell, a sour human smell. Not to mention all of the cigarette smoke. Being a smoker myself, it never bothered me. But Henry was always happiest when we were by ourselves and out-of-doors. As the weather grew warmer, we took our game outside. There was a picnic table under a large maple tree at the back of our building. The Baron sat in his chair. I sat on the bench across from him, and no one ever bothered us. If I'd had any doubts about the Baron's mind or whether his reasoning ability had been impaired, they were put to rest when I saw him play chess. He was a slow but ingenious player, with enormous concentration. There wasn't a move he made that wasn't deeply calculated, and in the end he always trounced me.

Often I'd stop in the middle of a game and go up to the building to fetch two Cokes from the machine. The smallest things delighted Henry. He gave me the feeling that playing chess and drinking Coke and sitting across from me under the open sky were all that he wanted in the world. When he leaned across the table, shook my arm, and smiled with all-out pleasure, it was as if he had no memory of suffering or injury, as if he had no past at all. It was strange how much his happiness, even the smallest evidence of it, affected me with pride, anxiety and even fear, and the more inseparable we became, the more I seemed to feel the power of his personality as if it were the atmosphere I breathed.

One afternoon, after Henry had played a brilliant game, we stayed at the table. The day was warm and the air so fresh it rose and danced for miles above, as if the winter sky had been a heavy roof that now was lifted. There was a soaring, endless feeling to the air. His head resting on one hand, Henry gazed at the view. His eyes appeared to be completely serene. I found myself staring at him, wondering what his problem was and why they'd put him on the psychiatric ward. There's little mystery about our chronics. Most of them have been here years. You know their fears and their obsessions as well as you'd know a normal man's opinions. I stared at Henry. His physical disability, his deformity, was obvious, but other than his initial fits of weeping, I'd seen no signs of his psychosis. Not once in the five months he'd been on the ward. Of course, I, too, had been unusually well the whole time I had known him. I wondered if, like me, his illness had a cycle. Like me and Ben Dimento who fought in Viet Nam. My cycle used to be as regular as Ben's. Six months of perfect health, six months of hell. Like clockwork. The doctors used to study me. I've read about myself in psychiatric journals. I wondered if the Baron was like me, if even now behind that calm facade he felt the signs, the subtle stirrings of his illness, as if it were a hibernating giant, half-roused by sounds and smells of spring. There wasn't a summer since the war when I hadn't been completely mad.

I studied Henry closely, whose upturned face still looked so satisfied. I thought of the way he relied on me more and more. He waited for me anxiously every morning. When I appeared, he took my arm with pleasure and relief. His growing dependence was flattering, but it worried me, sometimes to the point where my hands trembled when I thought of it. When Henry noticed the trembling, he sometimes took my hands in his and held them until the shaking stopped. He took my hands so naturally and with such ease, there was no embarrassment in it. I felt that I must warn him and prepare him for the worst, but I couldn't bring myself to do it yet.

II

When I think of my past, the early happy years are another life, a story that came to an end as final and complete as death. The child I was is a stranger about whom I know everything, a boy named Paul who showed an interest in the piano. When he'd come in from school, this little Paul would go straight to the living room, which in the afternoon was orderly and hushed. The sun poured silently through gleaming windows down on the spotless, yellow carpet, and the air was faintly scented with his father's pipe tobacco. He'd pass the flowered couch, the tables rubbed with lemon oil to shining, and slide across the slippery bench before the looming upright Steinway whose heavy ivory keys lay waiting, faintly yellowed to a color which seemed sanctified with mystery and beauty. Often he'd start to play with his hat and coat still on and stay there till his mother ordered him outside for an hour of fresh air. When he was six, he started lessons, and from that moment was so enchanted and possessed that had he been allowed he would have done nothing else but play. In the evenings after dinner he'd go back to practice. His father, if he were at home, would puff his pipe and read in his high-backed chair across the room. "That's *wonderful*, Paul," he'd sometimes say with real surprise. He had no musical ability himself and was slightly awed by the reports of the piano teacher, Adele Archer, who said she'd never had a pupil with such promise. His mother, too, was pleased, but not surprised. She seemed to expect her children would do wonders and was only amazed when they were rude or bad.

He learned to play his little Bach and Mozart pieces easily, played them over till the lurching notes smoothed together and rang out proudly from his hands. By the time he was eight he began to give recitals with several of Miss Archer's other pupils. He sat before a crowd without the slightest nervousness or fear, and while he played a silence louder than applause would build within the room inspired by the confidence and the natural bravado with which the child performed.

Throughout those early years Miss Archer's long horse face appeared to be continually wreathed with admiration. At their weekly lessons she listened to him play, her hands clasped tight against her chest, as if a miracle were happening in her living room. "It is *astonishing* the way he picks up everything so quickly," she told his parents in a voice that nearly trembled, her face becoming radiant when she looked down at her kindled student whose future rose before her like the sun. "I've been waiting for a child like Paul for thirty years," she said.

Something about Adele Archer's flushed cheeks, the long strands of her hair which came unpinned in her excitement and hung disheveled by her face, disturbed the father. The careless look of her clothes, the way her skirts hung on her bony frame, and the surprising feeling in her naked eyes, gave her a starved, unhealthy look. "I worry about that woman," he'd sometimes say to the mother in a burst of impatience. "I think she's pushing the boy too hard."

But it wasn't Miss Archer who drove Paul to practice longer and longer hours. It was the music, the subtlety and the difficulty of it which steadily increased, as if he'd been continually climbing, had passed the easy foothills and now found himself upon a startling slope which rose up with a steepness that required all of his skill. By the time he was twelve he began to dream of mountains, soaring alps which stretched before him in a chain of glory all the way to the horizon, each mountain higher than the last. The farthest peaks towards which he struggled were lost in clouds of unimaginable beauty.

One night, after a recital, Dr. Winslow, a friend of his father's, came up to congratulate him. "Tell me, Paul. What would you do if you couldn't play the piano anymore?" he said with a teasing smile. The question hung in the air while the child's face twisted with confusion. "I would die," he said at last, and he saw his own dismay reflected in the doctor's face.

Paul liked it best to practice in the summer, sunny days when his mother opened all the windows and the out-of-doors hummed like a great machine. From where he sat he had a view of his mother's terraced garden. Often she worked with her flowers or his father would appear at the door of the tool shed, the sun flashing in his glasses, and a world of sounds and smells rode through the room. He played to the noise of voices, footsteps, birds, and the steady whine of insects, as if the sounds of summer were his orchestra. And when he played his best, he disappeared into the music, drifted on the notes right out the window of the lonely room into the brilliant summer yard, rose above the buildings, moved in the heavy laden trees, or wafted out across the grass with an intensity that made his mother put her trowel down and turn to stare at the dark empty window.

After summer came dim afternoons when rain pelted the windows and the wind blew hard and wild outside while the room remained untouched. And winter days when the sky was a heavy, shifting veil of grey and the snow descended hour after hour, steadily and slowly, until the piano sounded loud and harsh in the vast accumulating silence. There were evenings when his concentration built like such an all-surrounding wall, it was a great relief to turn away from the piano, to find his mother knitting on the couch behind him, to see the colors of her sweater, pink or mauve or emerald green, and all the colors of the room leap forward with surprising brightness like a welcome. He'd rise with a sudden feeling of exhaustion, go to sit by his mother's feet, rest his head against her knee, and gaze into the cheerful, blazing fireplace like a traveler returning from a distance. He'd stare at the steadfast lamps and chairs and tables, feel the warmth of the fire and of his mother's love which flowed through the hand she placed on his shoulder, and he'd stay there till the sense of lostness, separateness had passed.

Already he'd felt the power of his mind, the way it could bewitch and hold him captive, lost to the world while his hands ran up and down the keys, enchanted little hands that moved so freely, of their own volition. And the more he disappeared into the music, the more important grew the moment when he'd turn away from the piano to face the solid beauty of the room. He came to count upon the impact of the room as if it were a healing blow that broke a spell releasing him from his mind back to the world. Years later, when he'd come home for a weekend visit, when he'd wander through the house as if he needed to inspect the rooms, he would avoid the living room. Home from the hospital for a long weekend, he'd climb the staircase to the second floor, follow the trail of rugs along the hall and stop at each open bedroom door. He'd tour the grounds, pause by his mother's garden, pass through the long dark dining room into the commotion of the kitchen or sit long hours on the veranda or the porch. But he never would go near the living room. The family was sure it must be the piano he avoided, that the sight of it was devastating to him. But they were wrong. It wasn't the piano, but the living room itself he couldn't bear to see, because it, too, had lost all impact, any power to bring him back, and now appeared, like all the world, to be a dream.

III

I have no memories of the war. Perhaps the heavy drugs I've taken have destroyed them. Whole years are gone as if they had been bombed into oblivion. I'm told that I saw action only for six months and that my company was at Anzio when I was declared mentally incompetent and unfit and shipped home to a psychiatric hospital. I remember little of the two years that I spent at Glenside Hospital. Only that I was disoriented and that my doctor discouraged me from playing the piano because it caused me too much stress. I was told that my prognosis was good and that with patience, time, and rest I would recover. I never believed this. In fact my weekend visits home convinced me I was growing steadily worse. I was twenty and I saw the world with the detachment and nostalgia of a dying man. All the most normal events and common sights developed poignancy and power. A table set for five became poetic. An easy chair, a rug, a pair of shoes, the faithful stars, the rising sun all developed extra meaning and importance. The world became a place of shining warmth within which normal people lived entirely immersed. I'd see them walking down the street at home with every shape or shade of color, temperature or change of weather, basking in familiar sounds and smells, unsurprised by anything. I'd see the way these people blindly ate their meals, conversed and sipped their drinks or calmly slept with an acceptance that made all human weaknesses and failings appear harmless and endearing for the innocence implied by such enormous faith, a faith which made a man belong entirely to the world the way a thoughtless tree belongs. While I, as I became more ill, became more outcast, saw all life with a clarity and distance which shattered innocence, with the loneliness of a voyeur who feels the shame of his detachment as if it were the greatest sin of all. Sometimes I was so overcome with consciousness that I could not remember how to hold a fork or walk across a room with any ease or grace.

Each summer there is a day when a trumpet blast cuts through the air. Then, if I strain my ears, I can hear the faintest sound of beating drums, the distant tramp of soldier's feet, and the rattle of their sabers. I can hear an army marching far away but on its way to me. It is a sound which used to chill my blood. In the early years I'd pace the floor for weeks while the steady tramp of feet grew louder. I'd moan, I'd cry, I'd pull my hair and beat my head against the floor until they'd have to put restraints on me. "Save me," I'd beg the orderlies and nurses. They'd look at me with pity and they'd drug me heavily, but nothing stopped the steady pounding feet which grew continually louder. Sometimes I passed out from the strain or fell into a swoon of fear on the hard floor. I'd see the hospital for days bathed in a brilliant shade of pink, then darkening to an ever deeper red until the nurses and the other patients all began to fade slowly and horribly. At last they disappeared in darkness.

Each year this sequence of events repeats itself with a hundred variations. Once the hospital has faded out I remain in a darkness more profound and deep than any in the living world. The stomp of feet is deafening by now and the rat-tat-tat of drums. I wait for the moment of total silence which comes just at the instant when I least expect it, that moment when the drums cease, when the feet come to a sudden halt, and when there is a rolling, awesome quiet more powerful than any sound. How long this pregnant silence lasts, this final moment of transition, I can't say. I wait in that hopeless blackness which is timeless.

Some years, at the boom of a single cannon, a scene completely formed bursts in a bloom of color all around me. I'm sure I'll never know the meaning of this stark, familiar scene, this panoramic grand display of symbols crucial to my soul. I stand at the edge of a skeletonic forest which has been entirely destroyed by fire. Before me lies a scorched field two miles wide which rises to a distant pointed ridge. All across this lifeless field the grass is blackened to the ground. No birds appear here, no brave surviving squirrel roots in the broken stubble of the forest. Not even the lowest insect lives or moves in this still land-scape. I search the view, hoping to find some hole in it, some weakness of imagination which will make it less believable. But everything I see is starkly real and rendered perfectly down to the last detail of distance and perspective. The more I look, the more the overwhelming authen-ticity of the scene wraps and seals itself around me in such a way that there is no escape.

Some years I see the army marching toward me over that conquered field with all the glamour of a history painting come to life in the smoky, hazy light. I see how antiquated their weapons are, all their swords, their cannons and equipment, as if this army had defeated time itself. The faces of the men are hard and white, their uniforms a brilliant red with yellow tassels at the shoulders, fringe along the sleeves. The boots they wear are shiny, black and high.

Sometimes I see the General himself who leads them on a skittish, prancing horse, his thick straight hair tossed back from his enormous, chisled face, his eyes steely and harsh above a twisted, cruel mouth. He rarely speaks to me as he approaches. He doesn't need to speak. He leads his men into my consciousness each summer. He plants the flag of his possession deep and makes my mind his camping place.

Some years I never see the men at all, but I know exactly how they look. The taste of them is like the taste of metal in my mouth. And it is suffering, pain enough to feel the bruising touch of all their striding, heedless feet. A mind is sacred ground. You cannot know this till the moment of a great invasion. You cannot know the awful pressure or the frightful strain as the men file in, toss all their weapons down and the heavy weight of their equipment. Yet still they keep arriving, pressing in until there isn't any inch of empty space left in me, and the tidal sound of them, the roaring chaos and the grand confusion of them rises to a pitch that shatters my last desperate concentration. Then I am nothing. I am theirs.

When I was first at Washington V.A., I used to fight each onset of my illness. At the sound of the trumpet blast in June, I picked up chairs and heaved them all the way across the dayroom. I broke windows. I put my fist through the television screen. The more I fought the more enormous my strength grew. One year I took on the whole cafeteria. I threw plates and trays. I flipped the trestle tables over and I flung them in the air light as balloons. I picked up cups and smashed them one by one against the ceilings, floors, and walls. No one could stop me. It took six orderlies to bring me down. They had to lock me in a padded cell from June to Christmas. I was a holy terror in those days. But the army was equally impressive. The men were young and fresh, invincible and fierce. They had no wounds or scars or any sign of weakness. Their uniforms were new and spotless, made of such a brilliant red it hurt the eyes to look at them.

They spoke to me. For half the year I heard their voices, loud and scornful, cold and haughty, or soft and silky and insinuating. Sometimes they spoke to me in choruses, in waves, and sometimes singly, individually using whatever tone was most effective at the time. I lay on a mat on the floor of my padded cell. The walls were white. One naked bulb hung down protected by a wire cage eight feet above. Their voices, dark and predatory, circled me, and in those days there was no end to the havoc they could cause.

Two weeks before my father died, he tried to visit me. Maybe he had a premonition of his heart attack. My mother drove up to the hospital with him. They came one afternoon just after lunch. The doctors wouldn't let them see me. I was far too ill for visitors, they were told. Of course nobody let me know that my parents had arrived. I was sitting in a chair on the ward, staring off in space, when something made me rise and walk across the room to the right window. I looked down at the parking lot and was surprised to see my father and mother walking to their car. It was warm. The window was barred, but it was open. I was going to call down to them. I was just about to when I saw my father stop. His face was in his hands. He was bent over, and my mother put her arm around his waist. She seemed to be supporting him. They looked so small, I felt I could have picked them up and held them in my hand. The cloudless sky was blue and vast above them and for just that moment I could truly see what I had done to them. Many times I have imagined and replayed this scene. My parents are in the parking lot with all the joy, the life gone out of them and I am at the high-barred window unable to call down to them. Did it ever really happen? I am never sure.

Some rare, cool-headed nights when I was in my twenties, I used to lie in the purest, soothing darkness of my room at 3 A.M. and glory in the silence of the hospital which seemed to match the quiet of my mind when sanity and privacy had been restored to it. In such a mood of gratitude I'd sometimes have to climb out of my bed, to walk about my room and feel the floor unshakeable and steady under my bare feet. I'd have to touch the metal bed post, to run my hand over the smooth-painted wall, to touch the light switch and to think that if I turned it on I'd see exactly what I would expect to see and nothing more. Sometimes the pleasure and the gratitude were so intense, I'd have to leave my room and step into the lighted hall where the shiny, checked linoleum was all that I saw or wanted to see and where the smudged green walls, the high grey ceilings and the iridescent lights above all waited unobtrusively and humbly, not caring whether I noticed them or not. By four A.M. over the whole ward the silence had a texture thick as soil. On nights like this I'd sometimes ask myself the meaning of my madness the way a normal man might hope to understand the stars or wonder at a stretch of strange, unseasonable weather, as if there had to be some explanation for it. I'd study my own illness with the coldness of a scientist who prides himself on his detachment. I'd ask myself the meaning of the General and the significance of the antiquated army. Why did they come specifically in June, and what was the reason for the six month cycle? Those brave, light-headed nights I'd feel quite sure that if I solved these riddles, my dread army would disintegrate and disappear forever. I'd be cured. But I never found a single answer to my questions. One thing only was clear; that the army's purpose was the purpose of all armies; to demoralize and to defeat the enemy, which was me.

My mother came to see me every year just after Christmas. "How are you, dear?" she'd ask, touching my cheek. "I'm fine," I'd tell her lightly, and I would produce the wide and carefree and preposterous smile I carefully prepared for every meeting with her, which by some miracle of love or mutual collusion was always effective. I saw my mother's face relax. Then we would limp through conversation. There was little to say. In the early years she brought me music scores and books; "The Principles of Composition," and heavy, hard-bound lives of Rimsky-Korsakoff and Charles Ives. I never had the heart to tell her that I could no longer read. I'd lost the concentration for it. "Have you been practicing at all?" she'd ask me hopefully. There was a "music room" in building 9. My first few years at Washington I sometimes practiced on the spinet in that room, though it was always out of tune. But there was never any pleasure in it. Since the war, by some odd twist of heightened nerves and over-sharp perceptions my ear had grown so piercingly acute that I could read a score and hear precisely how a piece should be interpreted down to the finest subtleties of tempo and dynamics. There was a simple Bartok piece I played for weeks hundreds of times a day and never once came close to the perfection of my ear. I went into such fits of fury and frustration banging on the keys that finally I was forbidden from further playing. Dr. Sewell must have spoken to my mother. After that she didn't bring me music anymore. Nor books either. She brought me cartons of the Marlboros I smoked one after another all day long, which were all that I wanted.

Each year, after the army had played out all of their tricks, there came a day in late December when they'd start to pack their gear. I'd watch them break camp in their slow, methodic way. This, too, was torture. It took them days and days. Each year the General came up to me as they were leaving. He came up close until his face was looming and immense. Then he turned his narrowed, knowing eyes hard on me. "You know the rules, Paul," was what he said. "You are to keep everything you've seen and heard here to yourself. One word, one slightest hint of it to anyone and there will be *hell* to pay." Then he mounted his great horse, he whirled away from me, and he was gone. I never wondered at his power, the sinking nausea and the instant terror that the sight of him always inspired. With lips sealed tight as if they had been welded by the General's command, I watched the men file slowly out behind him. It was always raining as they disappeared over the ridge, raining on them and on the muddy ground they'd left all littered and defiled.

I tested the General once, one night of a full moon when I was in my thirties. I started to tell Mrs. Davis, the night nurse, about my army of tormenters. It was a January night. I could see the swollen moon, enormous, cold, and white outside the window of my room. Mrs. Davis was leaning over me, wiping my face with a damp towel. I was lying on my bed. My arms were wrapped with gauze. I'd tried to cut my wrists.

"What is it, Paul?" she said. She could see that I wanted to speak. I took her arm and held it tightly. I planned to tell her everything. And yet when I tried to find words that would describe the army's tactics, and the meaning of those long kaleidoscopic months of nightmare images and darting scenes with which they'd held and punished and absorbed me, my mind appeared to melt into confusion.

"What is it, Paul?" said Mrs. Davis softly. "Can you tell me?" She leaned close over me, over my face which was pouring sweat.

"Try to tell me," she said gently. Her breasts just grazed my chest. A strong perfume came from her. I thought I heard the sound of drums begin, the steady roll and beat of them. I closed my eyes to concentrate and when I opened them I saw that Mrs. Davis was laughing. Her eyes were cruel slits and her white nurse's uniform was turning red. A cry escaped me, but it came out as a trumpet sound, long and high and shrill. I heard the General's voice beside my ear.

"I warned you, Paul," he said. I can remember Mrs. Davis's laughing face, her dress which seemed to float and shimmer red before my eyes, and how I watched her fade until she disappeared in a rising, swimming darkness. That was the last I saw of her for two years. The army kept me raving mad on the locked ward for two years as punishment for my attempted betrayal.

After I came back from that long siege, Bill was the first one in the family to visit me. When they brought me down to the visitor's room, he looked shocked. "You've lost so much weight, Paulie," he said. "You've got to eat more." I asked about Melina and the children and how his work was going. He looked uncomfortable the way he always did when he talked about himself in front of me. I wanted to say "For God's sake, Bill, I'm so far gone you couldn't pay me to be you."

There is a crossing point after long illness when a man begins to dread the possibility of ever being well again more than the prospect of remaining permanently ill. The hospital can recognize the signs; the glassy eyes, the aimless, shambling walk, the robot voice. The empty face without a human sign or message to convey makes a powerful impression, one that might be harmful to the other, healthier patients. This is what the hospital believes and why they've made a special building for the chronics to keep them hidden separate from the others.

When I was forty-two they put me with the chronics. By then it mattered little to me where I lived or slept. In the company of those milling, babbling men who drifted up and down the corridors with the vague directness of sleep-walkers, I sank into a numb obliviousness. Sometimes I was aware that weeks and months had disappeared without my noticing, as if once time had been detached from any purpose, it speeded up and rocketed like something that has been unleashed. Sometimes I watched the clock and felt the pulsing minutes flow unchecked out of my life as swiftly as the rush of blood escaping from a mortal wound.

In the dayroom we sat in chairs against the walls, a long curved row of bodies silent and entranced. The morning sun shone on the floor. It made a yellow square unnoticed and unseen by anyone. In the center of the room a man paced back and forth. All day from his small mouth there came a steady flood of gibberish which rose and fell and was monotonously soothing like the sound of bees.

They didn't have to lock me up in summer anymore. I found this out from Arthur Little. I asked him once whether I was ever violent anymore. "Hell, no, Paul. You're no trouble," he said. "When you're sick, you just sit in your chair all day. You don't talk to nobody and you don't do nothing. You're quiet as a lamb," he said. "Sometimes I walk you up and down the halls to exercise you. Come with me, Paul, is all I have to say. I lead you by the arm and you come right with me. You're no trouble to nobody, Paul," he said. "No trouble at all."

When I turned fifty, I noticed that the General was going grey, and I saw how much all of the men had aged along with me. The company grew slightly smaller every year, and the men appeared less strong and more obviously tired. There were more wounded and more who walked with canes, who limped, and some who had lost an arm or leg. The uniforms were soiled and patched. The boots were worn. Some had no boots and walked with painful feet bound up with cloth and tape. As they approached me over the ridge, their faces were more bored than hostile towards me. They rarely spoke to me or wanted my attention. They simply occupied me now. They dressed their wounds and they rested their weary bodies. For the most part they ignored me. One year I noticed that I'd almost lost my fear of them. I even spoke to the General once and I asked him a frivolous question. "You've kept me here all of these years. You've made me suffer any way you could. One thing has always puzzled me," I said. "Why did you let me smoke all of these years? Why did you allow me that one pleasure?"

"Because it was killing you," he replied.

I actually laughed when I heard that, which seemed to dismay the General. For a moment he looked quite shaken, and there was something grotesque about the uncertainty and the frailty I clearly saw in his softened, aging face. Then his expression changed. He smiled.

"I have to admire you, Paul," he said. "You've never betrayed us all of these years." The words were flattering and yet there was a razor tone of irony and scorn in them which made me suddenly look closely at the General's face. At his mouth, which was disdainful and amused. And in his narrowed eyes I saw the confidence and calculation of a player, who, far from finished, still holds a crushing trump card hidden in his hands.

My mother came to see me twice a year, just before the arrival of the army and shortly after their departure, the times I was expected to be well. I don't believe she ever knew how much I had deteriorated. Each time she came onto the ward, I was ready for her, smiling brightly. The nurses must have seen how much these visits cost me. They always warned me several days before my mother came. From whatever depths of illness I had gone to, I heard the nurses' far-off, faintly spoken message, and I would stir and strain to rouse myself from that dim, muffled place of ringing emptiness where I lay hidden and protected. Perhaps it was the place all chronics went to. Then, like a swimmer under heavy weights of water, I would rise to meet my mother on the surface, though the distance and the effort of that passage seemed more onerous each year. Also the pain. The pain of breaking through the surface into the roaring light of the dayroom where the din was overwhelming. I wondered how I ever had endured that brilliant light which bounded sharply off the walls like hurled knives aimed straight at me. And all the world's confusion and commotion. On all sides was shifting, dizzy motion. Such a blast of sharp, intruding smells. I gripped the arms of my hard chair as if I might be shaken free by all the forces in the room. I thought of Mother. I prepared myself to see her.

It was after one of Mother's visits that I first saw Henry Baron. I had walked Mother to the door and was on my way back to the dayroom full of a sense of fatigue so severe that I wondered if I could even make it to my chair. There was a farewell smile still plastered on my face as I passed Henry's room. I never paused. I continued on my way down the long corridor, and yet the image of the man I'd seen stayed right in front of me as if I'd stopped beside his door and still remained there staring at him.

IV

I arrived at Henry's room by eight o'clock each morning. He no longer liked to take his meals in bed. He enjoyed eating with me. I always found him wide awake and waiting eagerly for my arrival. His eyes lit up and shone with happiness when I appeared at his door. It is hard to describe the effect that this greeting had on me. I was not used to bringing joy to anybody. But then I was not used to any of the changes in my life since I'd known Henry. Often it seemed impossible that he was sitting across from me, that I'd just spoken to him. I kept expecting him to disappear. I was quite sure that some fine day I'd find his bed made up and empty. He'd be gone as suddenly as he'd come, and there would be no explanation for it. Perhaps the Baron had this same anxiety and that was why he greeted me with such enthusiasm every morning. He grasped my hand and held it tightly. Then I helped him into his chair and he wheeled himself down to the cafeteria where we had our breakfast. While we ate, we often planned what we would do that day. In the mornings we played chess or we sat together dozing in the sun. Hours would go by without a word or sign exchanged between us, yet there was a constant feeling of communion of a kind I'd never known with anyone before. It frightened me.

I could now sit comfortably in the morning sun. The light was soft. It wasn't painful to my eyes. I could look across the rolling lawn of shifting grass and swaying trees and passing cars without the slightest dizziness. Clouds inched across the sky, birds flew, and people walked among the buildings while I remained unmoved, perfectly still. The morning sounds of droning mowers, gardener's clippers, wind and birds and human voices seemed subdued and gentle to my ears.

I stopped playing cards with Mrs. Cooley. To sit with her seemed tiresome and pointless. In fact all talk with anyone but Henry was annoying. When I wrote my family not to visit me, I was surprised at how pleased I felt. More amazing was the tremendous improvement in my thinking the moment I stopped speaking with the staff. The very day I broke communications with them, my concentration sharpened to a point where I came very close to beating Henry at chess. My mind was suddenly so clear that I could see the fuzzy, muddying effect that my twice-daily dose of medications had on it. I began to hide the pills they gave me underneath my tongue and to dispose of them whatever way I could. In the days that followed, as I grew increasingly alert and energetic, it came as an unpleasant shock to think that all the drugs I'd swallowed since the war might have done more harm than good.

In the afternoons we took our walks. We headed down the path and the row of ominous brick buildings shrank behind us to the size of toys. I pushed the Baron in his chair when he grew tired. Often we went two miles to reach our favorite resting spot. At the top of a steeply winding path was a wide, sheer cliff with a spectacular view of checkered farms far down below. On a grassy knoll above the precipice someone had placed a wooden bench where one could rest and gaze out over the expanse of fields and buildings, woods and lakes, and mountains at the farthest distance. Henry always threw his arms up at the sight of this great liberating view, and I often thought that these wide gestures of his arms, the thousand signals of his delicate long hands and the sharp expressions in his eyes were far more powerfully explicit than words could ever be.

Not far from our cliff view was an old abandoned chapel, a grey stone building almost hidden in a crowd of juniper and pine. The heavy door was never locked and it was easy to push the Baron's chair over the low sill. More than once we went inside and sat in the silent oblong room of darkly varnished pews and stained glass windows. The air was cut with shafts of purple, red and green and had a musty, piney smell. A wooden cross hung from the wall above the empty marble altar. As we sat in the failing light of afternoon, there was a lonely echo to the bird cries outside of the building and a hollow feeling to the darkening surrounding woods which made me glad that the Baron was beside me.

By early May I felt so well, and I was convinced that all of it was my friend's doing, even the beauty of the Spring and my capacity to perceive it. The sky was a blue pastel day after perfect day. In the balmy warmth and the golden light everything was in bloom. The air that breezed across the grounds was heavily perfumed with lilacs and the banks and banks of lilies, hyacinths and nasturtium which the gardeners daily tended. Beside our building were blonde fountains of forsythia cascading with long sprays of yellow stars. For twenty years or more I'd never noticed spring at all. This year I was intoxicated.

One shadow fell through all of this exhilaration, which was the thought of my approaching army due to arrive in six short weeks or less. They'd always been on schedule. Why wouldn't they be now? And what would Henry think when I no longer showed up in the morning, and when I sat in the dayroom all day long like a vegetable in my chair, as Arthur Little had described it? I could imagine it so well, how Henry, having been so cruelly and inexplicably abandoned, would regress right back to the way he'd been when I first met him. Only this time maybe worse. And perhaps by Christmas when I came back to him, he'd have become unreachable himself. My hands shook when I thought of this. I knew that I must warn my friend and carefully prepare him for our separation, but each day I hesitated.

"I feel so well," I said to him instead, as if the saying of it made it so.

"I feel so amazingly well," I said repeatedly, and Henry nodded that he felt the same.

One morning Mrs. Cooley woke me early. She said she'd made an appointment for me to have a physical examination. Also a dental check. I hadn't been looking well, she thought, and I'd been holding my jaw as if a tooth were bothering me. She'd asked me repeatedly about the tooth as well as my health. Because I wouldn't answer any of her questions she'd felt it her duty to make the appointments for me.

"It won't take long, Paul," she insisted. "You'll feel much better when that tooth is fixed. It *has* been hurting, hasn't it?" she said.

I looked away from her, down at the floor. It was hard not speaking to Mrs. Cooley. I'd always been quite fond of her and thought she had a pleasant manner with the patients. When a man was well enough, she spoke to him as if he were an equal. It hurt me to be rude to her, but I didn't dare risk it yet. There was no denying the improvement in my head since I had limited all conversation to the Baron.

As I left the ward with Mrs. Cooley, I was tempted to tell Henry where I was going. But it was early, and when I passed his room he was sleeping so soundly that I couldn't bring myself to wake him. I would have liked to leave a message for him with one of the orderlies, but I didn't see how this could be accomplished without talk.

There was a line of patients waiting to see Dr. Barber. I had to wait more than an hour for the physical examination. Outside the window I noticed that the morning had gone dark. The lawn was a sharp, electric green, and black storm clouds were moving swiftly in over the sky with a look of spreading gloom. Mrs. Cooley brought me a cup of coffee and a muffin, but I didn't touch them. I thought of Henry lying in his bed waiting for me with a puzzled, lost expression in his eyes. I paced the floor and watched the clock with an increasing sense of worry and impatience.

It was ten o'clock before I was able to see the dentist. While I sat in his chair it began to thunder and lightning. A high wind splattered rain against the windows. I thought I'd never seen the rain come down so hard. The dentist did extract one of my teeth, but I felt no pain. I was thinking of Henry the whole time, knowing how worried he must be. I was half-sick thinking of it.

By the time I got back to the ward it was close to noon. The Baron's bed was empty and his chair was gone. I expected to find him in the dayroom, but he wasn't there. I checked all of the sleeping rooms along the hall, then went down to the cafeteria, stopped to look in the visitor's room and the recreation room. Two orderlies were playing ping pong, but no one else was there. I stepped outside. The rain had stopped and my heart jumped to see two deep wheel marks in the muddy ground by the front steps. It looked as if the Baron had shot his chair out the front door, cleared the steps, and landed violently on the rutted ground. I followed the wheel marks across the yard until they stopped at the driveway. The sky was beginning to clear and there was the sound of dripping by the buildings and the trees, and water rushing down the gutters by the road. The air was wonderfully fresh, as if it had been washed completely clean, and a strong wind blew with a surprising force. As I started down the hard top path we'd often taken, I was trying to imagine in what spirit Henry had set out on his own. Whether he was perturbed or calm, and whether he'd gone looking for me, which seemed likely. I walked at a fast pace, but the Baron had gotten a good start on me. It was a half hour before I saw him on the path about a quarter mile ahead of me, moving along in an unhurried way. I felt delighted as a child to see him. I called his name, but the wind was blowing in my face. It swallowed up my voice. The Baron couldn't hear me, but I could see where he was going. He was almost at the point where the path drops sharply into a long sloping hill. At the bottom of this hill was the turn off for the dirt path up to our cliff view. I walked faster and began to shout at him, but the Baron never slowed or turned in my direction. In fact to my dismay he picked up speed. There was a sudden urgency to the way he spun his wheels, and I saw the chair leap forward. As he started down the hill, he was racing. I was sure that he'd injure himself, and I began to run, still shouting to him. His head was bent so low that I could hardly see it, and he flew down the hill at a velocity that looked suicidal. I ran with all of my strength behind him and was relieved to see him make it safely to the bottom. "Henry, WAIT," I called to him, but he pressed ahead as hard as ever. He crossed the grass at a good clip and started up the high dirt path churning his wheels. The wind veered around and blew behind me then. It seemed to push my back with great harsh shoves. I doubled my speed and by the time the Baron had begun to falter halfway up the hill, I'd caught up with him, grabbed the chair, and pushed it with one long extended lunge up to the top and across the open patch of grass. My legs felt watery and strangely weak and I collapsed on the wooden bench with a feeling of exhaustion so acute, I thought I might be sick. The Baron was just as winded. We sat heaving and gasping, unable to speak. Our mountain view was buried in dense fog. It was impossible to see the valley. My lungs hurt me and I felt pain in my shoulders, gripping my neck and rising to my head where the blood was beating in my ears. The wind was even stronger on the cliff. It came at us in little blasts. The Baron's face was still bent forward. There was something dejected about the way his back remained curved over and his hands stayed holding the arms of his chair.

"Why did you run away from me?" I asked at last. Henry didn't look at me or move.

"I'm sorry about this morning," I said. "They sent me to the doctor and the dentist very early. You were asleep. I didn't want to wake you."

Henry raised his head. His eyes were red. The misery in them was so intense, it shocked me. He didn't look at me. He stared out over the foggy trough of nothingness below and I could see that under his sadness was a layer of coldness and unforgiving distance he had made between us.

"There are some things I have to tell you. I should have told you long ago," I said. But the Baron remained stony and his aloofness made my words sound strangely foolish. I could almost sense that he was growing more distant from me by the minute, as if he were running physically away from me again and I'd begun to chase him. A gust of wind blew in my face. It whipped my hair and tugged at the strip of loosened bandage by the Baron's ear. I felt light-headed and reckless. I thought I heard somebody whisper "Watch it, Paul. Just watch it." But the voice was pitiful and faint. The wind was stronger, lashing in my ears. It was blowing in my brain and all my thoughts were stirring, flying up and swirling in great arcs until my mind was spinning with them. I put my hands up to my face to stop the dizziness, the pressure and the knocking like great fists inside my head. I reached for the Baron's arm. I held onto it and I let my head fall down until it touched his sleeve. I began to speak to him. I was crying, and the voice I used was alien to me. It was a terrible voice, hoarse and low, which seemed to rise from some deep suffocating chasm and had to wrench and choke itself in order to escape. Yet once the voice had started, on and on it went like a machine switched on and driven separately from me. The words poured out with such a force, I felt I couldn't stop them if I tried. Words jumped out. Like things alive they leapt over each other in an effort for release. As they came, I heard the sound of drums begin, the noise of hurried marching feet, and a loud trumpet blast that sounded desperate, like a scream. Still my strange voice went on with the momentum of a river, and I told myself that if the army tried to overcome me, I would hurl myself over the cliff and wipe out the entire company in one grand explosion. Perhaps the General sensed the utter seriousness of my intention. The trumpet died away with a pathetic sigh, the drums and marching feet grew more remote and faint until I heard only the sound of my own stricken voice, this time more clearly. The grief was terrible in that weeping voice, so terrible that there was nothing I could do but listen with a sense of growing recognition. I listened and I saw a little white-washed farm house with two broken windows like two eyes, the door a gaping mouth wide open to the night. The house, set back from a dirt road, was vivid white under the moon which also bathed the wide surrounding fields and all the trees along the road in ghostly light. There was a soldier hurrying up the road with a carbine rifle tightly clutched against his chest. He was whimpering to himself and moaning, his darting eyes alarmed and wide with fear. The smells of the Italian countryside were an assault of sweetness to his nose, and the beauty of the night was something incomprehensible and appalling to the soldier, mad and AWOL, running from his men who even now were searching for him down the road. He stopped before the small abandoned house, the dismal face whose window eyes looked balefully at him while he stared back with every nerve alert, the moonlight pouring down, the rifle tightly pressed in two white hands that shook and trembled with a constant agitation. There was an unexpected noise within the house, a shuffling in the dark. The startled soldier sprang into a crouch, his rifle swung out from his chest, and when he saw a flash of white go by the door, he shot. He kept on shooting even when he heard a woman's scream and didn't stop until his gun was empty. The company commander, Captain Barker, was running up the road. And there were others, one who took away his gun, and one who ran up with a light and shone it on the dark-haired woman on the floor, thin and young, her white dress spattered with her blood, a child, a boy no more than nine, still clinging to her side, his body twitching, dying there before them. Captain Barker with a white ferocious face was saying "Christ, man, CHRIST look what you've done."

From a far distance I could feel the Baron's hand. It rested like protection on my head while my own ragged voice went on. It was the voice of an exhausted child, monotonous and flat, a voice that was familiar to me now.

V

Did I dream it that the rain began to pour while Henry and I were still up on the cliff? I could remember so well the feeling of icy rain soaking my back and how it fell like walls around us. I quickly pushed the Baron down the hill. The ground was slippery and muddy. The rain was blinding and I almost fell. Henry pointed to the chapel and we hurried into it for shelter. Once inside, the Baron wheeled himself right up the aisle. He pointed with excitement to the little organ by the altar, one that I'd never noticed before. He wanted to examine it more closely. I pushed him up the step and had to lift him to the organ bench. I was surprised to see how excited he was and pleased to see his old exuberance. When he pressed a G and heard the sound of it, he clapped his hands. He gestured to the little pew behind the organ, and I sat there. Then, to my amazement, he began to play. Not haltingly or poorly as you would expect of a man with a damaged brain who'd never indicated that he knew an instrument. He played that organ easily and brilliantly —while I sat there levitated and transfixed. It seemed to me that I had never heard Bach played so well or Messiaen or Dupré. He played piece after piece. I told myself perhaps the beauty of the music was so overwhelming because I hadn't heard real music since the war, only the canned sound they play over the speakers on the wards. I told myself that I had lost the critical ability to judge the quality of his playing. But the Baron had started a Bach toccata, one that I knew well, and I felt the power of that piece played to its fullest glory, so it was the genius of the music that came through the self-effacing ease and the excellence of Henry's playing. The rain had stopped and a ray of sun fell from the sacristy on Henry, shone on his greying head, flashed on his hands, and caught the dust that sparkled rising from the keys. He was playing flawlessly, and it was at that moment with a sense of creeping horror that I felt the hairs stand up on my neck. My eyes fell on the pumping feet and the helpless legs which leapt and danced over the pedals, and I had a sudden dead white feeling of pure fear that Henry Baron wasn't real.

I woke up in a strange room. The sun was shining in my eyes. There was an old man asleep in the bed next to me. He had two tubes in his nose and his arm was hooked up to an i.v. I was looking at him when my mother appeared beside my bed. Bill was standing behind her. She kissed my cheek and I smiled at her. "Don't try to speak, dear," she said, putting her hand over my mouth. "You've been very sick. The doctor wants you to rest and sleep as much as possible. Bill and I will be right here. Kathleen is coming too. You must try to sleep now."

I closed my eyes. I dreamed I was back on the ward in Henry's room. Two nurses were about to change his bandages. I was anxious to leave the room, but the Baron indicated urgently that he wanted me to stay. I stood at the end of his bed while the nurses removed the bandages strip by strip, starting at the forehead. Henry kept his eyes on me, and I was anxious not to show the slightest shock at anything revealed. His cheek bones were uncovered and I saw his nose. It was long and straight, without a sign of injury, an elegant, aristocratic nose. It was exactly the nose I would have expected the Baron to have. And yet when I saw the lower half of my friend's face, I gasped. Where was the sunken hollow of the cheek, the sheared-off chin, and the misshapen profile I'd so often seen? When the final swatch of bandage was removed, the face revealed was totally unmarred. I was reminded of Abe Lincoln when I saw the solemn dignity and the ugly beauty of the

Baron's face. I stared at him and shook my head uncomprehendingly. "But why the bandages?" I asked. The Baron only smiled. This amazing man. He smiled.

When I woke up, I was smiling too. The room was dark and the old man was snoring loudly in the bed beside me. I kept thinking of Henry. I was remembering the way he'd played the organ in the chapel. Surely I must have dreamed it and the Baron must be real, I told myself, but I was afraid. Why was Henry's face still bandaged more than thirty years after the war? It seemed preposterous that I had never questioned it before. And why was it that in all the five months I had known him I could not remember any orderly or nurse ever referring to him or once saying the name of Henry Baron? Perhaps the army had made the Baron up just so that they could take him away from me. I suffered with my thoughts and never slept the rest of that night. In the morning I was still awake when Mrs. Cooley walked into the room.

"I was on my way to work," she said cheerfully. "I'd have come to visit you sooner, but I've been on vacation." She came over to the bed. I watched her, holding my breath, hoping she might mention Henry. She looked at me, and her face became concerned. "Poor Paul. Have you been feeling awfully lonely?" She reached into her purse and dabbed my eyes and my face with a Kleenex. I strained to speak, but Mrs. Cooley gripped my shoulder. "Don't Paul. You mustn't talk," she said. She looked alarmed. "Haven't they told you?" she said. "You've had a stroke. You'll be fine, but you can't speak yet. Your speech has been affected." I listened, stunned, while she went on to tell me about the therapy they'd be starting. I felt strangely like laughing, the bitter laugh that comes after despair, when the mind is worn out with pain and turns away from it with irony and cold amusement, when the chain of human moods begins to roll again and life goes on and on and on.

The old man was gone from the bed beside me. I could hear my mother's voice out in the hall, talking to someone. The room was frightfully hot. A red-haired nurse came in and shut the window. "We're putting the air-conditioner on," she said. "You'll feel the difference soon." From where I lay the only view was one waving tree branch rising halfway up the window. The branch was heavy with dark leaves which were fully open and fully grown. I could see that it was a maple tree, and that it was well into summer. Time for my madness. Perhaps I was at this very moment mad, I thought. But then it came to me that there was no army, no sign of the army. The army was gone.

1984

JOYCE CAROL OATES

Theft

The semester Marya became acquainted with Imogene Skillman, a thief suddenly appeared in Maynard House, where Marya was rooming in her sophomore year at Port Oriskany: striking at odd, inspired, daring hours, sometimes in the early morning when a girl was out of her room and showering in the bathroom just down the corridor, sometimes late at night when some of the girls sat in the kitchen, drinking coffee, their voices kept low so that the resident adviser would not hear. (The kitchen was supposed to close officially at midnight. Maynard House itself "closed" at midnight—there were curfews in those days, in the women's residences.) A wristwatch stolen from one room, seven dollars from another, a physics textbook from yet another . . . the thief was clearly one of the residents, one of the twenty-six girls who roomed in the house, but no one knew who it was; no one wanted to speculate too freely. Naturally there were wild rumors, cruel rumors. Marya once heard the tail end of a conversation in which her own name—"Knauer" —was mentioned. She had brushed by, her expression neutral, stony. She wanted the girls to know she had heard—she scorned even confronting them.

One Saturday morning in November Marya returned to her room after having been gone less than five minutes—she'd run downstairs to check the mail, though she rarely received letters—to see, with a sickening pang, that the door was ajar.

Her wallet had been taken from her leather bag, which she'd left carelessly in sight, tossed on top of her bed.

Ever since the appearance of her first collection of short stories—By the North Gate (1963)— hardly a year has gone by without the publication of at least one book by Joyce Carol Oates. This prolific novelist, poet, and critic was born on Bloomsday (June 16) in 1938 in Lockport, New York. A graduate of Syracuse University and the University of Wisconsin and currently a professor at Princeton University, Oates combines the commonplace and the gothic, the naturalistic and the nightmarish. These intertwined tendencies figure in such novels as A Garden of Earthly Delights (1967) and them (1969, a National Book Award winner), both about American families trapped in cycles of poverty and violence. Consistent with Oates's almost unlimited range, more recent works turn both inward—the semiautobiographical You Must Remember This (1987), for example—and outward, as in her 1987 treatise, On Boxing, which examines the sport from a philosophical point of view.

Her lips shaped empty, angry prayers—Oh God please *no*—but of course it was too late. She felt faint, sickened. She had just cashed a check for forty-five dollars—a week's part-time wages from the university library—and she'd had time to spend only a few dollars; she needed the money badly. "No," she said aloud, baffled, chagrined. "God damn it, no."

Someone stood in the opened doorway behind her saying Marya? Is something wrong? but Marya paid her no notice. She was opening the drawers of her bureau one by one; she saw, disgusted, frightened, that the thief had been there too—rooting around in Marya's woollen socks and sweaters and frayed underwear. And her fountain pen was gone. She kept it in the top drawer of the bureau, a prize of her own, a handsome black Parker pen with a thick nub . . . now it was gone.

She had to resist the impulse to yank the drawer out and throw it to the floor—to yank all the drawers out—to give herself up to rage. A flame seemed to pass through her, white-hot, scalding. It was so unfair: she needed that money, every penny of that money, she'd worked in the library in that flickering fluorescent light until she staggered with exhaustion, and even then she'd been forced to beg her supervisor to allow her a few more hours. Her scholarships were only for tuition; she needed that money. And the pen—she could never replace the pen.

It was too much: something in her chest gave way: she burst into tears like an overgrown child. She had never heard such great gulping ugly sobs. And the girl in the doorway—Phyllis, whose room was across the hall—shy, timid, sweet-faced Phyllis—actually tried to hold her in her arms and comfort her. It's so unfair, it's so unfair, Marya wept, what am I going to *do*. . . .

Eventually the wallet was returned to Marya, having been found in a trash can up the street. Nothing was missing but the money, as it turned out: nothing but the money! Marya thought savagely. The wallet itself —simulated crocodile, black, with a fancy brass snap—now looked despoiled, worn, contemptible. It had been a present from Emmett two years before and she supposed she'd had it long enough.

She examined it critically inside and out. She wondered what the thief had thought. Marya Knauer's things, Marya Knauer's "personal" possessions: were they worth stealing, really?

For weeks afterward Marya dreaded returning to her room. Though she was careful to lock the door all the time now it always seemed, when she stepped inside, that someone had been there . . . that something was out of place. Sometimes when she was halfway up the long steep hill to Stafford Hall she turned impulsively and ran back to her dormitory seven blocks away, to see if she'd remembered to lock the door. You're breaking down, aren't you, she mocked herself as she ran, her heart pumping, perspiration itching beneath her arms,—this is how it begins, isn't it: cracking up.

In the early years of the century Maynard House must have been impressive: a small Victorian mansion with high handsome windows, a wide veranda rimmed with elaborate fretwork, a cupola, a half-dozen fireplaces, walnut paneling in several of the downstairs rooms. But now it had become dim and shabby. The outside needed painting; the wallpaper in most of the rooms was discolored. Because it was so far from the main campus, and because its rooms were so cramped (Marya could stand at her full height on only one side of her room, the ceiling on the other slanted so steeply) it was one of the lowest priced residences for women. The girls who roomed there were all scholarship students like Marya, and, like Marya, uneasily preoccupied with studies, grades, part-time employment, finances of a minute and degrading nature. They were perhaps not so humorless and unattractive as Maynard House's reputation would have it, but they did share a superficial family resemblance—they might have been cousins, grimly energetic, easily distracted, a little vain (for they *were* scholarship winners after all, competition for these scholarships was intense throughout the state), badly frightened at the prospect of failure. They were susceptible to tears at odd unprovoked moments, to eating binges, to outbursts of temper; several, including Marya, were capable of keeping their doors closed for days on end and speaking to no one when they did appear.

Before the theft Marya had rather liked Maynard House; she prized her cubbyhole of a room because it was *hers;* because in fact she could lock the door for days on end. The standard university furniture didn't displease her—the same minimal bed, desk, chair, bureau, bedside table, lamp in each room—and the sloped ceiling gave the room a cavelike, warmly intimate air, especially at night when only her desk lamp was burning. Though she couldn't really afford it Marya had bought a woven rug for the floor—Aztec colors, even more fierce than those in hers and Alice's rug at home—and a new lampshade edged with a festive gold braid; she had bought a Chagall print for ninety-eight cents (marked down because it was slightly shopworn) at the University Store. The walls were decorated with unframed charcoal drawings she had done, sketches of imaginary people, a few glowering self-portraits: when she was too tense or excited to sleep after hours of studying, or after having taken an exam, she took up a stick of charcoal and did whatever it seemed to wish to do—her fingers empowered with a curious sort of energy, twitchy, sporadic, often quite surprising. From the room's walls smudged and shadowy variants of her own sober face contemplated her. Strong cheekbones, dark eyes, thick dark censorious brows. . . . She had made the portraits uglier than she supposed she really was; that provided some comfort, it might be said to have been a reverse vanity. Who is *that?* one of the girls on the floor once asked, staring at Marya's own image,—is it a man?—a woman?

Marya prized her aloneness, her monastic isolation at the top of the house, tucked away in a corner. She could stay up all night if she wished, she could skip breakfast if she wished, she could fall into bed after her morning classes and sleep a heavy drugged sleep for much of the afternoon; and no one knew or cared. It seemed extraordinary to her now that for so many years—for all of her lifetime, in fact—she had had to submit to the routine schedule of Wilma's household: going to bed when she wasn't sleepy, getting up when the others did, eating meals with them, living her life as if it were nothing more than an extension of theirs. She loved to read for pleasure once her own assignments were completed: the reading she did late at night acquired an aura, a value, a mysterious sort of enchantment, that did not usually belong to daylight. It was illicit, precious beyond estimation. It seemed to her at such times that she was capable of slipping out of her own consciousness and into that of the writer's . . . into the very rhythms of another's prose. Bodiless, weightless, utterly absorbed, she traversed the landscape of another's mind and found it like her own yet totally unlike —surprising and jarring her, enticing her, leading her on. It was a secret process yet it was not criminal or forbidden—she made her way with the stealth of the thief, elated, subdued, through another's imagination, risking no harm, no punishment. The later the hour and the more exhausted she was, the greater, oddly, her powers of concentration; nothing in her resisted, nothing stood aside to doubt or ridicule; the books she read greedily seemed to take life through her, by way of her, with virtually no exertion of her own. It scarcely seemed to matter what she read, or whom—Nietzsche, William James, the Brontës, Wallace Stevens, Virginia Woolf, Stendhal, the early Greek philosophers—the experience of reading was electrifying, utterly mesmerizing, beyond anything she could recall from the past. She'd been, she thought severely, a superficial person in the past—how could anything that belonged to Innisfail, to those years, matter?

A writer's authentic self, she thought, lay in his writing and not in his life; it was the landscape of the imagination that endured, that was really real. Mere life was the husk, the actor's performance, negligible in the long run. . . . How could it be anything more than the vehicle by which certain works of art were transcribed . . . ? The thought frightened her, exhilarated her. She climbed out of her bed and leaned out her window as far as she could, her hair whipping in the wind. For long vacant minutes she stared at the sky; her vision absorbed without recording the illuminated water tower two miles north of the campus, the flickering red lights of a radio station, the passage of clouds blown livid across the moon. Standing in her bare feet, shivering, her head fairly ringing with fatigue and her eyes filling with tears, she thought her happiness almost too exquisite to be borne.

The first time Imogene Skillman climbed, uninvited, to Marya's room at the top of the old mansion, she stood in the doorway and exclaimed in her low throaty amused voice, "So *this* is where you hide out! . . . this depressing little hole."

Imogene was standing with her hands on her hips, her cheeks flushed, her eyes moving restlessly about. Why, Marya's room was a former maid's room, wasn't it, partitioned off from the others on the floor; and it had only that one window—no wonder the air was stale and close; and that insufferable Chagall print!—wasn't Marya aware that everyone on campus had one? And it was a poor reproduction at that. Then Imogene noticed the charcoal sketches; she came closer to investigate; she said, after a long moment, "At least these are interesting, I wouldn't mind owning one or two of them myself."

Marya had been taken by surprise, sitting at her desk, a book opened before her; she hadn't the presence of mind to invite Imogene in, or to tell her to go away.

"So this is where Marya Knauer lives," Imogene said slowly. Her eyes were a pellucid blue, blank and innocent as china. "All alone, of course. Who would *you* have roomed with—?"

The loss of the money and the Parker fountain pen was so upsetting to Marya, and so bitterly ironic, partly because Marya herself had become a casual thief.

She thought, I deserve this.

She thought, I will never steal anything again.

Alice had led her on silly little shoplifting expeditions in Woolworth's: plastic combs, spools of thread, lipsticks, useless items (hairnets, thumbtacks) pilfered for the sheer fun of it. Once, years ago, when she was visiting Bonnie Michalak, she made her way stealthily into Mrs. Michalak's bedroom and took—what had it been?—a button, a thimble, two or three pennies?—from the top of her dresser. A tube of much-used scarlet lipstick from the locker of a high school friend; a card-sized plastic calendar (an advertisement from a stationer's in town) from Mr. Schwilk's desk; stray nickels and dimes, quarters, fifty-cent pieces. . . . One of her prizes, acquired with great daring and trepidation, was a (fake) ruby ring belonging to someone's older sister, which Marya had found beneath carelessly folded clothing in a stall in the women's bathroom at Wolf's Head Lake, but had never dared to wear. The thefts were always impulsive and rather pointless. Marya saw her trembling hand dart out, saw the fingers close . . . and in that instant, wasn't the object hers?

There was a moment when an item passed over from belonging to another person to belonging to Marya; that moment interested her greatly. She felt excitement, near-panic, elation. A sense of having triumphed, in however petty a fashion.

(It had come to seem to her in retrospect that she'd stolen Father Shearing's wristwatch. She seemed to recall . . . unless it was a particularly vivid dream . . . she seemed to recall slipping the watch from his table into her bookbag, that old worn soiled bookbag she'd had for years. Father Shearing was asleep in his cranked-up bed. Though perhaps not . . . perhaps he was watching her all along through his eyelashes. Marya? Dear Marya? A common thief?)

Since coming to Port Oriskany she felt the impulse more frequently but she knew enough to resist. It was a childish habit, she thought, disgusted,—it wasn't even genuine theft, intelligently committed. Presumably she wanted to transgress; even to be punished; she *wanted* to be sinful.

Odd, Marya thought uneasily, that no one has ever caught me. When I haven't seemed to care. When I haven't seemed to have *tried*.

It happened that, in her classes, she found herself gazing at certain individuals, and at their belongings, day after day, week after week. What began as simple curiosity gradually shaded into intense interest. She might find herself, for instance, staring at a boy's spiral notebook in a lecture class . . . plotting a way to getting it for herself, leafing through it, seeing what he'd written. (For this boy, like Marya, was a daydreamer; an elaborate and tireless doodler, not without talent.) There was an antique opal ring belonging to a girl in her English literature class: the girl herself had waist-long brown hair, straight and coarse, and Marya couldn't judge whether she was striking, and very good-looking, or really quite repulsive. (Marya's own hair was growing long again—long and wavy and unruly—but it would never be that length again; the ends simply broke off.) Many of the students at Port

Oriskany were from well-to-do families, evidently, judging from their clothes and belongings: Marya's eye moved upon handtooled leather bags, and boots, and wristwatches, and earrings, and coats (suede, leather, fur-trimmed, camel's hair) half in scorn and half in envy. She did not want to steal these items, she did not *want* these items, yet, still, her gaze drifted onto them time and again, helplessly. . . .

She studied faces too, when she could. Profiles. That blonde girl in her political science class, for instance: smooth clear creamy skin, china-blue mocking eyes, a flawless nose, mouth: long hair falling over one shoulder. Knee-high leather boots, kid gloves, a handsome camel's hair coat, a blue cashmere muffler that hadn't been cleaned in some time. An engagement ring with a large square-cut diamond. . . . But it was the girl's other pieces of jewelry that drew Marya's interest. Sometimes she wore a big silver ring with a turquoise stone; and a long sporty necklace made of copper coins; and a succession of earrings in her pierced ears—gold loops that swung and caught the light, tiny iridescent-black stones, ceramic disks in which gold-burnished reds and blues flashed. Marya stared and stared, her heart quickening with—was it envy?—but envy of precisely what? It could not have been these expensive trinkets she coveted.

Imogene Skillman was a theater arts major; she belonged to one of the sororities on Masefield Avenue; Marya had even been able to discover that she was from Laurel Park, Long Island, and that she was engaged to a law student who had graduated from Port Oriskany several years ago. After she became acquainted with Imogene she would have been deeply humiliated if Imogene had known how much Marya knew of her beforehand. Not only her background, and her interest in acting, but that big leather bag, those boots, the silver ring, the ceramic earrings. . . .

It might have been Imogene's presence in class that inspired Marya to speak as she frequently did; answering their professor's questions in such detail, in such self-consciously structured sentences. (Marya thought of herself as shy, but, as it turned out, she could often speak at length if required—she became, suddenly, articulate and emphatic—even somewhat combative. The tenor of her voice caused people to turn around in their seats and often surprised, when it did not disconcert, her professors.) It wasn't that she spoke her mind—she rarely offered opinions—it seemed to her necessary to consider as many sides of an issue as possible, as many relevant points, presenting her case slowly and clearly and forcefully, showing no sign of the nervousness she felt. It was not simply that most of her professors solicited serious discussion —gave evidence, in fact, of being greatly dependent upon it to fill up fifty minutes of class time—or even that (so Marya reasoned, calculated) her precious grade might depend upon such contributions; she really became caught up in the subjects themselves. Conflicting theories of representative democracy, property rights, civil disobedience . . . the ethics of propaganda . . . revolution and counterrevolution . . . whether in fact terrorism might ever be justified. . . . Even when it seemed, as it sometimes did, that Marya's concern for these issues went beyond that of the professor's, she made her point; she felt a grudging approval throughout the room; and Imogene Skillman turned languidly in her seat to stare at her.

One afternoon Imogene left behind a little handwoven purse that must have slipped out of her leather bag. Marya snatched it up as if it were a prize. She followed after Imogene—followed her out of the building—that tall blonde girl in the camel's hair coat—striding along, laughing, in a high-spirited conversation with her friends. Marya approached her and handed her the purse, saying only, "You dropped this," in a neutral voice; she turned away without waiting for Imogene's startled thanks.

Afterward she felt both elated and unaccountably fatigued. As if she had experienced some powerful drain on her energy. As if, having returned Imogene's little purse to her, she now regretted having done so; and wondered if she had been a fool.

Marya's friendship with Imogene Skillman began, as it was to end, with a puzzling abruptness.

One day Imogene simply appeared beside Marya on one of the campus paths, asking if she was walking this way?—and falling comfortably in step with her. It was done as easily and as effortlessly as if they were old friends; as if Imogene had been reading Marya's most secret thoughts.

She began by flattering her, telling her she said "interesting" things in class; that she seemed to be the only person their professor really listened to. Then, almost coyly: "I should confess that it's your voice that really intrigues me. What if—so I ask myself, I'm always trying things on other people!—what if *she* was playing Hedda—Hedda Gabler—with that remarkable voice—and not mine — *mine* is so reedy — I've heard myself on tape and can barely stop from gagging. And there's something about your manner too — also your chin — when you speak — it looks as if you're gritting your teeth but you *are* making yourself perfectly audible, don't be offended! The thing is, I'm doing Hedda myself, I can't help but be jealous of how you might do her in my place though it's all *my* imagination of course. Are you free for lunch? No? Yes? We could have it at my sorority—no, better out — it's not so claustrophobic, out. We'll have to hurry, though, Marya, is it? — I have a class at one I don't *dare* cut again."

It gave Marya a feeling of distinct uneasiness, afterward, to think that Imogene had pursued *her*. Or, rather, that Imogene must have imagined herself the pursuer; and kept up for weeks the more active, the more charitably outgoing and inquisitive, of their two roles. (During their first conversation, for instance, Marya found herself stammering and blushing as she tried to answer Imogene's questions—Where are you from, what are you studying, where do you live on campus, what do you *think* of this place, isn't it disappointing?—put in so candid and ingenuous a manner, with that wide blue-eyed stare, Marya felt compelled to reply. She also felt vaguely criminal, guilty—as if she'd somehow drawn Imogene to her by the very intensity of her own interest, without Imogene's conscious knowledge.)

If Imogene reached out in friendship, at the beginning, Marya naturally drew back. She shared the Knauers' peasant shrewdness, or was it meanspiritedness: what does this person want from *me*, why on earth would this person seek out *me*? It was mysterious, puzzling, disconcerting. Imogene was so pretty, so popular and self-assured, a dominant campus personality; Marya had only a scattering of friends— friendly acquaintances, really. She hadn't, as she rather coolly explained to Imogene, time for "wasting" on people.

She also disapproved of Imogene's public manner, her air of flippancy, carelessness. In fact Imogene was quite intelligent—her swiftness of thought, her skill at repartee, made that clear—but she played at seeming otherwise, to Marya's surprise and annoyance. Imogene was always *Imogene*, always *on*. She was a master of sudden dramatic reversals: sunny warmth that shaded into chilling mockery; low-voiced serious conversations, on religion, perhaps (Imogene was an agnostic who feared, she said, lapsing into Anglicanism—it ran in her family), that deteriorated into wisecracks and bawdy jokes simply because one of her theater friends appeared. While Marya was too reserved to ask Imogene about herself, Imogene was pitiless in her interrogation of Marya, once the formality of their first meeting was out of the way. Has your family *always* lived in that part of the state, do you mean your father was really a *miner*, how old were you when he died, how old were you when your mother died, do you keep in touch with your high school friends, are you happy here, are you in love with anyone, have you ever been in love, are you a virgin, do you have any plans for this summer, what will you do after graduation?—what do you think your *life* will be?

Marya was dazed, disoriented. She answered as succinctly and curtly as she dared, never really telling the truth, yet not precisely lying; she had the idea that Imogene could detect a lie; she'd heard her challenge others when she doubted the sincerity of what they said. Half-truths went down very well, however. Half-truths, Marya had begun to think, were so much more reasonable—so much more convincing—than whole truths.

For surely brazen golden-haired Imogene Skillman didn't really want to know the truth about Marya's family—her father's death (of a heart attack, aged thirty-nine, wasn't that a possibility?—having had rheumatic fever, let's say, as a boy); her mother's disappearance that was, at least poetically, a kind of death too (automobile accident, Marya ten at the time, no one to blame). Marya was flattered, as who would not be, by Imogene's intense *interest* and *sympathy* ("You seem to have had such a hard life. . . .") but she was shrewd enough to know she must not push her friend's generosity of spirit too far: it was one thing to be moved, another thing to be repulsed.

So she was sparing with the truth. A little truth goes a long way, she thought, not knowing if the remark was an old folk saying, or something she'd coined herself.

She told herself that she resented Imogene's manner, her assumption of an easygoing informality that was all one-sided, or nearly; at the same time it couldn't be denied that Marya Knauer visibly brightened in Imogene Skillman's presence. She saw with satisfaction how Imogene's friends—meeting them in the student union, in the pub, in the restaurants and coffee shops along Fairfield Street—watched them with curiosity, and must have wondered who Imogene's new friend was.

Marya Knauer: but who is *she*?—where did Imogene pick up *her*?

Marya smiled cynically to herself, thinking that she understood at last the gratification a man must feel, in public, in the company of a beautiful woman. Better, really, than being the beautiful woman yourself.

They would have quarrelled, everything would have gone abrasive and sour immediately, if Marya hadn't chosen (consciously, deliberately) to admire Imogene's boldness, rather than to be insulted by it. (*Are you happy, are you lonely, have you ever been in love, are you a virgin?* —no one had ever dared ask Marya such questions. The Knauers were reticent, prudish, about such things as personal feelings: Wilma might haul off and slap her, and call her a little shit, but she'd have been convulsed with embarrassment to ask Marya if she was happy or unhappy, if she loved anyone, if, maybe, she knew how Wilma loved *her*.

Just as Lee and Everard might quarrel, and Lee might dare to tell his brawny hot-tempered father to go to hell, but he'd never have asked him—he'd never have even imagined asking him—how much money he made in a year, how much he had in the bank, what the property was worth, did he have a will, did he guess that, well, Lee sort of looked up to *him*, loved *him*, despite all these fights?)

Marya speculated that she'd come a great distance from Innisfail and the Canal Road—light-years, really, not two hundred miles—and she had to be careful, cautious, about speaking in the local idiom.

Imogene was nearly as tall as Marya, and her gold-gleaming hair and ebullient manner made her seem taller. Beside her, Marya knew herself shabby, undramatic, unattractive; it was not *her* prerogative to take offense, to recoil from her friend's extreme interest. After all—were so very many people interested in her, here in Port Oriskany? Did anyone really care if she lied, or told the truth, or invented ingenious half-truths . . . ? In any case, despite Imogene's high spirits, there was usually something harried about her. She hadn't studied enough for an exam, play rehearsals were going badly, she'd had an upsetting telephone call from home the night before, what in Christ's name was she to *do?* . . . Marya noted that beautiful white-toothed smile marred by tiny tics of vexation. Imogene was always turning the diamond ring round and round her finger, impatiently; she fussed with her earrings and hair; she was always late, always running—her coat unbuttoned and flapping about her, her tread heavy. Her eyes sometimes filled with tears that were, or were not, genuine.

Even her agitation, Marya saw, was enviable. There are certain modes of unhappiness with far more style than happiness.

Imogene insisted that Marya accompany her to a coffee shop on Fairfield —pretentiously called a coffee "house"—where all her friends gathered. These were her *real* friends, apart from her sorority sisters and her fraternity admirers. Marya steeled herself against their critical amused eyes; she didn't want to be one of their subjects for mimicry. (They did devastating imitations of their professors and even of one another— Marya had to admit, laughing, that they were really quite good. If only she'd known such people back in Innisfail!—in high school!—she might have been less singled out for disapproval; she might have been less lonely.)

Marya made certain that she gave her opinions in a quick flat unhesitating voice, since opinions tenuously offered were usually rejected. If she chose to talk with these people at all she made sure that she talked fast, so that she wouldn't be interrupted. (They were always interrupting one another, Imogene included.) With her excellent memory Marya could, if required, quote passages from the most difficult texts; her vocabulary blossomed wonderfully in the presence of a critical, slightly hostile audience she knew she *must* impress. (For Imogene prided herself on Marya Knauer's brilliance, Marya Knauer's knowledge and wit. Yes, that's right, she would murmur, laughing, nudging Marya in the ribs, go on, go *on*, you're absolutely right—you've got them now!) And Marya smoked cigarettes with the others, and drank endless cups of bitter black coffee, and flushed with pleasure when things went well . . . though she was wasting a great deal of time these days, wasn't she? . . . and wasn't time the precious element that would carry her along to her salvation?

The coffee shop was several blocks from the University's great stone archway, a tunnellike place devoid of obvious charm, where tables were crowded together and framed photographs of old, vanished athletes lined the walls. Everyone—Imogene's "everyone"—drifted there to escape from their living residences, and to sit for hours, talking loudly and importantly, about Strindberg, or Whitman, or Yeats, or the surrealists, or Prufrock, or Artaud, or *Ulysses*, or the Grand Inquisitor; or campus politics (who was in, who was out); or the theater department (comprised half of geniuses and saints, half of losers). Marya soon saw that several of the boys were in love with Imogene, however roughly they sometimes treated her. She didn't care to learn their names but of course she did anyway—Scott, and Andy, and Matthew (who took a nettlesome sort of dislike to Marya); there was a dark ferret-faced mathematics student named Brian whose manner was broadly theatrical and whose eyeglasses flashed with witty malice. The other girls in the group were attractive enough, in fact quite striking, but they were no match for Imogene when she was most herself.

Of course the love, even the puppyish affection, went unrequited. Imogene was engaged—the diamond ring was always in sight, glittering and winking; Imogene occasionally made reference to someone named Richard, whose opinion she seemed to value highly. (What is Imogene's fiancé like, Marya asked one of the girls, and was told he was "quiet" —"watchful"—that Imogene behaved a little differently around him; she was quieter herself.)

One wintry day when Marya should have been elsewhere she sat with Imogene's friends in a booth at the smoky rear of the coffee house, half-listening to their animated talk, wondering why Imogene cared so much for them. Her mind drifted loose; she found herself examining one of the photographs on the walls close by. It was sepia-tinted, and very old: the 1899 University rowing team. Beside it was a photograph

of the 1902 football team. How young those smiling athletes must have
felt, as the century turned, Marya thought. It must have seemed to them
. . . *theirs.*

She was too lazy to excuse herself and leave. She was too jealous
of Imogene. No, it was simply that her head ached; she hadn't slept well
the night before and wouldn't sleep well tonight. . . . Another rowing
team. Hopeful young men, standing so straight and tall; their costumes
slightly comical; their haircuts bizarre. An air of team spirit, hearty
optimism, doom. Marya swallowed hard, feeling suddenly strange. She
really should leave . . . She really shouldn't be here. . . .

Time had been a nourishing stream, a veritable sea, for those young
men. Like fish they'd swum in it without questioning it—without
knowing it was the element that sustained them and gave them life.
And then it had unaccountably withdrawn and left them exposed . . .
Forever youthful in those old photographs, in their outdated costumes;
long since aged, dead, disposed of.

Marya thought in a panic that she must leave; she must return to
her room and lock the door.

But when she rose Imogene lay a hand on her arm and asked
irritably what was wrong, why was she always jumping up and down:
couldn't she for Christ's sake sit *still?*

The vehemence of Imogene's response struck them all, it was in
such disproportion to Marya's behavior. Marya herself was too rushed,
too frightened, to take offense. She murmured, "Good-bye, Imogene,"
without looking at her; and escaped.

It was that night, not long before curfew, that Imogene dropped by for
the first time at Maynard House. She rapped on Marya's door, poked
her head in, seemed to fill the doorway, chattering brightly as if nothing
were wrong; as if they'd parted amiably. Of course she *was* rather rude
about the room—Marya hadn't realized it must have been a maid's
room, in the house's earliest incarnation—but her rudeness as always
passed by rather casually, in a sort of golden blue. She looked so pretty,
flushed with cold, her eyes inordinately damp. . . .

Tell me about these drawings, she said,—I didn't know you were
an artist. These are *good.*

But Marya wasn't in a mood for idle conversation. She said indifferently that she *wasn't* an artist; she was a student.

But Imogene insisted she was an artist. Because the sketches were
so rough, unfinished, yet they caught the eye, there was something
unnerving about them. "Do you see yourself like this, though?—

Marya?" Imogene asked almost wistfully. "So stern and ugly?—it *isn't* you, is it?"

"It isn't anyone," Marya said. "It's a few charcoal strokes on old paper."

She was highly excited that Imogene Skillman had come to her room: had anyone on the floor noticed?—had the girl downstairs at the desk, on telephone duty, noticed? At the same time she wished her gone, it was an intrusion into her privacy, insufferable. She had never invited Imogene to visit her—she never would.

"So this is where you live," Imogene said, drawing a deep breath. Her eyes darted mercilessly about; she would miss nothing, forget nothing. "You're alone and you don't mind, that's *just* like you. You have a whole other life, a sort of secret life, don't you," she said, with a queer pouting downward turn of her lips.

Friendship, Marya speculated in her journal,—the most enigmatic of all relationships.

In a sense it flourished unbidden; in another, it had to be cultivated, nurtured, sometimes even forced into existence. Though she was tirelessly active in most aspects of her life she'd always been quite passive when it came to friendship. She hadn't time, she told herself; she hadn't energy for something so . . . ephemeral.

Nothing was worthwhile, really worthwhile, except studying; getting high grades; and her own reading, her own work. Sometimes Marya found herself idly contemplating a young man—in one of her classes, in the library; sometimes, like most of her female classmates, she contemplated one or another of her male professors. But she didn't want a lover, not even a romance. To cultivate romance, Marya thought, you had to give over a great deal of time for daydreaming: she hadn't time to waste on *that*.

Since the first month of her freshman year Marya had acquired a reputation for being brilliant—the word wasn't hers but Imogene's: Do you know everyone thinks you're brilliant, everyone is afraid of you? —and it struck Marya as felicitous, a sort of glass barrier that would keep other people at a distance. . . . And then again she sometimes looked up from her reading, and noted that hours had passed; where was she and what was she doing to herself? (Had someone called her? Whispered her name? Marya, Marya. . . . You little savage, Marya. . . .) Suddenly she ached with the desire to see Wilma, and Everard; and her brothers; even Lee. She felt as if she must leave this airless little cubbyhole of a room—take a Greyhound bus to Innisfail—see that house on the Canal Road—sit at the kitchen table with the others—tell them she loved them, she loved them and couldn't help herself: what was happening?

Great handfuls of her life were being stolen from her and she would never be able to retrieve them.

To counteract Imogene Skillman's importance in her life, Marya made it a point to be friendly—if not, precisely, to *become friends*—with a number of Maynard House girls. She frequently ate meals with them in the dining hall a few blocks away, though she was inclined (yes, it was rude) to bring along a book or two just in case. And if the conversation went nowhere Marya would murmur, Do you mind?—I have so much reading to do.

Of course they didn't mind. Catherine or Phyllis or Sally or Diane. They too were scholarship students; they too were frightened, driven.

(Though Marya knew they discussed her behind her back. She was the only girl in the house with a straight-A average and they were waiting . . . were they perhaps hoping? . . . for her to slip down a notch or two. They were afraid of her sarcasm, her razorish wit. Then again, wasn't she sometimes very funny?—If you liked that sort of humor. As for the sorority girl Imogene Skillman: what did Marya see in *her?*—what did *she* see in Marya? It was also likely, wasn't it, that Marya was the house thief? For the thief still walked off with things sporadically. These were mean, pointless thefts—a letter from a mailbox, another textbook, a single angora glove, an inexpensive locket on a tarnished silver chain. Pack-rat sort of thievery, unworthy, in fact, of any girl who roomed in Maynard.)

When Marya told Imogene about the thief and the money she'd lost, Imogene said indifferently that there was a great deal of stealing on campus, and worse things too (this, with a sly twist of her lips), but no one wanted to talk about it; the student newspaper (the editors were all friends of hers, she knew such things) was forever being censored. For instance, last year a girl committed suicide by slashing her wrists in one of the off-campus senior houses and the paper wasn't allowed to publish the news, not even to *hint* at it, and the local newspaper didn't run anything either, it was all a sort of totalitarian kindergarten state, the university. As for theft: "*I've* never stolen anything in my life," Imogene said, smiling, brooding, "because why would I want anything that somebody else has already had?—something second-hand, used?"

Your friend Imogene, people began to say.

Your friend Imogene: she dropped by at noon, left this note for you.

Marya's pulses rang with pleasure, simple gratitude. She was flattered but—well, rather doubtful. Did she even *like* Imogene? Were they really friends? In a sense she liked one or two of the girls in Maynard better than she liked Imogene. Phyllis, for instance, a mathematics major, very sharp, very bright, though almost painfully shy; and a chunky farm girl named Diane from a tiny settlement north of Shaheen Falls, precociously matronly, with thick glasses and a heavy tread on the stairs and a perpetual odor of unwashed flesh, ill-laundered clothes. . . . But Diane was bright, very bright; Marya thought privately that here was her real competition at Port Oriskany, encased in baby fat, blinking through those thick lenses. (The residence buzzed with the rumor, however, that Diane was doing mysteriously poorly in her courses, had she a secret grief?—an unstated terror?) Marya certainly liked Phyllis and Diane, she recognized them as superior individuals, really much nicer, much kinder, than Imogene. Yet she had to admit it would not have deeply troubled her if she never saw them again. And the loss of Imogene would have been a powerful blow.

She went twice to see the production of *Hedda Gabler* in which Imogene starred. For she really did star, it was a one-woman show. That hard slightly drawling slightly nasal voice, that mercurial manner (cruel, seductive, mocksweet, languid, genuinely anguished by turns), certain odd tricks and mannerisms (the way she held her jaw, for instance: had she pilfered that from Marya?)—Imogene was *really* quite good; really a success. And they'd made her up to look even more beautiful on stage than she looked in life: her golden hair in a heavy Victorian twist, her cheeks subtly rouged, her eyes enormous. Only in the tense sparring scene with Judge Brack, when Hedda was forced to confront a personality as strong as her own, did Imogene's acting falter: her voice went strident, her manner became too broadly erotic.

Marya thought, slightly dazed,—Is she really talented? Is there some basis for her reputation, after all?

Backstage, Marya didn't care to compete for Imogene's attention; let the others hug and kiss her and shriek congratulations if they wished. It was all exaggerated, florid, embarrassing . . . so much emotion, such a *display*. . . . And Imogene looked wild, frenzied, her elaborate makeup now rather clownish, seen at close quarters. "Here's Marya," she announced, "—Marya will tell the truth—here's Marya—shut up, you idiots!—she'll tell the truth— *was* I any good, Marya? — *was* I really Hedda?" She pushed past her friends and gripped Marya's hands, staring at her with great shining painted eyes. She smelled of greasepaint and powder and perspiration; it seemed to Marya that Imogene towered over her.

"Of course you were good," Marya said flatly. "You know you were good."

Imogene gripped her hands tighter, her manner was feverish, outsized. "What are you saying?—you didn't care for the performance? It wasn't right? I failed?"

"Don't be ridiculous," Marya said, embarrassed, trying to pull away. "You don't need me to assess you, in any case. You *know* you were—"

"You didn't like it! Did you!"

"—you were perfect."

"*Perfect!*" Imogene said in a hoarse stage voice, "—but that doesn't sound like one of your words, Marya—you don't *mean* it."

It was some seconds before Marya, her face burning with embarrassment and resentment, could extricate her hands from Imogene's desperate grip. No, she couldn't come to the cast party; she had to get back to work. And yes, yes, for Christ's sake, *yes*—Imogene had been "perfect": or nearly.

Friendship, Marya wrote in her journal, her heart pounding with rage, —play-acting of an amateur type.

Friendship, she wrote,—a puzzle that demands too much of the imagination.

So she withdrew from Imogene, tried even to stop thinking about her, looking for her on campus. (That blue muffler, that camel's hair coat. And she had a new coat too: Icelandic shearling, with a black fur collar.) She threw herself into her work with more passion than before. Exams were upon her, papers were due, she felt the challenge with a sort of eager dread, an actual greed, knowing she could do well even if she didn't work hard; and she intended to work very, very hard. Even if she got sick, even if her eyes went bad.

Hour after hour of reading, taking notes, writing, rewriting. In her room, the lamp burning through the night; in one or another of her secret places in the library; in a corner of an old brick mansion a quarter-mile away that had been converted into the music school, where she might read and scribble notes and daydream, her heartbeat underscored by the muffled sounds of pianos, horns, violins, cellos, flutes, from the rows of practice rooms. The sounds—the various musics— were all rather harmonious, heard like this, in secret. Marya thought, closing her eyes: If you could only *be* music.

At the same time she had her job in the library, her ill-paid job, a drain on her time and spirit, a terrible necessity. She explained that she'd lost her entire paycheck—the money had been stolen out of her wallet —she *must* be allowed to work a little longer, to clock a few more hours each week. She intended (so she explained to her supervisor) to make up the loss she'd suffered by disciplining herself severely, spending no extra money if she could avoid it. She *must* be allowed a few hours extra work. . . . (The Parker pen could never be replaced, of course. As for the money: Marya washed her hair now once a week, and reasoned that she did not really need toothpaste, why did anyone *need* toothpaste? —she was sparing with her toiletries in general, and, if she could, used other girls', left in the third floor bathroom. She was always coming upon lost ballpoint pens, lost notebooks, even loose change; she could appropriate—lovely word, "appropriate"—cheap mimeograph paper from a supply room in the library; sometimes she even found half-empty packs of cigarettes—though her newest resolution was to stop smoking, since she resented every penny spent on so foolish a habit. Her puritan spirit blazed; she thought it an emblem of her purity, that the waistbands of her skirts were now too loose, her underwear was a size too large.)

After an evening of working in the library—her pay was approximately $1 an hour—she hurried home to Maynard, exhausted, yet exhilarated, eager to get to her schoolwork. Once she nearly fainted running up the stairs and Diane, who happened to be nearby, insisted that she come into her room for a few minutes. You look terrible, she said in awe—almost as bad as I do. But Marya brushed her aside, Marya hadn't time. She was light-headed from the stairs, that was all.

One night Imogene telephoned just before the switchboard was to close. What the hell was wrong, Imogene demanded, was Marya angry at her? She hurried out of class before Imogene could say two words to her—she never came down to Fairfield Street any longer—was she secretly in love?—was she working longer hours at the library?— would she like to come to dinner sometime this week, at the sorority? —or next week, before Christmas break?

Yes, thought Marya, bathed in gratitude, in golden splendor, "No," she said aloud, quietly, chastely, "—but thank you very much."

Schopenhauer, Dickens, Marx, Euripides. Oscar Wilde. Henry Adams. Sir Thomas More. Thomas Hobbes. And Shakespeare—of course. She read, she took notes, she daydreamed. It sometimes disturbed her that virtually nothing of what she read had been written by women (except Jane Austen, dear perennial Jane, *so* feminine!) but in her arrogance she told herself *she* would change all that.

Is this how it begins, she wondered, half-amused. Breaking down. Cracking up.

Why breaking *down* . . . but cracking *up* . . . ?

Her long periods of intense concentration began to be punctuated by bouts of directionless daydreaming, sudden explosions of *feeling*. At such times Shakespeare was too dangerous to be read closely—Hamlet whispered truths too cruel to be borne, every word in *Lear* hooked in

flesh and could not be dislodged. As for Wilde, Hobbes, Schopenhauer
. . . even cynicism, Marya saw, can't save you.

At such times she went for walks along Masefield Avenue, past the
enormous sorority and fraternity houses. They too were converted man-
sions but had retained much of their original glamor and stateliness.
Imogene's, for instance, boasted pretentious white columns, four of
them, in mock-Southern Colonial style. The cryptic Greek letters on the
portico struck an especially garish and irrelevant note. What did such
symbols mean, what did it mean (so Marya wondered, not quite bitterly) to be *clubbable*—? In the winter twilight, in the cold, these outsized houses appeared especially warm and secretive; every window of
their several storeys blazed. Marya thought, Why don't I feel anything,
can't I even feel envy . . . ? But the sororities were crudely discrimina-
tory (one was exclusively for Catholic girls, another exclusively for
Jewish girls, the sixteen others had quotas for Catholics and blackballed
all Jews who dared cross their threshold: the procedure was that blunt,
that childish). Dues and fees were absurdly high, beyond the inflated
price for room and board; the meetings involved pseudoreligious
"Greek" rituals (handshakes, secret passwords, special prayers). Imogene complained constantly, was always cutting activities and being
fined ($10 fine for missing a singing rehearsal!—the very thought made
Marya shiver in disbelief), always mocking the alumns, those well-to-
do matrons with too much time on their hands. Such assholes, all of
them, Imogene said loftily, such *pretentious* assholes. It was part of
Imogene's charm that she could be both contemptuous of pretension
and marvelously—shamelessly—pretentious herself.

Time is the element in which we exist, Marya noted solemnly in
her journal,—We are either borne along by it, or drowned in it.

It occurred to her with a chilling certitude that *every moment not
consciously devoted to her work* was an error, a blunder. As if you can kill
time, Thoreau said, without injuring Eternity.

Lying drowsily and luxuriously in bed after she'd wakened . . .
conversations with most people, or, indeed *all* people . . . spending too
long in the shower, or cleaning her room, or staring out the window,
or eating three meals a day (unless of course she brought along a book
to read) . . . daydreaming and brooding about Innisfail, or the Canal
Road, or that wretched little tarpaper-roofed shanty near Shaheen Falls
that had been her parents' house . . . crying over the past (though in
fact she rarely cried these days) as if the past were somehow present.
In high school she had been quite an athlete, especially at basketball
and field hockey; in college she hadn't time, hadn't the slightest interest.
It pleased her that she always received grades of A but at the same time
she wondered,—Are these *really* significant grades, do I *really* know

anything?—or is Port Oriskany one of the backwaters of the world, where nothing, even "excellence," greatly matters? She needed high grades in order to get into graduate school, however; beyond that she didn't allow herself to think. Though perhaps she wouldn't go to graduate school at all . . . perhaps she would try to write . . . her great problem being not that she hadn't anything to write about but that she had too much.

Unwisely, once, she confided in Imogene that she halfway feared to write anything that wasn't academic or scholarly or firmly rooted in the real world: once she began she wouldn't be able to stop: she was afraid of sinking too deep into her own head, cracking up, becoming lost.

Imogene said it once that Marya was just the type to be excessive, she needed reining in. "I know the symptoms," she said severely. Anyway, what good would academic success—or any kind of success —do her, if she destroyed her health?

"*You're* concerned about my health?" Marya asked incredulously.

"Of course. Yes, I *am*. Why shouldn't I be," Imogene said, "—aren't I a friend of yours?"

Marya stared at her, unable to reply. It struck her as wildly incongruous that Imogene Skillman, with her own penchant for abusing her health (she drank too much at fraternity parties, she stayed up all night doing hectic last-minute work) should be worrying about Marya.

"Aren't I a friend of yours?" Imogene asked less certainly. "Don't I have the right . . . ?"

Marya turned away with an indifferent murmur, perhaps because she was so touched.

"My health isn't of any use to me," she said, "if I don't get anything accomplished. If I fail."

Of course it was possible, Marya saw, to ruin one's health and fail anyway.

Several of her fellow residents in Maynard House were doing poorly in their courses, despite their high intelligence and the goading terror that energized them. One of them was Phyllis, who was failing an advanced calculus class; another, a chronically withdrawn and depressed girl named Mary, a physics major, whose deeply shadowed eyes and pale grainy skin, as well as her very name, struck a superstitious chord of dread in Marya—she avoided her as much as possible, and had the idea that Mary avoided *her.*

The University piously preached an ethic of knowledge for its own sake—knowledge and beauty being identical—the "entire person" was to be educated, not simply the mind; but of course it acted swiftly and pragmatically upon another ethic entirely. Performance was all, the grade-point average *was* everything. Marya, no idealist, saw that this was sound and just; but she felt an impatient sort of pity for those who fell by the wayside, or who, like the scholarship girls, in not being *best*, were to be judged *worthless*, and sent back home. (Anything below a B was failing for them.) She wanted only to be best, to be outstanding, to be . . . defined to herself as extraordinary . . . for, apart from being extraordinary, had she any essence at all?

The second semester of her freshman year she had come close to losing her perfect grade-point average. Unwisely, she signed up for a course in religion, having been attracted to the books on the syllabus and the supplementary reading list (the *Upanishads*; the *Bhagavad-Gita*; the *Bible*; the *Koran*; *Hymns of the Rigveda*; books on Gnosticism, and Taoism, and medieval Christianity, and the Christian heresies, and animism, magic, witchcraft, Renaissance ideas of Platonic love). It was all very promising, very heady stuff; quite the antidote to the catechismal Catholicism in which Marya no longer believed, and for which she had increasingly less tolerance. The professor, however turned out to be an ebullient balding popinjay who lectured from old notes in a florid and self-dramatizing style, presenting ideas in a melange clearly thrown together from others' books and articles. He wanted nothing more than these ideas (which were fairly simple, not at all metaphysical or troubling) given back to him on papers and examinations; and he did not encourage questions from the class. Marya would surely have done well —she transcribed notes faultlessly, even when contemptuous of their content—but she could not resist sitting in stony silence and refusing to laugh when the professor embarked upon one or another of his jocular anecdotes. It was a classroom mannerism of his, almost a sort of tic, that each time he alluded to something female he lowered his voice and added, as if off the cuff, a wry observation, meant not so much to be insulting as to be mildly teasing. He was a popular lecturer, well-liked by most, not taken seriously by the better students; even the girls laughed at his jokes, being grateful, as students are, for something —anything—to laugh at. Marya alone sat with her arms folded, her brow furrowed, staring. It was not until some years later that she realized, uncomfortably, how she must have appeared to that silly perspiring man—a sort of gorgon in the midst of his amiable little sea of admirers.

So it happened that, though Marya's grades for the course were all A's, the grade posted for her final examination was C; and the final grade for the course—a humiliating B +.

Marya was stunned, Marya was sickened—she would have had to reach back to her childhood—or to the night of that going-away party

—for an episode of equal mortification. That it was petty made it all the more mortifying.

I can forget this insult and forget him, Marya instructed herself,—or I can go to him and protest. To forget it seemed in a way noble, even Christian; to go to the man's office and humble herself in trying to get the grade raised (for she knew very well she hadn't written a C exam) somehow childish, degrading.

Of course she ran up to his office, made an appointment to see him; and, after a few minutes' clucking and fretting (he pretended she had failed to answer the last question, she hadn't handed in both examination booklets, but there the second booklet was, at the bottom of a heap of papers—ah, what a surprise!), he consented to raise the grade to A. And smiled roguishly at her, as if she had been caught out in mischief, or some sort of deception; for which he was forgiving her. "You seem like a rather grim young woman," he said, "you never smile—you look so *preoccupied.*" Marya stared at his swinging foot. He was a satyrish middle-aged man, red-brown tufts of hair in his ears, a paunch straining against his shirt front, a strangely vulnerable smile; a totally mediocre personality in every way—vain, uncertain, vindictive—yet Marya could see why others liked him; he was predictable, safe, probably decent enough. But she hated him. She simply wished him dead.

He continued as if not wanting to release her, waiting for her smile of blushing gratitude and her meek *thank you*—which assuredly was not going to come; he said again, teasing, "Are you *always* such an ungiving young woman, Miss Knauer?"—and Marya swallowed hard, and fixed her dark loathing stare on him, and said: "My mother is sick. She's been sick all semester. I know I shouldn't think about it so much . . . I shouldn't depress other people . . . but sometimes I can't help it. She isn't expected to live much longer, the cancer has metastasized to the brain. . . . I'm sorry if I offended you."

He stared at her; then began to stammer his apologies, rising from his desk, flushing deeply—the very image of chagrin and repentance. In an instant the entire atmosphere between them changed. He was sorry, he murmured, so very sorry . . . of course he couldn't have known . . .

A minute later Marya was striding down the corridor, her pulses beating hot, in triumph. In her coat pocket was the black fountain pen she had lifted from the man's cluttered desk.

An expensive pen, as it turned out. A Parker, with a squarish blunt nub, and the engraved initials E. W. S.

Marya used the pen to take notes in her journal, signing her name repeatedly, hypnotically: *Marya, Marya Knauer, Marya Marya Marya*

Marya Knauer, a name that eventually seemed to have been signed by someone else, a stranger.

The shame of having humbled herself before the ignorant man had been erased by the shame—what should have been shame—of theft.

So Marya speculated, thinking of that curious episode in her life. Eventually the pen ran out of ink and she didn't indulge herself in buying more—it was so old-fashioned a practice, a luxury she couldn't afford.

Phyllis began staying out late, violating curfew, returning to the residence drunk, dishevelled, tearful, angry—she couldn't stand the four walls of her room any longer, she told Marya; she couldn't stand shutting the door upon herself.

One night she didn't return at all. It was said afterward that she had been picked up by Port Oriskany police, wandering downtown, miles away, dazed and only partly clothed in the bitter cold—the temperature had gone as low as −5°F. She was taken at once to the emergency room of the city hospital; her parents, who lived upstate, were called; they came immediately the next morning to take her back home. No one at Maynard House was ever to see her again.

All the girls in the residence talked of Phyllis, somewhat dazed themselves, frightened. How quickly it had happened—how quickly Phyllis had disappeared. Marya was plied with questions about Phyllis (how many subjects she was failing, who were the boys she'd gone out with) but Marya didn't know; Marya grew vague, sullen.

And then the waters close over your head.—This phrase ran through Marya's mind repeatedly.

They talked about Phyllis for two or three days, then forgot her.

The following Saturday, however, Phyllis's mother and older sister arrived to pack up her things, clean out her room, fill out a half-dozen university forms. The resident advisor accompanied them; they looked confused, nervous, rather lost. Both women had Phyllis's pale blond limp hair, her rather small, narrow face. How is Phyllis, some of the girls asked, smiling, cautious, and Mrs. Myer said without looking at anyone, Oh Phyllis is fine, resting and eating and sleeping right again, sleeping good hours, she said, half-reproachfully, as if sleeping right hadn't been possible in Maynard House; and they were all to blame. Marya asked whether she might be returning second semester. No, not that soon, Mrs. Myer said quickly. She and the silent older sister were emptying drawers, packing suitcases briskly. Marya helped with Phyllis's books and papers, which lay in an untidy heap on her desk and on the floor surrounding the desk. There were dust balls everywhere. A great cobweb in which the desiccated corpses of insects hung, including that of the spider itself. Stiffened crumpled Kleenex wadded into balls, everywhere underfoot. An odor of grime and despair. . . . Marya discovered a calculus bluebook slashed heavily in red with a grade of D; a five-page paper on a subject that made no sense to her—Ring theory?—with a blunt red grade of F. It seemed to Marya that Phyllis was far more real now, more present, than she had been in the past . . . even when she'd tried to comfort Marya by taking her in her arms.

Marya supposed she had been Phyllis's closest friend at Port Oriskany. Yet Phyllis's mother and sister hadn't known her name, had no message for her . . . clearly Phyllis had never mentioned her to them at all. It was disappointing, sobering.

And the waters close over your head, Marya thought.

Then something remarkable happened: Marya rose from Phyllis's closet, a pile of books in her arms, her hair in her face, when she happened to see Mrs. Myer dumping loose items out of a drawer into a suitcase: a comb, ballpoint pens, coins, loose pieces of jewelry,—and her black fountain pen. *The* pen, unmistakable.

My God, Marya whispered.

No one heard. Marya stood rooted to the spot, staring, watching as her prize disappeared into Phyllis's suitcase, hidden now by a miscellany of socks and underwear. *The* pen—the emblem of her humiliation and triumph—disappearing forever.

It wasn't until months later that someone in Maynard made the observation that the thefts seemed to have stopped. . . . Since Phyllis moved out. . . . And the rest of the girls (they were at breakfast, eight or ten of them at a table) took it up, amazed, reluctant, wondering. Was it possible . . . *Phyllis* . . . ?

Marya said quietly that they shouldn't say such things since it couldn't be proved; that constituted slander.

Wednesday dinner, a "formal" dinner, in Imogene's sorority house, and Marya is seated beside Imogene, self-conscious, unnaturally shy, eating her food without tasting it. She *can* appreciate the thick slabs of roast beef, the small perfectly cooked parsley potatoes, the handsome giltedged china, the white linen tablecloth ("Oh it's Portuguese—from Portugal"), the crystal water goblets, the numerous tall candles, the silvery-green silk wallpaper, the house mother's poised social chatter at the head table . . . and the girls' stylized animation, their collective stylized beauty. For they *are* beautiful, without exception, as unlike the girls of Maynard House as one species is unlike another.

Imogene Skillman, in this dazzling context, isn't Marya's friend; she is clearly a sorority girl; even wearing her pin with its tiny diamonds and rubies just above her left breast. Her high delicate laughter echoes that of the others', . . . she isn't going to laugh coarsely here, or say anything witty and obscene . . . she can be a little mischievous, just a little cutting, at best. Marya notes how refined her table manners have become for the occasion; how practiced she is at passing things about, summoning one of the houseboys for assistance without quite looking at him. (The houseboy in his white uniform!—one of a subdued and faintly embarrassed little squadron of four or five boys, he turns out to be an acquaintance of Marya's from her Shakespeare class, who resolutely avoids her eye throughout the prolonged meal.)

Marya makes little effort to take part in the table's conversation, which swings from campus topics to vacation plans—Miami Beach, Sarasota, Bermuda, the Barbados, Trinidad, Switzerland ("for skiing"). Where are you going, Imogene asks Marya brightly, and Marya, with a pinched little smile says she will spend a few days at home, then return to school; she has work to do that must be done here. And Imogene's friends gaze upon her with faint neutral smiles. Is this the one Imogene boasted of, who is so intelligent and so well-spoken . . . ? So *witty* . . . ?

For days Marya has been anticipating this dinner, half in dread and half in simple childish excitement. She feared being ravenous with hunger and eating too much out of anxiety; she feared having no appetite at all. But everything is remote, detached, impersonal. Everything is taking place at a little distance from her. A mistake, my coming here, she thinks, my being invited. But she doesn't feel any great nervousness or discomfort. Like the uniformed houseboys who stand with such unnatural stiffness near the doorway to the kitchen, Marya is simply waiting for the meal to end.

She finds herself thinking of friendship, in the past tense. Phyllis, and Diane, and one or two others at Maynard; and, back in Innisfail, Bonnie Michalak, Erma Dietz. She *might* have been a close friend to any of these girls but of course she wasn't, isn't. As for Imogene—she knows she is disappointing Imogene but she can't seem to force herself to care. She halfway resents Imogene for having invited her—for having made a fool out of *herself,* in bringing Marya Knauer to dinner.

How pretty you look, Imogene said, very nearly puzzled, when Marya arrived at six-thirty,—what have you *done* to yourself?

Marya flushed with annoyance; then laughed; with such exuberance that Imogene laughed with her. For it *was* amusing, wasn't it?—Marya Knauer with her hair attractively up in a sort of French twist; Marya Knauer with her lips reddened, and her eyebrows plucked ("pruned," she might have said), Marya Knauer in a green-striped jersey dress that fitted her almost perfectly. A formal dinner meant high heels and stockings, which Marya detested; but she was wearing them none-theless. And all for Imogene.

Yet now, seated beside Imogene, she pays very little attention to her friend's chatter; she feels subdued, saddened; thinking instead of old friendships, old half-friendships, that year or so during which she'd imagined herself extraordinary, because it had seemed that Emmett Schroeder loved her. She had not loved him—she wasn't capable, she supposed, of loving anyone—but she had certainly basked in the sunny intensity of *his* love: she'd lapped it up eagerly, thirstily (so she very nearly saw herself, a dog lapping water) as if convinced that it had something to do with her. And now Imogene's friendship, which she knows she cannot keep for very long . . . Imogene who has a reputation for being as recklessly improvident with her female friends as with her male friends. . . . Why make the effort, Marya reasons, when all that matters in life is one's personal accomplishment? Work, success, that numbing grade-point average . . . that promise of a future, any future. . . .

While Imogene and several of the others are discussing (animatedly, severely) a sorority sister not present, Marya studies her face covertly; recalls an odd remark Imogene made some weeks ago. The measure of a person's love for you is the depth of his hurt at your betrayal; *that's* the only way you can know how much, or how little, you matter.

Imogene's face had fairly glowed in excited triumph, as she told Marya this bit of wisdom. Marya thought,—She knows from experi-ence, the bitch. She knows her own value.

Imogene is telling a silly convoluted story about a dear friend of hers (it turns out to be Matthew, devoted Matthew) who "helped" her with her term paper on Chekhov: she'd given him a messy batch of notes, he was kind enough to "arrange" them and "expand upon them" and "shape them into an 'A' paper." He's a saint, Imogene says sighing, laughing,—so sweet and so patient; so pathetic, really. But now Im-ogene is worried ("terrified") that their professor will call her into his office and interrogate her on her own paper, which she hadn't the time to read in its entirety; it was thirty pages long and heavy with footnotes. The girls assure her that if he marked it "A" it *is* an "A"; he'd never ask to see it again. Yes, says Imogene, opening her eyes wide,—but wait until he reads my final exam, and I say these ridiculous things about Chekhov!

Part of this is play-acting, Marya knows, because Imogene is quite intelligent enough, on the subject of Chekhov or anything else connected with drama; so Marya says, though not loudly enough for the entire table to hear: "That wasn't a very kind thing for *you* to do, was it?—and not very honest either."

Imogene chooses not to hear the tone of Marya's remark; she says gaily: "Oh you mean leading poor Matt on? Making him think—? But otherwise he wouldn't have written so *well*, there wouldn't have been so many impressive *footnotes*."

Marya doesn't reply. Marya draws her thumbnail hard against the linen tablecloth, making a secret indentation.

Imogene says, making a joke of it: "Marya's such a puritan—I know better than to ask help of *her*."

Marya doesn't rise to the bait; the conversation shifts onto other topics; in another fifteen minutes the lengthy dinner is over.

"You aren't going home immediately, are you?" Imogene says, surprised. She is smiling but there are strain lines around her mouth. "Come upstairs to my room for a while. Come on, we haven't had a chance to talk."

"Thank you for everything," says Marya. "But I really have to leave. I'm pressed for time these days. . . ."

"You *are* angry?—about that silly Matthew?" Imogene says.

Marya shrugs her shoulders, turns indifferently away.

"Well—are *you* so honest?" Imogene cries.

Marya gets her coat from the closet, her face burning. (Are *you* so honest! *You!*) Imogene is apologizing, talking of other things, laughing, while Marya thinks calmly that she will never see Imogene Skillman again.

"There's no reason why you shouldn't take this coat, it's a perfectly good coat," Imogene said in her "serious" voice—frank, level, un-emphatic. "I don't want it any longer because I have so many coats, I never get to wear it and it *is* perfectly lovely, it shouldn't just hang in the closet. . . . Anyway here it is; I think it would look wonderful on you."

Marya stared at the coat. It was the camel's hair she had long admired. Pleasantly scratchy beneath her fingers, belted in back, with a beautiful silky-beige lining: she estimated it would have cost $250 or more, new. And it was almost new.

(Marya's coat, bought two or three years before in Innisfail, had cost $45 on sale.)

Imogene insisted, and Marya tried on the coat, flicking her hair out from inside the collar, studying herself critically in Imogene's full-length mirror. Imogene was saying, "If you're worrying that people will know it's my coat—it *was* my coat—don't: camel's hair coats all look alike. Except they don't look like wool imitations."

Marya met Imogene's frank blue gaze in the mirror. "What about your parents, your mother?—won't someone wonder where the coat has gone?"

Imogene puckered her forehead quizzically. "What business is it of theirs?" she asked. "It's *my* coat. My things are mine, I do what I want with them."

Marya muttered that she just couldn't *take* the coat, and Imogene scolded her for talking with her jaw clenched, and Marya protested in a louder voice, yet still faintly, weakly. . . . "It's a beautiful coat," she said. She was thinking: It's too good for me, I can't accept and I can't refuse and I hate Imogene for this humiliation.

Imogene brought the episode to an end by saying rather coldly: "You'll hurt my feelings, Knauer, if you refuse it. If you're weighing your pride against mine, don't bother—mine is far, far more of a burden."

"So you are—Marya," Mrs. Skillman said in an ambiguous voice (warm? amused? doubtful?) in the drab front parlor of Maynard House, as Marya approached. She and Mr. Skillman and Imogene were taking Marya out to dinner, downtown at the Statler Chop House, one of the area's legendary good restaurants. "We've heard so much about you from Imogene," Mrs. Skillman said, "I think we were expecting someone more. . . ."

"Oh Mother, what on earth—!" Imogene laughed sharply.

". . . I was going to say *taller*, perhaps *older*," Mrs. Skillman said, clearly annoyed by her daughter's interruption.

Marya shook hands with both the Skillmans and saw to her relief that they appeared to be friendly well-intentioned people, attractive enough, surely, and very well-dressed, but nothing like their striking daughter. *She* might have been their daughter, brunette and subdued. (Except she hadn't dared wear the camel's hair coat, as Imogene had wanted. She was wearing her old plaid wool and her serviceable rubberized boots.)

In their presence Imogene was a subtly different person. Rather more disingenuous, childlike, sweet. Now and then at dinner Marya heard a certain self-mocking tone in her friend's voice ("am I playing this scene correctly?—how is it going down?") but neither of the Skillmans took notice; and perhaps it was Marya's imagination anyway.

Then, near the end of the meal, Imogene got suddenly high on white wine and said of her father's business: "It's a sophisticated form of theft."

She giggled, no one else laughed; Marya kept her expression carefully blank.

". . . I mean it *is*, you know . . . it's indirect . . . 'Savings and Loans' . . . and half the clients blacks who want their Dee-troit cars financed," Imogene said.

"Imogene, you aren't funny," Mrs. Skillman said.

"She's just teasing," Mr. Skillman said. "My little girl likes to tease."

"I do like to tease, don't I?—Marya knows," Imogene said, nudging her. Then, as if returning to her earlier sobriety, she said: "*I never mean a word of what I say and everybody knows it.*"

The subject leapt to Imogene's negligence about writing letters, or even telephoning home. "If we try to call," Mrs. Skillman said, "the line at the residence is busy for hours; and when we finally get through you aren't in; you're *never* in. And you never return our calls. . . ."

Imogene said carelessly that her sorority sisters were bad at taking down messages. Most of them were assholes, actually—

"Imogene!" Mrs. Skillman said.

"Oh Mother you know they *are*," Imogene said in a childlike voice.

After an awkward pause Mr. Skillman asked about Richard: Richard had evidently telephoned *them*, asking if something was wrong with Imogene because he couldn't get through to her either. "Your mother and I were hoping there wasn't some sort of . . . misunderstanding between you."

Imogene murmured that there weren't any misunderstandings at all between them.

"He seemed to think . . . to wonder . . ." Mrs. Skillman said. "That is, as long as we were driving up to visit. . . ."

Imogene finished off her glass of white wine and closed her eyes ecstatically. She said: "I really don't care to discuss my private matters in a restaurant.—Anyway Marya is here: why don't we talk about something lofty and intellectual? *She's* taking a philosophy course—if she can't tell us the meaning of life no one can."

"You and Richard haven't quarrelled, have you?" Mrs. Skillman said.

Imogene raised her left hand and showed the diamond ring to her mother, saying, "*Please* don't worry, I haven't given it back, it's safe." To Marya she said lightly: "Mother would be mortified if Dickie demanded it back. It's somebody's old dead socialite *grandmother's*."

"Imogene," Mr. Skillman said, his voice edged with impatience, "you really shouldn't tease so much. I've just read that teasing is a form of aggression . . . did you know that?"

"Not that I'd give it back if Dickie *did* demand it," Imogene laughed. "It's mine, I've earned it, let him *sue* to get it back—right, Marya?— he's going to be a hotshot lawyer after all. Let him *practice.*"

Everyone, including Marya, laughed as if Imogene had said something unusually witty; and Imogene, in the cool voice she used to summon the houseboys at her sorority, asked a passing waiter for more wine.

Richard.

"Dickie."

Am I jealous of someone called "Dickie," Marya wondered, lying sprawled and slovenly across her bed. She was doing rough, impatient charcoal sketches of imaginary faces—beetle-browed, glowering, defiantly ugly—that inevitably turned out to be forms of her own.

In Imogene's cluttered room on the second floor of the baronial sorority house Marya had come upon, to her astonishment, copies of *Bride* magazine. She leafed through them, jeering, while Imogene hid her face in laughing protestation. Wedding gowns! Satin and pearls! Veils made of antique lace! Orange blossoms! Shoes covered in white silk! And what is this, Marya said, flapping the pages in Imogene's direction,—a wedding-cake bridegroom to go with it all?—standing a little out of the range of the camera's focus, amiable and blurred.

"Ah, but you'll have to be a bridesmaid," Imogene said dryly. "Or a maid of honor."

Imogene showed her snapshots of the legendary Richard, flicking them like playing cards. Marya saw that, yes, Richard was a handsome young man—dark strong features, a slightly heavy chin, intelligent eyes. He was demanding, perhaps; an excellent match for Imogene. But it was difficult, Marya thought, to believe that the person in the snapshots —*this* person, standing with his hands on his hips, his hair lifting in the wind—would be capable of loving Imogene as much as she required being loved.

Imogene threw herself across her bed, lay on her back, let her long hair dangle to the floor. Her belly was stretched flat; her pelvic bones protruded. She smoothed her shirt across her abdomen with long nervous fingers. ". . . The first time I came with him," she said hesitantly, but with a breathy laugh, "it wasn't . . . you know . . . it wasn't with him inside me, the way you're supposed to . . . I was afraid of that then, I thought I might get pregnant. And he was so big, I thought he'd hurt me, they're *very* big compared to . . . compared to us. The first time it worked for me he was, well, you know, kissing me there . . . he'd gotten all crazy and wild and I couldn't stop him, and I never thought I would let anyone do that . . . I'd *heard* about that . . . because . . . oh Marya, am I embarrassing you? . . . because afterward," she said, laughing shrilly, "they only want to kiss you: and it's disgusting."

She rolled over amidst the tumble of things strewn on her bed and hid her face from Marya.

After a long time she said, her breath labored, her face still turned away: "Am I embarrassing you?"

Marya's throat and chest were so constricted, she couldn't reply.

A Marya Knauer anecdote, told by Imogene with peals of cruel ribald laughter. . . .

Imogene insisted that Marya accompany her on a date, yes a "date," an actual "date" (though it was generally thought that Marya shunned men because she imagined they weren't *serious* enough). Her escort was Matthew Fein, of all people—Matthew who had seemed to dislike Marya but who in fact (so Imogene revealed) had simply been afraid of her.

"Afraid of me?—you're being ridiculous," Marya said. She hardly knew whether to be hurt or flattered.

"Of course he's afraid of you, or was," Imogene said. "And my poor sorority sisters!—they told me afterward they'd never seen such eyes as yours—taking them all in and condemning them! *Those assholes!*"

It would be an ordinary evening, Imogene promised, no need to dress up, no *need* for the high-heels-stockings routine, though it was perfectly all right (so Imogene said innocently) if Marya wanted to comb her hair. Imogene's date for the evening was a senior in business administration and advertising whose name Marya never caught, or purposefully declined to hear. They drove out to a suburban mall to see a movie—in fact it was a pretentious French "film"—and then they went to a local Italian restaurant where everyone, excepting of course Marya, drank too much; and then they drove to the water-tower hill where numerous other cars were parked, their headlights off. Marya stiffened. Matthew had not yet touched her but she knew that he would be kissing her in another minute; and she had no idea of how to escape gracefully.

". . . Few minutes?" Imogene murmured from the front seat.

She was sending them away!—Marya saw with disbelief that, by the time she and Matthew climbed out of the car, Imogene and her date were locked in a ravenous embrace. One would have thought the two of them lovers; one would have thought them at least fond of each other. Marya's heart was beating frantically. That bitch! That bitch! Marya worried that she might suffocate—she couldn't seem to catch her breath.

Matthew took her cold unresisting hand. He slipped his arm around her shoulders.

They were meant to stroll for a few minutes along the darkened path, to contemplate, perhaps, the view of Port Oriskany below, all sparkling winking lights. A romantic sight, no doubt. Beautiful in its way. Matthew was saying something rather forced—making a joke of some kind—about the French movie?—about Imogene's reckless behavior?—but Marya interrupted. "Isn't she supposed to be engaged?" she asked. "Yes, I suppose so," Matthew said in resignation, "but she does this all the time. It's just Imogene." "She does this all the *time?*" Marya said, "but why—?" Matthew laughed uncomfortably. He was not quite Marya's height and his dark eyes shied away from hers. "I don't know," he said defensively, "—as I said, it's just Imogene, it's her business. Why shouldn't she do what she wants to do? Don't be angry with *me.*"

He was nervous yet keenly excited; Marya sensed his sexual agitation. Behind them, parked along the gravelled drive, were lovers' cars, one after another; from this distance, the car in which Imogene and her "date" were pawing at each other was undistinguishable from the others.

"You might not approve," Matthew said, his voice edged now with an air of authority, "—but Imogene is a free soul, she does what she wants, I don't suppose she actually *lies* to her fiancé. He'd have to allow her some freedom, you know, or she'd break off the engagement."

"You know a lot about her," Marya said.

"Imogene is a close friend of mine, we've worked together . . . I was stage manager for *Hedda Gabler,* don't you remember?"

"It's all so . . . trivial," Marya said slowly. "So degrading."

"What do you mean?"

"Oh—this."

"This—?"

Marya indicated the cars parked along the drive. Her expression was contemptuous.

"You take an awfully superior attitude, don't you," Matthew said, with an attempt at jocular irony. He tightened his arm around her shoulders; he drew nearer. Marya could hear his quickened breathing.

Is this idiot really going to kiss me, Marya wondered. Her heart was still beating heavily; she could see Imogene's profile, the cameo-clear outline of her face, illuminated for an instant as the headlights were extinguished. Then she moved into the young man's embrace, she kissed him, slid her arms around his neck. . . .

"Does she make love with them?" Marya asked.

"Them—?"

"Different boys. Men. One week after another."

"I don't know," Matthew said resentfully. "I suppose so—if she wants to."

"I thought *you* were in love with her," Marya said mockingly.

"We're just friends," Matthew said, offended.

"Oh no," said Marya, "—everyone knows you're in *love* with her."

Matthew drew away from Marya and walked beside her without speaking. There was nothing for them to do, suddenly; not a thing left to say. It was still March and quite cold. Their footsteps sounded dully on the crusted snow. Marya thought, The various ways we seek out our humiliations. . . .

After a few minutes Matthew said something conciliatory about the night, the stars, the city lights, "infinity," certain remarks of Pascal's; but Marya made no effort to listen. She kept seeing Imogene kissing that near-stranger, Imogene locking her arms about his neck *as if he mattered. As if they were lovers.*

She was going to observe aloud, cynically, that making love was as good a way as any of passing the time, if you hadn't anything better to do, when Matthew, brave Matthew, turned to her and took hold of her shoulders and tried to kiss her. It was a desperate gesture—his breath smelled of sweet red wine—but Marya would have none of it. She shoved him roughly in the chest.

"Marya, for Christ's sake grow up," Matthew said angrily. "You're a big girl now—"

"Why should you *kiss* me?" Marya said, equally angry, "—when you don't even *like* me? When you know I don't like you in the slightest, when we haven't anything to say to each other, when we're just waiting for the evening to get finished!—in fact we've been made fools of, both of us. And now you want to kiss me," she said, jeering, "—just for something to do."

He began to protest but Marya dismissed him with a derisory wave of her hand. She was going to walk back to the residence, she said; she was through with them all. Especially Imogene.

Matthew followed along behind her for a few minutes, trying to talk her into coming back to the car. It was almost midnight, he said; the campus was two miles away; what if something happened to her. . . . Marya ignored him and walked faster, descending the hill past a slow stream of cars that were ascending it, their headlights blinding her eyes. She lowered her head, tried to hide her face, her hands thrust deep in the pockets of her camel's hair coat. At first she was furious—almost sick with fury—her head rang with accusations against Imogene—but the cold still night air was so invigorating, so wonderfully cleansing, she felt quite good by the time she got to Maynard House, not very long after midnight. She felt *very* good.

Next day, Sunday, Imogene stood at the downstairs desk ringing Marya's buzzer repeatedly, one two three four, one two three four, and then one long rude ring, until Marya appeared at the top of the stairs, her hair in a towel. "Who the hell—?" she called down. She and Imogene stared at each other. Then Imogene said contemptuously, "Here's your purse, you left your purse in the car, Knauer. D'you know, Knauer, your behavior is getting eccentric; it isn't even amusing, just what if something had happened to you last night—walking back here all alone—a college girl, in some of those neighborhoods!—don't you think Lyle and Matt and I would feel responsible? But *you*," she said, her voice rising, "—*you* haven't the slightest sense of—of responsibility to other people—"

"Just leave the purse," Marya said, leaning over the bannister. "Leave it and go back to screwing what's-his-name—that's *your* responsibility—"

"Go screw yourself!" Imogene shouted. "Go fuck yourself!"

"Go fuck *yourself!*" Marya shouted.

As the stories sifted back to Marya, over a period of a week or ten days, they became increasingly disturbing, ugly.

In one version Marya Knauer had been almost attacked—that is, raped—in a black neighborhood near the foot of Tower Hill; and had run back to her residence hall, hysterical and sobbing. It was an even graver insult that her purse had been taken from her—her purse and all her money.

In another version, Marya was so panicked at being simply touched by her date (she was a virgin, she was frigid, she'd never been kissed before) that she ran from the car, hysterical and panting . . . ran all the way back to campus. The boy was a blind date, someone in drama, or maybe business administration, it was all a total surprise to him that Marya Knauer was so . . . crazy.

In a third improbable version it was Imogene Skillman's fiancé who offered to take Marya back to the residence, because she was so upset —having a breakdown of some kind—and when they were halfway there she threw herself on him in the car *while he was actually driving.*

And then, ashamed, she opened the car door and jumped out *while the car was still in motion.*

"It's Imogene," Marya said, licking her numbed lips. "She's making these things up . . . Why is she *doing* this to me . . . !"

There were vague rumors too that Marya had borrowed small sums of money from Imogene. And items of clothing as well—the camel's hair coat, for instance. (Because she hadn't a coat of her own. Because her coat had literally gone to shreds. Because she was so *poor,* a scholarship student from the hills, practically a *hillbilly.* . . .) As far as she was concerned, Imogene was reported saying, Marya Knauer could keep the coat if she was that desperate. Imogene no longer wanted it back.

Marya telephoned Imogene and accused her of telling lies, of telling slanderous tales. "Do you think I don't know who's behind this?" Marya cried. But Imogene hung up at once: Imogene was too wise to reply.

Marya began to see how people watched her . . . smiling covertly as she passed. They were pitying her, yet merciless. They knew. Marya Knauer with all her pretensions, Marya Knauer who had made a fool of herself with another girls' fiancé, Marya Knauer who was cracking up. . . .

In the fluorescent-lit dining hall she sat alone in an alcove, eating quickly, her head bowed; it was too much trouble to remove her plates and glass of water from the tray. Two boys passed near and she heard them laugh softly. . . . *That* the one? There? one of them whispered. She turned back to her book (. . . *the thought of suicide is a strong consolation, one can get through many a bad night with it*) but the print danced crazily in her eyes.

"Do you think I don't know who's behind this,—who's responsible?" Marya asked aloud, in anguish, in the privacy of her room. She tried to lock her door from the inside—as if there were any danger of being interrupted, invaded—but the doors in Maynard, as in university housing generally, did not lock in that direction.

At about this time Marya was notified that a short story she had submitted to a national competition had placed first; and, not long afterward—within a week or ten days, in fact—she learned that another story, sent out blindly and naively to a distinguished literary magazine, was accepted for publication.

She thought of telephoning Wilma and Everard . . . she thought of telephoning Imogene . . . running along the corridors of Maynard House, knocking on doors, sharing her good news. But her elation was tempered almost at once by a kind of sickened dread—she was going to be unequal to the task of whatever it was (so her panicked thoughts raced, veered) she might be expected to do.

Lately her "serious" writing frightened her. Not just the content itself —though the content was often wild, disturbing, unanticipated—but the emotional and psychological strain it involved. She could write all night long, sprawled across her bed, taking notes, drafting out sketches and scenes, narrating a story she seemed to be hearing in a kind of trance; she could write until her hand ached and her eyes filled with tears and she felt that another pulsebeat would push her over the brink —into despair, into madness, into sheer extinction. Nothing is worth this, she told herself early one morning, nothing can be worth this, she thought, staring at herself in the mirror of the third floor bathroom,— a ghastly hollowed-eyed death's head of a face, hardly recognizable as Marya, as a girl of nineteen.

Give up. Don't risk it. *Don't* risk it.

So she cautioned herself, so she gave and took warning. There was another kind of writing—highly conscious, cerebral, critical, discursive —which she found far easier; far less dangerous. She was praised for it lavishly, given the highest grades, the most splendid sort of encouragement. She should plan, her professors said, to go on to graduate school . . . they would advise her, help her get placed, help her make her way. . . . Don't risk this, she told herself, the waters will suck you down and close over your head: I know the symptoms.

And she did, she did. As if she had lived a previous life and could recall vividly the anguish of . . . whatever it was that might happen.

One windy morning at the end of March she saw Imogene Skillman walking with several of her friends. Imogene in sunglasses, her hair blowing wild, her laughter shrill and childish, Imogene in tight-fitting jeans and a bulky white ski sweater, overlong in the sleeves. That slatternly waifish affect. . . . Marya stood watching. Staring. Poor Marya Knauer, staring. Why did you lie about me! she wanted to cry. Why did you betray me! But she stood silent, paralyzed, watching. No doubt a figure of pathos—or of comedy—her snarled black hair blowing wild as Imogene's, her skin grainy and sallow.

Of course Imogene saw her; but Imogene's eyes were discreetly hidden by the dark-tinted glasses. No need for her to give any sign of recognition. No need.

Marya wrote Imogene a muddled little note, the first week in April. *Things aren't going well for me, I missed a philosophy exam & have no excuse*

& can't make myself lie. I don't know . . . am I unhappy (is it that simple?)
Why don't you drop by & see me sometime . . . or I could come over there &
see you. . . .

Yet she felt a revulsion for Imogene; she *really* disliked her. That
lazy drunken dip of her head, her lipstick smeared across her face,
sliding her arms around the neck of . . . whoever it had been: kissing
open-mouthed, simulating passion. Would you two let us alone for a
few minutes, Imogene drawled,—Would you two like to go for a stroll,
for a few minutes?

I'll come over there, Marya wrote, *and strangle you with that pretentious*
braid of yours.

In all she wrote a dozen notes, some by hand and some on the
typewriter. But she sent only the first ("why don't you drop by & see
me sometime . . . or I could come over there & see you"), not expecting,
and not receiving, an answer.

What is fictitious in a friendship, Marya pondered, and what is "real":
the world outside the head, the world *inside:* but whose world?—from
whose point of view?

If Imogene died. . . .

If Imogene were dying. . . .

She wouldn't lift a hand to prevent that death!—so she thought.

At the same time she quizzed herself about how to respond, should
Imogene really ask her to be a bridesmaid. (She had declined being a
bridesmaid at Alice's wedding; but then she had the excuse of school-
work, distance.) Imogene's wedding was going to be a costly affair held
in Long Beach, New York sometime the following year. The bridesmaid's
dress, the shoes . . . the shoes alone . . . would be staggeringly
expensive.

I can't afford it, Marya would say.

I can't afford *you.*

Though they hadn't any classes together this semester Marya learned
that Imogene had been absent from one of her lectures for three days
running. So she simply went, one rainy April afternoon, to Imogene's
residence—to that absurd white-columned "house" on Masefield Avenue—and rapped hard on Imogene's door; and let herself in before
Imogene could call out sleepily, who is it . . . ?

The shades were crookedly drawn. Clothes and towels and books
were strewn about. Imogene lay half-undressed on the bed with the
quilted spread pulled over her; the room smelled of something acrid and
medicinal.

"Oh Marya," Imogene said guiltily.

"Are you sick?" Marya asked.

They had both spoken at the same time.

". . . a headache, cramps, nothing worth mentioning," Imogene said hoarsely. ". . . the tail-end of this shitty flu that's been going around."

Marya stood with her hands on her hips, regarding Imogene in bed. Imogene's skin looked oddly coarse, her hair lay in spent greasy tangles on the pillow, spilling off the edge of the bed; her body was flat, curiously immobile. Without makeup she looked both young and rather ravaged. "If you're really sick, if you need a doctor, your sorority sisters will see to it," Marya said half-mockingly.

"I'm not really sick," said Imogene at once. "I'm resting."

After a long pause Marya said, as if incidentally: "You told so many lies about me."

Imogene coughed feebly. "They weren't exactly *lies,* there was an essence. . . ."

"They were lies," Marya said. "I wanted to strangle you."

Imogene lay without moving, her hands flat on her stomach. She said in a childish vague voice: "Oh nobody believed anything, it was just . . . talk . . . spinning tales. . . . You know, thinking 'What if' . . . that sort of thing. Anyway there was an *essence* that was true."

Marya was pacing about the room, the balls of her feet springy, the tendons of her calves strained. "I don't intend to let you destroy me," she said softly. "I don't even intend to do poorly in my courses." She brushed her hair out of her face and half-smiled at Imogene—a flash of hatred. "You won't make me lose my perfect record," she said.

"Won't I," said Imogene.

Marya laughed. She said: "But why did you concoct a story about your fiancé and me?—you know I've never even met him; I don't have any interest in meeting him."

"Yes you do," Imogene said, a little sharply. "You're jealous of him —of him and me."

"You're angry that I'm not jealous *enough,*" Marya said. "Do you think I'd want to sleep with your precious, 'Dickie'?"

"You think so goddam fucking highly of yourself, don't you," Imogene said, sitting up, adjusting a pillow impatiently behind her. "*You* can't be cracked open, can you?—a nut that can't be cracked," she said, laughing, yawning. "A tight little virgin, I suppose. And Catholic too! —what a joke! Very very proud of yourself."

"Why didn't you talk to me on the phone, why didn't you answer my note?" Marya asked quietly.

"Why did you avoid me on campus?"

"Avoid you when?"

"Why do you always look the other way?"

"Look the other way *when*—?"

"All the time."

Marya was striking her hands, her fists, lightly together. She drew a deep shaky breath. "As for the coat—you *gave* me the coat. Your precious Salvation Army gesture. You *gave* me the coat, you *forced* it on me."

"Oh Knauer, nobody forces anything on *you*," Imogene said, sneering. "What bullshit—!"

"I want to know why you've been spreading lies about me and ridiculing me behind my back," Marya said levelly.

Imogene pulled at her hair in a lazy, mawkishly theatrical gesture. "Hey. Did I tell you. I'm transferring out of here next year," she said. "I'm going to school somewhere in New York, N.Y.U. probably. The drama courses are too *restrained* here, there's too much crap about *tradition.* . . ."

"I said I want to know *why*."

"Oh for Christ's sweet sake what are you talking about!" Imogene cried. "I'm sick, my head is spinning, if you don't leave me alone I'm going to puke all over everything. I haven't been to a class in two weeks and I don't give a damn but I refuse to give *you* the satisfaction. . . . Transfer to New York, Marya, why don't you: you know you think you're too good for us *here*."

Marya stared at her, trembling. She had a vision of running at her friend and pummelling her with her fists—the two of them fighting, clawing, grunting in silence.

"Your jealousy, your morbid possessiveness. . . ." Imogene was saying wildly, her eyes wide, ". . . the way you sat in judgment of my parents . . . my poor father trying so hard to be *nice* to you, to be *kind*, because he felt *sorry* for you . . . and my mother too . . . .'Is she one of your strays and misfits?' Mother said, 'another one of that gang that will turn on you'. . . . As for my sorority sisters. . . ."

Marya said slowly, groping: "And what about you? You're spoiled, you're vicious. . . . And you don't even act that well: people here baby you, lie to you, tell you the kind of crap you want to hear."

At this Imogene threw herself back against the flattened pillows, laughing, half-sobbing. "Yes," she said. "Good. Now leave me alone."

"Do you think they tell you anything else?—anything else but crap?" Marya said carelessly, "—people who are in love with you? People who don't even know who you *are*?"

Imogene pawed at the bedspread and pulled it roughly over herself.

She lay very still but Marya could hear her labored breath. ". . . I took some aspirin before you came in, I want to sleep, maybe you'd better let me alone. I think you'd better let me alone."

She closed her eyes, she waved Marya away with a languid gesture. "Good-bye, Marya!" she whispered.

On the sidewalk outside the house Marya took out the earrings boldly to examine them.

The Aztec ones, the barbarian-princess ones, bronze and red and blue, burnished, gleaming. . . . Marya had seen her hand reach out to take them but she did not remember *taking* them from the room.

She tossed them in the palm of her hand as she strode along Masefield Avenue, smiling, grinning. No one, she thought in triumph, can keep me from my perfect record.

She went that day to an earring shop down on Fairfield Street; asked to have her ears pierced and Imogene's splendid earrings inserted. But the proprietor told her that wasn't the procedure; first, gold studs are inserted . . . then, after a few weeks, when the wounds are healed. . . .

No, Marya insisted, put in *these*. I don't have time to waste.

But there was the danger of infection, she was told. Everything has to be germ-free, antiseptic. . . .

"I don't give a damn about that," Marya said fiercely. "These earrings *are* gold. Put antiseptic on *them*. . . . Just pierce my ears and put them in and I'll pay you and that's all."

"Do you have five dollars?" the young man said curtly.

Crossing the quadrangle between Stafford Hall and the chapel one cold May afternoon, Marya caught sight of Imogene approaching her. It had been approximately two weeks since the theft of the earrings—two weeks during which Marya had worn the earrings everywhere, for everyone to see, to comment upon, to admire. She and Imogene had frequently noticed each other, usually at a distance, though once in rather close quarters on a crowded stairway; and Marya had been amused at Imogene's shocked expression; and the clumsy way she'd turned aside, pretending she hadn't seen Marya and Marya's new earrings.

Not a very good actress after all, Marya thought.

Now, however, Imogene was approaching her head-on, though her movements were rather forced, wooden. Marya didn't slacken her pace; she was headed for the library. She wore her raincoat half-unbuttoned, her head was bare, her hair loose, the earrings swung heavily as she walked, tugged at her earlobes. (Yes, her earlobes *were* sore. Probably infected, Marya thought indifferently, waking in the night to small stabs of pain.)

Imogene's face was dead white, and not very attractive. Something horsy about that face, after all, Marya thought. Her mouth was strained, and the tendons in her neck were clearly visible as, suddenly, she ran at Marya. She was screaming something about "hillbilly bitch"—"thief" —She grabbed at Marya's left ear, she would have ripped the earring out of Marya's flesh, but Marya was too quick for her: she knew instinctively what Imogene would try to do.

She struck Imogene's hand aside, and gave her a violent shove; Imogene slapped her hard across the face; Marya slapped *her.* "You bitch!" Imogene cried. "You won't get away with this! *I know you!*"

All their books had fallen to the sidewalk, Imogene's leather bag was tripping her up, passers-by stopped to stare, incredulous. What a sight, Imogene Skillman and Marya Knauer fighting, in front of the chapel,—both in blue jeans, both livid with rage. Marya was shouting, "Don't you touch me, you! What do you mean, touching *me!*" She was the better fighter, crouching with her knees bent, like a man, swinging at Imogene, striking her on the jaw. Not a slap but an actual punch: Marya's fist was unerring.

The blow was a powerful one, for Marya struck from the shoulder. Imogene's head snapped back—blood appeared on her mouth—she staggered backward and swayed, almost lost her balance. "Oh, Marya," she said.

Marya snatched up her things and turned away. Her long fast stride and the set of her shoulders, the set of her head, must have indicated confidence; angry assurance; but in fact she was badly shaken . . . it was some time before she could catch her breath. When she turned to look back Imogene was sitting on the ground and a small crowd had gathered around her. You'll be all right, Marya thought, someone will always take care of *you.*

After that, very little happened.

Marya kept the earrings, though her ears *were* infected and she had to give up wearing them; Imogene Skillman never approached her again, never pressed charges; nor did anyone dare bring the subject up to either of the girls.

Marya's record remained perfect but Imogene did poorly at the end of the semester, failing two subjects; and, in place of transferring to another university she quit college altogether.

That fall, Marya learned that Imogene was living in New York City. She had broken off her engagement over the summer; she had joined a troupe of semiprofessional actors, and lived in an apartment off St.

Mark's Square. It was said that she had a small role in an off-Broadway play scheduled to open sometime that winter but Marya never learned the title of the play, or when, precisely, it opened; or how successful it was.

1989

BHARATI MUKHERJEE

The Tenant

Maya Sanyal has been in Cedar Falls, Iowa, less than two weeks. She's come, books and clothes and one armchair rattling in the smallest truck that U-Haul would rent her, from New Jersey. Before that she was in North Carolina. Before that, Calcutta, India. Every place has something to give. She is sitting at the kitchen table with Fran drinking bourbon for the first time in her life. Fran Johnson found her the furnished apartment and helped her settle in. Now she's brought a bottle of bourbon which gives her the right to stay and talk for a bit. She's breaking up with someone named Vern, a pharmacist. Vern's father is also a pharmacist and owns a drugstore. Maya has seen Vern's father on TV twice already. The first time was on the local news when he spoke out against the selling of painkillers like Advil and Nuprin in supermarkets and gas stations. In the matter of painkillers, Maya is a universalist. The other time he was in a barbershop quartet. Vern gets along all right with his father. He likes the pharmacy business, as business goes, but

Bharati Mukherjee's life embodies many of the cultural confrontations and reconciliations that her novels and short stories so acutely describe. Mukherjee was born July 27, 1940, in Calcutta, India, lived much of her childhood with her family in London, and received academic degrees from the universities of Calcutta, Baroda, and Iowa (where she now teaches). For ten years she and her husband—the novelist Clark Blaise—lived and wrote in Canada, eventually returning to the United States in 1980. Accounts of the intricate process of becoming an "American" compose much of her recent fiction, such as the novel *Jasmine* (1989). Mukherjee's 1988 collection *The Middleman and Other Stories* received the National Book Critics Circle Award for fiction.

he wants to go back to graduate school and learn to make films. Maya is drinking her first bourbon tonight because Vern left today for San Francisco State.

"I understand totally," Fran says. She teaches Utopian Fiction and a course in Women's Studies and worked hard to get Maya hired. Maya has a Ph.D. in Comparative Literature and will introduce writers like R. K. Narayan and Chinua Achebe to three sections of sophomores at the University of Northern Iowa. "A person has to leave home. Try out his wings."

Fran has to use the bathroom. "I don't feel abandoned." She pushes her chair away from the table. "Anyway, it was a sex thing totally. We were good together. It'd be different if I'd loved him."

Maya tries to remember what's in the refrigerator. They need food. She hasn't been to the supermarket in over a week. She doesn't have a car yet and so she relies on a corner store—a longish walk—for milk, cereal, and frozen dinners. Someday these exigencies will show up as bad skin and collapsed muscle tone. No folly is ever lost. Maya pictures history as a net, the kind of safety net travelling trapeze artists of her childhood fell into when they were inattentive, or clumsy. Going to circuses in Calcutta with her father is what she remembers vividly. It is a banal memory, for her father, the owner of a steel company, is a complicated man.

Fran is out in the kitchen long enough for Maya to worry. They need food. Her mother believed in food. What is love, anger, inner peace, etc., her mother used to say, but the brain's biochemistry. Maya doesn't want to get into that, but she is glad she has enough stuff in the refrigerator to make an omelette. She realizes Indian women are supposed to be inventive with food, whip up exotic delights to tickle an American's palate, and she knows she should be meeting Fran's generosity and candor with some sort of bizarre and effortless countermove. If there's an exotic spice store in Cedar Falls or in neighboring Waterloo, she hasn't found it. She's looked in the phone book for common Indian names, especially Bengali, but hasn't yet struck up culinary intimacies. That will come—it always does. There's a six-pack in the fridge that her landlord, Ted Suminski, had put in because she'd be thirsty after unpacking. She was thirsty, but she doesn't drink beer. She probably should have asked him to come up and drink the beer. Except for Fran she hasn't had anyone over. Fran is more friendly and helpful than anyone Maya has known in the States since she came to North Carolina ten years ago, at nineteen. Fran is a Swede, and she is tall, with blue eyes. Her hair, however, is a dull, darkish brown.

"I don't think I can handle anything that heavy-duty," Fran says when she comes back to the room. She means the omelette. "I have to go home in any case." She lives with her mother and her aunt, two women in their mid-seventies, in a drafty farmhouse. The farmhouse now has a computer store catty-corner from it. Maya's been to the farm. She's been shown photographs of the way the corner used to be. If land values ever rebound, Fran will be worth millions.

Before Fran leaves she says, "Has Rab Chatterji called you yet?"

"No." She remembers the name, a good, reliable Bengali name, from the first night's study of the phone book. Dr. Rabindra Chatterji teaches Physics.

"He called the English office just before I left." She takes car keys out of her pocketbook. She reknots her scarf. "I bet Indian men are more sensitive than Americans. Rab's a Brahmin, that's what people say."

A Chatterji has to be a Bengali Brahmin—last names give ancestral secrets away—but Brahminness seems to mean more to Fran than it does to Maya. She was born in 1954, six full years after India became independent. Her India was Nehru's India: a charged, progressive place.

"All Indian men are wife beaters," Maya says. She means it and doesn't mean it. "That's why I married an American." Fran knows about the divorce, but nothing else. Fran is on the Hiring, Tenure, and Reappointment Committee.

Maya sees Fran down the stairs and to the car which is parked in the back in the spot reserved for Maya's car, if she had owned one. It will take her several months to save enough to buy one. She always pays cash, never borrows. She tells herself she's still recovering from the U-Haul drive halfway across the country. Ted Suminski is in his kitchen watching the women. Maya waves to him because waving to him, acknowledging him in that way, makes him seem less creepy. He seems to live alone though a sign, THE SUMINSKIS, hangs from a metal horse's head in the front yard. Maya hasn't seen Mrs. Suminski. She hasn't seen any children either. Ted always looks lonely. When she comes back from campus, he's nearly always in the back, throwing darts or shooting baskets.

"What's he like?" Fran gestures with her head as she starts up her car. "You hear these stories."

Maya doesn't want to know the stories. She has signed a year's lease. She doesn't want complications. "He's all right. I keep out of his way."

"You know what I'm thinking? Of all the people in Cedar Falls, you're the one who could understand Vern best. His wanting to try out his wings, run away, stuff like that."

"Not really." Maya is not being modest. Fran is being impulsively democratic, lumping her wayward lover and Indian friend together as headstrong adventurers. For Fran, a utopian and feminist, borders don't count. Maya's taken some big risks, made a break with her parents' ways. She's done things a woman from Ballygunge Park Road doesn't do, even in fantasies. She's not yet shared stories with Fran, apart from the divorce. She's told her nothing of men she picks up, the reputation she'd gained, before Cedar Falls, for "indiscretions." She has a job, equity, three friends she can count on for emergencies. She is an American citizen. But.

Fran's Brahmin calls her two nights later. On the phone he presents himself as Dr. Chatterji, not Rabindra or Rab. An old-fashioned Indian, she assumes. Her father still calls his closest friend, "Colonel." Dr. Chatterji asks her to tea on Sunday. She means to say no but hears herself saying, "Sunday? Fiveish? I'm not doing anything special this Sunday."

Outside, Ted Suminski is throwing darts into his garage door. The door has painted-on rings: orange, purple, pink. The bull's-eye is gray. He has to be fifty at least. He is a big, thick, lonely man about whom people tell stories. Maya pulls the phone cord as far as it'll go so she can look down more directly on her landlord's large, bald head. He has his back to her as he lines up a dart. He's in black running shoes, red shorts, he's naked to the waist. He hunches his right shoulder, he pulls the arm back; a big, lonely man shouldn't have so much grace. The dart is ready to cut through the September evening. But Ted Suminski doesn't let go. He swings on worn rubber soles, catches her eye in the window (she has to have imagined this), takes aim at her shadow. Could she have imagined the noise of the dart's metal tip on her windowpane?

Dr. Chatterji is still on the phone. "You are not having any mode of transportation, is that right?"

Ted Suminski has lost interest in her. Perhaps it isn't interest, at all; perhaps it's aggression. "I don't drive," she lies, knowing it sounds less shameful than not owning a car. She has said this so often she can get in the right degree of apology and Asian upper-class helplessness. "It's an awful nuisance."

"Not to worry, please." Then, "It is a great honor to be meeting Dr. Sanyal's daughter. In Calcutta business circles he is a legend."

On Sunday she is ready by four-thirty. She doesn't know what the afternoon holds; there are surely no places for "high tea"—a colonial tradition—in Cedar Falls, Iowa. If he takes her back to his place, it will mean he has invited other guests. From his voice she can tell Dr. Chatterji likes to do things correctly. She has dressed herself in a peach-colored nylon georgette sari, jade drop-earrings and a necklace. The color is good on dark skin. She is not pretty, but she does her best. Working at it is a part of self-respect. In the mid-seventies, when American women felt rather strongly about such things, Maya had been in trouble with her women's group at Duke. She was too feminine. She had tried to explain the world she came out of. Her grandmother had been married off at the age of five in a village now in Bangladesh. Her great-aunt had been burned to death over a dowry problem. She herself had been trained to speak softly, arrange flowers, sing, be pliant. If she were to seduce Ted Suminski, she thinks as she waits in the front yard for Dr. Chatterji, it would be minor heroism. She has broken with the past. But.

Dr. Chatterji drives up for her at about five ten. He is a hesitant driver. The car stalls, jumps ahead, finally slams to a stop. Maya has to tell him to back off a foot or so; it's hard to leap over two sacks of pruned branches in a sari. Ted Suminski is an obsessive pruner and gardener.

"My sincerest apologies, Mrs. Sanyal," Dr. Chatterji says. He leans across the wide front seat of his noisy, very old, very used car and unlocks the door for her. "I am late. But then, I am sure you're remembering that Indian Standard Time is not at all the same as time in the States." He laughs. He could be nervous—she often had that effect on Indian men. Or he could just be chatty. "These Americans are all the time rushing and rushing but where it gets them?" He moves his head laterally once, twice. It's the gesture made famous by Peter Sellers. When Peter Sellers did it, it had seemed hilarious. Now it suggests that Maya and Dr. Chatterji have three thousand years plus civilization, sophistication, moral virtue, over people born on this continent. Like her, Dr. Chatterji is a naturalized American.

"Call me Maya," she says. She fusses with the seat belt. She does it because she needs time to look him over. He seems quite harmless. She takes in the prominent teeth, the eyebrows that run together. He's in a blue shirt and a beige cardigan with the K-Mart logo that buttons tightly over the waist. It's hard to guess his age because he has dyed his hair and his moustache. Late thirties, early forties. Older than she had expected. "Not Mrs. Sanyal."

This isn't the time to tell about ex-husbands. She doesn't know where John is these days. He should have kept up at least. John had come into her life as a graduate student at Duke, and she, mistaking the brief breathlessness of sex for love, had married him. They had stayed together two years, maybe a little less. The pain that John had inflicted all those years ago by leaving her had subsided into a cozy feeling of loss. This isn't the time, but then she doesn't want to be a legend's daughter all evening. She's not necessarily on Dr. Chatterji's side is what she wants to get across early; she's not against America and Americans. She makes the story—of marriage outside the Brahminic pale, the divorce—quick, dull. Her unsentimentality seems to shock him. His stomach sags inside the cardigan.

"We've each had our several griefs," the physicist says. "We're each required to pay our karmic debts."

"Where are we headed?"

"Mrs. Chatterji has made some Indian snacks. She is waiting to meet you because she is knowing your cousin-sister who studied in Scottish Church College. My home is okay, no?"

Fran would get a kick out of this. Maya has slept with married men, with nameless men, with men little more than boys, but never with an Indian man. Never.

The Chatterjis live in a small blue house on a gravelly street. There are at least five or six other houses on the street; the same size but in different colors and with different front yard treatments. More houses are going up. This is the cutting edge of suburbia.

Mrs. Chatterji stands in the driveway. She is throwing a large plastic ball to a child. The child looks about four, and is Korean or Cambodian. The child is not hers because she tells it, "Chung-Hee, ta-ta, bye-bye. Now I play with guest," as Maya gets out of the car.

Maya hasn't seen this part of town. The early September light softens the construction pits. In that light the houses too close together, the stout woman in a striped cotton sari, the child hugging a pink ball, the two plastic lawn chairs by a tender young tree, the sheets and saris on the clothesline in the back, all seem miraculously incandescent.

"Go home now, Chung-Hee. I am busy." Mrs. Chatterji points the child homeward, then turns to Maya, who has folded her hands in traditional Bengali greeting. "It is an honor. We feel very privileged." She leads Maya indoors to a front room that smells of moisture and paint.

In her new, deliquescent mood, Maya allows herself to be backed into the best armchair—a low-backed, boxy Goodwill item draped over with a Rajasthani bedspread—and asks after the cousin Mrs. Chatterji knows. She doesn't want to let go of Mrs. Chatterji. She doesn't want husband and wife to get into whispered conferences about their guest's misadventures in America, as they make tea in the kitchen.

The coffee table is already laid with platters of mutton croquettes, fish chops, onion pakoras, ghugni with puris, samosas, chutneys. Mrs. Chatterji has gone to too much trouble. Maya counts four kinds of sweetmeats in Corning casseroles on an end table. She looks into a see-through lid; spongy, white dumplings float in rosewater syrup. Planets contained, mysteries made visible.

"What are you waiting for, Santana?" Dr. Chatterji becomes imperious, though not unaffectionate. He pulls a dining chair up close to the coffee table. "Make some tea." He speaks in Bengali to his wife, in English to Maya. To Maya he says, grandly, "We are having real Indian Green Label Lipton. A nephew is bringing it just one month back."

His wife ignores him. "The kettle's already on," she says. She wants to know about the Sanyal family. Is it true her great-grandfather was a member of the Star Chamber in England?

Nothing in Calcutta is ever lost. Just as her story is known to Bengalis all over America, so are the scandals of her family, the grandfather hauled up for tax evasion, the aunt who left her husband to act in films. This woman brings up the Star Chamber, the glories of the Sanyal family, her father's philanthropies, but it's a way of saying, *I know the dirt.*

The bedrooms are upstairs. In one of those bedrooms an unseen, tormented presence—Maya pictures it as a clumsy ghost that strains to shake off the body's shell—drops things on the floor. The things are heavy and they make the front room's chandelier shake. Light bulbs, shaped like tiny candle flames, flicker. The Chatterjis have said nothing about children. There are no tricycles in the hallway, no small sandals behind the doors. Maya is too polite to ask about the noise, and the Chatterjis don't explain. They talk just a little louder. They flip the embroidered cover off the stereo. What would Maya like to hear? Hemanta Kumar? Manna Dey? Oh, that young chap, Manna Dey! What sincerity, what tenderness he can convey!

Upstairs the ghost doesn't hear the music of nostalgia. The ghost throws and thumps. The ghost makes its own vehement music. Maya hears in its voice madness, self-hate.

Finally the water in the kettle comes to a boil. The whistle cuts through all fantasy and pretense. Dr. Chatterji says, "I'll see to it," and rushes out of the room. But he doesn't go to the kitchen. He shouts up the stairwell. "Poltoo, kindly stop this nonsense straightaway! We're having a brilliant and cultured lady-guest and you're creating earthquakes?" The kettle is hysterical.

Mrs. Chatterji wipes her face. The face that had seemed plump and cheery at the start of the evening now is flabby. "My sister's boy," the woman says.

So this is the nephew who has brought with him the cartons of Green Label tea, one of which will be given to Maya.

Mrs. Chatterji speaks to Maya in English as though only the alien language can keep emotions in check. "Such an intelligent boy! His father is government servant. Very highly placed."

Maya is meant to visualize a smart, clean-cut young man from south Calcutta, but all she can see is a crazy, thwarted, lost graduate student. Intelligence, proper family guarantee nothing. Even Brahmins can do self-destructive things, feel unsavory urges. Maya herself had been an excellent student.

"He was First Class First in B. Sc. from Presidency College," the woman says. "Now he's getting Master's in Ag. Science at Iowa State."

The kitchen is silent. Dr. Chatterji comes back into the room with a tray. The teapot is under a tea cozy, a Kashmiri one embroidered with the usual chinar leaves, loops, and chains. "*Her* nephew," he says. The dyed hair and dyed moustache are no longer signs of a man wishing to fight the odds. He is a vain man, anxious to cut losses. "Very unfortunate business."

The nephew's story comes out slowly, over fish chops and mutton croquettes. He is in love with a student from Ghana.

"Everything was A-Okay until the Christmas break. Grades, assistantship for next semester, everything."

"I blame the college. The office for foreign students arranged a Christmas party. And now, *baapre baap!* Our poor Poltoo wants to marry a Negro Muslim."

Maya is known for her nasty, ironic one-liners. It has taken her friends weeks to overlook her malicious, un-American pleasure in others' misfortunes. Maya would like to finish Dr. Chatterji off quickly. He is pompous; he is reactionary; he wants to live and work in America but give back nothing except taxes. The confused world of the immigrant—the lostness that Maya and Poltoo feel—that's what Dr. Chatterji wants to avoid. She hates him. But.

Dr. Chatterji's horror is real. A good Brahmin boy in Iowa is in love with an African Muslim. It shouldn't be a big deal. But the more she watches the physicist, the more she realizes that "Brahmin" isn't a caste; it's a metaphor. You break one small rule, and the constellation collapses. She thinks suddenly that John Cheever—she is teaching him as a "world writer" in her classes, cheek-by-jowl with Africans and West Indians—would have understood Dr. Chatterji's dread. Cheever had been on her mind, ever since the late afternoon light slanted over Mrs.

Chatterji's drying saris. She remembers now how full of a soft, Cheeverian light Durham had been the summer she had slept with John Hadwen; and how after that, her tidy graduate-student world became monstrous, lawless. All men became John Hadwen; John became all men. Outwardly, she retained her poise, her Brahminical breeding. She treated her crisis as a literary event; she lost her moral sense, her judgment, her power to distinguish. Her parents had behaved magnanimously. They had cabled from Calcutta: WHAT'S DONE IS DONE, WE ARE CONFIDENT YOU WILL HANDLE NEW SITUATIONS WELL. ALL LOVE. But she knows more than do her parents. Love is anarchy.

Poltoo is Mrs. Chatterji's favorite nephew. She looks as though it is her fault that the Sunday has turned unpleasant. She stacks the empty platters methodically. To Maya she says, "It is the goddess who pulls the strings. We are puppets. I know the goddess will fix it. Poltoo will not marry that African woman." Then she goes to the coat closet in the hall and staggers back with a harmonium, the kind sold in music stores in Calcutta, and sets it down on the carpeted floor. "We're nothing but puppets," she says again. She sits at Maya's feet, her pudgy hands on the harmonium's shiny, black bellows. She sings, beautifully, in a virgin's high voice, "Come, goddess, come, muse, come to us hapless peoples' rescue."

Maya is astonished. She has taken singing lessons at Dakshini Academy in Calcutta. She plays the sitar and the tanpur, well enough to please Bengalis, to astonish Americans. But stout Mrs. Chatterji is a devotee, talking to God.

A little after eight, Dr. Chatterji drops her off. It's been an odd evening and they are both subdued.

"I want to say one thing," he says. He stops her from undoing her seat belt. The plastic sacks of pruned branches are still at the corner.

"You don't have to get out," she says.

"Please. Give me one more minute of your time."

"Sure."

"Maya is my favorite name."

She says nothing. She turns away from him without making her embarrassment obvious.

"Truly speaking, it is my favorite. You are sometimes lonely, no? But you are lucky. Divorced women can date, they can go to bars and discos. They can see mens, many mens. But inside marriage there is so much loneliness." A groan, low, horrible, comes out of him.

She turns back toward him, to unlatch the seat belt and run out of the car. She sees that Dr. Chatterji's pants are unzipped. One hand works hard under his Jockey shorts; the other rests, limp, penitential, on the steering wheel.

"Dr. Chatterji— *really!*" she cries.

The next day, Monday, instead of getting a ride home with Fran—Fran says she *likes* to give rides, she needs the chance to talk, and she won't share gas expenses, absolutely not—Maya goes to the periodicals room of the library. There are newspapers from everywhere, even from Madagascar and New Caledonia. She thinks of the periodicals room as an asylum for homesick aliens. There are two aliens already in the room, both Orientals, both absorbed in the politics and gossip of their far off homes.

She goes straight to the newspapers from India. She bunches her raincoat like a bolster to make herself more comfortable. There's so much to catch up on. A village headman, a known Congress-Indira party worker, has been shot at by scooter-riding snipers. An Indian pugilist has won an international medal—in Nepal. A child drawing well water—the reporter calls the child "a neo-Buddhist, a convert from the now-outlawed untouchable caste"—has been stoned. An editorial explains that the story about stoning is not a story about caste but about failed idealism; a story about promises of green fields and clean, potable water broken, a story about bribes paid and wells not dug. But no, thinks Maya, it's about caste.

Out here, in the heartland of the new world, the India of serious newspapers unsettles. Maya longs again to feel what she had felt in the Chatterjis' living room: virtues made physical. It is a familiar feeling, a longing. Had a suitable man presented himself in the reading room at that instant, she would have seduced him. She goes on to the stack of *India Abroads,* reads through matrimonial columns, and steals an issue to take home.

Indian men want Indian brides. Married Indian men want Indian mistresses. All over America, "handsome, tall, fair" engineers, doctors, data processors—the new pioneers—cry their eerie love calls.

Maya runs a finger down the first column; her fingertip, dark with newsprint, stops at random.

> Hello! Hi! Yes, you *are* the one I'm looking for. You are the new emancipated Indo-American woman. You have a zest for life. You are at ease in USA and yet your ethics are rooted in Indian tradition. The man of your dreams has come. Yours truly is handsome,

ear-nose-throat specialist, well-settled in Connecticut. Age is 41 but never married, physically fit, sportsmanly, and strong. I adore idealism, poetry, beauty. I abhor smugness, passivity, caste system. Write with recent photo. Better still, call!!!

Maya calls. Hullo, hullo, hullo! She hears immigrant lovers cry in crowded shopping malls. Yes, you who are at ease in both worlds, you are the one. She feels she has a fair chance.

A man answers. "Ashoke Mehta speaking."

She speaks quickly into the bright-red mouthpiece of her telephone. He will be in Chicago, in transit, passing through O'Hare. United counter, Saturday, two P.M. As easy as that.

"Good," Ashoke Mehta says. "For these encounters I, too, prefer a neutral zone."

On Saturday at exactly two o'clock the man of Maya's dreams floats toward her as lovers used to in shampoo commercials. The United counter is a loud, harrassed place but passengers and piled-up luggage fall away from him. Full-cheeked and fleshy-lipped, he is handsome. He hasn't lied. He is serene, assured, a Hindu god touching down in Illinois.

She can't move. She feels ugly and unworthy. Her adult life no longer seems miraculously rebellious; it is grim, it is perverse. She has accomplished nothing. She has changed her citizenship but she hasn't broken through into the light, the vigor, the *bustle* of the New World. She is stuck in dead space.

"Hullo, Hullo!" Their fingers touch.

Oh, the excitement! Ashoke Mehta's palm feels so right in the small of her back. Hullo, hullo, hullo. He pushes her out of the reach of anti-Khomeini Iranians, Hare Krishnas, American Fascists, men with fierce wants, and guides her to an empty gate. They have less than an hour.

"What would you like, Maya?"

She knows he can read her mind, she knows her thoughts are open to him. *You,* she's almost giddy with the thought, with simple desire. "From the snack bar," he says, as though to clarify. "I'm afraid I'm starved."

Below them, where the light is strong and hurtful, a Boeing is being serviced. "Nothing," she says.

He leans forward. She can feel the nap of his scarf—she recognizes the Cambridge colors—she can smell the wool of his Icelandic sweater.

She runs her hand along the scarf, then against the flesh of his neck. "Only the impulsive ones call," he says.

The immigrant courtship proceeds. It's easy, he's good with facts. He knows how to come across to a stranger who may end up a lover, a spouse. He makes over a hundred thousand. He owns a house in Hartford, and two income properties in Newark. He plays the market but he's cautious. He's good at badminton but plays handball to keep in shape. He watches all the sports on television. Last August he visited Copenhagen, Helsinki and Leningrad. Once upon a time he collected stamps but now he doesn't have hobbies, except for reading. He counts himself an intellectual, he spends too much on books. Ludlum, Forsyth, MacInnes; other names she doesn't catch. She supresses a smile, she's told him only she's a graduate student. He's not without his vices. He's a spender, not a saver. He's a sensualist: good food—all foods, but easy on the Indian—good wine. Some temptations he doesn't try to resist.

And I, she wants to ask, do I tempt?

"Now tell me about yourself, Maya." He makes it easy for her. "Have you ever been in love?"

"No."

"But many have loved you, I can see that." He says it not unkindly. It is the fate of women like her, and men like him. Their karmic duty, to be loved. It is expected, not judged. She feels he can see them all, the sad parade of need and demand. This isn't the time to reveal all.

And so the courtship enters a second phase.

When she gets back to Cedar Falls, Ted Suminski is standing on the front porch. It's late at night, chilly. He is wearing a down vest. She's never seen him on the porch. In fact there's no chair to sit on. He looks chilled through. He's waited around a while.

"Hi." She has her keys ready. This isn't the night to offer the six-pack in the fridge. He looks expectant, ready to pounce.

"Hi." He looks like a man who might have aimed the dart at her. What has he done to his wife, his kids? Why isn't there at least a dog? "Say, I left a note upstairs."

The note is written in Magic Marker and thumb-tacked to her apartment door. DUE TO PERSONAL REASONS, NAMELY REMARRIAGE, I RE-QUEST THAT YOU VACATE MY PLACE AT THE END OF THE SEMESTER.

Maya takes the note down and retacks it to the kitchen wall. The whole wall is like a bulletin board, made of some new, crumbly build-ing-material. Her kitchen, Ted Suminski had told her, was once a child's bedroom. Suminski in love: the idea stuns her. She has misread her landlord. The dart at her window speaks of no twisted fantasy. The landlord wants the tenant out.

She gets a glass out of the kitchen cabinet, gets out a tray of ice, pours herself a shot of Fran's bourbon. She is happy for Ted Suminski. She is. She wants to tell someone how moved she'd been by Mrs. Chatterji's singing. How she'd felt in O'Hare, even about Dr. Rab Chatterji in the car. But Fran is not the person. No one she's ever met is the person. She can't talk about the dead space she lives in. She wishes Ashoke Mehta would call. Right now.

Weeks pass. Then two months. She finds a new room, signs another lease. Her new landlord calls himself Fred. He has no arms, but he helps her move her things. He drives between Ted Suminski's place and his twice in his station wagon. He uses his toes the way Maya uses her fingers. He likes to do things. He pushes garbage sacks full of Maya's clothes up the stairs.

"It's all right to stare," Fred says. "Hell, I would."

That first afternoon in Fred's rooming house, they share a Chianti. Fred wants to cook her pork chops but he's a little shy about Indians and meat. Is it beef, or pork? Or any meat? She says it's okay, any meat, but not tonight. He has an ex-wife in Des Moines, two kids in Portland, Oregon. The kids are both normal; he's the only freak in the family. But he's self-reliant. He shops in the supermarket like anyone else, he carries out the garbage, shovels the snow off the sidewalk. He needs Maya's help with one thing. Just one thing. The box of Tide is a bit too heavy to manage. Could she get him the giant size every so often and leave it in the basement?

The dead space need not suffocate. Over the months, Fred and she will settle into companionship. She has never slept with a man without arms. Two wounded people, he will joke during their nightly contortions. It will shock her, this assumed equivalence with a man so strikingly deficient. She knows she is strange, and lonely, but being Indian is not the same, she would have thought, as being a freak.

One night in spring, Fred's phone rings. "Ashoke Mehta speaking." None of this "do you remember me?" nonsense. The god has tracked her down. He hasn't forgotten. "Hullo," he says, in their special way. And because she doesn't answer back, "Hullo, hullo, hullo." She is aware of Fred in the back of the room. He is lighting a cigarette with his toes.

"Yes," she says, "I remember."

"I had to take care of a problem," Ashoke Mehta says. "You know that I have my vices. That time at O'Hare I was honest with you."

She is breathless.

"Who is it, May?" asks Fred.

"You also have a problem," says the voice. His laugh echoes. "You will come to Hartford, I know."

When she moves out, she tells herself, it will not be the end of Fred's world.

1986

AMY TAN

Rules of the Game

I was six when my mother taught me the art of invisible strength. It was a strategy for winning arguments, respect from others, and eventually, though neither of us knew it at the time, chess games.

"Bite back your tongue," scolded my mother when I cried loudly, yanking her hand toward the store that sold bags of salted plums. At home, she said, "Wise guy, he not go against wind. In Chinese we say, Come from South, blow with wind—poom!—North will follow. Strongest wind cannot be seen."

The next week I bit back my tongue as we entered the store with

The Joy Luck Club (1989), Amy Tan's first novel, comprises various tales of cross-cultural experience, each told from a different narrative viewpoint. The author's own life embodies this structure of shifting perspectives. Born in Oakland, California, in 1952, Tan is the child of Chinese-born parents who had emigrated only two and a half years earlier. When she was fifteen, she and her family moved to Montreux, Switzerland. Her displacement and her standing in Europe as, in Tan's own words, "a novelty," helped to clarify her cultural position as both Chinese and American. A visit to China in 1987 reinforced this dual status and, after thirty-five years, allowed her to celebrate it. Tan now lives and writes in San Francisco. Her latest novel is *The Kitchen God's Wife* (1991).

the forbidden candies. When my mother finished her shopping, she quietly plucked a small bag of plums from the rack and put it on the counter with the rest of the items.

My mother imparted her daily truths so she could help my older brothers and me rise above our circumstances. We lived in San Francisco's Chinatown. Like most of the other Chinese children who played in the back alleys of restaurants and curio shops, I didn't think we were poor. My bowl was always full, three five-course meals every day, beginning with a soup full of mysterious things I didn't want to know the names of.

We lived on Waverly Place, in a warm, clean, two-bedroom flat that sat above a small Chinese bakery specializing in steamed pastries and dim sum. In the early morning, when the alley was still quiet, I could smell fragrant red beans as they were cooked down to a pasty sweetness. By daybreak, our flat was heavy with the odor of fried sesame balls and sweet curried chicken crescents. From my bed, I would listen as my father got ready for work, then locked the door behind him, one-two-three clicks.

At the end of our two-block alley was a small sandlot playground with swings and slides well-shined down the middle with use. The play area was bordered by wood-slat benches where old-country people sat cracking roasted watermelon seeds with their golden teeth and scattering the husks to an impatient gathering of gurgling pigeons. The best playground, however, was the dark alley itself. It was crammed with daily mysteries and adventures. My brothers and I would peer into the medicinal herb shop, watching old Li dole out onto a stiff sheet of white paper the right amount of insect shells, saffron-colored seeds, and pungent leaves for his ailing customers. It was said that he once cured a woman dying of an ancestral curse that had eluded the best of American doctors. Next to the pharmacy was a printer who specialized in gold-embossed wedding invitations and festive red banners.

Farther down the street was Ping Yuen Fish Market. The front window displayed a tank crowded with doomed fish and turtles struggling to gain footing on the slimy green-tiled sides. A hand-written sign informed tourists, "Within this store, is all for food, not for pet." Inside, the butchers with their bloodstained white smocks deftly gutted the fish while customers cried out their orders and shouted, "Give me your freshest," to which the butchers always protested, "All are freshest." On less crowded market days, we would inspect the crates of live frogs and crabs which we were warned not to poke, boxes of dried cuttlefish, and row upon row of iced prawns, squid, and slippery fish. The sanddabs made me shiver each time; their eyes lay on one flattened side and reminded me of my mother's story of a careless girl who ran into a crowded street and was crushed by a cab. "Was smash flat," reported my mother.

At the corner of the alley was Hong Sing's, a four-table café with a recessed stairwell in front that led to a door marked "Tradesmen." My brothers and I believed the bad people emerged from this door at night. Tourists never went to Hong Sing's, since the menu was printed only in Chinese. A Caucasian man with a big camera once posed me and my playmates in front of the restaurant. He had us move to the side of the picture window so the photo would capture the roasted duck with its head dangling from a juice-covered rope. After he took the picture, I told him he should go into Hong Sing's and eat dinner. When he smiled and asked me what they served, I shouted, "Guts and duck's feet and octopus gizzards!" Then I ran off with my friends, shrieking with laughter as we scampered across the alley and hid in the entryway grotto of the China Gem Company, my heart pounding with hope that he would chase us.

My mother named me after the street that we lived on: Waverly Place Jong, my official name for important American documents. But my family called me Meimei, "Little Sister." I was the youngest, the only daughter. Each morning before school, my mother would twist and yank on my thick black hair until she had formed two tightly wound pigtails. One day, as she struggled to weave a hard-toothed comb through my disobedient hair, I had a sly thought.

I asked her, "Ma, what is Chinese torture?" My mother shook her head. A bobby pin was wedged between her lips. She wetted her palm and smoothed the hair above my ear, then pushed the pin in so that it nicked sharply against my scalp.

"Who say this word?" she asked without a trace of knowing how wicked I was being. I shrugged my shoulders and said, "Some boy in my class said Chinese people do Chinese torture."

"Chinese people do many things," she said simply. "Chinese people do business, do medicine, do painting. Not lazy like American people. We do torture. Best torture."

My older brother Vincent was the one who actually got the chess set. We had gone to the annual Christmas party held at the First Chinese Baptist Church at the end of the alley. The missionary ladies had put together a Santa bag of gifts donated by members of another church.

None of the gifts had names on them. There were separate sacks for boys and girls of different ages.

One of the Chinese parishioners had donned a Santa Claus costume and a stiff paper beard with cotton balls glued to it. I think the only children who thought he was the real thing were too young to know that Santa Claus was not Chinese. When my turn came up, the Santa man asked me how old I was. I thought it was a trick question; I was seven according to the American formula and eight by the Chinese calendar. I said I was born on March 17, 1951. That seemed to satisfy him. He then solemnly asked if I had been a very, very good girl this year and did I believe in Jesus Christ and obey my parents. I knew the only answer to that. I nodded back with equal solemnity.

Having watched the other children opening their gifts, I already knew that the big gifts were not necessarily the nicest ones. One girl my age got a large coloring book of biblical characters, while a less greedy girl who selected a smaller box received a glass vial of lavender toilet water. The sound of the box was also important. A ten-year-old boy had chosen a box that jangled when he shook it. It was a tin globe of the world with a slit for inserting money. He must have thought it was full of dimes and nickels, because when he saw that it had just ten pennies, his face fell with such undisguised disappointment that his mother slapped the side of his head and led him out of the church hall, apologizing to the crowd for her son who had such bad manners he couldn't appreciate such a fine gift.

As I peered into the sack, I quickly fingered the remaining presents, testing their weight, imagining what they contained. I chose a heavy, compact one that was wrapped in shiny silver foil and a red satin ribbon. It was a twelve-pack of Life Savers and I spent the rest of the party arranging and rearranging the candy tubes in the order of my favorites. My brother Winston chose wisely as well. His present turned out to be a box of intricate plastic parts; the instructions on the box proclaimed that when they were properly assembled he would have an authentic miniature replica of a World War II submarine.

Vincent got the chess set, which would have been a very decent present to get at a church Christmas party, except it was obviously used and, as we discovered later, it was missing a black pawn and a white knight. My mother graciously thanked the unknown benefactor, saying, "Too good. Cost too much." At which point, an old lady with fine white, wispy hair nodded toward our family and said with a whistling whisper, "Merry, merry Christmas."

When we got home, my mother told Vincent to throw the chess set away. "She not want it. We not want it." she said, tossing her head stiffly to the side with a tight, proud smile. My brothers had deaf ears. They were already lining up the chess pieces and reading from the dog-eared instruction book.

I watched Vincent and Winston play during Christmas week. The chessboard seemed to hold elaborate secrets waiting to be untangled. The chessmen were more powerful than old Li's magic herbs that cured ancestral curses. And my brothers wore such serious faces that I was sure something was at stake that was greater than avoiding the tradesmen's door to Hong Sing's.

"Let me! Let me!" I begged between games when one brother or the other would sit back with a deep sigh of relief and victory, the other annoyed, unable to let go of the outcome. Vincent at first refused to let me play, but when I offered my Life Savers as replacements for the buttons that filled in for the missing pieces, he relented. He chose the flavors: wild cherry for the black pawn and peppermint for the white knight. Winner could eat both.

As our mother sprinkled flour and rolled out small doughy circles for the steamed dumplings that would be our dinner that night, Vincent explained the rules, pointing to each piece. "You have sixteen pieces and so do I. One king and queen, two bishops, two knights, two castles, and eight pawns. The pawns can only move forward one step, except on the first move. Then they can move two. But they can only take men by moving crossways like this, except in the beginning, when you can move ahead and take another pawn."

"Why?" I asked as I moved my pawn. "Why can't they move more steps?"

"Because they're pawns," he said.

"But why do they go crossways to take other men? Why aren't there any women and children?"

"Why is the sky blue? Why must you always ask stupid questions?" asked Vincent. "This is a game. These are the rules. I didn't make them up. See. Here. In the book." He jabbed a page with a pawn in his hand. "Pawn. P-A-W-N. Pawn. Read it yourself."

My mother patted the flour off her hands. "Let me see book," she said quietly. She scanned the pages quickly, not reading the foreign English symbols, seeming to search deliberately for nothing in particular.

"This American rules," she concluded at last. "Every time people come out from foreign country, must know rules. You not know, judge say, Too bad, go back. They not telling you why so you can use their way go forward. They say, Don't know why, you find out yourself. But they knowing all the time. Better you take it, find out why yourself." She tossed her head back with a satisfied smile.

I found out about all the whys later. I read the rules and looked up all the big words in a dictionary. I borrowed books from the Chinatown library. I studied each chess piece, trying to absorb the power each contained.

I learned about opening moves and why it's important to control the center early on; the shortest distance between two points is straight down the middle. I learned about the middle game and why tactics between two adversaries are like clashing ideas; the one who plays better has the clearest plans for both attacking and getting out of traps. I learned why it is essential in the endgame to have foresight, a mathematical understanding of all possible moves, and patience; all weaknesses and advantages become evident to a strong adversary and are obscured to a tiring opponent. I discovered that for the whole game one must gather invisible strengths and see the endgame before the game begins.

I also found out why I should never reveal "why" to others. A little knowledge withheld is a great advantage one should store for future use. That is the power of chess. It is a game of secrets in which one must show and never tell.

I loved the secrets I found within the sixty-four black and white squares. I carefully drew a handmade chessboard and pinned it to the wall next to my bed, where at night I would stare for hours at imaginary battles. Soon I no longer lost any games or Life Savers, but I lost my adversaries. Winston and Vincent decided they were more interested in roaming the streets after school in their Hopalong Cassidy cowboy hats.

On a cold spring afternoon, while walking home from school, I detoured through the playground at the end of our alley. I saw a group of old men, two seated across a folding table playing a game of chess, others smoking pipes, eating peanuts, and watching. I ran home and grabbed Vincent's chess set, which was bound in a cardboard box with rubber bands. I also carefully selected two prized rolls of Life Savers. I came back to the park and approached a man who was observing the game.

"Want to play?" I asked him. His face widened with surprise and he grinned as he looked at the box under my arm.

"Little sister, been a long time since I play with dolls," he said, smiling benevolently. I quickly put the box down next to him on the bench and displayed my retort.

Lau Po, as he allowed me to call him, turned out to be a much better player than my brothers. I lost many games and many Life Savers.

But over the weeks, with each diminishing roll of candies, I added new secrets. Lau Po gave me the names. The Double Attack from the East and West Shores. Throwing Stones on the Drowning Man. The Sudden Meeting of the Clan. The Surprise from the Sleeping Guard. The Humble Servant Who Kills the King. Sand in the Eyes of Advancing Forces. A Double Killing Without Blood.

There were also the fine points of chess etiquette. Keep captured men in neat rows, as well-tended prisoners. Never announce "Check" with vanity, lest someone with an unseen sword slit your throat. Never hurl pieces into the sandbox after you have lost a game, because then you must find them again, by yourself, after apologizing to all around you. By the end of the summer, Lau Po had taught me all he knew, and I had become a better chess player.

A small weekend crowd of Chinese people and tourists would gather as I played and defeated my opponents one by one. My mother would join the crowds during these outdoor exhibition games. She sat proudly on the bench, telling my admirers with proper Chinese humility, "Is luck."

A man who watched me play in the park suggested that my mother allow me to play in local chess tournaments. My mother smiled graciously, an answer that meant nothing. I desperately wanted to go, but I bit back my tongue. I knew she would not let me play among strangers. So as we walked home I said in a small voice that I didn't want to play in the local tournament. They would have American rules. If I lost, I would bring shame on my family.

"Is shame you fall down nobody push you," said my mother.

During my first tournament, my mother sat with me in the front row as I waited for my turn. I frequently bounced my legs to unstick them from the cold metal seat of the folding chair. When my name was called, I leapt up. My mother unwrapped something in her lap. It was her *chang*, a small tablet of red jade which held the sun's fire. "Is luck," she whispered, and tucked it into my dress pocket. I turned to my opponent, a fifteen-year-old boy from Oakland. He looked at me, wrinkling his nose.

As I began to play, the boy disappeared, the color ran out of the room, and I saw only my white pieces and his black ones waiting on the other side. A light wind began blowing past my ears. It whispered secrets only I could hear.

"Blow from the South," it murmured. "The wind leaves no trail." I saw a clear path, the traps to avoid. The crowd rustled. "Shhh! Shhh!" said the corners of the room. The wind blew stronger. "Throw sand from the East to distract him." The knight came forward ready for the sacrifice. The wind hissed, louder and louder. "Blow, blow, blow. He cannot see. He is blind now. Make him lean away from the wind so he is easier to knock down."

"Check," I said, as the wind roared with laughter. The wind died down to little puffs, my own breath.

My mother placed my first trophy next to a new plastic chess set that the neighborhood Tao society had given to me. As she wiped each piece with a soft cloth, she said, "Next time win more, lose less."

"Ma, it's not how many pieces you lose," I said. "Sometimes you need to lose pieces to get ahead."

"Better to lose less, see if you really need."

At the next tournament, I won again, but it was my mother who wore the triumphant grin.

"Lost eight piece this time. Last time was eleven. What I tell you? Better off lose less!" I was annoyed, but I couldn't say anything.

I attended more tournaments, each one farther away from home. I won all games, in all divisions. The Chinese bakery downstairs from our flat displayed my growing collection of trophies in its window, amidst the dust-covered cakes that were never picked up. The day after I won an important regional tournament, the window encased a fresh sheet cake with whipped-cream frosting and red script saying "Congratulations, Waverly Jong, Chinatown Chess Champion." Soon after that, a flower shop, headstone engraver, and funeral parlor offered to sponsor me in national tournaments. That's when my mother decided I no longer had to do the dishes. Winston and Vincent had to do my chores.

"Why does she get to play and we do all the work," complained Vincent.

"Is new American rules," said my mother. "Meimei play, squeeze all her brains out for win chess. You play, worth squeeze towel."

By my ninth birthday, I was a national chess champion. I was still some 429 points away from grand-master status, but I was touted as the Great American Hope, a child prodigy and a girl to boot. They ran a photo of me in *Life* magazine next to a quote in which Bobby Fischer said, "There will never be a woman grand master." "Your move, Bobby," said the caption.

The day they took the magazine picture I wore neatly plaited braids clipped with plastic barrettes trimmed with rhinestones. I was playing in a large high school auditorium that echoed with phlegmy coughs and the squeaky rubber knobs of chair legs sliding across freshly waxed wooden floors. Seated across from me was an American man, about the same age as Lau Po, maybe fifty. I remember that his sweaty brow seemed to weep at my every move. He wore a dark, malodorous suit. One of his pockets was stuffed with a great white kerchief on which he wiped his palm before sweeping his hand over the chosen chess piece with great flourish.

In my crisp pink-and-white dress with scratchy lace at the neck, one of two my mother had sewn for these special occasions, I would clasp my hands under my chin, the delicate points of my elbows poised lightly on the table in the manner my mother had shown me for posing for the press. I would swing my patent leather shoes back and forth like an impatient child riding on a school bus. Then I would pause, suck in my lips, twirl my chosen piece in midair as if undecided, and then firmly plant it in its new threatening place, with a triumphant smile thrown back at my opponent for good measure.

I no longer played in the alley of Waverly Place. I never visited the playground where the pigeons and old men gathered. I went to school, then directly home to learn new chess secrets, cleverly concealed advantages, more escape routes.

But I found it difficult to concentrate at home. My mother had a habit of standing over me while I plotted out my games. I think she thought of herself as my protective ally. Her lips would be sealed tight, and after each move I made, a soft "Hmmmmph" would escape from her nose.

"Ma, I can't practice when you stand there like that," I said one day. She retreated to the kitchen and made loud noises with the pots and pans. When the crashing stopped, I could see out of the corner of my eye that she was standing in the doorway. "Hmmmph!" Only this one came out of her tight throat.

My parents made many concessions to allow me to practice. One time I complained that the bedroom I shared was so noisy that I couldn't think. Thereafter, my brothers slept in a bed in the living room facing the street. I said I couldn't finish my rice; my head didn't work right when my stomach was too full. I left the table with half-finished bowls and nobody complained. But there was one duty I couldn't avoid. I had to accompany my mother on Saturday market days when I had no tournament to play. My mother would proudly walk with me, visiting many shops, buying very little. "This my daughter Wave-ly Jong," she said to whoever looked her way.

One day after we left a shop I said under my breath, "I wish you wouldn't do that, telling everybody I'm your daughter." My mother stopped walking. Crowds of people with heavy bags pushed past us on the sidewalk, bumping into first one shoulder, then another.

"Aiii-ya. So shame be with mother?" She grasped my hand even tighter as she glared at me.

I looked down. "It's not that, it's just so obvious. It's just so embarrassing."

"Embarrass you be my daughter?" Her voice was cracking with anger.

"That's not what I meant. That's not what I said."

"What you say?"

I knew it was a mistake to say anything more, but I heard my voice speaking, "Why do you have to use me to show off? If you want to show off, then why don't you learn to play chess?"

My mother's eyes turned into dangerous black slits. She had no words for me, just sharp silence.

I felt the wind rushing around my hot ears. I jerked my hand out of my mother's tight grasp and spun around, knocking into an old woman. Her bag of groceries spilled to the ground.

"Aii-ya! Stupid girl!" my mother and the woman cried. Oranges and tin cans careened down the sidewalk. As my mother stooped to help the old woman pick up the escaping food, I took off.

I raced down the street, dashing between people, not looking back as my mother screamed shrilly, "Meimei! Meimei!" I fled down an alley, past dark, curtained shops and merchants washing the grime off their windows. I sped into the sunlight, into a large street crowded with tourists examining trinkets and souvenirs. I ducked into another dark alley, down another street, up another alley. I ran until it hurt and I realized I had nowhere to go, that I was not running from anything. The alleys contained no escape routes.

My breath came out like angry smoke. It was cold. I sat down on an upturned plastic pail next to a stack of empty boxes, cupping my chin with my hands, thinking hard. I imagined my mother, first walking briskly down one street or another looking for me, then giving up and returning home to await my arrival. After two hours, I stood up on creaking legs and slowly walked home.

The alley was quiet and I could see the yellow lights shining from our flat like two tiger's eyes in the night. I climbed the sixteen steps to the door, advancing quietly up each so as not to make any warning sounds. I turned the knob; the door was locked. I heard a chair moving, quick steps, the locks turning—click! click! click!—and then the door opened.

"About time you got home," said Vincent. "Boy, are you in trouble."

He slid back to the dinner table. On a platter were the remains of a large fish, its fleshy head still connected to bones swimming upstream in vain escape. Standing there waiting for my punishment, I heard my mother speak in a dry voice.

"We not concerning this girl. This girl not have concerning for us."

Nobody looked at me. Bone chopsticks clinked against the inside of bowls being emptied into hungry mouths.

I walked into my room, closed the door, and lay down on my bed. The room was dark, the ceiling filled with shadows from the dinnertime lights of neighboring flats.

In my head, I saw a chessboard with sixty-four black and white squares. Opposite me was my opponent, two angry black slits. She wore a triumphant smile. "Strongest wind cannot be seen," she said.

Her black men advanced across the plane, slowly marching to each successive level as a single unit. My white pieces screamed as they scurried and fell off the board one by one. As her men drew closer to my edge, I felt myself growing light. I rose up into the air and flew out the window. Higher and higher, above the alley, over the tops of tiled roofs, where I was gathered up by the wind and pushed up toward the night sky until everything below me disappeared and I was alone.

I closed my eyes and pondered my next move.

1989

LOUISE ERDRICH

Love Medicine

(1982)

LIPSHA MORRISSEY

I never really done much with my life, I suppose. I never had a television. Grandma Kashpaw had one inside her apartment at the Senior Citizens, so I used to go there and watch my favorite shows. For a while she used to call me the biggest waste on the reservation and hark back to how she saved me from my own mother, who wanted to tie me in a potato sack and throw me in a slough. Sure, I was grateful to Grandma Kashpaw for saving me like that, for raising me, but gratitude gets old. After a while, stale. I had to stop thanking her. One day I told her I had paid her back in full by staying at her beck and call. I'd do anything for Grandma. She knew that. Besides, I took care of Grandpa like nobody else could, on account of what a handful he'd gotten to be.

But that was nothing. I know the tricks of mind and body inside out without ever having trained for it, because I got the touch. It's a thing you got to be born with. I got secrets in my hands that nobody ever knew to ask. Take Grandma Kashpaw with her tired veins all knotted up in her legs like clumps of blue snails. I take my fingers and I snap them on the knots. The medicine flows out of me. The touch. I run my fingers up the maps of those rivers of veins or I knock very gentle above their hearts or I make a circling motion on their stomachs, and it helps them. They feel much better. Some women pay me five dollars.

I couldn't do the touch for Grandpa, though. He was a hard nut. You know, some people fall right through the hole in their lives. It's invisible, but they come to it after time, never knowing where. There is

In 1984, Louise Erdrich received the National Book Critics Circle Award for her first novel, *Love Medicine*. A tale of families living on a Chippewa reservation in western North Dakota, this and many subsequent novels spring from the writer's own acquaintance with the area and its people. Born in 1954 in Little Falls, Minnesota, Erdrich—herself of Chippewa and German descent—spent much of her youth on the Native American lands in North Dakota with her parents, both of whom worked for the Bureau of Indian Affairs. She now teaches at Dartmouth College, where she lives with her husband (and sometimes co-writer), Michael Dorris.

this woman here, Lulu Lamartine, who always had a thing for Grandpa. She loved him since she was a girl and always said he was a genius. Now she says that his mind got so full it exploded.

How can I doubt that? I know the feeling when your mental power builds up too far. I always used to say that's why the Indians got drunk. Even statistically we're the smartest people on the earth. Anyhow with Grandpa I couldn't hardly believe it, because all my youth he stood out as a hero to me. When he started getting toward second childhood he went through different moods. He would stand in the woods and cry at the top of his shirt. It scared me, scared everyone, Grandma worst of all.

Yet he was so smart—do you believe it?—that he *knew* he was getting foolish.

He said so. He told me that December I failed school and come back on the train to Hoopdance. I didn't have nowhere else to go. He picked me up there and he said it straight out: "I'm getting into my second childhood." And then he said something else I still remember: "I been chosen for it. I couldn't say no." So I figure that a man so smart all his life—tribal chairman and the star of movies and even pictured in the statehouse and on cans of snuff—would know what he's doing by saying yes. I think he was called to second childhood like anybody else gets a call for the priesthood or the army or whatever. So I really did not listen too hard when the doctor said this was some kind of disease old people got eating too much sugar. You just can't tell me that a man who went to Washington and gave them bureaucrats what for could lose his mind from eating too much Milky Way. No, he put second childhood on himself.

Behind those songs he sings out in the middle of Mass, and back of those stories that everybody knows by heart, Grandpa is thinking hard about life. I know the feeling. Sometimes I'll throw up a smokescreen to think behind. I'll hitch up to Winnipeg and play the Space Invaders for six hours, but all the time there and back I will be thinking some fairly deep thoughts that surprise even me, and I'm used to it. As for him, if it was just the thoughts there wouldn't be no problem. Smokescreen is what irritates the social structure, see, and Grandpa has done things that just distract people to the point they want to throw him in the cookie jar where they keep the mentally insane. He's far from that, I know for sure, but even Grandma had trouble keeping her patience once he started sneaking off to Lamartine's place. He's not supposed to have his candy, and Lulu feeds it to him. That's *one* of the reasons why he goes.

Grandma tried to get me to put the touch on Grandpa soon after he began stepping out. I didn't want to, but before Grandma started telling me again what a bad state my bare behind was in when she first took me home, I thought I should at least pretend.

I put my hands on either side of Grandpa's head. You wouldn't look at him and say he was crazy. He's a fine figure of a man, as Lamartine would say, with all his hair and half his teeth, a beak like a hawk, and cheeks like the blades of a hatchet. They put his picture on all the tourist guides to North Dakota and even copied his face for artistic paintings. I guess you could call him a monument all of himself. He started grinning when I put my hands on his templates, and I knew right then he knew how come I touched him. I knew the smokescreen was going to fall.

And I was right: just for a moment it fell.

"Let's pitch whoopee," he said across my shoulder to Grandma.

They don't use that expression much around here anymore, but for damn sure it must have meant something. It got her goat right quick.

She threw my hands off his head herself and stood in front of him, overmatching him pound for pound, and taller too, for she had a growth spurt in middle age while he had shrunk, so now the length and breadth of her surpassed him. She glared up and spoke her piece into his face about how he was off at all hours tomcatting and chasing Lamartine again and making a damn old fool of himself.

"And you got no more whoopee to pitch anymore anyhow!" she yelled at last, surprising me so my jaw just dropped, for us kids all had pretended for so long that those rustling sounds we heard from their side of the room at night never happened. She sure had pretended it, up till now, anyway. I saw that tears were in her eyes. And that's when I saw how much grief and love she felt for him. And it gave me a real shock to the system. You see I thought love got easier over the years so it didn't hurt so bad when it hurt, or feel so good when it felt good. I thought it smoothed out and old people hardly noticed it. I thought it curled up and died, I guess. Now I saw it rear up like a whip and lash.

She loved him. She was jealous. She mourned him like the dead.

And he just smiled into the air, trapped in the seams of his mind.

So I didn't know what to do. I was in a laundry then. They was like parents to me, the way they had took me home and reared me. I could see her point for wanting to get him back the way he was so at least she could argue with him, sleep with him, not be shamed out by Lamartine. She'd always love him. That hit me like a ton of bricks. For one whole day I felt this odd feeling that cramped my hands. When you have the touch, that's where longing gets you. I never loved like that. It made me feel all inspired to see them fight, and I wanted to go out and find a woman who I would love until one of us died or went crazy. But I'm not like that really. From time to time I heal a person all up good inside, however when it comes to the long shot I doubt that I got staying power.

And you need that, staying power, going out to love somebody. I knew this quality was not going to jump on me with no effort. So I turned my thoughts back to Grandma and Grandpa. I felt her side of it with my hands and my tangled guts, and I felt his side of it within the stretch of my mentality. He had gone out to lunch one day and never came back. He was fishing in the middle of Lake Turcot. And there was big thoughts on his line, and he kept throwing them back for even bigger ones that would explain to him, say, the meaning of how we got here and why we have to leave so soon. All in all, I could not see myself treating Grandpa with the touch, bringing him back, when the real part of him had chose to be off thinking somewhere. It was only the rest of him that stayed around causing trouble, after all, and we could handle most of it without any problem.

Besides, it was hard to argue with his reasons for doing some things. Take Holy Mass. I used to go there just every so often, when I got frustrated mostly, because even though I know the Higher Power dwells everyplace, there's something very calming about the cool greenish inside of our mission. Or so I thought, anyway. Grandpa was the one who stripped off my delusions in this matter, for it was he who busted right through what Father Upsala calls the sacred serenity of the place.

We filed in that time. Me and Grandpa. We sat down in our pews. Then the rosary got started up pre-Mass and that's when Grandpa filled up his chest and opened his mouth and belted out them words.

HAIL MARIE FULL OF GRACE.

He had a powerful set of lungs.

And he kept on like that. He did not let up. He hollered and he yelled them prayers, and I guess people was used to him by now, because they only muttered theirs and did not quit and gawk like I did. I was getting red-faced, I admit. I give him the elbow once or twice, but that wasn't nothing to him. He kept on. He shrieked to heaven and he pleaded like a movie actor and he pounded his chest like Tarzan in the Lord I Am Not Worthies. I thought he might hurt himself. Then after a while I guess I got used to it, and that's when I wondered: how come?

So afterwards I out and asked him. "How come? How come you yelled?"

"God don't hear me otherwise," said Grandpa Kashpaw.

I sweat. I broke right into a little cold sweat at my hairline because I knew this was perfectly right and for years not one damn other person had noticed it. God's been going deaf. Since the Old Testament, God's been deafening up on us. I read, see. Besides the dictionary, which I'm constantly in use of, I had this Bible once. I read it. I found there was discrepancies between then and now. It struck me. Here God used to raineth bread from clouds, smite the Phillipines, sling fire down on red-light districts where people got stabbed. He even appeared in person every once in a while. God used to pay attention, is what I'm saying.

Now there's your God in the Old Testament and there is Chippewa Gods as well. Indian Gods, good and bad, like tricky Nanabozho or the water monster, Missepeshu, who lives over in Lake Turcot. That water monster was the last God I ever heard to appear. It had a weakness for young girls and grabbed one of the Blues off her rowboat. She got to shore all right, but only after this monster had its way with her. She's an old lady now. Old Lady Blue. She still won't let her family fish that lake.

Our Gods aren't perfect, is what I'm saying, but at least they come around. They'll do a favor if you ask them right. You don't have to yell. But you do have to know, like I said, how to ask in the right way. That makes problems, because to ask proper was an art that was lost to the Chippewas once the Catholics gained ground. Even now, I have to wonder if Higher Power turned it back, if we got to yell, or if we just don't speak its language.

I looked around me. How else could I explain what all I had seen in my short life—King smashing his fist in things, Gordie drinking himself down to the Bismarck hospitals, or Aunt June left by a white man to wander off in the snow. How else to explain the times my touch don't work, and farther back, to the old-time Indians who was swept away in the outright germ warfare and dirty-dog killing of the whites. In those times, us Indians was so much kindlier than now.

We took them in.

Oh yes, I'm bitter as an old cutworm just thinking of how they done to us and doing still.

So Grandpa Kashpaw just opened my eyes a little there. Was there any sense relying on a God whose ears was stopped? Just like the government? I says then, right off, maybe we got nothing but ourselves. And that's not much, just personally speaking. I know I don't got the cold hard potatoes it takes to understand everything. Still, there's things I'd like to do. For instance, I'd like to help some people like my Grandpa and Grandma Kashpaw get back some happiness within the tail ends of their lives.

I told you once before I couldn't see my way clear to putting the direct touch on Grandpa's mind, and I kept my moral there, but something soon happened to make me think a little bit of mental adjustment wouldn't do him and the rest of us no harm.

It was after we saw him one afternoon in the sunshine courtyard of the Senior Citizens with Lulu Lamartine. Grandpa used to like to dig there. He had his little dandelion fork out, and he was prying up them dandelions right and left while Lamartine watched him.

"He's scratching up the dirt, all right," said Grandma, watching Lamartine watch Grandpa out the window.

Now Lamartine was about half the considerable size of Grandma, but you would never think of sizes anyway. They were different in an even more noticeable way. It was the difference between a house fixed up with paint and picky fence, and a house left to weather away into the soft earth, is what I'm saying. Lamartine was jacked up, latticed, shuttered, and vinyl sided, while Grandma sagged and bulged on her slipped foundations and let her hair go the silver gray of rain-dried lumber. Right now, she eyed the Lamartine's pert flowery dress with such a look it despaired me. I knew what this could lead to with Grandma. Alternating tongue storms and rock-hard silences was hard on a man, even one who didn't notice, like Grandpa. So I went fetching him.

But he was gone when I popped through the little screen door that led out on the courtyard. There was nobody out there either, to point which way they went. Just the dandelion fork quibbling upright in the ground. That gave me an idea. I snookered over to the Lamartine's door and I listened in first, then knocked. But nobody. So I went walking through the lounges and around the card tables. Still nobody. Finally it was my touch that led me to the laundry room. I cracked the door. I went in. There they were. And he was really loving her up good, boy, and she was going hell for leather. Sheets was flapping on the lines above, and washcloths, pillowcases, shirts was also flying through the air, for they was trying to clear out a place for themselves in a high-heaped but shallow laundry cart. The washers and the dryers was all on, chock full of quarters, shaking and moaning. I couldn't hear what Grandpa and the Lamartine was billing and cooing, and they couldn't hear me.

I didn't know what to do, so I went inside and shut the door.

The Lamartine wore a big curly light-brown wig. Looked like one of them squeaky little white-people dogs. Poodles they call them. Anyway, that wig is what saved us from the worse. For I could hardly shout and tell them I was in there, no more could I try and grab him. I was trapped where I was. There was nothing I could really do but hold the door shut. I was scared of somebody else upsetting in and really getting an eyeful. Turned out though, in the heat of the clinch, as I was trying to avert my eyes you see, the Lamartine's curly wig jumped off her head. And if you ever been in the midst of something and had a big change like that occur in someone, you can't help know how it devastates your basic urges. Not only that, but her wig was almost with a life of its own. Grandpa's eyes were bugging at the change already, and swear to God if the thing didn't rear up and pop him in the face like it was going to start something. He scrambled up, Grandpa did, and the Lamartine jumped up after him all addled looking. They just stared at each other, huffing and puffing, with quizzical expression. The surprise seemed to drive all sense completely out of Grandpa's mind.

"The letter was what started the fire," he said. "I never would have done it."

"What letter?" said the Lamartine. She was stiff-necked now, and elegant, even bald, like some alien queen. I gave her back the wig. The Lamartine replaced it on her head, and whenever I saw her after that, I couldn't help thinking of her bald, with special powers, as if from another planet.

"That was a close call," I said to Grandpa after she had left.

But I think he had already forgot the incident. He just stood there all quiet and thoughtful. You really wouldn't think he was crazy. He looked like he was just about to say something important, explaining himself. He said something, all right, but it didn't have nothing to do with anything that made sense.

He wondered where the heck he put his dandelion fork. That's when I decided about the mental adjustment.

Now what was mostly our problem was not so much that he was not all there, but that what was there of him often hankered after Lamartine. If we could put a stop to that, I thought, we might be getting someplace. But here, see, my touch was of no use. For what could I snap my fingers at to make him faithful to Grandma? Like the quality of staying power, this faithfulness was invisible. I know it's something that you got to acquire, but I never known where from. Maybe there's no rhyme or reason to it, like my getting the touch, and then again maybe it's a kind of magic.

It was Grandma Kashpaw who thought of it in the end. She knows things. Although she will not admit she has a scrap of Indian blood in her, there's no doubt in my mind she's got some Chippewa. How else would you explain the way she'll be sitting there, in front of her TV story, rocking in her armchair and suddenly she turns on me, her brown eyes hard as lake-bed flint.

"Lipsha Morrissey," she'll say, "you went out last night and got drunk."

How did she know that? I'll hardly remember it myself. Then she'll say she just had a feeling or ache in the scar of her hand or a creak in her shoulder. She is constantly being told things by little aggravations in her joints or by her household appliances. One time she told Gordie never to ride with a crazy Lamartine boy. She had seen something in the polished-up tin of her bread toaster. So he didn't. Sure enough, the time came we heard how Lyman and Henry went out of control in their car, ending up in the river. Lyman swam to the top, but Henry never made it.

Thanks to Grandma's toaster, Gordie was probably spared.

Someplace in the blood Grandma Kashpaw knows things. She also remembers things, I found. She keeps things filed away. She's got a memory like them video games that don't forget your score. One reason she remembers so many details about the trouble I gave her in early life is so she can flash back her total when she needs to.

Like now. Take the love medicine. I don't know where she remembered that from. It came tumbling from her mind like an asteroid off the corner of the screen.

Of course she starts out by mentioning the time I had this accident in church and did she leave me there with wet overhalls? No she didn't. And ain't I glad? Yes I am. Now what you want now, Grandma?

But when she mentions them love medicines, I feel my back prickle at the danger. These love medicines is something of an old Chippewa specialty. No other tribe has got them down so well. But love medicines is not for the layman to handle. You don't just go out and get one without paying for it. Before you get one, even, you should go through one hell of a lot of mental condensation. You got to think it over. Choose the right one. You could really mess up your life grinding up the wrong little thing.

So anyhow, I said to Grandma I'd give this love medicine some thought. I knew the best thing was to go ask a specialist like Old Man Pillager, who lives up in a tangle of bush and never shows himself. But the truth is I was afraid of him, like everyone else. He was known for putting the twisted mouth on people, seizing up their hearts. Old Man Pillager was serious business, and I have always thought it best to steer clear of that whenever I could. That's why I took the powers in my own hands. That's why I did what I could.

I put my whole mentality to it, nothing held back. After a while I started to remember things I'd heard gossiped over.

I heard of this person once who carried a charm of seeds that looked like baby pearls. They was attracted to a metal knife, which made them powerful. But I didn't know where them seeds grew. Another love charm I heard about I couldn't go along with, because how was I suppose to catch frogs in the act, which it required. Them little creatures is slippery and fast. And then the powerfullest of all, the most extreme, involved nail clips and such. I wasn't anywhere near asking Grandma to provide me all the little body bits that this last love recipe called for. I went walking around for days just trying to think up something that would work.

Well I got it. If it hadn't been the early fall of the year, I never would have got it. But I was sitting underneath a tree one day down near the school just watching people's feet go by when something tells me, look up! Look up! So I look up, and I see two honkers, Canada geese, the kind with little masks on their faces, a bird what mates for life. I see them flying right over my head naturally preparing to land in some slough on the reservation, which they certainly won't get off of alive.

It hits me, anyway. Them geese, they mate for life. And I think to myself, just what if I went out and got a pair? And just what if I fed some part—say the goose heart—of the female to Grandma and Grandpa ate the other heart? Wouldn't that work? Maybe it's all invisible, and then maybe again it's magic. Love is a stony road. We know that for sure. If it's true that the higher feelings of devotion get lodged in the heart like people say, then we'd be home free. If not, eating goose heart couldn't harm nobody anyway. I thought it was worth my effort, and Grandma Kashpaw thought so, too. She had always known a good idea when she heard one. She borrowed me Grandpa's gun.

So I went out to this particular slough, maybe the exact same slough I never got thrown in by my mother, thanks to Grandma Kashpaw, and I hunched down in a good comfortable pile of rushes. I got my gun loaded up. I ate a few of these soft baloney sandwiches Grandma made me for lunch. And then I waited. The cattails blown back and forth above my head. Them stringy blue herons was spearing up their prey. The thing I know how to do best in this world, the thing I been training for all my life, is to wait. Sitting there and sitting there was no hardship on me. I got to thinking about some funny things that happened. There was this one time that Lulu Lamartine's little blue tweety bird, a paraclete, I guess you'd call it, flown up inside her dress and got lost within there. I recalled her running out into the hallway trying to yell something, shaking. She was doing a right good jig there, cutting the rug for sure, and the thing is it *never* flown out. To this day people speculate where it went. They fear she might perhaps of crushed it in her corsets. It sure hasn't ever yet been seen alive. I thought of funny things for a while, but then I used them up, and strange things that happened started weaseling their way into my mind.

I got to thinking quite naturally of the Lamartine's cousin named Wristwatch. I never knew what his real name was. They called him Wristwatch because he got his father's broken wristwatch as a young boy when his father passed on. Never in his whole life did Wristwatch take his father's watch off. He didn't care if it worked, although after a while he got sensitive when people asked what time it was, teasing him. He often put it to his ear like he was listening to the tick. But it was broken for good and forever, people said so, at least that's what they thought.

Well I saw Wristwatch smoking in his pickup one afternoon and by nine that evening he was dead.

He died sitting at the Lamartine's table, too. As she told it, Wristwatch had just eaten himself a good-size dinner and she said would he take seconds on the hot dish when he fell over to the floor. They turnt him over. He was gone. But here's the strange thing: when the Senior Citizen's orderly took the pulse he noticed that the wristwatch Wristwatch wore was now working. The moment he died the wristwatch started keeping perfect time. They buried him with the watch still ticking on his arm.

I got to thinking. What if some gravediggers dug up Wristwatch's casket in two hundred years and that watch was still going? I thought what question they would ask and it was this: Whose hand wound it?

I started shaking like a piece of grass at just the thought.

Not to get off the subject or nothing. I was still hunkered in the slough. It was passing late into the afternoon and still no honkers had touched down. Now I don't need to tell you that the waiting did not get to me, it was the chill. The rushes was very soft, but damp. I was getting cold and debating to leave, when they landed. Two geese swimming here and there as big as life, looking deep into each other's little pinhole eyes. Just the ones I was looking for. So I lifted Grandpa's gun to my shoulder and I aimed perfectly, and *blam! Blam!* I delivered two accurate shots. But the thing is, them shots missed. I couldn't hardly believe it. Whether it was that the stock had warped or the barrel got bent someways, I don't quite know, but anyway them geese flown off into the dim sky, and Lipsha Morrissey was left there in the rushes with evening fallen and his two cold hands empty. He had before him just the prospect of another day of bone-cracking chill in them rushes, and the thought of it got him depressed.

Now it isn't my style, in no way, to get depressed.

So I said to myself, Lipsha Morrissey, you're a happy S.O.B. who could be covered up with weeds by now down at the bottom of this slough, but instead you're alive to tell the tale. You might have problems in life, but you still got the touch. You got the power, Lipsha Morrissey. Can't argue that. So put your mind to it and figure out how not to be depressed.

I took my advice. I put my mind to it. But I never saw at the time how my thoughts led me astray toward a tragic outcome none could have known. I ignored all the danger, all the limits, for I was tired of sitting in the slough and my feet were numb. My face was aching. I was chilled, so I played with fire. I told myself love medicine was simple. I told myself the old superstitions was just that—strange beliefs. I told myself to take the ten dollars Mary MacDonald had paid me for putting the touch on her arthritis joint, and the other five I hadn't spent yet from winning bingo last Thursday. I told myself to go down to the Red Owl store.

And here is what I did that made the medicine backfire. I took an evil shortcut. I looked at birds that was dead and froze.

All right. So now I guess you will say, "Slap a malpractice suit on Lipsha Morrissey."

I heard of those suits. I used to think it was a color clothing quack doctors had to wear so you could tell them from the good ones. Now I know better that it's law.

As I walked back from the Red Owl with the rock-hard, heavy turkeys, I argued to myself about malpractice. I thought of faith. I thought to myself that faith could be called belief against the odds and whether or not there's any proof. How does that sound? I thought how we might have to yell to be heard by Higher Power, but that's not saying it's not *there*. And that is faith for you. It's belief even when the goods don't deliver. Higher Power makes promises we all know they can't back up, but anybody ever go and slap an old malpractice suit on God? Or the U.S. government? No they don't. Faith might be stupid, but it gets us through. So what I'm heading at is this. I finally convinced myself that the real actual power to the love medicine was not the goose heart itself but the faith in the cure.

I didn't believe it, I knew it was wrong, but by then I had waded so far into my lie I was stuck there. And then I went one step further.

The next day, I cleaned the hearts away from the paper packages of gizzards inside the turkeys. Then I wrapped them hearts with a clean hankie and brung them both to get blessed up at the mission. I wanted to get official blessings from the priest, but when Father answered the door to the rectory, wiping his hands on a little towel, I could tell he was a busy man.

"Booshoo, Father," I said. "I got a slight request to make of you this afternoon."

"What is it?" he said.

"Would you bless this package?" I held out the hankie with the hearts tied inside it.

He looked at the package, questioning it.

"It's turkey hearts," I honestly had to reply.

A look of annoyance crossed his face.

"Why don't you bring this matter over to Sister Martin," he said. "I have duties."

And so, although the blessing wouldn't be as powerful, I went over to the Sisters with the package.

I rung the bell, and they brought Sister Martin to the door. I had her as a music teacher, but I was always so shy then. I never talked out loud. Now, I had grown taller than Sister Martin. Looking down, I saw that she was not feeling up to snuff. Brown circles hung under her eyes.

"What's the matter?" she said, not noticing who I was.

"Remember me, Sister?"

She squinted up at me.

"Oh yes," she said after a moment. "I'm sorry, you're the youngest of the Kashpaws. Gordie's brother."

Her face warmed up.

"Lipsha," I said, "that's my name."

"Well, Lipsha," she said, smiling broad at me now, "what can I do for you?"

They always said she was the kindest-hearted of the Sisters up the hill, and she was. She brought me back into their own kitchen and made me take a big yellow wedge of cake and a glass of milk.

"Now tell me," she said, nodding at my package. "What have you got wrapped up so carefully in those handkerchiefs?"

Like before, I answered honestly.

"Ah," said Sister Martin. "Turkey hearts." She waited.

"I hoped you could bless them."

She waited some more, smiling with her eyes. Kindhearted though she was, I began to sweat. A person could not pull the wool down over Sister Martin. I stumbled through my mind for an explanation, quick, that wouldn't scare her off.

"They're a present," I said, "for Saint Kateri's statue."

"She's not a saint yet."

"I know," I stuttered on, "in the hopes they will crown her."

"Lipsha," she said, "I never heard of such a thing."

So I told her. "Well the truth is," I said, "it's a kind of medicine."

"For what?"

"Love."

"Oh Lipsha," she said after a moment, "you don't need any medicine. I'm sure any girl would like you exactly the way you are."

I just sat there. I felt miserable, caught in my pack of lies.

"Tell you what," she said, seeing how bad I felt, "my blessing won't make any difference anyway. But there is something you can do."

I looked up at her, hopeless.

"Just be yourself."

I looked down at my plate. I knew I wasn't much to brag about right then, and I shortly became even less. For as I walked out the door I stuck my fingers in the cup of holy water that was sacred from their touches. I put my fingers in and blessed the hearts, quick, with my own hand.

I went back to Grandma and sat down in her little kitchen at the Senior Citizens. I unwrapped them hearts on the table, and her hard agate eyes went soft. She said she wasn't even going to cook those hearts up but eat them raw so their power would go down strong as possible.

I couldn't hardly watch when she munched hers. Now that's true love. I was worried about how she would get Grandpa to eat his, but she told me she'd think of something and don't worry. So I did not. I was supposed to hide off in her bedroom while she put dinner on a plate for Grandpa and fixed up the heart so he'd eat it. I caught a glint of the plate she was making for him. She put that heart smack on a piece of lettuce like in a restaurant and then attached to it a little heap of boiled peas.

He sat down. I was listening in the next room.

She said, "Why don't you have some mash potato?" So he had some mash potato. Then she gave him a little piece of boiled meat. He ate that. Then she said, "Why you don't never touch your salad yet. See that heart? I'm feeding you it because the doctor said your blood needs building up."

I couldn't help it, at that point I peeked through a crack in the door.

I saw Grandpa picking at that heart on his plate with a certain look. He didn't look appetized at all, is what I'm saying. I doubted our plan was going to work. Grandma was getting worried, too. She told him one more time, loudly, that he had to eat that heart.

"Swallow it down," she said, "You'll hardly notice it."

He just looked at her straight on. The way he looked at her made me think I was going to see the smokescreen drop a second time, and sure enough it happened.

"What you want me to eat this for so bad?" he asked her uncannily.

Now Grandma knew the jig was up. She knew that he knew she was working medicine. He put his fork down. He rolled the heart around his saucer plate.

"I don't want to eat this," he said to Grandma. "It don't look good."

"Why it's fresh grade-A," she told him. "One hundred percent."

He didn't ask percent what, but his eyes took on an even more warier look.

"Just go on and try it," she said, taking the salt shaker up in her hand. She was getting annoyed. "Not tasty enough? You want me to salt it for you?" She waved the shaker over his plate.

"All right, skinny white girl!" She had got Grandpa mad. Oopsy-daisy, he popped the heart into his mouth. I was about to yawn loudly and come out of the bedroom. I was about ready for this crash of wills to be over, when I saw he was still up to his old tricks. First he rolled it into one side of his cheek. "Mmmmm," he said. Then he rolled it into the other side of his cheek. "Mmmmmmmm," again. Then he stuck his tongue out with the heart on it and put it back, and there was no time to react. He had pulled Grandma's leg once too far. Her goat was got. She was so mad she hopped up quick as a wink and slugged him between the shoulderblades to make him swallow.

Only thing is, he choked.

He choked real bad. A person can choke to death. You ever sit down at a restaurant table and up above you there is a list of instructions what to do if something slides down the wrong pipe? It sure makes you chew slow, that's for damn sure. When Grandpa fell off his chair better believe me that little graphic illustrated poster fled into my mind. I jumped out the bedroom. I done everything within my power that I could do to unlodge what was choking him. I squeezed underneath his ribcage. I socked him in the back. I was desperate. But here's the factor of decision: he wasn't choking on the heart alone. There was more to it than that. It was other things that choked him as well. It didn't seem like he wanted to struggle or fight. Death came and tapped his chest, so he went just like that. I'm sorry all through my body at what I done to him with that heart, and there's those who will say Lipsha Morrissey is just excusing himself off the hook by giving song and dance about how Grandpa gave up.

Maybe I can't admit what I did. My touch had gone worthless, that is true. But here is what I seen while he lay in my arms.

You hear a person's life will flash before their eyes when they're in danger. It was him in danger, not me, but it was *his* life come over me. I saw him dying, and it was like someone pulled the shade down in a room. His eyes clouded over and squeezed shut, but just before that I looked in. He was still fishing in the middle of Lake Turcot. Big thoughts was on his line and he had half a case of beer in the boat. He waved at me, grinned, and then the bobber went under.

Grandma had gone out of the room crying for help. I bunched my force up in my hands and I held him. I was so wound up I couldn't even breathe. All the moments he had spent with me, all the times he had hoisted me on his shoulders or pointed into the leaves was concentrated in that moment. Time was flashing back and forth like a pinball machine. Lights blinked and balls hopped and rubber bands chirped, until suddenly I realized the last ball had gone down the drain and there was nothing. I felt his force leaving him, flowing out of Grandpa never to return. I felt his mind weakening. The bobber going under in the lake. And I felt the touch retreat back into the darkness inside my body, from where it came.

One time, long ago, both of us were fishing together. We caught a big old snapper what started towing us around like it was a motor. "This here fishline is pretty damn good," Grandpa said. "Let's keep this turtle on and see where he takes us." So we rode along behind the turtle, watching as from time to time it surfaced. The thing was just about the size of a washtub. It took us all around the lake twice, and as it was traveling, Grandpa said something as a joke. "Lipsha," he said, "we are glad your mother didn't want you because we was always looking for a boy like you who would tow us around the lake."

"I ain't no snapper. Snappers is so stupid they stay alive when their head's chopped off," I said.

"That ain't stupidity," said Grandpa. "Their brain's just in their heart, like yours is."

When I looked up, I knew the fuse had blown between my heart and my mind and that a terrible understanding was to be given.

Grandma got back into the room and I saw her stumble. And then she went down too. It was like a house you can't hardly believe has stood so long, through years of record weather, suddenly goes down in the worst yet. It makes sense, is what I'm saying, but you still can't hardly believe it. You think a person you know has got through deaths and illness and being broke and living on commodity rice will get through anything. Then they fold and you see how fragile were the stones that underpinned them. You see how instantly the ground can shift you thought was solid. You see the stop signs and the yellow dividing markers of roads you traveled and all the instructions you had played according to vanish. You see how all the everyday things you counted on was just a dream you had been having by which you run your whole life. She had been over me, like a sheer overhang of rock dividing Lipsha Morrissey from outer space. And now she went underneath. It was as though the banks gave way on the shores of Lake Turcot, and where Grandpa's passing was just the bobber swallowed under by his biggest thought, her fall was the house and the rock under it sliding after, sending half the lake splashing up to the clouds.

Where there was nothing.

You play them games never knowing what you see. When I fell into the dream alongside of both of them I saw that the dominions I had defended myself from anciently was but delusions of the screen. Blips of light. And I was scot-free now, whistling through space.

I don't know how I come back. I don't know from where. They was slapping my face when I arrived back at Senior Citizens and they was oxygenating her. I saw her chest move, almost unwilling. She sighed the way she would when somebody bothered her in the middle of a row of beads she was counting. I think it irritated her to no end that they brought her back. I knew from the way she looked after they took the mask off, she was not going to forgive them disturbing her restful peace. Nor was she forgiving Lipsha Morrissey. She had been stepping out onto the road of death, she told the children later at the funeral. I asked was there any stop signs or dividing markers on that road, but she clamped her lips in a vise the way she always done when she was mad.

Which didn't bother me. I knew when things had cleared out she wouldn't have no choice. I was not going to speculate where the blame was put for Grandpa's death. We was in it together. She had slugged him between the shoulders. My touch had failed him, never to return.

All the blood children and the took-ins, like me, came home from Minneapolis and Chicago, where they had relocated years ago. They stayed with friends on the reservation or with Aurelia or slept on Grandma's floor. They were struck down with grief and bereavement to be sure, every one of them. At the funeral I sat down in the back of the church with Albertine. She had gotten all skinny and ragged haired from cramming all her years of study into two or three. She had decided that to be a nurse was not enough for her so she was going to be a doctor. But the way she was straining her mind didn't look too hopeful. Her eyes were bloodshot from driving and crying. She took my hand. From the back we watched all the children and the mourners as they hunched over their prayers, their hands stuffed full of Kleenex. It was someplace in that long sad service that my vision shifted. I began to see things different, more clear. The family kneeling down turned to rocks in a field. It struck me how strong and reliable grief was, and death. Until the end of time, death would be our rock.

So I had perspective on it all, for death gives you that. All the Kashpaw children had done various things to me in their lives—shared their folks with me, loaned me cash, beat me up in secret—and I decided, because of death, then and there I'd call it quits. If I ever saw King again, I'd shake his hand. Forgiving somebody else made the whole thing easier to bear.

Everybody saw Grandpa off into the next world. And then the Kashpaws had to get back to their jobs, which was numerous and impressive. I had a few beers with them and I went back to Grandma, who had sort of got lost in the shuffle of everybody being sad about Grandpa and glad to see one another.

Zelda had sat beside her the whole time and was sitting with her now. I wanted to talk to Grandma, say how sorry I was, that it wasn't her fault, but only mine. I would have, but Zelda gave me one of her looks of strict warning as if to say, "I'll take care of Grandma. Don't horn in on the women."

If only Zelda knew, I thought, the sad realities would change her. But of course I couldn't tell the dark truth.

It was evening, late. Grandma's light was on underneath a crack in the door. About a week had passed since we buried Grandpa. I knocked first but there wasn't no answer, so I went right in. The door was unlocked. She was there but she didn't notice me at first. Her hands were tied up in her rosary, and her gaze was fully absorbed in the easy chair opposite her, the one that had always been Grandpa's favorite. I stood there, staring with her, at the little green nubs in the cloth and plastic armrest covers and the sad little hair-tonic stain he had made on the white doily where he laid his head. For the life of me I couldn't figure what she was staring at. Thin space. Then she turned.

"He ain't gone yet," she said.

Remember that chill I luckily didn't get from waiting in the slough? I got it now. I felt it start from the very center of me, where fear hides, waiting to attack. It spiraled outward so that in minutes my fingers and teeth were shaking and clattering. I knew she told the truth. She seen Grandpa. Whether or not he had been there is not the point. She had *seen* him, and that meant anybody else could see him, too. Not only that but, as is usually the case with these here ghosts, he had a certain uneasy reason to come back. And of course Grandma Kashpaw had scanned it out.

I sat down. We sat together on the couch watching his chair out of the corner of our eyes. She had found him sitting in his chair when she walked in the door.

"It's the love medicine, my Lipsha," she said. "It was stronger than we thought. He came back even after death to claim me to his side."

I was afraid. "We shouldn't have tampered with it," I said. She agreed. For a while we sat still. I don't know what she thought, but my head felt screwed on backward. I couldn't accurately consider the situation, so I told Grandma to go to bed. I would sleep on the couch keeping my eye on Grandpa's chair. Maybe he would come back and maybe he wouldn't. I guess I feared the one as much as the other, but I got to thinking, see, as I lay there in darkness, that perhaps even through my terrible mistakes some good might come. If Grandpa did come back, I thought he'd return in his right mind. I could talk with him. I could tell him it was all my fault for playing with power I did not understand. Maybe he'd forgive me and rest in peace. I hoped this. I calmed myself and waited for him all night.

He fooled me though. He knew what I was waiting for, and it wasn't what he was looking to hear. Come dawn I heard a bloodsplitting cry from the bedroom and I rushed in there. Grandma turnt the lights on. She was sitting on the edge of the bed and her face looked harsh, pinched-up, gray.

"He was here," she said. "He came and laid down next to me in bed. And he touched me."

Her heart broke down. She cried. His touch was so cold. She laid back in bed after a while, as it was morning, and I went to the couch. As I lay there, falling asleep, I suddenly felt Grandpa's presence and the barrier between us like a swollen river. I felt how I had wronged him. How awful was the place where I had sent him. Behind the wall of death, he'd watched the living eat and cry and get drunk. He was lonesome, but I understood he meant no harm.

"Go back, " I said to the dark, afraid and yet full of pity. "You got to be with your own kind now," I said. I felt him retreating, like a sigh, growing less. I felt his spirit as it shrunk back through the walls, the blinds, the brick courtyard of Senior Citizens. "Look up Aunt June," I whispered as he left.

I slept late the next morning, a good hard sleep allowing the sun to rise and warm the earth. It was past noon when I awoke. There is nothing, to my mind, like a long sleep to make those hard decisions that you neglect under stress of wakefulness. Soon as I woke up that morning, I saw exactly what I'd say to Grandma. I had gotten humble in the past week, not just losing the touch but getting jolted into the understanding that would prey on me from here on out. Your life feels different on you, once you greet death and understand your heart's position. You wear your life like a garment from the mission bundle sale ever after— lightly because you realize you never paid nothing for it, cherishing because you know you won't ever come by such a bargain again. Also you have the feeling someone wore it before you and someone will after. I can't explain that, not yet, but I'm putting my mind to it.

"Grandma," I said, "I got to be honest about the love medicine."

She listened. I knew from then on she would be listening to me the way I had listened to her before. I told her about the turkey hearts and how I had them blessed. I told her what I used as love medicine was purely a fake, and then I said to her what my understanding brought me.

"Love medicine ain't what brings him back to you, Grandma. No, it's something else. He loved you over time and distance, but he went off so quick he never got the chance to tell you how he loves you, how he doesn't blame you, how he understands. It's true feeling, not no magic. No supermarket heart could have brung him back."

She looked at me. She was seeing the years and days I had no way of knowing, and she didn't believe me. I could tell this. Yet a look came on her face. It was like the look of mothers drinking sweetness from their children's eyes. It was tenderness.

"Lipsha," she said, "you was always my favorite."

She took the beads off the bedpost, where she kept them to say at night, and she told me to put out my hand. When I did this, she shut the beads inside of my fist and held them there a long minute, tight, so my hand hurt. I almost cried when she did this. I don't really know why. Tears shot up behind my eyelids, and yet it was nothing. I didn't understand, except her hand was so strong, squeezing mine.

The earth was full of life and there were dandelions growing out the window, thick as thieves, already seeded, fat as big yellow plungers. She let my hand go. I got up. "I'll go out and dig a few dandelions," I told her.

Outside, the sun was hot and heavy as a hand on my back. I felt it flow down my arms, out my fingers, arrowing through the ends of the fork into the earth. With every root I prized up there was return, as if

I was kin to its secret lesson. The touch got stronger as I worked through the grassy afternoon. Uncurling from me like a seed out of the blackness where I was lost, the touch spread. The spiked leaves full of bitter mother's milk. A buried root. A nuisance people dig up and throw in the sun to wither. A globe of frail seeds that's indestructible.

1984

FOUR

Stories of Speech,
Stories of Silence

CHARLOTTE PERKINS GILMAN, The
   Yellow Wallpaper
TONI CADE BAMBARA, Maggie of the
   Green Bottles
ANTON CHEKHOV, The Darling
D. H. LAWRENCE, The Lovely Lady
HENRY JAMES, Paste
WILLA CATHER, The Way of the World

One of the signs of an autonomous existence is being able to tell one's own story, or to speak for oneself. Infants and children and animals need others to speak for them; sometimes even adults are reduced to infancy when others assume the power to tell their stories. Historically women have often been denied the power of speaking for themselves. The stories in this chapter are of women losing, regaining, and voicing their powers of speech.

In "The Yellow Wallpaper," the narrator—whom we know only as she is referred to by her husband, his "little girl"—is virtually imprisoned: she is forbidden to write, to read, to have intellectual companionship, to speak for herself, all of which sends her into madness by the end of the story. Charlotte Perkins Gilman details the chilling consequences of this silencing of a voice; prohibiting stories can be dangerous; forbidding stories can destroy worlds.

Stories can also build new worlds, as Toni Cade Bambara shows in "Maggie of the Green Bottles," in which telling stories and fortunes and horoscopes is how knowledge is passed down in the female line. Inspired by her place in the chain, the great-granddaughter sees herself as "the hope of the Aries line." But in the midst of this hope, the grandmother suffers. Although the child sees her as wise and funny and strong—as well as magical—she is actually a drunkard. The green bottles that are supposed to hold magic really hold gin.

In some of the stories, women do not seem to have any stories of their own to tell; they are simply parasites. In "The Darling," Anton Chekhov portrays a character, Olenka, who has no ideas of her own, but who assumes, in turn, those of the men in her life; she sheds ideas with each new relationship. D. H. Lawrence, in "The Lovely Lady," paints a much more malevolent portrait of an aging beauty who, like a vampire, "put a sucker into one's soul and sucked up one's essential life." Her dreadful power over other people comes from stealing their stories and using them as her own.

Women have always had a restricted repertoire from which to choose their selves, limited roles to play, few speeches to declaim. The stepson in Henry James's "Paste" cannot believe his stepmother's pearls, given to her before her marriage, are genuine, since that would destroy his sense of her virtue; rather, paste pearls—the false—better mark the truth of her nature. By confining her life and character within rigid limits, the son reveals his own character as paste. "The Way of the World" (Willa Cather) presents a little girl victorious in her independence; before she is allowed to join the wholly male play-town, how-ever, even her champion—Speckle—wonders about whether a girl "could meet the large demands on the imagination requisite to citizenship in Speckle-ville." Of course, Mary Eliza ultimately displaces Speckle himself as the center of this imaginary town, capable of rewriting and transforming the story of their world.

Mary Eliza can prod and persuade until she changes the script she's been given. And in speaking her own lines, she is able to change the way of the world itself. Although most of the women in this chapter are silenced, locked up, locked out, and condemned, the stories themselves give them back their voices.

CHARLOTTE PERKINS GILMAN

The Yellow Wallpaper

It is very seldom that mere ordinary people like John and myself secure ancestral halls for the summer.

A colonial mansion, a hereditary estate, I would say a haunted house and reach the height of romantic felicity—but that would be asking too much of fate!

Still I will proudly declare that there is something queer about it.

Else, why should it be let so cheaply? And why have stood so long untenanted?

John laughs at me, of course, but one expects that.

John is practical in the extreme. He has no patience with faith, an intense horror of superstition, and he scoffs openly at any talk of things not to be felt and seen and put down in figures.

John is a physician, and *perhaps*—(I would not say it to a living soul, of course, but this is dead paper and a great relief to my mind)— *perhaps* that is one reason I do not get well faster.

Charlotte Perkins Gilman was born in 1860 in Hartford, Connecticut, and grew up in Rhode Island. When Gilman was very young, her father abandoned the family. The ensuing economic and psychological effects of this event on both her own and her mother's life forced Gilman to confront at an early age the position to which women were consigned in western society. With the beginning of her literary career in the 1890s, Gilman's point of view was reflected in numerous speeches, socioeconomic analyses, and short stories, including "The Yellow Wallpaper" (1892). From 1909 to 1916, she argued for the emancipation of women and social reorganization in *The Forerunner*, a journal that she founded and edited and for which she wrote almost all the material. In 1935, residing in Pasadena, California, and suffering from breast cancer, Gilman took her own life.

You see, he does not believe I am sick! And what can one do?

If a physician of high standing, and one's own husband, assures friends and relatives that there is really nothing the matter with one but temporary nervous depression—a slight hysterical tendency—what is one to do?

My brother is also a physician, and also of high standing, and he says the same thing.

So I take phosphates or phosphites—whichever it is—and tonics, and air and exercise, and journeys, and am absolutely forbidden to "work" until I am well again.

Personally, I disagree with their ideas.

Personally, I believe that congenial work, with excitement and change, would do me good.

But what is one to do?

I did write for a while in spite of them; but it *does* exhaust me a good deal—having to be so sly about it, or else meet with heavy opposition.

I sometimes fancy that in my condition, if I had less opposition and more society and stimulus—but John says the very worst thing I can do is to think about my condition, and I confess it always makes me feel bad.

So I will let it alone and talk about the house.

The most beautiful place! It is quite alone, standing well back from the road, quite three miles from the village. It makes me think of English places that you read about, for there are hedges and walls and gates that lock, and lots of separate little houses for the gardeners and people.

There is a *delicious* garden! I never saw such a garden—large and shady, full of box-bordered paths, and lined with long grape-covered arbors with seats under them.

There were greenhouses, but they are all broken now.

There was some legal trouble, I believe, something about the heirs and co-heirs; anyhow, the place has been empty for years.

That spoils my ghostliness, I am afraid, but I don't care—there is something strange about the house—I can feel it.

I even said so to John one moonlight evening, but he said what I felt was a draught, and shut the window.

I get unreasonably angry with John sometimes. I'm sure I never used to be so sensitive. I think it is due to this nervous condition.

But John says if I feel so I shall neglect proper self-control; so I take pains to control myself—before him, at least, and that makes me very tired.

I don't like our room a bit. I wanted one downstairs that opened onto the piazza and had roses all over the window, and such pretty old-fashioned chintz hangings! But John would not hear of it.

He said there was only one window and not room for two beds, and no near room for him if he took another.

He is very careful and loving, and hardly lets me stir without special direction.

I have a schedule prescription for each hour in the day; he takes all care from me, and so I feel basely ungrateful not to value it more.

He said he came here solely on my account, that I was to have perfect rest and all the air I could get. "Your exercise depends on your strength, my dear," said he, "and your food somewhat on your appetite; but air you can absorb all the time." So we took the nursery at the top of the house.

It is a big, airy room, the whole floor nearly, with windows that look all ways, and air and sunshine galore. It was nursery first, and then playroom and gymnasium, I should judge, for the windows are barred for little children, and there are rings and things in the walls.

The paint and paper look as if a boys' school had used it. It is stripped off—the paper—in great patches all around the head of my bed, about as far as I can reach, and in a great place on the other side of the room low down. I never saw a worse paper in my life. One of those sprawling, flamboyant patterns committing every artistic sin.

It is dull enough to confuse the eye in following, pronounced enough constantly to irritate and provoke study, and when you follow the lame uncertain curves for a little distance they suddenly commit suicide—plunge off at outrageous angles, destroy themselves in unheard-of contradictions.

The color is repellent, almost revolting: a smouldering unclean yellow, strangely faded by the slow-turning sunlight. It is a dull yet lurid orange in some places, a sickly sulphur tint in others.

No wonder the children hated it! I should hate it myself if I had to live in this room long.

There comes John, and I must put this away—he hates to have me write a word.

We have been here two weeks, and I haven't felt like writing before, since that first day.

I am sitting by the window now, up in this atrocious nursery, and there is nothing to hinder my writing as much as I please, save lack of strength.

John is away all day, and even some nights when his cases are serious.

I am glad my case is not serious!

But these nervous troubles are dreadfully depressing.

John does not know how much I really suffer. He knows there is no reason to suffer, and that satisfies him.

Of course it is only nervousness. It does weigh on me so not to do my duty in any way!

I meant to be such a help to John, such a real rest and comfort, and here I am a comparative burden already!

Nobody would believe what an effort it is to do what little I am able —to dress and entertain, and order things.

It is fortunate Mary is so good with the baby. Such a dear baby!

And yet I *cannot* be with him, it makes me so nervous.

I suppose John never was nervous in his life. He laughs at me so about this wallpaper!

At first he meant to repaper the room, but afterward he said that I was letting it get the better of me, and that nothing was worse for a nervous patient than to give way to such fancies.

He said that after the wallpaper was changed it would be the heavy bedstead, and then the barred windows, and then that gate at the head of the stairs, and so on.

"You know the place is doing you good," he said, "and really, dear, I don't care to renovate the house just for a three months' rental."

"Then do let us go downstairs," I said. "There are such pretty rooms there."

Then he took me in his arms and called me a blessed little goose, and said he would go down cellar, if I wished, and have it whitewashed into the bargain.

But he is right enough about the beds and windows and things.

It is as airy and comfortable a room as anyone need wish, and, of course, I would not be so silly as to make him uncomfortable just for a whim.

I'm really getting quite fond of the big room, all but that horrid paper.

Out of one window I can see the garden—those mysterious deep-shaded arbors, the riotous old-fashioned flowers, and bushes and gnarly trees.

Out of another I get a lovely view of the bay and a little private wharf belonging to the estate. There is a beautiful shaded lane that runs down there from the house. I always fancy I see people walking in these numerous paths and arbors, but John has cautioned me not to give way to fancy in the least. He says that with my imaginative power and habit of story-making, a nervous weakness like mine is sure to lead to all manner of excited fancies, and that I ought to use my will and good sense to check the tendency. So I try.

I think sometimes that if I were only well enough to write a little it would relieve the press of ideas and rest me.

But I find I get pretty tired when I try.

It is so discouraging not to have any advice and companionship about my work. When I get really well, John says we will ask Cousin Henry and Julia down for a long visit; but he says he would as soon put fireworks in my pillow-case as to let me have those stimulating people about now.

I wish I could get well faster.

But I must not think about that. This paper looks to me as if it *knew* what a vicious influence it had!

There is a recurrent spot where the pattern lolls like a broken neck and two bulbous eyes stare at you upside down.

I get positively angry with the impertinence of it and the everlastingness. Up and down and sideways they crawl, and those absurd unblinking eyes are everywhere. There is one place where two breadths didn't match, and the eyes go all up and down the line, one a little higher than the other.

I never saw so much expression in an inanimate thing before, and we all know how much expression they have! I used to lie awake as a child and get more entertainment and terror out of blank walls and plain furniture than most children could find in a toy-store.

I remember what a kindly wink the knobs of our big old bureau used to have, and there was one chair that always seemed like a strong friend.

I used to feel that if any of the other things looked too fierce I could always hop into that chair and be safe.

The furniture in this room is no worse than inharmonious, however, for we had to bring it all from downstairs. I suppose when this was used as a playroom they had to take the nursery things out, and no wonder! I never saw such ravages as the children have made here.

The wallpaper, as I said before, is torn off in spots, and it sticketh closer than a brother—they must have had perseverance as well as hatred.

Then the floor is scratched and gouged and splintered, the plaster itself is dug out here and there, and this great heavy bed, which is all we found in the room, looks as if it had been through the wars.

But I don't mind it a bit—only the paper.

There comes John's sister. Such a dear girl as she is, and so careful of me! I must not let her find me writing.

She is a perfect and enthusiastic housekeeper, and hopes for no better profession. I verily believe she thinks it is the writing which made me sick!

But I can write when she is out, and see her a long way off from these windows.

There is one that commands the road, a lovely shaded winding road, and one that just looks off over the country. A lovely country, too, full of great elms and velvet meadows.

This wallpaper has a kind of subpattern in a different shade, a particularly irritating one, for you can only see it in certain lights, and not clearly then.

But in the places where it isn't faded and where the sun is just so —I can see a strange, provoking, formless sort of figure that seems to skulk about behind that silly and conspicuous front design.

There's sister on the stairs!

Well, the Fourth of July is over! The people are all gone, and I am tired out. John thought it might do me good to see a little company, so we just had Mother and Nellie and the children down for a week.

Of course I didn't do a thing. Jennie sees to everything now.

But it tired me all the same.

John says if I don't pick up faster he shall send me to Weir Mitchell in the fall.

But I don't want to go there at all. I had a friend who was in his hands once, and she says he is just like John and my brother, only more so!

Besides, it is such an undertaking to go so far.

I don't feel as if it was worthwhile to turn my hand over for anything, and I'm getting dreadfully fretful and querulous.

I cry at nothing, and cry most of the time.

Of course I don't when John is here, or anybody else, but when I am alone.

And I am alone a good deal just now. John is kept in town very often by serious cases, and Jennie is good and lets me alone when I want her to.

So I walk a little in the garden or down that lovely lane, sit on the porch under the roses, and lie down up here a good deal.

I'm getting really fond of the room in spite of the wallpaper. Perhaps *because* of the wallpaper.

It dwells in my mind so!

I lie here on this great immovable bed—it is nailed down, I believe —and follow that pattern about by the hour. It is as good as gymnastics, I assure you. I start, we'll say, at the bottom, down in the corner over there where it has not been touched, and I determine for the thousandth time that I *will* follow that pointless pattern to some sort of a conclusion.

I know a little of the principle of design, and I know this thing was not arranged on any laws of radiation, or alternation, or repetition, or symmetry, or anything else that I ever heard of.

It is repeated, of course, by the breadths, but not otherwise.

Looked at in one way, each breadth stands alone; the bloated curves and flourishes—a kind of "debased Romanesque" with delirium tremens go waddling up and down in isolated columns of fatuity.

But, on the other hand, they connect diagonally, and the sprawling outlines run off in great slanting waves of optic horror, like a lot of wallowing sea-weeds in full chase.

The whole thing goes horizontally, too, at least it seems so, and I exhaust myself trying to distinguish the order of its going in that direction.

They have used a horizontal breadth for a frieze, and that adds wonderfully to the confusion.

There is one end of the room where it is almost intact, and there, when the crosslights fade and the low sun shines directly upon it, I can almost fancy radiation after all—the interminable grotesque seems to form around a common center and rush off in headlong plunges of equal distraction.

It makes me tired to follow it. I will take a nap, I guess.

I don't know why I should write this.

I don't want to.

I don't feel able.

And I know John would think it absurd. But I *must* say what I feel and think in some way—it is such a relief!

But the effort is getting to be greater than the relief.

Half the time now I am awfully lazy, and lie down ever so much. John says I mustn't lose my strength, and has me take cod liver oil and lots of tonics and things, to say nothing of ale and wines and rare meat.

Dear John! He loves me very dearly, and hates to have me sick. I tried to have a real earnest reasonable talk with him the other day, and tell him how I wish he would let me go and make a visit to Cousin Henry and Julia.

But he said I wasn't able to go, nor able to stand it after I got there; and I did not make out a very good case for myself, for I was crying before I had finished.

It is getting to be a great effort for me to think straight. Just this nervous weakness, I suppose.

And dear John gathered me up in his arms, and just carried me upstairs and laid me on the bed, and sat by me and read to me till it tired my head.

He said I was his darling and his comfort and all he had, and that I must take care of myself for his sake, and keep well.

He says no one but myself can help me out of it, that I must use my will and self-control and not let any silly fancies run away with me.

There's one comfort—the baby is well and happy, and does not have to occupy this nursery with the horrid wallpaper.

If we had not used it, that blessed child would have! What a fortunate escape! Why, I wouldn't have a child of mine, an impressionable little thing, live in such a room for worlds.

I never thought of it before, but it is lucky that John kept me here after all; I can stand it so much easier than a baby, you see.

Of course I never mention it to them any more—I am too wise—but I keep watch for it all the same.

There are things in the wallpaper that nobody knows about but me, or ever will.

Behind that outside pattern the dim shapes get clearer every day.

It is always the same shape, only very numerous.

And it is like a woman stooping down and creeping about behind that pattern. I don't like it a bit. I wonder—I begin to think—I wish John would take me away from here!

It is so hard to talk with John about my case, because he is so wise, and because he loves me so.

But I tried it last night.

It was moonlight. The moon shines in all around just as the sun does.

I hate to see it sometimes, it creeps so slowly, and always comes in by one window or another.

John was asleep and I hated to waken him, so I kept still and watched the moonlight on that undulating wallpaper till I felt creepy.

The faint figure behind seemed to shake the pattern, just as if she wanted to get out.

I got up softly and went to feel and see if the paper *did* move, and when I came back John was awake.

"What is it, little girl?" he said. "Don't go walking about like that —you'll get cold."

I thought it was a good time to talk, so I told him that I really was not gaining here, and that I wished he would take me away.

"Why, darling!" said he. "Our lease will be up in three weeks, and I can't see how to leave before.

"The repairs are not done at home, and I cannot possibly leave town just now. Of course, if you were in any danger, I could and would, but you really are better, dear, whether you can see it or not. I am a doctor, dear, and I know. You are gaining flesh and color, your appetite is better, I feel really much easier about you."

"I don't weigh a bit more," said I, "nor as much; and my appetite may be better in the evening when you are here but it is worse in the morning when you are away!"

"Bless her little heart!" said he with a big hug. "She shall be as sick as she pleases! But now let's improve the shining hours by going to sleep, and talk about it in the morning!"

"And you won't go away?" I asked gloomily.

"Why, how can I, dear? It is only three weeks more and then we will take a nice little trip for a few days while Jennie is getting the house ready. Really, dear, you are better!"

"Better in body perhaps—" I began, and stopped short, for he sat up straight and looked at me with such a stern, reproachful look that I could not say another word.

"My darling," said he, "I beg you, for my sake and for our child's sake, as well as for your own, that you will never for one instant let that idea enter your mind! There is nothing so dangerous, so fascinating, to a temperament like yours. It is a false and foolish fancy. Can you trust me as a physician when I tell you so?"

So of course I said no more on that score, and we went to sleep before long. He thought I was asleep first, but I wasn't, and lay there for hours trying to decide whether that front pattern and the back pattern really did move together or separately.

On a pattern like this, by daylight, there is a lack of sequence, a defiance of law, that is a constant irritant to a normal mind.

The color is hideous enough, and unreliable enough, and infuriating enough, but the pattern is torturing.

You think you have mastered it, but just as you get well under way in following, it turns a back-somersault and there you are. It slaps you in the face, knocks you down, and tramples upon you. It is like a bad dream.

The outside pattern is a florid arabesque, reminding one of a fungus. If you can imagine a toadstool in joints, an interminable string of toadstools, budding and sprouting in endless convolutions—why, that is something like it.

That is, sometimes!

There is one marked peculiarity about this paper, a thing nobody seems to notice but myself, and that is that it changes as the light changes.

When the sun shoots in through the east window—I always watch for that first long, straight ray—it changes so quickly that I never can quite believe it.

That is why I watch it always.

By moonlight—the moon shines in all night when there is a moon —I wouldn't know it was the same paper.

At night in any kind of light, in twilight, candlelight, lamplight, and worst of all by moonlight, it becomes bars! The outside pattern, I mean, and the woman behind it is as plain as can be.

I didn't realize for a long time what the thing was that showed behind, that dim subpattern, but now I am quite sure it is a woman.

By daylight she is subdued, quiet. I fancy it is the pattern that keeps her so still. It is so puzzling. It keeps me quiet by the hour.

I lie down ever so much now. John says it is good for me, and to sleep all I can.

Indeed he started the habit by making me lie down for an hour after each meal.

It is a very bad habit, I am convinced, for you see, I don't sleep.

And that cultivates deceit, for I don't tell them I'm awake—oh, no!

The fact is I am getting a little afraid of John.

He seems very queer sometimes, and even Jennie has an inexplicable look.

It strikes me occasionally, just as a scientific hypothesis, that perhaps it is the paper!

I have watched John when he did not know I was looking, and come into the room suddenly on the most innocent excuses, and I've caught him several times *looking at the paper!* And Jennie too. I caught Jennie with her hand on it once.

She didn't know I was in the room, and when I asked her in a quiet, a very quiet voice, with the most restrained manner possible, what she was doing with the paper, she turned around as if she had been caught stealing, and looked quite angry—asked me why I should frighten her so!

Then she said that the paper stained everything it touched, that she had found yellow smooches on all my clothes and John's and she wished we would be more careful!

Did not that sound innocent? But I know she was studying that pattern, and I am determined that nobody shall find it out but myself!

Life is very much more exciting now than it used to be. You see, I have something more to expect, to look forward to, to watch. I really do eat better, and am more quiet than I was.

John is so pleased to see me improve! He laughed a little the other day, and said I seemed to be flourishing in spite of my wallpaper.

I turned it off with a laugh. I had no intention of telling him it was *because* of the wallpaper—he would make fun of me. He might even want to take me away.

I don't want to leave now until I have found it out. There is a week more, and I think that will be enough.

I'm feeling so much better!

I don't sleep much at night, for it is so interesting to watch developments; but I sleep a good deal during the daytime.

In the daytime it is tiresome and perplexing.

There are always new shoots on the fungus, and new shades of yellow all over it. I cannot keep count of them, though I have tried conscientiously.

It is the strangest yellow, that wallpaper! It makes me think of all the yellow things I ever saw—not beautiful ones like buttercups, but old, foul, bad yellow things.

But there is something else about that paper—the smell! I noticed it the moment we came into the room, but with so much air and sun it was not bad. Now we have had a week of fog and rain, and whether the windows are open or not, the smell is here.

It creeps all over the house.

I find it hovering in the dining-room, skulking in the parlor, hiding in the hall, laying in wait for me on the stairs.

It gets into my hair.

Even when I go to ride, if I turn my head suddenly and surprise it —there is that smell!

Such a peculiar odor, too! I have spent hours in trying to analyze it, to find what it smelled like.

It is not bad—at first—and very gentle, but quite the subtlest, most enduring odor I ever met.

In this damp weather it is awful. I wake up in the night and find it hanging over me.

It used to disturb me at first. I thought seriously of burning the house —to reach the smell.

But now I am used to it. The only thing I can think of that it is like is the *color* of the paper! A yellow smell.

There is a very funny mark on this wall, low down, near the mopboard. A streak that runs round the room. It goes behind every piece of furniture, except the bed, a long, straight, even *smooch,* as if it had been rubbed over and over.

I wonder how it was done and who did it, and what they did it for.

Round and round and round—round and round and round—it makes me dizzy!

I really have discovered something at last.

Through watching so much at night, when it changes so, I have finally found out.

The front pattern *does* move—and no wonder! The woman behind shakes it!

Sometimes I think there are a great many women behind, and sometimes only one, and she crawls around fast, and her crawling shakes it all over.

Then in the very bright spots she keeps still, and in the very shady spots she just takes hold of the bars and shakes them hard.

And she is all the time trying to climb through. But nobody could climb through that pattern—it strangles so; I think that is why it has so many heads.

They get through and then the pattern strangles them off and turns them upside down, and makes their eyes white!

If those heads were covered or taken off it would not be half so bad.

I think that woman gets out in the daytime!

And I'll tell you why—privately—I've seen her!

I can see her out of every one of my windows!

It is the same woman, I know, for she is always creeping, and most women do not creep by daylight.

I see her in that long shaded lane, creeping up and down. I see her in those dark grape arbors, creeping all round the garden.

I see her on that long road under the trees, creeping along, and when a carriage comes she hides under the blackberry vines.

I don't blame her a bit. It must be very humiliating to be caught creeping by daylight!

I always lock the door when I creep by daylight. I can't do it at night, for I know John would suspect something at once.

And John is so queer now that I don't want to irritate him. I wish he would take another room! Besides, I don't want anybody to get that woman out at night but myself.

I often wonder if I could see her out of all the windows at once.

But, turn as fast as I can, I can only see out of one at one time.

And though I always see her, she *may* be able to creep faster than I can turn! I have watched her sometimes away off in the open country, creeping as fast as a cloud shadow in a wind.

If only that top pattern could be gotten off from the under one! I mean to try it, little by little.

Why, there's John at the door!

It is no use, young man, you can't open it!

How he does call and pound!

Now he's crying to Jennie for an axe.

It would be a shame to break down that beautiful door!

"John, dear!" said I in the gentlest voice. "The key is down by the front steps, under a plantain leaf!"

That silenced him for a few moments.

Then he said, very quietly indeed, "Open the door, my darling!"

"I can't," said I. "The key is down by the front door under a plantain leaf!" And then I said it again, several times, very gently and slowly, and said it so often that he had to go and see, and he got it of course, and came in. He stopped short by the door.

"What is the matter?" he cried. "For God's sake, what are you doing!"

I kept on creeping just the same, but I looked at him over my shoulder.

"I've got out at last," said I, "in spite of you and Jane. And I've pulled off most of the paper, so you can't put me back!"

Now why should that man have fainted? But he did, and right across my path by the wall, so that I had to creep over him every time!

1892

TONI CADE BAMBARA

Maggie of the Green Bottles

Maggie had not intended to get sucked in on this thing, sleeping straight through the christening, steering clear of the punch bowl, and refusing to dress for company. But when she glanced over my grandfather's shoulder and saw "Aspire, Enspire, Perspire" scrawled across the first page in that hard-core Protestant hand, and a grease stain from the fried chicken too, something snapped in her head. She snatched up the book and retired rapidly to her room, locked my mother out, and explained through the door that my mother was a fool to encourage a lot of misspelled nonsense from Mr. Tyler's kin, and an even bigger fool for having married the monster in the first place.

I imagine that Maggie sat at her great oak desk, rolled the lace cuffs gently back, and dipped her quill into the lavender ink pot with all the ceremony due the Emancipation Proclamation, which was, after all, exactly what she was drafting. Writing to me, she explained, was serious business, for she felt called upon to liberate me from all historical and genealogical connections except the most divine. In short, the family was a disgrace, degrading Maggie's and my capacity for wings, as they say. I can only say that Maggie was truly inspired. And she probably ruined my life from the get-go.

There is a photo of the two of us on the second page. There's Maggie in Minnie Mouse shoes and a long polka-dot affair with her stockings rolled up at the shins, looking like muffins. There's me with nothing much at all on, in her arms, and looking almost like a normal, mortal, everyday-type baby—raw, wrinkled, ugly. Except that it must be clearly understood straightaway that I sprang into the world full wise and

To list Toni Cade Bambara's achievements as a novelist and short-story writer, composer of screenplays, and editor of anthologies would hardly exhaust the many-faceted nature of her career. Born in New York City in 1939, Bambara followed up her education at Queens College with positions such as social investigator for the city's Department of Welfare, director of recreation in the psychiatry department of the Metropolitan Hospital, and others that affirmed her status as a socially committed writer and respected civil-rights advocate. Works like *Gorilla, My Love* (1972), *The Sea Birds Are Still Alive* (1977), and *The Salt Eaters* (1980) are praised for their poetic and engaging depiction of African American life and culture. Bambara lives in Philadelphia.

invulnerable and gorgeous like a goddess. Behind us is the player piano with the spooky keys. And behind that, the window outlining Maggie's crosshatched face and looking out over the yard, overgrown even then, where later I lay lost in the high grass, never hoping to be found till Maggie picked me up into her hair and told me all about the earth's moons.

Once just a raggedy thing holding telegrams from well-wishers, the book was pleasant reading on those rainy days when I didn't risk rusting my skates, or maybe just wasn't up to trailing up and down the city streets with the kids, preferring to study Maggie's drawings and try to grab hold of the fearsome machinery which turned the planets and coursed the stars and told me in no uncertain terms that as an Aries babe I was obligated to carry on the work of other Aries greats from Alexander right on down to anyone you care to mention. I could go on to relate all the wise-alecky responses I gave to Maggie's document as an older child rummaging in the trunks among the canceled checks and old sheet music, looking for some suspicioned love letters or some small proof that my mother had once had romance in her life, and finding instead the raggedy little book I thought was just a raggedy little book. But it is much too easy to smile at one's ignorant youth just to flatter one's present wisdom, but I digress.

Because, on my birthday, Saturn was sitting on its ass and Mars was taken unawares, getting bumped by Jupiter's flunkies, I would not be into my own till well past twenty. But according to the cards, and my palm line bore it out, the hangman would spare me till well into my hundredth year. So all in all, the tea leaves having had their say and the coffee-ground patterns being what they were, I was destined for greatness. She assured me. And I was certain of my success, as I was certain that my parents were not my parents, that I was descended, anointed and ready to gobble up the world from urgent, noble Olympiads.

I am told by those who knew her, whose memories consist of something more substantial than a frantic gray lady who poured coffee into her saucer, that Margaret Cooper Williams wanted something she could not have. And it was the sorrow of her life that all her children and theirs and theirs were uncooperative—worse, squeamish. Too busy taking in laundry, buckling at the knees, putting their faith in Jesus, mute and sullen in their sorrow, too squeamish to band together and take the world by storm, make history, or even to appreciate the calling of Maggie the Ram, or the Aries that came after. Other things they told me too, things I put aside to learn later though I always knew, perhaps, but never quite wanted to, the way you hold your breath and steady yourself to the knowledge secretly, but never let yourself understand. They called her crazy.

It is to Maggie's guts that I bow forehead to the floor and kiss her hand, because she'd tackle the lot of them right there in the yard, blood kin or by marriage, and neighbors or no. And anybody who'd stand up to my father, gross Neanderthal that he was, simply had to be some kind of weird combination of David, Aries, and lunatic. It began with the cooking usually, especially the pots of things Maggie concocted. Witchcraft, he called it. Home cooking, she'd counter. Then he'd come over to the stove, lift a lid with an incredible face, and comment about cesspools and fertilizers. But she'd remind him of his favorite dish, chitlins, addressing the bread box, though. He'd turn up the radio and make some remark about good church music and her crazy voodoo records. Then she'd tell the curtains that some men, who put magic down with nothing to replace it and nothing much to recommend them in the first place but their magic wand, lived a runabout life, practicing black magic on other men's wives. Then he'd say something about freeloading relatives and dancing to the piper's tune. And she'd whisper to the kettles that there wasn't no sense in begging from a beggar. Depending on how large an audience they drew, this could go on for hours until my father would cock his head to the side, listening, and then try to make his getaway.

"Ain't nobody calling you, Mr. Tyler, cause don't nobody want you." And I'd feel kind of bad about my father like I do about the wolf man and the phantom of the opera. Monsters, you know, more than anybody else, need your pity cause they need beauty and love so bad.

One day, right about the time Maggie would say something painful that made him bring up freeloaders and piper's tunes, he began to sputter so bad it made me want to cry. But Maggie put the big wooden spoon down and whistled for Mister T—at least that's what Maggie and my grandmother, before she died, insisted on calling him. The dog, always hungry, came bounding through the screen door, stopped on a dime by the sink, and slinked over to Maggie's legs the way beat-up dogs can do, their tails all confused as to just what to do, their eyes unblinkingly watchful. Maggie offered him something from the pot. And when Mister T had finished, he licked Maggie's hand. She began to cackle. And then, before I could even put my milk down, up went Maggie's palm, and *bam*, Mister T went skidding across the linoleum and banged all the seltzer bottles down.

"Damn-fool mutt," said Maggie to her wooden spoon, "too dumb to even know you're supposed to bite the hand that feeds you."

My father threw his hand back and yelled for my mother to drop whatever she was doing, which was standing in the doorway shaking her head, and pack up the old lady's things posthaste. Maggie went right on laughing and talking to the spoon. And Mister T slinked over to the table so Baby Jason could pet him. And then it was name-calling time. And again I must genuflect and kiss her ring, because my father was no slouch when it came to names. He could malign your mother and work your father's lineage over in one short breath, describing in absolute detail all the incredible alliances made between your ancestors and all sorts of weird creatures. But Maggie had him beat there too, old lady in lace talking to spoons or no.

My mother came in weary and worn and gave me a nod. I slid my peanut-butter sandwich off the icebox, grabbed Baby Jason by his harness, and dragged him into our room, where I was supposed to read to him real loud. But I listened, I always listened to my mother's footfalls on the porch to the gravel path and down the hard mud road to the woodshed. Then I could give my attention to the kitchen, for "Goldilocks," keep in mind, never was enough to keep the brain alive. Then, right in the middle of some fierce curse or other, my father did this unbelievable thing. He stomped right into Maggie's room—that sanctuary of heaven charts and incense pots and dream books and magic stuffs. Only Jason, hiding from an August storm, had ever been allowed in there, and that was on his knees crawling. But in he stomped all big and bad like some terrible giant, this man whom Grandma Williams used to say was just the sort of size man put on this earth for the "'spress purpose of clubbing us all to death." And he came out with these green bottles, one in each hand, snorting and laughing at the same time. And I figured, peeping into the kitchen, that these bottles were enchanted, for they had a strange effect on Maggie, she shut right up. They had a strange effect on me too, gleaming there up in the air, nearly touching the ceiling, glinting off the shots of sunshine, grasped in the giant's fist. I was awed.

Whenever I saw them piled in the garbage out back I was tempted to touch them and make a wish, knowing all the while that the charm was all used up and that that was why they were in the garbage in the first place. But there was no doubt that they were special. And whenever Baby Jason managed to drag one out from under the bed, there was much whispering and shuffling on my mother's part. And when Sweet Basil, the grocer's boy, delivered these green bottles to Maggie, it was all hush-hush and backdoor and in the corner dealings, slipping it in and out of innumerable paper bags, holding it up to the light, then off she'd run to her room and be gone for hours, days sometimes, and when she did appear, looking mysterious and in a trance, her face all full of shadows. And she'd sit at the sideboard with that famous cup from the World's Fair, pouring coffee into the saucer and blowing on it very carefully, nodding and humming and swirling the grinds. She called me over once to look at the grinds.

"What does this look like, Peaches?"

"Looks like a star with a piece out of it."

"Hmm," she mumbled, and swirled again. "And now?"

Me peering into the cup and lost for words. "Looks like a face that lost its eyes."

"Hmm," again, as she thrust the cup right under my nose, and me wishing it was a box of falling glass I could look at where I knew what was what instead of looking into the bottom of a fat yellow cup at what looked like nothing but coffee grinds.

"Looks like a mouth losing its breath, Great Granny."

"Let's not get too outrageous, Peaches. This is serious business."

"Yes ma'am." Peering again and trying to be worthy of Alexander and the Ram and all my other forebears. "What it really seems to be" —stalling for time and praying for inspiration—"is an upside-down bird, dead on its back with his heart chopped out and the hole bleeding."

She flicked my hand away when I tried to point the picture out which by now I was beginning to believe. "Go play somewhere, girl," she said. She was mad. "And quit calling me Granny."

"What happened here today?" my mother kept asking all evening, thumping out the fragrant dough and wringing the dishtowel, which was supposed to help the dough rise, wringing it to pieces. I couldn't remember anything particular, following her gaze to Maggie's door. "Was Sweet Basil here this afternoon?" Couldn't remember that either, but tried to show I was her daughter by staring hard at the closed door too. "Was Great Granny up and around at all today?" My memory failed me there too. "You ain't got much memory to speak of at all, do you?" said my father. I hung onto my mother's apron and helped her wring the dishtowel to pieces.

They told me she was very sick, so I had to drag Baby Jason out to the high grass and play with him. It was a hot day and the smell of the kerosene soaking the weeds that were stubborn about dying made my eyes tear. I was face down in the grass just listening, waiting for the afternoon siren which last year I thought was Judgment Day because it blew so long to say that the war was over and that we didn't have to eat Spam any more and that there was a circus coming and a parade and Uncle Bubba too, but with only one leg to show for it all. Maggie came into the yard with her basket of vegetables. She sat down at the edge of the gravel path and began stringing the peppers, red and green, red and green. And, like always, she was humming one of those weird songs of hers which always made her seem holier and blacker than she could've been. I tied Baby Jason to a tree so he wouldn't crawl into her lap, which always annoyed her. Maggie didn't like baby boys, or any kind of boys I'm thinking, but especially baby boys born in Cancer and Pisces or anything but in Aries.

"Look here, Peaches," she called, working the twine through the peppers and dropping her voice real low. "I want you to do this thing for your Great Granny."

"What must I do?" I waited a long time till I almost thought she'd fallen asleep, her head rolling around on her chest and her hands fumbling with the slippery peppers, ripping them.

"I want you to go to my room and pull out the big pink box from under the bed." She looked around and woke up a bit. "This is a secret you-and-me thing now, Peaches." I nodded and waited some more. "Open the box and you'll see a green bottle. Wrap this apron around it and tuck it under your arm like so. Then grab up the mushrooms I left on the sideboard like that's what you came for in the first place. But get yourself back here right quick." I repeated the instructions, flopped a necklace of peppers around me, and dashed into the hot and dusty house. When I got back she dumped the mushrooms into her lap, tucked the bottle under her skirt, and smiled at the poor little peppers her nervous hands had strung. They hung wet and ruined off the twine like broken-necked little animals.

I was down in the bottoms playing with the state-farm kids when Uncle Bubba came sliding down the sand pile on his one good leg. Jason was already in the station wagon hanging onto my old doll. We stayed at Aunt Min's till my father came to get us in the pickup. Everybody was in the kitchen dividing up Maggie's things. The linen chest went to Aunt Thelma. And the souvenirs from Maggie's honeymoons went to the freckle-faced cousins from town. The clothes were packed for the church. And Reverend Elson was directing the pianist's carrying from the kitchen window. The scattered sopranos, who never ever seemed to get together on their high notes or on their visits like this, were making my mother drink tea and kept nodding at me, saying she was sitting in the mourner's seat, which was just like all the other chairs in the set; same as the amen corner was no better or any less dusty than the rest of the church and not even a corner. Then Reverend Elson turned to say that no matter how crazy she'd been, no matter how hateful she'd acted toward the church in general and him in particular, no matter how spiteful she'd behaved towards her neighbors and even her blood kin, and even though everyone was better off without her, seeing how she died as proof of her heathen character, and right there in the front yard too, with a bottle under her skirts, the sopranos joined in scattered as ever, despite all that, the Reverend Elson continued, God rest her soul, if He saw fit, that is.

The china darning egg went into Jason's overalls. And the desk went into my room. Bubba said he wanted the books for his children. And they all gave him such a look. My mother just sat in the kitchen chair called the mourner's seat and said nothing at all except that they were selling the house and moving to the city.

"Well, Peaches," my father said. "You were her special, what you want?"

"I'll take the bottles," I said.

"Let us pray," said the Reverend.

That night I sat at the desk and read the baby book for the first time. It sounded like Maggie for the world, holding me in her lap and spreading the charts on the kitchen table. I looked my new bottle collection over. There were purple bottles with glass stoppers and labels. There were squat blue bottles with squeeze tops but nothing in them. There were flat red bottles that could hold only one flower at a time. I had meant the green bottles. I was going to tell them and then I didn't. I was too small for so much enchantment anyway. I went to bed feeling much too small. And it seemed a shame that the hope of the Aries line should have to sleep with a light on still, and blame it on Jason and cry with balled fists in the eyes just like an ordinary, mortal, everyday-type baby.

1967

ANTON CHEKHOV

The Darling

Olenka, the daughter of the retired collegiate assessor, Plemyanniakov, was sitting in her back porch, lost in thought. It was hot, the flies were persistent and teasing, and it was pleasant to reflect that it would soon be evening. Dark rainclouds were gathering from the east, and bringing from time to time a breath of moisture in the air.

Kukin, who was the manager of an open-air theatre called the Tivoli, and who lived in the lodge, was standing in the middle of the garden looking at the sky.

"Again!" he observed despairingly. "It's going to rain again! Rain every day, as though to spite me. I might as well hang myself! It's ruin! Fearful losses every day."

He flung up his hands, and went on, addressing Olenka:

"There! that's the life we lead, Olga Semyonovna. It's enough to make one cry. One works and does one's utmost; one wears oneself out, getting no sleep at night, and racks one's brain what to do for the best. And then what happens? To begin with, one's public is ignorant, boorish. I give them the very best operetta, a dainty masque, first rate music-hall artists. But do you suppose that's what they want! They don't understand anything of that sort. They want a clown; what they ask for is vulgarity. And then look at the weather! Almost every evening it rains. It started on the tenth of May, and it's kept it up all May and June. It's simply awful! The public doesn't come, but I've to pay the rent just the same, and pay the artists."

Anton Chekhov was born in Taganrog, Russia, on January 29, 1860. Educated in the town gymnasium (a secondary school that prepares students for the university), he bore for most of his life the burden of supporting his family, eventually becoming a doctor in Moscow in order to continue fulfilling this obligation. To supplement his income, Chekhov began writing jokes and comic sketches, publishing them in local journals. These humorous pieces—more than a hundred appeared in 1886 alone—gained a certain popularity for the author. With this encouragement he began composing more studied and serious works, culminating in stories such as "My Life" (1896) and "Peasants" (1897). Chekhov's spare plots, coupled with his attention to character and to the oppressive details of everyday life, found their fullest expression in dramas composed during his last years. The Cherry Orchard—his masterpiece—was first performed in January 1904, only months before his death on July 14.

The next evening the clouds would gather again, and Kukin would say with an hysterical laugh:

"Well, rain away, then! Flood the garden, drown me! Damn my luck in this world and the next! Let the artists have me up! Send me to prison!—to Siberia!—the scaffold! Ha, ha, ha!"

And next day the same thing.

Olenka listened to Kukin with silent gravity, and sometimes tears came into her eyes. In the end his misfortunes touched her; she grew to love him. He was a small thin man, with a yellow face, and curls combed forward on his forehead. He spoke in a thin tenor; as he talked his mouth worked on one side, and there was always an expression of despair on his face; yet he aroused a deep and genuine affection in her. She was always fond of some one, and could not exist without loving. In earlier days she had loved her papa, who now sat in a darkened room, breathing with difficulty; she had loved her aunt who used to come every other year from Bryansk; and before that, when she was at school, she had loved her French master. She was a gentle, soft-hearted, compassionate girl, with mild, tender eyes and very good health. At the sight of her full rosy cheeks, her soft white neck with a little dark mole on it, and the kind, naïve smile, which came into her face when she listened to anything pleasant, men thought, "Yes, not half bad," and smiled too, while lady visitors could not refrain from seizing her hand in the middle of a conversation, exclaiming in a gush of delight, "You darling!"

The house in which she had lived from her birth upwards, and which was left her in her father's will, was at the extreme end of the town, not far from the Tivoli. In the evenings and at night she could hear the band playing, and the crackling and banging of fireworks, and it seemed to her that it was Kukin struggling with his destiny, storming the entrenchments of his chief foe, the indifferent public; there was a sweet thrill at her heart, she had no desire to sleep, and when he returned home at daybreak, she tapped softly at her bedroom window, and showing him only her face and one shoulder through the curtain, she gave him a friendly smile. . . .

He proposed to her, and they were married. And when he had a closer view of her neck and her plump, fine shoulders, he threw up his hands, and said:

"You darling!"

He was happy, but as it rained on the day and night of his wedding, his face still retained an expression of despair.

They got on very well together. She used to sit in his office, to look after things in the Tivoli, to put down the accounts and pay the wages.

And her rosy cheeks, her sweet, naïve, radiant smile, were to be seen now at the office window, now in the refreshment bar or behind the scenes of the theatre. And already she used to say to her acquaintances that the theatre was the chief and most important thing in life, and that it was only through the drama that one could derive true enjoyment and become cultivated and humane.

"But do you suppose the public understands that?" she used to say. "What they want is a clown. Yesterday we gave 'Faust Inside Out,' and almost all the boxes were empty; but if Vanitchka and I had been producing some vulgar thing, I assure you the theatre would have been packed. Tomorrow Vanitchka and I are doing 'Orpheus in Hell.' Do come."

And what Kukin said about the theatre and the actors she repeated. Like him she despised the public for their ignorance and their indifference to art; she took part in the rehearsals, she corrected the actors, she kept an eye on the behaviour of the musicians, and when there was an unfavourable notice in the local paper, she shed tears, and then went to the editor's office to set things right.

The actors were fond of her and used to call her "Vanitchka and I," and "the darling"; she was sorry for them and used to lend them small sums of money, and if they deceived her, she used to shed a few tears in private, but did not complain to her husband.

They got on well in the winter too. They took the theatre in the town for the whole winter, and let it for short terms to a Little Russian company, or to a conjurer, or to a local dramatic society. Olenka grew stouter, and was always beaming with satisfaction, while Kukin grew thinner and yellower, and continually complained of their terrible losses, although he had not done badly all the winter. He used to cough at night, and she used to give him hot raspberry tea or lime-flower water, to rub him with eau-de-Cologne and to wrap him in her warm shawls.

"You're such a sweet pet!" she used to say with perfect sincerity, stroking his hair. "You're such a pretty dear!"

Towards Lent he went to Moscow to collect a new troupe, and without him she could not sleep, but sat all night at her window, looking at the stars, and she compared herself with the hens, who are awake all night and uneasy when the cock is not in the hen-house. Kukin was detained in Moscow, and wrote that he would be back at Easter, adding some instructions about the Tivoli. But on the Sunday before Easter, late in the evening, came a sudden ominous knock at the gate; some one was hammering on the gate as though on a barrel—boom, boom, boom! The drowsy cook went flopping with her bare feet through the puddles, as she ran to open the gate.

"Please open," said some one outside in a thick bass. "There is a telegram for you."

Olenka had received telegrams from her husband before, but this time for some reason she felt numb with terror. With shaking hands she opened the telegram and read as follows:

"Ivan Petrovitch died suddenly to-day. Awaiting immate instructions fufuneral Tuesday."

That was how it was written in the telegram—"fufuneral," and the utterly incomprehensible word "immate." It was signed by the stage manager of the operatic company.

"My darling!" sobbed Olenka. "Vanitchka, my precious, my darling! Why did I ever meet you! Why did I know you and love you! Your poor heart-broken Olenka is all alone without you!"

Kukin's funeral took place on Tuesday in Moscow, Olenka returned home on Wednesday, and as soon as she got indoors she threw herself on her bed and sobbed so loudly that it could be heard next door, and in the street.

"Poor darling!" the neighbours said, as they crossed themselves. "Olga Semyonovna, poor darling! How she does take on!"

Three months later Olenka was coming home from mass, melancholy and in deep mourning. It happened that one of her neighbours, Vassily Andreitch Pustovalov, returning home from church, walked back beside her. He was the manager at Babakayev's the timber merchant's. He wore a straw hat, a white waistcoat, and a gold watch-chain, and looked more like a country gentleman than a man in trade.

"Everything happens as it is ordained, Olga Semyonovna," he said gravely, with a sympathetic note in his voice; "and if any of our dear ones die, it must be because it is the will of God, so we ought to have fortitude and bear it submissively."

After seeing Olenka to her gate, he said good-bye and went on. All day afterwards she heard his sedately dignified voice, and whenever she shut her eyes she saw his dark beard. She liked him very much. And apparently she had made an impression on him too, for not long afterwards an elderly lady, with whom she was only slightly acquainted, came to drink coffee with her, and as soon as she was seated at table began to talk about Pustovalov, saying that he was an excellent man whom one could thoroughly depend upon, and that any girl would be glad to marry him. Three days later Pustovalov came himself. He did not stay long, only about ten minutes, and he did not say much, but when he left, Olenka loved him—loved him so much that she lay awake all night in a perfect fever, and in the morning she sent for the elderly lady. The match was quickly arranged, and then came the wedding.

Pustovalov and Olenka got on very well together when they were married.

Usually he sat in the office till dinner-time, then he went out on business, while Olenka took his place, and sat in the office till evening, making up accounts and booking orders.

"Timber gets dearer every year; the price rises twenty per cent," she would say to her customers and friends. "Only fancy we used to sell local timber, and now Vassitchka always has to go for wood to the Mogilev district. And the freight!" she would add, covering her cheeks with her hands in horror. "The freight!"

It seemed to her that she had been in the timber trade for ages and ages, and that the most important and necessary thing in life was timber; and there was something intimate and touching to her in the very sound of words such as "baulk," "post," "beam," "pole," "scantling," "batten," "lath," "plank," etc.

At night when she was asleep she dreamed of perfect mountains of planks and boards, and long strings of wagons, carting timber somewhere far away. She dreamed that a whole regiment of six-inch beams forty feet high, standing on end, was marching upon the timber-yard; that logs, beams, and boards knocked together with the resounding crash of dry wood, kept falling and getting up again, piling themselves on each other. Olenka cried out in her sleep, and Pustovalov said to her tenderly: "Olenka, what's the matter, darling? Cross yourself!"

Her husband's ideas were hers. If he thought the room was too hot, or that business was slack, she thought the same. Her husband did not care for entertainments, and on holidays he stayed at home. She did likewise.

"You are always at home or in the office," her friends said to her. "You should go to the theatre, darling, or to the circus."

"Vassitchka and I have no time to go to theatres," she would answer sedately. "We have no time for nonsense. What's the use of these theatres?"

On Saturdays Pustovalov and she used to go to the evening service; on holidays to early mass, and they walked side by side with softened faces as they came home from church. There was a pleasant fragrance about them both, and her silk dress rustled agreeably. At home they drank tea, with fancy bread and jams of various kinds, and afterwards they ate pie. Every day at twelve o'clock there was a savoury smell of beet-root soup and of mutton or duck in their yard, and on fast-days of fish, and no one could pass the gate without feeling hungry. In the office the samovar was always boiling, and customers were regaled with tea and cracknels. Once a week the couple went to the baths and returned side by side, both red in the face.

"Yes, we have nothing to complain of, thank God," Olenka used to say to her acquaintances. "I wish every one were as well off as Vassitchka and I."

When Pustovalov went away to buy wood in the Mogilev district, she missed him dreadfully, lay awake and cried. A young veterinary surgeon in the army, called Smirnin, to whom they had let their lodge, used sometimes to come in in the evening. He used to talk to her and play cards with her, and this entertained her in her husband's absence. She was particularly interested in what he told her of his home life. He was married and had a little boy, but was separated from his wife because she had been unfaithful to him, and now he hated her and used to send her forty roubles a month for the maintenance of their son. And hearing of all this, Olenka sighed and shook her head. She was sorry for him.

"Well, God keep you," she used to say to him at parting, as she lighted him down the stairs with a candle. "Thank you for coming to cheer me up, and may the Mother of God give you health."

And she always expressed herself with the same sedateness and dignity, the same reasonableness, in imitation of her husband. As the veterinary surgeon was disappearing behind the door below, she would say:

"You know, Vladimir Platonitch, you'd better make it up with your wife. You should forgive her for the sake of your son. You may be sure the little fellow understands."

And when Pustovalov came back, she told him in a low voice about the veterinary surgeon and his unhappy home life, and both sighed and shook their heads and talked about the boy, who, no doubt, missed his father, and by some strange connection of ideas, they went up to the holy ikons, bowed to the ground before them and prayed that God would give them children.

And so the Pustovalovs lived for six years quietly and peaceably in love and complete harmony.

But behold! one winter day after drinking hot tea in the office, Vassily Andreitch went out into the yard without his cap on to see about sending off some timber, caught cold, and was taken ill. He had the best doctors, but he grew worse and died after four months' illness. And Olenka was a widow once more.

"I've nobody, now you've left me, my darling," she sobbed, after her husband's funeral. "How can I live without you, in wretchedness and misery! Pity me, good people, all alone in the world!"

She went about dressed in black with long "weepers," and gave up wearing hat and gloves for good. She hardly ever went out, except to church, or to her husband's grave, and led the life of a nun. It was not till six months later that she took off the weepers and opened the shutters of the windows. She was sometimes seen in the mornings, going with her cook to market for provisions, but what went on in her house and how she lived now could only be surmised. People guessed, from seeing her drinking tea in her garden with the veterinary surgeon, who read the newspaper aloud to her, and from the fact that, meeting a lady she knew at the post-office, she said to her:

"There is no proper veterinary inspection in our town, and that's the cause of all sorts of epidemics. One is always hearing of people's getting infection from the milk supply, or catching diseases from horses and cows. The health of domestic animals ought to be as well cared for as the health of human beings."

She repeated the veterinary surgeon's words, and was of the same opinion as he about everything. It was evident that she could not live a year without some attachment, and had found new happiness in the lodge. In any one else this would have been censured, but no one could think ill of Olenka; everything she did was so natural. Neither she nor the veterinary surgeon said anything to other people of the change in their relations, and tried, indeed, to conceal it, but without success, for Olenka could not keep a secret. When he had visitors, men serving in his regiment, and she poured out tea or served the supper, she would begin talking of the cattle plague, of the foot and mouth disease, and of the municipal slaughter-houses. He was dreadfully embarrassed, and when the guests had gone, he would seize her by the hand and hiss angrily:

"I've asked you before not to talk about what you don't understand. When we veterinary surgeons are talking among ourselves, please don't put your word in. It's really annoying."

And she would look at him with astonishment and dismay, and ask him in alarm: "But, Voloditchka, what *am* I to talk about?"

And with tears in her eyes she would embrace him, begging him not to be angry, and they were both happy.

But this happiness did not last long. The veterinary surgeon departed, departed for ever with his regiment, when it was transferred to a distant place—to Siberia, it may be. And Olenka was left alone.

Now she was absolutely alone. Her father had long been dead, and his armchair lay in the attic, covered with dust and lame of one leg. She got thinner and plainer, and when people met her in the street they did not look at her as they used to, and did not smile to her; evidently her best years were over and left behind, and now a new sort of life had begun for her, which did not bear thinking about. In the evening Olenka sat in the porch, and heard the band playing and the fireworks popping in the Tivoli, but now the sound stirred no response. She looked into her yard without interest, thought of nothing, wished for nothing, and afterwards, when night came on she went to bed and dreamed of her empty yard. She ate and drank as it were unwillingly.

And what was worst of all, she had no opinions of any sort. She saw the objects about her and understood what she saw, but could not form any opinion about them, and did not know what to talk about. And how awful it is not to have any opinions! One sees a bottle, for instance, or the rain, or a peasant driving in his cart, but what the bottle is for, or the rain, or the peasant, and what is the meaning of it, one can't say, and could not even for a thousand roubles. When she had Kukin, or Pustovalov, or the veterinary surgeon, Olenka could explain everything, and give her opinion about anything you like, but now there was the same emptiness in her brain and in her heart as there was in her yard outside. And it was as harsh and as bitter as wormwood in the mouth.

Little by little the town grew in all directions. The road became a street, and where the Tivoli and the timber-yard had been, there were new turnings and houses. How rapidly time passes! Olenka's house grew dingy, the roof got rusty, the shed sank on one side, and the whole yard was overgrown with docks and stinging-nettles. Olenka herself had grown plain and elderly; in summer she sat in the porch, and her soul, as before, was empty and dreary and full of bitterness. In winter she sat at her window and looked at the snow. When she caught the scent of spring, or heard the chime of the church bells, a sudden rush of memories from the past came over her, there was a tender ache in her heart, and her eyes brimmed over with tears; but this was only for a minute, and then came emptiness again and the sense of the futility of life. The black kitten, Briska, rubbed against her and purred softly, but Olenka was not touched by these feline caresses. That was not what she needed. She wanted a love that would absorb her whole being, her whole soul and reason—that would give her ideas and an object in life, and would warm her old blood. And she would shake the kitten off her skirt and say with vexation:

"Get along; I don't want you!"

And so it was, day after day and year after year, and no joy, and no opinions. Whatever Mavra, the cook, said she accepted.

One hot July day, towards evening, just as the cattle were being driven away, and the whole yard was full of dust, some one suddenly knocked at the gate. Olenka went to open it herself and was dumbfounded when she looked out: she saw Smirnin, the veterinary surgeon, grey-headed, and dressed as a civilian. She suddenly remembered everything. She could not help crying and letting her head fall on his breast without uttering a word, and in the violence of her feeling she did not notice how they both walked into the house and sat down to tea.

"My dear Vladimir Platonitch! What fate has brought you?" she muttered, trembling with joy.

"I want to settle here for good, Olga Semyonovna," he told her. "I have resigned my post, and have come to settle down and try my luck on my own account. Besides, it's time for my boy to go to school. He's a big boy. I am reconciled with my wife, you know."

"Where is she?" asked Olenka.

"She's at the hotel with the boy, and I'm looking for lodgings."

"Good gracious, my dear soul! Lodgings? Why not have my house? Why shouldn't that suit you? Why, my goodness, I wouldn't take any rent!" cried Olenka in a flutter, beginning to cry again. "You live here, and the lodge will do nicely for me. Oh dear! how glad I am!"

Next day the roof was painted and the walls were whitewashed, and Olenka, with her arms akimbo, walked about the yard giving directions. Her face was beaming with her old smile, and she was brisk and alert as though she had waked from a long sleep. The veterinary's wife arrived—a thin, plain lady, with short hair and a peevish expression. With her was her little Sasha, a boy of ten, small for his age, blue-eyed, chubby, with dimples in his cheeks. And scarcely had the boy walked into the yard when he ran after the cat, and at once there was the sound of his gay, joyous laugh.

"Is that your puss, auntie?" he asked Olenka. "When she has little ones, do give us a kitten. Mamma is awfully afraid of mice."

Olenka talked to him, and gave him tea. Her heart warmed and there was a sweet ache in her bosom, as though the boy had been her own child. And when he sat at the table in the evening, going over his lessons, she looked at him with deep tenderness and pity as she murmured to herself:

"You pretty pet! . . . my precious! . . . Such a fair little thing, and so clever."

"'An island is a piece of land which is entirely surrounded by water,'" he read aloud.

"An island is a piece of land," she repeated, and this was the first opinion to which she gave utterance with positive conviction after so many years of silence and dearth of ideas.

Now she had opinions of her own, and at supper she talked to

Sasha's parents, saying how difficult the lessons were at the high schools, but that yet the high-school was better than a commercial one, since with a high-school education all careers were open to one, such as being a doctor or an engineer.

Sasha began going to the high school. His mother departed to Harkov to her sister's and did not return; his father used to go off every day to inspect cattle, and would often be away from home for three days together, and it seemed to Olenka as though Sasha was entirely abandoned, that he was not wanted at home, that he was being starved, and she carried him off to her lodge and gave him a little room there.

And for six months Sasha had lived in the lodge with her. Every morning Olenka came into his bedroom and found him fast asleep, sleeping noiselessly with his hand under his cheek. She was sorry to wake him.

"Sashenka," she would say mournfully, "get up, darling. It's time for school."

He would get up, dress and say his prayers, and then sit down to breakfast, drink three glasses of tea, and eat two large cracknels and half a buttered roll. All this time he was hardly awake and a little ill-humoured in consequence.

"You don't quite know your fable, Sashenka," Olenka would say, looking at him as though he were about to set off on a long journey. "What a lot of trouble I have with you! You must work and do your best, darling, and obey your teachers."

"Oh, do leave me alone!" Sasha would say.

Then he would go down the street to school, a little figure, wearing a big cap and carrying a satchel on his shoulder. Olenka would follow him noiselessly.

"Sashenka!" she would call after him, and she would pop into his hand a date or a caramel. When he reached the street where the school was, he would feel ashamed of being followed by a tall, stout woman; he would turn round and say:

"You'd better go home, auntie. I can go the rest of the way alone."

She would stand still and look after him fixedly till he had disappeared at the school-gate.

Ah, how she loved him! Of her former attachments not one had been so deep; never had her soul surrendered to any feeling so spontaneously, so disinterestedly, and so joyously as now that her maternal instincts were aroused. For this little boy with the dimple in his cheek and the big school cap, she would have given her whole life, she would have given it with joy and tears of tenderness. Why? Who can tell why?

When she had seen the last of Sasha, she returned home, contented and serene, brimming over with love; her face, which had grown younger during the last six months, smiled and beamed; people meeting her looked at her with pleasure.

"Good-morning, Olga Semyonovna, darling. How are you, darling?"

"The lessons at the high school are very difficult now," she would relate at the market. "It's too much; in the first class yesterday they gave him a fable to learn by heart, and a Latin translation and a problem. You know it's too much for a little chap."

And she would begin talking about the teachers, the lessons, and the school books, saying just what Sasha said.

At three o'clock they had dinner together: in the evening they learned their lessons together and cried. When she put him to bed, she would stay a long time making the Cross over him and murmuring a prayer; then she would go to bed and dream of that far-away misty future when Sasha would finish his studies and become a doctor or an engineer, would have a big house of his own with horses and a carriage, would get married and have children. . . . She would fall asleep still thinking of the same thing, and tears would run down her cheeks from her closed eyes, while the black cat lay purring beside her: "Mrr, mrr, mrr."

Suddenly there would come a loud knock at the gate.

Olenka would wake up breathless with alarm, her heart throbbing. Half a minute later would come another knock.

"It must be a telegram from Harkov," she would think, beginning to tremble from head to foot. "Sasha's mother is sending for him from Harkov. . . . Oh, mercy on us!"

She was in despair. Her head, her hands, and her feet would turn chill, and she would feel that she was the most unhappy woman in the world. But another minute would pass, voices would be heard: it would turn out to be the veterinary surgeon coming home from the club.

"Well, thank God!" she would think.

And gradually the load in her heart would pass off, and she would feel at ease. She would go back to bed thinking of Sasha, who lay sound asleep in the next room, sometimes crying out in his sleep:

"I'll give it you! Get away! Shut up!"

1899

D. H. LAWRENCE

The Lovely Lady

At seventy-two, Pauline Attenborough could still sometimes be mistaken, in the half-light, for thirty. She really was a wonderfully preserved woman, of perfect *chic*. Of course, it helps a great deal to have the right frame. She would be an exquisite skeleton, and her skull would be an exquisite skull, like that of some Etruscan woman, with feminine charm still in the swerve of the bone and the pretty naïve teeth.

Mrs. Attenborough's face was of the perfect oval, and slightly flat type that wears best. There is no flesh to sag. Her nose rode serenely, in its finely bridged curve. Only her big grey eyes were a tiny bit prominent on the surface of her face, and they gave her away most. The bluish lids were heavy, as if they ached sometimes with the strain of keeping the eyes beneath them arch and bright; and at the corners of the eyes were fine little wrinkles which would slacken with haggardness, then be pulled up tense again, to that bright, gay look like a Leonardo woman who really could laugh outright.

Her niece Cecilia was perhaps the only person in the world who was aware of the invisible little wire which connected Pauline's eye-wrinkles with Pauline's will-power. Only Cecilia *consciously* watched the eyes go haggard and old and tired, and remain so, for hours; until Robert came home. Then ping!—the mysterious little wire that worked between Pauline's will and her face went taut, the weary, haggard, prominent eyes suddenly began to gleam, the eyelids arched, the queer curved eyebrows which floated in such frail arches on Pauline's forehead began to gather a mocking significance, and you had the *real* lovely lady, in all her charm.

One of the most important and controversial English writers of the twentieth century, D. H. Lawrence was born in 1885 in Nottinghamshire. In 1912 the aspiring writer met the aristocratic Frieda Weekley and traveled with her throughout Europe for the next two years, before they married in 1914. In his novels, short stories, and poems, as well as his rather unsettled life-style, Lawrence attempted to escape from what he saw as the horrors of modern existence. Visions of an ideal, more natural alternative—embodied in such works as *The Rainbow* (1915) and *Lady Chatterley's Lover* (1928)—were often banned as obscene. Plagued by deteriorating health, Lawrence spent much of his life outside of England until his death in 1930 in a sanatorium near Antibes, France.

She really had the secret of everlasting youth; that is to say, she could don her youth again like an eagle. But she was sparing of it. She was wise enough not to try being young for too many people. Her son Robert, in the evenings, and Sir Wilfred Knipe sometimes in the afternoon to tea: then occasional visitors on Sunday, when Robert was home: for these she was her lovely and changeless self, that age could not wither, nor custom stale: so bright and kindly and yet subtly mocking, like Mona Lisa, who knew a thing or two. But Pauline knew more, so she needn't be smug at all, she could laugh that lovely mocking Bacchante laugh of hers, which was at the same time never malicious, always good-naturedly tolerant, both of virtues and vices. The former, of course, taking much more tolerating. So she suggested, roguishly.

Only with her niece Cecilia she did not trouble to keep up the glamour. Ciss was not very observant, anyhow: and more than that, she was plain: more still, she was in love with Robert: and most of all, she was thirty, and dependent on her Aunt Pauline. Oh, Cecilia! Why make music for her!

Cecilia, called by her aunt and by her cousin Robert just Ciss, like a cat spitting, was a big dark-complexioned, pug-faced young woman who very rarely spoke, and when she did, couldn't get it out. She was the daughter of a poor Congregational minister who had been, while he lived, brother to Ronald, Aunt Pauline's husband. Ronald and the Congregational minister were both well dead, and Aunt Pauline had had charge of Ciss for the last five years.

They lived all together in a quite exquisite though rather small Queen Anne house some twenty-five miles out of town, secluded in a little dale, and surrounded by small but very quaint and pleasant grounds. It was an ideal place and an ideal life for Aunt Pauline, at the age of seventy-two. When the kingfishers flashed up the little stream in the garden, going under the alders, something still flashed in her heart. She was that kind of woman.

Robert, who was two years older than Ciss, went every day to town, to his chambers in one of the Inns. He was a barrister, and, to his secret but very deep mortification, he earned about a hundred pounds a year. He simply *couldn't* get above that figure, though it was rather easy to get below it. Of course, it didn't matter. Pauline had money. But then what was Pauline's was Pauline's, and though she could give almost lavishly, still, one was always aware of having a *lovely* and *undeserved* present made to one: presents are so much nicer when they are undeserved, Aunt Pauline would say.

Robert too was plain, and almost speechless. He was medium-sized, rather broad and stout, though not fat. Only his creamy, clean-shaven face was rather fat, and sometimes suggestive of an Italian priest, in its silence and its secrecy. But he had grey eyes like his mother, but very shy and uneasy, not bold like hers. Perhaps Ciss was the only person who fathomed his awful shyness and *malaise*, his habitual feeling that he was in the wrong place: almost like a soul that has got into the wrong body. But he never did anything about it. He went up to his chambers and read law. It was, however, all the weird old processes that interested him. He had, unknown to everybody but his mother, a quite extraordinary collection of old Mexican legal documents, reports of processes and trials, pleas, accusations, the weird and awful mixture of ecclesiastical law and common law in seventeenth-century Mexico. He had started a study in this direction through coming across a report of a trial of two English sailors, for murder, in Mexico in 1620, and he had gone on, when the next document was an accusation against a Don Miguel Estrada for seducing one of the nuns of the Sacred Heart Convent in Oaxaca in 1680.

Pauline and her son Robert had wonderful evenings with these old papers. The lovely lady knew a little Spanish. She even looked a trifle Spanish herself, with a high comb and a marvellous dark brown shawl embroidered in thick silvery silk embroidery. So she would sit at the perfect old table, soft as velvet in its deep brown surface, a high comb in her hair, ear-rings with dropping pendants in her ears, her arms bare and still beautiful, a few strings of pearls round her throat, a puce velvet dress on and this or another beautiful shawl, and by candle-light she looked, yes, a Spanish highbred beauty of thirty-two or three. She set the candles to give her face just the chiaroscuro she knew suited her; her high chair that rose behind her face was done in old green brocade, against which her face emerged like a Christmas rose.

They were always three at table; and they always drank a bottle of champagne: Pauline two glasses, Ciss two glasses, Robert the rest. The lovely lady sparkled and was radiant. Ciss, her black hair bobbed, her broad shoulders in a very nice and becoming dress that Aunt Pauline had helped her to make, stared from her aunt to her cousin and back again, with rather confused, mute, hazel eyes, and played the part of an audience suitably impressed. She *was* impressed, somewhere, all the time. And even rendered speechless by Pauline's brilliancy, even after five years. But at the bottom of her consciousness were the data of as weird a document as Robert ever studied: all the things she knew about her aunt and cousin.

Robert was always a gentleman, with an old-fashioned punctilious courtesy that covered his shyness quite completely. He was, and Ciss knew it, more confused than shy. He was worse than she was. Cecilia's own confusion dated from only five years back—Robert's must have started before he was born. In the lovely lady's womb he must have felt *very* confused.

He paid all his attention to his mother, drawn to her as a humble flower to the sun. And yet, priest-like, he was all the time aware, with the tail of his consciousness, that Ciss was there, and that she was a bit shut out of it, and that something wasn't right. He was aware of the third consciousness in the room. Whereas to Pauline, her niece Cecilia was an appropriate part of her own setting, rather than a distinct consciousness.

Robert took coffee with his mother and Ciss in the warm drawing-room, where all the furniture was so lovely, all collectors' pieces—Mrs. Attenborough had made her own money, dealing privately in pictures and furniture and rare things from barbaric countries—and the three talked desultorily till about eight or half-past. It was very pleasant, very cosy, very homely even: Pauline made a real home cosiness out of so much elegant material. The chat was simple, and nearly always bright. Pauline was her *real* self, emanating a friendly mockery and an odd, ironic gaiety. Till there came a little pause.

At which Ciss always rose and said good night and carried out the coffee-tray, to prevent Burnett from intruding any more.

And then! Oh, then, the lovely glowing intimacy of the evening, between mother and son, when they deciphered manuscripts and discussed points, Pauline with that eagerness of a girl, for which she was famous. And it was quite genuine. In some mysterious way she had *saved up* her power for being thrilled, in connection with a man. Robert, solid, rather quiet and subdued, seemed like the elder of the two: almost like a priest with a young girl pupil. And that was rather how he felt.

Ciss had a flat for herself just across the courtyard, over the old coach-house and stables. There were no horses. Robert kept his car in the coach-house. Ciss had three very nice rooms up there, stretching along in a row one after another, and she had got used to the ticking of the stable clock.

But sometimes she did not go up to her rooms. In the summer she would sit on the lawn, and from the open window of the drawing-room upstairs she would hear Pauline's wonderful heart-searching laugh. And in the winter the young woman would put on a thick coat and walk slowly to the little balustraded bridge over the stream, and then look back at the three lighted windows of that drawing-room where mother and son were so happy together.

Ciss loved Robert, and she believed that Pauline intended the two of them to marry: when she was dead. But poor Robert, he was so convulsed with shyness already, with man or woman. What would he be when his mother was dead—in a dozen more years? He would be just a shell, the shell of a man who had never lived.

The strange unspoken sympathy of the young with one another, when they are overshadowed by the old, was one of the bonds between Robert and Ciss. But another bond, which Ciss did not know how to draw tight, was the bond of passion. Poor Robert was by nature a passionate man. His silence and his agonised, though hidden, shyness were both the result of a secret physical passionateness. And how Pauline could play on this! Ah, Ciss was not blind to the eyes which he fixed on his mother, eyes fascinated yet humiliated, full of shame. He was ashamed that he was not a man. And he did not love his mother. He was fascinated by her. Completely fascinated. And for the rest, paralysed in a life-long confusion.

Ciss stayed in the garden till the lights leapt up in Pauline's bedroom —about ten o'clock. The lovely lady had retired. Robert would now stay another hour or so, alone. Then he too would retire. Ciss, in the dark outside, sometimes wished she could creep up to him and say: "Oh, Robert! It's all wrong!" But Aunt Pauline would hear. And, any-how, Ciss couldn't do it. She went off to her own rooms once more, and so for ever.

In the morning coffee was brought up on a tray to each of the three relatives. Ciss had to be at Sir Wilfred Knipe's at nine o'clock, to give two hours' lessons to his little granddaughter. It was her sole serious occupation, except that she played the piano for the love of it. Robert set off to town about nine. And, as a rule, Aunt Pauline appeared at lunch, though sometimes not until tea-time. When she appeared, she looked fresh and young. But she was inclined to fade rather quickly, like a flower without water, in the day-time. Her hour was the candle hour.

So she always rested in the afternoon. When the sun shone, if possible she took a sun-bath. This was one of her secrets. Her lunch was very light, she could take her sun-and-air-bath before noon or after, as it pleased her. Often it was in the afternoon, when the sun shone very warmly into a queer little yew-walled square just behind the stables. Here Ciss stretched out the lying-chair and rugs, and put the light parasol in the silent little enclosure of thick dark yew hedges beyond the red walls of the unused stables. And hither came the lovely lady with her book. Ciss then had to be on guard in one of her own rooms, should her aunt, who was very keen-eared, hear a footstep.

One afternoon it occurred to Cecilia that she herself might while away this rather long afternoon by taking a sun-bath. She was growing restive. The thought of the flat roof of the stable buildings, to which she could climb from a loft at the end, started her on a new adventure. She often went on to the roof: she had to, to wind up the stable clock, which was a job she had assumed to herself. Now she took a rug, climbed out under the heavens, looked at the sky and the great elm-tops, looked at the sun, then took off her things and lay down perfectly serenely, in a corner of the roof under the parapet, full in the sun.

It was rather lovely, to bask all one's length like this in warm sun and air. Yes, it was very lovely! It even seemed to melt some of the hard bitterness of her heart, some of that core of unspoken resentment which never dissolved. Luxuriously, she spread herself, so that the sun should touch her limbs fully, fully. If she had no other lover, she should have the sun! She rolled voluptuously. And suddenly her heart stood still in her body, and her hair almost rose on end as a voice said very softly, musingly in her ear:

"No, Henry dear! It was not my fault you died instead of marrying that Claudia. No darling. I was quite, quite willing for you to marry her, unsuitable though she was."

Cecilia sank down on her rug powerless and perspiring with dread. That awful voice, so soft, so musing, yet so unnatural. Not a human voice at all. Yet there must, there must be someone on the roof! Oh! how unspeakably awful!

She lifted her weak head and peeped across the sloping leads. Nobody! The chimneys were far too narrow to shelter anybody. There was nobody on the roof. Then it must be someone in the trees, in the elms. Either that, or terror unspeakable, a bodiless voice! She reared her head a little higher.

And as she did so, came the voice again:

"No, darling! I told you you would tire of her in six months. And you see, it was true, dear. It was true, true, true! I wanted to spare you that. So it wasn't I who made you feel weak and disabled, wanting that very silly Claudia; poor thing, she looked so woebegone afterwards! Wanting her and not wanting her, you got *yourself* into that perplexity, my dear. I only warned you. What else could I do? And you lost your spirit and died without ever knowing me again. It was bitter, bitter—"

The voice faded away. Cecilia subsided weakly on to her rug, after the anguished tension of listening. Oh, it was awful. The sun shone, the sky was blue, all seemed so lovely and afternoony and summery. And yet, oh, horror!—she was going to be forced to believe in the supernatural! And she loathed the supernatural, ghosts and voices and rappings and all the rest.

But that awful creepy bodiless voice, with its rusty sort of whisper of an overtone! It had something so fearfully familiar in it too! and yet was so utterly uncanny. Poor Cecilia could only lie there unclothed, and so all the more agonisingly helpless, inert, collapsed in sheer dread.

And then she heard the thing sigh! A deep sigh that seemed weirdly familiar, yet was not human. "Ah, well; ah, well, the heart must bleed! Better it should bleed than break. It is grief, grief! But it wasn't my fault, dear. And Robert could marry our poor dull Ciss to-morrow, if he wanted her. But he doesn't care about it, so why force him into anything!" The sounds were very uneven, sometimes only a husky sort of whisper. Listen! Listen!

Cecilia was about to give vent to loud and piercing screams of hysteria, when the last two sentences arrested her. All her caution and her cunning sprang alert. It was Aunt Pauline! It must be Aunt Pauline, practising ventriloquism or something like that! What a devil she was!

Where was she? She must be lying down there, right below where Cecilia herself was lying. And it was either some fiend's trick of ventriloquism, or else thought transference that conveyed itself like sound. The sounds were very uneven. Sometimes quite inaudible, sometimes only a brushing sort of noise. Ciss listened intently. No, it could not be ventriloquism. It was worse, some form of thought transference. Some horror of that sort. Cecilia still lay weak and inert, terrified to move, but she was growing calmer with suspicion. It was some diabolic trick of that unnatural woman.

But *what a devil* of a woman! She even knew that she, Cecilia, had mentally accused her of killing her son Henry. Poor Henry was Robert's elder brother, twelve years older than Robert. He had died suddenly when he was twenty-two, after an awful struggle with himself, because he was passionately in love with a young and very good-looking actress, and his mother had humorously despised him for the attachment. So he had caught some sudden ordinary disease, but the poison had gone to his brain and killed him before he ever regained consciousness. Ciss knew the few facts from her own father. And lately she had been thinking that Pauline was going to kill Robert as she had killed Henry. It was clear murder: a mother murdering her sensitive sons, who were fascinated by her: the Circe!

"I suppose I may as well get up," murmured the dim, unbreaking voice. "Too much sun is as bad as too little. Enough sun, enough love thrill, enough proper food, and not too much of any of them, and a woman might live for ever. I verily believe for ever. If she absorbs as much vitality as she expends! Or perhaps a trifle more!"

It was certainly Aunt Pauline! How, how horrible! She, Ciss, was hearing Aunt Pauline's thoughts. Oh, how ghastly! Aunt Pauline was sending out her thoughts in a sort of radio, and she, Ciss, had to *hear* what her aunt was thinking. How ghastly! How insufferable! One of them would surely have to die.

She twisted and she lay inert and crumpled, staring vacantly in front of her. Vacantly! Vacantly! And her eyes were staring almost into a hole. She was staring into it unseeing, a hole going down in the corner from the lead gutter. It meant nothing to her. Only it frightened her a little more.

When suddenly out of the hole came a sigh and a last whisper. "Ah, well! Pauline! Get up, it's enough for today!" Good God! Out of the hole of the rain-pipe! The rain-pipe was acting as a speaking-tube! Impossible! No, quite possible. She had read of it even in some book. And Aunt Pauline, like the old and guilty woman she was, talked aloud to herself. That was it!

A sullen exultance sprang into Ciss's breast. *That* was why she would never have anybody, not even Robert, in her bedroom. That was why she never dozed in a chair, never sat absent-minded anywhere, but went to her room, and kept to her room, except when she roused herself to be alert. When she slackened off, she talked to herself! She talked in a soft little crazy voice to herself. But she was not crazy. It was only her thoughts murmuring themselves aloud.

So she had qualms about poor Henry! Well she might have! Ciss believed that Aunt Pauline had loved her big, handsome, brilliant first-born much more than she loved Robert, and that his death had been a terrible blow and a chagrin to her. Poor Robert had been only ten years old when Henry died. Since then he had been the substitute.

Ah, how awful!

But Aunt Pauline was a strange woman. She had left her husband when Henry was a small child, some years even before Robert was born. There was no quarrel. Sometimes she saw her husband again, quite amicably, but a little mockingly. And she even gave him money.

For Pauline earned all her own. Her father had been a consul in the East and in Naples: and a devoted collector of beautiful and exotic things. When he died, soon after his grandson Henry was born, he left his collection of treasures to his daughter. And Pauline, who had really a passion and a genius for loveliness, whether in texture or form or colour, had laid the basis of her fortune on her father's collection. She had gone on collecting, buying where she could, and selling to collectors and to museums. She was one of the first to sell old, weird African wooden figures to the museums, and ivory carvings from New Guinea. She bought Renoir as soon as she saw his pictures. But not Rousseau. And all by herself she made a fortune.

After her husband died, she had not married again. She was not even *known* to have had lovers. If she did have lovers, it was not among the men who admired her most and paid her devout and open attendance. To these she was a "friend."

Cecilia slipped on her clothes and caught up her rug, hastened carefully down the ladder to the loft. As she descended she heard the ringing musical call: "All right, Ciss!" which meant that the lovely lady was finished, and returning to the house. Even her voice was marvellously young and sonorous, beautifully balanced and self-possessed. So different from the little voice in which she talked to herself. *That* was much more the voice of an old woman.

Ciss hastened round to the yew enclosure, where lay the comfortable chaise-longue with the various delicate rugs. Everything Pauline had was choice, to the fine straw mat on the floor. The great yew walls were beginning to cast long shadows. Only in the corner, where the rugs tumbled their delicate colours, was there hot, still sunshine.

The rugs folded up, the chair lifted away, Cecilia stooped to look at the mouth of the rain-pipe. There it was, in the corner, under a little hood of masonry and just projecting from the thick leaves of the creeper on the wall. If Pauline, lying there, turned her face towards the wall, she would speak into the very mouth of the hole. Cecilia was reassured. She had heard her aunt's thoughts indeed, but by no uncanny agency.

That evening, as if aware of something, Pauline was a little quicker than usual, though she looked her own serene, rather mysterious self. And after coffee she said to Robert and Ciss: "I'm so sleepy. The sun has made me so sleepy. I feel full of sunshine like a bee. I shall go to bed, if you don't mind. You two sit and have a talk."

Cecilia looked quickly at her cousin.

"Perhaps you would rather be alone," she said to him.

"No, no," he replied. "Do keep me company for a while, if it doesn't bore you."

The windows were open, the scent of the honeysuckle wafted in with the sound of an owl. Robert smoked in silence. There was a sort of despair in the motionless, rather squat body. He looked like a caryatid bearing a weight.

"Do you remember Cousin Henry?" Cecilia asked him suddenly.

He looked up in surprise.

"Yes, very well," he said.

"What did he look like?" she said, glancing into her cousin's big, secret-troubled eyes, in which there was so much frustration.

"Oh, he was handsome: tall and fresh-coloured, with mother's soft brown hair." As a matter of fact, Pauline's hair was grey. "The ladies admired him very much; he was at all the dances."

"And what kind of character had he?"

"Oh, very good-natured and jolly. He liked to be amused. He was rather quick and clever, like mother, and very good company."

"And did he love your mother?"

"Very much. She loved him too—better than she does me, as a matter of fact. He was so much more nearly her idea of a man."

"Why was he more her idea of a man?"

"Tall—handsome—attractive, and very good company—and would, I believe, have been very successful at law. I'm afraid I am merely negative in all those respects."

Ciss looked at him attentively, with her slow-thinking hazel eyes. Under his impassive mask, she knew he suffered.

"Do you think you are so much more negative than he?" she said.

He did not lift his face. But after a few moments he replied:

"My life, certainly, is a negative affair."

She hesitated before she dared ask him:

"And do you mind?"

He did not answer her at all. Her heart sank.

"You see, I am afraid my life is as negative as yours is," she said. "And I'm beginning to mind bitterly. I'm thirsty."

She saw his creamy, well-bred hand tremble.

"I suppose," he said, without looking at her, "one will rebel when it is too late."

That was queer, from him.

"Robert," she said, "do you like me at all?"

She saw his dusky, creamy face, so changeless in its folds, go pale.

"I am very fond of you," he murmured.

"Won't you kiss me? Nobody ever kisses me," she said pathetically.

He looked at her, his eyes strange with fear and a certain haughtiness. Then he rose and came softly over to her and kissed her gently on the cheek.

"It's an awful shame, Ciss!" he said softly.

She caught his hand and pressed it to her breast.

"And sit with me some time in the garden," she said, murmuring with difficulty. "Won't you?"

He looked at her anxiously and searchingly.

"What about mother?" he said.

Ciss smiled a funny little smile, and looked into his eyes. He suddenly flushed crimson, turning aside his face. It was a painful sight.

"I know," he said, "I am no lover of women."

He spoke with sarcastic stoicism against himself, but even she did not know the shame it was to him.

"You never try to be!" she said.

Again his eyes changed uncannily.

"Does one have to try?" he said.

"Why, yes! One never does anything if one doesn't try."

He went pale again.

"Perhaps you are right," he said.

In a few minutes she left him and went to her room. At least, she had tried to take off the everlasting lid from things.

The weather continued sunny, Pauline continued her sun-baths, and Ciss lay on the roof eavesdropping in the literal sense of the word. But Pauline was not to be heard. No sound came up the pipe. She must be lying with her face away into the open. Ciss listened with all her might. She could just detect the faintest, faintest murmur away below, but no audible syllable.

And at night, under the stars, Cecilia sat and waited in silence, on the seat which kept in view the drawing-room windows and the side door into the garden. She saw the light go up in her aunt's room. She saw the lights at last go out in the drawing-room. And she waited. But he did not come. She stayed on in the darkness half the night, while the owl hooted. But she stayed alone.

Two days she heard nothing, her aunt's thoughts were not revealed and at evening nothing happened. Then the second night, as she sat with heavy, helpless persistence in the garden, suddenly she started. He had come out. She rose and went softly over the grass to him.

"Don't speak," he murmured.

And in silence, in the dark, they walked down the garden and over the little bridge to the paddock, where the hay, cut very late, was in cock. There they stood disconsolate under the stars.

"You see," he said, "how can I ask for love, if I don't feel any love in myself. You know I have a real regard for you—"

"How can you feel any love, when you never feel anything?" she said.

"That is true," he replied.

And she waited for what next.

"And how can I marry?" he said. "I am a failure even at making money. I can't ask my mother for money."

She sighed deeply.

"Then don't bother yet about marrying," she said. "Only love me a little. Won't you?"

He gave a short laugh.

"It sounds so atrocious, to say it is hard to begin," he said.

She sighed again. He was so stiff to move.

"Shall we sit down a minute," she said. And then as they sat on the hay, she added: "May I touch you? Do you mind?"

"Yes, I mind! But do as you wish," he replied, with that mixture of shyness and queer candour which made him a little ridiculous, as he knew quite well. But in his heart there was almost murder.

She touched his black, always tidy hair with her fingers.

"I suppose I shall rebel one day," he said again, suddenly.

They sat some time, till it grew chilly. And he held her hand fast, but he never put his arms round her. At last she rose and went indoors, saying good night.

The next day, as Cecilia lay stunned and angry on the roof, taking her sun-bath, and becoming hot and fierce with sunshine, suddenly she started. A terror seized her in spite of herself. It was the voice.

"*Caro, caro, tu non l'hai visto!*" it was murmuring away, in a language Cecilia did not understand. She lay and writhed her limbs in the sun, listening intently to words she could not follow. Softly, whisperingly, with infinite caressiveness and yet with that subtle, insidious arrogance under its velvet, came the voice, murmuring in Italian: "*Bravo, si molto bravo, poverino, ma uomo come te non lo sara mai, mai, mai!*" Oh, especially in Italian Cecilia heard the poisonous charm of the voice, so caressive, so soft and flexible, yet so utterly egoistic. She hated it with intensity as it sighed and whispered out of nowhere. Why, why should it be so delicate, so subtle and flexible and beautifully controlled, while she herself was so clumsy! Oh, poor Cecilia, she writhed in the afternoon sun, knowing her own clownish clumsiness and lack of suavity, in comparison.

"No, Robert dear, you will never be the man your father was, though you have some of his looks. He was a marvellous lover, soft as a flower, yet piercing as a humming-bird. No, Robert dear, you will never know how to serve a woman as Monsignor Mauro did. *Cara, cara mia bellissima, ti ho aspettato come l'agonizzante aspetta la morte, morte deliziosa, quasi quasi troppo deliziosa per un' anima humana*—Soft as a flower, yet probing like a humming-bird. He gave himself to a woman as he gave himself to God. Mauro! Mauro! How you loved me!"

The voice ceased in reverie, and Cecilia knew what she had guessed before, that Robert was not the son of her Uncle Ronald, but of some Italian.

"I am disappointed in you, Robert. There is no poignancy in you. Your father was a Jesuit, but he was the most perfect and poignant lover in the world. You are a Jesuit like a fish in a tank. And that Ciss of yours is the cat fishing for you. It is less edifying even than poor Henry."

Cecilia suddenly bent her mouth down to the tube, and said in a deep voice:

"Leave Robert alone! Don't kill him as well."

There was a dead silence, in the hot July afternoon that was lowering for thunder. Cecilia lay prostrate, her heart beating in great thumps. She was listening as if her whole soul were an ear. At last she caught the whisper:

"Did someone speak?"

She leaned again to the mouth of the tube.

"Don't kill Robert as you killed me," she said with slow enunciation, and a deep but small voice.

"Ah!" came the sharp little cry. "Who is that speaking?"

"Henry!" said the deep voice.

There was a dead silence. Poor Cecilia lay with all the use gone out of her. And there was dead silence. Till at last came the whisper:

"I didn't kill Henry. No, NO! Henry, surely you can't blame me! I loved you, dearest. I only wanted to help you."

"You killed me!" came the deep, artificial, accusing voice. "Now, let Robert live. Let him go! Let him marry!"

There was a pause.

"How very, very awful!" mused the whispering voice. "Is it possible, Henry, you are a spirit, and you condemn me?"

"Yes! I condemn you!"

Cecilia felt all her pent-up rage going down that rain-pipe. At the same time, she almost laughed. It was awful.

She lay and listened and listened. No sound! As if time had ceased, she lay inert in the weakening sun. The sky was yellowing. Quickly she dressed herself, went down, and out to the corner of the stables.

"Aunt Pauline!" she called discreetly. "Did you hear thunder?"

"Yes! I am going in. Don't wait," came a feeble voice.

Cecilia retired, and from the loft watched, spying, as the figure of the lovely lady, wrapped in a lovely wrap of old blue silk, went rather totteringly to the house.

The sky gradually darkened, Cecilia hastened in with the rugs. Then the storm broke. Aunt Pauline did not appear to tea. She found the thunder trying. Robert also did not arrive till after tea, in the pouring rain. Cecilia went down the covered passage to her own house, and dressed carefully for dinner, putting some white columbines at her breast.

The drawing-room was lit with a softly-shaded lamp. Robert, dressed, was waiting, listening to the rain. He too seemed strangely cracking and on edge. Cecilia came in with the white flowers nodding at her breast. Robert was watching her curiously, a new look on his face. Cecilia went to the bookshelves near the door, and was peering for something, listening acutely. She heard a rustle, then the door softly opening. And as it opened, Ciss suddenly switched on the strong electric light by the door.

Her aunt, in a dress of black lace over ivory colour, stood in the doorway. Her face was made up, but haggard with a look of unspeakable irritability, as if years of suppressed exasperation and dislike of her fellow-men had suddenly crumpled her into an old witch.

"Oh, aunt!" cried Cecilia.

"Why, mother, you're a little old lady!" came the astounded voice of Robert: like an astonished boy: as if it were a joke.

"Have you only just found it out?" snapped the old woman venomously.

"Yes! Why, I thought—" his voice tailed out in misgiving.

The haggard, old Pauline, in a frenzy of exasperation, said: "Aren't we going down?"

She had never even noticed the excess of light, a thing she shunned. And she went downstairs almost tottering.

At table she sat with her face like a crumpled mask of unspeakable irritability. She looked old, very old, and like a witch. Robert and Cecilia fetched furtive glances at her. And Ciss, watching Robert, saw that he was so astonished and repelled by his mother's looks, that he was another man.

"What kind of drive home did you have?" snapped Pauline, with an almost gibbering irritability.

"It rained, of course," he said.

"How clever of you to have found that out!" said his mother, with the grisly grin of malice that had succeeded her arch smirk.

"I don't understand," he said with quiet suavity.

"It's apparent," said his mother, rapidly and sloppily eating her food.

She rushed through the meal like a crazy dog, to the utter consternation of the servant. And the moment it was over, she darted in a queer, crab-like way upstairs. Robert and Cecilia followed her, thunderstruck, like two conspirators.

"You pour the coffee. I loathe it! I'm going! Good night!" said the old woman, in a succession of sharp shots. And she scrambled out of the room.

There was a dead silence. At last he said:

"I'm afraid mother isn't well. I must persuade her to see a doctor."

"Yes!" said Cecilia.

The evening passed in silence. Robert and Ciss stayed on in the drawing-room, having lit a fire. Outside was cold rain. Each pretended to read. They did not want to separate. The evening passed with ominous mysteriousness, yet quickly.

At about ten o'clock, the door suddenly opened, and Pauline appeared in a blue wrap. She shut the door behind her, and came to the fire. Then she looked at the two young people in hate, real hate.

"You two had better get married quickly," she said in an ugly voice. "It would look more decent; such a passionate pair of lovers!"

Robert looked up at her quietly.

"I thought you believed that cousins should not marry, mother," he said.

"I do! But you're not cousins. Your father was an Italian priest." Pauline held her daintily-slippered foot to the fire, in an old coquettish gesture. Her body tried to repeat all the old graceful gestures. But the nerve had snapped, so it was a rather dreadful caricature.

"Is that really true, mother?" he asked.

"True! What do you think? He was a distinguished man, or he wouldn't have been my lover. He was far too distinguished a man to have had you for a son. But that joy fell to me."

"How unfortunate all round," he said slowly.

"Unfortunate for you? You were lucky. It was *my* misfortune," she said acidly to him.

She was really a dreadful sight, like a piece of lovely Venetian glass that has been dropped, and gathered up again in horrible, sharp-edged fragments.

Suddenly she left the room again.

For a week it went on. She did not recover. It was as if every nerve in her body had suddenly started screaming in an insanity of discordance. The doctor came, and gave her sedatives, for she never slept. Without drugs, she never slept at all, only paced back and forth in her room, looking hideous and evil, reeking with malevolence. She could not bear to see either her son or her niece. Only when either of them came, she asked in pure malice:

"Well! When's the wedding! Have you celebrated the nuptials yet?"

At first Cecilia was stunned by what she had done. She realised vaguely that her aunt, once a definite thrust of condemnation had penetrated her beautiful armour, had just collapsed squirming inside her shell. It was too terrible. Ciss was almost terrified into repentance. Then she thought: This is what she always was. Now let her live the rest of her days in her true colours.

But Pauline would not live long. She was literally shrivelling away. She kept to her room, and saw no one. She had her mirrors taken away.

Robert and Cecilia sat a good deal together. The jeering of the mad Pauline had not driven them apart, as she had hoped. But Cecilia dared not confess to him what she had done.

"Do you think your mother ever loved anybody?" Ciss asked him tentatively, rather wistfully, one evening.

He looked at her fixedly.

"Herself!" he said at last.

"She didn't even *love* herself," said Ciss. "It was something else—what was it?" She lifted a troubled, utterly puzzled face to him.

"Power!" he said curtly.

"But what power?" she asked. "I don't understand."

"Power to feed on other lives," he said bitterly. "She was beautiful, and she fed on life. She has fed on me as she fed on Henry. She put a sucker into one's soul and sucked up one's essential life."

"And don't you forgive her?"

"No."

"Poor Aunt Pauline!"

But even Ciss did not mean it. She was only aghast.

"I *know* I've got a heart," he said, passionately striking his breast. "But it's almost sucked dry. I *know* people who want power over others."

Ciss was silent; what was there to say?

And two days later, Pauline was found dead in her bed, having taken too much veronal, for her heart was weakened. From the grave even she hit back at her son and her niece. She left Robert the noble sum of one thousand pounds; and Ciss one hundred. All the rest, with the nucleus of her valuable antiques, went to form the "Pauline Attenborough Museum."

1933

HENRY JAMES

Paste

"I've found a lot more things," her cousin said to her the day after the second funeral; "they're up in her room—but they're things I wish *you'd* look at."

The pair of mourners, sufficiently stricken, were in the garden of the vicarage together, before luncheon, waiting to be summoned to that meal, and Arthur Prime had still in his face the intention, she was moved to call it rather than the expression, of feeling something or other. Some such appearance was in itself of course natural within a week of his stepmother's death, within three of his father's; but what was most present to the girl, herself sensitive and shrewd, was that he seemed somehow to brood without sorrow, to suffer without what she in her own case would have called pain. He turned away from her after this last speech—it was a good deal his habit to drop an observation and leave her to pick it up without assistance. If the vicar's widow, now in her turn finally translated, had not really belonged to him it was not for want of her giving herself, so far as he ever would take her; and she had lain for three days all alone at the end of the passage, in the great cold chamber of hospitality, the dampish, greenish room where visitors slept and where several of the ladies of the parish had, without effect, offered, in pairs and successions, piously to watch with her. His personal connection with the parish was now slighter than ever, and he had really not waited for this opportunity to show the ladies what he thought of them. She felt that she herself had, during her doleful month's leave from Bleet, where she was governess, rather taken her place in the same

Henry James is considered by many to have taken the American novel to its highest form. His career and art, though, are singularly transatlantic. Born into a wealthy New York family in 1843, James spent much of his youth in the shadow of his elder brother, William (who would later gain recognition as one of the country's leading psychologists and philosophers). After dropping out of Harvard Law School, Henry James began to write. By his midtwenties he was a leader of American realism, and eventually became the exemplar of psychological realism. In 1875 he settled permanently in Europe, in many ways living out the confrontation of New and Old World cultures that eventually appeared in novels like *The American* (1877) and *The Ambassadors* (1903). A year before his death in 1916, James became a subject of the British crown.

snubbed order; but it was presently, none the less, with a better little hope of coming in for some remembrance, some relic, that she went up to look at the things he had spoken of, the identity of which, as a confused cluster of bright objects on a table in the darkened room, shimmered at her as soon as she had opened the door.

They met her eyes for the first time, but in a moment, before touching them, she knew them as things of the theatre, as very much too fine to have been, with any verisimilitude, things of the vicarage. They were too dreadfully good to be true, for her aunt had had no jewels to speak of, and these were coronets and girdles, diamonds, rubies, and sapphires. Flagrant tinsel and glass, they looked strangely vulgar, but if, after the first queer shock of them, she found herself taking them up, it was for the very proof, never yet so distinct to her, of a far-off faded story. An honest widowed cleric with a small son and a large sense of Shakespeare had, on a brave latitude of habit as well as of taste—since it implied his having in very fact dropped deep into the "pit"—conceived for an obscure actress, several years older than himself, an admiration of which the prompt offer of his reverend name and hortatory hand was the sufficiently candid sign. The response had perhaps, in those dim years, in the way of eccentricity, even bettered the proposal, and Charlotte, turning the tale over, had long since drawn from it a measure of the career renounced by the undistinguished *comédienne*— doubtless also tragic, or perhaps pantomimic, at a pinch—of her late uncle's dreams. This career could not have been eminent and must much more probably have been comfortless.

"You see what it is—old stuff of the time she never liked to mention."

Our young woman gave a start; her companion had, after all, rejoined her and had apparently watched a moment her slightly scared recognition. "So I said to myself," she replied. Then, to show intelligence, yet keep clear of twaddle: "How peculiar they look!"

"They look awful," said Arthur Prime. "Cheap gilt, diamonds as big as potatoes. These are trappings of a ruder age than ours. Actors do themselves better now."

"Oh now," said Charlotte, not to be less knowing, "actresses have real diamonds."

"Some of them." Arthur spoke drily.

"I mean the bad ones—the nobodies too."

"Oh, some of the nobodies have the biggest. But mamma wasn't of that sort."

"A nobody?" Charlotte risked.

"Not a nobody to whom somebody—well, not a nobody with diamonds. It isn't all worth, this trash, five pounds."

There was something in the old gewgaws that spoke to her, and she continued to turn them over. "They're relics. I think they have their melancholy and even their dignity."

Arthur observed another pause. "Do you care for them?" he then asked. "I mean," he promptly added, "as a souvenir."

"Of you?" Charlotte threw off.

"Of me? What have I to do with it? Of your poor dead aunt who was so kind to you," he said with virtuous sternness.

"Well, I would rather have them than nothing."

"Then please take them," he returned in a tone of relief which expressed somehow more of the eager than of the gracious.

"Thank you." Charlotte lifted two or three objects up and set them down again. Though they were lighter than the materials they imitated they were so much more extravagant that they struck her in truth as rather an awkward heritage, to which she might have preferred even a matchbox or a penwiper. They were indeed shameless pinchbeck. "Had you any idea she had kept them?"

"I don't at all believe she had kept them or knew they were there, and I'm very sure my father didn't. They had quite equally worked off any tenderness for the connection. These odds and ends, which she thought had been given away or destroyed, had simply got thrust into a dark corner and been forgotten."

Charlotte wondered. "Where then did you find them?"

"In that old tin box"—and the young man pointed to the receptacle from which he had dislodged them and which stood on a neighbouring chair. "It's rather a good box still, but I'm afraid I can't give you *that*."

The girl gave the box no look; she continued only to look at the trinkets. "What corner had she found?"

"She hadn't 'found' it," her companion sharply insisted; "she had simply lost it. The whole thing had passed from her mind. The box was on the top shelf of the old schoolroom closet, which, until one put one's head into it from a stepladder, looked, from below, quite cleared out. The door is narrow and the part of the closet to the left goes well into the wall. The box had stuck there for years."

Charlotte was conscious of a mind divided and a vision vaguely troubled, and once more she took up two or three of the subjects of this revelation; a big bracelet in the form of a gilt serpent with many twists and beady eyes, a brazen belt studded with emeralds and rubies, a chain, of flamboyant architecture, to which, at the Theatre Royal Little

Peddlington, Hamlet's mother had probably been careful to attach the portrait of the successor to Hamlet's father. "Are you very sure they're not really worth something? Their mere weight alone—!" she vaguely observed, balancing a moment a royal diadem that might have crowned one of the creations of the famous Mrs. Jarley.

But Arthur Prime, it was clear, had already thought the question over and found the answer easy. "If they had been worth anything to speak of she would long ago have sold them. My father and she had unfortunately never been in a position to keep any considerable value locked up." And while his companion took in the obvious force of this he went on with a flourish just marked enough not to escape her: "If they're worth anything at all—why, you're only the more welcome to them."

Charlotte had now in her hand a small bag of faded, figured silk— one of those antique conveniences that speak to us, in the terms of evaporated camphor and lavender, of the part they have played in some personal history; but, though she had for the first time drawn the string, she looked much more at the young man than at the questionable treasure it appeared to contain. "I shall like them. They're all I have."

"All you have—?"

"That belonged to her."

He swelled a little, then looked about him as if to appeal—as against her avidity—to the whole poor place. "Well, what else do you want?"

"Nothing. Thank you very much." With which she bent her eyes on the article wrapped, and now only exposed, in her superannuated satchel—a necklace of large pearls, such as might once have graced the neck of a provincial Ophelia and borne company to a flaxen wig. "This perhaps *is* worth something. Feel it." And she passed him the necklace, the weight of which she had gathered for a moment into her hand.

He measured it in the same way with his own, but remained quite detached. "Worth at most thirty shillings."

"Not more?"

"Surely not if it's paste?"

"But *is* it paste?"

He gave a small sniff of impatience. "Pearls nearly as big as filberts?"

"But they're heavy," Charlotte declared.

"No heavier than anything else." And he gave them back with an allowance for her simplicity. "Do you imagine for a moment they're real?"

She studied them a little, feeling them, turning them round. "Mightn't they possibly be?"

"Of that size—stuck away with that trash?"

"I admit it isn't likely," Charlotte presently said. "And pearls are so easily imitated."

"That's just what—to a person who knows—they're not. These have no lustre, no play."

"No—they *are* dull. They're opaque."

"Besides," he lucidly inquired, "how could she ever have come by them?"

"Mightn't they have been a present?"

Arthur stared at the question as if it were almost improper. "Because actresses are exposed—?" He pulled up, however, not saying to what, and before she could supply the deficiency had, with the sharp ejaculation of "No, they mightn't!" turned his back on her and walked away. His manner made her feel that she had probably been wanting in tact, and before he returned to the subject, the last thing that evening, she had satisfied herself of the ground of his resentment. They had been talking of her departure the next morning, the hour of her train and the fly that would come for her, and it was precisely these things that gave him his effective chance. "I really can't allow you to leave the house under the impression that my stepmother was at *any* time of her life the sort of person to allow herself to be approached—"

"With pearl necklaces and that sort of thing?" Arthur had made for her somehow the difficulty that she couldn't show him she understood him without seeming pert.

It at any rate only added to his own gravity. "That sort of thing, exactly."

"I didn't think when I spoke this morning—but I see what you mean."

"I mean that she was beyond reproach," said Arthur Prime.

"A hundred times yes."

"Therefore if she couldn't, out of her slender gains, ever have paid for a row of pearls—"

"She couldn't, in that atmosphere, ever properly have had one? Of course she couldn't. I've seen perfectly since our talk," Charlotte went on, "that that string of beads isn't even, as an imitation, very good. The little clasp itself doesn't seem even gold. With false pearls, I suppose," the girl mused, "it naturally wouldn't be."

"The whole thing's rotten paste," her companion returned as if to have done with it. "If it were *not*, and she had kept it all these years hidden—"

"Yes?" Charlotte sounded as he paused.

"Why, I shouldn't know what to think!"

"Oh, I see." She had met him with a certain blankness, but adequately enough, it seemed, for him to regard the subject as dismissed; and there was no reversion to it between them before, on the morrow, when she had with difficulty made a place for them in her trunk, she carried off these florid survivals.

At Bleet she found small occasion to revert to them and, in an air charged with such quite other references, even felt, after she had laid them away, much enshrouded, beneath various piles of clothing, as if they formed a collection not wholly without its note of the ridiculous. Yet she was never, for the joke, tempted to show them to her pupils, though Gwendolen and Blanche, in particular, always wanted, on her return, to know what she had brought back; so that without an accident by which the case was quite changed they might have appeared to enter on a new phase of interment. The essence of the accident was the sudden illness, at the last moment, of Lady Bobby, whose advent had been so much counted on to spice the five days' feast laid out for the coming of age of the eldest son of the house; and its equally marked effect was the despatch of a pressing message, in quite another direction, to Mrs. Guy, who, could she by a miracle be secured—she was always engaged ten parties deep—might be trusted to supply, it was believed, an element of exuberance scarcely less active. Mrs. Guy was already known to several of the visitors already on the scene, but she was not yet known to our young lady, who found her, after many wires and counter-wires had at last determined the triumph of her arrival, a strange, charming little red-haired, black-dressed woman, with the face of a baby and the authority of a commodore. She took on the spot the discreet, the exceptional young governess into the confidence of her designs and, still more, of her doubts; intimating that it was a policy she almost always promptly pursued.

"To-morrow and Thursday are all right," she said frankly to Charlotte on the second day, "but I'm not half satisfied with Friday."

"What improvement then do you suggest?"

"Well, my strong point, you know, is *tableaux vivants*."

"Charming. And what is your favourite character?"

"Boss!" said Mrs. Guy with decision; and it was very markedly under that ensign that she had, within a few hours, completely planned her campaign and recruited her troop. Every word she uttered was to the point, but none more so than, after a general survey of their equipment, her final inquiry of Charlotte. She had been looking about, but half appeased, at the muster of decoration and drapery. "We shall be dull. We shall want more colour. You've nothing else?"

Charlotte had a thought. "No—I've *some* things."

"Then why don't you bring them?"

The girl hesitated. "Would you come to my room?"

"No," said Mrs. Guy—"bring them to-night to mine."

So Charlotte, at the evening's end, after candlesticks had flickered through brown old passages bedward, arrived at her friend's door with the burden of her aunt's relics. But she promptly expressed a fear. "Are they too garish?"

When she had poured them out on the sofa Mrs. Guy was but a minute, before the glass, in clapping on the diadem. "Awfully jolly— we can do Ivanhoe!"

"But they're only glass and tin."

"Larger than life they are, *rather!*—which is exactly what, for tab-leaux, is wanted. Our jewels, for historic scenes, don't tell—the real thing falls short. Rowena must have rubies as big as eggs. Leave them with me," Mrs. Guy continued—"they'll inspire me. Good-night."

The next morning she was in fact—yet very strangely—inspired. "Yes, *I'll* do Rowena. But I don't, my dear, understand."

"Understand what?"

Mrs. Guy gave a very lighted stare. "How you come to have such things."

Poor Charlotte smiled. "By inheritance."

"Family jewels?"

"They belonged to my aunt, who died some months ago. She was on the stage a few years in early life, and these are a part of her trappings."

"She left them to you?"

"No; my cousin, her stepson, who naturally has no use for them, gave them to me for remembrance of her. She was a dear kind thing, always so nice to me, and I was fond of her."

Mrs. Guy had listened with visible interest. "But it's *he* who must be a dear kind thing!"

Charlotte wondered. "You think so?"

"Is *he,*" her friend went on, "also 'always so nice' to you?"

The girl, at this, face to face there with the brilliant visitor in the deserted breakfast-room, took a deeper sounding. "What is it?"

"Don't you know?"

Something came over her. "The pearls—?" But the question fainted on her lips.

"Doesn't *he* know?"

Charlotte found herself flushing. "They're *not* paste?"

"Haven't you looked at them?"

She was conscious of two kinds of embarrassment. "*You* have?"

"Very carefully."

"And they're real?"

Mrs. Guy became slightly mystifying and returned for all answer: "Come again, when you've done with the children, to my room."

Our young woman found she had done with the children, that morning, with a promptitude that was a new joy to them, and when she reappeared before Mrs. Guy this lady had already encircled a plump white throat with the only ornament, surely, in all the late Mrs. Prime's —the effaced Miss Bradshaw's—collection, in the least qualified to raise a question. If Charlotte had never yet once, before the glass, tied the string of pearls about her own neck, this was because she had been capable of no such condescension to approved "imitation"; but she had now only to look at Mrs. Guy to see that, so disposed, the ambiguous objects might have passed for frank originals. "What in the world have you done to them?"

"Only handled them, understood them, admired them, and put them on. That's what pearls want; they want to be worn—it wakes them up. They're alive, don't you see? How *have* these been treated? They must have been buried, ignored, despised. They were half dead. Don't you *know* about pearls?" Mrs. Guy threw off as she fondly fingered the necklace.

"How *should* I? Do *you?*"

"Everything. These were simply asleep, and from the moment I really touched them—well," said their wearer lovingly, "it only took one's eye!"

"It took more than mine—though I did just wonder; and than Arthur's," Charlotte brooded. She found herself almost panting. "Then their value—?"

"Oh, their value's excellent."

The girl, for a deep moment, took another plunge into the wonder, the beauty and mystery, of them. "Are you *sure?*"

Her companion wheeled round for impatience. "Sure? For what kind of an idiot, my dear, do you take me?"

It was beyond Charlotte Prime to say. "For the same kind as Arthur —and as myself," she could only suggest. "But my cousin didn't know. He thinks they're worthless."

"Because of the rest of the lot? Then your cousin's an ass. But what —if, as I understood you, he gave them to you—has he to do with it?"

"Why, if he gave them to me as worthless and they turn out precious—"

"You must give them back? I don't see that—if he was such a fool. He took the risk."

Charlotte fed, in fancy, on the pearls, which, decidedly, were exquisite, but which at the present moment somehow presented themselves much more as Mrs. Guy's than either as Arthur's or as her own. "Yes—he did take it; even after I had distinctly hinted to him that they looked to me different from the other pieces."

"Well, then!" said Mrs. Guy with something more than triumph—with a positive odd relief.

But it had the effect of making our young woman think with more intensity. "Ah, you see he thought they couldn't be different, because—so peculiarly—they shouldn't be."

"Shouldn't? I don't understand."

"Why, how would she have got them?"—so Charlotte candidly put it.

"She? Who?" There was a capacity in Mrs. Guy's tone for a sinking of persons—!

"Why, the person I told you of: his stepmother, my uncle's wife—among whose poor old things, extraordinarily thrust away and out of sight, he happened to find them."

Mrs. Guy came a step nearer to the effaced Miss Bradshaw. "Do you mean she may have stolen them?"

"No. But she had been an actress."

"Oh, well then," cried Mrs. Guy, "wouldn't that be just how?"

"Yes, except that she wasn't at all a brilliant one, nor in receipt of large pay." The girl even threw off a nervous joke. "I'm afraid she couldn't have been our Rowena."

Mrs. Guy took it up. "Was she very ugly?"

"No. She may very well, when young, have looked rather nice."

"Well, then!" was Mrs. Guy's sharp comment and fresh triumph.

"You mean it was a present? That's just what he so dislikes the idea of her having received—a present from an admirer capable of going such lengths."

"Because she wouldn't have taken it for nothing? *Speriamo*—that she wasn't a brute. The 'length' her admirer went was the length of a whole row. Let us hope she was just a little kind!"

"Well," Charlotte went on, "that she was 'kind' might seem to be shown by the fact that neither her husband, nor his son, nor I, his niece, knew or dreamed of her possessing anything so precious; by her having kept the gift all the rest of her life beyond discovery—out of sight and protected from suspicion."

"As if, you mean"—Mrs. Guy was quick—"she had been wedded to it and yet was ashamed of it? Fancy," she laughed while she manipulated the rare beads, "being ashamed of these!"

"But you see she had married a clergyman."

"Yes, she must have been 'rum.' But at any rate he had married *her*. What did he suppose?"

"Why, that she had never been of the sort by whom such offerings are encouraged."

"Ah, my dear, the sort by whom they are *not*—!" But Mrs. Guy caught herself up. "And her stepson thought the same?"

"Overwhelmingly."

"Was he, then if only her stepson—"

"So fond of her as that comes to? Yes; he had never known, consciously, his real mother, and, without children of her own, she was very patient and nice with him. And I liked her so," the girl pursued, "that at the end of ten years, in so strange a manner, to 'give her away'—"

"Is impossible to you? Then don't!" said Mrs. Guy with decision.

"Ah, but if they're real I can't keep them!" Charlotte, with her eyes on them, moaned in her impatience. "It's too difficult."

"Where's the difficulty, if he has such sentiments that he would rather sacrifice the necklace than admit it, with the presumption it carries with it, to be genuine? You've only to be silent."

"And keep it? How can *I* ever wear it?"

"You'd have to hide it, like your aunt?" Mrs. Guy was amused. "You can easily sell it."

Her companion walked round her for a look at the affair from behind. The clasp was certainly, doubtless intentionally, misleading, but everything else was indeed lovely. "Well, I must think. Why didn't *she* sell them?" Charlotte broke out in her trouble.

Mrs. Guy had an instant answer. "Doesn't that prove what they secretly recalled to her? You've only to be silent!" she ardently repeated.

"I must think—I must think!"

Mrs. Guy stood with her hands attached but motionless. "Then you want them back?"

As if with the dread of touching them Charlotte retreated to the door. "I'll tell you to-night."

"But may I wear them?"

"Meanwhile?"

"This evening—at dinner."

It was the sharp, selfish pressure of this that really, on the spot, determined the girl; but for the moment, before closing the door on the question, she only said: "As you like!"

They were busy much of the day with preparation and rehearsal, and at dinner, that evening, the concourse of guests was such that a place among them for Miss Prime failed to find itself marked. At the time the company rose she was therefore alone in the schoolroom, where, towards eleven o'clock, she received a visit from Mrs. Guy. This lady's white shoulders heaved, under the pearls, with an emotion that the very red lips which formed, as if for the full effect, the happiest opposition of colour, were not slow to translate. "My dear, you should have seen the sensation—they've had a success!"

Charlotte, dumb a moment, took it all in. "It *is* as if they knew it —they're more and more alive. But so much the worse for both of us! I can't," she brought out with an effort, "be silent."

"You mean to return them?"

"If I don't I'm a thief."

Mrs. Guy gave her a long, hard look: what was decidedly not of the baby in Mrs. Guy's face was a certain air of established habit in the eyes. Then, with a sharp little jerk of her head and a backward reach of her bare beautiful arms, she undid the clasp and, taking off the necklace, laid it on the table. "If you do, you're a goose."

"Well, of the two—!" said our young lady, gathering it up with a sigh. And as if to get it, for the pang it gave, out of sight as soon as possible, she shut it up, clicking the lock, in the drawer of her own little table; after which, when she turned again, her companion, without it, looked naked and plain. "But what will you say?" it then occurred to her to demand.

"Downstairs—to explain?" Mrs. Guy was, after all, trying at least to keep her temper. "Oh, I'll put on something else and say that clasp is broken. And you won't of course name *me* to him," she added.

"As having undeceived me? No—I'll say that, looking at the thing more carefully, it's my own private idea."

"And does he know how little you really know?"

"As an expert—surely. And he has much, always, the conceit of his own opinion."

"Then he won't believe you—as he so hates to. He'll stick to his judgment and maintain his gift, and we shall have the darlings back!" With which reviving assurance Mrs. Guy kissed for good-night.

She was not, however, to be gratified or justified by any prompt event, for, whether or no paste entered into the composition of the ornament in question, Charlotte shrank from the temerity of despatching it to town by post. Mrs. Guy was thus disappointed of the hope of seeing the business settled—"by return," she had seemed to expect— before the end of the revels. The revels, moreover, rising to a frantic pitch, pressed for all her attention, and it was at last only in the general confusion of leave-taking that she made, parenthetically, a dash at her young friend.

"Come, what will you take for them?"

"The pearls! Ah, you'll have to treat with my cousin."

Mrs. Guy, with quick intensity, lent herself. "Where then does he live?"

"In chambers in the Temple. You can find him."

"But what's the use, if *you* do neither one thing nor the other?"

"Oh, I *shall* do the 'other,'" Charlotte said: "I'm only waiting till I go up. You want them so awfully?" She curiously, solemnly again, sounded her.

"I'm dying for them. There's a special charm in them—I don't know what it is: they tell so their history."

"But what do you know of that?"

"Just what they themselves say. It's all *in* them—and it comes out. They breathe a tenderness—they have the white glow of it. My dear," hissed Mrs. Guy in supreme confidence and as she buttoned her glove —"they're things of love!"

"Oh!" our young woman vaguely exclaimed.

"They're things of passion!"

"Mercy!" she gasped, turning short off. But these words remained, though indeed their help was scarce needed, Charlotte being in private face to face with a new light, as she by this time felt she must call it, on the dear dead, kind, colourless lady whose career had turned so sharp a corner in the middle. The pearls had quite taken their place as a revelation. She might have received them for nothing—admit that; but she couldn't have kept them so long and so unprofitably hidden, couldn't have enjoyed them only in secret, for nothing; and she had mixed them, in her reliquary, with false things, in order to put curiosity and detection off the scent. Over this strange fact poor Charlotte interminably mused: it became more touching, more attaching for her than she could now confide to any ear. How bad, or how happy—in the sophisticated sense of Mrs. Guy and the young man at the Temple— the effaced Miss Bradshaw must have been to have had to be so mute! The little governess at Bleet put on the necklace now in secret sessions; she wore it sometimes under her dress; she came to feel, verily, a haunting passion for it. Yet in her penniless state she would have parted with it for money; she gave herself also to dreams of what in this direction it would do for her. The sophistry of her so often saying to herself that Arthur had after all definitely pronounced her welcome to any gain from his gift that might accrue—this trick remained innocent, as she perfectly knew it for what it was. Then there was always the possibility of his—as she could only picture it—rising to the occasion. Mightn't he have a grand magnanimous moment?—mightn't he just say: "Oh, of course I couldn't have afforded to let you have it if I had known; but since you *have* got it, and have made out the truth by your own wit, I really can't screw myself down to the shabbiness of taking it back"?

She had, as it proved, to wait a long time—to wait till, at the end of several months, the great house of Bleet had, with due deliberation, for the season, transferred itself to town; after which, however, she fairly snatched at her first freedom to knock, dressed in her best and armed with her disclosure, at the door of her doubting kinsman. It was still with doubt and not quite with the face she had hoped that he listened to her story. He had turned pale, she thought, as she produced the necklace, and he appeared, above all, disagreeably affected. Well, perhaps there was reason, she more than ever remembered; but what on earth was one, in close touch with the fact, to do? She had laid the pearls on his table, where, without his having at first put so much as a finger to them, they met his hard, cold stare.

"I don't believe in them," he simply said at last.

"That's exactly then," she returned with some spirit, "what I wanted to hear!"

She fancied that at this his colour changed; it was indeed vivid to her afterwards—for she was to have a long recall of the scene—that she had made him quite angrily flush. "It's a beastly unpleasant imputation, you know!"—and he walked away from her as he had always walked at the vicarage.

"It's none of *my* making, I'm sure," said Charlotte Prime. "If you're afraid to believe they're real—"

"Well?"—and he turned, across the room, sharp round at her.

"Why, it's not my fault."

He said nothing more, for a moment, on this; he only came back to the table. "They're what I originally said they were. They're rotten paste."

"Then I may keep them?"

"No. I want a better opinion."

"Than your own?"

"Than *your* own." He dropped on the pearls another queer stare, then, after a moment, bringing himself to touch them, did exactly what she had herself done in the presence of Mrs. Guy at Bleet—gathered them together, marched off with them to a drawer, put them in, and clicked the key. "You say I'm afraid," he went on as he again met her; "but I shan't be afraid to take them to Bond Street."

"And if the people say they're real—?"

He hesitated—then had his strangest manner. "They won't say it! They shan't!"

There was something in the way he brought it out that deprived poor Charlotte, as she was perfectly aware, of any manner at all. "Oh!" she simply sounded, as she had sounded for her last word to Mrs. Guy; and, within a minute, without more conversation, she had taken her departure.

A fortnight later she received a communication from him, and towards the end of the season one of the entertainments in Eaton Square was graced by the presence of Mrs. Guy. Charlotte was not at dinner, but she came down afterwards, and this guest, on seeing her, abandoned a very beautiful young man on purpose to cross and speak to her. The guest had on a lovely necklace and had apparently not lost her habit of overflowing with the pride of such ornaments.

"Do you see?" She was in high joy.

"They were indeed splendid pearls—so far as poor Charlotte could feel that she knew, after what had come and gone, about such mysteries. Charlotte had a sickly smile. "They're almost as fine as Arthur's."

"Almost? Where, my dear, are your eyes? They *are* 'Arthur's!'" After which, to meet the flood of crimson that accompanied her young friend's start: "I tracked them—after your folly, and, by miraculous luck, recognised them in the Bond Street window to which he had disposed of them."

"*Disposed* of them?" the girl gasped. "He wrote me that I had insulted his mother and that the people had shown him he was right— had pronounced them utter paste."

Mrs. Guy gave a stare. "Ah, I told you he wouldn't bear it! No. But I had, I assure you," she wound up, "to drive my bargain!"

Charlotte scarce heard or saw; she was full of her private wrong. "He wrote me," she panted, "that he had smashed them."

Mrs. Guy could only wonder and pity. "He's really morbid!" But it was not quite clear which of the pair she pitied; though Charlotte felt really morbid too after they had separated and she found herself full of thought. She even went the length of asking herself what sort of a bargain Mrs. Guy had driven and whether the marvel of the recognition in Bond Street had been a veracious account of the matter. Hadn't she perhaps in truth dealt with Arthur directly? It came back to Charlotte almost luridly that she had had his address.

1899

WILLA CATHER

The Way of the World

O! the world was full of the summer time,
  And the year was always June,
When we two played together
  In the days that were done too soon.

O! every hand was an honest hand,
  And every heart was true.
When you were the king of the cornlands
  And I was a queen with you.

When I could believe in the fairies still,
  And our elf in the cottonwood tree,
And the pot of gold at the rainbow's end
  And you could believe in me.

Speckle Burnham sat on Mary Eliza's front porch waiting until she finished her practicing. Apparently he was not in a hurry for her to do so. He shuffled his bare feet uneasily over the splintery boards when the dragging, hopeless thumping within quickened in tempo to a rapid, hurried volley of sounds, telling that Mary Eliza's "hour" was nearly over and that she was prodding the lagging moments with fiery impatience.

Indeed, cares of state were weighing heavily upon Speckle, and he had some excuse for gravity, for Speckle was a prince in his own right and a ruler of men.

In Speckle Burnham's back yard were half-a-dozen store boxes of large dimensions, placed evenly in a row against the side of the barn, and there was Speckle's empire. It had long been a cherished project of the boys on Speckle's street to collect their scattered lemonade stands

Willa Cather was born in 1873 into a well-established Virginia farming family. At the age of nine, however, she and her parents resettled in the harsh and imposing prairies of Nebraska, near the small village of Red Cloud. Even after Cather moved back east, filling various positions as writer, teacher, and editor, her experiences on the Great Plains remained in her mind and her fiction, most notably her hallmark novel *My Ántonia* (1918). Throughout her lengthy and successful career, Cather positioned herself as, in the words of the critic Maxwell Geismar, "a defender of spiritual graces in the midst of an increasingly materialistic culture." Cather died in New York City in 1947.

and sidewalk booths and organize a community; but without Speckle's wonderful executive ability the thing would never have been possible.

In the first place, Speckle had the most disreputable back yard in the community. It would have been quite out of the question to have littered up any other yard on the street with half-a-dozen store boxes and the assorted chattels of their respective occupants. But Speckle's folks had been farming people, and regarded their back yard as the natural repository for such encumbrances as were in the way in the house; and Speckle was among them. Speckle had offered his yard as a possible site for a flourishing town, and the other boys brought their store boxes and called the town Speckleville in honor of the founder.

Now it must not be thought that Speckleville was a transient town, such as boys often found in the morning and destroy in the evening. Speckle's especial point was organization. No boy was allowed to change his business or his place of business without due permission from the assembled council of Speckleville. Jimmy Templeton kept a grocery stocked with cinnamon barks, soda crackers, ginger snaps, and "Texas Mixed"—a species of cheap candy which came in big wooden buckets; these he pilfered from his father's store. Tommy Sanders was proprietor of a hardware store, stocked with bows and arrows, sling-shots, pea shooters, and ammunition for the same. "Shorty" Thompson kept a pool room with a table covered with one of his mother's com-forters. Dick Hutchinson ran the dime museum where he fearlessly handled live bull snakes for the sum of a few pins and exhibited snap-ping turtles, pocket gophers, bullets from Chattanooga, rusty firearms, and a piece of the rope with which a horse thief had been lynched. Reinholt Birkner was the son of the village undertaker and was a youth of a dolorous turn of mind and insisted upon keeping a marble shop, where he made little tombstones and neat caskets for the boys' deceased woodpeckers and prairie dogs, and for such of the museum specimens as sought early and honored graves.

Speckle, by reason of inventive genius and real estate monopoly, held all the important offices in the town. He was mayor and postmaster, and he conducted a bank, wherein he compelled the citizens to deposit their pins, charging them heavily for that privilege and lending out their own funds to them at a ruinous usury, taking mortgages on the stock and business houses of such unfortunates as failed to meet their obliga-tions promptly. His father was a chattel broker in the days when money changed hands quickly in the country beyond the Missouri, and from his tenderest years Speckle had been initiated into the nefarious arts of the business. But although his threats many a time caused poor delin-quents to tremble, I never heard of him actually foreclosing on any one, and I can assert on good authority that when Dick Hutchinson's father failed in business, causing great consternation throughout the village, Speckle went to Dick privately and offered to lend him a few hundred pins gratis to tide him over any present difficulties.

But certainly Speckle had a right to be autocratic, for it was Speckle's fecund fancy more than his back yard that was the real site of that town, and his imagination was the coin current of the realm, and made those store boxes seem temples of trade to more eyes than his own. A really creative imagination was Speckle's—one that could invent occupations for half-a-dozen boys, metamorphize an express wagon into a street-car line, a rubber hose into city water works, devise feast days and circuses and public rejoicings, railway accidents and universal disasters, even invent a Fourth of July in the middle of June and cause the hearts of his fellow townsmen to beat high with patriotism. For Speckle, by a species of innocent hypnotism, colored the mental visions of his fellow townsmen until his fancies seemed weighty realities to them, just as a clever play actor makes you tremble and catch your breath when he draws his harmless rapier. And, like the play actors, Speckle was the willing victim of his own conceit. What matter if he had to peddle milk to the neighbor women at night? What matter even if he were chastised because he had lost the hatchet or forgotten to dig around the trees on his father's lots? Tomorrow he was the founder of a city and a king of men!

So the inhabitants of Speckleville had dwelt together in all peace and concord until Mary Eliza Jenkins had peered at them through the morning-glory vines on her back porch and had envied these six male beings their happiness; for although Mary Eliza was the tomboy of the street, the instincts of her sex were strong in her, and that six male beings should dwell together in ease and happiness seemed to her an unnatural and a monstrous thing. Furthermore, she and Speckle had played together ever since the days when he had been father to all her dolls and had rocked them to sleep, and until the founding of Speckleville he had openly preferred her to any boy on the street, and she bitterly resented his desertion.

Once, in a moment of rashness, the boys invited her over to a circus in Speckle's barn, and after that Speckle knew no peace of his life. Night and day Mary Eliza importuned him for admittance to his town. She hung around his back porch as soon as she was through practicing in the morning; she nudged him and whispered to him as she sat next to him at Sunday school; she waylaid him while he was taking his cow out to pasture and sprang upon him from ambush when he was taking his milk in the evening, even offering to accompany him and carry one of the tin pails. Taking his milk was the prime curse of Speckle's life and he weakly accepted her company, especially to the house of the old woman who kept the big dog. When Speckle went there alone he usually played he was a burglar.

Now Speckle himself had really no objection to granting Mary Eliza naturalization papers and full rights of citizenship, but the other boys would not hear of it.

"She'll try to boss us all just like she bosses you," objected Tommy Sanders.

"Anyhow, she's a girl and this ain't a girl's play. I suppose she'd keep a dressmaking shop and dress our dolls for us," snorted Dick Hutchinson contemptuously.

"Put it any way you like, she'll spoil the town," said Jimmy Templeton.

"You began it all yourself, Temp. You asked her to the circus, you know you did," retorted Speckle.

Poor Speckle! He had never heard of that old mud-walled town in Latium that was also founded by a boy, and where so many good fellows dwelt together in jovial comradeship until they invited some ladies from the Sabine hills to a party, with such disastrous results.

On this particular morning Speckle had come over to, if possible, persuade Mary Eliza to desist from her appeals, and he sat in the sunshine gloomily awaiting the interview. Presently a triumphant "one, two, three, FOUR," and a triumphant bang announced that her hour of penal servitude was over for the day, and she dashed out on the porch.

"Well, have you made them?" she demanded.

Speckle braced himself and came directly to the point.

"I can't make them, Mary 'Liza, and they say you'd get tired and spoil the town."

"O stuff! What makes them say that?"

"Well, it's 'cause you're a girl, I guess," said Speckle reflectively, wrinkling the big yellow freckle on his nose that was accountable for his nickname.

"Girl nothin'! I'd play I was a man, and that's all you do. M. E. Jenkins—that's what I'll have over my store. I've got the signs already made. 'Delmonico Resteraunt, M. E. Jenkins, Prop.' Come, Speckle, you know I can skin a cat as well as you can and I can beat Hutch running, can't I now?"

"Course you can. I'd like to have you in, Mary 'Liza," remonstrated Speckle.

"O well, I don't care so much about getting in your old town anyhow, only my father keeps the bakery and I could have cookies and cream puffs and candy to sell in my store, chocolates and things, none of your old Texas Mixed, and I thought I could be a good deal of use in your town."

"Say, Mary 'Liza, do you mean that? I guess I'd better tell them. I guess I'll tell them tonight," said Speckle, with a new interest.

"O do, Speckle, and do get me in!" cried Mary Eliza, as she hopped gleefully about on one foot. "You know you can if you want to, 'cause it's in your yard. And we can have Strawberry for a ring horse when we have circuses. His tail isn't all rubbed off like your Billy's and he can be a pony in the side show, too."

Speckle did not reply at once. He was wondering whether Mary Eliza could meet the large demands on the imagination requisite to citizenship in Speckleville. He was not wholly certain as to the enduring qualities of feminine imagination, but he did not know exactly how to express his doubts, so he remained silent.

"What are you thinking about now?" demanded Mary Eliza.

"O nothing. I'll see them about it tonight."

"And if they don't let me in I'll know it's all your fault," called Mary Eliza threateningly, as she dashed into the house.

That evening after Speckle had taken his milk he hung the empty pails on the fence and went around to interview each of the boys privately. He suspected that by seeing them separately he could best appeal to their individual weaknesses. He bribed Dick Hutchinson with a dozen of his rarest tin tobacco tags, all with euphuistic names such as "Rose Leaf" and "Lily of the Valley," which his uncle had sent him from Florida. He won Reinholt Birkner with promises of many a solemn funeral cortege for Mary Eliza's deceased pets, and charmed "Shorty" Thompson's ears with stories of the cream puffs from old Jenkins' bakery. Over Jimmy Templeton he had no hold, Jimmy being of that peculiarly odious species of humanity that is thoroughly upright and without secret weakness. So he merely told him of the consent of the other boys and used his personal influence for all it was worth.

"All right, if you fellows say so," Temp replied gravely. He was soaking cattails in the kerosene can preparatory to a torchlight procession of the Speckleville Republican Club. "I won't be the man to kick, but you mark my word, Speckle, she'll spoil the town. Girls always spoil everything a boy's got if you give 'em a chance."

That night after Speckle's mother had anointed his sunburned face with cold cream and he had climbed into bed and was reposing peacefully on his stomach, enjoying the only real comfort he had had that day, he heard a violent "tic-tac" at the window at the head of his bed.

"Hello, Temp, is that you?" he called.

"No, Speckle, it's me. Did you make them?" whispered Mary Eliza.

"Yes, I made them," replied Speckle, rather wearily.

"O, Speckle, you are a dandy! I just love you, Speckle!" and Mary Eliza pounded and scratched joyfully at the screen as she departed.

The next day Speckle vacated his piano box, the largest and most commodious structure in his town, and fitted it up for Mary Eliza with a lavishness which astonished his comrades. In the afternoon Mary Eliza made her triumphant entry into Speckleville with an old-fashioned carpet sack in one hand and a Japanese umbrella in the other.

She was all smiles and sweetmeats and showed neither resentment nor embarrassment at her chilling reception. She set forth her cream puffs and chocolates and in half an hour the Delmonico Restaurant was the center of interest and commercial activity.

I shall not attempt to rehearse all the arts and wiles by which Mary Eliza deposed Speckle and made herself sole imperatrix of Speckleville. She made it her business to appeal to every masculine instinct in the boys, beginning with their stomachs. When first a woman tempted a man she said unto him, "Eat." The cream puffs alone would have assured her victory, but she did not stop there. She possessed cunning of hand and could make wonderful neckties of colored tissue paper, and stiff hats of pasteboard covered with black paper and polished with white of egg, which she disposed of for a number of pins. She became the star of the circus ring, and it was considered a great sight to behold Mary Eliza attired in blue cambric tights with an abundance of blonde locks, made by unraveling a few feet of new heavy rope, flowing about her shoulders, executing feats of marvelous dexterity upon the flying trapeze.

Indeed, Mary Eliza possessed certain talents which peculiarly fitted her to dwell and rule in a boys' town. Otherwise she could never have brought disaster and ruin upon the town of Speckleville. For all boys will admit that there are some girls who would make the best boys in the world—if they were not girls.

It soon befell that Mary Eliza's word, her lightest wish, was law in Speckleville. Half the letters that went through Speckle's post office were for her, and even the phlegmatic Reinholt Birkner made her a beautiful little tombstone with a rose carved on it as an ornament for her center table.

Meanwhile Speckle—poor, deposed Speckle—sat by without demur and without more than an occasional pang of jealousy and watched the success of his protégée, learning, as many another monarch had done before him, how pleasant it sometimes is to serve.

Now, alas! it is time to introduce the tragic motif in this simple chronicle of Speckleville, to bring about the advent of the heavy villain into the comedy. He came in the form of a boy from Chicago, to spend the summer with his aunt just across the street from Speckle's home. From the first he found small favor in the eyes of the Speckleville boys. To begin with, he invariably wore shoes and stockings, a habit disgustingly effeminate to any true and loyal Specklevillian. To this he added the grievance of a stiff hat, and on Sundays even sunk to the infamy of kid gloves. He also smoked many cubeb cigarettes—corn-silks were considered the only manly smoke in Speckleville—and ate some odorous confection to conceal his guilt from his mamma. The good citizens of Speckleville all looked with horror upon these gilded vices—all, save one, perhaps.

The first time the New Boy visited the town he bought a cream puff of Mary Eliza, and on being told that the price of the same was ten pins, he laughed scornfully, saying that he did not carry a pincushion and had not brought his workbox with him. He then threw down a nickel upon the counter. Now to offer money to a citizen of Speckleville was an insult, like offering a bribe, and the boys were painfully surprised when Mary Eliza accepted that shameful coin, bestowing upon the purchaser a smile more desirable than many cream puffs.

After that the New Boy came often, usually confining his trade to the Delmonico Restaurant, where he hung about telling of his trip on Lake Michigan and his outings in Lincoln Park, while the proprietor listened with greedy ears. He persisted in paying for his purchases in coppers and nickels, and Mary Eliza persisted in accepting the despised currency, while the Speckleville boys went about with a secret shame in their hearts, feeling that somehow she had disgraced herself and them. They began to wonder as to just what a girl's notion of the square thing was, a question that has sometimes vexed older heads.

As for Mary Eliza, although she sometimes joined with the boys in a laugh at his expense, she by no means shared the general dislike of the New Boy. She thought his city clothes and superior manners very impressive, and felt more grown up and important when in his company. Even his letters, which were always written on real note paper with a monogram at the top and signed SEMPER IDEM seemed vastly more dignified than the rude scrawls of the other boys.

She had tact enough to know that this fine young gentleman would never wear tissue paper neckties, so she made him a red paper rose, which he wore, daily perfuming it with Florida water. Speckle had noted the growing discontent in his town, and sought to conceal Mary Eliza's disgraceful conduct and shield her from open contempt by asking her to make him a paper rose. But she laughed heartlessly with a wink at the New Boy and said she had no more paper. I doubt if any of the rebuffs his gallantry may have received in after years ever cut Speckle as that wink did.

Matters hastened from bad to worse in the town. The days came and went as days will, but over Mary Eliza's throne there was the shadow of the New Boy. The crisis came at last when in a meeting of the city council Mary Eliza boldly proposed admitting the New Boy to the town. Her motion was greeted by indignant howls and hisses and Speckle blushed to the roots of his red hair.

"Very well," said Mary Eliza, "if you won't have him in then I won't be in either. Him and me'll start another town over in his yard."

"You can just go and do it, then! We won't have that Chicago dude hanging around here any longer!" howled councilman Sanders, knocking over his chair.

To this all the rest echoed a wrathful assent. It was the utterance of an old grievance.

Mary Eliza arose with great dignity and began to pack her wares into her carpetbag. She made no display of ill humor, and talked cheerfully of her new town as she wrapped up her candies in tissue paper; the boys stood by and watched her, they did not believe she would go. But Mary Eliza departed even as she had come, with her carpetbag in her hand and her Japanese parasol tilted gaily over her head, while Speckle held the gate open for her, feeling that his illusions were vanishing fast.

"I'll send over for my box in the morning, Speckle, and you must all come over to our town and buy things, and we'll come over and buy things at yours," she called after him.

The treachery, the infamy of her deception never seemed to have occurred to her. It was as though Coriolanus, when he deserted Rome for the camp of the Volscians, had asked the Conscript Fathers to call on him and bring their families!

"She'll be back tomorrow all right enough," said Speckle.

But on the morrow the New Boy came for the piano box, and by noon Mary Eliza was fairly installed across the street, making paper neckties for the New Boy and canvassing the neighborhood for the New Boy's town. There could be no doubt that she had transferred her allegiance.

The Speckleville boys went resolutely to their stores and bought and sold and made a great show, but they had little heart in it all. They missed the cream puffs and the paper ties, and they missed something else more than these—something they could not name. If Speckle had chanced to confide in his young uncle, who was in the rapturous tortures of his first love affair, he would have been told that it was the "eternal feminine" they missed, and he would have been as much in the dark as before.

Mary Eliza had put herself at the head of everything, and now nothing went on without her. After the manner of her kind, she had come where she was not wanted, made herself indispensable, and gone again, taking with her, oh, so much more than her parasol and chocolate creams!

Everything went wrong in Speckleville that afternoon, and after the day was over the citizens of that passing village were quarreling violently, not, as in former times, because every one wanted to do something in a different way, but because no one wanted to do anything at all.

"It's all your fault, Speckle. We ought never to have [had] her in, and we wouldn't if it hadn't been for you."

"Well, now she's gone." protested Speckle, "so why can't we go on like we did before?"

No one attempted to answer. It was scarcely a wise question to ask.

"I always told you she'd spoil the town, Speckle, and now she's done it," said Jimmy Templeton.

"Well, you fellows seemed mighty glad to get her after she came, anyway, and you needn't put your lip in, Temp; you loafed around her store like a ninny," retorted Speckle, who felt that his persecution was more than he could bear.

Jimmy was not in a mood to endure a jibe at his weakness and by way of an answer he biffed Speckle one on the side of his nose, and it required the united strength of their fellow citizens to part them.

"I'm not going to stay in your old town any longer. I can have more fun in my own yard, and I'm going to take my things home," announced Dick Hutchinson, as he began pocketing the properties of his museum.

"I'll be darned if I do!" cried Jimmy Templeton. "And I'll thank you to give me my pins out of your old tin box, Mr. Speckle."

Speckle had woes enough without a run on his bank, but when Providence helps a man to trouble it is usually generous and dishes out all manner of calamities, regardless of what he may already have on his plate. Speckle sat there until he had paid out the last pin from his spice box. The boys all fell to packing their belongings as though fleeing from a doomed city, and they ceased not from making unkind remarks as they did so. Even Reinholt Birkner gathered up his chisels and monuments, all save one big block of granite that was too heavy for him, and that stood by his store box like a white tombstone. Under Speckle's very eyes his town vanished as many another western town has done since then.

"It's all your fault, Speckle!" bawled Jimmy Templeton, as he vaulted over the back fence, and Speckle, after having said all the swear words he knew, went off to the barn to smoke innumerable corn-silk cigarettes and to wonder at the queer way things are run down here.

After he had taken his milk that night he heard Mary Eliza laughing as she played tag with the New Boy under the electric light, and he sat down with his empty pails in his deserted town, as Caius Marius once sat among the ruins of Carthage.

                                                                    1898

FIVE

Domesticity and Desire

This chapter assembles love stories that explore the bonds between husbands and wives and parents and children. These stories concentrate on transformations in apparently stable relationships, the flux that occurs within the sameness of family bonds, and the continual mystery of the separateness of the other person in the most intimate relationships.

Virginia Woolf's husband and wife create an elaborate fantasy world in which they are transformed into King Lappin and Queen Lapinova. These alter egos allow them access to their essential selves and sharing that revelation with each other confers on their marriage the transcendental status of soul mates. The man and woman in "The Gilded Six-Bits" also place play at the center of their marriage, and their games are the sign of their communion. In both stories, when the ability to share these games with one another becomes strained or lost, so do the husband and wife become lost to each other.

So, too, can everyday intimacy dull people to their own, and to the other's, mysteriously separate being. In James Joyce's "The Dead," Gabriel Conroy suddenly comes upon a wellspring of his wife's history and emotional life—the death of a boy who loved her long ago—that shocks him into recognizing the basic solitude of all beings, which exists despite the closeness of their shared lives.

In Doris Lessing's "To Room Nineteen," Matthew and Susan Rawlings try to control their emotional life so rigidly that they end by prohibiting any emotional range at all; they forbid "quarrelling, sulking, anger, silences of withdrawal, accusations, and tears." They deny themselves "the dramatic words 'unfaithful,' 'forgive.'" But in disowning her emotional life, Susan loses her spiritual heart; she is emptied of "a centre of life and a reason for being." Gradually, she severs her bonds with her husband, her children, and even herself, becoming almost insensible to the wavering line between life and death.

Both Raymond Carver and Tillie Olsen focus on the bonds between mothers and children. In Olsen's "I Stand Here Ironing," we are privy to a mother's interior monologue, in which she reviews her daughter's harsh years growing up. Her love for her daughter is expressed directly, but it's also evident, more subtly, in the wealth of minute detail that spills out like jewels from a fairy-tale casket. The son in Carver's "Boxes" considers the flawed nature of love and the obscure arrangements we make with life to be able to endure it. An aging mother has spent her life rootless, moving from place to place, putting her whole life in boxes and simply moving on. She, her son, and the woman with whom he lives have never achieved a happy domesticity, yet all three of them—in different ways and equipped only with the smallest of gestures—are trying to find the path toward a home life in which they feel "less afraid, more hopeful about the future."

All of these characters share a desire for a domestic life that includes love, that offers both freedom and safety. Some of them only realize that life inchoately; they yearn for something, something they can only measure by their sense of its absence. All of these stories, however, recognize the frailty of our spiritual connection with other beings, and yet acknowledge that our desire to forge that link is as strong as iron.

VIRGINIA WOOLF

Lappin and Lapinova

They were married. The wedding march pealed out. The pigeons fluttered. Small boys in Eton jackets threw rice; a fox terrier sauntered across the path; and Ernest Thorburn led his bride to the car through that small inquisitive crowd of complete strangers which always collects in London to enjoy other people's happiness or unhappiness. Certainly he looked handsome and she looked shy. More rice was thrown, and the car moved off.

That was on Tuesday. Now it was Saturday. Rosalind had still to get used to the fact that she was Mrs. Ernest Thorburn. Perhaps she never would get used to the fact that she was Mrs. Ernest Anybody, she thought, as she sat in the bow window of the hotel looking over the

Virginia Woolf was born in London in 1882 and educated at home in both her father's extensive library (her father, Leslie Stephen, was an esteemed literary critic and editor of the *Cornhill Magazine* and the *Dictionary of National Biography*) and in the company of many of the notable intellectual and cultural figures of the day. She carried on the tradition of such gatherings, hosting with her sister Vanessa the meetings of what would be called the Bloomsbury Group—a coterie of friends, writers, and preeminent thinkers all sharing a dedication to the arts, one of whom, Leonard Woolf, she married in 1912. In *Mrs. Dalloway* (1925), *To the Lighthouse* (1927), and other works, Woolf applied interior monologue and stream of consciousness to psychological experiences of her characters and their reactions even to their most restricted actions. In 1941, suffering from recurring mental illness, Woolf drowned herself outside her Sussex home.

lake to the mountains, and waited for her husband to come down to breakfast. Ernest was a difficult name to get used to. It was not the name she would have chosen. She would have preferred Timothy, Antony, or Peter. He did not look like Ernest either. The name suggested the Albert Memorial, mahogany sideboards, steel engravings of the Prince Consort with his family—her mother-in-law's dining-room in Porchester Terrace in short.

But here he was. Thank goodness he did not look like Ernest—no. But what did he look like? She glanced at him sideways. Well, when he was eating toast he looked like a rabbit. Not that anyone else would have seen a likeness to a creature so diminutive and timid in this spruce, muscular young man with the straight nose, the blue eyes, and the very firm mouth. But that made it all the more amusing. His nose twitched very slightly when he ate. So did her pet rabbit's. She kept watching his nose twitch; and then she had to explain, when he caught her looking at him, why she laughed.

"It's because you're like a rabbit, Ernest," she said. "Like a rabbit," she added, looking at him. "A hunting rabbit; a King Rabbit; a rabbit that makes laws for all the other rabbits."

Ernest had no objection to being that kind of rabbit, and since it amused her to see him twitch his nose—he had never known that his nose twitched—he twitched it on purpose. And she laughed and laughed; and he laughed too, so that the maiden ladies and fishing man and the Swiss waiter in his greasy black jacket all guessed right; they were very happy. But how long does such happiness last? they asked themselves; and each answered according to his own circumstances.

At lunch time, seated on a clump of heather beside the lake; "Lettuce, rabbit?" said Rosalind, holding out the lettuce that had been provided to eat with the hard-boiled eggs. "Come and take it out of my hand," she added, and he stretched out and nibbled the lettuce and twitched his nose.

"Good rabbit, nice rabbit," she said, patting him, as she used to pat her tame rabbit at home. But that was absurd. He was not a tame rabbit, whatever he was. She turned it into French. "Lapin," she called him. But whatever he was, he was not a French rabbit. He was simply and solely English—born at Porchester Terrace, educated at Rugby; now a clerk in His Majesty's Civil Service. So she tried "Bunny" next; but that was worse. "Bunny" was someone plump and soft and comic; he was thin and hard and serious. Still, his nose twitched. "Lappin," she exclaimed suddenly; and gave a little cry as if she had found the very word she looked for.

"Lappin, Lappin, King Lappin," she repeated. It seemed to suit him exactly; he was not Ernest, he was King Lappin. Why? She did not know.

When there was nothing new to talk about on their long solitary walks—and it rained, as everyone had warned them that it would rain; or when they were sitting over the fire in the evening, for it was cold, and the maiden ladies had gone and the fishing man, and the waiter only came if you rang the bell for him, she let her fancy play with the story of the Lappin tribe. Under her hands—she was sewing; he was reading—they became very real, very vivid, very amusing. Ernest put down the paper and helped her. There were the black rabbits and the red; there were the enemy rabbits and the friendly. There were the wood in which they lived and the outlying prairies and the swamp. Above all there was King Lappin, who, far from having only the one trick—that he twitched his nose—became as the days passed an animal of the greatest character; Rosalind was always finding new qualities in him. But above all he was a great hunter.

"And what," said Rosalind, on the last day of the honeymoon, "did the King do to-day?"

In fact they had been climbing all day; and she had worn a blister on her heel; but she did not mean that.

"To-day," said Ernest, twitching his nose as he bit the end off his cigar, "he chased a hare." He paused; struck a match, and twitched again.

"A woman hare," he added.

"A white hare!" Rosalind exclaimed, as if she had been expecting this. "Rather a small hare; silver grey; with big bright eyes?"

"Yes," said Ernest, looking at her as she had looked at him, "a smallish animal; with eyes popping out of her head, and two little front paws dangling." It was exactly how she sat, with her sewing dangling in her hands; and her eyes, that were so big and bright, were certainly a little prominent.

"Ah, Lapinova," Rosalind murmured.

"Is that what she's called?" said Ernest—"the real Rosalind?" He looked at her. He felt very much in love with her.

"Yes; that's what she's called," said Rosalind. "Lapinova." And before they went to bed that night it was all settled. He was King Lappin; she was Queen Lapinova. They were the opposite of each other; he was bold and determined; she wary and undependable. He ruled over the busy world of rabbits; her world was a desolate, mysterious place, which she ranged mostly by moonlight. All the same, their territories touched; they were King and Queen.

Thus when they came back from their honeymoon they possessed a private world, inhabited, save for the one white hare, entirely by rabbits. No one guessed that there was such a place, and that of course made it all the more amusing. It made them feel, more even than most young married couples, in league together against the rest of the world. Often they looked slyly at each other when people talked about rabbits and woods and traps and shooting. Or they winked furtively across the table when Aunt Mary said that she could never bear to see a hare in a dish—it looked so like a baby: or when John, Ernest's sporting brother, told them what price rabbits were fetching that autumn in Wiltshire, skins and all. Sometimes when they wanted a gamekeeper, or a poacher or a Lord of the Manor, they amused themselves by distributing the parts among their friends. Ernest's mother, Mrs. Reginald Thorburn, for example, fitted the part of the Squire to perfection. But it was all secret—that was the point of it; nobody save themselves knew that such a world existed.

Without that world, how, Rosalind wondered, that winter could she have lived at all? For instance, there was the golden-wedding party, when all the Thorburns assembled at Porchester Terrace to celebrate the fiftieth anniversary of that union which had been so blessed—had it not produced Ernest Thorburn? and so fruitful—had it not produced nine other sons and daughters into the bargain, many themselves married and also fruitful? She dreaded that party. But it was inevitable. As she walked upstairs she felt bitterly that she was an only child and an orphan at that; a mere drop among all those Thorburns assembled in the great drawing-room with the shiny satin wallpaper and the lustrous family portraits. The living Thorburns much resembled the painted; save that instead of painted lips they had real lips; out of which came jokes; jokes about schoolrooms, and how they had pulled the chair from under the governess; jokes about frogs and how they had put them between the virgin sheets of maiden ladies. As for herself, she had never even made an apple-pie bed. Holding her present in her hand she advanced toward her mother-in-law sumptuous in yellow satin; and toward her father-in-law decorated with a rich yellow carnation. All round them on tables and chairs there were golden tributes, some nestling in cotton wool; others branching resplendent—candlesticks; cigar boxes; chains; each stamped with the goldsmith's proof that it was solid gold, hallmarked, authentic. But her present was only a little pinchbeck box pierced with holes; an old sand caster, an eighteenth-century relic, once used to sprinkle sand over wet ink. Rather a senseless present she felt —in an age of blotting paper; and as she proffered it, she saw in front of her the stubby black handwriting in which her mother-in-law when they were engaged had expressed the hope that "My son will make you happy." No, she was not happy. Not at all happy. She looked at Ernest, straight as a ramrod with a nose like all the noses in the family portraits; a nose that never twitched at all.

Then they went down to dinner. She was half hidden by the great chrysanthemums that curled their red and gold petals into large tight balls. Everything was gold. A gold-edged card with gold initials intertwined recited the list of all the dishes that would be set one after another before them. She dipped her spoon in a plate of clear golden fluid. The raw white fog outside had been turned by the lamps into a golden mesh that blurred the edges of the plates and gave the pineapples a rough golden skin. Only she herself in her white wedding dress peering ahead of her with her prominent eyes seemed insoluble as an icicle.

As the dinner wore on, however, the room grew steamy with heat. Beads of perspiration stood out on the men's foreheads. She felt that her icicle was being turned to water. She was being melted; dispersed; dissolved into nothingness; and would soon faint. Then through the surge in her head and the din in her eyes she heard a woman's voice exclaim, "But they breed so!"

The Thorburns—yes; they breed so, she echoed; looking at all the round red faces that seemed doubled in the giddiness that overcame her; and magnified in the gold mist that enhaloed them. "They breed so." Then John bawled:

"Little devils! . . . Shoot'em! Jump on'em with big boots! That's the only way to deal with 'em . . . rabbits!"

At that word, that magic word, she revived. Peeping between the chrysanthemums she saw Ernest's nose twitch. It rippled, it ran with successive twitches. And at that a mysterious catastrophe befell the Thorburns. The golden table became a moor with the gorse in full bloom; the din of voices turned to one peal of lark's laughter ringing down from the sky. It was a blue sky—clouds passed slowly. And they had all been changed—the Thorburns. She looked at her father-in-law, a furtive little man with dyed moustaches. His foible was collecting things—seals, enamel boxes, trifles from eighteenth-century dressing tables which he hid in the drawers of his study from his wife. Now she saw him as he was—a poacher, stealing off with his coat bulging with pheasants and partridges to drop them stealthily into a three-legged pot in his smoky little cottage. That was her real father-in-law—a poacher. And Celia, the unmarried daughter, who always nosed out other people's secrets, the little things they wished to hide—she was a white ferret with pink eyes, and a nose clotted with earth from her horrid underground nosings and pokings. Slung round men's shoulders, in a net, and thrust down a hole—it was a pitiable life—Celia's; it was none

of her fault. So she saw Celia. And then she looked at her mother-in-law
—whom they dubbed The Squire. Flushed, coarse, a bully—she was
all that, as she stood returning thanks, but now that Rosalind—that is
Lapinova—saw her, she saw behind her the decayed family mansion,
the plaster peeling off the walls, and heard her, with a sob in her voice,
giving thanks to her children (who hated her) for a world that had
ceased to exist. There was a sudden silence. They all stood with their
glasses raised; they all drank; then it was over.

"Oh, King Lappin!" she cried as they went home together in the
fog, "if your nose hadn't twitched just at that moment, I should have
been trapped!"

"But you're safe," said King Lappin, pressing her paw.

"Quite safe," she answered.

And they drove back through the Park, King and Queen of the
marsh, of the mist, and of the gorse-scented moor.

Thus time passed; one year; two years of time. And on a winter's
night, which happened by a coincidence to be the anniversary of the
golden-wedding party—but Mrs. Reginald Thorburn was dead; the
house was to let; and there was only a caretaker in residence—Ernest
came home from the office. They had a nice little home; half a house
above a saddler's shop in South Kensington, not far from the tube
station. It was cold, with fog in the air, and Rosalind was sitting over
the fire, sewing.

"What d'you think happened to me to-day?" she began as soon as
he had settled himself down with his legs stretched to the blaze. "I was
crossing the stream when—"

"What stream?" Ernest interrupted her.

"The stream at the bottom, where our wood meets the black wood,"
she explained.

Ernest looked completely blank for a moment.

"What the deuce are you talking about?" he asked.

"My dear Ernest!" she cried in dismay, "King Lappin," she added,
dangling her little front paws in the firelight. But his nose did not twitch.
Her hands—they turned to hands—clutched the stuff she was holding;
her eyes popped half out of her head. It took him five minutes at least
to change from Ernest Thorburn to King Lappin; and while she waited
she felt a load on the back of her neck, as if somebody were about to
wring it. At last he changed to King Lappin; his nose twitched; and they
spent the evening roaming the woods much as usual.

But she slept badly. In the middle of the night she woke, feeling as
if something strange had happened to her. She was stiff and cold. At
last she turned on the light and looked at Ernest lying beside her. He

was sound asleep. He snored. But even though he snored, his nose remained perfectly still. It looked as if it had never twitched at all. Was it possible that he was really Ernest; and that she was really married to Ernest? A vision of her mother-in-law's dining-room came before her; and there they sat, she and Ernest, grown old, under the engravings, in front of the sideboard. . . . It was their golden-wedding day. She could not bear it.

"Lappin, King Lappin!" she whispered, and for a moment his nose seemed to twitch of its own accord. But he still slept. "Wake up, Lappin, wake up!" she cried.

Ernest woke; and seeing her sitting bolt upright beside him he asked:

"What's the matter?"

"I thought my rabbit was dead!" she whimpered. Ernest was angry.

"Don't talk such rubbish, Rosalind," he said. "Lie down and go to sleep."

He turned over. In another moment he was sound asleep and snoring.

But she could not sleep. She lay curled up on her side of the bed, like a hare in its form. She had turned out the light, but the street lamp lit the ceiling faintly, and the trees outside made a lacy network over it as if there were a shadowy grove on the ceiling in which she wandered, turning, twisting, in and out, round and round, hunting, being hunted, hearing the bay of hounds and horns; flying, escaping . . . until the maid drew the blinds and brought their early tea.

Next day she could settle to nothing. She seemed to have lost something. She felt as if her body had shrunk; it had grown small, and black and hard. Her joints seemed stiff too, and when she looked in the glass, which she did several times as she wandered about the flat, her eyes seemed to burst out of her head, like currants in a bun. The rooms also seemed to have shrunk. Large pieces of furniture jutted out at odd angles and she found herself knocking against them. At last she put on her hat and went out. She walked along the Cromwell Road; and every room she passed and peered into seemed to be a dining-room where people sat eating under steel engravings, with thick yellow lace curtains, and mahogany sideboards. At last she reached the Natural History Museum; she used to like it when she was a child. But the first thing she saw when she went in was a stuffed hare standing on sham snow with pink glass eyes. Somehow it made her shiver all over. Perhaps it would be better when dusk fell. She went home and sat over the fire, without a light, and tried to imagine that she was out alone on a moor; and there was a stream rushing; and beyond the stream a dark wood.

But she could get no further than the stream. At last she squatted down on the bank on the wet grass, and sat crouched in her chair, with her hands dangling empty, and her eyes glazed, like glass eyes, in the firelight. Then there was the crack of a gun. . . . She started as if she had been shot. It was only Ernest, turning his key in the door. She waited, trembling. He came in and switched on the light. There he stood, tall, handsome, rubbing his hands that were red with cold.

"Sitting in the dark?" he said.

"Oh, Ernest, Ernest!" she cried, starting up in her chair.

"Well, what's up now?" he asked briskly, warming his hands at the fire.

"It's Lapinova . . ." she faltered, glancing wildly at him out of her great started eyes. "She's gone, Ernest. I've lost her!"

Ernest frowned. He pressed his lips tight together.

"Oh, that's what's up, is it?" he said, smiling rather grimly at his wife. For ten seconds he stood there, silent; and she waited, feeling hands tightening at the back of her neck.

"Yes," he said at length. "Poor Lapinova . . ." He straightened his tie at the looking-glass over the mantelpiece.

"Caught in a trap," he said, "killed," and sat down and read the newspaper.

So that was the end of that marriage.

1938

ZORA NEALE HURSTON

The Gilded Six-Bits

It was a Negro yard around a Negro house in a Negro settlement that looked to the payroll of the G and G Fertilizer works for its support.

But there was something happy about the place. The front yard was parted in the middle by a sidewalk from gate to doorstep, a sidewalk edged on either side by quart bottles driven neck down to the ground on a slant. A mess of homey flowers planted without a plan but blooming cheerily from their helter-skelter places. The fence and house were whitewashed. The porch and steps scrubbed white.

The front door stood open to the sunshine so that the floor of the front room could finish drying after its weekly scouring. It was Saturday. Everything clean from the front gate to the privy house. Yard raked so that the strokes of the rake would make a pattern. Fresh newspaper cut in fancy-edge on the kitchen shelves.

Missie May was bathing herself in the galvanized washtub in the bedroom. Her dark-brown skin glistened under the soapsuds that skittered down from her wash rag. Her stiff young breasts thrust forward aggressively like broad-based cones with the tips lacquered in black.

She heard men's voices in the distance and glanced at the dollar clock on the dresser.

"Humph! Ah'm way behind time t'day! Joe gointer be heah 'fore Ah git mah clothes on if Ah don't make haste."

She grabbed the clean meal sack at hand and dried herself hurriedly and began to dress. But before she could tie her slippers, there came the ring of singing metal on wood. Nine times.

Missie May grinned with delight. She had not seen the big tall man come stealing in the gate and creep up the walk grinning happily at the joyful mischief he was about to commit. But she knew that it was her

Zora Neale Hurston was born in the town of Eatonville, Florida, in 1903. Her writing career, however, blossomed in New York City, where she arrived during the height of the Harlem Renaissance. She proceeded to study anthropology at Columbia University under Franz Boas. These experiences led to a variety of work, both in her analyses of Haitian voodoo and American folklore and such fictional explorations and celebrations of southern black heritage as *Their Eyes Were Watching God* (1937). In the later years of her life, Hurston returned to Florida, where she died, unknown and penniless, in 1960.

husband throwing silver dollars in the door for her to pick up and pile beside her plate at dinner. It was this way every Saturday afternoon. The nine dollars hurled into the open door, he scurried to a hiding place behind the cape jasmine bush and waited.

Missie May promptly appeared at the door in mock alarm.

"Who dat chunkin' money in mah do'way?" she demanded. No answer from the yard. She leaped off the porch and began to search the shrubbery. She peeped under the porch and hung over the gate to look up and down the road. While she did this, the man behind the jasmine darted to the chinaberry tree. She spied him and gave chase.

"Nobody ain't gointer be chunkin' money at me and Ah not do'em nothin'," she shouted in mock anger. He ran around the house with Missie May at his heels. She overtook him at the kitchen door. He ran inside but could not close it after him before she crowded in and locked with him in a rough and tumble. For several minutes the two were a furious mass of male and female energy. Shouting, laughing, twisting, turning, and Joe trying, but not too hard, to get away.

"Missie May, take yo' hand out mah pocket!" Joe shouted out between laughs.

"Ah ain't, Joe, not lessen you gwine gimme whateve' it is good you got in yo' pocket. Turn it go Joe, do Ah'll tear yo' clothes."

"Go on tear 'em. You de one dat pushes de needles round heah. Move yo' hand Missie May."

"Lemme git dat paper sack out yo' pocket. Ah bet its candy kisses."

"Tain't. Move yo' hand. Woman ain't got no business in a man's clothes nohow. Go 'way."

Missie May gouged way down and gave an upward jerk and triumphed.

"Unhhunh! Ah got it. It 'tis so candy kisses. Ah knowed you had somethin' for me in yo' clothes. Now Ah got to see whut's in every pocket you got."

Joe smiled indulgently and let his wife go through all of his pockets and take out the things that he had hidden there for her to find. She bore off the chewing gum, the cake of sweet soap, the pocket handkerchief as if she had wrested them from him, as if they had not been bought for the sake of this friendly battle.

"Whew! dat play-fight done got me all warmed up," Joe exclaimed. "Got me some water in de kittle?"

"Yo' water is on de fire and yo' clean things is cross de bed. Hurry up and wash yo'self and git changed so we kin eat. Ah'm hongry." As Missie said this, she bore the steaming kettle into the bedroom.

"You ain't hongry, sugar," Joe contradicted her. "Youse jes's little empty. Ah'm de one whut's hongry. Ah could eat up camp meetin', back off 'ssociation, and drink Jurdan dry. Have it on de table when Ah git out de tub."

"Don't you mess wid mah business, man. You git in yo' clothes. Ah'm a real wife, not no dress and breath. Ah might not look lak one, but if you burn me, you won't git a thing but wife ashes."

Joe splashed in the bedroom and Missie May fanned around in the kitchen. A fresh red and white checked cloth on the table. Big pitcher of buttermilk beaded with pale drops of butter from the churn. Hot fried mullet, crackling bread, ham hocks atop a mound of string beans and new potatoes, and perched on the window-sill a pone of spicy potato pudding.

Very little talk during the meal but that little consisted of banter that pretended to deny affection but in reality flaunted it. Like when Missie May reached for a second helping of the tater pone. Joe snatched it out of her reach. After Missie May had made two of three unsuccessful grabs at the pan, she begged, "Aw, Joe gimme some mo' dat tater pone."

"Nope, sweetenin' is for us men-folks. Y'all pritty li'l frail eels don't need nothin' lak dis. You too sweet already."

"Please, Joe."

"Naw, naw. Ah don't want you to git no sweeter than whut you is already. We goin' down de road al li'l piece t'night so you go put on yo' Sunday-go-to-meetin' things."

Missie May looked at her husband to see if he was playing some prank. "Sho 'nuff, Joe?"

"Yeah. We goin' to de ice cream parlor."

"Where de ice cream parlor at, Joe?"

"A new man done come heah from Chicago and he done got a place and took and opened it up for a ice cream parlor, and bein' as it's real swell, Ah wants you to be one de first ladies to walk in dere and have some set down."

"Do Jesus, Ah ain't knowed nothin' 'bout it. Who de man done it?"

"Mister Otis D. Slemmons, of spots and places—Memphis, Chicago, Jacksonville, Philadelphia and so on."

"Dat heavy-set man wid his mouth full of gold teethes?"

"Yeah. Where did you see 'im at?"

"Ah went down to de sto' tuh git a box of lye and Ah seen 'im standin' on de corner talkin' to some of de mens, and Ah come on back and went to scrubbin' de floor, and he passed and tipped his hat whilst Ah was scourin' de steps. Ah thought never Ah seen *him* befo'."

Joe smiled pleasantly. "Yeah, he's up to date. He got de finest clothes Ah ever seen on a colored man's back."

"Aw, he don't look no better in his clothes than you do in yourn. He got a puzzlegut on 'im and he so chuckle-headed, he got a pone behind his neck."

Joe looked down at his own abdomen and said wistfully, "Wisht Ah had a build on me lak he got. He ain't puzzlegutted, honey. He jes' got a corperation. Dat make 'm look lak a rich white man. All rich mens is got some belly on 'em."

"Ah seen de pitchers of Henry Ford and he's a spare-built man and Rockefeller look lak he ain't got but one gut. But Ford and Rockefeller and dis Slemmons and all de rest kin be as many-gutted as dey please, ah'm satisfied wid you jes' lak you is, baby. God took pattern after a pine tree and built you noble. Youse a pritty still man, and if Ah knowed any way to make you mo' pritty still Ah'd take and do it."

Joe reached over gently and toyed with Missie May's ear. "You jes' say dat cause you love me, but Ah know Ah can't hold no light to Otis D. Slemmons. Ah ain't never been nowhere and Ah ain't got nothin' but you."

"How you know dat, Joe."

"He tole us hisself."

"Dat don't make it so. His mouf is cut cross-ways, ain't it? Well, he kin lie jes' lak anybody els."

"Good Lawd, Missie! You womens sho' is hard to sense into things. He's got a five-dollar gold piece for a stick-pin and he got a ten-dollar gold piece on his watch chain and his mouf is jes' crammed full of gold teethes. Sho' wisht it wuz mine. And whut make it so cool, he got money 'cumulated. And womens give it all to 'im."

"Ah don't see whut de womens see on 'im. Ah wouldn't give 'im a wind if de sherff wuz after 'im."

"Well, he tole us how de white womens in Chicago give 'im all dat gold money. So he don't 'low nobody to touch it at all. Not even put dey finger on it. Dey tole 'im not to. You kin make 'miration at it, but don't tetch it."

"Whyn't he stay up dere where dey so crazy 'bout im?"

"Ah reckon dey done made 'im vast-rich and he wants to travel some. He say dey wouldn't leave 'im hit a lick of work. He got mo' lady people crazy 'bout him than he kin shake a stick at."

"Joe, Ah hates to see you so dumb. Dat stray nigger jes' tell y'all anything and y'all b'lieve it."

"Go 'head on now, honey and put on yo' clothes. He talkin' 'bout his pritty womens—Ah want 'im to see *mine*."

Missie May went off to dress and Joe spent the time trying to make his stomach punch out like Slemmons' middle. He tried the rolling swagger of the stranger, but found that his tall bone-and-muscle stride fitted ill with it. He just had time to drop back into his seat before Missie May came in dressed to go.

On the way home that night Joe was exultant. "Didn't Ah say ole Otis was swell? Can't he talk Chicago talk? Wuzn't dat funny whut he said when great big fat ole Ida Armstrong come in? He asted me, "'Who is dat broad wid de forty shake?' Dat's a new word. Us always thought forty was a set of figgers but he showed us where it means a whole heap of things. Sometimes he don't say forty, he jes' say thirty-eight and two and dat mean de same thing. Know whut he tole me when Ah was payin' for our ice cream? He say, 'Ah have to hand it to you, Joe. Dat wife of yours is jes' thirty-eight and two. Yessuh, she's forty!' Ain't he killin'?"

"He'll do in case of a rush. But he sho' is got uh heap uh gold on 'im. Dat's de first time Ah ever seed gold money. It lookted good on him sho' nuff, but it'd look a whole heap better on you."

"Who, me? Missie May was youse crazy! Where would a po' man lak me git gold money from?"

Missie May was silent for a minute, then she said, "Us might find some goin' long de road some time. Us could."

"Who would be losin' gold money 'round heah? We ain't even seen none dese white folks wearin' no gold money on dey watch chain. You must be figgeren' Mister Packard or Mister Cadillac goin' pass through heah . . ."

"You don't know whut been lost 'round heah. Maybe somebody way back in memorial times lost they gold money and went on off and it ain't never been found. And then if we wuz to find it, you could wear some 'thout havin' no gang of womens lak dat Slemmons say he got."

Joe laughed and hugged her. "Don't be so wishful 'bout me. Ah'm satisfied de way Ah is. So long as Ah be yo' husband, ah don't keer 'bout nothin' else. Ah'd ruther all de other womens in de world to be dead than for you to have de toothache. Less we go to bed and git our night rest."

It was Saturday night once more before Joe could parade his wife in Slemmons' ice cream parlor again. He worked the night shift and Saturday was his only night off. Every other evening around six o'clock he left home, and dying dawn saw him hustling home around the lake where the challenging sun flung a flaming sword from east to west across the trembling water.

That was the best part of life—going home to Missie May. Their whitewashed house, the mock battle on Saturday, the dinner and ice cream parlor afterwards, church on Sunday nights when Missie out-dressed any woman in town—all, everything was right.

One night around eleven the acid ran out at the G and G. The foreman knocked off the crew and let the steam die down. As Joe rounded the lake on his way home, a lean moon rode the lake in a silver boat. If anybody had asked Joe about the moon on the lake, he would have said he hadn't paid it any attention. But he saw it with his feelings. It made him yearn painfully for Missie. Creation obsessed him. He thought about children. They had been married for more than a year now. They had money put away. They ought to be making little feet for shoes. A little boy child would be about right.

He saw a dim light in the bedroom and decided to come in through the kitchen door. He could wash the fertilizer dust off himself before presenting himself to Missie May. It would be nice for her not to know that he was there until he slipped into his place in bed and hugged her back. She always liked that.

He eased the kitchen door open slowly and silently, but when he went to set his dinner bucket on the table he bumped it into a pile of dishes, and something crashed to the floor. He heared his wife gasp in fright and hurried to reassure her.

"Iss me, honey. Don't get skeered."

There was a quick, large movement in the bedroom. A rustle, a thud, and a stealthy silence. The light went out.

What? Robbers? Murderers? Some varmint attacking his helpless wife, perhaps. He struck a match, threw himself on guard and stepped over the door-sill into the bedroom.

The great belt on the wheel of Time slipped and eternity stood still. By the match light he could see the man's legs fighting with his breeches in his frantic desire to get them on. He had both chance and time to kill the intruder in his helpless condition—half-in and half-out of his pants —but he was too weak to take action. The shapeless enemies of hu-manity that live in the hours of Time had waylaid Joe. He was assaulted in his weakness. Like Samson awakening after his haircut. So he just opened his mouth and laughed.

The match went out and he struck another and lit the lamp. A howling wind raced across his heart, but underneath its fury he heard his wife sobbing and Slemmons pleading for his life. Offering to buy it with all that he had. "Please, suh, don't kill me. Sixty-two dollars at de sto' gold money."

Joe just stood. Slemmons looked at the window, but it was

screened. Joe stood out like a rough-backed mountain between him and the door. Barring him from escape, from sunrise, from life.

He considered a surprise attack upon the big clown that stood there laughing like a chessy cat. But before his fist could travel an inch, Joe's own rushed out to crush him like a battering ram. Then Joe stood over him.

"Git into yo' damn rags, Slemmons, and dat quick."

Slemmons scrambled to his feet and into his vest and coat. As he grabbed his hat, Joe's fury overrode his intentions and he grabbed at Slemmons with his left hand and struck at him with his right. The right landed. The left grazed the front of his vest. Slemmons was knocked a somersault into the kitchen and fled through the open door. Joe found himself alone with Missie May, with the golden watch charm clutched in his left fist. A short bit of broken chain dangled between his fingers.

Missie May was sobbing. Wails of weeping without words. Joe stood, and after awhile she found out that he had something in his hand. And then he stood and felt without thinking and without seeing with his natural eyes. Missie May kept on crying and Joe kept on feeling so much and not knowing what to do with all his feelings, he put Slemmons' watch charm in his pants pocket and took a good laugh and went to bed.

"Missie May, whut you crying for?"

"Cause Ah love you so hard and Ah know you don't love *me* no mo'."

Joe sank his face into the pillow for a spell then he said huskily, "You don't know de feelings of dat yet, Missie May."

"Oh Joe, honey, he said he wuz gointer gimme dat gold money and he jes' kept on after me—"

Joe was very still and silent for a long time. Then he said, "Well, don't cry no mo', Missie May. Ah got yo' gold piece for you."

The hours went past on their rusty ankles. Joe still and quiet on one bed-rail and Missie May wrung dry of sobs on the other. Finally the sun's tide crept upon the shore of night and drowned all its hours. Missie May with her face stiff and streaked towards the window saw the dawn come into her yard. It was day. Nothing more. Joe wouldn't be coming home as usual. No need to fling open the front door and sweep off the porch, making it nice for Joe. Never no more breakfast to cook; no more washing and starching of Joe's jumper-jackets and pants. No more nothing. So why get up?

With this strange man in her bed, she felt embarrassed to get up and dress. She decided to wait till he had dressed and gone. Then she would get up, dress quickly and be gone forever beyond reach of Joe's looks and laughs. But he never moved. Red light turned to yellow, then white.

From beyond the no-man's land between them came a voice. A strange voice that yesterday had been Joe's.

"Missie May, ain't you gonna fix me no breakfus'?"

She sprang out of bed. "Yeah, Joe. Ah didn't reckon you wuz hongry."

No need to die today. Joe needed her for a few more minutes anyhow.

Soon there was a roaring fire in the cook stove. Water bucket full and two chickens killed. Joe loved fried chicken and rice. She didn't deserve a thing and good Joe was letting her cook him some breakfast. She rushed hot biscuits to the table as Joe took his seat.

He ate with his eyes on his plate. No laughter, no banter.

"Missie May, you ain't eatin' yo' breakfus'."

"Ah don't choose none, Ah thank yuh."

His coffee cup was empty. She sprang to refill it. When she turned from the stove and bent to set the cup beside Joe's plate, she saw the yellow coin on the table between them.

She slumped into her seat and wept into her arms.

Presently Joe said calmly, "Missie May, you cry too much. Don't look back lak Lot's wife and turn to salt."

The sun, the hero of every day, the impersonal old man that beams as brightly on death as on birth, came up every morning and raced across the blue dome and dipped into the sea of fire every evening. Water ran down hill and birds nested.

Missie knew why she didn't leave Joe. She couldn't. She loved him too much. But she couldn't understand why Joe didn't leave her. He was polite, even kind at times, but aloof.

There were no more Saturday romps. No ringing silver dollars to stack beside her plate. No pockets to rifle. In fact the yellow coin in his trousers was like a monster hiding in the cave of his pockets to destroy her.

She often wondered if he still had it, but nothing could have induced her to ask nor yet to explore his pockets to see for herself. Its shadow was in the house whether or no.

One night Joe came home around midnight and complained of pains in the back. He asked Missie to rub him down with liniment. It had been three months since Missie had touched his body and it all seemed strange. But she rubbed him. Grateful for the chance. Before morning, youth triumphed and Missie exulted. But the next day, as she joyfully made up their bed, beneath her pillow she found the piece of money with the bit of chain attached.

Alone to herself, she looked at the thing with loathing, but look she must. She took it into the hands with trembling and saw first thing that it was no gold piece. It was a gilded half-dollar. Then she knew why Slemmons had forbidden anyone to touch his gold. He trusted village eyes at a distance not to recognize his stick-pin as a gilded quarter, and his watch charm as a four-bit piece.

She was glad at first that Joe had left it there. Perhaps he was through with her punishment. They were man and wife again. Then another thought came clawing at her. He had come home to buy from her as if she were any woman in the long house. Fifty cents for her love. As if to say that he could pay as well as Slemmons. She slid the coin into his Sunday pants pocket and dressed herself and left his house.

Halfway between her house and the quarters she met her husband's mother, and after a short talk she turned and went back home. If she had not the substance of marriage, she had the outside show. Joe must leave *her*. She let him see she didn't want his old gold four-bits too.

She saw no more of the coin for some time though she knew that Joe could not help finding it in his pocket. But his health kept poor, and he came home at least every ten days to be rubbed.

The sun swept around the horizon, trailing its robes of weeks and days. One morning as Joe came in from work, he found Missie May chopping wood. Without a word he took the ax and chopped a huge pile before he stopped.

"You ain't got no business choppin' wood, and you know it."

"How come? Ah been choppin' it for de last longest."

"Ah ain't blind. You makin' feet for shoes."

"Won't you be glad to have a li'l baby chile, Joe?"

"You know dat 'thout astin' me."

"Iss gointer be a boy chile and de very spit of you."

"You reckon, Missie May?"

"Who else could it look lak?"

Joe said nothing, but he thrust his hand deep into his pocket and fingered something there.

· It was almost six months later Missie May took to bed and Joe went and got his mother to come wait on the house.

Missie May delivered a fine boy. Her travail was over when Joe came in from work one morning. His mother and the old women were drinking great bowls of coffee around the fire in the kitchen.

The minute Joe came into the room his mother called him aside.

"How did Missie May make out?" he asked quickly.

"Who, dat gal? She strong as a ox. She gointer have plenty mo'. We done fixed her wid de sugar and lard to sweeten her for de nex' one."

Joe stood silent awhile.

"You ain't ast 'bout de baby, Joe. You oughter be mighty proud cause he sho' is de spittin' image of yuh, son. Dat's yourn all right, if you never git another on, dat un is yourn. And you know Ah'm mighty proud too, son, cause Ah never thought well of you marryin' Missie May cause her make used tuh fan her foot 'round right smart and Ah been mighty skeered dat Missie May wuz gointer git misput on her road."

Joe said nothing. He fooled around the house till late in the day then just before he went to work, he went and stood at the foot of the bed and asked his wife how she felt. He did this every day during the week.

On Saturday he went to Orlando to make his market. It had been a long time since he had done that.

Meat and lard, meal and flour, soap and starch. Cans of corn and tomatoes. All the staples. He fooled around town for a while and bought bananas and apples. Way after while he went around to the candy store.

"Hellow, Joe," the clerk greeted him. "Ain't seen you in a long time."

"Nope, Ah ain't been heah. Been 'round spots and places."

"Want some of them molasses kisses you always buy?"

"Yessuh." He threw the gilded half-dollar on the counter. "Will dat spend?"

"Whut is it, Joe? Well, I'll be doggone! A gold-plated four-bit piece. Where'd you git it, Joe?"

"Offen a stray nigger dat come through Eatonville. He had it on his watch chain for a charm—goin' 'round making out iss gold money. Ha ha! He had a quarter on his tie pin and it wuz all golded up too. Tryin' to fool people. Makin' out he is rich and everything. Ha! Ha! Tryin' to tole off folkses wives from home."

"How did you git it, Joe? Did he fool you, too?"

"Who, me? Naw suh! He ain't fooled me none. Know whut Ah done? He come 'round me wid his smart talk. Ah hauled off and knocked 'im down and took his old four-bits 'way from 'im. Gointer buy my wife some good ole 'lasses kisses wid it. Gimme fifty cents worth of dem candy kisses."

"Fifty cents buys a mightly lot of candy kisses, Joe. Why don't you split it up and take some chocolate bars, too. They eat good, too."

"Yessuh, dey do, but Ah wants all dat in kisses. Ah got a li'l boy chile home now. Tain't a week old yet, but he kin suck a sugar tit and maybe eat one them kisses hisself."

Joe got his candy and left the store. The clerk turned to the next customer. "Wisht I could be like these darkies. Laughin' all the time. Nothin' worries 'em."

Back in Eatonville, Joe reached his own front door. There was the ring of singing metal on wood. Fifteen times. Missie May couldn't run to the door, but she crept there as quickly as she could.

"Joe Banks, Ah hear you chunkin' money in mah do'way. You wait till Ah got mah strength back and Ah'm gointer fix you for dat."

1925

JAMES JOYCE

The Dead

Lily, the caretaker's daughter, was literally run off her feet. Hardly had she brought one gentleman into the little pantry behind the office on the ground floor and helped him off with his overcoat than the wheezy hall-door bell clanged again and she had to scamper along the bare hallway to let in another guest. It was well for her she had not to attend to the ladies also. But Miss Kate and Miss Julia had thought of that and had converted the bedroom upstairs into a ladies' dressing-room. Miss

James Joyce was born in Dublin, Ireland, in 1882 into a Roman Catholic, often poverty-stricken family. After attending Jesuit boarding schools and Dublin's University College, Joyce left his home country in 1940 with Nora Barnacle, who would later become his wife. Although he spent the rest of his life in Trieste, Paris, and Zurich, this novelist, playwright, and short-story writer never abandoned either Ireland or Dublin. Through his experiments in form and stream-of-consciousness narration, his complex wordplay and reworking of classical mythology, Joyce refigured the world's understanding of these places. Ulysses (1922) and Finnegans Wake (1939) remain for many the acme of European high modernism. Depressed by the contemporary reception of his work and nearly blind, Joyce died in Zurich in 1941.

Kate and Miss Julia were there, gossiping and laughing and fussing, walking after each other to the head of the stairs, peering down over the banisters and calling down to Lily to ask her who had come.

It was always a great affair, the Misses Morkan's annual dance. Everybody who knew them came to it, members of the family, old friends of the family, the members of Julia's choir, any of Kate's pupils that were grown up enough and even some of Mary Jane's pupils too. Never once had it fallen flat. For years and years it had gone off in splendid style as long as anyone could remember; ever since Kate and Julia, after the death of their brother Pat, had left the house in Stoney Batter and taken Mary Jane, their only niece, to live with them in the dark gaunt house on Usher's Island, the upper part of which they had rented from Mr. Fulham, the corn-factor on the ground floor. That was a good thirty years ago if it was a day. Mary Jane, who was then a little girl in short clothes, was now the main prop of the household for she had the organ in Haddington Road. She had been through the Academy and gave a pupils' concert every year in the upper room of the Antient Concert Rooms. Many of her pupils belonged to better-class families on the Kingstown and Dalkey line. Old as they were, her aunts also did their share. Julia, though she was quite grey, was still the leading soprano in Adam and Eve's, and Kate, being too feeble to go about much, gave music lessons to beginners on the old square piano in the back room. Lily, the caretaker's daughter, did housemaid's work for them. Though their life was modest they believed in eating well; the best of everything: diamond-bone sirloins, three-shilling tea and the best bottled stout. But Lily seldom made a mistake in the orders so that she got on well with her three mistresses. They were fussy, that was all. But the only thing they would not stand was back answers.

Of course they had good reason to be fussy on such a night. And then it was long after ten o'clock and yet there was no sign of Gabriel and his wife. Besides they were dreadfully afraid that Freddy Malins might turn up screwed. They would not wish for worlds that any of Mary Jane's pupils should see him under the influence; and when he was like that it was sometimes very hard to manage him. Freddy Malins always came late but they wondered what could be keeping Gabriel: and that was what brought them every two minutes to the banisters to ask Lily had Gabriel or Freddy come.

—O, Mr. Conroy, said Lily to Gabriel when she opened the door for him, Miss Kate and Miss Julia thought you were never coming. Good-night, Mrs. Conroy.

—I'll engage they did, said Gabriel, but they forget that my wife here takes three mortal hours to dress herself.

He stood on the mat, scraping the snow from his goloshes, while Lily led his wife to the foot of the stairs and called out:

—Miss Kate, here's Mrs. Conroy.

Kate and Julia came toddling down the dark stairs at once. Both of them kissed Gabriel's wife, said she must be perished alive and asked was Gabriel with her.

—Here I am as right as the mail, Aunt Kate! Go on up. I'll follow, called out Gabriel from the dark.

He continued scraping his feet vigorously while the three women went upstairs, laughing, to the ladies' dressing-room. A light fringe of snow lay like a cape on the shoulders of his overcoat and like toecaps on the toes of his goloshes; and, as the buttons of his overcoat slipped with a squeaking noise through the snow-stiffened frieze, a cold fragrant air from out-of-doors escaped from crevices and folds.

—Is it snowing again, Mr. Conroy? asked Lily.

She had preceded him into the pantry to help him off with his overcoat. Gabriel smiled at the three syllables she had given his surname and glanced at her. She was a slim, growing girl, pale in complexion and with hay-coloured hair. The gas in the pantry made her look still paler. Gabriel had known her when she was a child and used to sit on the lowest step nursing a rag doll.

—Yes, Lily, he answered, and I think we're in for a night of it.

He looked up at the pantry ceiling, which was shaking with the stamping and shuffling of feet on the floor above, listened for a moment to the piano and then glanced at the girl, who was folding his overcoat carefully at the end of a shelf.

—Tell me, Lily, he said in a friendly tone, do you still go to school?

—O no, sir, she answered, I'm done schooling this year and more.

—O, then, said Gabriel gaily, I suppose we'll be going to your wedding one of these fine days with your young man, eh?

The girl glanced back at him over her shoulder and said with great bitterness:

—The men that is now is only all palaver and what they can get out of you.

Gabriel coloured as if he felt he had made a mistake and, without looking at her, kicked off his goloshes and flicked actively with his muffler at his patent-leather shoes.

He was a stout tallish young man. The high colour of his cheeks pushed upwards even to his forehead where it scattered itself in a few formless patches of pale red; and on his hairless face there scintillated restlessly the polished lenses and the bright gilt rims of the glasses which screened his delicate and restless eyes. His glossy black hair was parted

in the middle and brushed in a long curve behind his ears where it
curled slightly beneath the groove left by his hat.

When he had flicked lustre into his shoes he stood up and pulled
his waistcoat down more tightly on his plump body. Then he took a
coin rapidly from his pocket.

—O Lily, he said, thrusting it into her hands, it's Christmas-time,
isn't it? Just . . . here's a little. . . .

He walked rapidly towards the door.

—O no, sir! cried the girl, following him. Really, sir, I wouldn't
take it.

—Christmas-time! Christmas-time! said Gabriel, almost trotting to
the stairs and waving his hand to her in deprecation.

The girl, seeing that he had gained the stairs, called out after him:

—Well, thank you, sir.

He waited outside the drawing-room door until the waltz should
finish, listening to the skirts that swept against it and to the shuffling of
feet. He was still discomposed by the girl's bitter and sudden retort. It
had cast a gloom over him which he tried to dispel by arranging his
cuffs and the bows of his tie. Then he took from his waistcoat pocket a
little paper and glanced at the headings he had made for his speech.
He was undecided about the lines from Robert Browning for he feared
they would be above the heads of his hearers. Some quotation that
they could recognise from Shakespeare or from the Melodies would
be better. The indelicate clacking of the men's heels and the shuffling
of their soles reminded him that their grade of culture differed from
his. He would only make himself ridiculous by quoting poetry to
them which they could not understand. They would think that he
was airing his superior education. He would fail with them just as
he had failed with the girl in the pantry. He had taken up a
wrong tone. His whole speech was a mistake from first to last, an utter
failure.

Just then his aunts and his wife came out of the ladies' dressing-
room. His aunts were two small plainly dressed old women. Aunt Julia
was an inch or so the taller. Her hair, drawn low over the tops of her
ears, was grey; and grey also, with darker shadows, was her large flaccid
face. Though she was stout in build and stood erect her slow eyes and
parted lips gave her the appearance of a woman who did not know
where she was or where she was going. Aunt Kate was more vivacious.
Her face, healthier than her sister's, was all puckers and creases, like a
shrivelled red apple, and her hair, braided in the same old-fashioned
way, had not lost its ripe nut colour.

They both kissed Gabriel frankly. He was their favourite nephew, the son of their dead elder sister, Ellen, who had married T. J. Conroy of the Port and Docks.

—Gretta tells me you're not going to take a cab back to Monkstown to-night, Gabriel, said Aunt Kate.

—No, said Gabriel, turning to his wife, we had quite enough of that last year, hadn't we. Don't you remember, Aunt Kate, what a cold Gretta got out of it? Cab windows rattling all the way, and the east wind blowing in after we passed Merrion. Very jolly it was. Gretta caught a dreadful cold.

Aunt Kate frowned severely and nodded her head at every word.

—Quite right, Gabriel, quite right, she said. You can't be too careful.

—But as for Gretta there, said Gabriel, she'd walk home in the snow if she were let.

Mrs. Conroy laughed.

—Don't mind him, Aunt Kate, she said. He's really an awful bother, what with green shades for Tom's eyes at night and making him do the dumb-bells, and forcing Eva to eat the stirabout. The poor child! And she simply hates the sight of it! . . . O, but you'll never guess what he makes me wear now!

She broke out into a peal of laughter and glanced at her husband, whose admiring and happy eyes had been wandering from her dress to her face and hair. The two aunts laughed heartily too, for Gabriel's solicitude was a standing joke with them.

—Goloshes! said Mrs. Conroy. That's the latest. Whenever it's wet underfoot I must put on my goloshes. To-night even he wanted me to put them on, but I wouldn't. The next thing he'll buy me will be a diving suit.

Gabriel laughed nervously and patted his tie reassuringly while Aunt Kate nearly doubled herself, so heartily did she enjoy the joke. The smile soon faded from Aunt Julia's face and her mirthless eyes were directed towards her nephew's face. After a pause she asked:

—And what are goloshes, Gabriel?

—Goloshes, Julia! exclaimed her sister. Goodness me, don't you know what goloshes are? You wear them over your . . . over your boots, Gretta, isn't it?

—Yes, said Mrs. Conroy. Guttapercha things. We both have a pair now. Gabriel says everyone wears them on the continent.

—O, on the continent, murmured Aunt Julia, nodding her head slowly.

Gabriel knitted his brows and said, as if he were slightly angered:

—It's nothing very wonderful but Gretta thinks it very funny because she says the word reminds her of Christy Minstrels.

—But tell me, Gabriel, said Aunt Kate, with brisk tact. Of course, you've seen about the room. Gretta was saying . . .

—O, the room is all right, replied Gabriel. I've taken one in the Gresham.

—To be sure, said Aunt Kate, by far the best thing to do. And the children, Gretta, you're not anxious about them?

—O, for one night, said Mrs. Conroy. Besides, Bessie will look after them.

—To be sure, said Aunt Kate again. What a comfort it is to have a girl like that, one you can depend on! There's that Lily, I'm sure I don't know what has come over her lately. She's not the girl she was at all.

Gabriel was about to ask his aunt some questions on this point but she broke off suddenly to gaze after her sister who had wandered down the stairs and was craning her neck over the banisters.

—Now, I ask you, she said, almost testily, where is Julia going? Julia! Julia! Where are you going?

Julia, who had gone halfway down one flight, came back and announced blandly:

—Here's Freddy.

At the same moment a clapping of hands and a final flourish of the pianist told that the waltz had ended. The drawing-room door was opened from within and some couples came out. Aunt Kate drew Gabriel aside hurriedly and whispered into his ear:

—Slip down, Gabriel, like a good fellow and see if he's all right, and don't let him up if he's screwed. I'm sure he's screwed. I'm sure he is.

Gabriel went to the stairs and listened over the banisters. He could hear two persons talking in the pantry. Then he recognised Freddy Malins' laugh. He went down the stairs noisily.

—It's such a relief, said Aunt Kate to Mrs. Conroy, that Gabriel is here. I always feel easier in my mind when he's here. . . . Julia, there's Miss Daly and Miss Power will take some refreshment. Thanks for your beautiful waltz, Miss Daly. It made lovely time.

A tall wizen-faced man, with a stiff grizzled moustache and swarthy skin, who was passing out with his partner said:

—And may we have some refreshment, too, Miss Morkan?

—Julia, said Aunt Kate summarily, and here's Mr. Browne and Miss Furlong. Take them in, Julia, with Miss Daly and Miss Power.

—I'm the man for the ladies, said Mr. Browne, pursing his lips until his moustache bristled and smiling in all his wrinkles. You know, Miss Morkan, the reason they are so fond of me is—

He did not finish his sentence, but, seeing that Aunt Kate was out of earshot, at once led the three young ladies into the back room. The middle of the room was occupied by two square tables placed end to end, and on these Aunt Julia and the caretaker were straightening and smoothing a large cloth. On the sideboard were arrayed dishes and plates, and glasses and bundles of knives and forks and spoons. The top of the closed square piano served also as a sideboard for viands and sweets. At a smaller sideboard in one corner two young men were standing, drinking hop-bitters.

Mr. Browne led his charges thither and invited them all, in jest, to some ladies' punch, hot, strong, and sweet. As they said they never took anything strong he opened three bottles of lemonade for them. Then he asked one of the young men to move aside, and, taking hold of the decanter, filled out for himself a goodly measure of whisky. The young men eyed him respectfully while he took a trial sip.

—God help me, he said, smiling, it's the doctor's orders.

His wizened face broke into a broad smile, and the three young ladies laughed in musical echo to his pleasantry, swaying their bodies to and fro, with nervous jerks of their shoulders. The boldest said:

—O, now, Mr. Browne, I'm sure the doctor never ordered anything of the kind.

Mr. Browne took another sip of his whisky and said, with sidling mimicry:

—Well, you see, I'm like the famous Mrs. Cassidy, who is reported to have said: *Now, Mary Grimes, if I don't take it, make me take it, for I feel I want it.*

His hot face had leaned forward a little too confidentially and he had assumed a very low Dublin accent so that the young ladies, with one instinct, received his speech in silence. Miss Furlong, who was one of Mary Jane's pupils, asked Miss Daly what was the name of the pretty waltz she had played; and Mr. Browne, seeing that he was ignored, turned promptly to the two young men who were more appreciative.

A red-faced young woman, dressed in pansy, came into the room, excitedly clapping her hands and crying:

—Quadrilles! Quadrilles!

Close on her heels came Aunt Kate, crying:

—Two gentlemen and three ladies, Mary Jane!

—O, here's Mr. Bergin and Mr. Kerrigan, said Mary Jane. Mr. Kerrigan, will you take Miss Power? Miss Furlong, may I get you a partner, Mr. Bergin. O, that'll just do now.

—Three ladies, Mary Jane, said Aunt Kate.

The two young gentlemen asked the ladies if they might have the pleasure, and Mary Jane turned to Miss Daly.

—O, Miss Daly, you're really awfully good, after playing for the last two dances, but really we're so short of ladies to-night.

—I don't mind in the least, Miss Morkan.

—But I've a nice partner for you, Mr. Bartell D'Arcy, the tenor. I'll get him to sing later on. All Dublin is raving about him.

—Lovely voice, lovely voice! said Aunt Kate.

As the piano had twice begun the prelude to the first figure Mary Jane led her recruits quickly from the room. They had hardly gone when Aunt Julia wandered slowly into the room, looking behind her at something.

—What is the matter, Julia? asked Aunt Kate anxiously. Who is it?

Julia, who was carrying in a column of table-napkins, turned to her sister and said, simply, as if the question had surprised her.

—It's only Freddy, Kate, and Gabriel with him.

In fact right behind her Gabriel could be seen piloting Freddy Malins across the landing. The latter, a young man of about forty, was of Gabriel's size and build, with very round shoulders. His face was fleshy and pallid, touched with colour only at the thick hanging lobes of his ears and at the wide wings of his nose. He had coarse features, a blunt nose, a convex and receding brow, tumid and protruded lips. His heavy-lidded eyes and the disorder of his scanty hair made him look sleepy. He was laughing heartily in a high key at a story which he had been telling Gabriel on the stairs and at the same time rubbing the knuckles of his left fist backwards and forwards into his left eye.

—Good-evening, Freddy, said Aunt Julia.

Freddy Malins bade the Misses Morkan good-evening in what seemed an offhand fashion by reason of the habitual catch in his voice and then, seeing that Mr. Browne was grinning at him from the side-board, crossed the room on rather shaky legs and began to repeat in an undertone the story he had just told to Gabriel.

—He's not so bad, is he? said Aunt Kate to Gabriel.

Gabriel's brows were dark but he raised them quickly and answered:

—O no, hardly noticeable.

—Now, isn't he a terrible fellow! she said. And his poor mother made him take the pledge on New Year's Eve. But come on, Gabriel, into the drawing-room.

Before leaving the room with Gabriel she signalled to Mr. Browne by frowning and shaking her forefinger in warning to and fro. Mr. Browne nodded in answer and, when she had gone, said to Freddy Malins:

—Now, then, Teddy, I'm going to fill you out a good glass of lemonade just to buck you up.

Freddy Malins, who was nearing the climax of his story, waved the offer aside impatiently but Mr. Browne, having first called Freddy Malins' attention to a disarray in his dress, filled out and handed him a full glass of lemonade. Freddy Malins' left hand accepted the glass mechanically, his right hand being engaged in the mechanical readjustment of his dress. Mr. Browne, whose face was once more wrinkling with mirth, poured out for himself a glass of whisky while Freddy Malins exploded, before he had well reached the climax of his story, in a kink of high-pitched bronchitic laughter and, setting down his untasted and overflowing glass, began to rub the knuckles of his left fist backwards and forwards into his left eye, repeating words of his last phrase as well as his fit of laughter would allow him.

Gabriel could not listen while Mary Jane was playing her Academy piece, full of runs and difficult passages, to the hushed drawing-room. He liked music but the piece she was playing had no melody for him and he doubted whether it had any melody for the other listeners, though they had begged Mary Jane to play something. Four young men, who had come from the refreshment-room to stand in the doorway at the sound of the piano, had gone away quietly in couples after a few minutes. The only persons who seemed to follow the music were Mary Jane herself, her hands racing along the key-board or lifted from it at the pauses like those of a priestess in momentary imprecation, and Aunt Kate standing at her elbow to turn the page.

Gabriel's eyes, irritated by the floor, which glittered with beeswax under the heavy chandelier, wandered to the wall above the piano. A picture of the balcony scene in *Romeo and Juliet* hung there and beside it was a picture of the two murdered princes in the Tower which Aunt Julia had worked in red, blue, and brown wools when she was a girl. Probably in the school they had gone to as girls that kind of work had been taught, for one year his mother had worked for him as a birthday present a waistcoat of purple tabinet, with little foxes' heads upon it, lined with brown satin and having round mulberry buttons. It was strange that his mother had had no musical talent though Aunt Kate used to call her the brains carrier of the Morkan family. Both she and Julia had always seemed a little proud of their serious and matronly sister. Her photograph stood before the pierglass. She held an open book on her knees and was pointing out something in it to Constantine who, dressed in a man-o'-war suit, lay at her feet. It was she who had chosen the names for her sons for she was very sensible of the dignity of family life. Thanks to her, Constantine was now senior curate in Balbriggan and, thanks to her Gabriel himself had taken his degree in the Royal University. A shadow passed over his face as he remembered her sullen opposition to his marriage. Some slighting phrases she had used still rankled in his memory; she had once spoken of Gretta as being country cute and that was not true of Gretta at all. It was Gretta who had nursed her during all her last long illness in their house at Monkstown.

He knew that Mary Jane must be near the end of her piece for she was playing again the opening melody with runs of scales after every bar and while he waited for the end the resentment died down in his heart. The piece ended with a trill of octaves in the treble and a final deep octave in the bass. Great applause greeted Mary Jane as, blushing and rolling up her music nervously, she escaped from the room. The most vigorous clapping came from the four young men in the doorway who had gone away to the refreshment-room at the beginning of the piece but had come back when the piano had stopped.

Lancers were arranged. Gabriel found himself partnered with Miss Ivors. She was a frank-mannered talkative young lady, with a freckled face and prominent brown eyes. She did not wear a low-cut bodice and the large brooch which was fixed in the front of her collar bore on it an Irish device.

When they had taken their places she said abruptly:

—I have a crow to pluck with you.

—With me? said Gabriel.

She nodded her head gravely.

—What is it? asked Gabriel, smiling at her solemn manner.

—Who is G. C.? answered Miss Ivors, turning her eyes upon him.

Gabriel coloured and was about to knit his brows, as if he did not understand, when she said bluntly.

—O, innocent Amy! I have found out that you write for *The Daily Express.* Now, aren't you ashamed of yourself?

—Why should I be ashamed of myself? asked Gabriel, blinking his eyes and trying to smile.

—Well, I'm ashamed of you, said Miss Ivors frankly. To say you'd write for a rag like that. I didn't think you were a West Briton.

A look of perplexity appeared on Gabriel's face. It was true that he wrote a literary column every Wednesday in *The Daily Express*, for which he was paid fifteen shillings. But that did not make him a West Briton surely. The books he received for review were almost more welcome than the paltry cheque. He loved to feel the covers and turn over the pages of newly printed books. Nearly every day when his teaching in the college was ended he used to wander down the quays to the second-hand booksellers, to Hickey's on Bachelor's Walk, to Webb's or Massey's on Aston's Quay, or to O'Clohissey's in the by-street. He did not know how to meet her charge. He wanted to say that literature was above politics. But they were friends of many years' standing and their careers had been parallel, first at the University and then as teachers: he could not risk a grandiose phrase with her. He continued blinking his eyes and trying to smile and murmured lamely that he saw nothing political in writing reviews of books.

When their turn to cross had come he was still perplexed and inattentive. Miss Ivors promptly took his hand in a warm grasp and said in a soft friendly tone:

—Of course, I was only joking. Come, we cross now.

When they were together again she spoke of the University question and Gabriel felt more at ease. A friend of hers had shown her his review of Browning's poems. That was how she had found out the secret: but she liked the review immensely. Then she said suddenly:

—O, Mr. Conroy, will you come for an excursion to the Aran Isles this summer? We're going to stay there a whole month. It will be splendid out in the Atlantic. You ought to come. Mr. Clancy is coming, and Mr. Kilkelly and Kathleen Kearney. It would be splendid for Gretta too if she'd come. She's from Connacht, isn't she?

—Her people are, said Gabriel shortly.

—But you will come, won't you? said Miss Ivors, laying her warm hand eagerly on his arm.

—The fact is, said Gabriel, I have already arranged to go—

—Go where? asked Miss Ivors.

—Well, you know, every year I go for a cycling tour with some fellows and so—

—But where? asked Miss Ivors.

—Well, we usually go to France or Belgium or perhaps Germany, said Gabriel awkwardly.

—And why do you go to France and Belgium, said Miss Ivors, instead of visiting your own land?

—Well, said Gabriel, it's partly to keep in touch with the languages and partly for a change.

—And haven't you your own language to keep in touch with— Irish? asked Miss Ivors.

—Well, said Gabriel, if it comes to that, you know, Irish is not my language.

Their neighbours had turned to listen to the cross-examination. Gabriel glanced right and left nervously and tried to keep his good

humour under the ordeal which was making a blush invade his forehead.

—And haven't you your own land to visit, continued Miss Ivors,
that you know nothing of, your own people, and your own country?

—O, to tell you the truth, retorted Gabriel suddenly, I'm sick of my
own country, sick of it!

—Why? asked Miss Ivors.

Gabriel did not answer for his retort had heated him.

—Why? repeated Miss Ivors.

They had to go visiting together and, as he had not answered her,
Miss Ivors said warmly:

—Of course, you've no answer.

Gabriel tried to cover his agitation by taking part in the dance with
great energy. He avoided her eyes for he had seen a sour expression on
her face. But when they met in the long chain he was surprised to feel
his hand firmly pressed. She looked at him from under her brows for a
moment quizzically until he smiled. Then, just as the chain was about
to start again, she stood on tiptoe and whispered into his ear:

—West Briton!

When the lancers were over Gabriel went away to a remote corner
of the room where Freddy Malins' mother was sitting. She was a stout
feeble old woman with white hair. Her voice had a catch in it like her
son's and she stuttered slightly. She had been told that Freddy had come
and that he was nearly all right. Gabriel asked her whether she had had
a good crossing. She lived with her married daughter in Glasgow and
came to Dublin on a visit once a year. She answered placidly that she
had had a beautiful crossing and that the captain had been most attentive to her. She spoke also of the beautiful house her daughter kept in
Glasgow, and of all the nice friends they had there. While her tongue
rambled on Gabriel tried to banish from his mind all memory of the
unpleasant incident with Miss Ivors. Of course the girl or woman, or
whatever she was, was an enthusiast but there was a time for all things.
Perhaps he ought not to have answered her like that. But she had no
right to call him a West Briton before people, even in joke. She had
tried to make him ridiculous before people, heckling him and staring at
him with her rabbit's eyes.

He saw his wife making her way towards him through the waltzing
couples. When she reached him she said into his ear:

—Gabriel, Aunt Kate wants to know won't you carve the goose as
usual. Miss Daly will carve the ham and I'll do the pudding.

—All right, said Gabriel.

—She's sending in the younger ones first as soon as this waltz is
over so that we'll have the table to ourselves.

—Were you dancing? asked Gabriel.

—Of course I was. Didn't you see me? What words had you with Molly Ivors?

—No words. Why? Did she say so?

—Something like that. I'm trying to get that Mr. D'Arcy to sing. He's full of conceit, I think.

—There were no words, said Gabriel moodily, only she wanted me to go for a trip to the west of Ireland and I said I wouldn't.

His wife clasped her hands excitedly and gave a little jump.

—O, do go, Gabriel, she cried. I'd love to see Galway again.

—You can go if you like, said Gabriel coldly.

She looked at him for a moment, then turned to Mrs. Malins and said:

—There's a nice husband for you, Mrs. Malins.

While she was threading her way back across the room Mrs. Malins, without adverting to the interruption, went on to tell Gabriel what beautiful places there were in Scotland and beautiful scenery. Her son-in-law brought them every year to the lakes and they used to go fishing. Her son-in-law was a splendid fisher. One day he caught a fish, a beautiful big big fish, and the man in the hotel boiled it for their dinner.

Gabriel hardly heard what she said. Now that supper was coming near he began to think again about his speech and about the quotation. When he saw Freddy Malins coming across the room to visit his mother Gabriel left the chair free for him and retired into the embrasure of the window. The room had already cleared and from the back room came the clatter of plates and knifes. Those who still remained in the drawing-room seemed tired of dancing and were conversing quietly in little groups. Gabriel's warm trembling fingers tapped the cold pane of the window. How cool it must be outside! How pleasant it would be to walk out alone, first along by the river and then through the park! The snow would be lying on the branches of the trees and forming a bright cap on the top of the Wellington Monument. How much more pleasant it would be there than at the supper-table!

He ran over the headings of his speech: Irish hospitality, sad memories, the Three Graces, Paris, the quotation from Browning. He repeated to himself a phrase he had written in his review: *One feels that one is listening to a thought-tormented music.* Miss Ivors had praised the review. Was she sincere? Had she really any life of her own behind all her propagandism? There had never been any ill-feeling between them until that night. It unnerved him to think that she would be at the supper-table, looking up at him while he spoke with her critical quizzing eyes. Perhaps she would not be sorry to see him fail in his speech. An idea came into his mind and gave him courage. He would say, alluding to

Aunt Kate and Aunt Julia: *Ladies and Gentlemen, the generation which is now on the wane among us may have had its faults but for my part I think it had certain qualities of hospitality, of humour, of humanity, which the new and very serious and hypereducated generation that is growing up around us seems to me to lack.* Very good: that was one for Miss Ivors. What did he care that his aunts were only two ignorant old women?

A murmur in the room attracted his attention. Mr. Browne was advancing from the door, gallantly escorting Miss Julia, who leaned upon his arm, smiling and hanging her head. An irregular musketry of applause escorted her also as far as the piano and then, as Mary Jane seated herself on the stool, and Aunt Julia, no longer smiling, half turned so as to pitch her voice fairly into the room, gradually ceased. Gabriel recognised the prelude. It was that of an old song of Aunt Julia's —*Arrayed for the Bridal.* Her voice, strong and clear in tone, attacked with great spirit the runs which embellish the air and though she sang very rapidly she did not miss even the smallest of the grace notes. To follow the voice, without looking at the singer's face, was to feel and share the excitement of swift and secure flight. Gabriel applauded loudly with all the others at the close of the song and loud applause was borne in from the invisible supper-table. It sounded so genuine that a little colour struggled into Aunt Julia's face as she bent to replace in the music-stand the old leather-bound song-book that had her initials on the cover. Freddy Malins, who had listened with his head perched sideways to hear her better, was still applauding when everyone else had ceased and talking animatedly to his mother who nodded her head gravely and slowly in acquiescence. At last, when he could clap no more, he stood up suddenly and hurried across the room to Aunt Julia whose hand he seized and held in both his hands, shaking it when words failed him or the catch in his voice proved too much for him.

—I just was telling my mother, he said, I never heard you sing so well, never. No, I never heard your voice so good as it is to-night. Now! Would you believe that now? That's the truth. Upon my word and honour that's the truth. I never heard your voice sound so fresh and so . . . so clear and fresh, never.

Aunt Julia smiled broadly and murmured something about compliments as she released her hand from his grasp. Mr. Browne extended his open hand towards her and said to those who were near him in the manner of a showman introducing a prodigy to an audience:

—Miss Julia Morkan, my latest discovery!

He was laughing very heartily at this himself when Freddy Malins turned to him and said:

—Well, Browne, if you're serious you might make a worse discovery. All I can say is I never heard her sing half so well as long as I am coming here. And that's the honest truth.

—Neither did I, said Mr. Browne. I think her voice has greatly improved.

Aunt Julia shrugged her shoulders and said with meek pride:

—Thirty years ago I hadn't a bad voice as voices go.

—I often told Julia, said Aunt Kate emphatically, that she was simply thrown away in that choir. But she never would be said by me.

She turned as if to appeal to the good sense of the others against a refractory child while Aunt Julia gazed in front of her, a vague smile of reminiscence playing on her face.

—No, continued Aunt Kate, she wouldn't be said or led by anyone, slaving there in that choir night and day, night and day. Six o'clock on Christmas morning! And all for what?

—Well, isn't it for the honour of God, Aunt Kate? asked Mary Jane, twisting round on the piano-stool and smiling.

Aunt Kate turned fiercely on her niece and said:

—I know all about the honour of God, Mary Jane, but I think it's not at all honourable for the pope to turn out the women out of the choirs that have slaved there all their lives and put little whipper-snappers of boys over their heads. I suppose it is for the good of the Church if the pope does it. But it's not just, Mary Jane, and it's not right.

She had worked herself into a passion and would have continued in defence of her sister for it was a sore subject with her but Mary Jane, seeing that all the dancers had come back, intervened pacifically:

—Now, Aunt Kate, you're giving scandal to Mr. Browne who is of the other persuasion.

Aunt Kate turned to Mr. Browne, who was grinning at this allusion to his religion, and said hastily:

—O, I don't question the pope's being right. I'm only a stupid old woman and I wouldn't presume to do such a thing. But there's such a thing as common everyday politeness and gratitude. And if I were in Julia's place I'd tell that Father Healy straight up to his face . . .

—And besides, Aunt Kate, said Mary Jane, we really are all hungry and when we are hungry we are all very quarrelsome.

—And when we are thirsty we are also quarrelsome, added Mr. Browne.

—So that we had better go to supper, said Mary Jane, and finish the discussion afterwards.

On the landing outside the drawing-room Gabriel found his wife and Mary Jane trying to persuade Miss Ivors to stay for supper. But Miss Ivors, who had put on her hat and was buttoning her cloak, would not stay. She did not feel in the least hungry and she had already overstayed her time.

—But only for ten minutes, Molly, said Mrs. Conroy. That won't delay you.

—To take a pick itself, said Mary Jane, after all your dancing.

—I really couldn't, said Miss Ivors.

—I am afraid you didn't enjoy yourself at all, said Mary Jane hopelessly.

—Ever so much, I assure you, said Miss Ivors, but you really must let me run off now.

—But how can you get home? asked Mrs. Conroy.

—O, it's only two steps up the quay.

Gabriel hesitated a moment and said:

—If you will allow me, Miss Ivors, I'll see you home if you really are obliged to go.

But Miss Ivors broke away from them.

—I won't hear of it, she cried. For goodness sake go in to your suppers and don't mind me. I'm quite well able to take care of myself.

—Well, you're the comical girl, Molly, said Mrs. Conroy frankly.

—*Beannacht libh, cried Miss Ivors, with a laugh, as she ran down the staircase.*

Mary Jane gazed after her, a moodily puzzled expression on her face, while Mrs. Conroy leaned over the banisters to listen for the hall-door. Gabriel asked himself was he the cause of her abrupt departure. But she did not seem to be in ill humour: she had gone away laughing. He stared blankly down the staircase.

At that moment Aunt Kate came toddling out of the supper-room, almost wringing her hands in despair.

—Where is Gabriel? she cried. Where on earth is Gabriel? There's everyone waiting in there, stage to let, and nobody to carve the goose!

—Here I am, Aunt Kate! cried Gabriel, with sudden animation, ready to carve a flock of geese, if necessary.

A fat brown goose lay at one end of the table and at the other end, on a bed of creased paper strewn with sprigs of parsley, lay a great ham, stripped of its outer skin and peppered over with crust crumbs, a neat paper frill round its shin and beside this was a round of spiced beef. Between these rival ends ran parallel lines of side-dishes: two little minsters of jelly, red and yellow; a shallow dish full of blocks of blanc-mange and red jam, a large green leaf-shaped dish with a stalk-shaped handle, on which lay bunches of purple raisins and peeled almonds, a companion dish on which lay a solid rectangle of Smyrna figs, a dish of custard topped with grated nutmeg, a small bowl full of chocolates and sweets wrapped in gold and silver papers and a glass vase in which stood some tall celery stalks. In the centre of the table there stood, as sentries to a fruit-stand which upheld a pyramid of oranges and American apples, two squat old-fashioned decanters of cut glass, one containing port and the other dark sherry. On the closed square piano a pudding in a huge yellow dish lay in waiting and behind it were three squads of bottles of stout and ale and minerals, drawn up according to the colours of their uniforms, the first two black, with brown and red labels, the third and smallest squad white, with transverse green sashes.

Gabriel took his seat boldly at the head of the table and, having looked at the edge of the carver, plunged his fork firmly into the goose. He felt quite at ease now for he was an expert carver and liked nothing better than to find himself at the head of a well-laden table.

—Miss Furlong, what shall I send you? he asked. A wing or a slice of the breast?

—Just a small slice of the breast.

—Miss Higgins, what for you?

—O, anything at all, Mr. Conroy.

While Gabriel and Miss Daly exchanged plates of goose and plates of ham and spiced beef Lily went from guest to guest with a dish of hot floury potatoes wrapped in a white napkin. This was Mary Jane's idea and she had also suggested apple sauce for the goose but Aunt Kate had said that plain roast goose without apple sauce had always been good enough for her and she hoped she might never eat worse. Mary Jane waited on her pupils and saw that they got the best slices and Aunt Kate and Aunt Julia opened and carried across from the piano bottles of stout and ale for the gentlemen and bottles of minerals for the ladies. There was a great deal of confusion and laughter and noise, the noise of orders and counter-orders, of knives and forks, of corks and glass-stoppers. Gabriel began to carve second helpings as soon as he had finished the first round without serving himself. Everyone protested loudly so that he compromised by taking a long draught of stout for he had found the carving hot work. Mary Jane settled down quietly to her supper but Aunt Kate and Aunt Julia were still toddling round the table, walking on each other's heels, getting in each other's way and giving each other unheeded orders. Mr. Browne begged of them to sit down and eat their suppers and so did Gabriel but they said there was time enough so that, at last, Freddy Malins stood up and, capturing Aunt Kate, plumped her down on her chair amid general laughter.

When everyone had been well served Gabriel said, smiling:

—Now, if anyone wants a little more of what vulgar people call stuffing let him or her speak.

A chorus of voices invited him to begin his own supper and Lily came forward with three potatoes which she had reserved for him.

—Very well, said Gabriel amiably, as he took another preparatory draught, kindly forget my existence, ladies and gentlemen, for a few minutes.

He set to his supper and took no part in the conversation with which the table covered Lily's removal of the plates. The subject of talk was the opera company which was then at the Theatre Royal. Mr. Bartell D'Arcy, the tenor, a dark-complexioned young man with a smart moustache, praised very highly the leading contralto of the company but Miss Furlong thought she had a rather vulgar style of production. Freddy Malins said there was a negro chieftain singing in the second part of the Gaiety pantomime who had one of the finest tenor voices he had ever heard.

—Have you heard him? he asked Mr. Bartell D'Arcy across the table.

—No, answered Mr. Bartell D'Arcy carelessly.

—Because, Freddy Malins explained, now I'd be curious to hear your opinion of him. I think he has a grand voice.

—It takes Teddy to find out the really good things, said Mr. Browne familiarly to the table.

—And why couldn't he have a voice too? asked Freddy Malins sharply. Is it because he's only a black?

Nobody answered this question and Mary Jane led the table back to the legitimate opera. One of her pupils had given her a pass for *Mignon*. Of course it was very fine, she said, but it made her think of poor Georgina Burns. Mr. Browne could go back further still, to the old Italian companies that used to come to Dublin—Tietjens, Ilma de Murzka, Campanini, the great Trebelli, Giuglini, Ravelli, Aramburo. Those were the days, he said, when there was something like singing to be heard in Dublin. He told too of how the top galley of the old Royal used to be packed night after night, of how one night an Italian tenor had sung five encores to *Let Me Like a Soldier Fall*, introducing a high C every time, and of how the gallery boys would sometimes in their enthusiasm unyoke the horses from the carriage of some great *prima donna* and pull her themselves through the streets to her hotel. Why did they never play the grand old operas now, he asked, *Dinorah*, *Lucrezia Borgia*? Because they could not get the voices to sing them: that was why.

—O, well, said Mr. Bartell D'Arcy, I presume there are as good singers to-day as there were then.

—Where are they? asked Mr. Browne defiantly.

—In London, Paris, Milan, said Mr. Bartell D'Arcy warmly. I suppose Caruso, for example, is quite as good, if not better than any of the men you have mentioned.

—Maybe so, said Mr. Browne. But I may tell you I doubt it strongly.

—O, I'd give anything to hear Caruso sing, said Mary Jane.

—For me, said Aunt Kate, who had been picking a bone, there was only one tenor. To please me, I mean. But I suppose none of you ever heard of him.

—Who was he, Miss Morkan? asked Mr. Bartell D'Arcy politely.

—His name, said Aunt Kate, was Parkinson. I heard him when he was in his prime and I think he had then the purest tenor voice that was ever put into a man's throat.

—Strange, said Mr. Bartell D'Arcy. I never even heard of him.

—Yes, yes, Miss Morkan is right, said Mr. Browne. I remember hearing of old Parkinson but he's too far back for me.

—A beautiful pure sweet mellow English tenor, said Aunt Kate with enthusiasm.

Gabriel having finished, the huge pudding was transferred to the table. The clatter of forks and spoons began again. Gabriel's wife served out spoonfuls of the pudding and passed the plates down the table. Midway down they were held up by Mary Jane, who replenished them with raspberry or orange jelly or with blancmange and jam. The pudding was of Aunt Julia's making and she received praises for it from all quarters. She herself said that it was not quite brown enough.

—Well, I hope, Miss Morkan, said Mr. Browne, that I'm brown enough for you because, you know, I'm all brown.

All the gentlemen, except Gabriel, ate some of the pudding out of compliment to Aunt Julia. As Gabriel never ate sweets the celery had been left for him. Freddy Malins also took a stalk of celery and ate it with his pudding. He had been told that celery was a capital thing for the blood and he was just then under doctor's care. Mrs. Malins, who had been silent all through the supper, said that her son was going down to Mount Melleray in a week or so. The table then spoke of Mount Melleray, how bracing the air was down there, how hospitable the monks were, and how they never asked for a penny-piece from their guests.

—And do you mean to say, asked Mr. Browne incredulously, that a chap can go down there and put up there as if it were a hotel and live on the fat of the land and then come away without paying a farthing?

—O, most people give some donation to the monastery when they leave, said Mary Jane.

—I wish we had an institution like that in our Church, said Mr. Browne candidly.

He was astonished to hear that the monks never spoke, got up at two in the morning and slept in their coffins. He asked what they did it for.

—That's the rule of the order, said Aunt Kate firmly.

—Yes, but why? asked Mr. Browne.

Aunt Kate repeated that it was the rule, that was all. Mr. Browne still seemed not to understand. Freddy Malins explained to him, as best he could, that the monks were trying to make up for the sins committed by all the sinners in the outside world. The explanation was not very clear for Mr. Browne grinned and said:

—I like that idea very much but wouldn't a comfortable spring bed do them as well as a coffin?

—The coffin, said Mary Jane, is to remind them of their last end.

As the subject had grown lugubrious it was buried in a silence of the table during which Mrs. Malins could be heard saying to her neighbour in an indistinct undertone:

—They are very good men, the monks, very pious men.

The raisins and almonds and figs and apples and oranges and chocolates and sweets were now passed about the table and Aunt Julia invited all the guests to have either port or sherry. At first Mr. Bartell D'Arcy refused to take either but one of his neighbours nudged him and whispered something to him upon which he allowed his glass to be filled. Gradually as the last glasses were being filled the conversation ceased. A pause followed, broken only by the noise of the wine and by unsettlings of chairs. The Misses Morkan, all three, looked down at the tablecloth. Someone coughed once or twice and then a few gentlemen patted the table gently as a signal for silence. The silence came and Gabriel pushed back his chair and stood up.

The patting at once grew louder in encouragement and then ceased altogether. Gabriel leaned his ten trembling fingers on the tablecloth and smiled nervously at the company. Meeting a row of upturned faces he raised his eyes to the chandelier. The piano was playing a waltz tune and he could hear the skirts sweeping against the drawing-room door. People, perhaps, were standing in the snow on the quay outside, gazing up at the lighted windows and listening to the waltz music. The air was pure there. In the distance lay the park where the trees were weighted with snow. The Wellington Monument wore a gleaming cap of snow that flashed westward over the white field of Fifteen Acres.

He began:

—Ladies and Gentlemen.

—It has fallen to my lot this evening, as in years past, to perform a very pleasing task but a task for which I am afraid my poor powers as a speaker are all too inadequate.

—No, no! said Mr. Browne.

—But, however that may be, I can only ask you to-night to take the will for the deed and to lend me your attention for a few moments while I endeavour to express to you in words what my feelings are on this occasion.

—Ladies and Gentlemen. It is not the first time that we have gathered together under this hospitable roof, around this hospitable board. It is not the first time that we have been the recipients—or perhaps, I had better say, the victims—of the hospitality of certain good ladies.

He made a circle in the air with his arm and paused. Everyone laughed or smiled at Aunt Kate and Aunt Julia and Mary Jane who all turned crimson with pleasure. Gabriel went on more boldly:

—I feel more strongly with every recurring year that our country has no tradition which does it so much honour and which it should guard so jealously as that of its hospitality. It is a tradition that is unique as far as my experience goes (and I have visited not a few places abroad) among the modern nations. Some would say, perhaps, that with us it is rather a failing than anything to be boasted of. But granted even that, it is, to my mind, a princely failing, and one that I trust will long be cultivated among us. Of one thing, at least, I am sure. As long as this one roof shelters the good ladies aforesaid—and I wish from my heart it may do so for many and many a long year to come—the tradition of genuine warm-hearted courteous Irish hospitality, which our forefathers have handed down to us and which we in turn must hand down to our descendants, is still alive among us.

A hearty murmur of assent ran round the table. It shot through Gabriel's mind that Miss Ivors was not there and that she had gone away discourteously: and he said with confidence in himself:

—Ladies and Gentlemen.

—A new generation is growing up in our midst, a generation actuated by new ideas and new principles. It is serious and enthusiastic for these new ideas and its enthusiasm, even when it is misdirected, is, I believe, in the main sincere. But we are living in a skeptical and, if I may use the phrase, a thought-tormented age: and sometimes I fear that this new generation, educated or hypereducated as it is, will lack those qualities of humanity, of hospitality, of kindly humour which belonged to an older day. Listening to-night to the names of all those great singers of the past it seemed to me, I must confess, that we were living in a less spacious age. Those days might, without exaggeration, be called spacious days: and if they are gone beyond recall let us hope, at least, that in gatherings such as this we shall still speak of them with pride and affection, still cherish in our hearts the memory of those dead and gone great ones whose fame the world will not willingly let die.

—Hear, hear! said Mr. Browne loudly.

—But yet, continued Gabriel, his voice falling into a softer inflection, there are always in gatherings such as this sadder thoughts that will recur to our minds: thoughts of the past, of youth, of changes, of absent faces that we miss here to-night. Our path through life is strewn with many such sad memories: and were we to brood upon them always we could not find the heart to go on bravely with our work among the living. We have all of us living duties and living affections which claim, and rightly claim, our strenuous endeavours.

—Therefore, I will not linger on the past. I will not let any gloomy moralising intrude upon us here to-night. Here we are gathered together for a brief moment from the bustle and rush of our everyday routine. We are met here as friends, in the spirit of good-fellowship, as colleagues, also to a certain extent, in the true spirit of *camaraderie,* and as the guests of—what shall I call them?—the Three Graces of the Dublin musical world.

The table burst into applause and laughter at this sally. Aunt Julia vainly asked each of her neighbours in turn to tell her what Gabriel had said.

—He says we are the Three Graces, Aunt Julia, said Mary Jane.

Aunt Julia did not understand but she looked up, smiling, at Gabriel, who continued in the same vein:

—Ladies and Gentlemen.

—I will not attempt to play to-night the part that Paris played on another occasion. I will not attempt to choose between them. The task would be an invidious one and one beyond my poor powers. For when I view them in turn, whether it be our chief hostess herself, whose good heart, whose too good heart, has become a byword with all who know her, or her sister, who seems to be gifted with perennial youth and whose singing must have been a surprise and a revelation to us all to-night, or, last but not least, when I consider our youngest hostess, talented, cheerful, hard-working, and the best of nieces, I confess, Ladies and Gentlemen, that I do not know to which of them I should award the prize.

Gabriel glanced down at his aunts and, seeing the large smile on Aunt Julia's face and the tears which had risen to Aunt Kate's eyes, hastened to his close. He raised his glass of port gallantly, while every member of the company fingered a glass expectantly, and said loudly:

—Let us toast them all three together. Let us drink to their health, wealth, long life, happiness, and prosperity and may they long continue to hold the proud and self-won position which they hold in their profession and the position of honour and affection which they hold in our hearts.

All the guests stood up, glass in hand, and, turning towards the three seated ladies, sang in unison, with Mr. Browne as leader:

For they are jolly gay fellows,
For the are jolly gay fellows,
For they are jolly gay fellows,
Which nobody can deny.

Aunt Kate was making frank use of her handkerchief and even Aunt Julia seemed moved. Freddy Malins beat time with his pudding-fork and the singers turned towards one another, as if in melodious conference, while they sang, with emphasis:

Unless he tells a lie,
Unless he tells a lie.

Then, turning once more towards their hostesses, they sang:

For they are jolly gay fellows,
For they are jolly gay fellows,
For they are jolly gay fellows,
Which nobody can deny.

The acclamation which followed was taken up beyond the door of the supper-room by many of the other guests and renewed time after time, Freddy Malins acting as officer with his fork on high.

The piercing morning air came into the hall where they were standing so that Aunt Kate said:

—Close the door, somebody. Mrs. Malins will get her death of cold.

—Browne is out there, Aunt Kate, said Mary Jane.

—Browne is everywhere, said Aunt Kate, lowering her voice.

Mary Jane laughed at her tone.

—Really, she said archly, he is very attentive.

—He has been laid on here like the gas, said Aunt Kate in the same tone, all during the Christmas.

She laughed herself this time good-humouredly and then added quickly:

—But tell him to come in, Mary Jane, and close the door. I hope to goodness he didn't hear me.

At that moment the hall-door was opened and Mr. Browne came in from the doorstep, laughing as if his heart would break. He was dressed in a long green overcoat with mock astrakhan cuffs and collar and wore on his head an oval fur cap. He pointed down the snow-covered quay from where the sound of shrill prolonged whistling was borne in.

—Teddy will have all the cabs in Dublin out, he said.

Gabriel advanced from the little pantry behind the office, struggling into his overcoat and, looking round the hall, said:

—Gretta not down yet?

—She's getting on her things, Gabriel, said Aunt Kate.

—Who's playing up there? asked Gabriel.

—Nobody. They're all gone.

—O, no, Aunt Kate, said Mary Jane. Bartell D'Arcy and Miss O'Callaghan aren't gone yet.

—Someone is strumming at the piano, anyhow, said Gabriel.

Mary Jane glanced at Gabriel and Mr. Browne and said with a shiver:

—It makes me feel cold to look at you two gentlemen muffled up like that. I wouldn't like to face your journey home at this hour.

—I'd like nothing better this minute, said Mr. Browne stoutly, than a rattling fine walk in the country or a fast drive with a good spanking goer between the shafts.

—We used to have a very good horse and trap at home, said Aunt Julia sadly.

—The never-to-be-forgotten Johnny, said Mary Jane, laughing.

Aunt Kate and Gabriel laughed too.

—Why, what was wonderful about Johnny? asked Mr. Browne.

—The late lamented Patrick Morkan, our grandfather, that is, explained Gabriel, commonly known in his later years as the old gentleman, was a glue-boiler.

—O, now, Gabriel, said Aunt Kate, laughing, he had a starch mill.

—Well, glue or starch, said Gabriel, the old gentleman had a horse by the name of Johnny. And Johnny used to work in the old gentleman's mill, walking round and round in order to drive the mill.

That was all very well; but now comes the tragic part about Johnny. One fine day the old gentleman thought he'd like to drive out with the quality to a military review in the park.

—The Lord have mercy on his soul, said Aunt Kate compassionately.

—Amen, said Gabriel. So the old gentleman, as I said, harnessed Johnny and put on his very best tall hat and his very best stock collar and drove out in grand style from his ancestral mansion somewhere near Back Lane, I think.

Everyone laughed, even Mrs. Malins, at Gabriel's manner and Aunt Kate said:

—O now, Gabriel, he didn't live in Back Lane, really. Only the mill was there.

—Out from the mansion of his forefathers, continued Gabriel, he drove with Johnny. And everything went on beautifully until Johnny came in sight of King Billy's statue: and whether he fell in love with the horse King Billy sits on or whether he thought he was back again in the mill, anyhow he began to walk round the statue.

Gabriel paced in a circle round the hall in his goloshes amid the laughter of the others.

—Round and round he went, said Gabriel, and the old gentleman, who was a very pompous old gentleman, was highly indignant. *Go on, sir! What do you mean, sir? Johnny! Johnny! Most extraordinary conduct! Can't understand the horse!*

The peals of laughter which followed Gabriel's imitation of the incident were interrupted by a resounding knock at the hall-door. Mary Jane ran to open it and let in Freddy Malins. Freddy Malins, with his hat well back on his head and his shoulders humped with cold, was puffing and steaming after his exertions.

—I could only get one cab, he said.

—O, we'll find another along the quay, said Gabriel.

—Yes, said Aunt Kate. Better not keep Mrs. Malins standing in the draught.

Mrs. Malins was helped down the front steps by her son and Mr. Browne and, after many manœuvers, hoisted into the cab. Freddy Malins clambered in after her and spent a long time settling her on the seat. Mr. Browne helping him with advice. At last she was settled comfortably and Freddy Malins invited Mr. Browne into the cab. There was a good deal of confused talk, and then Mr. Browne got into the cab. The cabman settled his rug over his knees, and bent down for the address. The confusion grew greater and the cabman was directed differently by Freddy Malins and Mr. Browne, each of whom had his head out through a window of the cab. The difficulty was to know where to drop Mr. Browne along the route and Aunt Kate, Aunt Julia, and Mary Jane helped the discussion from the doorstep with cross-directions and contradictions and abundance of laughter. As for Freddy Malins he was speechless with laughter. He popped his head in and out of the window every moment, to the great danger of his hat, and told his mother how the discussion was progressing till at last Mr. Browne shouted to the bewildered cabman above the din of everybody's laughter:

—Do you know Trinity College?

—Yes, sir, said the cabman.

—Well, drive bang up against Trinity College gates, said Mr. Browne, and then we'll tell you where to go. You understand now?

—Yes, sir, said the cabman.

—Make like a bird for Trinity College.

—Right, sir, cried the cabman.

The horse was whipped up and the cab rattled off along the quay amid a chorus of laughter and adieus.

Gabriel had not gone to the door with the others. He was in a dark part of the hall gazing up the staircase. A woman was standing near the top of the first flight, in the shadow also. He could not see her face but he could see the terracotta and salmonpink panels of her skirt which the shadow made appear black and white. It was his wife. She was leaning on the banisters, listening to something. Gabriel was surprised at her stillness and strained his ear to listen also. But he could hear little save the noise of laughter and dispute on the front steps, a few chords struck on the piano, and a few notes of a man's voice singing.

He stood still in the gloom of the hall, trying to catch the air that the voice was singing and gazing up at his wife. There was grace and mystery in her attitude as if she were a symbol of something. He asked himself what is a woman standing on the stairs in the shadow, listening to distant music, a symbol of. If he were a painter he would paint her in that attitude. Her blue felt hat would show off the bronze of her hair against the darkness and the dark panels of her skirt would show off the light ones. *Distant Music* he would call the picture if he were a painter.

The hall-door was closed; and Aunt Kate, Aunt Julia, and Mary Jane came down the hall, still laughing.

—Well, isn't Freddy terrible? said Mary Jane. He's really terrible.

Gabriel said nothing but pointed up the stairs towards where his wife was standing. Now that the hall-door was closed the voice and the piano could be heard more clearly. Gabriel held up his hand for them to be silent. The song seemed to be in the old Irish tonality and the singer seemed uncertain both of his words and of his voice. The voice, made plaintive by distance and by the singer's hoarseness, faintly illuminated the cadence of the air with words expressing grief:

> *O, the rain falls on my heavy locks*
> *And the dew wets my skin,*
> *My babe lies cold . . .*

—O, exclaimed Mary Jane. It's Bartell D'Arcy singing and he wouldn't sing all the night. O, I'll get him to sing a song before he goes.

—O do, Mary Jane, said Aunt Kate.

Mary Jane brushed past the others and ran to the staircase but before she reached it the singing stopped and the piano was closed abruptly.

—O, what a pity! she cried. Is he coming down, Gretta?

Gabriel heard his wife answer yes and saw her come down towards them. A few steps behind her were Mr. Bartell D'Arcy and Miss O'Callaghan.

—O, Mr. D'Arcy, cried Mary Jane, it's downright mean of you to break off like that when we were all in raptures listening to you.

—I have been at him all the evening, said Miss O'Callaghan, and Mrs. Conroy too and he told us he had a dreadful cold and couldn't sing.

—O, Mr. D'Arcy, said Aunt Kate, now that was a great fib to tell.

—Can't you see that I'm as hoarse as a crow? said Mr. D'Arcy roughly.

He went into the pantry hastily and put on his overcoat. The others, taken aback by his rude speech, could find nothing to say. Aunt Kate wrinkled her brows and made signs to the others to drop the subject. Mr. D'Arcy stood swathing his neck carefully and frowning.

—It's the weather, said Aunt Julia, after a pause.

—Yes, everybody has colds, said Aunt Kate readily, everybody.

—They say, said Mary Jane, we haven't had snow like it for thirty years; and I read this morning in the newspapers that the snow is generally all over Ireland.

—I love the look of snow, said Aunt Julia sadly.

—So do I, said Miss O'Callaghan. I think Christmas is never really Christmas unless we have the snow on the ground.

—But poor Mr. D'Arcy doesn't like the snow, said Aunt Kate, smiling.

Mr. D'Arcy came from the pantry, fully swathed and buttoned, and in a repentant tone told them the history of his cold. Everyone gave him advice and said it was a great pity and urged him to be very careful of his throat in the night air. Gabriel watched his wife who did not join in the conversation. She was standing right under the dusty fanlight and the flame of the gas lit up the rich bronze of her hair which he had seen her drying at the fire a few days before. She was in the same attitude and seemed unaware of the talk about her. At last she turned towards them and Gabriel saw that there was colour on her cheeks and that her eyes were shining. A sudden tide of joy went leaping out of his heart.

—Mr. D'Arcy, she said, what is the name of that song you were singing?

—It's called *The Lass of Aughrim,* said Mr. D'Arcy, but I couldn't remember it properly. Why? Do you know it?

—*The Lass of Aughrim,* she repeated. I couldn't think of the name.

—It's a very nice air, said Mary Jane. I'm sorry you were not in voice to-night.

—Now, Mary Jane, said Aunt Kate, don't annoy Mr. D'Arcy. I won't have him annoyed.

Seeing that all were ready to start she shepherded them to the door where good-night was said:

—Well, good-night, Aunt Kate, and thanks for the pleasant evening.

—Good-night, Gabriel. Good-night, Gretta!

—Good-night, Aunt Kate, and thanks ever so much. Good-night, Aunt Julia.

—O, good-night, Gretta, I didn't see you.

—Good-night, Mr. D'Arcy. Good-night, Miss O'Callaghan.

—Good-night, Miss Morkan.

—Good-night, again.

—Good-night, all. Safe home.

—Good-night. Good-night.

The morning was still dark. A dull yellow light brooded over the houses and the river; and the sky seemed to be descending. It was slushy underfoot; and only streaks and patches of snow lay on the roofs, on the parapets of the quay, and on the area railings. The lamps were still burning redly in the murky air and, across the river, the palace of the Four Courts stood out menacingly against the heavy sky.

She was walking on before him with Mr. Bartell D'Arcy, her shoes in a brown parcel tucked under one arm and her hands holding her skirt up from the slush. She had no longer any grace of attitude but Gabriel's eyes were still bright with happiness. The blood went bounding along his veins; and the thoughts went rioting through his brain, proud, joyful, tender, valorous.

She was walking on before him so lightly and so erect that he longed to run after her noiselessly, catch her by the shoulders, and say something foolish and affectionate into her ear. She seemed to him so frail that he longed to defend her against something and then to be alone with her. Moments of their secret life together burst like stars upon his memory. A heliotrope envelope was lying beside his breakfast-cup and he was caressing it with his hand. Birds were twittering in the ivy and the sunny web of the curtain was shimmering along the floor: he could not eat for happiness. They were standing on the crowded platform and he was placing a ticket inside the warm palm of her glove. He was standing with her in the cold, looking in through a grated window at a man making bottles in a roaring furnace. It was very cold. Her face, fragrant in the cold air, was quite close to his; and suddenly she called out to the man at the furnace:

—Is the fire hot, sir?

But the man could not hear her with the noise of the furnace. It was just as well. He might have answered rudely.

A wave of yet more tender joy escaped from his heart and went coursing in warm flood along his arteries. Like the tender fires of stars moments of their life together, that no one knew of or would ever know of, broke upon and illumined his memory. He longed to recall to her those moments, to make her forget the years of their dull existence together and remember only their moments of ecstasy. For the years, he felt, had not quenched his soul or hers. Their children, his writing, her household chores had not quenched all their souls' tender fire. In one letter that he had written to her then he had said: *Why is it that words like these seem to me so dull and cold? Is it because there is no word tender enough to be your name?*

Like distant music these words that he had written years before were borne towards him from the past. He longed to be alone with her. When the others had gone away, when he and she were in their room in the hotel, then they would be alone together. He would call her softly:

—Gretta!

Perhaps she would not hear at once: she would be undressing. Then something in his voice would strike her. She would turn and look at him. . . .

At the corner of Winetavern Street they met a cab. He was glad of its rattling noise as it saved him from conversation. She was looking out of the window and seemed tired. The others spoke only a few words, pointing out some building or street. The horse galloped along wearily under the murky morning sky, dragging his old rattling box after his heels, and Gabriel was again in a cab with her, galloping to catch the boat, galloping to their honeymoon.

As the cab drove across O'Connell Bridge Miss O'Callaghan said:

—They say you never cross O'Connell Bridge without seeing a white horse.

—I see a white man this time, said Gabriel.

—Where? asked Mr. Bartell D'Arcy.

Gabriel pointed to the statue, on which lay patches of snow. Then he nodded familiarly to it and waved his hand.

—Good-night, Dan, he said gaily.

When the cab drew up before the hotel Gabriel jumped out and, in spite of Mr. Bartell D'Arcy's protest, paid the driver. He gave the man a shilling over his fare. The man saluted and said:

—A prosperous New Year to you, sir.

—The same to you, said Gabriel cordially.

She leaned for a moment on his arm in getting out of the cab and while standing at the curbstone, bidding the others good-night. She leaned lightly on his arm, as lightly as when she had danced with him a few hours before. He had felt proud and happy then, happy that she was his, proud of her grace and wifely carriage. But now, after the kindling again of so many memories, the first touch of her body, musical and strange and perfumed, sent through him a keen pang of lust. Under cover of her silence he pressed her arm closely to his side; and, as they stood at the hotel door, he felt that they had escaped from their lives and duties, escaped from home and friends and run away together with wild and radiant hearts to a new adventure.

An old man was dozing in a great hooded chair in the hall. He lit a candle in the office and went before them to the stairs. They followed him in silence, their feet falling in soft thuds on the thickly carpeted stairs. She mounted the stairs behind the porter, her head bowed in the ascent, her frail shoulders curved as with a burden, her skirt girt tightly about her. He could have flung his arms about her hips and held her still for his arms were trembling with desire to seize her and only the stress of his nails against the palms of his hands held the wild impulse of his body in check. The porter halted on the stairs to settle his guttering candle. They halted too on the steps below him. In the silence Gabriel could hear the falling of the molten wax into the tray and the thumping of his own heart against his ribs.

The porter led them along a corridor and opened a door. Then he set his unstable candle down on a toilet-table and asked at what hour they were to be called in the morning.

—Eight, said Gabriel.

The porter pointed to the tap of the electric-light and began a muttered apology but Gabriel cut him short.

—We don't want any light. We have light enough from the street. And I say, he added, pointing to the candle, you might remove that handsome article, like a good man.

The porter took up his candle again, but slowly for he was surprised by such a novel idea. Then he mumbled good-night and went out. Gabriel shot the lock to.

A ghostly light from the street lamp lay in a long shaft from one window to the door. Gabriel threw his overcoat and hat on a couch and crossed the room towards the window. He looked down into the street in order that his emotion might calm a little. Then he turned and leaned against a chest of drawers with his back to the light. She had taken off her hat and cloak and was standing before a large swinging mirror, unhooking her waist. Gabriel paused for a few moments, watching her, and then said:

—Gretta!

She turned as well as from the mirror slowly and walked along the shaft of light towards him. Her face looked so serious and weary that the words would not pass Gabriel's lips. No, it was not the moment yet.

—You looked tired, he said.

—I am a little, she answered.

—You don't feel ill or weak?

—No, tired: that's all.

She went on to the window and stood there, looking out. Gabriel waited again and then, fearing that diffidence was about to conquer him, he said abruptly:

—By the way, Gretta!

—What is it?

—You know that poor fellow Malins? he said quickly.

—Yes. What about him?

—Well, poor fellow, he's a decent sort of chap after all, continued Gabriel in a false voice. He gave me back that sovereign I lent him and I didn't expect it really. It's a pity he wouldn't keep away from that Browne, because he's not a bad fellow at heart.

He was trembling now with annoyance. Why did she seem so abstracted? He did not know how he could begin. Was she annoyed, too, about something? If she would only turn to him or come to him or her own accord! To take her as she was would be brutal. No, he must see some ardour in her eyes first. He longed to be master of her strange mood.

—When did you lend him the pound? she asked, after a pause.

Gabriel strove to restrain himself from breaking out into brutal language about the sottish Malins and his pound. He longed to cry to her from his soul, to crush her body against his, to overmaster her. But he said:

—O, at Christmas, when he opened that little Christmas-card shop in Henry Street.

He was in such a fever of rage and desire that he did not hear her come from the window. She stood before him for an instant, looking at him strangely. Then, suddenly raising herself on tiptoe and resting her hands lightly on his shoulders, she kissed him.

—You are a very generous person, Gabriel, she said.

Gabriel, trembling with delight at her sudden kiss and at the quaintness of her phrase, put his hands on her hair and began smoothing it back, scarcely touching it with his fingers. The washing had made it fine, and brilliant. His heart was brimming over with happiness. Just when he was wishing for it she had come to him of her own accord. Perhaps her thoughts had been running with his. Perhaps she had felt the impetuous desire that was in him and then the yielding mood had come upon her. Now that she had fallen to him so easily he wondered why he had been so diffident.

He stood, holding her head between his hands. Then, slipping one arm swiftly about her body and drawing her towards him, he said softly:

—Gretta, dear, what are you thinking about?

She did not answer nor yield wholly to his arm. He said again, softly.

—Tell me what it is, Gretta. I think I know what is the matter. Do I know?

She did not answer at once. Then she said in an outburst of tears:

—O, I am thinking about that song, *The Lass of Aughrim.*

She broke loose from him and ran to the bed and, throwing her arms across the bed-rail, hid her face. Gabriel stood stock-still for a moment in astonishment and then followed her. As he passed in the way of the cheval-glass he caught sight of himself in full length, his broad, well-filled shirt-front, the face whose expression always puzzled him when he saw it in a mirror and his glimmering gilt-rimmed eyeglasses. He halted a few paces from her and said:

—What about the song? Why does that make you cry?

She raised her head from her arms and dried her eyes with the back of her hand like a child. A kinder note than he had intended went into his voice.

—Why, Gretta? he asked.

—I am thinking about a person long ago who used to sing that song.

—And who was the person long ago? asked Gabriel, smiling.

—It was a person I used to know in Galway when I was living with my grandmother, she said.

The smile passed away from Gabriel's face. A dull anger began to gather again at the back of his mind and the dull fires of his lust began to glow angrily in his veins.

—Someone you were in love with? he asked ironically.

—It was a young boy I used to know, she answered, named Michael Furey. He used to sing that song, *The Lass of Aughrim*. He was very delicate.

Gabriel was silent. He did not wish her to think that he was interested in this delicate boy.

—I can see him so plainly, she said after a moment. Such eyes as he had: big dark eyes! And such an expression in them—an expression! ·

—O then, you were in love with him? said Gabriel.

—I used to go out walking with him, she said, when I was in Galway.

A thought flew across Gabriel's mind.

—Perhaps that was why you wanted to go to Galway with that Ivors girl? he said coldly.

She looked at him and asked in surprise:

—What for?

Her eyes made Gabriel feel awkward. He shrugged his shoulders and said:

—How do I know? To see him perhaps.

She looked away from him along the shaft of light towards the window in silence.

—He is dead, she said at length. He died when he was only seventeen. Isn't it a terrible thing to die so young as that?

—What was he? asked Gabriel, still ironically.

—He was in the gasworks, she said.

Gabriel felt humiliated by the failure of this irony and by the evocation of this figure from the dead, a boy in the gasworks. While he had been full of memories of their secret life together, full of tenderness and joy and desire, she had been comparing him in her mind with another. A shameful consciousness of his own person assailed him. He saw himself as a ludicrous figure, acting as a pennyboy for his aunts, a nervous well-meaning sentimentalist, orating to vulgarians and idealising his own clownish lusts, the pitiable fatuous fellow he had caught a glimpse of in the mirror. Instinctively he turned his back more to the light lest she might see the shame that burned upon his forehead.

He tried to keep up his tone of cold interrogation but his voice when he spoke was humble and indifferent.

—I suppose you were in love with this Michael Furey, Gretta, he said.

—I was great with him at that time, she said.

Her voice was veiled and sad. Gabriel, feeling now how vain it would be to try to lead her whither he had purposed, caressed one of her hands and said, also sadly:

—And what did he die of so young, Gretta? Consumption, was it?

—I think he died for me, she answered.

A vague terror seized Gabriel at this answer as if, at that hour when he had hoped to triumph, some impalpable and vindictive being was coming against him, gathering forces against him in its vague world. But he shook himself free of it with an effort of reason and continued to caress her hand. He did not question her again for he felt that she would tell him of herself. Her hand was warm and moist: it did not respond to his touch but he continued to caress it just as he had caressed her first letter to him that spring morning.

—It was in the winter, she said, about the beginning of the winter when I was going to leave my grandmother's and come up here to the convent. And he was ill at the time in his lodgings in Galway and wouldn't be let out and his people in Oughterard were written to. He was in decline, they said, or something like that. I never knew rightly.

She paused for a moment and sighed.

—Poor fellow, she said. He was very fond of me and he was such a gentle boy. We used to go out together, walking, you know, Gabriel, like the way they do in the country. He was going to study singing only for his health. He had a very good voice, poor Michael Furey.

—Well; and then? asked Gabriel.

—And then when it came to the time for me to leave Galway and come up to the convent he was much worse and I wouldn't be let see him so I wrote a letter saying I was going up to Dublin and would be back in the summer and hoping he would be better then.

She paused for a moment to get her voice under control and then went on:

—Then the night before I left I was in my grandmother's house in Nuns' Island, packing up, and I heard gravel thrown up against the window. The window was so wet I couldn't see so I ran downstairs as I was and slipped out the back into the garden and there was the poor fellow at the end of the garden, shivering.

—And did you not tell him to go back? asked Gabriel.

—I implored of him to go home at once and told him he would get his death in the rain. But he said he did not want to live. I can see his eyes as well as well! He was standing at the end of the wall where there was a tree.

—And did he go home? asked Gabriel.

—Yes, he went home. And when I was only a week in the convent he died and he was buried in Oughterard where his people came from. O, the day I heard that, that he was dead!

She stopped, choking with sobs, and, overcome by emotion, flung herself downward on the bed, sobbing in the quilt. Gabriel held her hand for a moment longer, irresolutely, and then, shy of intruding on her grief, let it fall gently and walked quietly to the window.

She was fast asleep.

Gabriel, leaning on his elbow, looked for a few moments un-resentfully on her tangled hair and half-open mouth, listening to her deep-drawn breath. So she had had that romance in her life: a man had died for her sake. It hardly pained him now to think how poor a part he, her husband, had played in her life. He watched her while she slept as though he and she had never lived together as man and wife. His curious eyes rested long upon her face and on her hair: and, as he thought of what she must have been then, in that time of her first girlish beauty, a strange friendly pity for her entered his soul. He did not like to say even to himself that her face was no longer beautiful but he knew that it was no longer the face for which Michael Furey had braved death.

Perhaps she had not told him all the story. His eyes moved to the chair over which she had thrown some of her clothes. A petticoat string dangled to the floor. One boot stood upright, its limp upper fallen down: the fellow of it lay upon its side. He wondered at his riot of emotions of an hour before. From what had it proceeded? From his aunt's supper, from his own foolish speech, from the wine and dancing, the merry-making when saying good-night in the hall, the pleasure of the walk along the river in the snow. Poor Aunt Julia! She, too, would soon be a shade with the shade of Patrick Morkan and his horse. He caught that haggard look upon her face for a moment when she was singing *Arrayed for the Bridal.* Soon, perhaps, he would be sitting in that same drawing-room, dressed in black, his silk hat on his knees. The blinds would be drawn down and Aunt Kate would be sitting beside him, crying and blowing her nose and telling him how Julia had died. He would cast about in his mind for some words that might console her, and would find only lame and useless ones. Yes, yes: that would happen very soon.

The air of the room chilled his shoulders. He stretched himself cautiously along under the sheets and lay down beside his wife. One by one they were all becoming shades. Better pass boldly into that other world, in the full glory of some passion, than fade and wither dismally with age. He thought of how she who lay beside him had locked in her heart for so many years that image of her lover's eyes when he had told her that he did not wish to live.

Generous tears filled Gabriel's eyes. He had never felt like that himself towards any woman but he knew that such a feeling must be love. The tears gathered more thickly in his eyes and in the partial darkness he imagined he saw the form of a young man standing under a dripping tree. Other forms were near. His soul had approached that region where dwell the vast hosts of the dead. He was conscious of, but could not apprehend, their wayward and flickering existence. His own identity was fading out into a grey impalpable world: the solid world itself which these dead had one time reared and lived in was dissolving and dwindling.

A few light taps upon the pane made him turn to the window. It had begun to snow again. He watched sleepily the flakes, silver and dark, falling obliquely against the lamplight. The time had come for him to set out on his journey westward. Yes, the newspapers were right: snow was general all over Ireland. It was falling on every part of the dark central plain, on the treeless hills, falling softly upon the Bog of Allen and, farther westward, softly falling into the dark mutinous Shannon waves. It was falling, too, upon every part of the lonely churchyard on the hill where Michael Furey lay buried. It lay thickly drifted on the crooked crosses and headstones, on the spears of the little gate, on the barren thorns. His soul swooned slowly as he heard the snow falling faintly through the universe and faintly falling, like the descent of their last end, upon all the living and the dead.

1916

DORIS LESSING

To Room Nineteen

This is a story, I suppose, about a failure in intelligence: the Rawlings' marriage was grounded in intelligence.

They were older when they married than most of their married friends: in their well-seasoned late twenties. Both had had a number of affairs, sweet rather than bitter; and when they fell in love—for they did fall in love—had known each other for some time. They joked that they had saved each other "for the real thing." That they had waited so long (but not too long) for this real thing was to them a proof of their sensible discrimination. A good many of their friends had married young, and now (they felt) probably regretted lost opportunities; while others, still unmarried, seemed to them arid, self-doubting, and likely to make desperate or romantic marriages.

Not only they, but others, felt they were well-matched: their friends' delight was an additional proof of their happiness. They had played the same roles, male and female, in this group or set, if such a wide, loosely connected, constantly changing constellation of people could be called a set. They had both become, by virtue of their moderation, their humour, and their abstinence from painful experience, people to whom others came for advice. They could be, and were, relied on. It was one of those cases of a man and a woman linking themselves whom no one else had ever thought of linking, probably because of their similarities. But then everyone exclaimed: Of course! How right! How was it we never thought of it before!

And so they married amid general rejoicing, and because of their

Doris Lessing, one of England's most celebrated contemporary novelists, did not actually live in the British Isles until she was thirty. Born on October 22, 1919, in Kermanshah, Persia (now Iran), she spent much of her childhood and early adult life in the farmlands of Southern Rhodesia (today Zimbabwe). It was in these colonial spaces—and her shock, upon her first visit to England, at the conditions of this imperial center—that this high-school dropout's still evolving commitments to socialism, feminism, and racial equality first took shape. Since her first novel, The Grass Is Singing (1950), Lessing has published entire series of political novels (Children of Violence) and of mystically inspired science fiction (Canopus in Argos: Archives) as well as the highly acclaimed study of sexual and artistic exploration The Golden Notebook (1962). She lives in London.

foresight and their sense for what was probable, nothing was a surprise to them.

Both had well-paid jobs. Matthew was a subeditor on a large London newspaper, and Susan worked in an advertising firm. He was not the stuff of which editors or publicised journalists were made, but he was much more than "a subeditor," being one of the essential background people who in fact steady, inspire, and make possible the people in the limelight. He was content with this position. Susan had a talent for commercial drawing. She was humorous about the advertisements she was responsible for, but she did not feel strongly about them one way or the other.

Both, before they married, had had pleasant flats, but they felt it unwise to base a marriage on either flat, because it might seem like a submission of personality on the part of the one whose flat it was not. They moved into a new flat in South Kensington on the clear understanding that when their marriage had settled down (a process they knew would not take long, and was in fact more a humorous concession to popular wisdom than what was due to themselves) they would buy a house and start a family.

And this is what happened. They lived in their charming flat for two years, giving parties and going to them, being a popular young married couple, and then Susan became pregnant, she gave up her job, and they bought a house in Richmond. It was typical of this couple that they had a son first, then a daughter, then twins, son and daughter. Everything right, appropriate, and what everyone would wish for, if they could choose. But people did feel these two had chosen; this balanced and sensible family was no more than what was due to them because of their infallible sense for *choosing* right.

And so they lived with their four children in their gardened house in Richmond and were happy. They had everything they had wanted and had planned for.

And yet . . .

Well, even this was expected, that there must be a certain flatness. . . .

Yes, yes, of course, it was natural they sometimes felt like this. Like what?

Their life seemed to be like a snake biting its tail. Matthew's job for the sake of Susan, children, house, and garden—which caravanserai needed a well-paid job to maintain it. And Susan's practical intelligence for the sake of Matthew, the children, the house, and the garden— which unit would have collapsed in a week without her.

But there was no point about which either could say: "For the sake of *this* is all the rest." Children? But children can't be a centre of life and a reason for being. They can be a thousand things that are delightful, interesting, satisfying, but they can't be a wellspring to live from. Or they shouldn't be. Susan and Matthew knew that well enough.

Matthew's job? Ridiculous. It was an interesting job, but scarcely a reason for living. Matthew took pride in doing it well, but he could hardly be expected to be proud of the newspaper; the newspaper he read, *his* newspaper, was not the one he worked for.

Their love for each other? Well, that was nearest it. If this wasn't a centre, what was? Yes, it was around this point, their love, that the whole extraordinary structure revolved. For extraordinary it certainly was. Both Susan and Matthew had moments of thinking so, of looking in secret disbelief at this thing they had created: marriage, four children, big house, garden, charwomen, friends, cars . . . and this *thing*, this entity, all of it had come into existence, been blown into being out of nowhere, because Susan loved Matthew and Matthew loved Susan. Extraordinary. So that was the central point, the wellspring.

And if one felt that it simply was not strong enough, important enough, to support it all, well whose fault was that? Certainly neither Susan's nor Matthew's. It was in the nature of things. And they sensibly blamed neither themselves nor each other.

On the contrary, they used their intelligence to preserve what they had created from a painful and explosive world: they looked around them, and took lessons. All around them, marriages collapsing, or breaking, or rubbing along (even worse, they felt). They must not make the same mistakes, they must not.

They had avoided the pitfall so many of their friends had fallen into —of buying a house in the country *for the sake of the children,* so that the husband became a weekend husband, a weekend father, and the wife always careful not to ask what went on in the town flat which they called (in joke) a bachelor flat. No, Matthew was a full-time husband, a full-time father, and at night, in the big married bed in the big married bedroom (which had an attractive view of the river), they lay beside each other talking and he told her about his day, and what he had done, and whom he had met; and she told him about her day (not as interesting, but that was not her fault), for both knew of the hidden resentments and deprivations of the woman who has lived her life—and above all, has earned her own living—and is now dependent on a husband for outside interests and money.

Nor did Susan make the mistake of taking a job for the sake of her independence, which she might very well have done, since her old firm, missing her qualities of humour, balance, and sense, invited her often to go back. Children needed their mother to a certain age, that both parents knew and agreed on; and when these four healthy wisely brought up children were of the right age, Susan would work again, because she knew, and so did he, what happened to women of fifty at the height of their energy and ability, with grownup children who no longer needed their full devotion.

So here was this couple, testing their marriage, looking after it, treating it like a small boat full of helpless people in a very stormy sea. Well, of course, so it was. . . . The storms of the world were bad, but not too close—which is not to say they were selfishly felt: Susan and Matthew were both well-informed and responsible people. And the inner storms and quicksands were understood and charted. So everything was all right. Everything was in order. Yes, things were under control.

So what did it matter if they felt dry, flat? People like themselves, fed on a hundred books (psychological, anthropological, sociological), could scarcely be unprepared for the dry, controlled wistfulness which is the distinguishing mark of the intelligent marriage. Two people, endowed with education, with discrimination, with judgement, linked together voluntarily from their will to be happy together and to be of use to others—one sees them everywhere, one knows them, one even is that thing oneself: sadness because so much is after all so little. These two, unsurprised, turned towards each other with even more courtesy and gentle love: this was life, that two people, no matter how carefully chosen, could not be everything to each other. In fact, even to say so, to think in such a way, was banal; they were ashamed to do it.

It was banal, too, when one night Matthew came home late and confessed he had been to a party, taken a girl home, and slept with her. Susan forgave him, of course. Except that forgiveness is hardly the word. Understanding, yes. But if you understand something, you don't forgive it, you are the thing itself: forgiveness is for what you *don't* understand. Nor had he *confessed*—what sort of word is that?

The whole thing was not important. After all, years ago they had joked: Of course I'm not going to be faithful to you, no one can be faithful to one other person for a whole lifetime. (And there was the word "faithful"—stupid, all these words, stupid, belonging to a savage old world.) But the incident left both of them irritable. Strange, but they were both bad-tempered, annoyed. There was something unassimilable about it.

Making love splendidly after he had come home that night, both had felt that the idea that Myra Jenkins, a pretty girl met at a party, could be even relevant was ridiculous. They had loved each other for over a decade, would love each other for years more. Who, then, was Myra Jenkins?

Except, thought Susan, unaccountably bad-tempered, she was (is?) the first. In ten years. So either the ten years' fidelity was not important, or she isn't. (No, no, there is something wrong with this way of thinking, there must be.) But if she isn't important, presumably it wasn't important either when Matthew and I first went to bed with each other that afternoon whose delight even now (like a very long shadow at sundown) lays a long, wandlike finger over us. (Why did I say sundown?) Well, if what we felt that afternoon was not important, nothing is important, because if it hadn't been for what we felt, we wouldn't be Mr. and Mrs. Rawlings with four children, et cetera, et cetera. The whole thing is absurd—for him to have come home and told me was absurd. For him not to have told me was absurd. For me to care or, for that matter, not to care, is absurd . . . and who is Myra Jenkins? Why, no one at all.

There was only one thing to do, and of course these sensible people did it; they put the thing behind them, and consciously, knowing what they were doing, moved forward into a different phase of their marriage, giving thanks for past good fortune as they did so.

For it was inevitable that the handsome, blond, attractive, manly man, Matthew Rawlings, should be at times tempted (oh, what a word!) by the attractive girls at parties she could not attend because of the four children; and that sometimes he would succumb (a word even more repulsive, if possible) and that she, a goodlooking woman in the big well-tended garden at Richmond, would sometimes be pierced as by an arrow from the sky with bitterness. Except that bitterness was not in order, it was out of court. Did the casual girls touch the marriage? They did not. Rather it was they who knew defeat because of the handsome Matthew Rawlings' marriage body and soul to Susan Rawlings.

In that case why did Susan feel (though luckily not for longer than a few seconds at a time) as if life had become a desert, and that nothing mattered, and that her children were not her own?

Meanwhile her intelligence continued to assert that all was well. What if her Matthew did have an occasional sweet afternoon, the odd affair? For she knew quite well, except in her moments of aridity, that they were very happy, that the affairs were not important.

Perhaps that was the trouble? It was in the nature of things that the adventures and delights could no longer be hers, because of the four children and the big house that needed so much attention. But perhaps she was secretly wishing, and even knowing that she did, that the wildness and the beauty could be his. But he was married to her. She was married to him. They were married inextricably. And therefore the gods could not strike him with the real magic, not really. Well, was it Susan's fault that after he came home from an adventure he looked harassed rather than fulfilled? (In fact, that was how she knew he had been unfaithful, because of his sullen air, and his glances at her, similar to hers at him: What is it that I share with this person that shields all delight from me?) But none of it by anybody's fault. (But what did they feel ought to be somebody's fault?) Nobody's fault, nothing to be at fault, no one to blame, no one to offer or to take it . . . and nothing wrong, either, except that Matthew never was really struck, as he wanted to be, by joy; and that Susan was more and more often threatened by emptiness. (It was usually in the garden that she was invaded by this feeling: she was coming to avoid the garden, unless the children or Matthew were with her.) There was no need to use the dramatic words "unfaithful," "forgive," and the rest: intelligence forbade them. Intelligence barred, too, quarrelling, sulking, anger, silences of withdrawal, accusations, and tears. Above all, intelligence forbids tears.

A high price has to be paid for the happy marriage with the four healthy children in the large white gardened house.

And they were paying it, willingly, knowing what they were doing. When they lay side by side or breast to breast in the big civilised bedroom overlooking the wild sullied river, they laughed, often, for no particular reason; but they knew it was really because of these two small people, Susan and Matthew, supporting such an edifice on their intelligent love. The laugh comforted them; it saved them both, though from what, they did not know.

They were now both fortyish. The older children, boy and girl, were ten and eight, at school. The twins, six, were still at home. Susan did not have nurses or girls to help her: childhood is short; and she did not regret the hard work. Often enough she was bored, since small children can be boring; she was often very tired; but she regretted nothing. In another decade, she would turn herself back into being a woman with a life of her own.

Soon the twins would go to school, and they would be away from home from nine until four. These hours, so Susan saw it, would be the preparation for her own slow emancipation away from the role of hub-of-the-family into woman-with-her-own-life. She was already planning for the hours of freedom when all the children would be "off her hands." That was the phrase used by Matthew and by Susan and by their friends, for the moment when the youngest child went off to school. "They'll be off your hands, darling Susan, and you'll have time to yourself." So said Matthew, the intelligent husband, who had often enough commended and consoled Susan, standing by her in spirit during the years when her soul was not her own, as she said, but her children's.

What it amounted to was that Susan saw herself as she had been at twenty-eight, unmarried; and then again somewhere about fifty, blossoming from the root of what she had been twenty years before. As if the essential Susan were in abeyance, as if she were in cold storage. Matthew said something like this to Susan one night: and she agreed that it was true—she did feel something like that. What, then, was this essential Susan? She did not know. Put like that it sounded ridiculous, and she did not really feel it. Anyway, they had a long discussion about the whole thing before going off to sleep in each other's arms.

So the twins went off to their school, two bright affectionate children who had no problems about it, since their older brother and sister had trodden this path so successfully before them. And now Susan was going to be alone in the big house, every day of the school term, except for the daily woman who came in to clean.

It was now, for the first time in this marriage, that something happened which neither of them had foreseen.

This is what happened. She returned, at nine-thirty, from taking the twins to the school by car, looking forward to seven blissful hours of freedom. On the first morning she was simply restless, worrying about the twins "naturally enough" since this was their first day away at school. She was hardly able to contain herself until they came back. Which they did happily, excited by the world of school, looking forward to the next day. And the next day Susan took them, dropped them, came back, and found herself reluctant to enter her big and beautiful home because it was as if something was waiting for her there that she did not wish to confront. Sensibly, however, she parked the car in the garage, entered the house, spoke to Mrs. Parkes, the daily woman, about her duties, and went up to her bedroom. She was possessed by a fever which drove her out again, downstairs, into the kitchen, where Mrs. Parkes was making cake and did not need her, and into the garden. There she sat on a bench and tried to calm herself looking at trees, at a brown glimpse of the river. But she was filled with tension, like a panic: as if an enemy was in the garden with her. She spoke to herself severely, thus: All this is quite natural. First, I spent twelve years of my adult life working, *living my own life*. Then I married, and from the moment I became pregnant for the first time I signed myself over, so to speak, to other people. To the children. Not for one moment in twelve years have I been alone, had time to myself. So now I have to learn to be myself again. That's all.

And she went indoors to help Mrs. Parkes cook and clean, and found some sewing to do for the children. She kept herself occupied every day. At the end of the first term she understood she felt two contrary emotions: First: secret astonishment and dismay that during those weeks when the house was empty of children she had in fact been more occupied (had been careful to keep herself occupied) than ever she had been when the children were around her needing her continual attention. Second: that now she knew the house would be full of them, and for five weeks, she resented the fact she would never be alone. She was already looking back at those hours of sewing, cooking (but by herself) as at a lost freedom which would not be hers for five long weeks. And the two months of term which would succeed the five weeks stretched alluringly open to her—freedom. But what freedom—when in fact she had been so careful *not* to be free of small duties during the last weeks? She looked at herself, Susan Rawlings, sitting in a big chair by the window in the bedroom, sewing shirts or dresses, which she might just as well have bought. She saw herself making cakes for hours at a time in the big family kitchen: yet usually she bought cakes. What she saw was a woman alone, that was true, but she had not felt alone. For instance, Mrs. Parkes was always somewhere in the house. And she did not like being in the garden at all, because of the closeness there of the enemy—irritation, restlessness, emptiness, whatever it was —which keeping her hands occupied made less dangerous for some reason.

Susan did not tell Matthew of these thoughts. They were not sensible. She did not recognise herself in them. What should she say to her dear friend and husband, Matthew? "When I go into the garden, that is, if the children are not there, I feel as if there is an enemy there waiting to invade me." "What enemy, Susan darling?" "Well, I don't know, really. . . ." "Perhaps you should see a doctor?"

No, clearly this conversation should not take place. The holidays began and Susan welcomed them. Four children, lively, energetic, intelligent, demanding: she was never, not for a moment of her day, alone. If she was in a room, they would be in the next room, or waiting for her to do something for them; or it would soon be time for lunch or tea, or to take one of them to the dentist. Something to do: five weeks of it, thank goodness.

On the fourth day of these so welcome holidays, she found she was storming with anger at the twins; two shrinking beautiful children who (and this is what checked her) stood hand in hand looking at her with sheer dismayed disbelief. This was their calm mother, shouting at them. And for what? They had come to her with some game, some bit of nonsense. They looked at each other, moved closer for support, and went off hand in hand, leaving Susan holding on to the windowsill of the livingroom, breathing deep, feeling sick. She went to lie down, telling the older children she had a headache. She heard the boy Harry telling the little ones: "It's all right, Mother's got a headache." She heard that *It's all right* with pain.

That night she said to her husband: "Today I shouted at the twins, quite unfairly." She sounded miserable, and he said gently: "Well, what of it?"

"It's more of an adjustment than I thought, their going to school."

"But Susie, Susie darling. . . ." For she was crouched weeping on the bed. He comforted her: "Susan, what is all this about? You shouted at them? What of it? If you shouted at them fifty times a day it wouldn't be more than the little devils deserve." But she wouldn't laugh. She wept. Soon he comforted her with his body. She became calm. Calm, she wondered what was wrong with her, and why she should mind so much that she might, just once, have behaved unjustly with the children. What did it matter? They had forgotten it all long ago: Mother had a headache and everything was all right.

It was a long time later that Susan understood that that night, when she had wept and Matthew had driven the misery out of her with his big solid body, was the last time, ever in their married life, that they had been—to use their mutual language—with each other. And even that was a lie, because she had not told him of her real fears at all.

The five weeks passed, and Susan was in control of herself, and good and kind, and she looked forward to the holidays with a mixture of fear and longing. She did not know what to expect. She took the twins off to school (the elder children took themselves to school) and she returned to the house determined to face the enemy wherever he was, in the house, or the garden or—where?

She was again restless, she was possessed by restlessness. She cooked and sewed and worked as before, day after day, while Mrs. Parkes remonstrated: "Mrs. Rawlings, what's the need for it? I can do that, it's what you pay me for."

And it was so irrational that she checked herself. She would put the car into the garage, go up to her bedroom, and sit, hands in her lap, forcing herself to be quiet. She listened to Mrs. Parkes moving around the house. She looked out into the garden and saw the branches shake the trees. She sat defeating the enemy, restlessness. Emptiness. She ought to be thinking about her life, about herself. But she did not. Or perhaps she could not. As soon as she forced her mind to think about Susan (for what else did she want to be alone for?), it skipped off to thoughts of butter or school clothes. Or it thought of Mrs. Parkes. She realised that she sat listening for the movements of the cleaning woman, following her every turn, bend, thought. She followed her in mind from kitchen to bathroom, from table to oven, and it was as if the duster, the cleaning cloth, the saucepan, were in her own hand. She would hear herself saying: No, not like that, don't put that there. . . . Yet she did not give a damn what Mrs. Parkes did, or if she did it at all. Yet she could not prevent herself from being conscious of her, every minute. Yet, this was what was wrong with her: she needed, when she was alone, to be really alone, with no one near. She could not endure the knowledge that in ten minutes or in half an hour Mrs. Parkes would call up the stairs: "Mrs. Rawlings, there's no silver polish. Madam, we're out of flour."

So she left the house and went to sit in the garden where she was screened from the house by trees. She waited for the demon to appear and claim her, but he did not.

She was keeping him off, because she had not, after all, come to an end of arranging herself.

She was planning how to be somewhere where Mrs. Parkes would not come after her with a cup of tea, or a demand to be allowed to telephone (always irritating, since Susan did not care who she telephoned or how often), or just a nice talk about something. Yes, she needed a place, or a state of affairs, where it would not be necessary to keep reminding herself: In ten minutes I must telephone Matthew about . . . and at half past three I must leave early for the children because the car needs cleaning. And at ten o'clock tomorrow I must remember. . . . She was possessed with resentment that the seven hours of freedom in every day (during weekdays in the school term) were not free, that never, not for one second, ever, was she free from the pressure of time, from having to remember this or that. She could never forget herself; never really let herself go into forgetfulness.

Resentment. It was poisoning her. (She looked at this emotion and thought it was absurd. Yet she felt it.) She was a prisoner. (She looked at this thought too, and it was no good telling herself it was a ridiculous one.) She must tell Matthew—but what? She was filled with emotions that were utterly ridiculous, that she despised, yet that nevertheless she was feeling so strongly she could not shake them off.

The school holidays came round, and this time they were for nearly two months, and she behaved with a conscious controlled decency that nearly drove her crazy. She would lock herself in the bathroom, and sit on the edge of the bath, breathing deep, trying to let go into some kind of calm. Or she went up into the spare room, usually empty, where no one would expect her to be. She heard the children calling, "Mother, Mother," and kept silent, feeling guilty. Or she went to the very end of the garden, by herself, and looked at the slow-moving brown river; she looked at the river and closed her eyes and breathed slow and deep, taking it into her being, into her veins.

Then she returned to the family, wife and mother, smiling and responsible, feeling as if the pressure of these people—four lively children and her husband—were a painful pressure on the surface of her skin, a hand pressing on her brain. She did not once break down into irritation during these holidays, but it was like living out a prison sentence, and when the children went back to school, she sat on a white stone near the flowing river, and she thought: It is not even a year since the twins went to school, since *they were off my hands* (What on earth did I think I meant when I used that stupid phrase?), and yet I'm a different person. I'm simply not myself. I don't understand it.

Yet she had to understand it. For she knew that this structure—big white house, on which the mortgage still cost four hundred a year, a husband, so good and kind and insightful; four children, all doing so nicely; and the garden where she sat; and Mrs. Parkes, the cleaning woman—all this depended on her, and yet she could not understand why, or even what it was she contributed to it.

She said to Matthew in their bedroom: "I think there must be something wrong with me."

And he said: "Surely not, Susan? You look marvellous—you're as lovely as ever."

She looked at the handsome blond man, with his clear, intelligent, blue-eyed face, and thought: Why is it I can't tell him? Why not? And she said: "I need to be alone more than I am."

At which he swung his slow blue gaze at her, and she saw what she had been dreading: Incredulity. Disbelief. And fear. An incredulous blue stare from a stranger who was her husband, as close to her as her own breath.

He said: "But the children are at school and off your hands."

She said to herself: I've got to force myself to say: Yes, but do you realize that I never feel free? There's never a moment when I can say to myself: There's nothing I have to remind myself about, nothing I have to do in half an hour, or an hour, or two hours. . . .

But she said: "I don't feel well."

He said: "Perhaps you need a holiday."

She said, appalled: "But not without you, surely?" For she could not imagine herself going off without him. Yet that was what he meant. Seeing her face, he laughed, and opened his arms, and she went into them, thinking: Yes, yes, but why can't I say it? And what is it I have to say?

She tried to tell him, about never being free. And he listened and said: "But Susan, what sort of freedom can you possibly want—short of being dead! Am I ever free? I go to the office, and I have to be there at ten—all right, half past ten, sometimes. And I have to do this or that, don't I? Then I've got to come home at a certain time—I don't mean it, you know I don't—but if I'm not going to be back home at six I telephone you. When can I ever say to myself: I have nothing to be responsible for in the next six hours?"

Susan, hearing this, was remorseful. Because it was true. The good marriage, the house, the children, depended just as much on his voluntary bondage as it did on hers. But why did he not feel bound? Why didn't he chafe and become restless? No, there was something really wrong with her and this proved it.

And that word "bondage"—why had she used it? She had never felt marriage, or the children, as bondage. Neither had he, or surely they wouldn't be together lying in each other's arms content after twelve years of marriage.

No, her state (whatever it was) was irrelevant, nothing to do with her real good life with her family. She had to accept the fact that, after all, she was an irrational person and to live with it. Some people had to live with crippled arms, or stammers, or being deaf. She would have to live knowing she was subject to a state of mind she could not own.

Nevertheless, as a result of this conversation with her husband, there was a new regime next holidays.

The spare room at the top of the house now had a cardboard sign saying: PRIVATE! DO NOT DISTURB! on it. (This sign had been drawn in coloured chalks by the children, after a discussion between the parents in which it was decided this was psychologically the right thing.) The family and Mrs. Parkes knew this was "Mother's Room" and that she was entitled to her privacy. Many serious conversations took place between Matthew and the children about not taking Mother for granted. Susan overheard the first, between father and Harry, the older boy, and was surprised at her irritation over it. Surely she could have a room somewhere in that big house and retire into it without such a fuss being made? Without it being so solemnly discussed? Why couldn't she simply have announced: "I'm going to fit out the little top room for myself, and when I'm in it I'm not to be disturbed for anything short of fire"? Just that, and finished; instead of long earnest discussions. When she heard Harry and Matthew explaining it to the twins with Mrs. Parkes coming in—"Yes, well, a family sometimes gets on top of a woman"—

she had to go right away to the bottom of the garden until the devils of exasperation had finished their dance in her blood.

But now there was a room, and she could go there when she liked, she used it seldom: she felt even more caged there than in her bedroom. One day she had gone up there after a lunch for ten children she had cooked and served because Mrs. Parkes was not there, and had sat alone for a while looking into the garden. She saw the children stream out from the kitchen and stand looking up at the window where she sat behind the curtains. They were all—her children and their friends— discussing Mother's Room. A few minutes later, the chase of children in some game came pounding up the stairs, but ended as abruptly as if they had fallen over a ravine, so sudden was the silence. They had remembered she was there, and had gone silent in a great gale of "Hush! Shhhhhh! Quiet, you'll disturb her. . . ." And they went tiptoeing downstairs like criminal conspirators. When she came down to make tea for them, they all apologised. The twins put their arms around her, from front to back, making a human cage of loving limbs, and promised it would never occur again. "We forgot, Mummy, we forgot all about it!"

What it amounted to was that Mother's Room, and her need for privacy, had become a valuable lesson in respect for other people's rights. Quite soon Susan was going up to the room only because it was a lesson it was a pity to drop. Then she took sewing up there, and the children and Mrs. Parkes came in and out: it had become another family room.

She sighed, and smiled, and resigned herself—she made jokes at her own expense with Matthew over the room. That is, she did from the self she liked, she respected. But at the same time, something inside her howled with impatience, with rage. . . . And she was frightened. One day she found herself kneeling by her bed and praying: "Dear God, keep it away from me, keep him away from me." She meant the devil, for she now thought of it, not caring if she was irrational, as some sort of demon. She imagined him, or it, as a youngish man, or perhaps a middleaged man pretending to be young. Or a man young-looking from immaturity? At any rate, she saw the young-looking face which, when she drew closer, had dry lines about mouth and eyes. He was thinnish, meagre in build. And he had a reddish complexion, and ginger hair. That was he—a gingery, energetic man, and he wore a reddish hairy jacket, unpleasant to the touch.

Well, one day she saw him. She was standing at the bottom of the garden, watching the river ebb past, when she raised her eyes and saw this person, or being, sitting on the white stone bench. He was looking at her, and grinning. In his hand was a long crooked stick, which he had picked off the ground, or broken off the tree above him. He was absent-mindedly, out of an absent-minded or freakish impulse of spite, using the stick to stir around in the coils of a blindworm or a grass snake (or some kind of snakelike creature: it was whitish and unhealthy to look at, unpleasant). The snake was twisting about, flinging its coils from side to side in a kind of dance of protest against the teasing prodding stick.

Susan looked at him, thinking: Who is the stranger? What is he doing in our garden? Then she recognised the man around whom her terrors had crystallised. As she did so, he vanished. She made herself walk over to the bench. A shadow from a branch lay across thin emerald grass, moving jerkily over its roughness, and she could see why she had taken it for a snake, lashing and twisting. She went back to the house thinking: Right, then, so I've seen him with my own eyes, so I'm not crazy after all—there *is* a danger because I've seen him. He is lurking in the garden and sometimes even in the house, and he wants to *get into me and take me over.*

She dreamed of having a room or a place, anywhere, where she could go and sit, by herself, no one knowing where she was.

Once, near Victoria, she found herself outside a news agent that had Rooms to Let advertised. She decided to rent a room, telling no one. Sometimes she could take the train in to Richmond and sit alone in it for an hour or two. Yet how could she? A room would cost three or four pounds a week, and she earned no money, and how could she explain to Matthew that she needed such a sum? What for? It did not occur to her that she was taking it for granted she wasn't going to tell him about the room.

Well, it was out of the question, having a room; yet she knew she must.

One day, when a school term was well established, and none of the children had measles or other ailments, and everything seemed in order, she did the shopping early, explained to Mrs. Parkes she was meeting an old school friend, took the train to Victoria, searched until she found a small quiet hotel, and asked for a room for the day. They did not let rooms by the day, the manageress said, looking doubtful, since Susan so obviously was not the kind of woman who needed a room for unrespectable reasons. Susan made a long explanation about not being well, being unable to shop without frequent rests for lying down. At last she was allowed to rent the room provided she paid a full night's price for it. She was taken up by the manageress and a maid, both concerned over the state of her health . . . which must be pretty bad if, living in Richmond (she had signed her name and address in the register), she needed a shelter at Victoria.

The room was ordinary and anonymous, and was just what Susan needed. She put a shilling in the gas fire, and sat, eyes shut, in a dingy armchair with her back to a dingy window. She was alone. She was alone. She was alone. She could feel pressures lifting off her. First the sounds of traffic came very loud; then they seemed to vanish; she might even have slept a little. A knock on the door: it was Miss Townsend, the manageress, bringing her a cup of tea with her own hands, so concerned was she over Susan's long silence and possible illness.

Miss Townsend was a lonely woman of fifty, running this hotel with all the rectitude expected of her, and she sensed in Susan the possibility of understanding companionship. She stayed to talk. Susan found herself in the middle of a fantastic story about her illness, which got more and more impossible as she tried to make it tally with the large house at Richmond, well-off husband, and four children. Suppose she said instead: Miss Townsend, I'm here in your hotel because I need to be alone for a few hours, above all *alone and with no one knowing where I am*. She said it mentally, and saw, mentally, the look that would inevitably come on Miss Townsend's elderly maiden's face. "Miss Townsend, my four children and my husband are driving me insane, do you understand that? Yes, I can see from the gleam of hysteria in your eyes that comes from loneliness controlled but only just contained that I've got everything in the world you've ever longed for. Well, Miss Townsend, I don't want any of it. You can have it, Miss Townsend. I wish I was absolutely alone in the world, like you. Miss Townsend, I'm besieged by seven devils, Miss Townsend, Miss Townsend, let me stay here in your hotel where the devils can't get me. . . ." Instead of saying all this, she described her anaemia, agreed to try Miss Townsend's remedy for it, which was raw liver, minced, between whole-meal bread, and said yes, perhaps it would be better if she stayed at home and let a friend do shopping for her. She paid her bill and left the hotel, defeated.

At home Mrs. Parkes said she didn't really like it, no, not really, when Mrs. Rawlings was away from nine in the morning until five. The teacher had telephoned from school to say Joan's teeth were paining her, and she hadn't known what to say; and what was she to make for the children's tea, Mrs. Rawlings hadn't said.

All this was nonsense, of course. Mrs. Parkes's complaint was that Susan had withdrawn herself spiritually, leaving the burden of the big house on her.

Susan looked back at her day of "freedom" which had resulted in her becoming a friend of the lonely Miss Townsend, and in Mrs. Parkes's remonstrances. Yet she remembered the short blissful hour of being alone, really alone. She was determined to arrange her life, no matter what it cost, so that she could have that solitude more often. An absolute solitude, where no one knew her or cared about her.

But how? She thought of saying to her old employer: I want you to back me up in a story with Matthew that I am doing part-time work for you. The truth is that . . . But she would have to tell him a lie too, and which lie? She could not say: I want to sit by myself three or four times a week in a rented room. And besides, he knew Matthew, and she could not really ask him to tell lies on her behalf, apart from being bound to think it meant a lover.

Suppose she really took a part-time job, which she could get through fast and efficiently, leaving time for herself. What job? Addressing envelopes? Canvassing?

And there was Mrs. Parkes, working widow, who knew exactly what she was prepared to give to the house, who knew by instinct when her mistress withdrew in spirit from her responsibilities. Mrs. Parkes was one of the servers of this world, but she needed someone to serve. She had to have Mrs. Rawlings, her madam, at the top of the house or in the garden, so that she could come and get support from her: "Yes, the bread's not what it was when I was a girl. . . . Yes, Harry's got a wonderful appetite, I wonder where he puts it all. . . . Yes, it's lucky the twins are so much of a size, they can wear each other's shoes, that's a saving in these hard times. . . . Yes, the cherry jam from Switzerland is not a patch on the jam from Poland, and three times the price . . ." And so on. That sort of talk Mrs. Parkes must have, every day, or she would leave, not knowing herself why she left.

Susan Rawlings, thinking these thoughts, found that she was prowling through the great thicketed garden like a wild cat: she was walking up the stairs, down the stairs, through the rooms into the garden, along the brown running river, back, up through the house, down again. . . . It was a wonder Mrs. Parkes did not think it strange. But, on the contrary, Mrs. Rawlings could do what she liked, she could stand on her head if she wanted, provided she was *there*. Susan Rawlings prowled and muttered through her house, hating Mrs. Parkes, hating poor Miss Townsend, dreaming of her hour of solitude in the dingy respectability of Miss Townsend's hotel bedroom, and she knew quite well she was mad. Yes, she was mad.

She said to Matthew that she must have a holiday. Matthew agreed with her. This was not as things had been once—how they had talked in each other's arms in the marriage bed. He had, she knew, diagnosed her finally as *unreasonable.* She had become someone outside himself that he had to manage. They were living side by side in this house like two tolerably friendly strangers.

Having told Mrs. Parkes—or rather, asked for her permission—she went off on a walking holiday in Wales. She chose the remotest place she knew of. Every morning the children telephoned her before they went off to school, to encourage and support her, just as they had over Mother's Room. Every evening she telephoned them, spoke to each child in turn, and then to Matthew. Mrs. Parkes, given permission to telephone for instructions or advice, did so every day at lunchtime. When, as happened three times, Mrs. Rawlings was out on the mountainside, Mrs. Parkes asked that she should ring back at such-and-such a time, for she would not be happy in what she was doing without Mrs. Rawlings' blessing.

Susan prowled over wild country with the telephone wire holding her to her duty like a leash. The next time she must telephone, or wait to be telephoned, nailed her to her cross. The mountains themselves seemed trammelled by her unfreedom. Everywhere on the mountains, where she met no one at all, from breakfast time to dusk, excepting sheep, or a shepherd, she came face to face with her own craziness, which might attack her in the broadest valleys, so that they seemed too small, or on a mountain top from which she could see a hundred other mountains and valleys, so that they seemed too low, too small, with the sky pressing down too close. She would stand gazing at a hillside brilliant with ferns and bracken, jewelled with running water, and see nothing but her devil, who lifted inhuman eyes at her from where he leaned negligently on a rock, switching at his ugly yellow boots with a leafy twig.

She returned to her home and family, with the Welsh emptiness at the back of her mind like a promise of freedom.

She told her husband she wanted to have an *au pair* girl.

They were in their bedroom, it was late at night, the children slept. He sat, shirted and slippered, in a chair by the window, looking out. She sat brushing her hair and watching him in the mirror. A time-hallowed scene in the connubial bedroom. He said nothing, while she heard the arguments coming into his mind, only to be rejected because every one was *reasonable.*

"It seems strange to get one now; after all, the children are in school most of the day. Surely the time for you to have help was when you were stuck with them day and night. Why don't you ask Mrs. Parkes to cook for you? She's even offered to—I can understand if you are tired of cooking for six people. But you know that an *au pair* girl means all kinds of problems; it's not like having an ordinary char in during the day. . . ."

Finally he said carefully: "Are you thinking of going back to work?"

"No," she said, "no, not really." She made herself sound vague, rather stupid. She went on brushing her black hair and peering at herself so as to be oblivious of the short uneasy glances her Matthew kept giving her. "Do you think we can't afford it?" she went on vaguely, not at all the old efficient Susan who knew exactly what they could afford.

"It's not that," he said, looking out of the window at dark trees, so as not to look at her. Meanwhile she examined a round, candid, pleasant face with clear dark brows and clear grey eyes. A sensible face. She brushed thick healthy black hair and thought: Yet that's the reflection of a madwoman. How very strange! Much more to the point if what looked back at me was the gingery green-eyed demon with his dry meagre smile. . . . Why wasn't Matthew agreeing? After all, what else could he do? She was breaking her part of the bargain and there was no way of forcing her to keep it: that her spirit, her soul, should live in this house, so that the people in it could grow like plants in water, and Mrs. Parkes remain content in their service. In return for this, he would be a good loving husband, and responsible towards the children. Well, nothing like this had been true of either of them for a long time. He did his duty, perfunctorily; she did not even pretend to do hers. And he had become like other husbands, with his real life in his work and the people he met there, and very likely a serious affair. All this was her fault.

At last he drew heavy curtains, blotting out the trees, and turned to force her attention: "Susan, are you really sure we need a girl?" But she would not meet his appeal at all. She was running the brush over her hair again and again, lifting fine black clouds in a small hiss of electricity. She was peering in and smiling as if she were amused at the clinging hissing hair that followed the brush.

"Yes, I think it would be a good idea, on the whole," she said, with the cunning of a madwoman evading the real point.

In the mirror she could see her Matthew lying on his back, his hands behind his head, staring upwards, his face sad and hard. She felt her heart (the old heart of Susan Rawlings) soften and call out to him. But she set it to be indifferent.

He said: "Susan, the children?" It was an appeal that *almost* reached her. He opened his arms, lifting them palms up, empty. She had only to run across and fling herself into them, onto his hard, warm chest, and melt into herself, into Susan. But she could not. She would not see his lifted arms. She said vaguely: "Well, surely it'll be even better for them? We'll get a French or a German girl and they'll learn the language."

In the dark she lay beside him, feeling frozen, a stranger. She felt as if Susan had been spirited away. She disliked very much this woman who lay here, cold and indifferent beside a suffering man, but she could not change her.

Next morning she set about getting a girl, and very soon came Sophie Traub from Hamburg, a girl of twenty, laughing, healthy, blue-eyed, intending to learn English. Indeed, she already spoke a good deal. In return for a room—"Mother's Room"—and her food, she undertook to do some light cooking, and to be with the children when Mrs. Rawlings asked. She was an intelligent girl and understood perfectly what was needed. Susan said: "I go off sometimes, for the morning or for the day—well, sometimes the children run home from school, or they ring up, or a teacher rings up. I should be here, really. And there's the daily woman. . . ." And Sophie laughed her deep fruity *Fräulein's* laugh, showed her fine white teeth and her dimples, and said: "You want some person to play mistress of the house sometimes, not so?"

"Yes, that is just so," said Susan, a bit dry, despite herself, thinking in secret fear how easy it was, how much nearer to the end she was than she thought. Healthy Fräulein Traub's instant understanding of their position proved this to be true.

The *au pair* girl, because of her own commonsense, or (as Susan said to herself, with her new inward shudder) because she had been *chosen* so well by Susan, was a success with everyone, the children liking her, Mrs. Parkes forgetting almost at once that she was German, and Matthew finding her "nice to have around the house." For he was now taking things as they came, from the surface of life, withdrawn both as a husband and a father from the household.

One day Susan saw how Sophie and Mrs. Parkes were talking and laughing in the kitchen, and she announced that she would be away until tea time. She knew exactly where to go and what she must look for. She took the District Line to South Kensington, changed to the Circle, got off at Paddington, and walked around looking at the smaller hotels until she was satisfied with one which had FRED'S HOTEL painted on windowpanes that needed cleaning. The facade was a faded shiny yellow, like unhealthy skin. A door at the end of a passage said she must knock; she did, and Fred appeared. He was not at all attractive, not in any way, being fattish, and run-down, and wearing a tasteless striped suit. He had small sharp eyes in a white creased face, and was quite prepared to let Mrs. Jones (she chose the farcical name ately, staring him out) have a room three days a week from ten until six. Provided of course that she paid in advance each time she came? Susan produced fifteen shillings (no price had been set by him) and held it out, still fixing him with a bold unblinking challenge she had not known until then she could use at will. Looking at her still, he took up a ten-shilling note from her palm between thumb and forefinger, fingered it; then shuffled up two half-crowns, held out his own palm with these bits of money displayed thereon, and let his gaze lower broodingly at them. They were standing in the passage, a red-shaded light above, bare boards beneath, and a strong smell of floor polish rising about them. He shot his gaze up at her over the still-extended palm, and smiled as if to say: What do you take me for? "I shan't," said Susan, "be using this room for the purpose of making money." He still waited. She added another five shillings, at which he nodded and said: "You pay, and I ask no questions." "Good," said Susan. He now went past her to the stairs, and there waited a moment: the light from the street door being in her eyes, she lost sight of him momentarily. Then she saw a sober-suited, white-faced, white-balding little man trotting up the stairs like a waiter, and she went after him. They proceeded in utter silence up the stairs of this house where no questions were asked—Fred's Hotel, which could afford the freedom for its visitors that poor Miss Townsend's hotel could not. The room was hideous. It had a single window, with thin green brocade curtains, a three-quarter bed that had a cheap green satin bedspread on it, a fireplace with a gas fire and a shilling meter by it, a chest of drawers, and a green wicker armchair.

"Thank you," said Susan, knowing that Fred (if this was Fred, and not George, or Herbert or Charlie) was looking at her, not so much with curiosity, an emotion he would not own to, for professional reasons, but with a philosophical sense of what was appropriate. Having taken her money and shown her up and agreed to everything, he was clearly disapproving of her for coming here. She did not belong here at all, so his look said. (But she knew, already, how very much she did belong: the room had been waiting for her to join it.) "Would you have me called at five o'clock, please?" and he nodded and went downstairs.

It was twelve in the morning. She was free. She sat in the armchair, she simply sat, she closed her eyes and sat and let herself be alone. She was alone and no one knew where she was. When a knock came on the door she was annoyed, and prepared to show it: but it was Fred himself; it was five o'clock and he was calling her as ordered. He flicked his sharp little eyes over the room—bed, first. It was undisturbed. She might never have been in the room at all. She thanked him, said she would be returning the day after tomorrow, and left. She was back home in time to cook supper, to put the children to bed, to cook a second supper for her husband and herself later. And to welcome Sophie back from the pictures where she had gone with a friend. All these things she did cheerfully, willingly. But she was thinking all the time of the hotel room; she was longing for it with her whole being.

Three times a week. She arrived promptly at ten, looked Fred in the eyes, gave him twenty shillings, followed him up the stairs, went into the room, and shut the door on him with gentle firmness. For Fred, disapproving of her being here at all, was quite ready to let friendship, or at least acquaintanceship, follow his disapproval, if only she would let him. But he was content to go off on her dismissing nod, with the twenty shillings in his hand.

She sat in the armchair and shut her eyes.

What did she *do* in the room? Why, nothing at all. From the chair, when it had rested her, she went to the window, stretching her arms, smiling, treasuring her anonymity, to look out. She was no longer Susan Rawlings, mother of four, wife of Matthew, employer of Mrs. Parkes and of Sophie Traub, with these and those relations with friends, school-teachers, tradesmen. She no longer was mistress of the big white house and garden, owning clothes suitable for this and that activity or occasion. She was Mrs. Jones, and she was alone, and she had no past and no future. Here I am, she thought, after all these years of being married and having children and playing those roles of responsibility—and I'm just the same. Yet there have been times I thought that nothing existed for me except the roles that went with being Mrs. Matthew Rawlings. Yes, here I am, and if I never saw any of my family again, here I would still be . . . how very strange that is! And she leaned on the sill, and looked into the street, loving the men and women who passed, because she did not know them. She looked at the downtrodden buildings over the street, and at the sky, wet and dingy, or sometimes blue, and she felt she had never seen buildings or sky before. And then she went back to the chair, empty, her mind a blank. Sometimes she talked aloud, saying nothing—an exclamation, meaningless, followed by a comment about the floral pattern on the thin rug, or a stain on the green satin coverlet. For the most part, she wool-gathered—what word is there for it?—brooded, wandered, simply went dark, feeling emptiness run deliciously through her veins like the movement of her blood.

This room had become more her own than the house she lived in. One morning she found Fred taking her a flight higher than usual. She stopped, refusing to go up, and demanded her usual room, Number 19. "Well, you'll have to wait half an hour, then," he said. Willingly she descended to the dark disinfectant-smelling hall, and sat waiting until the two, man and woman, came down the stairs, giving her swift indifferent glances before they hurried out into the street, separating at the door. She went up to the room, *her* room, which they had just vacated. It was no less hers, though the windows were set wide open, and a maid was straightening the bed as she came in.

After these days of solitude, it was both easy to play her part as mother and wife, and difficult—because it was so easy: she felt an imposter. She felt as if her shell moved here, with her family, answering to Mummy, Mother, Susan, Mrs. Rawlings. She was surprised no one saw through her, that she wasn't turned out of doors, as a fake. On the contrary, it seemed the children loved her more; Matthew and she "got on" pleasantly, and Mrs. Parkes was happy in her work under (for the most part, it must be confessed) Sophie Traub. At night she lay beside her husband, and they made love again, apparently just as they used to, when they were really married. But she, Susan, or the being who answered so readily and improbably to the name of Susan, was not there: she was in Fred's Hotel, in Paddington, waiting for the easing hours of solitude to begin.

Soon she made a new arrangement with Fred and with Sophie. It was for five days a week. As for the money, five pounds, she simply asked Matthew for it. She saw that she was not even frightened he might ask what for: he would give it to her, she knew that, and yet it was terrifying it could be so, for this close couple, these partners, had once known the destination of every shilling they must spend. He agreed to give her five pounds a week. She asked for just so much, not a penny more. He sounded indifferent about it. It was as if he were paying her, she thought: *paying her off*—yes, that was it. Terror came back for a moment when she understood this, but she stilled it: things had gone too far for that. Now, every week, on Sunday nights, he gave her five pounds, turning away from her before their eyes could meet on the transaction. As for Sophie Traub, she was to be somewhere in or near the house until six at night, after which she was free. She was not to cook, or to clean; she was simply to be there. So she gardened or sewed, and asked friends in, being a person who was bound to have a lot of friends. If the children were sick, she nursed them. If teachers telephoned, she answered them sensibly. For the five daytimes in the school week, she was altogether the mistress of the house.

One night in the bedroom, Matthew asked: "Susan, I don't want to interfere—don't think that, please—but are you sure you are well?"

She was brushing her hair at the mirror. She made two more strokes on either side of her head, before she replied: "Yes, dear, I am sure I am well."

He was again lying on his back, his blond head on his hands, his elbows angled up and part-concealing his face. He said: "Then Susan, I have to ask you this question, though you must understand, I'm not putting any sort of pressure on you." (Susan heard the word "pressure" with dismay, because this was inevitable; of course she could not go on like this.) "Are things going to go on like this?"

"Well," she said, going vague and bright and idiotic again, so as to escape: "Well, I don't see why not."

He was jerking his elbows up and down, in annoyance or in pain, and, looking at him, she saw he had got thin, even gaunt; and restless angry movements were not what she remembered of him. He said: "Do you want a divorce, is that it?"

At this, Susan only with the greatest difficulty stopped herself from laughing: she could hear the bright bubbling laughter she *would* have emitted, had she let herself. He could only mean one thing: she had a lover, and that was why she spent her days in London, as lost to him as if she had vanished to another continent.

Then the small panic set in again: she understood that he hoped she did have a lover, he was begging her to say so, because otherwise it would be too terrifying.

She thought this out as she brushed her hair, watching the fine black stuff fly up to make its little clouds of electricity, hiss, hiss, hiss. Behind her head, across the room, was a blue wall. She realised she was absorbed in watching the black hair making shapes against the blue. She should be answering him. "Do *you* want a divorce, Matthew?"

He said: "That surely isn't the point, is it?"

"You brought it up, I didn't," she said, brightly, suppressing meaningless tinkling laughter.

Next day she asked Fred: "Have enquiries been made for me?"

He hesitated, and she said: "I've been coming here a year now. I've made no trouble, and you've been paid every day. I have a right to be told."

"As a matter of fact, Mrs. Jones, a man did come asking."

"A man from a detective agency?"

"Well, he could have been, couldn't he?"

"I was asking you. . . . Well, what did you tell him?"

"I told him a Mrs. Jones came every weekday from ten until five or six and stayed in Number 19 by herself."

"Describing me?"

"Well, Mrs. Jones, I had no alternative. Put yourself in my place."

"By rights I should deduct what that man gave you for the information."

He raised shocked eyes: she was not the sort of person to make jokes like this! Then he chose to laugh: a pinkish wet slit appeared across his white crinkled face; his eyes positively begged her to laugh, otherwise he might lose some money. She remained grave, looking at him.

He stopped laughing and said: "You want to go up now?"—returning to the familiarity, the comradeship, of the country where no questions are asked, on which (and he knew it) she depended completely.

She went up to sit in her wicker chair. But it was not the same. Her husband had searched her out. (The world had searched her out.) The pressures were on her. She was here with his connivance. He might walk in at any moment, here, into Room 19. She imagined the report from the detective agency: "A woman calling herself Mrs. Jones, fitting the description of your wife (et cetera, et cetera, et cetera), stays alone all day in Room No. 19. She insists on this room, waits for it if it is engaged. As far as the proprietor knows, she receives no visitors there, male or female." A report something on these lines Matthew must have received.

Well, of course he was right: Things couldn't go on like this. He had put an end to it all simply by sending the detective after her.

She tried to shrink herself back into the shelter of the room, a snail pecked out of its shell and trying to squirm back. But the peace of the room had gone. She was trying consciously to revive it, trying to let go into the dark creative trance (or whatever it was) that she had found there. It was no use, yet she craved for it, she was as ill as a suddenly deprived addict.

Several times she returned to the room, to look for herself there, but instead she found the unnamed spirit of restlessness, a pricking fevered hunger for movement, an irritable self-consciousness that made her brain feel as if it had coloured lights going on and off inside it. Instead of the soft dark that had been the room's air, were now waiting for her demons that made her dash blindly about, muttering words of hate; she was impelling herself from point to point like a moth dashing itself against a windowpane, sliding to the bottom, fluttering off on broken wings, then crashing into the invisible barrier again. And again and again. Soon she was exhausted, and she told Fred that for a while she would not be needing the room, she was going on holiday. Home she went, to the big white house by the river. The middle of a weekday, and she felt guilty at returning to her own home when not expected. She stood unseen, looking in at the kitchen window. Mrs. Parkes, wearing a discarded floral overall of Susan's, was stooping to slide something into the oven. Sophie, arms folded, was leaning her back against a cupboard and laughing at some joke made by a girl not seen before by Susan—a dark foreign girl, Sophie's visitor. In an armchair Molly, one of the twins, lay curled, sucking her thumb and watching the grownups. She must have some sickness, to be kept from school. The child's listless face, the dark circles under her eyes, hurt Susan: Molly was looking at the three grownups working and talking in exactly the same way Susan looked at the four through the kitchen window: she was remote, shut off from them.

But then, just as Susan imagined herself going in, picking up the little girl, and sitting in an armchair with her, stroking her probably heated forehead, Sophie did just that: she had been standing on one leg, the other knee flexed, its foot set against the wall. Now she let her foot in its ribbon-tied red shoe slide down the wall, stood solid on two feet, clapping her hands before and behind her, and sang a couple of lines in German, so that the child lifted her heavy eyes at her and began to smile. Then she walked, or rather skipped, over to the child, swung her up, and let her fall into her lap at the same moment she sat herself. She said "Hopla! Hopla! Molly . . ." and began stroking the dark untidy young head that Molly laid on her shoulder for comfort.

Well. . . . Susan blinked the tears of farewell out of her eyes, and went quietly up through the house to her bedroom. There she sat looking at the river through the trees. She felt at peace, but in a way that was new to her. She had no desire to move, to talk, to do anything at all. The devils that had haunted the house, the garden, were not there; but she knew it was because her soul was in Room 19 in Fred's Hotel; she was not really here at all. It was a sensation that should have been frightening: to sit at her own bedroom window, listening to Sophie's rich young voice sing German nursery songs to her child, listening to Mrs. Parkes clatter and move below, and to know that all this had nothing to do with her: she was already out of it.

Later, she made herself go down and say she was home: it was unfair to be here unannounced. She took lunch with Mrs. Parkes, Sophie, Sophie's Italian friend Maria, and her daughter Molly, and felt like a visitor.

A few days later, at bedtime, Matthew said: "Here's your five pounds," and pushed them over to her. Yet he must have known she had not been leaving the house at all.

She shook her head, gave it back to him, and said, in explanation, not in accusation: "As soon as you knew where I was, there was no point."

He nodded, not looking at her. He was turned away from her: thinking, she knew, how best to handle this wife who terrified him.

He said: "I wasn't trying to . . . It's just that I was worried."

"Yes, I know."

"I must confess that I was beginning to wonder . . ."

"You thought I had a lover?"

"Yes, I am afraid I did."

She knew that he wished she had. She sat wondering how to say: "For a year now I've been spending all my days in a very sordid hotel room. It's the place where I'm happy. In fact, without it I don't exist." She heard herself saying this, and understood how terrified he was that she might. So instead she said: "Well, perhaps you're not far wrong."

Probably Matthew would think the hotel proprietor lied: he would want to think so.

"Well," he said, and she could hear his voice spring up, so to speak, with relief, "in that case I must confess I've got a bit of an affair on myself."

She said, detached and interested: "Really? Who is she?" and saw Matthew's startled look because of this reaction.

"It's Phil. Phil Hunt."

She had known Phil Hunt well in the old unmarried days. She was thinking: No, she won't do, she's too neurotic and difficult. She's never been happy yet. Sophie's much better. Well, Matthew will see that himself, as sensible as he is.

This line of thought went on in silence, while she said aloud: "It's no point telling you about mine, because you don't know him."

Quick, quick, invent, she thought. Remember how you invented all that nonsense for Miss Townsend.

She began slowly, careful not to contradict herself: "His name is Michael" (*Michael What?*) — "Michael Plant." (What a silly name!) "He's rather like you—in looks, I mean." And indeed, she could imagine herself being touched by no one but Matthew himself. "He's a publisher." (Really? Why?) "He's got a wife already and two children."

She brought out this fantasy, proud of herself.

Matthew said: "Are you two thinking of marrying?"

She said, before she could stop herself: "Good God, *no!*"

She realised, if Matthew wanted to marry Phil Hunt, that this was too emphatic, but apparently it was all right, for his voice sounded relieved as he said: "It is a bit impossible to imagine oneself married to anyone else, isn't it?" With which he pulled her to him, so that her head lay on his shoulder. She turned her face into the dark of his flesh and listened to the blood pounding through her ears saying: I am alone, I am alone, I am alone.

In the morning Susan lay in bed while he dressed.

He had been thinking things out in the night, because now he said: "Susan, why don't we make a foursome?"

Of course, she said to herself, of course he would be bound to say that. If one is sensible, if one is reasonable, if one never allows oneself a base thought or an envious emotion, naturally one says: Let's make a foursome!

"Why not?" she said.

"We could all meet for lunch. I mean, it's ridiculous, you sneaking off to filthy hotels, and me staying late at the office, and all the lies everyone has to tell."

What on earth did I say his name was?—she panicked, then said: "I think it's a good idea, but Michael is away at the moment. When he comes back, though—and I'm sure you two would like each other."

"He's away, is he? So that's why you've been . . . " Her husband put his hand to the knot of his tie in a gesture of male coquetry she would not before have associated with him; and he bent to kiss her cheek with the expression that goes with the words: Oh you naughty little puss! And she felt its answering look, naughty and coy, come onto her face.

Inside she was dissolving in horror at them both, at how far they had both sunk from honesty of emotion.

So now she was saddled with a lover, and he had a mistress! How ordinary, how reassuring, how jolly! And now they would make a foursome of it, and go about to theatres and restaurants. After all, the Rawlings could well afford that sort of thing, and presumably the publisher Michael Plant could afford to do himself and his mistress quite well. No, there was nothing to stop the four of them developing the most intricate relationship of civilised tolerance, all enveloped in a charming afterglow of autumnal passion. Perhaps they would all go off on holidays together? She had known people who did. Or perhaps Matthew would draw the line there? Why should he, though, if he was capable of talking about "foursomes" at all?

She lay in the empty bedroom, listening to the car drive off with Matthew in it, off to work. Then she heard the children clattering off to school to the accompaniment of Sophie's cheerfully ringing voice. She slid down into the hollow of the bed, for shelter against her own irrelevance. And she stretched out her hand to the hollow where her husband's body had lain, but found no comfort there: he was not her husband. She curled herself up in a small tight ball under the clothes: she could stay here all day, all week, indeed, all her life.

But in a few days she must produce Michael Plant, and—but how?

She must presumably find some agreeable man prepared to impersonate a publisher called Michael Plant. And in return for which she would—what? Well, for one thing they would make love. The idea made her want to cry with sheer exhaustion. Oh no, she had finished with all that —the proof of it was that the words "make love," or even imagining it, trying hard to revive no more than the pleasures of sensuality, let alone affection, or love, made her want to run away and hide from the sheer effort of the thing. . . . Good Lord, why make love at all? Why make love with anyone? Or if you are going to make love, what does it matter who with? Why shouldn't she simply walk into the street, pick up a man, and have a roaring sexual affair with him? Why not? Or even with Fred? What difference did it make?

But she had let herself in for it—an interminable stretch of time with a lover, called Michael, as part of a gallant civilised foursome. Well, she could not, and she would not.

She got up, dressed, went down to find Mrs. Parkes, and asked her for the loan of a pound, since Matthew, she said, had forgotten to leave her money. She exchanged with Mrs. Parkes variations on the theme that husbands are all the same, they don't think, and without saying a word to Sophie, whose voice could be heard upstairs from the telephone, walked to the underground, travelled to South Kensington, changed to the Inner Circle, got out at Paddington, and walked to Fred's Hotel. There she told Fred that she wasn't going on holiday after all, she needed the room. She would have to wait an hour, Fred said. She went to a busy tearoom-cum-restaurant around the corner, and sat watching the people flow in and out the door that kept swinging open and shut, watched them mingle and merge, and separate, felt her being flow into them, into their movement. When the hour was up, she left a half-crown for her pot of tea, and left the place without looking back at it, just as she had left her house, the big, beautiful white house, without another look, but silently dedicating it to Sophie. She returned to Fred, received the key of Number 19, now free, and ascended the grimy stairs slowly, letting floor after floor fall away below her, keeping her eyes lifted, so that floor after floor descended jerkily to her level of vision, and fell away out of sight.

Number 19 was the same. She saw everything with an acute, narrow, checking glance: the cheap shine of the satin spread, which had been replaced carelessly after the two bodies had finished their convulsions under it; a trace of powder on the glass that topped the chest of drawers; an intense green shade in a fold of the curtain. She stood at the window, looking down, watching people pass and pass and pass until her mind went dark from the constant movement. Then she sat in the wicker chair, letting herself go slack. But she had to be careful, because she did not want, today, to be surprised by Fred's knock at five o'clock.

The demons were not here. They had gone forever, because she was buying her freedom from them. She was slipping already into the dark fructifying dream that seemed to caress her inwardly, like the movement of her blood . . . but she had to think about Matthew first. Should she write a letter for the coroner? But what should she say? She would like to leave him with the look on his face she had seen this morning—banal, admittedly, but at least confidently healthy. Well, that was impossible, one did not look like that with a wife dead from suicide. But how to leave him believing she was dying because of a man—because of the fascinating publisher Michael Plant? Oh, how ridiculous! How absurd! How humiliating! But she decided not to trouble about it, simply not to think about the living. If he wanted to believe she had a lover, he would believe it. And he *did* want to believe it. Even when he found out that there was no publisher in London called Michael Plant, he would think: Oh poor Susan, she was afraid to give me his real name.

And what did it matter whether he married Phil Hunt or Sophie? Though it ought to be Sophie, who was already the mother of those children . . . and what hypocrisy to sit here worrying about the children, when she was going to leave them because she had not got the energy to stay.

She had about four hours. She spent them delightfully, darkly, sweetly, letting herself slide gently, gently, to the edge of the river. Then, with hardly a break of consciousness, she got up, pushed the thin rug against the door, made sure the windows were tight shut, put two shillings in the meter, and turned on the gas. For the first time since she had been in the room she lay on the hard bed that smelled stale, that smelled of sweat and sex.

She lay on her back on the green satin cover, but her legs were chilly. She got up, found a blanket folded in the bottom of the chest of drawers, and carefully covered her legs with it. She was quite content lying there, listening to the faint soft hiss of the gas that poured into the room, into her lungs, into her brain, as she drifted off into the dark river.

1963

TILLIE OLSEN

I Stand Here Ironing

I stand here ironing, and what you asked me moves tormented back and forth with the iron.

"I wish you would manage the time to come in and talk with me about your daughter. I'm sure you can help me understand her. She's a youngster who needs help and whom I'm deeply interested in helping."

"Who needs help." . . . Even if I came, what good would it do? You think because I am her mother I have a key, or that in some way you could use me as a key? She has lived for nineteen years. There is all that life that has happened outside of me, beyond me.

And when is there time to remember, to sift, to weigh, to estimate, to total? I will start and there will be an interruption and I will have to gather it all together again. Or I will become engulfed with all I did or did not do, with what should have been and what cannot be helped.

She was a beautiful baby. The first and only one of our five that was beautiful at birth. You do not guess how new and uneasy her tenancy in her now-loveliness. You did not know her all those years she was thought homely, or see her poring over her baby pictures, making me tell her over and over how beautiful she had been—and would be, I would tell her—and was now, to the seeing eye. But the seeing eyes were few or nonexistent. Including mine.

I nursed her. They feel that's important nowadays, I nursed all the children, but with her, with all the fierce rigidity of first motherhood, I did like the books then said. Though her cries battered me to trembling and my breasts ached with swollenness, I waited till the clock decreed.

Although born in Omaha, Nebraska, in 1913, Tillie Olsen has been a San Franciscan for most of her life. She wrote as a girl, but was forced to abandon this luxury with the arrival of the depression and four children. She did not take up writing again until her midforties. In 1961 Olsen published her first collection of stories, *Tell Me a Riddle*, receiving the O. Henry Award for the best American short story for the title story. She has even returned to manuscripts written in her youth, reworking them with her fluid prose style. A former Guggenheim fellow, Olsen has taught at Amherst and Stanford, among other places.

Why do I put that first? I do not even know if it matters, or if it explains anything.

She was a beautiful baby. She blew shining bubbles of sound. She loved motion, loved light, loved color and music and textures. She would lie on the floor in her blue overalls patting the surface so hard in ecstasy her hands and feet would blur. She was a miracle to me, but when she was eight months old I had to leave her daytimes with the woman downstairs to whom she was no miracle at all, for I worked or looked for work and for Emily's father, who "could no longer endure" (he wrote in his good-bye note) "sharing want with us."

I was nineteen. It was pre-relief, pre-WPA world of the depression. I would start running as soon as I got off the streetcar, running up the stairs, the place smelling sour, and awake or asleep to startle awake, when she saw me she would break into a clogged weeping that could not be comforted, a weeping I can hear yet.

After a while I found a job hashing at night so I could be with her days, and it was better. But it came to where I had to bring her to his family and leave her.

It took a long time to raise the money for her fare back. Then she got chicken pox and I had to wait longer. When she finally came, I hardly knew her, walking quick and nervous like her father, looking like her father, thin, and dressed in a shoddy red that yellowed her skin and glared at the pockmarks. All the baby loveliness gone.

She was two. Old enough for nursery school they said, and I did not know then what I know now—the fatigue of the long day, and the lacerations of group life in the kinds of nurseries that are only parking places for children.

Except that it would have made no difference if I had known. It was the only place there was. It was the only way we could be together, the only way I could hold a job.

And even without knowing, I knew. I knew the teacher that was evil because all these years it has curdled into my memory, the little boy hunched in the corner, her rasp, "why aren't you outside, because Alvin hits you? that's no reason, go out, scaredy." I knew Emily hated it even if she did not clutch and implore "don't go Mommy" like the other children, mornings.

She always had a reason why we should stay home. Momma, you look sick. Momma, I feel sick. Momma, the teachers aren't there today, they're sick. Momma, we can't go, there was a fire last night. Momma, it's a holiday today, no school, they told me.

But never a direct protest, never rebellion. I think of our others in their three-, four-year-oldness—the explosions, the tempers, the denunciations, the demands—and I feel suddenly ill. I put the iron down. What in me demanded that goodness in her? And what was the cost, the cost to her of such goodness?

The old man living in the back once said in his gentle way: "You should smile at Emily more when you look at her." What *was* in my face when I looked at her? I loved her. There were all the acts of love.

It was only with the others I remembered what he said, and it was the face of joy, and not of care or tightness or worry I turned to them —too late for Emily. She does not smile easily, let alone almost always as her brothers and sisters do. Her face is closed and sombre, but when she wants, how fluid. You must have seen it in her pantomimes, you spoke of her rare gift for comedy on the stage that rouses laughter out of the audience so dear they applaud and applaud and do not want to let her go.

Where does it come from, that comedy? There was none of it in her when she came back to me that second time, after I had to send her away again. She had a new daddy now to learn to love, and I think perhaps it was a better time.

Except when we left her alone nights, telling ourselves she was old enough.

"Can't you go some other time, Mommy, like tomorrow?" she would ask. "Will it be just a little while you'll be gone? Do you promise?"

The time we came back, the front door open, the clock on the floor in the hall. She rigid awake. "It wasn't just a little while. I didn't cry. Three times I called you, just three times, and then I ran downstairs to open the door so you could come faster. The clock talked loud. I threw it away, it scared me what it talked."

She said the clock talked loud again that night I went to the hospital to have Susan. She was delirious with the fever that comes before red measles, but she was fully conscious all the week I was gone and the week after we were home when she could not come near the new baby or me.

She did not get well. She stayed skeleton thin, not wanting to eat, and night after night she had nightmares. She would call for me, and I would rouse from exhaustion to sleepily call back: "You're all right, darling, go to sleep, it's just a dream," and if she still called, in a sterner voice, "now go to sleep, Emily, there's nothing to hurt you." Twice, only twice, when I had to get up for Susan anyhow, I went in to sit with her.

Now when it is too late (as if she would let me hold her and comfort her like I do the others) I get up and go to her at once at her moan or restless stirring. "Are you awake, Emily? Can I get you something?" And the answer is always the same: "No, I'm all right, go back to sleep, Mother."

They persuaded me at the clinic to send her away to a convalescent home in the country where "she can have the kind of food and care you can't manage for her, and you'll be free to concentrate on the new baby." They still send children to that place. I see pictures on the society page of sleek young women planning affairs to raise money for it, or dancing at the affairs, or decorating Easter eggs or filling Christmas stockings for the children.

They never have a picture of the children so I do not know if the girls still wear those gigantic red bows and the ravaged looks on the every other Sunday when parents can come to visit "unless otherwise notified"—as we were notified the first six weeks.

Oh it is a handsome place, green lawns and tall trees and fluted flower beds. High up on the balconies of each cottage the children stand, the girls in their red bows and white dresses, the boys in white suits and giant red ties. The parents stand below shrieking up to be heard and the children shriek down to be heard, and between them the invisible wall "Not To Be Contaminated by Parental Germs or Physical Affection."

There was a tiny girl who always stood hand in hand with Emily. Her parents never came. One visit she was gone. "They moved her to Rose Cottage," Emily shouted in explanation. "They don't like you to love anybody here."

She wrote once a week, the labored writing of a seven-year-old. "I am fine. How is the baby. If I write my letter nicly I will have a star. Love." There never was a star. We wrote every other day, letters she could never hold or keep but only hear read—once. "We simply do not have room for children to keep any personal possessions," they patiently explained when we pieced one Sunday's shrieking together to plead how much it would mean to Emily, who loved so to keep things, to be allowed to keep her letters and cards.

Each visit she looked frailer. "She isn't eating," they told us.

(They had runny eggs for breakfast or mush with lumps, Emily said later, I'd hold it in my mouth and not swallow. Nothing ever tasted good, just when they had chicken.)

It took us eight months to get her released home, and only the fact that she gained back so little of her seven lost pounds convinced the social worker.

I used to try to hold and love her after she came back, but her body would stay stiff, and after a while she'd push away. She ate little. Food sickened her, and I think much of life too. Oh she had physical lightness and brightness, twinkling by on skates, bouncing like a ball up and down up and down over the jump rope, skimming over the hill; but these were momentary.

She fretted about her appearance, thin and dark and foreign-looking at a time when every little girl was supposed to look or thought she should look a chubby blonde replica of Shirley Temple. The doorbell sometimes rang for her, but no one seemed to come and play in the house or to be a best friend. Maybe because we moved so much.

There was a boy she loved painfully through two school semesters. Months later she told me how she had taken pennies from my purse to buy him candy. "Licorice was his favorite and I brought him some every day, but he still liked Jennifer better'n me. Why, Mommy?" The kind of question for which there is no answer.

School was a worry for her. She was not glib or quick in a world where glibness and quickness were easily confused with ability to learn. To her overworked and exasperated teachers she was an overconscientious "slow learner" who kept trying to catch up and was absent entirely too often.

I let her be absent, though sometimes the illness was imaginary. How different from my now-strictness about attendance with the others. I wasn't working. We had a new baby. I was home anyhow. Sometimes, after Susan grew old enough, I would keep her home from school, too, to have them all together.

Mostly Emily had asthma, and her breathing, harsh and labored, would fill the house with a curiously tranquil sound. I would bring the two old dresser mirrors and her boxes of collections to her bed. She would select beads and single earrings, bottle tops and shells, dried flowers and pebbles, old postcards and scraps, all sorts of oddments; then she and Susan would play Kingdom, setting up landscapes and furniture, peopling them with action.

Those were the only times of peaceful companionship between her and Susan. I have edged away from it, that poisonous feeling between them, that terrible balancing of hurts and needs I had to do between the two, and did so badly, those earlier years.

Oh there were conflicts between the others too, each one human, needing, demanding, hurting, taking—but only between Emily and Susan, no, Emily toward Susan that corroding resentment. It seems so obvious on the surface, yet it is not obvious; Susan, the second child, Susan, golden- and curly-haired and chubby, quick and articulate and assured, everything in appearance and manner Emily was not; Susan, not able to resist Emily's precious things, losing or sometimes clumsily breaking them; Susan telling jokes and riddles to company for applause while Emily sat silent (to say to me later: that was *my* riddle, Mother, I told it to Susan); Susan, who for all the five years' difference in age was just a year behind Emily in developing physically.

I am glad for that slow physical development that widened the difference between her and her contemporaries, though she suffered over it. She was too vulnerable for that terrible world of youthful competition, of preening and parading, of constant measuring of yourself against every other, of envy, "If I had that copper hair," "If I had that skin. . . ." She tormented herself enough about not looking like the others, there was enough of unsureness, the having to be conscious of words before you speak, the constant caring—what are they thinking of me? without having it all magnified by the merciless physical drives.

Ronnie is calling. He is wet and I change him. It is rare there is such a cry now. That time of motherhood is almost behind me when the ear is not one's own but must always be racked and listening for the child cry, the child call. We sit for a while and I hold him, looking out over the city spread in charcoal with its soft aisles of light. *"Shoogily,"* he breathes and curls closer. I carry him back to bed, asleep. *Shoogily.* A funny word, a family word, inherited from Emily, invented by her to say: *comfort.*

In this and other ways she leaves her seal, I say aloud. And startle at my saying it. What do I mean? What did I start to gather together, to try and make coherent? I was at the terrible, growing years. War years. I do not remember them well. I was working, there were four smaller ones now, there was not time for her. She had to help be a mother, and housekeeper, and shopper. She had to get her seal. Mornings of crisis and near hysteria trying to get lunches packed, hair combed, coats and shoes found, everyone to school or Child Care on time, the baby ready for transportation. And always the paper scribbled on by a smaller one, the book looked at by Susan then mislaid, the homework not done. Running out to that huge school where she was one, she was lost, she was a drop; suffering over the unpreparedness, stammering and unsure in her classes.

There was so little time left at night after the kids were bedded down. She would struggle over books, always eating (it was in those years she developed her enormous appetite that is legendary in our family) and I would be ironing, or preparing food for the next day, or writing V-mail to Bill, or tending the baby. Sometimes, to make me laugh, or out of her despair, she would imitate happenings or types at school.

I think I said once: "Why don't you do something like this in the school amateur show?" One morning she phoned me at work, hardly understandable through the weeping: "Mother, I did it. I won, I won; they gave me first prize; they clapped and clapped and wouldn't let me go."

Now suddenly she was Somebody, and as imprisoned in her difference as she had been in anonymity.

She began to be asked to perform at other high schools, even in colleges, then at city and statewide affairs. The first one we went to, I only recognized her that first moment when thin, shy, she almost drowned herself into the curtains. Then: Was this Emily? The control, the command, the convulsing and deadly clowning, the spell, then the roaring, stamping audience, unwilling to let this rare and precious laughter out of their lives.

Afterwards: You ought to do something about her with a gift like that—but without money or knowing how, what does one do? We have left it all to her, and the gift has so often eddied inside, clogged and clotted, as been used and growing.

She is coming. She runs up the stairs two at a time with her light graceful step, and I know she is happy tonight. Whatever it was that occasioned your call did not happen today.

"Aren't you ever going to finish the ironing, Mother? Whistler painted his mother in a rocker. I'd have to paint mine standing over an ironing board." This is one of her communicative nights and she tells me everything and nothing as she fixes herself a plate of food out of the icebox.

She is so lovely. Why did you want me to come in at all? Why were you concerned? She will find her way.

She starts up the stairs to bed. "Don't get me up with the rest in the morning." "But I thought you were having midterms." "Oh, those," she comes back in, kisses me, and says quite lightly, "in a couple of years when we'll all be atom-dead they won't matter a bit."

She has said it before. She *believes* it. But because I have been dredging the past, and all that compounds a human being is so heavy and meaningful in me, I cannot endure it tonight.

I will never total it all. I will never come in to say: She was a child seldom smiled at. Her father left me before she was a year old. I had to work her first six years when there was work, or I sent her home and to his relatives. There were years she had care she hated. She was dark and thin and foreign-looking in a world where the prestige went to blondeness and curly hair and dimples, she was slow where glibness was prized. She was a child of anxious, not proud, love. We were poor and could not afford for her the soil of easy growth. I was a young mother, I was a distracted mother. There were other children pushing up, demanding. Her younger sister seemed all that she was not. There were years she did not want me to touch her. She kept too much in herself, her life was such she had to keep too much in herself. My wisdom came too late. She has much to her and probably little will come of it. She is a child of her age, of depression, of war, of fear.

Let her be. So all that is in her will not bloom—but in how many does it? There is still enough left to live by. Only help her to know— help make it so there is cause for her to know—that she is more than this dress on the ironing board, helpless before the iron.

1961

RAYMOND CARVER

Boxes

My mother is packed and ready to move. But Sunday afternoon, at the last minute, she calls and says for us to come eat with her. "My icebox is defrosting," she tells me. "I have to fry up this chicken before it rots." She says we should bring our own plates and some knives and forks. She's packed most of her dishes and kitchen things. "Come on and eat with me one last time," she says. "You and Jill."

I hang up the phone and stand at the window for a minute longer, wishing I could figure this thing out. But I can't. So finally I turn to Jill and say, "Let's go to my mother's for a good-bye meal."

The art of Raymond Carver is mainly set in the Pacific Northwest, where Carver was born in 1938 in the logging town of Clatskanie, Oregon. Husband and father of two before the age of twenty, Carver spent much of his early life holding down a series of odd jobs. In the 1970s, though, his fiction and poetry began to receive widespread attention. Critics praised the short stories in such collections as *Will You Please Be Quiet, Please* (1976) and *What We Talk About When We Talk About Love* (1981) for their direct and uncomplicated depiction of the American lower middle class. Carver also taught writing at a number of academic institutions, including the University of Iowa. He died in 1988 in Port Angeles, Washington.

Jill is at the table with the Sears catalogue in front of her, trying to find us some curtains. But she's been listening. She makes a face. "Do we have to?" she says. She bends down the corner of a page and closes the catalogue. She sighs. "God, we been over there to eat two or three times in this last month alone. Is she ever actually going to leave?"

Jill always says what's on her mind. She's thirty-five years old, wears her hair short, and grooms dogs for a living. Before she became a groomer, something she likes, she used to be a housewife and mother. Then all hell broke loose. Her two children were kidnapped by her first husband and taken to live in Australia. Her second husband, who drank, left her with a broken eardrum before he drove their car through a bridge into the Elwha River. He didn't have life insurance, not to mention property-damage insurance. Jill had to borrow money to bury him, and then—can you beat it?—she was presented with a bill for the bridge repair. Plus, she had her own medical bills. She can tell this story now. She's bounced back. But she has run out of patience with my mother. I've run out of patience, too. But I don't see my options.

"She's leaving day after tomorrow," I say. "Hey, Jill, don't do any favors. Do you want to come with me or not?" I tell her it doesn't matter to me one way or the other. I'll say she has a migraine. It's not like I've never told a lie before.

"I'm coming," she says. And like that she gets up and goes into the bathroom, where she likes to pout.

We've been together since last August, about the time my mother picked to move up here to Longview from California. Jill tried to make the best of it. But my mother pulling into town just when we were trying to get our act together was nothing either of us had bargained for. Jill said it reminded her of the situations with her first husband's mother. "She was a clinger," Jill said. "You know what I mean? I thought I was going to suffocate."

It's fair to say that my mother sees Jill as an intruder. As far as she's concerned, Jill is just another girl in a series of girls who have appeared in my life since my wife left me. Someone, to her mind, likely to take away affection, attention, maybe even some money that might otherwise come to her. But someone deserving of respect? No way. I remember—how can I forget it?—she called my wife a whore before we were married, and then called her a whore fifteen years later, after she left me for someone else.

Jill and my mother act friendly enough when they find themselves together. They hug each other when they say hello or good-bye. They talk about shopping specials. But Jill dreads the time she has to spend in my mother's company. She claims my mother bums her out. She says my mother is negative about everything and everybody and ought to find an outlet, like other people in her age bracket. Crocheting, maybe, or card games at the Senior Citizens Center, or else going to church. Something, anyway, so that she'll leave us in peace. But my mother had her own way of solving things. She announced she was moving back to California. The hell with everything and everybody in this town. What a place to live! She wouldn't continue the live in this town if they gave her the place and six more like it.

Within a day or two of deciding to move, she'd packed her things into boxes. That was last January. Or maybe it was February. Anyway, last winter sometime. Now it's the end of June. Boxes have been sitting around inside her house for months. You have to walk around them or step over them to get from one room to another. This is no way for anyone's mother to live.

After a while, ten minutes or so, Jill comes out of the bathroom. I've found a roach and am trying to smoke that and drink a bottle of ginger ale while I watch one of the neighbors change the oil in his car. Jill doesn't look at me. Instead, she goes back into the kitchen and puts some plates and utensils into a paper sack. But when she comes back through the living room I stand up, and we hug each other. Jill says, "It's okay." What's okay, I wonder. As far as I can see, nothing's okay. But she holds me and keeps patting my shoulder. I can smell the pet shampoo on her. She comes home from work wearing the stuff. It's everywhere. Even when we're in bed together. She gives me a final pat. Then we go out to the car and drive across town to my mother's.

I like where I live. I didn't when I first moved here. There was nothing to do at night, and I was lonely. Then I met Jill. Pretty soon, after a few weeks, she brought her things over and started living with me. We didn't set any long-term goals. We were happy and we had a life together. We told each other we'd finally got lucky. But my mother didn't have anything going in her life. So she wrote me and said she'd decided on moving here. I wrote her back and said I didn't think it was such a good idea. The weather's terrible in the winter, I said. They're building a prison a few miles from town, I told her. The place is bumper-to-bumper tourists all summer, I said. But she acted as if she never got any letters, and came anyway. Then, after she'd been in town a little less than a month, she told me she hated the place. She acted as if it were my fault she'd moved here and my fault she found everything so disagreeable. She started calling me up and telling me how crummy the place was. "Laying guilt trips," Jill called it. She told me the bus service was terrible and the drivers unfriendly. As for the people at the Senior Citizens—

well, she didn't want to play casino. "They can go to hell," she said, "And take their card games with them." The clerks at the supermarket were surly, the guys in the service station didn't give a damn about her or her car. And she'd made up her mind about the man she rented from, Larry Hadlock. King Larry, she called him. "He thinks he's *superior* to everyone because he has some shacks for rent and a few dollars. I wish to God I'd never laid eyes on him."

It was too hot for her when she arrived, in August, and in September it started to rain. It rained almost every day for weeks. In October it turned cold. There was snow in November and December. But long before that she began to put the bad mouth on the place and the people to the extent that I didn't want to hear about it anymore, and I told her so finally. She cried, and I hugged her and thought that was the end of it. But a few days later she started in again, same stuff. Just before Christmas she called to see when I was coming by with her presents. She hadn't put up a tree and didn't intend to, she said. Then she said something else. She said if this weather didn't improve she was going to kill herself.

"Don't talk crazy," I said.

She said, "I mean it, honey. I don't want to see this place again except from my coffin. I hate this g.d. place. I don't know why I moved here. I wish I could just die and get it over with."

I remember hanging on to the phone and watching a man high up on a pole doing something to a power line. Snow whirled around his head. As I watched, he leaned out from the pole, supported only by his safety belt. Suppose he falls, I thought. I didn't have any idea what I was going to say next. I had to say something. But I was filled with unworthy feelings, thoughts no son should admit to. "You're my mother," I said finally. "What can I do to help?"

"Honey, you can't do anything," she said. "The time for doing anything has come and gone. It's too late to do anything. I wanted to like it here. I thought we'd go on picnics and take drives together. But none of that happened. You're always busy. You're off working, you and Jill. You're never at home. Or else if you are at home you have the phone off the hook all day. Anyway, I never see you," she said.

"That's not true," I said. And it wasn't. But she went on as if she hadn't heard me. Maybe she hadn't.

"Besides," she said, "this weather's killing me. It's too damned cold here. Why didn't you tell me this was the North Pole? If you had, I'd never have come. I want to go back to California, honey. I can get out and go places there. I don't know anywhere to go here. There are people back in California. I've got friends there who care what happens to me. Nobody gives a damn here. Well, I just pray I can get through to June.

If I can make it that long, if I can last to June, I'm leaving this place forever. This is the worst place I've ever lived in."

What could I say? I didn't know what to say. I couldn't even say anything about the weather. Weather was a real sore point. We said good-bye and hung up.

Other people take vacations in the summer, but my mother moves. She started moving years ago, after my dad lost his job. When that happened, when he was laid off, they sold their home, as if this were what they should do, and went to where they thought things would be better. But things weren't any better there, either. They moved again. They kept on moving. They lived in rented houses, apartments, mobile homes, and motel units then. They kept moving, lightening their load with each move they made. A couple of times they landed in a town where I lived. They'd move in with my wife and me for a while and then they'd move on again. They were like migrating animals in this regard, except the was no pattern to their movement. They moved around for years, sometimes even leaving the state for what they thought would be greener pastures. But mostly they stayed in Northern California and did their moving there. Then my dad died, and I thought my mother would stop moving and stay in one place for a while. But she didn't. She kept moving. I suggested once that she go to a psychiatrist. I even said I'd pay for it. But she wouldn't hear of it. She packed and moved out of town instead. I was desperate about things or I wouldn't have said that about the psychiatrist.

She was always in the process of packing or else unpacking. Sometimes she'd move two or three times in the same year. She talked bitterly about the place she was leaving and optimistically about the place she was going to. Her mail got fouled up, her benefit checks went off somewhere else, and she spent hours writing letters, trying to get it all straightened out. Sometimes she'd move out of an apartment house, move to another one a few blocks away, and then, a month later, move back to the place she'd left, only to a different floor or a different side of the building. That's why when she moved here I rented a house for her and saw to it that it was furnished to her liking. "Moving around keeps her alive," Jill said. "It gives her something to do. She must get some kind of weird enjoyment out of it, I guess." But enjoyment or not, Jill thinks my mother must be losing her mind. I think so, too. But how do you tell your mother this? How do you deal with her if this is the case? Crazy doesn't stop her from planning and getting on with her next move.

She is waiting at the back door for us when we pull in. She's seventy years old, has gray hair, wears glasses with rhinestone frames, and has never been sick a day in her life. She hugs Jill, and then she hugs me. Her eyes are bright, as if she's been drinking. But she doesn't drink. She quit years ago, after my dad went on the wagon. We finish hugging and go inside. It's around five in the afternoon. I smell whatever it is drifting out of her kitchen and remember I haven't eaten since breakfast. My buzz has worn off.

"I'm starved," I say.

"Something smells good," Jill says.

"I hope it tastes good," my mother says. "I hope this chicken's done." She raises the lid on a fry pan and pushes a fork into a chicken breast. "If there's anything I can't stand, it's raw chicken. I think it's done. Why don't you sit down? Sit anyplace. I still can't regulate my stove. The burners heat up too fast. I don't like electric stoves and never have. Move that junk off the chair, Jill. I'm living here like a damned gypsy. But not for much longer, I hope." She sees me looking around for the ashtray. "Behind you," she says. "On the windowsill, honey. Before you sit down, why don't you pour us some of that Pepsi? You'll have to use these paper cups. I should have told you to bring some glasses. Is the Pepsi cold? I don't have any ice. This icebox won't keep anything cold. It isn't worth a damn. My ice cream turns to soup. It's the worst icebox I've ever had."

She forks the chicken into a plate and puts the plate on the table along with beans and coleslaw and white bread. Then she looks to see if there is anything she's forgetting. Salt and pepper! "Sit down," she says.

We draw our chairs up to the table, and Jill takes the plates out of the sack and hands them around the table to us. "Where are you going to live when you go back?" she says. "Do you have a place lined up?"

My mother passes the chicken to Jill and says, "I wrote that lady I rented from before. She wrote back and said she had a nice first-floor place I could have. It's close to the bus stop and there's lots of stores in the area. There's a bank and a Safeway. It's the nicest place. I don't know why I left there." She says that and helps herself to some coleslaw.

"Why'd you leave then?" Jill says. "If it was so nice and all." She picks up her drumstick, looks at it, and takes a bite of the meat.

"I'll tell you why. There was an old alcoholic woman who lived next door to me. She drank from morning to night. The walls were so thin I could hear her munching ice cubes all day. She had to use a walker to get around, but that still didn't stop her. I'd hear that walker *scrape, scrape* against the floor from morning to night. That and her icebox door closing." She shakes her head at all she had to put up with. "I had to get out of there. *Scrape, scrape* all day. I couldn't stand it. I just couldn't live like that. This time I told the manager I didn't want to be next to any alcoholics. And I didn't want anything on the second floor. The second floor looks out on the parking lot. Nothing to see from there." She waits for Jill to say something more. But Jill doesn't comment. My mother looks over at me.

I'm eating like a wolf and don't say anything, either. In any case, there's nothing more to say on the subject. I keep chewing and look over at the boxes stacked against the fridge. Then I help myself to more coleslaw.

Pretty soon I finish and push my chair back. Larry Hadlock pulls up in back of the house, next to my car, and takes a lawn mower out of his pickup. I watch him through the window behind the table. He doesn't look in our direction.

"What's he want?" my mother says and stops eating.

"He's going to cut your grass, it looks like," I say.

"It doesn't need cutting," she says. "He cut it last week. What's there for him to cut?"

"It's for the new tenant," Jill says. "Whoever that turns out to be."

My mother takes this in and then goes back to eating.

Larry Hadlock starts his mower and begins to cut the grass. I know him a little. He lowered the rent twenty-five a month when I told him it was my mother. He is a widower—a big fellow, mid-sixties. An unhappy man with a good sense of humor. His arms are covered with white hair, and white hair stands out from under his cap. He looks like a magazine illustration of a farmer. But he isn't a farmer. He is a retired construction worker who's saved a little money. For a while, in the beginning, I let myself imagine that he and my mother might take some meals together and become friends.

"There's the king," my mother says. "King Larry. Not everyone has as much money as he does and can live in a big house and charge other people high rents. Well, I hope I never see his cheap old face again once I leave here. Eat the rest of this chicken," she says to me. But I shake my head and light a cigarette. Larry pushes his mower past the window.

"You won't have to look at it much longer," Jill says.

"I'm sure glad of that, Jill. But I know he won't give me my deposit back."

"How do you know that?" I say.

"I just know," she says. "I've had dealings with his kind before. They're out for all they can get."

Jill says, "It won't be long now and you won't have to have anything more to do with him."

"I'll be so glad."

"But it'll be somebody just like him," Jill says.

"I don't want to think that, Jill," my mother says.

She makes coffee while Jill clears the table. I rinse the cups. Then I pour coffee, and we step around a box marked "Knickknacks" and take our cups into the living room.

Larry Hadlock is at the side of the house. Traffic moves slowly on the street out in front, and the sun has started down over the trees. I can hear the commotion the mower makes. Some crows leave the phone line and settle onto the newly cut grass in the front yard.

"I'm going to miss you, honey," my mother says. Then she says, "I'll miss you, too, Jill. I'm going the miss both of you."

Jill sips from her coffee and nods. Then she says, "I hope you have a safe trip back and find the place you're looking for at the end of the road."

"When I get settled—and this is my last move, so help me—I hope you'll come and visit," my mother says. She looks at me and waits to be reassured.

"We will," I say. But even as I say it I know it isn't true. My life caved in on me down there, and I won't be going back.

"I wish you could have been happier here," Jill says. "I wish you'd been able to stick it out or something. You know what? Your son is worried sick about you."

"Jill," I say.

But she gives her head a little shake and goes on. "Sometimes he can't sleep over it. He wakes up sometimes in the night and says, 'I can't sleep. I'm thinking about my mother.' There," she says and looks at me. "I've said it. But it was on my mind."

"How do you think I must feel?" my mother says. Then she says, "Other women my age can be happy. Why can't I be like other women? All I want is a house and a town to live in that will make me happy. That isn't a crime, is it? I hope not. I hope I'm not asking too much out of life." She puts her cup on the floor next to her chair and waits for Jill to tell her she isn't asking for too much. But Jill doesn't say anything, and in a minute my mother begins to outline her plans to be happy.

After a time Jill lowers her eyes to her cup and has some more coffee. I can tell she's stopped listening. But my mother keeps talking anyway. The crows work their way through the grass in the front yard. I hear the mower howl and then thud as it picks up a clump of grass in the blade and comes to a stop. In a minute, after several tries, Larry gets it going again. The crows fly off, back to their wire. Jill picks at a fingernail. My mother is saying that the secondhand-furniture dealer is coming around the next morning to collect the things she isn't going to send on the bus or carry with her in the car. The table and chairs, TV, sofa, and bed are going with the dealer. But he's told her he doesn't have any use for the card table, so my mother is going to throw it out unless we want it.

"We'll take it," I say. Jill looks over. She starts to say something but changes her mind.

I will drive the boxes to the Greyhound station the next afternoon and start them on the way to California. My mother will spend the last night with us, as arranged. And then, early the next morning, two days from now, she'll be on her way.

She continues to talk. She talks on and on as she describes the trip she is about to make. She'll drive until four o'clock in the afternoon and then take a motel room for the night. She figures to make Eugene by dark. Eugene is a nice town—she stayed there once before, on the way up here. When she leaves the motel, she'll leave at sunrise and should, if God is looking out for her, be in California that afternoon. And God *is* looking out for her, she knows he is. How else explain her being kept around on the face of the earth? He has a plan for her. She's been praying a lot lately. She's been praying for me, too.

"Why are you praying for him?" Jill wants to know.

"Because I feel like it. Because he's my son," my mother says. "Is there anything the matter with that? Don't we all need praying for sometimes? Maybe some people don't. I don't know. What do I know anymore?" She brings a hand to her forehead and rearranges some hair that's come loose from a pin.

The mower sputters off, and pretty soon we see Larry go around the house pulling the hose. He sets the hose out and then goes slowly back around the house to turn the water on. The sprinkler begins to turn.

My mother starts listing the ways she imagines Larry has wronged her since she's been in the house. But now I'm not listening, either. I am thinking how she is about to go down the highway again, and nobody can reason with her or do anything to stop her. What can I do? I can't tie her up, or commit her, though it may come to that eventually. I worry for her, and she is a heartache to me. She is all the family I have left. I'm sorry she didn't like it here and wants to leave. But I'm never going back to California. And when that's clear to me I understand something else, too. I understand that after she leaves I'm probably never going to see her again.

I look over at my mother. She stops talking. Jill raises her eyes. Both of them look at me.

"What is it, honey?" my mother says.

"What's wrong?" Jill says.

I lean forward in the chair and cover my face with my hands. I sit like that for a minute, feeling bad and stupid for doing it. But I can't help it. And the woman who brought me into this life, and this other woman I picked up with less than a year ago, they exclaim together and rise and come over to where I sit with my head in my hands like a fool. I don't open my eyes. I listen to the sprinkler whipping the grass.

"What's wrong? What's the matter?" they say.

"It's okay," I say. And in a minute it is. I open my eyes and bring my head up. I reach for a cigarette.

"See what I mean?" Jill says. "You're driving him crazy. He's going crazy with worry over you." She is on one side of my chair, and my mother is on the other side. They could tear me apart in no time at all.

"I wish I could die and get out of everyone's way," my mother says quietly. "So help me Hannah, I can't take much more of this."

"How about some more coffee?" I say. "Maybe we ought to catch the news," I say. "Then I guess Jill and I better head for home."

Two days later, early in the morning, I say good-bye to my mother for what may be the last time. I've let Jill sleep. It won't hurt if she's late to work for a change. The dogs can wait for their baths and trimmings and such. My mother holds my arm as I walk her down the steps to the driveway and open the car door for her. She is wearing white slacks and a white blouse and white sandals. Her hair is pulled back and tied with a scarf. That's white, too. It's going to be a nice day, and the sky is clear and already blue.

On the front seat of the car I see maps and a thermos of coffee. My mother looks at these things as if she can't recall having come outside with them just a few minutes ago. She turns to me then and says, "Let me hug you once more. Let me love your neck. I know I won't see you for a long time." She puts an arm around my neck, draws me to her, and then begins to cry. But she stops almost at once and steps back, pushing the heel of her hand against her eyes. "I said I wouldn't do that, and I won't. But let me get a last look at you anyway. I'll miss you, honey," she says. "I'm just going to have to live through this. I've already lived through things I didn't think were possible. But I'll live through this, too, I guess." She gets into the car, starts it, and runs the engine for a minute. She rolls her window down.

"I'm going to miss you," I say. And I *am* going to miss her. She's my mother, after all, and why shouldn't I miss her? But, God forgive me, I'm glad, too, that it's finally time and that she is leaving.

"Good-bye," she says. "Tell Jill thanks for supper last night. Tell her I said good-bye."

"I will," I say. I stand there wanting to say something else. But I don't know what. We keep looking at each other, trying to smile and reassure each other. Then something comes into her eyes, and I believe she is thinking about the highway and how far she is going to have to drive that day. She takes her eyes off me and looks down the road. Then she rolls her window up, puts the car into gear, and drives to the intersection, where she has to wait for the light to change. When I see she's made it into traffic and headed toward the highway, I go back in the house and drink some coffee. I feel sad for a while, and then the sadness goes away and I start thinking about other things.

A few nights later my mother calls to say she is in her new place. She is busy fixing it up, the way she does when she has a new place. She tells me I'll be happy to know she likes it just fine to be back in sunny California. But she says there's something in the air where she is living, maybe it's pollen, that is causing her to sneeze a lot. And the traffic is heavier than she remembers from before. She doesn't recall there being so much traffic in her neighborhood. Naturally, everyone still drives like crazy down there. "California drivers," she says. "What else can you expect?" She says it's hot for this time of the year. She doesn't think the air-conditioning unit in her apartment is working right. I tell her she should talk to the manager. "She's never around when you need her," my mother says. She hopes she hasn't made a mistake in moving back to California. She waits before she says anything else.

I'm standing at the window with the phone pressed to my ear, looking out at the lights from town and at the lighted houses closer by. Jill is at the table with the catalogue, listening.

"Are you still there?" my mother asks. "I wish you'd say something."

I don't know why, but it's then I recall the affectionate name my dad used sometimes when he was talking nice to my mother—those times, that is, when he wasn't drunk. It was a long time ago, and I was a kid, but always, hearing it, I felt better, less afraid, more hopeful about the future. "*Dear,*" he'd say. He called her "dear" sometimes—a sweet name. "Dear," he'd say, "if you're going to the store, will you bring me some cigarettes?" or "Dear, is your cold any better?" "Dear, where is my coffee cup?"

The word issues from my lips before I can think what else I want to say to go along with it. "Dear." I say it again. I call her "dear." "Dear, try not to be afraid," I say. I tell my mother I love her and I'll write to her, yes. Then I say good-bye, and I hang up.

For a while I don't move from the window. I keep standing there, looking out at the lighted houses in our neighborhood. As I watch, a car turns off the road and pulls into a driveway. The porch light goes on. The door to the house opens and someone comes out on the porch and stands there waiting.

Jill turns the pages of her catalogue, and then she stops turning them. "This is what we want," she says. "This is more like what I had in mind. Look at this, will you." But I don't look. I don't care five cents for curtains. "What is it you see out there, honey?" Jill says. "Tell me."

What's there to tell? The people over there embrace for a minute, and then they go inside the house together. They leave the light burning. Then they remember, and it goes out.

1986

SIX

Decolonizing the Imagination

Part of being alive is discovering that the attitudes that we thought "natural" between people—between men and women, blacks and whites, people of all cultures, races, and religions—are actually socially constructed. Human beings, for the most part, do not have an enviable history in dealing with others whom they perceive to be different. Difference, whether sexual or racial, cultural or religious, tends to incite the dominant culture to banish the Other, and treat him (or her) as the conquerors did the people of the colonies, just as the Boers in South Africa used apartheid to banish the indigenous peoples to the ironically titled "homelands." The power of the story, however, allows us to decolonize our imaginations and to integrate the Other within ourselves.

The stories in this chapter set their characters within an arena of prejudice, persecution, suspicion, and oppression. When a lesbian couple moves into Gloria Naylor's Brewster Place ("The Two"), they are greeted with hostility: "Confronted with the difference that had been thrust into their predictable world," the neighbors piece together prejudice out "of their secret fears and lingering childhood nightmares." The presence of prejudice marks an absence in their hearts.

In some of these stories, the point of view belongs to the people who are perpetrating the cruelty. Shirley Jackson, in "Flower Garden," puts us in the mind of the persecutor, who recognizes that her own delight in being cruel is exactly the same pleasure that her mother-in-law takes in her oppression of the narrator. The narrator persecutes because of her own weakness: she is afraid of being cast out of her society along with the transgressor.

Other stories place us in the minds of the victims, who can see the likeness between themselves and their tormentors that the tormentors seem to deny. For example, in Reginald McKnight's "The Kind of Light That Shines on Texas," the young African American is taught in school that "the color of the thing isn't what you see, but the light that's reflected off it," but he wonders if a light exists that would reveal the sameness between him and his classmates.

Helena María Viramontes, in "The Cariboo Cafe," gives us access to both the victim and the victimizer. Her story shows the almost unimaginable cruelty of a political regime, especially in its practices against women and children. The point of view shifts from the woman—shattered by her son's torture and death —to the man who betrays her, who is damaged by his own losses.

In "Fever" John Edgar Wideman juxtaposes fragments of persecution, slavery, and sickness to form a collagelike narrative about the yellow fever epidemic burning through Philadelphia in 1793. The African Americans were punished by three lies: first, they were blamed for the pestilence; second, they were declared immune and were forced into caring for the dying white population while their own families and friends suffered their last agonies alone; and third, their labors were derided and denied. "Fever" repudiates these lies and replaces them with a fiery gaze into the nature of oppression.

Of all these stories, Anna Lee Walters's "The Warriors" allows her characters the most hope, but even they don't escape unscathed. Two young Pawnee girls are taught about their culture, customs, and etiquette by their uncle. Yet even these oral tribal lessons aren't powerful enough to defeat Uncle Ralph's alcoholism, and the traditions aren't strong enough to save the teller from losing his people and his life. Despite these losses, the girls grow into warriors who follow their tradition and do battle to "live beautifully or not live at all"—and who are strengthened by exchanging stories about their cultural identity.

Historically, the prejudiced dominant culture has sentenced the Other, either literally or metaphorically, to uncharted colonies. But stories provide some means by which that Other can return to the designated center. Stories take us inside the Other, inside the victim and the victimizer, inside the oppressor and the oppressed. People have been literally erased because of their difference, effectively effaced from dominant accounts of history and culture. Writing has the power to bring those erased selves back into being.

GLORIA NAYLOR

The Two

At first they seemed like such nice girls. No one could remember exactly when they had moved into Brewster. It was earlier in the year before Ben was killed—of course, it had to be before Ben's death. But no one remembered if it was in the winter or spring of that year that the two had come. People often came and went on Brewster Place like a restless

Gloria Naylor once asserted that she hoped through her fiction to present the experiences of African American women without suggesting that her artistic perspective is in some way "definitive." In realizing this project, she drew on her own wide-ranging experiences, from her youth in New York—where she was born on January 25, 1950, and still lives today—to her missionary work for the Jehovah's Witnesses in North Carolina and Florida. Naylor's award-winning first novel, *The Women of Brewster Place* (1982), embraces a spectrum of differing viewpoints, which intertwine to show how the lives of seven women are shaped by racial, sexual, and economic divisions. Later novels, such as *Linden Hills* (1985), expand this purview, spinning off from places and themes introduced in her first novel. In the words of one reviewer, "Gloria Naylor is building a world."

night's dream, moving in and out in the dark to avoid eviction notices or neighborhood bulletins about the dilapidated condition of their furnishings. So it wasn't until the two were clocked leaving in the mornings and returning in the evenings at regular intervals that it was quietly absorbed that they now claimed Brewster as home. And Brewster waited, cautiously prepared to claim them, because you never knew about young women, and obviously single at that. But when no wild music or drunken friends careened out of the corner building on weekends, and especially, when no slightly eager husbands were encouraged to linger around that first-floor apartment and run errands for them, a suspended sigh of relief floated around the two when they dumped their garbage, did their shopping, and headed for the morning bus.

The women of Brewster had readily accepted the lighter, skinny one. There wasn't much threat in her timid mincing walk and the slightly protruding teeth she seemed so eager to show everyone in her bell-like good mornings and evenings. Breaths were held a little longer in the direction of the short dark one—too pretty, and too much behind. And she insisted on wearing those thin Qiana dresses that the summer breeze molded against the maddening rhythm of the twenty pounds of rounded flesh that she swung steadily down the street. Through slitted eyes, the women watched their men watching her pass, knowing the bastards were praying for a wind. But since she seemed oblivious to whether these supplications went answered, their sighs settled around her shoulders too. Nice girls.

And so no one even cared to remember exactly when they had moved into Brewster Place, until the rumor started. It had first spread through the block like a sour odor that's only faintly perceptible and easily ignored until it starts growing in strength from the dozen mouths it had been lying in, among clammy gums and scum-coated teeth. And then it was everywhere—lining the mouths and whitening the lips of everyone as they wrinkled up their noses at its pervading smell, unable to pinpoint the source or time of its initial arrival. Sophie could—she had been there.

It wasn't that the rumor had actually begun with Sophie. A rumor needs no true parent. It only needs a willing carrier, and it found one in Sophie. She had been there—on one of those August evenings when the sun's absence is a mockery because the heat leaves the air so heavy it presses the naked skin down on your body, to the point that a sheet becomes unbearable and sleep impossible. So most of Brewster was outside that night when the two had come in together, probably from one of those air-conditioned movies downtown, and had greeted the ones who were loitering around their building. And they had started up the steps when the skinny one tripped over a child's ball and the darker one had grabbed her by the arm and around the waist to break her fall. "Careful, don't wanna lose you now." And the two of them had laughed into each other's eyes and went into the building.

The smell had begun there. It outlined the image of the stumbling woman and the one who had broken her fall. Sophie and a few other women sniffed at the spot and then, perplexed, silently looked at each other. Where had they seen that before? They had often laughed and touched each other—held each other in joy or its dark twin—but where had they seen *that* before? It came to them as the scent drifted down the steps and entered their nostrils on the way to their inner mouths. They had seen that—done that—with their men. That shared moment of invisible communion reserved for two and hidden from the rest of the world behind laughter or tears or a touch. In the days before babies, miscarriages, and other broken dreams, after stolen caresses in barn stalls and cotton houses, after intimate walks from church and secret kisses with boys who were now long forgotten or permanently fixed in their lives—that was where. They could almost feel the odor moving about in their mouths, and they slowly knitted themselves together and let it out into the air like a yellow mist that began to cling to the bricks on Brewster.

So it got around that the two in 312 were *that* way. And they had seemed like such nice girls. Their regular exits and entrances to the block were viewed with a jaundiced eye. The quiet that rested around their door on the weekends hinted of all sorts of secret rituals, and their friendly indifference to the men on the street was an insult to the women as a brazen flaunting of unnatural ways.

Since Sophie's apartment windows faced theirs from across the air shaft, she became the official watchman for the block, and her opinions were deferred to whenever the two came up in conversation. Sophie took her position seriously and was constantly alert for any telltale signs that might creep out around their drawn shades, across from which she kept a religious vigil. An entire week of drawn shades was evidence enough to send her flying around with reports that as soon as it got dark they pulled their shades down and put on the lights. Heads nodded in knowing unison—a definite sign. If doubt was voiced with a "But I pull my shades down at night too," a whispered "Yeah, but you're not *that* way" was argument enough to win them over.

Sophie watched the lighter one dumping their garbage, and she went outside and opened the lid. Her eyes darted over the crushed tin cans, vegetable peelings, and empty chocolate chip cookie boxes. What do they do with all them chocolate chip cookies? It was surely a sign, but it would take some time to figure that one out. She saw Ben go into their apartment, and she waited and blocked his path as he came out, carrying his toolbox.

"What ya see?" She grabbed his arm and whispered wetly in his face.

Ben stared at her squinted eyes and drooping lips and shook his head slowly. "Uh, uh, uh, it was terrible."

"Yeah?" She moved in a little closer.

"Worst busted faucet I seen in my whole life." He shook her hand off his arm and left her standing in the middle of the block.

"You old sop bucket," she muttered, as she went back up on her stoop. A broken faucet, huh? Why did they need to use so much water?

Sophie had plenty to report that day. Ben had said it was terrible in there. No, she didn't know exactly what he had seen, but you can imagine—and they did. Confronted with the difference that had been thrust into their predictable world, they reached into their imaginations and, using an ancient pattern, weaved themselves a reason for its existence. Out of necessity they stitched all of their secret fears and lingering childhood nightmares into this existence, because even though it was deceptive enough to try and look as they looked, talk as they talked, and do as they did, it had to have some hidden stain to invalidate it— it was impossible for them both to be right. So they leaned back, supported by the sheer weight of their numbers and comforted by the woven barrier that kept them protected from the yellow mist that enshrouded the two as they came and went on Brewster Place.

Lorraine was the first to notice the change in the people on Brewster Place. She was a shy but naturally friendly woman who got up early, and had read the morning paper and done fifty sit-ups before it was time to leave for work. She came out of her apartment eager to start her day by greeting any of her neighbors who were outside. But she noticed that some of the people who had spoken to her before made a point of having something else to do with their eyes when she passed, although she could almost feel them staring at her back as she moved on. The ones who still spoke only did so after an uncomfortable pause, in which they seemed to be peering through her before they begrudged her a good morning or evening. She wondered if it was all in her mind and she thought about mentioning it to Theresa, but she didn't want to be accused of being too sensitive again. And how would Tee even notice anything like that anyway? She had a lousy attitude and hardly ever spoke to people. She stayed in that bed until the last moment and rushed out of the house fogged-up and grumpy, and she was used to being stared at—by men at least—because of her body.

Lorraine thought about these things as she came up the block from work, carrying a large paper bag. The group of women on her stoop parted silently and let her pass.

"Good evening," she said, as she climbed the steps.

Sophie was standing on the top step and tried to peek into the bag. "You been shopping, huh? What ya buy?" It was almost an accusation.

"Groceries." Lorraine shielded the top of the bag from view and squeezed past her with a confused frown. She saw Sophie throw a knowing glance to the others at the bottom of the stoop. What was wrong with this old woman? Was she crazy or something?

Lorraine went into her apartment. Theresa was sitting by the window, reading a copy of *Mademoiselle.* She glanced up from her magazine. "Did you get my chocolate chip cookies?"

"Why good evening to you, too, Tee. And how was my day? Just wonderful." She sat the bag down on the couch. "The little Baxter boy brought in a puppy for show-and-tell, and the damn thing pissed all over the floor and then proceeded to chew the heel off my shoe, but, yes, I managed to hobble to the store and bring you your chocolate chip cookies."

Oh, Jesus, Theresa thought, she's got a bug up her ass tonight.

"Well, you should speak to Mrs. Baxter. She ought to train her kid better than that." She didn't wait for Lorraine to stop laughing before she tried to stretch her good mood. "Here, I'll put those things away. Want me to make dinner so you can rest? I only worked half a day, and the most tragic thing that went down was a broken fingernail and that got caught in my typewriter."

Lorraine followed Theresa into the kitchen. "No, I'm not really tired, and fair's fair, you cooked last night. I didn't mean to tick off like that; it's just that . . . well, Tee, have you noticed that people aren't as nice as they used to be?"

Theresa stiffened. Oh, God, here she goes again. "What people, Lorraine? Nice in what way?"

"Well, the people in this building and on the street. No one hardly speaks anymore. I mean, I'll come in and say good evening—and just silence. It wasn't like that when we first moved in. I don't know, it just makes you wonder; that's all. What are they thinking?"

"I personally don't give a shit what they're thinking. And their good evenings don't put any bread on my table."

"Yeah, but you didn't see the way that woman looked at me

out there. They must feel something or know something. They probably—"

"They, they, they!" Theresa exploded. "You know, I'm not starting
up with this again, Lorraine. Who in the hell are they? And where in
the hell are we? Living in some dump of a building in this God-forsaken
part of town around a bunch of ignorant niggers with the cotton still
under their fingernails because of you and your theys. They knew
something in Linden Hills, so I gave up an apartment for you that I'd
been in for the last four years. And then they knew in Park Heights,
and you made me so miserable there we had to leave. Now these
mysterious theys are on Brewster Place. Well, look out the window, kid.
There's a big wall down that block, and this is the end of the line for
me. I'm not moving anymore, so if that's what you're working yourself
up to—save it!"

When Theresa became angry she was like a lump of smoldering
coal, and her fierce bursts of temper always unsettled Lorraine.

"You see, that's why I didn't want to mention it." Lorraine began
to pull at her fingers nervously. "You're always flying up and jumping
to conclusions—no one said anything about moving. And I didn't know
your life has been so miserable since you met me. I'm sorry about that,"
she finished tearfully.

Theresa looked at Lorraine, standing in the kitchen door like a
wilted leaf, and she wanted to throw something at her. Why didn't she
ever fight back? The very softness that had first attracted her to Lorraine
was now a frequent cause for irritation. Smoked honey. That's what
Lorraine had reminded her of, sitting in her office clutching that application. Dry autumn days in Georgia woods, thick bloated smoke under
a beehive, and the first glimpse of amber honey just faintly darkened
about the edges by the burning twigs. She had flowed just that heavily
into Theresa's mind and had stuck there with a persistent sweetness.

But Theresa hadn't known then that this softness filled Lorraine up
to the very middle and that she would bend at the slightest pressure,
would be constantly seeking to surround herself with the comfort of
everyone's goodwill, and would shrivel up at the least touch of disapproval. It was becoming a drain to be continually called upon for this
nurturing and support that she just didn't understand. She had supplied
it at first out of love for Lorraine, hoping that she would harden eventually, even as honey does when exposed to the cold. Theresa was
growing tired of being clung to—of being the one who was leaned on.
She didn't want a child—she wanted someone who could stand toe to
toe with her and be willing to slug it out at times. If they practiced that
way with each other, then they could turn back to back and beat the

hell out of the world for trying to invade their territory. But she had found no such sparring partner in Lorraine, and the strain of fighting alone was beginning to show on her.

"Well, if it was that miserable, I would have been gone a long time ago," she said, watching her words refresh Lorraine like a gentle shower.

"I guess you think I'm some sort of a sick paranoid, but I can't afford to have people calling my job or writing letters to my principal. You know I've already lost a position like that in Detroit. And teaching is my whole life, Tee."

"I know," she sighed, not really knowing at all. There was no danger of that ever happening on Brewster Place. Lorraine taught too far from this neighborhood for anyone here to recognize her in that school. No, it wasn't her job she feared losing this time, but their approval. She wanted to stand out there and chat and trade makeup secrets and cake recipes. She wanted to be secretary of their block association and be asked to mind their kids while they ran to the store. And none of that was going to happen if they couldn't even bring themselves to accept her good evenings.

Theresa silently finished unpacking the groceries. "Why did you buy cottage cheese? Who eats that stuff?"

"Well, I thought we should go on a diet."

"If *we* go on a diet, then you'll disappear. You've got nothing to lose but your hair."

"Oh, I don't know. I thought that we might want to try and reduce our hips or something." Lorraine shrugged playfully.

"No, thank you. We are very happy with our hips the way they are," Theresa said, as she shoved the cottage cheese to the back of the refrigerator. "And even when I lose weight, it never comes off there. My chest and arms just get smaller, and I start looking like a bottle of salad dressing."

The two women laughed, and Theresa sat down to watch Lorraine fix dinner. "You know, this behind has always been my downfall. When I was coming up in Georgia with my grandmother, the boys used to promise me penny candy if I would let them pat my behind. And I used to love those jawbreakers—you know, the kind that lasted all day and kept changing colors in your mouth. So I was glad to oblige them, because in one afternoon I could collect a whole week's worth of jawbreakers."

"Really. That's funny to you? Having some boy feeling all over you."

Theresa sucked her teeth. "We were only kids, Lorraine. You know, you remind me of my grandmother. That was one straight-laced old lady. She had a fit when my brother told her what I was doing. She called me into the smokehouse and told me in this real scary whisper that I could get pregnant from letting little boys pat my butt and that I'd end up like my cousin Willa. But Willa and I had been thick as fleas, and she had already given me a step-by-step summary of how she'd gotten into her predicament. But I sneaked around to her house that night just to double-check her story, since that old lady had seemed so earnest. 'Willa, are you sure?' I whispered through her bedroom window. 'I'm tellin' ya, Tee,' she said. 'Just keep both feet on the ground and you home free.' Much later I learned that advice wasn't too biologically sound, but it worked in Georgia because those country boys didn't have much imagination."

Theresa's laughter bounced off of Lorraine's silent, rigid back and died in her throat. She angrily tore open a pack of the chocolate chip cookies. "Yeah," she said, staring at Lorraine's back and biting down hard into the cookie, "it wasn't until I came up north to college that I found out there's a whole lot of things that a dude with a little imagination can do to you even with both feet on the ground. You see, Willa forgot to tell me not to bend over or squat or—"

"Must you!" Lorraine turned around from the stove with her teeth clenched tightly together.

"Must I what, Lorraine? Must I talk about things that are as much a part of life as eating or breathing or growing old? Why are you always so uptight about sex or men?"

"I'm not uptight about anything. I just think it's disgusting when you go on and on about—"

"There's nothing disgusting about it, Lorraine. You've never been with a man, but I've been with quite a few—some better than others. There were a couple who I still hope to this day will die a slow, painful death, but then there were some who were good to me—in and out of bed."

"If they were so great, then why are you with me?" Lorraine's lips were trembling.

"Because—" Theresa looked steadily into her eyes and then down at the cookie she was twirling on the table. "Because," she continued slowly, "you can take a chocolate chip cookie and put holes in it and attach it to your ears and call it an earring, or hang it around your neck on a silver chain and pretend it's a necklace—but it's still a cookie. See —you can toss it in the air and call it a Frisbee or even a flying saucer, if the mood hits you, and it's still just a cookie. Send it spinning on a table—like this—until it's a wonderful blur of amber and brown light that you can imagine to be a topaz or rusted gold or old crystal, but the law of gravity has got to come into play, sometime, and it's got to come to rest—sometime. Then all the spinning and pretending and hoopla is over with. And you know what you got?"

"A chocolate chip cookie," Lorraine said.

"Uh-huh." Theresa put the cookie in her mouth and winked. "A lesbian." She got up from the table. "Call me when dinner's ready, I'm going back to read." She stopped at the kitchen door. "Now, why are you putting gravy on that chicken, Lorraine? You know it's fattening."

1983

SHIRLEY JACKSON

Flower Garden

After living in an old Vermont manor house together for almost eleven years, the two Mrs. Winnings, mother and daughter-in-law, had grown to look a good deal alike, as women will who live intimately together, and work in the same kitchen and get things done around the house in the same manner. Although young Mrs. Winning had been a Talbot, and had dark hair which she wore cut short, she was now officially a Winning, a member of the oldest family in town and her hair was beginning to grey where her mother-in-law's hair had greyed first, at the temples; they both had thin sharp-featured faces with eloquent hands, and sometimes when they were washing dishes or shelling peas

Born in San Francisco on December 14, 1919, Shirley Jackson's promise as a writer stretched as far back as the age of twelve, when she received a prize for her poetry. Conscientious application of this talent accompanied Jackson through her school years and, by her own account, helped her recover from repeated bouts of depression. In 1937 the young writer entered Syracuse University, where she received her degree and met the literary critic Stanley Edgar Hyman, whom she married in 1940. Jackson spent the rest of her life in North Bennington, Vermont, writing humorous stories for national periodicals, satiric fictionalized memoirs (*Raising Demons*, 1957), brooding and pessimistic novels (*The Sundial*, 1958), and of course her 1948 tale of violence, tradition, and small towns, "The Lottery."

or polishing silverware together, their hands, moving so quickly and similarly, communicated more easily and sympathetically than their minds ever could. Young Mrs. Winning thought sometimes, when she sat at the breakfast table next to her mother-in-law, with her baby girl in the high-chair close by, that they must resemble some stylized block print for a New England wallpaper; mother, daughter, and granddaughter, with perhaps Plymouth Rock or Concord Bridge in the background.

On this, as on other cold mornings, they lingered over their coffee, unwilling to leave the big kitchen with the coal stove and the pleasant atmosphere of food and cleanliness, and they sat together silently sometimes until the baby had long finished her breakfast and was playing quietly in the special baby corner, where uncounted Winning children had played with almost identical toys from the same heavy wooden box.

"It seems as though spring would never come," young Mrs. Winning said. "I get so tired of the cold."

"Got to be cold some of the time," her mother-in-law said. She began to move suddenly and quickly, stacking plates, indicating that the time for sitting was over and the time for working had begun. Young Mrs. Winning, rising immediately to help, thought for the thousandth time that her mother-in-law would never relinquish the position of authority in her own house until she was too old to move before anyone else.

"And I wish someone would move into the old cottage," young Mrs. Winning added. She stopped halfway to the pantry with the table napkins and said longingly, "If only *someone* would move in before spring." Young Mrs. Winning had wanted, long ago, to buy the cottage herself, for her husband to make with his own hands into a home where they could live with their children, but now, accustomed as she was to the big old house at the top of the hill where her husband's family had lived for generations, she had only a great kindness left toward the little cottage, and a wistful anxiety to see some happy young people living there. When she heard it was sold, as all the old houses were being sold in these days when no one could seem to find a newer place to live, she had allowed herself to watch daily for a sign that someone new was coming; every morning she glanced down from the back porch to see if there was smoke coming out of the cottage chimney, and every day going down the hill on her way to the store she hesitated past the cottage, watching carefully for the least movement within. The cottage had been sold in January and now, nearly two months later, even though it seemed prettier and less worn with the snow gently covering the overgrown garden and icicles in front of the blank windows, it was still forlorn and empty, despised since the day long ago when Mrs. Winning had given up all hope of ever living there.

Mrs. Winning deposited the napkins in the pantry and turned to tear the leaf off the kitchen calendar before selecting a dish towel and joining her mother-in-law at the sink. "March already," she said despondently.

"They *did* tell me down at the store yesterday," her mother-in-law said, "that they were going to start painting the cottage this week."

"Then that *must* mean someone's coming!"

"Can't take more than a couple of weeks to paint inside that little house," old Mrs. Winning said.

It was almost April, however, before the new people moved in. The snow had almost melted and was running down the street in icy, half-solid rivers. The ground was slushy and miserable to walk on, the skies grey and dull. In another month the first amazing green would start in the trees and on the ground, but for the better part of April there would be cold rain and perhaps more snow. The cottage had been painted inside, and new paper put on the walls. The front steps had been repaired and new glass put into the broken windows. In spite of the grey sky and the patches of dirty snow the cottage looked neater and firmer, and the painters were coming back to do the outside when the weather cleared. Mrs. Winning, standing at the foot of the cottage walk, tried to picture the cottage as it stood now, against the picture of the cottage she had made years ago, when she had hoped to live there herself. She had wanted roses by the porch; that could be done, and the neat colorful garden she had planned. She would have painted the outside white, and that too might still be done. Since the cottage had been sold she had not gone inside, but she remembered the little rooms, with the windows over the garden that could be so bright with gay curtains and window boxes, the small kitchen she would have painted yellow, the two bedrooms upstairs with slanting ceilings under the eaves. Mrs. Winning looked at the cottage for a long time, standing on the wet walk, and then went slowly on down to the store.

The first news she had of the new people came, at last, from the grocer a few days later. As he was tieing the string around the three pounds of hamburger the large Winning family would consume in one meal, he asked cheerfully, "Seen your new neighbors yet?"

"Have they moved in?" Mrs. Winning asked. "The people in the cottage?"

"Lady in here this morning," the grocer said. "Lady and a little boy, seem like nice people. They say her husband's dead. Nice-looking lady."

Mrs. Winning had been born in the town and the grocer's father had given her jawbreakers and licorice in the grocery store while the present grocer was still in high school. For a while, when she was twelve and the grocer's son was twenty, Mrs. Winning had hoped secretly that he would want to marry her. He was fleshy now, and middle-aged, and although he still called her Helen and she still called him Tom, she belonged now to the Winning family and had to speak critically to him, no matter how unwillingly, if the meat were tough or the butter price too high. She knew that when he spoke of the new neighbor as a "lady" he meant something different than if he had spoken of her as a "woman" or a "person." Mrs. Winning knew that he spoke of the two Mrs. Winnings to his other customers as "ladies." She hesitated and then asked, "Have they really moved in to stay?"

"She'll have to stay for a while," the grocer said drily. "Bought a week's worth of groceries."

Going back up the hill with her packages, Mrs. Winning watched all the way to detect some sign of the new people in the cottage. When she reached the cottage walk she slowed down and tried to watch not too obviously. There was no smoke coming from the chimney, and no sign of furniture near the house, as there might have been if people were still moving in, but there was a middle-aged car parked in the street before the cottage and Mrs. Winning thought she could see figures moving past the windows. On a sudden irresistible impulse she turned and went up the walk to the front porch, and then, after debating for a moment, on up the steps to the door. She knocked, holding her bag of groceries in one arm, and then the door opened and she looked down on a little boy, about the same age, she thought happily, as her own son.

"Hello," Mrs. Winning said.

"Hello," the boy said. He regarded her soberly.

"Is your mother here?" Mrs. Winning asked. "I came to see if I could help her move in."

"We're all moved in," the boy said. He was about to close the door, but a woman's voice said from somewhere in the house, "Davey? Are you talking to someone?"

"That's my mommy," the little boy said. The woman came up behind him and opened the door a little wider. "Yes?" she said.

Mrs. Winning said, "I'm Helen Winning. I live about three houses up the street, and I thought perhaps I might be able to help you."

"Thank you," the woman said doubtfully. She's younger than I am, Mrs. Winning thought, she's about thirty. And pretty. For a clear minute Mrs. Winning saw why the grocer had called her a lady.

"It's so nice to have someone living in this house," Mrs. Winning said shyly. Past the other woman's head she could see the small hallway, with the larger living-room beyond and the door on the left going into the kitchen, the stairs on the right, with the delicate stair-rail newly painted; they had done the hall in light green, and Mrs. Winning smiled with friendship at the woman in the doorway, thinking, She *has* done it right; this is the way it should look after all, she knows about pretty houses.

After a minute the other woman smiled back, and said, "Will you come in?"

As she stepped back to let Mrs. Winning in, Mrs. Winning wondered with a suddenly stricken conscience if perhaps she had not been too forward, almost pushing herself in. . . . "I hope I'm not making a nuisance of myself," she said unexpectedly, turning to the other woman. "It's just that I've been wanting to live here myself for so long." Why did I say that, she wondered; it had been a very long time since young Mrs. Winning had said the first thing that came into her head.

"Come see *my* room," the little boy said urgently, and Mrs. Winning smiled down at him.

"I have a little boy just about your age," she said. "What's your name?"

"Davey," the little boy said, moving closer to his mother. "Davey William MacLane."

"My little boy," Mrs. Winning said soberly, "is named Howard Talbot Winning."

The little boy looked up at his mother uncertainly, and Mrs. Winning, who felt ill at ease and awkward in this little house she so longed for, said, "How old are you? My little boy is five."

"I'm five," the little boy said, as though realizing it for the first time. He looked again at his mother and she said graciously, "Will you come in and see what we've done to the house?"

Mrs. Winning put her bag of groceries down on the slim-legged table in the green hall, and followed Mrs. MacLane into the living-room, which was L-shaped and had the windows Mrs. Winning would have fitted with gay curtains and flower-boxes. As she stepped into the room Mrs. Winning realized, with a quick wonderful relief, that it was really going to be all right, after all. Everything, from the andirons in the fireplace to the books on the table, was exactly as Mrs. Winning might have done if she were eleven years younger; a little more informal, perhaps, nothing of quite such good quality as young Mrs. Winning might have chosen, but still richly, undeniably right. There was a picture of Davey on the mantel, flanked by a picture which Mrs. Winning supposed was Davey's father; there was a glorious blue bowl on the low coffee table, and around the corner of the L stood a row of orange plates on a shelf, and a polished maple table and chairs.

"It's lovely," Mrs. Winning said. This could have been mine, she was thinking, and she stood in the doorway and said again, "It's perfectly lovely."

Mrs. MacLane crossed over to the low armchair by the fireplace and picked up the soft blue material that lay across the arm. "I'm making curtains," she said, and touched the blue bowl with the tip of one finger. "Somehow I always make my blue bowl the center of the room," she said. "I'm having the curtains the same blue, and my rug—when it comes!—will have the same blue in the design."

"It matches Davey's eyes," Mrs. Winning said, and when Mrs. MacLane smiled again she saw that it matched Mrs. MacLane's eyes too. Helpless before so much that was magic to her, Mrs. Winning said "*Have* you painted the kitchen yellow?"

"Yes," Mrs. MacLane said, surprised. "Come and see." She led the way through the L, around past the orange plates to the kitchen, which caught the late morning sun and shone with clean paint and bright aluminum; Mrs. Winning noticed the electric coffeepot, the waffle iron, the toaster, and thought, *she* couldn't have too much trouble cooking, not with just the two of them.

"When I have a garden," Mrs. MacLane said, "we'll be able to see it from almost all the windows." She gestured to the broad kitchen windows, and added, "I love gardens. I imagine I'll spend most of my time working in this one, as soon as the weather is nice."

"It's a good house for a garden," Mrs. Winning said. "I've heard that it used to be one of the prettiest gardens on the block."

"I thought so too," Mrs. MacLane said. "I'm going to have flowers on all four sides of the house. With a cottage like this you can, you know."

Oh, I know, I know, Mrs. Winning thought wistfully, remembering the neat charming garden she could have had, instead of the row of nasturtiums along the side of the Winning house, which she tended so carefully; no flowers would grow well around the Winning house, because of the heavy old maple trees which shaded all the yard and which had been tall when the house was built.

Mrs. MacLane had had the bathroom upstairs done in yellow, too, and the two small bedrooms with overhanging eaves were painted green and rose. "All garden colors," she told Mrs. Winning gaily, and Mrs. Winning, thinking of the oddly matched, austere bedrooms in the big Winning house, sighed and admitted that it would be wonderful to have window seats under the eaved windows. Davey's bedroom was the green one, and his small bed was close to the window. "This morning," he told Mrs. Winning solemnly, "I looked out and there were four icicles hanging by my bed."

Mrs. Winning stayed in the cottage longer than she should have; she felt certain, although Mrs. MacLane was pleasant and cordial, that her visit was extended past courtesy and into curiosity. Even so, it was only her sudden guilt about the three pounds of hamburger and dinner for the Winning men that drove her away. When she left, waving good-bye to Mrs. MacLane and Davey as they stood in the cottage doorway, she had invited Davey up to play with Howard, Mrs. MacLane up for tea, both of them to come for lunch some day, and all without the permission of her mother-in-law.

Reluctantly she came to the big house and turned past the bolted front door to go up the walk to the back door, which all the family used in the winter. Her mother-in-law looked up as she came into the kitchen and said irritably, "I called the store and Tom said you left an hour ago."

"I stopped off at the old cottage," Mrs. Winning said. She put the package of groceries down on the table and began to take things out quickly, to get the doughnuts on to a plate and the hamburger into the pan before too much time was lost. With her coat still on and her scarf over her head she moved as fast as she could while her mother-in-law, slicing bread at the kitchen table, watched her silently.

"Take your coat off," her mother-in-law said finally. "Your husband will be home in a minute."

By twelve o'clock the house was noisy and full of mud tracked across the kitchen floor. The oldest Howard, Mrs. Winning's father-in-law, came in from the farm and went silently to hang his hat and coat in the dark hall before speaking to his wife and daughter-in-law; the younger Howard, Mrs. Winning's husband, came in from the barn after putting the truck away and nodded to his wife and kissed his mother; and the youngest Howard, Mrs. Winning's son, crashed into the kitchen, home from kindergarten, shouting, "Where's dinner?"

The baby, anticipating food, banged on her high-chair with the silver cup which had first been used by the oldest Howard Winning's mother. Mrs. Winning and her mother-in-law put plates down on the table swiftly, knowing after many years the exact pause between the latest arrival and the serving of food, and with a minimum of time three generations of the Winning family were eating silently and efficiently, all anxious to be back about their work: the farm, the mill, the electric train; the dishes; the sewing, the nap. Mrs. Winning, feeding the baby, trying to anticipate her mother-in-law's gestures of serving, thought, today more poignantly than ever before, that she had at least given them another Howard, with the Winning eyes and mouth, in exchange for her food and her bed.

After dinner, after the men had gone back to work and the children were in bed, the baby for her nap and Howard resting with crayons and coloring book, Mrs. Winning sat down with her mother-in-law over their sewing and tried to describe the cottage.

"It's just perfect," she said helplessly. "Everything is so pretty. She invited us to come down some day and see it when it's all finished, the curtains and everything."

"I was talking to Mrs. Blake," the elder Mrs. Winning said, as though in agreement. "She says the husband was killed in an automobile accident. *She* had some money in her own name and I guess she decided to settle down in the country for the boy's health. Mrs. Blake said he looked peakish."

"She loves gardens," Mrs. Winning said, her needle still in her hand for a moment. "She's going to have a big garden all around the house."

"She'll need help," the elder woman said humorlessly, "that's a mighty big garden she'll have."

"She has the *most* beautiful blue bowl, Mother Winning. You'd love it, it's almost like silver."

"Probably," the elder Mrs. Winning said after a pause, "probably her people came from around here a ways back, and *that's* why she's settled in these parts."

The next day Mrs. Winning walked slowly past the cottage, and slowly the next, and the day after, and the day after that. On the second day she saw Mrs. MacLane at the window, and waved, and on the third day she met Davey on the sidewalk. "When are you coming to visit my little boy?" she asked him, and he stared at her solemnly and said, "Tomorrow."

Mrs. Burton, next-door to the MacLanes, ran over on the third day they were there with a fresh apple pie, and then told all the neighbors about the yellow kitchen and the bright electric utensils. Another neighbor, whose husband had helped Mrs. MacLane start her furnace, explained that Mrs. MacLane was only very recently widowed. One or another of the townspeople called on the MacLanes almost daily, and frequently, as young Mrs. Winning passed, she saw familiar faces at the windows, measuring the blue curtains with Mrs. MacLane, or she waved to acquaintances who stood chatting with Mrs. MacLane on the now firm front steps. After the MacLanes had been in the cottage for about a week Mrs. Winning met them one day in the grocery and they walked up the hill together, and talked about putting Davey into the kingergarten. Mrs. MacLane wanted to keep him home as long as possible, and Mrs. Winning asked her, "Don't you feel terribly tied down, having him with you all the time?"

"I like it," Mrs. MacLane said cheerfully, "we keep each other company," and Mrs. Winning felt clumsy and ill-mannered, remembering Mrs. MacLane's widowhood.

As the weather grew warmer and the first signs of green showed on the trees and on the wet ground, Mrs. Winning and Mrs. MacLane became better friends. They met almost daily at the grocery and walked up the hill together, and twice Davey came up to play with Howard's electric train, and once Mrs. MacLane came up to get him and stayed for a cup of coffee in the great kitchen while the boys raced round and round the table and Mrs. Winning's mother-in-law was visiting a neighbor.

"It's such an old house," Mrs. MacLane said, looking up at the dark ceiling. "I love old houses; they feel so secure and warm, as though lots of people had been perfectly satisfied with them and they *knew* how useful they were. You don't get that feeling with a new house."

"This dreary old place," Mrs. Winning said. Mrs. MacLane, with a rose-colored sweater and her bright soft hair, was a spot of color in the kitchen that Mrs. Winning knew she could never duplicate. "I'd give anything in the world to live in your house," Mrs. Winning said.

"*I* love it," Mrs. MacLane said. "I don't think I've ever been so happy. Everyone around here is so nice, and the house is so pretty, and I planted a lot of bulbs yesterday." She laughed. "I used to sit in that apartment in New York and dream about planting bulbs again."

Mrs. Winning looked at the boys, thinking how Howard was half-a-head taller, and stronger, and how Davey was small and weak and loved his mother adoringly. "It's been good for Davey already," she said. "There's color in his cheeks."

"Davey loves it," Mrs. MacLane agreed. Hearing his name Davey came over and put his head in her lap and she touched his hair, bright like her own. "We'd better be getting on home, Davey boy," she said.

"Maybe our flowers have grown some since yesterday," said Davey.

Gradually the days became miraculously long and warm, and Mrs. MacLane's garden began to show colors and became an ordered thing, still very young and unsure, but promising rich brilliance for the end of the summer, and the next summer, and summers ten years from now.

"It's even better than I hoped," Mrs. MacLane said to Mrs. Winning, standing at the garden gate. "Things grow so much better here than almost anywhere else."

Davey and Howard played daily after the school was out for the summer, and Howard was free all day. Sometimes Howard stayed at Davey's house for lunch, and they planted a vegetable patch together in the MacLane back yard. Mrs. Winning stopped for Mrs. MacLane on her way to the store in the mornings and Davey and Howard frolicked ahead of them down the street. They picked up their mail together and read it walking back up the hill, and Mrs. Winning went more cheerfully back to the big Winning house after walking most of the way home with Mrs. MacLane.

One afternoon Mrs. Winning put the baby in Howard's wagon and with the two boys they went for a long walk in the country. Mrs. MacLane picked Queen Anne's lace and put it into the wagon with the baby, and the boys found a garter snake and tried to bring it home. On the way up the hill Mrs. MacLane helped pull the wagon with the baby and the Queen Anne's lace, and they stopped halfway to rest and Mrs. MacLane said, "Look, I believe you can see my garden all the way from here."

It was a spot of color almost at the top of the hill and they stood looking at it while the baby threw the Queen Anne's lace out of the wagon. Mrs. MacLane said, "I always want to stop here to look at it," and then, "Who is that *beautiful* child?"

Mrs. Winning looked and then laughed. "He *is* attractive, isn't he," she said. "It's Billy Jones." She looked at him herself, carefully, trying to see him as Mrs. MacLane would. He was a boy about twelve, sitting quietly on a wall across the street, with his chin in his hands, silently watching Davey and Howard.

"He's like a young statue," Mrs. MacLane said. "So brown, and will you look at that face?" She started to walk again to see him more clearly, and Mrs. Winning followed her. "Do I know his mother and fath——?"

"The Jones children are half-Negro," Mrs. Winning said hastily. "But they're all beautiful children; you should see the girl. They live just outside town."

Howard's voice reached them clearly across the summer air. "Nigger," he was saying, "nigger, nigger boy."

"Nigger," Davey repeated, giggling.

Mrs. MacLane gasped, and then said, "*Davey*," in a voice that made Davey turn his head apprehensively; Mrs. Winning had never heard her friend use such a voice, and she too watched Mrs. MacLane.

"Davey," Mrs. MacLane said again, and Davey approached slowly. "What did I hear you say?"

"Howard," Mrs. Winning said, "leave Billy alone."

"Go tell that boy you're sorry," Mrs. MacLane said. "Go at once and tell him you're sorry."

Davey blinked tearfully at his mother and then went to the curb and called across the street, "I'm sorry."

Howard and Mrs. Winning waited uneasily, and Billy Jones across the street raised his head from his hands and looked at Davey and then, for a long time, at Mrs. MacLane. Then he put his chin on his hands again.

Suddenly Mrs. MacLane called, "Young man—Will you come here a minute, please?"

Mrs. Winning was surprised, and stared at Mrs. MacLane, but when the boy across the street did not move Mrs. Winning said sharply, "Billy! Billy Jones! Come here at once!"

The boy raised his head and looked at them, and then slid slowly down from the wall and started across the street. When he was across the street and about five feet from them he stopped, waiting.

"Hello," Mrs. MacLane said gently, "what's your name?"

The boy looked at her for a minute and then at Mrs. Winning, and Mrs. Winning said, "He's Billy Jones. Answer when you're spoken to, Billy."

"Billy," Mrs. MacLane said, "I'm sorry my little boy called you a name, but he's very little and he doesn't always know what he's saying. But he's sorry, too."

"Okay," Billy said, still watching Mrs. Winning. He was wearing an old pair of blue jeans and a torn white shirt, and he was barefoot. His skin and hair were the same color, the golden shade of a very heavy tan, and his hair curled lightly; he had the look of a garden statue.

"Billy," Mrs. MacLane said, "how would you like to come and work for me? Earn some money?"

"Sure," Billy said.

"Do you like gardening?" Mrs. MacLane asked. Billy nodded soberly. "Because," Mrs. MacLane went on enthusiastically, "I've been needing someone to help me with my garden, and it would be just the thing for you to do." She waited a minute and then said, "Do you know where I live?"

"Sure," Billy said. He turned his eyes away from Mrs. Winning and for a minute looked at Mrs. MacLane, his brown eyes expressionless. Then he looked back at Mrs. Winning, who was watching Howard up the street.

"Fine," Mrs. MacLane said. "Will you come tomorrow?"

"Sure," Billy said. He waited for a minute, looking from Mrs. MacLane to Mrs. Winning, and then ran back across the street and vaulted over the wall where he had been sitting. Mrs. MacLane watched him admiringly. Then she smiled at Mrs. Winning and gave the wagon a tug to start it up the hill again. They were nearly at the MacLane cottage before Mrs. MacLane finally spoke. "I just can't stand that," she said, "to hear children attacking people for things they can't help."

"They're strange people, the Joneses," Mrs. Winning said readily. "The father works around as a handyman; maybe you've seen him. You see—" she dropped her voice—"the mother was white, a girl from around here. A local girl," she said again, to make it more clear to a foreigner. "She left the whole litter of them when Billy was about two, and went off with a white man."

"Poor children," Mrs. MacLane said.

"*They're* all right," Mrs. Winning said. "The church takes care of them, of course, and people are always giving them things. The girl's old enough to work now, too. She's sixteen, but. . . ."

"But what?" Mrs. MacLane said, when Mrs. Winning hesitated.

"Well, people talk about her a lot, you know," Mrs. Winning said. "Think of her mother, after all. And there's another boy, couple of years older than Billy."

They stopped in front of the MacLane cottage and Mrs. MacLane touched Davey's hair. "Poor unfortunate child," she said.

"Children *will* call names," Mrs. Winning said. "There's not much you can do."

"Well . . ." Mrs. MacLane said. "Poor child."

The next day, after the dinner dishes were washed, and while Mrs. Winning and her mother-in-law were putting them away, the elder Mrs. Winning said casually, "Mrs. Blake tells me your friend Mrs. MacLane was asking around the neighbors how to get hold of the Jones boy."

"She wants someone to help in the garden, I think," Mrs. Winning said weakly. "She needs help in that big garden."

"Not *that* kind of help," the elder Mrs. Winning said. "You tell her about them?"

"She seemed to feel sorry for them," Mrs. Winning said, from the depths of the pantry. She took a long time settling the plates in even stacks in order to neaten her mind. She *shouldn't* have done it, she was thinking, but her mind refused to tell her why. She should have asked me first, though, she thought finally.

The next day Mrs. Winning stopped off at the cottage with Mrs. MacLane after coming up the hill from the store. They sat in the yellow kitchen and drank coffee, while the boys played in the back yard. While they were discussing the possibilities of hammocks between the apple trees there was a knock at the kitchen door and when Mrs. MacLane opened it she found a man standing there, so that she said, "Yes?" politely, and waited.

"Good morning," the man said. He took off his hat and nodded his head at Mrs. MacLane. "Billy told me you was looking for someone to work your garden," he said.

"Why . . ." Mrs. MacLane began, glancing sideways uneasily at Mrs. Winning.

"I'm Billy's father," the man said. He nodded his head toward the back yard and Mrs. MacLane saw Billy Jones sitting under one of the apple trees, his arms folded in front of him, his eyes on the grass at his feet.

"How do you do," Mrs. MacLane said inadequately.

"Billy told me you said for him to come work your garden," the man said. "Well, now, I think maybe a summer job's too much for a boy his age, he ought to be out playing in the good weather. And that's the kind of work I do anyway, so's I thought I'd just come over and see if you found anyone yet."

He was a big man, very much like Billy, except that where Billy's hair curled only a little, his father's hair curled tightly, with a line around his head where his hat stayed constantly and where Billy's skin was a golden tan, his father's skin was darker, almost bronze. When he moved, it was gracefully, like Billy, and his eyes were the same fathomless brown. "Like to work this garden," Mr. Jones said, looking around. "Could be a mighty nice place."

"You were very nice to come," Mrs. MacLane said. "I certainly do need help."

Mrs. Winning sat silently, not wanting to speak in front of Mr. Jones. She was thinking, I wish she'd ask me first, this is impossible . . . and Mr. Jones stood silently, listening courteously, with his dark eyes on Mrs. MacLane while she spoke. "I guess a lot of the work would be too much for a boy like Billy," she said. "There are a lot of things I can't even do myself, and I was sort of hoping I could get someone to give me a hand."

"That's fine, then," Mr. Jones said. "Guess I can manage most of it," he said, and smiled.

"Well," Mrs. MacLane said, "I guess that's all settled, then. When do you want to start?"

"How about right now?" he said.

"Grand," Mrs. MacLane said enthusiastically, and then, "Excuse me for a minute," to Mrs. Winning over her shoulder. She took down her gardening gloves and wide straw hat from the shelf by the door. "Isn't it a lovely day?" she asked Mr. Jones as she stepped out into the garden while he stood back to let her pass.

"You go along home now, Bill," Mr. Jones called as they went toward the side of the house.

"Oh, why not let him stay?" Mrs. MacLane said. Mrs. Winning heard her voice going on as they went out of sight. "He can play around the garden, and he'd probably enjoy . . ."

For a minute, Mrs. Winning sat looking at the garden, at the corner around which Mr. Jones had followed Mrs. MacLane, and then Howard's face appeared around the side of the door and he said, "Hi, is it nearly time to eat?"

"Howard," Mrs. Winning said quietly, and he came in through the door and came over to her. "It's time for you to run along home," Mrs. Winning said. "I'll be along in a minute."

Howard started to protest, but she added, "I want you to go right away. Take my bag of groceries if you think you can carry it."

Howard was impressed by her conception of his strength, and he lifted down the bag of groceries; his shoulders, already broad out of proportion, like his father's and his grandfather's, strained under the weight, and then he steadied on his feet. "Aren't I strong?" he asked exultantly.

"*Very* strong," Mrs. Winning said. "Tell Grandma I'll be right up. I'll just say good-bye to Mrs. MacLane."

Howard disappeared through the house; Mrs. Winning heard him walking heavily under the groceries, out through the open front door and down the steps. Mrs. Winning rose and was standing by the kitchen door when Mrs. MacLane came back.

"You're not ready to go?" Mrs. MacLane exclaimed when she saw Mrs. Winning with her jacket on. "Without finishing your coffee?"

"I'd better catch Howard," Mrs. Winning said. "He ran along ahead."

"I'm sorry I left you like that," Mrs. MacLane said. She stood in the doorway beside Mrs. Winning looking out into the garden. "How *wonderful* it all is," she said, and laughed happily.

They walked together through the house; the blue curtains were up by now, and the rug with the touch of blue in the design was on the floor.

"Good-bye," Mrs. Winning said on the front steps.

Mrs. MacLane was smiling, and following her look Mrs. Winning turned and saw Mr. Jones, his shirt off and his strong back shining in the sun as he bent with a scythe over the long grass at the side of the house. Billy lay nearby, under the shade of the bushes; he was playing with a grey kitten. "I'm going to have the finest garden in town," Mrs. MacLane said proudly.

"You won't have him working here past today, will you?" Mrs. Winning asked. "Of course you won't have him any longer than just today?"

"But surely—" Mrs. MacLane began, with a tolerant smile, and Mrs. Winning, after looking at her for an incredulous minute, turned and started, indignant and embarrassed, up the hill.

Howard had brought the groceries safely home and her mother-in-law was already setting the table.

"Howard says you sent him home from MacLanes," her mother-in-law said, and Mrs. Winning answered briefly, "I thought it was getting late."

The next morning when Mrs. Winning reached the cottage on her way down to the store she saw Mr. Jones swinging the scythe expertly against the side of the house, and Billy Jones and Davey sitting on the front steps watching him. "Good morning, Davey," Mrs. Winning called, "is your mother ready to go downstreet?"

"Where's Howard?" Davey asked, not moving.

"He stayed home with his grandma today," Mrs. Winning said brightly. "Is your mother ready?"

"She's making lemonade for Billy and me," Davey said. "We're going to have it in the garden."

"Then tell her," Mrs. Winning said quickly, "tell her that I said I was in a hurry and that I had to go on ahead. I'll see her later." She hurried on down the hill.

In the store she met Mrs. Harris, a lady whose mother had worked for the elder Mrs. Winning nearly forty years before. "Helen," Mrs. Harris said, "you get greyer every year. You ought to stop all this running around."

Mrs. Winning, in the store without Mrs. MacLane for the first time in weeks, smiled shyly and said that she guessed she needed a vacation.

"Vacation!" Mrs. Harris said. "Let that husband of yours do the housework for a change. He doesn't have nuthin' else to do."

She laughed richly, and shook her head. "Nuthin' else to do," she said. "The Winnings!"

Before Mrs. Winning could step away Mrs. Harris added, her laughter penetrated by a sudden sharp curiosity: "Where's that dressed-up friend of yours get to? Usually downstreet together, ain't you?"

Mrs. Winning smiled courteously, and Mrs. Harris said, laughing again, "Just couldn't believe those shoes of hers, first time I seen them. Them shoes!"

While she was laughing again Mrs. Winning escaped to the meat counter and began to discuss the potentialities of pork shoulder earnestly with the grocer. Mrs. Harris only says what everyone else says, she was thinking, are they talking like that about Mrs. MacLane? Are they laughing at her? When she thought of Mrs. MacLane she thought of the quiet house, the soft colors, the mother and son in the garden; Mrs. MacLane's shoes were green and yellow platform sandals, odd-looking certainly next to Mrs. Winning's solid white oxfords, but so inevitably right for Mrs. MacLane's house, and her garden. . . . Mrs. Harris came up behind her and said, laughing again, "What's she got, that Jones fellow working for her now?"

When Mrs. Winning reached home, after hurrying up the hill past the cottage, where she saw no one, her mother-in-law was waiting for her in front of the house, watching her come the last few yards. "Early enough today," her mother-in-law said. "MacLane out of town?"

Resentful, Mrs. Winning said only, "Mrs. Harris nearly drove me out of the store, with her jokes."

"Nothing wrong with Lucy Harris getting away from that man of hers wouldn't cure," the elder Mrs. Winning said. Together, they began to walk around the house to the back door. Mrs. Winning, as they walked, noticed that the grass under the trees had greened up nicely, and that the nasturtiums beside the house were bright.

"I've got something to say to you, Helen," the elder Mrs. Winning said finally.

"Yes?" her daughter-in-law said.

"It's the MacLane girl, about her, I mean. You know her well, you ought to talk to her about that colored man working there."

"I suppose so," Mrs. Winning said.

"You *sure* you told her? You told her about those people?"

"I told her," Mrs. Winning said.

"He's there every blessed day," her mother-in-law said. "And working out there without his shirt on. He goes in the house."

And that evening Mr. Burton, next-door neighbor to Mrs. MacLane, dropped in to see the Howard Winnings about getting a new lot of shingles at the mill; he turned, suddenly, to Mrs. Winning, who was sitting sewing next to her mother-in-law at the table in the front room, and raised his voice a little when he said, "Helen, I wish you'd tell your friend Mrs. MacLane to keep that kid of hers out of my vegetables."

"Davey?" Mrs. Winning said involuntarily.

"No," Mr. Burton said, while all the Winnings looked at the younger Mrs. Winning, "no, the other one, the colored boy. He's been running loose through our back yard. Makes me sort of mad, that kid coming in spoiling other people's property. You know," he added, turning to the Howard Winnings, "you know, that does make a person mad." There was a silence, and then Mr. Burton added, rising heavily, "Guess I'll say good-night to you people."

They all attended him to the door and came back to their work in silence. I've got to do something, Mrs. Winning was thinking, pretty soon they'll stop coming to me first, they'll tell someone else to speak to *me*. She looked up, found her mother-in-law looking at her, and they both looked down quickly.

Consequently Mrs. Winning went to the store the next morning earlier than usual, and she and Howard crossed the street just above the MacLane house, and went down the hill on the other side.

"Aren't we going to see Davey?" Howard asked once, and Mrs. Winning said carelessly, "Not today, Howard. Maybe your father will take you out to the mill this afternoon."

She avoided looking across the street at the MacLane house, and hurried to keep up with Howard.

Mrs. Winning met Mrs. MacLane occasionally after that at the store or the post office, and they spoke pleasantly. When Mrs. Winning passed the cottage after the first week or so, she was no longer embarrassed about going by, and even looked at it frankly once or twice. The garden was going beautifully; Mr. Jones's broad back was usually visible through the bushes, and Billy Jones sat on the steps or lay on the grass with Davey.

One morning on her way down the hill Mrs. Winning heard a conversation between Davey MacLane and Billy Jones; they were in the bushes together and she heard Davey's high familiar voice saying, "Billy, you want to build a house with me today?"

"Okay," Billy said. Mrs. Winning slowed her steps a little to hear.

"We'll build a big house out of branches," Davey said excitedly, "and when it's finished we'll ask my mommy if we can have lunch out there."

"You can't build a house just out of branches," Billy said. "You ought to have wood, and boards."

"And chairs and tables and dishes," Davey agreed. "And walls."

"Ask your mommy can we have two chairs out here," Billy said. "Then we can pretend the whole garden is our house."

"And I'll get us some cookies, too," Davey said. "And we'll ask my mommy and your daddy to come to our house." Mrs. Winning heard them shouting as she went down along the sidewalk.

You have to admit, she told herself as though she were being strictly just, you have to admit that he's doing a lot with that garden; it's the prettiest garden on the street. And Billy acts as though he had as much right there as Davey.

As the summer wore on into long hot days undistinguishable one from another, so that it was impossible to tell with any accuracy whether the light shower had been yesterday or the day before, the Winnings moved out into their yard to sit after supper, and in the warm darkness Mrs. Winning sometimes found an opportunity of sitting next to her husband so that she could touch his arm; she was never able to teach Howard to run to her and put his head in her lap, or inspire him with other than the perfunctory Winning affection, but she consoled herself with the thought that at least they were a family, a solid respectable thing.

The hot weather kept up, and Mrs. Winning began to spend more time in the store, postponing the long aching walk up the hill in the sun. She stopped and chatted with the grocer, with other young mothers in the town, with older friends of her mother-in-law's, talking about the weather, the work that had to be done before school started in the fall, chickenpox, the P.T.A. One morning she met Mrs. Burton in the store, and they spoke of their husbands, the heat, and the hot-weather occupations of their children before Mrs. Burton said: "By the way, Johnny will be six on Saturday and he's having a birthday party; can Howard come?"

"Wonderful," Mrs. Winning said, thinking, His good white shorts, the dark blue shirt, a carefully-wrapped present.

"Just about eight children," Mrs. Burton said, with the loving care-lessness mothers use in planning the birthday parties of their children. "They'll stay for supper, of course—send Howard down about three-thirty."

"That sounds so nice," Mrs. Winning said. "He'll be delighted when I tell him."

"I thought I'd have them all play outdoors most of the time," Mrs. Burton said. "In this weather. And then perhaps a few games indoors, and supper. Keep it simple—*you* know." She hesitated, running her finger around and around the top rim of a can of coffee. "Look," she said, "I hope you won't mind me asking, but would it be all right with you if I didn't invite the MacLane boy?"

Mrs. Winning felt sick for a minute, and had to wait for her voice to even out before she said lightly, "It's all right with me if it's all right with *you;* why do you have to ask *me?*"

Mrs. Burton laughed. "I just thought you might mind if he didn't come."

Mrs. Winning was thinking. Something bad has happened, somehow people think they know something about me that they won't say, they all pretend it's nothing, but this never happened to me before; I live with the Winnings, don't I? "Really," she said, putting the weight of the old Winning house into her voice, "why in the *world* would it bother me?" Did I take it too seriously, she was wondering, did I seem too anxious, should I have let it go?

Mrs. Burton was embarrassed, and she set the can of coffee down on the shelf and began to examine the other shelves studiously. "I'm sorry I mentioned it at all," she said.

Mrs. Winning felt that she had to say something further, something to state her position with finality, so that no longer would Mrs. Burton, at least, dare to use such a tone to a Winning, presume to preface a question with "I hope you don't mind me asking." "After all," Mrs. Winning said carefully, weighing the words, "she's like a second mother to Billy."

Mrs. Burton, turning to look at Mrs. Winning for confirmation, grimaced and said, "Good Lord, Helen!"

Mrs. Winning shrugged and then smiled and Mrs. Burton smiled and then Mrs. Winning said, "I do feel sorry for the little boy, though."

Mrs. Burton said, "Such a sweet little thing, too."

Mrs. Winning had just said, "He and Billy are together *all* the time now," when she looked up and saw Mrs. MacLane regarding her from the end of the aisle of shelves; it was impossible to tell whether she had heard them or not. For a minute Mrs. Winning looked steadily back at Mrs. MacLane, and then she said, with just the right note of cordiality, "Good morning, Mrs. MacLane. Where is your little boy this morning?"

"Good morning, Mrs. Winning," Mrs. MacLane said, and moved on past the aisle of shelves, and Mrs. Burton caught Mrs. Winning's arm and made a desperate gesture of hiding her face and, unable to help themselves, both she and Mrs. Winning began to laugh.

Soon after that, although the grass in the Winning yard under the maple trees stayed smooth and green, Mrs. Winning began to notice in her daily trips past the cottage that Mrs. MacLane's garden was suffering from the heat. The flowers wilted under the morning sun, and no longer stood up fresh and bright; the grass was browning slightly and the rose bushes Mrs. MacLane had put in so optimistically were noticeably dying. Mr. Jones seemed always cool, working steadily; sometimes bent down with his hands in the earth, sometimes tall against the side of the house, setting up a trellis or pruning a tree, but the blue curtains hung lifelessly at the windows. Mrs. MacLane still smiled at Mrs. Winning in the store, and then one day they met at the gate of Mrs. MacLane's garden and, after hesitating for a minute, Mrs. MacLane said, "Can you come in for a few minutes? I'd like to have a talk, if you have time."

"Surely," Mrs. Winning said courteously, and followed Mrs. Mac-Lane up the walk, still luxuriously bordered with flowering bushes, but somehow disenchanted, as though the summer heat had baked away the vivacity from the ground. In the familiar living-room Mrs. Winning sat down on a straight chair, holding herself politely stiff, while Mrs. MacLane sat as usual in her armchair.

"How is Davey?" Mrs. Winning asked finally, since Mrs. MacLane did not seem disposed to start any conversation.

"He's very well," Mrs. MacLane said, and smiled as she always did when speaking of Davey. "He's out back with Billy."

There was a quiet minute, and then Mrs. MacLane said, staring at the blue bowl on the coffee table, "What I wanted to ask you is, what on earth is gone wrong?"

Mrs. Winning had been holding herself stiff in readiness for some such question, and when she said, "I don't know what you mean," she thought, I sound exactly like Mother Winning, and realized, I'm enjoying this, just as *she* would; and no matter what she thought of herself she was unable to keep from adding, "*Is* something wrong?"

"Of course," Mrs. MacLane said. She stared at the blue bowl, and said slowly, "When I first came, everyone was so nice, and they seemed to like Davey and me and want to help us."

That's wrong, Mrs. Winning was thinking, you mustn't ever talk about whether people like you, that's bad taste.

"And the garden was going so well," Mrs. MacLane said helplessly. "And now, no one ever does more than just speak to us—I used to say 'Good morning' over the fence to Mrs. Burton, and now she just says 'Morning' and goes in the house—and no one ever smiles, or anything."

This is dreadful, Mrs. Winning thought, this is childish, this is complaining. People treat you as you treat them, she thought; she wanted desperately to go over and take Mrs. MacLane's hand and ask her to come back and be one of the nice people again; but she only sat straighter in the chair and said, "I'm sure you must be mistaken. I've never heard anyone speak of it."

"*Are* you sure?" Mrs. MacLane turned and looked at her. "Are you sure it isn't because of Mr. Jones working here?"

Mrs. Winning lifted her chin a little higher and said, "Why on earth would anyone around here be rude to you because of Jones?"

Mrs. MacLane came with her to the door, both of them planning vigorously for the days some time next week, when they would all go swimming, when they would have a picnic, and Mrs. Winning went down the hill thinking, The nerve of her, trying to blame the colored folks.

Toward the end of the summer there was a bad thunderstorm, breaking up the prolonged hot spell. It raged with heavy wind and rain over the town all night, sweeping without pity through the trees, pulling up young bushes and flowers ruthlessly; a barn was struck on one side of town, the wires pulled down on another. In the morning Mrs. Winning opened the back door to find the Winning yard littered with small branches from the maples, the grass bent almost flat to the ground.

Her mother-in-law came to the door behind her. "Quite a storm," she said, "did it wake you?"

"I woke up once and went to look at the children," Mrs. Winning said. "It must have been about three o'clock."

"I was up later," her mother-in-law said. "I looked at the children too; they were both asleep."

They turned together and went in to start breakfast.

Later in the day Mrs. Winning started down to the store; she had almost reached the MacLane cottage when she saw Mrs. MacLane standing in the front garden with Mr. Jones standing beside her and Billy Jones with Davey in the shadows of the front porch. They were all looking silently at a great branch from one of the Burtons' trees that lay across the center of the garden, crushing most of the flowering bushes and pinning down what was to have been a glorious tulip bed. As Mrs. Winning stopped, watching, Mrs. Burton came out on to her front porch to survey the storm-damage, and Mrs. MacLane called to her, "Good morning, Mrs. Burton, it looks like we have part of your tree over here."

"Looks so," Mrs. Burton said, and she went back into her house and closed the door flatly.

Mrs. Winning watched while Mrs. MacLane stood quietly for a minute. Then she looked up at Mr. Jones almost hopefully and she and Mr. Jones looked at one another for a long time. Then Mrs. MacLane said, her clear voice carrying lightly across the air washed clean by the storm: "Do you think I ought to give it up, Mr. Jones? Go back to the city where I'll never have to see another garden?"

Mr. Jones shook his head despondently, and Mrs. MacLane, her shoulders tired, went slowly over and sat on her front steps and Davey came and sat next to her. Mr. Jones took hold of the great branch angrily and tried to move it, shaking it and pulling until his shoulders tensed with the strength he was bringing to bear, but the branch only gave slightly and stayed, clinging to the garden.

"Leave it alone, Mr. Jones," Mrs. MacLane said finally. "Leave it for the next people to move!"

But still Mr. Jones pulled against the branch, and then suddenly Davey stood up and cried out, "There's Mrs. Winning! Hi, Mrs. Winning!"

Mrs. MacLane and Mr. Jones both turned, and Mrs. MacLane waved and called out, "Hello!"

Mrs. Winning swung around without speaking and started, with great dignity, back up the hill toward the old Winning house.

1948

REGINALD McKNIGHT

The Kind of Light That Shines on Texas

I never liked Marvin Pruitt. Never liked him, never knew him, even though there were only three of us in the class. Three black kids. In our school there were fourteen classrooms of thirty-odd white kids (in '66, they considered Chicanos provisionally white) and three or four black kids. Primary school in primary colors. Neat division. Alphabetized. They didn't stick us in the back, or arrange us by degrees of hue, apartheidlike. This was real integration, a ten-to-one ratio as tidy as upper-class landscaping. If it all worked, you could have ten white kids all to yourself. They could talk to you, get the feel of you, scrutinize you bone deep if they wanted to. They seldom wanted to, and that was fine with me for two reasons. The first was that their scrutiny was irritating. How do you comb your hair—why do you comb your hair—may I please touch your hair—were the kinds of questions they asked. This is no way to feel at home. The second reason was Marvin. He embarrassed me. He smelled bad, was at least two grades behind, was hostile, dark skinned, homely, closemouthed. I feared him for his size, pitied him for his dress, watched him all the time. Marveled at him, mystified, astonished, uneasy.

He had the habit of spitting on his right arm, juicing it down till it would glisten. He would start in immediately after taking his seat when we'd finished with the Pledge of Allegiance, "The Yellow Rose of Texas," "The Eyes of Texas Are upon You," and "Mistress Shady." Marvin would rub his spit-flecked arm with his left hand, rub and roll as if polishing an ebony pool cue. Then he would rest his head in the crook of his arm, sniffing, huffing deep like blackjacket boys huff bagsful of

It was the unpredictability of Reginald McKnight's upbringing—born in Germany in 1958 and raised as an Air Force brat in half a dozen different places—that gave this award-winning novelist and short-story writer a "strong sense of myself as an individual." Yet McKnight's sense of himself as an artist did not come to fruition until he visited Senegal in the early 1980s. That country became the setting (both literally and psychologically) for much of his later fiction, including his first novel, *I Get on the Bus* (1990), and many of the entries in his 1988 collection, *Moustapha's Eclipse*. This story is taken from his most recent collection, *The Kind of Light That Shines on Texas* (1992). McKnight teaches writing at Carnegie-Mellon University in Pittsburgh.

acrylics. After ten minutes or so, his eyes would close, heavy. He would sleep till recess. Mrs. Wickham would let him.

There was one other black kid in our class, a girl they called Ah-so. I never learned what she did to earn this name. There was nothing Asian about this big-shouldered girl. She was the tallest, heaviest kid in school. She was quiet, but I don't think any one of us was subtle or sophisticated enough to nickname our classmates according to any but physical attributes. Fat kids were called Porky or Butterball; skinny ones were called Stick or Ichabod. Ah-so was big, thick, and African. She would impassively sit, sullen, silent as Marvin. She wore the same dark blue pleated skirt every day, the same ruffled white blouse every day. Her skin always shone as if worked by Marvin's palms and fingers. I never spoke one word to her, nor she to me.

Of the three of us, Mrs. Wickham called only on Ah-so and me. Ah-so never answered one question, correctly or incorrectly, so far as I can recall. She wasn't stupid. When asked to read aloud she read well, seldom stumbling over long words, reading with humor and expression. But when Wickham asked her about Farmer Brown and how many cows, or the capital of Vermont, or the date of this war or that, Ah-so never spoke. Not one word. But you always felt she could have answered those questions if she'd wanted to. I sensed no tension, embarrassment, or anger in Ah-so's reticence. She simply refused to speak. There was something unshakable about her, some core so impenetrably solid, you got the feeling that if you stood too close to her she could eat your thoughts like a black star eats light. I didn't despise Ah-so as I despised Marvin. There was nothing malevolent about her. She sat like a great icon in the back of the classroom, tranquil, guarded, sealed up, watchful. She was close to sixteen, and it was my guess she'd given up on school. Perhaps she was just obliging the wishes of her family, sticking it out till the law could no longer reach her.

There were at least half a dozen older kids in our class. Besides Marvin and Ah-so there was Oakley, who sat behind me, whispering threats into my ear; Varna Willard with the large breasts; Eddie Limon, who played bass for a high school rock band; and Lawrence Ridderbeck, whom everyone said had a kid and a wife. You couldn't expect me to know anything about Texan educational practices of the 1960s, so I never knew why there were so many older kids in my sixth grade class. After all, I was just a boy and had transferred into the school around midyear. My father, an air force sergeant, had been sent to Viet Nam. The air force sent my mother, my sister Claire, and me to Connolly Air Force Base, which during the war housed "unaccompanied wives." I'd been to so many different schools in my short life that I ceased wondering about their differences. All I knew about the Texas schools is that they weren't afraid to flunk you.

Yet though I was only twelve then, I had a good idea why Wickham never once called on Marvin, why she let him snooze in the crook of his polished arm. I knew why she would press her lips together, and narrow her eyes at me whenever I correctly answered a question, rare as that was. I knew why she badgered Ah-so with questions everyone knew Ah-so would never even consider answering. Wickham didn't like us. She wasn't gross about it, but it was clear she didn't want us around. She would prove her dislike day after day with little stories and jokes. "I just want to share with you all," she would say, "a little riddle my daughter told me at the supper table th'other day. Now, where do you go when you injure your knee?" Then one, two, or all three of her pets would say for the rest of us, "We don't know, Miz Wickham," in that skin-chilling way suckasses speak, "where?" "Why, to Africa," Wickham would say, "where the knee grows."

The thirty-odd white kids would laugh, and I would look across the room at Marvin. He'd be asleep. I would glance back at Ah-so. She'd be sitting still as a projected image, staring down at her desk. I, myself, would smile at Wickham's stupid jokes, sometimes fake a laugh. I tried to show her that at least one of us was alive and alert, even though her jokes hurt. I sucked ass, too, I suppose. But I wanted her to understand more than anything that I was not like her other nigra children, that I was worthy of more than the nonattention and the negative attention she paid Marvin and Ah-so. I hated her, but never showed it. No one could safely contradict that woman. She knew all kinds of tricks to demean, control, and punish you. And she could swing her two-foot paddle as fluidly as a big league slugger swings a bat. You didn't speak in Wickham's class unless she spoke to you first. You didn't chew gum, or wear "hood" hair. You didn't drag your feet, curse, pass notes, hold hands with the opposite sex. Most especially, you didn't say anything bad about the Aggies, Governor Connolly, LBJ, Sam Houston, or Waco. You did the forbidden and she would get you. It was that simple.

She never got me, though. Never gave her reason to. But she could have invented reasons. She did a lot of that. I can't be sure, but I used to think she pitied me because my father was in Viet Nam and my uncle A.J. had recently died there. Whenever she would tell one of her racist jokes, she would always glance at me, preface the joke with, "Now don't you nigra children take offense. This is all in fun, you know. I just want to share with you all something Coach Gilchrest told me th'other day." She would tell her joke, and glance at me again. I'd giggle, feeling a little queasy. "I'm half Irish," she would chuckle, "and you should hear some of those Irish jokes." She never told any, and I never really expected her to. I just did my Tom-thing. I kept my shoes shined, my desk neat, answered her questions as best I could, never brought gum to school, never cursed, never slept in class. I wanted to show her we were not all the same.

I tried to show them all, all thirty-odd, that I was different. It worked to some degree, but not very well. When some article was stolen from someone's locker or desk, Marvin, not I, was the first accused. I'd be second. Neither Marvin, nor Ah-so nor I were ever chosen for certain classroom honors—"Pledge leader," "flag holder," "noise monitor," "paper passer outer," but Mrs. Wickham once let me be "eraser duster." I was proud. I didn't even care about the cracks my fellow students made about my finally having turned the right color. I had done something that Marvin, in the deeps of his never-ending sleep, couldn't even dream of doing. Jack Preston, a kid who sat in front of me, asked me one day at recess whether I was embarrassed about Marvin. "Can you believe that guy?" I said. "He's like a pig or something. Makes me sick."

"Does it make you ashamed to be colored?"

"No," I said, but I meant yes. Yes, if you insist on thinking us all the same. Yes, if his faults are mine, his weaknesses inherent in me.

"I'd be," said Jack.

I made no reply. I was ashamed. Ashamed for not defending Marvin and ashamed that Marvin even existed. But if it had occurred to me, I would have asked Jack whether he was ashamed of being white because of Oakley. Oakley, "Oak Tree," Kelvin "Oak Tree" Oakley. He was sixteen and proud of it. He made it clear to everyone, including Wickham, that his life's ambition was to stay in school one more year, till he'd be old enough to enlist in the army. "Them slopes got my brother," he would say. "I'mna sign up and git me a few slopes. Gonna kill them bastards deader'n shit." Oakley, so far as anyone knew, was and always had been the oldest kid in his family. But no one contradicted him. He would, as anyone would tell you, "snap yer neck jest as soon as look at you." Not a boy in class, excepting Marvin and myself, had been able to avoid Oakley's pink bellies, Texas titty twisters, moon pie punches, or worse. He didn't bother Marvin, I suppose, because Marvin was closer to his size and age, and because Marvin spent five-sixths of the school day asleep. Marvin probably never crossed Oakley's mind. And to say that Oakley hadn't bothered me is not to say he had no intention of ever doing so. In fact, this haphazard sketch of hairy fingers, slash of eyebrow, explosion of acne, elbows, and crooked teeth, swore almost daily that he'd like to kill me.

Naturally, I feared him. Though we were about the same height, he outweighed me by no less than forty pounds. He talked, stood, smoked, and swore like a man. No one, except for Mrs. Wickham, the principal, and the coach, ever laid a finger on him. And even Wickham knew that the hot lines she laid on him merely amused him. He would smile out at the classroom, goofy and bashful, as she laid down the two, five or maximum ten strokes on him. Often he would wink, or surreptitiously flash us the thumb as Wickham worked on him. When she was finished, Oakley would walk so cool back to his seat you'd think he was on wheels. He'd slide into his chair, sniff the air, and say, "Somethin's burnin. Do y'all smell smoke? I swanee, I smell smoke and fahr back here." If he made these cracks and never threatened me, I might have grown to admire Oakley, even liked him a little. But he hated me, and took every opportunity during the six-hour school day to make me aware of this. "Some Sambo's gittin his ass broke open one of these days," he'd mumble. "I wanna fight somebody. Need to keep in shape till I git to Nam."

I never said anything to him for the longest time. I pretended not to hear him, pretended not to notice his sour breath on my neck and ear. "Yep," he'd whisper. "Coonies keep ya in good shape for slope killin." Day in, day out, that's the kind of thing I'd pretend not to hear. But one day when the rain dropped down like lead balls, and the cold air made your skin look plucked, Oakley whispered to me, "My brother tells me it rains like this in Nam. Maybe I oughta go out at recess and break your ass open today. Nice and cool so you don't sweat. Nice and wet to clean up the blood." I said nothing for at least half a minute, then I turned half right and said, "Thought you said your brother was dead." Oakley, silent himself, for a time, poked me in the back with his pencil and hissed, "*Yer* dead." Wickham cut her eyes our way, and it was over.

It was hardest avoiding him in gym class. Especially when we played murderball. Oakley always aimed his throws at me. He threw with unblinking intensity, his teeth gritting, his neck veining, his face flushing, his black hair sweeping over one eye. He could throw hard, but the balls were squishy and harmless. In fact, I found his misses more intimidating than his hits. The balls would whizz by, thunder against the folded bleachers. They rattled as though a locomotive were passing through them. I would duck, dodge, leap as if he were throwing grenades. But he always hit me, sooner or later. And after a while I noticed that the other boys would avoid throwing at me, as if I belonged to Oakley.

One day, however, I was surprised to see that Oakley was throwing at everyone else but me. He was uncommonly accurate, too; kids were falling like tin cans. Since no one was throwing at me, I spent most of the game watching Oakley cut this one and that one down. Finally, he and I were the only ones left on the court. Try as he would, he couldn't hit me, nor I him. Coach Gilchrest blew his whistle and told Oakley and me to bring the red rubber balls to the equipment locker. I was relieved I'd escaped Oakley's stinging throws for once. I was feeling triumphant, full of myself. As Oakley and I approached Gilchrest, I thought about saying something friendly to Oakley: Good game, Oak Tree, I would say. Before I could speak, though, Gilchrest said, "All right boys, there's five minutes left in the period. Y'all are so good, looks like, you're gonna have to play like men. No boundaries, no catch outs, and you gotta hit your opponent three times in order to win. Got me?"

We nodded.

"And you're gonna use these," said Gilchrest, pointing to three volleyballs at his feet. "And you better believe they're pumped full. Oates, you start at that end of the court. Oak Tree, you're at th'other end. Just like usual, I'll set the balls at mid-court, and when I blow my whistle I want y'all to haul your cheeks to the middle and th'ow for all you're worth. Got me?" Gilchrest nodded at our nods, then added, "Remember, no boundaries, right?"

I at my end, Oakley at his, Gilchrest blew his whistle. I was faster than Oakley and scooped up a ball before he'd covered three quarters of his side. I aimed, threw, and popped him right on the knee. "One-zip!" I heard Gilchrest shout. The ball bounced off his knee and shot right back into my hands. I hurried my throw and missed. Oakley bent down, clutched the two remaining balls. I remember being amazed that he could palm each ball, run full out, and throw left-handed or right-handed without a shade of awkwardness. I spun, ran, but one of Oakley's throws glanced off the back of my head. "One-one!" hollered Gilchrest. I fell and spun on my ass as the other ball came sailing at me. I caught it. "He's out!" I yelled. Gilchrest's voice boomed, "No catch outs. Three hits. Three hits." I leapt to my feet as Oakley scrambled across the floor for another ball. I chased him down, leapt, and heaved the ball hard as he drew himself erect. The ball hit him dead in the face, and he went down flat. He rolled around, cupping his hands over his nose. Gilchrest sped to his side, helped him to his feet, asked him whether he was OK. Blood flowed from Oakley's nose, dripped in startlingly bright spots on the floor, his shoes, Gilchrest's shirt. The coach removed Oakley's T-shirt and pressed it against the big kid's nose to stanch the bleeding. As they walked past me toward the office I mumbled an apology to Oakley, but couldn't catch his reply. "You watch your filthy mouth, boy," said Gilchrest to Oakley.

The locker room was unnaturally quiet as I stepped into its steamy atmosphere. Eyes clicked in my direction, looked away. After I was out of my shorts, had my towel wrapped around me, my shower kit in hand,

Jack Preston and Brian Nailor approached me. Preston's hair was combed slick and plastic looking. Nailor's stood up like frozen flames. Nailor smiled at me with his big teeth and pale eyes. He poked my arm with a finger. "You fucked up," he said.

"I tried to apologize."

"Won't do you no good," said Preston.

"I swanee," said Nailor.

"It's part of the game," I said. "It was an accident. Wasn't my idea to use volleyballs."

"Don't matter," Preston said. "He's jest lookin for an excuse to fight you."

"I never done nothing to him."

"Don't matter," said Nailor. "He don't like you."

"Brian's right, Clint. He'd jest as soon kill you as look at you."

"I never done nothing to him."

"Look," said Preston, "I know him pretty good. And jest between you and me, it's cause you're a city boy—"

"Whadda you mean? I've never—"

"He don't like your clothes—"

"And he don't like the fancy way you talk in class."

"What fancy—"

"I'm tellin him, if you don't mind, Brian."

"Tell him then."

"He don't like the way you say 'tennis shoes' instead of sneakers. He don't like coloreds. A whole bunch of things, really."

"I never done nothing to him. He's got no reason—"

"*And*," said Nailor, grinning, "*and*, he says you're a stuck-up rich kid." Nailor's eyes had crow's-feet, bags beneath them. They were a man's eyes.

"My dad's a sergeant," I said.

"You chicken to fight him?" said Nailor.

"Yeah, Clint, don't be chicken. Jest go on and git it over with. He's whupped pert near ever'body else in the class. It ain't so bad."

"Might as well, Oates."

"Yeah, yer pretty skinny, but yer jest about his height. Jest git im in a headlock and don't let go."

"Goddamn," I said, "he's got no reason to—"

Their eyes shot right and I looked over my shoulder. Oakley stood at his locker, turning its tumblers. From where I stood I could see that a piece of cotton was wedged up one of his nostrils, and he already had the makings of a good shiner. His acne burned red like a fresh abrasion. He snapped the locker open and kicked his shoes off without sitting. Then he pulled off his shorts, revealing two paddle stripes on his ass.

They were fresh red bars speckled with white, the white speckles being the reverse impression of the paddle's suction holes. He must not have watched his filthy mouth while in Gilchrest's presence. Behind me, I heard Preston and Nailor pad to their lockers.

Oakley spoke without turning around. "Somebody's gonna git his skinny black ass kicked, right today, right after school." He said it softly. He slipped his jock off, turned around. I looked away. Out of the corner of my eye I saw him stride off, his hairy nakedness a weapon clearing the younger boys from his path. Just before he rounded the corner of the shower stalls, I threw my toilet kit to the floor and stammered, "I —I never did nothing to you, Oakley." He stopped, turned, stepped closer to me, wrapping his towel around himself. Sweat streamed down my rib cage. It felt like ice water. "You wanna go at it right now, boy?"

"I never did nothing to you." I felt tears in my eyes. I couldn't stop them even though I was blinking like mad. "Never."

He laughed. "You busted my nose, asshole."

"What about before? What'd I ever do to you?"

"See you after school, Coonie." Then he turned away, flashing his acne-spotted back like a semaphore. "Why?" I shouted. "Why you wanna fight me?" Oakley stopped and turned, folded his arms, leaned against a toilet stall. "Why you wanna fight *me*, Oakley?" I stepped over the bench. "What'd I do? Why me?" And then unconsciously, as if scratching, as if breathing, I walked toward Marvin, who stood a few feet from Oakley, combing his hair at the mirror. "Why not him?" I said. "How come you're after *me* and not *him?*" The room froze. Froze for a moment that was both evanescent and eternal, somewhere between an eye blink and a week in hell. No one moved, nothing happened; there was no sound at all. And then it was as if all of us at the same moment looked at Marvin. He just stood there, combing away, the only body in motion, I think. He combed his hair and combed it, as if seeing only his image, hearing only his comb scraping his scalp. I knew he'd heard me. There's no way he could not have heard me. But all he did was slide the comb into his pocket and walk out the door.

"I got no quarrel with Marvin," I heard Oakley say. I turned toward his voice, but he was already in the shower.

I was able to avoid Oakley at the end of the school day. I made my escape by asking Mrs. Wickham if I could go to the restroom.

"'Restroom,'" Oakley mumbled. "It's a damn toilet, sissy."

"Clinton," said Mrs. Wickham. "Can you *not* wait till the bell rings? It's almost three o'clock."

"No ma'am," I said. "I won't make it."

"Well, I should make you wait just to teach you to be more mindful about . . . hygiene . . . uh things." She sucked in her cheeks, squinted.

"But I'm feeling charitable today. You may go." I immediately left the building, and got on the bus. "Ain't you a little early?" said the bus driver, swinging the door shut. "Just left the office," I said. The driver nodded, apparently not giving me a second thought. I had no idea why I'd told her I'd come from the office, or why she found it a satisfactory answer. Two minutes later the bus filled, rolled and shook its way to Connolly Air Base.

When I got home, my mother was sitting in the living room, smoking her Slims, watching her soap opera. She absently asked me how my day had gone and I told her fine. "Hear from Dad?" I said.

"No, but I'm sure he's fine." She always said that when we hadn't heard from him in a while. I suppose she thought I was worried about him, or that I felt vulnerable without him. It was neither. I just wanted to discuss something with my mother that we both cared about. If I spoke with her about things that happened at school, or on my weekends, she'd listen with half an ear, say something like, "Is that so?" or "You don't say?" I couldn't stand that sort of thing. But when I mentioned my father, she treated me a bit more like an adult, or at least someone who was worth listening to. I didn't want to feel like a boy that afternoon. As I turned from my mother and walked down the hall I thought about the day my father left for Viet Nam. Sharp in his uniform, sure behind his aviator specs, he slipped a cigar from his pocket and stuck it in mine. "Not till I get back," he said. "We'll have us one when we go fishing. Just you and me, out on the lake all day, smoking and casting and sitting. Don't let Mamma see it. Put it in y'back pocket." He hugged me, shook my hand, and told me I was the man of the house now. He told me he was depending on me to take good care of my mother and sister. "Don't you let me down, now, hear?" And he tapped his thick finger on my chest. "You almost as big as me. Boy, you something else." I believed him when he told me those things. My heart swelled big enough to swallow my father, my mother, Claire. I loved, feared, and respected myself, my manhood. That day I could have put all of Waco, Texas, in my heart. And it wasn't till about three months later that I discovered I really wasn't the man of the house, that my mother and sister, as they always had, were taking care of me.

For a brief moment I considered telling my mother about what had happened at school that day, but for one thing, she was deep down in the halls of "General Hospital," and never paid you much mind till it was over. For another thing, I just wasn't the kind of person—I'm still not, really—to discuss my problems with anyone. Like my father I kept things to myself, talked about my problems only in retrospect. Since my father wasn't around, I consciously wanted to be like him, doubly like him, I could say. I wanted to be the man of the house in some respect, even if it had to be in an inward way. I went to my room, changed my clothes, and laid out my homework. I couldn't focus on it. I thought about Marvin, what I'd said about him or done to him—I couldn't tell which. I'd done something to him, said something about him; said something about and done something to myself. *How come you're after me and not* him? I kept trying to tell myself I hadn't meant it that way. *That* way. I thought about approaching Marvin, telling him what I really meant was that he was more Oakley's age and weight than I. I would tell him I meant I was no match for Oakley. *See, Marvin, what I meant was that he wants to fight a colored guy, but is afraid to fight you cause you could beat him.* But try as I did, I couldn't for a moment convince myself that Marvin would believe me. I meant it *that* way and no other. Everybody heard. Everybody knew. That afternoon I forced myself to confront the notion that tomorrow I would probably have to fight both Oakley and Marvin. I'd have to be two men.

I rose from my desk and walked to the window. The light made my skin look orange, and I started thinking about what Wickham had told us once about light. She said that oranges and apples, leaves and flowers, the whole multi-colored world, was not what it appeared to be. The colors we see, she said, look like they do only because of the light or ray that shines on them. "The color of the thing isn't what you see, but the light that's reflected off it." Then she shut out the lights and shone a white light lamp on a prism. We watched the pale splay of colors on the projector screen; some people ooohed and aaahed. Suddenly, she switched on a black light and the color of everything changed. The prism colors vanished, Wickham's arms were purple, the buttons of her dress were as orange as hot coals, rather than the blue they had been only seconds before. We were all very quiet. "Nothing," she said after a while, "is really what it appears to be." I didn't really understand then. But as I stood at the window, gazing at my orange skin, I wondered what kind of light I could shine on Marvin, Oakley, and me that would reveal us as the same.

I sat down and stared at my arms. They were dark brown again. I worked up a bit of saliva under my tongue and spat on my left arm. I spat again, then rubbed the spittle into it, polishing, working till my arm grew warm. As I spat, and rubbed, I wondered why Marvin did this weird, nasty thing to himself, day after day. Was he trying to rub away the black, or deepen it, doll it up? And if he did this weird nasty thing for a hundred years, would he spit-shine himself invisible, rolling away the eggplant skin, revealing the scarlet muscle, blue vein, pink and yellow tendon, white bone? Then disappear? Seen through, all colors, no colors. Spitting and rubbing. Is this the way you do it? I leaned forward, sniffed the arm. It smelled vaguely of mayonnaise. After an hour or so, I fell asleep.

I saw Oakley the second I stepped off the bus the next morning. He stood outside the gym in his usual black penny loafers, white socks, high water jeans, T-shirt, and black jacket. Nailor stood with him, his big teeth spread across his bottom lip like playing cards. If there was anyone I felt like fighting, that day, it was Nailor. But I wanted to put off fighting for as long as I could. I stepped toward the gymnasium, thinking that I shouldn't run, but if I hurried I could beat Oakley to the door and secure myself near Gilchrest's office. But the moment I stepped into the gym, I felt Oakley's broad palm clap down on my shoulder. "Might as well stay out here, Coonie," he said. "I need me a little target practice." I turned to face him and he slapped me, one-two, with the back, then the palm of his hand, as I'd seen Bogart do to Peter Lorre in "The Maltese Falcon." My heart went wild. I could scarcely breathe. I couldn't swallow.

"Call me a nigger," I said. I have no idea what made me say this. All I know is that it kept me from crying. "Call me a nigger, Oakley."

"Fuck you, ya black ass slope." He slapped me again, scratching my eye. "I don't do what coonies tell me."

"Call me a nigger."

"Outside, Coonie."

"Call me one. Go ahead."

He lifted his hand to slap me again, but before his arm could swing my way, Marvin Pruitt came from behind me and calmly pushed me aside. "Git out my way, boy," he said. And he slugged Oakley on the side of his head. Oakley stumbled back, stiff-legged. His eyes were big. Marvin hit him twice more, once again to the side of the head, once to the nose. Oakley went down and stayed down. Though blood was drawn, whistles blowing, fingers pointing, kids hollering, Marvin just stood there, staring at me with cool eyes. He spat on the ground, licked his lips, and just stared at me, till Coach Gilchrest and Mr. Calderon tackled him and violently carried him away. He never struggled, never took his eyes off me.

Nailor and Mrs. Wickham helped Oakley to his feet. His already fattened nose bled and swelled so that I had to look away. He looked around, bemused, wall-eyed, maybe scared. It was apparent he had no idea how bad he was hurt. He didn't even touch his nose. He didn't look like he knew much of anything. He looked at me, looked me dead in the eye in fact, but didn't seem to recognize me.

That morning, like all other mornings, we said the Pledge of Allegiance, sang "The Yellow Rose of Texas," "The Eyes of Texas Are upon You," and "Mistress Shady." The room stood strangely empty without Oakley, and without Marvin, but at the same time you could feel their presence more intensely somehow. I felt like I did when I'd walk into my mother's room and could smell my father's cigars, or cologne. He was more palpable, in certain respects, than when there in actual flesh. For some reason, I turned to look at Ah-so, and just this once I let my eyes linger on her face. She had a very gentle-looking face, really. That surprised me. She must have felt my eyes on her because she glanced up at me for a second and smiled, white teeth, downcast eyes. Such a pretty smile. That surprised me too. She held it for a few seconds, then let it fade. She looked down at her desk, and sat still as a photograph.

1989

HELENA MARÍA VIRAMONTES

The Cariboo Cafe

I

They arrived in the secrecy of night, as displaced people often do, stopping over for a week, a month, eventually staying a lifetime. The plan was simple. Mother would work too until they saved enough to move into a finer future where the toilet was one's own and the children needn't be frightened. In the meantime, they played in the back allies,

Helena María Viramontes's fiction describes the resilience and courage of women who confront daily the oppression of poverty, women whose voices resonate with those who surrounded this Latina writer throughout her childhood. Viramontes was born in 1954 in East Los Angeles, California, and grew up in an extended Spanish-speaking family. She began writing fiction in 1975 and since then has promoted the work of her literary compeers in her capacity as literary editor on the journal 201: Homenaje a la Cuidad de Los Angeles and as former coordinator of the L.A. Latino Writers Association. In 1988 Viramontes coedited Chicana Creativity and Criticism: Charting New Frontiers in American Literature. The Moths and Other Stories (1985) is her first collection.

among the broken glass, wise to the ways of the streets. Rule one: never talk to strangers, not even the neighbor who paced up and down the hallways talking to himself. Rule two: the police, or "polie" as Sonya's popi pronounced the word, was La Migra in disguise and thus should always be avoided. Rule three: keep your key with you at all times—the four walls of the apartment were the only protection against the streets until Popi returned home.

Sonya considered her key a guardian saint and she wore it around her neck as such until this afternoon. Gone was the string with the big knot. Gone was the key. She hadn't noticed its disappearance until she picked up Macky from Mrs. Avila's house and walked home. She remembered playing with it as Amá walked her to school. But lunch break came, and Lalo wrestled her down so that he could see her underwear, and it probably fell somewhere between the iron rings and sandbox. Sitting on the front steps of the apartment building, she considered how to explain the missing key without having to reveal what Lalo had seen, for she wasn't quite sure which offense carried the worse penalty.

She watched people piling in and spilling out of the buses, watched an old man asleep on the bus bench across the street. He resembled a crumbled ball of paper, huddled up in the security of a tattered coat. She became aware of their mutual loneliness and she rested her head against her knees blackened by the soot of the playground asphalt.

The old man eventually awoke, yawned like a lion's roar, unfolded his limbs, and staggered to the alley where he urinated between two trash bins. (She wanted to peek, but it was Macky who turned to look.) He zipped up, drank from a paper bag and she watched him until he disappeared around the corner. As time passed, buses came less frequently, and every other person seemed to resemble Popi. Macky became bored. He picked through the trash barrel; later, and to Sonya's fright, he ran into the street after a pigeon. She understood his restlessness for waiting was as relentless as long lines to the bathroom. When a small boy walked by, licking away at a scoop of vanilla ice cream, Macky ran after him. In his haste to outrun Sonya's grasp, he fell and tore the knee of his denim jeans. He began to cry, wiping snot against his sweater sleeve.

"See?" she asked, dragging him back to the porch steps by his wrist. "See? God punished you!" It was a thing she always said because it seemed to work. Terrified by the scrawny tortured man on the cross, Macky wanted to avoid his wrath as much as possible. She sat him on the steps in one gruff jerk. Seeing his torn jeans, and her own scraped knees, she wanted to join in his sorrow, and cry. Instead she snuggled so close to him, she could hear his stomach growling.

"Coke," he asked. Mrs. Avila gave him an afternoon snack which usually held him over until dinner. But sometimes Macky got lost in the midst of her own six children and . . .

Mrs. Avila! It took Sonya a few moments to realize the depth of her idea. They could wait there, at Mrs. Avila's. And she'd probably have a stack of flour tortillas, fresh off the comal, ready to eat with butter and salt. She grabbed his hand. "Mrs. Avila has Coke."

"Coke!" He jumped up to follow his sister. "Coke," he cooed.

At the major intersection, Sonya quietly calculated their next move while the scores of adults hurried to their own destinations. She scratched one knee as she tried retracing her journey home in the labyrinth of her memory. Things never looked the same when backwards and she searched for familiar scenes. She looked for the newspaperman who sat in a little house with a little T.V. on and selling magazines with naked girls holding beach balls. But he was gone. What remained was a little closet-like shed with chains and locks, and she wondered what happened to him, for she thought he lived there with the naked ladies.

They finally crossed the street at a cautious pace, the colors of the street lights brighter as darkness descended, a stereo store blaring music from two huge, blasting speakers. She thought it was the disco store she passed, but she didn't remember if the sign was green or red. And she didn't remember it flashing like it was now. Studying the neon light, she bumped into a tall, lanky dark man. Maybe it was Raoul's Popi. Raoul was a dark boy in her class that she felt sorry for because everyone called him sponge head. Maybe she could ask Raoul's Popi where Mrs. Avila lived, but before she could think it all out, red sirens flashed in their faces and she shielded her eyes to see the polie.

The polie is men in black who get kids and send them to Tijuana, says Popi. Whenever you see them, run, because they hate you, says Popi. She grabs Macky by his sleeve and they crawl under a table of bargain cassettes. Macky's nose is running, and when he sniffles, she puts her finger to her lips. She peeks from behind the poster of Vincente Fernandez to see Raoul's father putting keys and stuff from his pockets onto the hood of the polie car. And it's true, they're putting him in the car and taking him to Tijuana. Popi, she murmured to herself. Mamá.

"Coke." Macky whispered, as if she had failed to remember.

"Ssssh. Mi'jo, when I say run, you run, okay?" She waited for the tires to turn out, and as the black and white drove off, she whispered "Now," and they scurried out from under the table and ran across the street, oblivious to the horns.

They entered a maze of allies and dead ends, the long, abandoned warehouses shadowing any light. Macky stumbled and she continued to drag him until his crying, his untied sneakers, and his raspy breathing finally forced her to stop. She scanned the boarded up boxcars, the rows of rusted rails to make sure the polie wasn't following them. Tired, her heart bursting, she leaned him against a tall, chainlink fence. Except for the rambling of some railcars, silence prevailed, and she could hear Macky sniffling in the darkness. Her mouth was parched and she swallowed to rid herself of the metallic taste of fear. The shadows stalked them, hovering like nightmares. Across the tracks, in the distance, was a room with a yellow glow, like a beacon light at the end of a dark sea. She pinched Macky's nose with the corner of her dress, took hold of his sleeve. At least the shadows will be gone, she concluded, at the zero zero place.

II

Don't look at me. I didn't give it the name. It was passed on. Didn't even know what it meant until I looked it up in some library dictionary. But I kinda liked the name. It's, well, romantic, almost like the name of a song, you know, so I kept it. That was before JoJo turned fourteen even. But now if you take a look at the sign, the paint's peeled off 'cept for the two O's. The double zero cafe. Story of my life. But who cares, right? As long as everyone 'round the factories know I run an honest business.

The place is clean. That's more than I can say for some people who walk through that door. And I offer the best prices on double burger deluxes this side of Main Street. Okay, so its not pure beef. Big deal, most meat markets do the same. But I make no bones 'bout it. I tell them up front, "yeah, it ain't dogmeat, but it ain't sirloin either." Cause that's the sort of guy I am. Honest.

That's the trouble. It never pays to be honest. I tried scrubbing the stains off the floor, so that my customers won't be reminded of what happened. But they keep walking as if my cafe ain't fit for lepers. And that's the thanks I get for being a fair guy.

Not once did I hang up all those stupid signs. You know, like "We reserve the right to refuse service to anyone," or "No shirt, no shoes, no service." To tell you the truth—which is what I always do though it don't pay—I wouldn't have nobody walking through that door. The streets are full of scum, but scum gotta eat too is the way I see it. Now, listen. I ain't talkin 'bout out-of-luckers, weirdos, whores, you know. I'm talking 'bout five-to-lifers out of some tech. I'm talking Paulie.

I swear Paulie is thirty-five, or six. JoJo's age if he were still alive, but he don't look a day over ninety. Maybe why I let him hang out 'cause he's JoJo's age. Shit, he's okay as long as he don't bring his wigged out friends whose voices sound like a record at low speed. Paulie's got too many stories and they all get jammed up in his mouth so I can't make out what he's saying. He scares the other customers too, acting like he is shadow boxing, or like a monkey hopping on a frying pan. You know, nervous, jumpy, his jaw all falling and his eyes bulgy and dirt yellow. I give him the last booth, coffee and yesterday's donut holes to keep him quiet. After a few minutes, out he goes, before lunch. I'm too old, you know, too busy making ends meet to be nursing the kid. And so is Delia.

That Delia's got these unique titties. One is bigger than another. Like an orange and grapefruit. I kid you not. They're like that on account of when she was real young she had some babies, and they all sucked only one favorite tittie. So one is bigger than the other, and when she used to walk in with Paulie, huggy huggy and wearing those tight leotard blouses that show the nipple dots, you could see the difference. You could tell right off that Paulie was proud of them, the way he'd hang his arm over her shoulder and squeeze the grapefruit. They kill me, her knockers. She'd come in real queen-like, smacking gum and chewing the fat with the illegals who work in that garment warehouse. They come in real queen-like too, sitting in the best booth near the window, and order cokes. That's all. Cokes. Hey, but I'm a nice guy, so what if they mess up my table, bring their own lunches and only order small cokes, leaving a dime as tip? So sometimes the place ain't crawling with people, you comprende buddy? A dime's a dime as long as its in my pocket.

Like I gotta pay my bills too, I gotta eat. So like I serve anybody whose got the greens, including that crazy lady and the two kids that started all the trouble. If only I had closed early. But I had to wash the dinner dishes on account of I can't afford a dishwasher. I was scraping off some birdshit glue stuck to this plate, see, when I hear the bells jingle against the door. I hate those fucking bells. That was Nell's idea. Nell's my wife; my ex-wife. So people won't sneak up on you, says my ex. Anyway, I'm standing behind the counter staring at this short woman. Already I know that she's bad news because she looks street to me. Round face, burnt toast color, black hair that hangs like straight ropes. Weirdo, I've had enough to last me a lifetime. She's wearing a shawl and a dirty slip is hanging out. Shit if I have to dish out a free meal. Funny thing, but I didn't see the two kids 'til I got to the booth. All of a sudden I see these big eyes looking over the table's edge at me. It shook me up, the way they kinda appeared. Aw, maybe they were there all the time.

The boy's a sweetheart. Short Order don't look nothing like his mom. He's got dried snot all over his dirty cheeks and his hair ain't seen a comb for years. She can't take care of herself, much less him or the doggie of a sister. But he's a tough one, and I pinch his nose 'cause he's a real sweetheart like JoJo. You know, my boy.

It's his sister I don't like. She's got these poking eyes that follow you 'round 'cause she don't trust no one. Like when I reach for Short Order, she flinches like I'm 'bout to tear his nose off, gives me a nasty, squinty look. She's maybe five, maybe six, I don't know, and she acts like she owns him. Even when I bring the burgers, she doesn't let go of his hand. Finally, the fellow bites it and I wink at him. A real sweetheart.

In the next booth, I'm twisting the black crud off the top of the ketchup bottle when I hear the lady saying something in Spanish. Right off I know she's illegal, which explains why she looks like a weirdo. Anyway, she says something nice to them 'cause it's in the same tone that Nell used when I'd rest my head on her lap. I'm surprised the illegal's got a fiver to pay, but she and her tail leave no tip. I see Short Order's small bites on the bun.

You know, a cafe's the kinda business that moves. You get some regulars but most of them are on the move, so I don't pay much attention to them. But this lady's face sticks like egg yolk on a plate. It ain't 'til I open a beer and sit in front of the B & W to check out the wrestling matches that I see this news bulletin 'bout two missing kids. I recognize the mugs right away. Short Order and his doggie sister. And all of a sudden her face is out of my mind. Aw fuck, I say, and put my beer down so hard that the foam spills onto last months *Hustler*. Aw fuck.

See, if Nell was here, she'd know what to do: call the cops. But I don't know. Cops ain't exactly my friends, and all I need is for bacon to be crawling all over my place. And seeing how her face is vague now, I decide to wait 'til the late news. Short Order don't look right neither. I'll have another beer and wait for the late news.

The alarm rings at four and I have this headache, see, from the sixpak, and I gotta get up. I was supposed to do something, but I got all suck-faced and forgot. Turn off the T.V., take a shower, but that don't help my memory any.

Hear sirens near the railroad tracks. Cops. I'm supposed to call the cops. I'll do it after I make the coffee, put away the eggs, get the donuts out. But Paulie strolls in looking partied out. We actually talk 'bout last night's wrestling match between BoBo Brazil and the Crusher. I slept through it, you see. Paulie orders an O.J. on account of he's catching a cold. I open up my big mouth and ask about De. Drinks the rest of his O.J., says real calm like, that he caught her eaglespread with the Vegetable fatso down the block. Then, very polite like, Paulie excuses himself. That's one thing I gotta say about Paulie. He may be one big Fuck-up, but he's got manners. Juice gave him shit cramps, he says.

Well, leave it to Paulie. Good ole Mr. Fuck-Up himself to help me with the cops. The prick O.D.'s in my crapper; vomits and shits are all over—I mean all over the fuckin' walls. That's the thanks I get for being Mr. Nice Guy. I had the cops looking up my ass for the stash; says one, the one wearing a mortician's suit, We'll be back, we'll be back when you ain't looking. If I was pushing, would I be burning my goddamn balls off with spitting grease? So fuck 'em, I think. I ain't gonna tell you nothing 'bout the lady. Fuck you, I say to them as they drive away. Fuck your mother.

That's why Nell was good to have 'round. She could be a pain in the ass, you know, like making me hang those stupid bells, but mostly she knew what to do. See, I go bananas. Like my mind fries with the potatoes and by the end of the day, I'm deader than dogshit. Let me tell you what I mean. A few hours later, after I swore I wouldn't give the fuckin' pigs the time of day, the green vans roll up across the street. While I'm stirring the chili con carne I see all these illegals running out of the factory to hide, like roaches when the lightswitch goes on. I taste the chile, but I really can't taste nothing on account of I've lost my appetite after cleaning out the crapper, when three of them run into the Cariboo. They look at me as if I'm gonna stop them, but when I go on stirring the chile, they run to the bathroom. Now look, I'm a nice guy, but I don't like to be used, you know? Just 'cause they're regulars don't mean jackshit. I run an honest business. And that's what I told them Agents. See, by that time, my stomach being all dizzy, and the cops all over the place, and the three illegals running in here, I was all confused, you know. That's how it was, and well, I haven't seen Nell for years, and I guess that's why I pointed to the bathroom.

I don't know. I didn't expect handcuffs and them agents putting their hands up and down their thighs. When they walked passed me, they didn't look at me. That is the two young ones. The older one, the one that looked silly in the handcuffs on account of she's old enough to be my grandma's grandma, looks straight at my face with the same eyes Short Order's sister gave me yesterday. What a day. Then, to top off the potatoes with the gravy, the bells jingle against the door and in enters the lady again with the two kids.

III

He's got lice. Probably from living in the detainers. Those are the rooms where they round up the children and make them work for their food.

I saw them from the window. Their eyes are cut glass, and no one looks for sympathy. They take turns, sorting out the arms from the legs, heads from the torsos. Is that one your mother? one guard asks, holding a mummified head with eyes shut tighter than coffins. But the children no longer cry. They just continue sorting as if they were salvaging cans from a heap of trash. They do this until time is up and they drift into a tunnel, back to the womb of sleep, while a new group comes in. It is all very organized. I bite my fist to keep from retching. Please God, please don't let Geraldo be there.

For you see, they took Geraldo. By mistake, of course. It was my fault. I shouldn't have sent him out to fetch me a mango. But it was just to the corner. I didn't even bother to put his sweater on. I hear his sandals flapping against the gravel. I follow him with my eyes, see him scratching his buttocks when the wind picks up swiftly, as it often does at such unstable times, and I have to close the door.

The darkness becomes a serpent's tongue, swallowing us whole. It is the night of La Llorona. The women come up from the depths of sorrow to search for their children. I join them, frantic, desperate, and our eyes become scrutinizers, our bodies opiated with the scent of their smiles. Descending from door to door, the wind whips our faces. I hear the wailing of the women and know it to be my own. Geraldo is nowhere to be found.

Dawn is not welcomed. It is a drunkard wavering between consciousness and sleep. My life is fleeing, moving south towards the sea. My tears are now hushed and faint.

The boy, barely a few years older than Geraldo, lights a cigarette, rests it on the edge of his desk, next to all the other cigarette burns. The blinds are down to keep the room cool. Above him hangs a single bulb that shades and shadows his face in such a way as to mask his expressions. He is not to be trusted. He fills in the information, for I cannot write. Statements delivered, we discuss motives.

"Spies," says he, flicking a long burning ash from the cigarette onto the floor, then wolfing the smoke in as if his lungs had an unquenchable thirst for nicotine. "We arrest spies. Criminals." He says this with cigarette smoke spurting out from his nostrils like a nose bleed.

"Spies? Criminal?" My shawl falls to the ground. "He is only five and a half years old." I plead for logic with my hands. "What kind of crimes could a five year old commit?"

"Anyone who so willfully supports the contras in any form must be arrested and punished without delay." He knows the line by heart.

I think about moths and their stupidity. Always attracted by light, they fly into fires, or singe their wings with the heat of the single bulb and fall on his desk, writhing in pain. I don't understand why nature has been so cruel as to prevent them from feeling warmth. He dismisses them with a sweep of a hand. "This," he continues, "is what we plan to do with the contras, and those who aid them." He inhales again.

"But, Señor, he's just a baby."

"Contras are tricksters. They exploit the ignorance of people like you. Perhaps they convinced your son to circulate pamphlets. You should be talking to them, not us." The cigarette is down to his yellow finger tips, to where he can no longer continue to hold it without burning himself. He throws the stub on the floor, crushes it under his boot. "This," he says, screwing his boot into the ground, "is what the contras do to people like you."

"Señor. I am a washer woman. You yourself see I cannot read or write. There is my X. Do you think my son can read?" How can I explain to this man that we are poor, that we live as best we can? "If such a thing has happened, perhaps he wanted to make a few centavos for his mamá. He's just a baby."

"So you are admitting his guilt?"

"So you are admitting he is here?" I promise, once I see him, hold him in my arms again, I will never, never scold him for wanting more than I can give. "You see, he needs his sweater . . ." The sweater lies limp on my lap.

"Your assumption is incorrect."

"May I check the detainers for myself?"

"In time."

"And what about my Geraldo?"

"In time." He dismisses me, placing the forms in a big envelope crinkled by the day's humidity.

"When?" I am wringing the sweater with my hands.

"Don't be foolish, woman. Now off with your nonsense. We will try to locate your Pedro."

"Geraldo."

Maria came by today with a bowl of hot soup. She reports, in her usual excited way, that the soldiers are now eating the brains of their victims. It is unlike her to be so scandalous. So insane. Geraldo must be cold without his sweater.

"Why?" I ask as the soup gets cold. I will write Tavo tonight.

At the plaza a group of people are whispering. They are quiet when I pass, turn to one another and put their finger to their lips to cage their voices. They continue as I reach the church steps. To be associated with me is condemnation.

Today I felt like killing myself, Lord. But I am too much of a coward. I am a washer woman, Lord. My mother was one, and hers too. We have lived as best we can, washing other people's laundry, rinsing off other people's dirt until our hands crust and chap. When my son wanted to hold my hand, I held soap instead. When he wanted to play, my feet were in pools of water. It takes such little courage, being a washer woman. Give me strength, Lord.

What have I done to deserve this, Lord? Raising a child is like building a kite. You must bend the twigs enough, but not too much, for you might break them. You must find paper that is delicate and light enough to wave on the breath of the wind, yet must withstand the ravages of a storm. You must tie the strings gently but firmly so that it may not fall apart. You must let the string go, eventually, so that the kite will stretch its ambition. It is such delicate work, Lord, being a mother. This I understand, Lord, because I am, but you have snapped the cord, Lord. It was only a matter of minutes and my life is lost somewhere in the clouds. I don't know, I don't know what games you play, Lord.

These four walls are no longer my house, the earth beneath it, no longer my home. Weeds have replaced all good crops. The irrigation ditches are clodded with bodies. No matter where we turn, there are rumors facing us and we try to live as best we can, under the rule of men who rape women, then rip their fetuses from their bellies. Is this our home? Is this our country? I ask Maria. Don't these men have mothers, lovers, babies, sisters? Don't they see what they are doing? Later, Maria says, these men are babes farted out from the Devil's ass. We check to make sure no one has heard her say this.

Without Geraldo, this is not my home, the earth beneath it, not my country. This is why I have to leave. Maria begins to cry. Not because I am going, but because she is staying.

Tavo. Sweet Tavo. He has sold his car to send me the money. He has just married and he sold his car for me. Thank you, Tavo. Not just for the money. But also for making me believe in the goodness of people again . . . The money is enough to buy off the border soldiers. The rest will come from the can. I have saved for Geraldo's schooling and it is enough for a bus ticket to Juarez. I am to wait for Tavo there.

I spit. I do not turn back.

Perhaps I am wrong in coming. I worry that Geraldo will not have a home to return to, no mother to cradle his nightmares away, soothe the scars, stop the hemorrhaging of his heart. Tavo is happy I am here, but it is crowded, the three of us, and I hear them arguing behind their closed door. There is only so much a nephew can provide. I must find work. I have two hands willing to work. But the heart. The heart wills only to watch the children playing in the street.

The machines, their speed and dust, make me ill. But I can clean.

I clean toilets, dump trash cans, sweep. Disinfect the sinks. I will gladly do whatever is necessary to repay Tavo. The baby is due any time and money is tight. I volunteer for odd hours, weekends, since I really have very little to do. When the baby comes I know Tavo's wife will not let me hold it, for she thinks I am a bad omen. I know it.

Why would God play such a cruel joke, if he isn't my son? I jumped the curb, dashed out into the street, but the street is becoming wider and wider. I've lost him once and can't lose him again and to hell with the screeching tires and the horns and the headlights barely touching my hips. I can't take my eyes off him because, you see, they are swift and cunning and can take your life with a snap of a finger. But God is a just man and His mistakes can be undone.

My heart pounds in my head like a sledge hammer against the asphalt. What if it isn't Geraldo? What if he is still in the detainer waiting for me? A million questions, one answer: Yes. Geraldo, yes. I want to touch his hand first, have it disappear in my own because it is so small. His eyes look at me in total bewilderment. I grab him because the earth is crumbling beneath us and I must save him. We both fall to the ground.

A hot meal is in store. A festival. The cook, a man with shrunken cheeks and the hands of a car mechanic, takes a liking to Geraldo. Its like birthing you again, mi'jo. My baby.

I bathe him. He flutters in excitement, the water grey around him. I scrub his head with lye to kill off the lice, comb his hair out with a fine tooth comb. I wash his rubbery penis, wrap him in a towel and he stands in front of the window, shriveling and sucking milk from a carton, his hair shiny from the dampness.

He finally sleeps. So easily, she thinks. On her bed next to the open window he coos in the night. Below the sounds of the city become as monotonous as the ocean waves. She rubs his back with warm oil, each stroke making up for the days of his absence. She hums to him softly so that her breath brushes against his face, tunes that are rusted and crack in her throat. The hotel neon shines on his back and she covers him.

All the while the young girl watches her brother sleeping. She removes her sneakers, climbs into the bed, snuggles up to her brother, and soon her breathing is raspy, her arms under her stomach.

The couch is her bed tonight. Before switching the light off, she checks once more to make sure this is not a joke. Tomorrow she will make arrangements to go home. Maria will be the same, the mango stand on the corner next to the church plaza will be the same. It will all be the way it was before. But enough excitement. For the first time in years, her mind is quiet of all noise and she has the desire to sleep.

The bells jingle when the screen door slaps shut behind them. The cook wrings his hands in his apron, looking at them. Geraldo is in the middle, and they sit in the booth farthest away from the window, near the hall where the toilets are, and right away the small boy, his hair now neatly combed and split to the side like an adult, wrinkles his nose at the peculiar smell. The cook wipes perspiration off his forehead with the corner of his apron, finally comes over to the table.

She looks so different, so young. Her hair is combed slick back into one thick braid and her earrings hang like baskets of golden pears on her finely sculptured ears. He can't believe how different she looks. Almost beautiful. She points to what she wants on the menu with a white, clean fingernail. Although confused, the cook is sure of one thing —it's Short Order all right, pointing to him with a commanding finger, saying his only English word: coke.

His hands tremble as he slaps the meat on the grill; the patties hiss instantly. He feels like vomiting. The chile overboils and singes the fires, deep red trail of chile crawling to the floor and puddling there. He grabs the handles, burns himself, drops the pot on the wooden racks of the floor. He sucks his fingers, the patties blackening and sputtering grease. He flips them, and the burgers hiss anew. In some strange way he hopes they have disappeared, and he takes a quick look only to see Short Order's sister, still in the same dress, still holding her brother's hand. She is craning her neck to peek at what is going on in the kitchen.

Aw, fuck, he says, in a fog of smoke his eyes burning tears. He can't believe it, but he's crying. For the first time since JoJo's death, he's crying. He becomes angry at the lady for returning. At JoJo. At Nell for leaving him. He wishes Nell here, but doesn't know where she's at or what part of Vietnam JoJo is all crumbled up in. Children gotta be with their parents, family gotta be together, he thinks. It's only right. The emergency line is ringing.

Two black and whites roll up and skid the front tires against the curb. The flashing lights carousel inside the cafe. She sees them opening the screen door, their guns taut and cold like steel erections. Something is wrong, and she looks to the cowering cook. She has been betrayed, and her heart is pounding like footsteps running, faster, louder, faster and she can't hear what they are saying to her. She jumps up from the table, grabs Geraldo by the wrist, his sister dragged along because, like her, she refuses to release his hand. Their lips are mouthing words she can't hear, can't comprehend. Run, Run is all she can think of to do, Run through the hallway, out to the alley, Run because they will never take him away again.

But her legs are heavy and she crushes Geraldo against her, so tight, as if she wants to conceal him in her body again, return him to her belly so that they will not castrate him and hang his small, blue penis on her door, not crush his face so that he is unrecognizable, not bury him among the heaps of bones, and ears, and teeth, and jaws, because no one, but she, cared to know that he cried. For years he cried and she could hear him day and night. Screaming, howling, sobbing, shriveling and crying because he is only five years old, and all she wanted was a mango.

But the crying begins all over again. In the distance, she hears crying.

She refuses to let go. For they will have to cut her arms off to take him, rip her mouth off to keep her from screaming for help. Without thinking, she reaches over to where two pots of coffee are brewing and throws the streaming coffee into their faces. Outside, people begin to gather, pressing their faces against the window glass to get a good view. The cook huddles behind the counter, frightened, trembling. Their faces become distorted and she doesn't see the huge hand that takes hold of Geraldo and she begins screaming all over again, screaming so that the walls shake, screaming enough for all the women of murdered children, screaming, pleading for help from the people outside, and she pushes an open hand against an officer's nose, because no one will stop them and he pushes the gun barrel to her face.

And I laugh at his ignorance. How stupid of him to think that I will let them take my Geraldo away, just because he waves that gun like a flag. Well, to hell with you, you pieces of shit, do you hear me? Stupid, cruel pigs. To hell with you all, because you can no longer frighten me. I will fight you for my son until I have no hands left to hold a knife. I will fight you all because you're all farted out of the Devil's ass, and you'll not take us with you. I am laughing, howling at their stupidity. Because they should know by now that I will never let my son go and then I hear something crunching like broken glass against my forehead and I am blinded by the liquid darkness. But I hold onto his hand. That I can feel, you see, I'll never let go. Because we are going home. My son and I.

1985

JOHN EDGAR WIDEMAN

Fever

TO MATTHEW CAREY, ESQ., who fled Philadelphia
in its hour of need and upon his return
published a libelous account of the behavior of black
nurses and undertakers, thereby injuring all
people of my race and especially those without
whose unselfish, courageous labours the city
could not have survived the late calamity.

Consider Philadelphia from its centrical situation,
the extent of its commerce, the number of
its artificers, manufacturers and other circumstances,
to be to the United States what the heart
is to the human body in circulating the blood.
                                    Robert Morris, 1777

He stood staring through a tall window at the last days of November.
The trees were barren women starved for love and they'd stripped off
all their clothes, but nobody cared. And not one of them gave a fuck
about him, sifting among them, weightless and naked, knowing just as
well as they did, no hands would come to touch them, warm them,
pick leaves off the frozen ground and stick them back in place. Before
he'd gone to bed a flutter of insects had stirred in the dark outside his
study. Motion worrying the corner of his eye till he turned and focused
where light pooled on the deck, a cone in which he could trap slants
of snow so they materialized into wet, gray feathers that blotted against
the glass, the planks of the deck. If he stood seven hours, dark would
come again. At some point his reflection would hang in the glass, a ship
from the other side of the world, docked in the ether. Days were shorter

Oxford graduate and Rhodes scholar, as well as All-Ivy basketball player at the University of
Pennsylvania, John Edgar Wideman was born in Washington, D.C., in 1941. He grew up in a poor,
predominantly black neighborhood of Pittsburgh—an area that Wideman would later transpose
into a group of novels known as The Homewood Trilogy. One of this trio of works, *Sent for You
Yesterday* (1983), won its author the 1984 PEN/Faulkner Award for fiction. In a highly literary style
often compared to that of William Faulkner, Wideman explores the shaping influences of African
American urban experience. In 1975 Wideman moved to the city of Laramie, where he teaches
literature at the University of Wyoming.

now. A whole one spent wondering what goes wrong would fly away, fly in the blink of an eye.

Perhaps, *perhaps it may be acceptable to the reader to know how we found the sick affected by the sickness; our opportunities of hearing and seeing them have been very great. They were taken with a chill, a headache, a sick stomach, with pains in their limbs and back, this was the way the sickness in general began, but all were not affected alike, some appeared but slightly affected with some of these symptoms, what confirmed us in the opinion of a person being smitten was the colour of their eyes.*

Victims in this low-lying city perished every year, and some years were worse than others, but the worst by far was the long hot dry summer of '93, when the dead and dying wrested control of the city from the living. Most who were able, fled. The rich to their rural retreats, others to relatives and friends in the countryside or neighboring towns. Some simply left, with no fixed destination, the prospect of privation or starvation on the road preferable to cowering in their homes awaiting the fever's fatal scratching at their door. Busy streets deserted, commerce halted, members of families shunning one another, the sick abandoned to suffer and die alone. Fear ruled. From August when the first cases of fever appeared below Water Street, to November when merciful frosts ended the infestation, the city slowly deteriorated, as if it, too, could suffer the terrible progress of the disease: fever, enfeeblement, violent vomiting and diarrhea, helplessness, delirium, settled dejection when patients *concluded they must go (so the phrase for dying was), and therefore in a kind of fixed determined state of mind went off.*

In some it raged more furiously than in others—some have languished for seven and ten days, and appeared to get better the day, or some hours before they died, while others were cut off in one, two, or three days, but their complaints were similar. Some lost their reason and raged with all the fury madness could produce, and died in strong convulsions. Others retained their reason to the last, and seemed rather to fall asleep than die.

Yellow fever: an acute infectious disease of subtropical and tropical New World areas, caused by a filterable virus transmitted by a mosquito of the genus *Aëdes* and characterized by jaundice and dark colored vomit resulting from hemorrhages. Also called *yellow jack.*

Dengue: an infectious, virulent tropical and subtropical disease transmitted by mosquitos and characterized by fever, rash, and severe pains in the joints. Also called *breakbone fever, dandy.* [Spanish, of African origin, akin to Swahili *kindinga.*]

Curled in the black hold of the ship he wonders why his life on solid green earth had to end, why the gods had chosen this new habitation for him, floating, chained to other captives, no air, no light, the wooden walls shuddering, battered, as if some madman is determined to destroy even this last pitiful refuge where he skids in foul puddles of waste, bumping other bodies, skinning himself on splintery beams and planks, always moving, shaken and spilled like palm nuts in the diviner's fist, and Esu casts his fate, constant motion, tethered to an iron ring.

In the darkness he can't see her, barely feels her light touch on his fevered skin. Sweat thick as oil but she doesn't mind, straddles him, settles down to do her work. She enters him and draws his blood up into her belly. When she's full, she pauses, dreamy, heavy. He could kill her then; she wouldn't care. But he doesn't. Listens to the whine of her wings lifting till the whimper is lost in the roar and crash of waves, creaking wood, prisoners groaning. If she returns tomorrow and carries away another drop of him, and the next day and the next, a drop each day, enough days, he'll be gone. Shrink to nothing, slip out of this iron noose and disappear.

Aëdes aegypti: a mosquito of the family *Culicidae,* genus *Aëdes* in which the female is distinguished by a long proboscis for sucking blood. This winged insect is a vector (an organism that carries pathogens from one host to another) of yellow fever and dengue. [New Latin *Aëdes,* from Greek *aedes,* unpleasant: *a-,* not + *edos,* pleasant . . .]

All things arrive in the waters and waters carry all things away. So there is no beginning or end, only the waters' flow, ebb, flood, trickle, tides emptying and returning, salt seas and rivers and rain and mist and blood, the sun drowning in an ocean of night, wet sheen of dawn washing darkness from our eyes. This city is held in the water's palm. A captive as surely as I am captive. Long fingers of river, Schuylkill, Delaware, the rest of the hand invisible; underground streams and channels feed the soggy flesh of marsh, clay pit, sink, gutter, stagnant pool. What's not seen is heard in the suck of footsteps through spring mud of unpaved streets. Noxious vapors that sting your eyes, cause you to gag, spit, and wince are evidence of a presence, the dead hand cupping this city, the poisons that circulate through it, the sweat on its rotting flesh.

No one has asked my opinion. No one will. Yet I have seen this fever before, and though I can prescribe no cure, I could tell stories of other visitations, how it came and stayed and left us, the progress of disaster, its several stages, its horrors and mitigations. My words would not save one life, but those mortally affrighted by the fever, by the prospect of universal doom, might find solace in knowing there are limits to the power of this scourge that has befallen us, that some, yea, most will survive, that this condition is temporary, a season, that the fever must disappear with the first deep frosts and its disappearance is as certain as the fact it will come again.

They say the rat's-nest ships from Santo Domingo brought the fever. Frenchmen and their black slaves fleeing black insurrection. Those who've seen Barbados's distemper say our fever is its twin born in the tropical climate of the hellish Indies. I know better. I hear the drum, the forest's heartbeat, pulse of the sea that chains the moon's wandering, the spirit's journey. Its throb is source and promise of all things being connected, a mirror storing everything, forgetting nothing. To explain the fever we need no boatloads of refugees, ragged and wracked with killing fevers, bringing death to our shores. We have bred the affliction within our breasts. Each solitary heart contains all the world's tribes, and its precarious dance echoes the drum's thunder. We are our ancestors and our children, neighbors and strangers to ourselves. Fever descends when the waters that connect us are clogged with filth. When our seas are garbage. The waters cannot come and go when we are shut off one from the other, each in his frock coat, wig, bonnet, apron, shop, shoes, skin, behind locks, doors, sealed faces, our blood grows thick and sluggish. Our bodies void infected fluids. Then we are dry and cracked as a desert country, vital parts wither, all dust and dry bones inside. Fever is a drought consuming us from within. Discolored skin caves in upon itself, we burn, expire.

I regret there is so little comfort in this explanation. It takes into account neither climatists nor contagionists, flies in the face of logic and reason, the good doctors of the College of Physicians who would bleed us, purge us, quarantine, plunge us in icy baths, starve us, feed us elixirs of bark and wine, sprinkle us with gunpowder, drown us in vinegar according to the dictates of their various healing sciences. Who, then, is this foolish, old man who receives his wisdom from pagan drums in pagan forests? Are these the delusions of one whose brain the fever has already begun to gnaw? Not quite. True, I have survived other visitations of the fever, but while it prowls this city, I'm in jeopardy again as you are, because I claim no immunity, no magic. The messenger who bears the news of my death will reach me precisely at the stroke determined when it was determined I should tumble from the void and taste air the first time. Nothing is an accident. Fever grows in the secret places of our hearts, planted there when one of us decided to sell one of us to another. The drum must pound ten thousand years to drive that evil away.

Fires burn on street corners. Gunshots explode inside wooden houses. Behind him a carter's breath expelled in low, labored pants warns him to edge closer to housefronts forming one wall of a dark, narrow, twisting lane. Thick wheels furrow the unpaved street. In the fire glow the cart stirs a shimmer of dust, faint as a halo, a breath smear on a mirror. Had the man locked in the traces of the cart cursed him or was it just a wheeze of exertion, a complaint addressed to the unforgiving weight of his burden? Creaking wheels, groaning wood, plodding footsteps, the cough of dust, bulky silhouette blackened as it lurches into brightness at the block's end. All gone in a moment. Sounds, motion, sight extinguished. What remained, as if trapped by a lid clamped over the lane, was the stench of dead bodies. A stench cutting through the ubiquitous pall of vinegar and gunpowder. Two, three, four corpses being hauled to Potter's Field, trailed by the unmistakable wake of decaying flesh. He'd heard they raced their carts to the burial ground. Two or three entering Potter's Field from different directions would acknowledge one another with challenges, raised fists, gather their strength for a last dash to the open trenches where they tip their cargoes. Their brethren would wager, cheer, toast the victor with tots of rum. He could hear the rumble of coffins crashing into a common grave, see the comical chariots bouncing, the men's legs pumping, faces contorted by fires that blazed all night at the burial ground. Shouting and curses would hang in the torpid night air, one more nightmare troubling the city's sleep.

He knew this warren of streets as well as anyone. Night or day he could negotiate the twists and turnings, avoid cul-de-sacs, find the river even if his vision was obscured in tunnel-like alleys. He anticipated when to duck a jutting signpost, knew how to find doorways where he was welcome, wooden steps down to a cobbled terrace overlooking the water where his shod foot must never trespass. Once beyond the grand houses lining one end of Water Street, in this quarter of hovels, beneath these wooden sheds leaning shoulder to shoulder were cellars and caves dug into the earth, poorer men's dwellings under these houses of the poor, an invisible region where his people burrow, pull earth like blanket and quilt round themselves to shut out cold and dampness, sleeping multitudes to a room, stacked and crosshatched and spoon fashion, themselves the only fuel, heat of one body passed to others and passed back from all to see. Can he blame the lucky ones who are strong enough to pull the death carts, who celebrate and leap and roar all night around the bonfires? Why should they return here? Where living and dead, sick and well must lie face to face, shivering or sweltering on the same dank floor.

Below Water Street the alleys proliferate. Named and nameless. He knows where he's going but fever has transformed even the familiar. He'd been waiting in Dr. Rush's entrance hall. An English mirror, oval framed in scalloped brass, drew him. He watched himself glide closer, a shadow, a blur, then the huge shape of his face materialized from silken depths. A mask he did not recognize. He took the thing he saw and murmured to it. Had he once been in control? Could he tame it again? Like a garden ruined overnight, pillaged, overgrown, trampled by marauding beasts. He stares at the chaos until he can recall familiar contours of earth, seasons of planting, harvesting, green shoots, nodding blossoms, scraping, digging, watering. Once upon a time he'd cultivated this thing, this plot of flesh and blood and bone, but what had it become? Who owned it now? He'd stepped away. His eyes constructed another face and set it there, between him and the wizened old man in the glass. He'd aged twenty years in a glance and the fever possessed the same power to alter suddenly what it touched. This city had grown ancient and fallen into ruin in two months since early August, when the first cases of fever appeared. Something in the bricks, mortar, beams, and stones had gone soft, had lost its permanence. When he entered sickrooms, walls fluttered, floors buckled. He could feel roofs pressing down. Putrid heat expanding. In the bodies of victims. In rooms, buildings, streets, neighborhoods. Membranes that preserved the integrity of substances and shapes, kept each in its proper place, were worn thin. He could poke his finger through yellowed skin. A stone wall. The eggshell of his skull. What should be separated was running together. Threatened to burst. Nothing contained the way it was supposed to be. No clear lines of demarcation. A mongrel city. Traffic where there shouldn't be traffic. An awful void opening around him, preparing itself to hold explosions of bile, vomit, gushing bowels, ooze, sludge, seepage.

Earlier in the summer, on a July afternoon, he'd tried to escape the heat by walking along the Delaware. The water was unnaturally calm, isolated into stagnant pools by outcroppings of wharf and jetty. A shelf of rotting matter paralleled the river edge. As if someone had attempted to sweep what was unclean and dead from the water. Bones, skins, entrails, torn carcasses, unrecognizable tatters and remnants broomed into a neat ridge. No sigh of the breeze he'd sought, yet fumes from the rim of garbage battered him in nauseating waves, a palpable medium intimate as wind. Beyond the tidal line of refuge, a pale margin lapped clean by receding waters. Then the iron river itself, flat, dark, speckled by scores of foam that puckered and swirled, worrying the stillness with a life of their own.

Spilled. Spoiled. Those words repeated themselves endlessly as he made his rounds. Dr. Rush had written out his portion, his day's share from the list of dead and dying. He'd purged, bled, comforted and buried victims of the fever. In and out of homes that had become tombs, prisons, charnel houses. Dazed children wandering the streets, searching for their parents. How can he explain to a girl, barely more than an infant, that the father and mother she sobs for are gone from this earth? Departed. Expired. They are resting, child. Asleep forever. In a far, far better place, my sweet, dear, suffering one. In God's bosom. Wrapped in His incorruptible arms. A dead mother with a dead baby at her breast. Piteous cries of the helpless offering all they own for a drink of water. How does he console the delirious boy who pummels him, fastens himself on his leg because he's put the boy's mother in a box and now must nail shut the lid?

Though light-headed from exhaustion, he's determined to spend a few hours here, among his own people. But were these lost ones really his people? The doors of his church were open to them, yet these were the ones who stayed away, wasting their lives in vicious pastimes of the idle, the unsaved, the ignorant. His benighted brethren who'd struggle to reach this city of refuge and then, once inside the gates, had fallen prisoners again, trapped by chains of dissolute living as they'd formerly been snared in the bonds of slavery. He'd come here and preached to them. Thieves, beggars, loose women, debtors, fugitives, drunkards, gamblers, the weak, crippled and outcast with nowhere else to go. They spurned his church so he'd brought church to them, preaching in gin mills, whoring dens, on street corners. He'd been jeered and hooted, spat upon, clods of unnameable filth had spattered his coat. But a love for them, as deep and unfathomable as his sorrow, his pity, brought him back again and again, exhorting them, setting the gospel before them so they might partake of its bounty, the infinite goodness, blessed sustenance therein. Jesus had toiled among the wretched, the outcast, that flotsam and jetsam deposited like a ledge of filth on the banks of the city. He understood what had brought the dark faces of his brethren north, to the Quaker promise of this town, this cradle and capital of a New World, knew the misery they were fleeing, the bright star in the Gourd's handle that guided them, the joy leaping in their hearts when at last, at last the opportunity to be viewed as men instead of things was theirs. He'd dreamed such dreams himself, oh yes, and prayed that the light of hope would never be extinguished. He'd been praying for deliverance, for peace and understanding when God had granted him a vision, hordes of sable bondsmen throwing off their chains, marching, singing, a path opening in the sea, the sea shaking its shaggy shoulders, resplendent with light and power. A radiance sparkling in this walkway through the water, pearls, diamonds, spears of light. This was the glistening way home. Waters parting, glory blinking and winking. Too intense to stare at, a promise shimmering, a rainbow arching over the end of the path. A hand tapped him. He'd waited for it to blend into the vision, for its meaning to shine forth in the language neither word nor thought, God was speaking in His visitation. Tapping became a grip. Someone was shoving him. He was being pushed off his knees, hauled to his feet. Someone was snatching him from the honeyed dream of salvation. When his eyes popped open he knew the name of each church elder manhandling him. Pale faces above a wall of black cloth belonged to his fellow communicants. He knew without looking the names of the men whose hands touched him gently, steering, coaxing, and those whose hands dug into his flesh, the impatient, imperious, rough hands that shunned any contact with him except as overseer or master.

Allen, Allen. Do you hear me? You and your people must not kneel at the front of the gallery. On your feet. Come. Come. Now. On your feet.

Behind the last row of pews. There ye may fall down on your knees and give praise.

And so we built our African house of worship. But its walls could not imprison the Lord's word. Go forth. Go forth. And he did so. To this sinful quarter. Tunnels, cellars, and caves. Where no sunlight penetrates. Where wind off the river cuts like a knife. Chill of icy spray channeled here from the ocean's wintry depths. Where each summer the brackish sea that is mouth and maw and bowel deposits its waste in puddles stinking to high heaven.

Water Street becomes what it's named, rises round his ankles, soaks his boots, threatens to drag him down. Patrolling these murky depths he's predator, scavenger, the prey of some dagger-toothed creature whose shadow closes over him like a net.

When the first settlers arrived here they'd scratched caves into the soft earth of the riverbank. Like ants. Rats. Gradually they'd pushed inland, laying out a geometrical grid of streets, perpendicular, true angled and straight edged, the mirror of their rectitude. Black Quaker coats and dour visages were remembrances of mud, darkness, the place of their lying in, cocooned like worms, propagating dreams of a holy city. The latest comers must always start here, on this dotted line, in this riot of alleys, lanes, tunnels. Wave after wave of immigrants unloaded here, winnowed here, dying in these shanties, grieving in strange languages. But white faces move on, bury their dead, bear their children, negotiate the invisible reef between this broken place and the foursquare town. Learn enough of their new tongue to say to the blacks they've left behind, *thou shalt not pass.*

I watched him bring the scalding liquid to his lips and thought to myself that's where his color comes from. The black brew he drinks every morning. Coloring him, changing him. A hue I had not considered until that instant as other than absence, something nonwhite and therefore its opposite, what light would be if extinguished, sky or sea drained of the color blue when the sun disappears, the blackness of cinders. As he sips, steam rises. I peer into the cup that's become mine, at the moon in its center, waxing, waning. A light burning in another part of the room caught there, as my face would be if I leaned over the cup's hot mouth. But I have no wish to see my face. His is what I study as I stare into my cup and see not absence, but the presence of wood darkly stained, wet plowed earth, a boulder rising from a lake, blackly glistening as it sheds crowns and beards and necklaces of water. His color neither neglect nor abstention, nor mystery, but a swelling tide in his skin of this bitter morning beverage it is my habit to imbibe.

We were losing, clearly losing the fight. One day in mid-September fifty-seven were buried before noon.

He'd begun with no preamble. Our conversation taken up again directly as if the months since our last meeting were no more than a cobweb his first words lightly brush away. I say conversation but a better word would be soliloquy because I was only a listener, a witness learning his story, a story buried so deeply he couldn't recall it, but dreamed pieces, a conversation with himself, a reverie with the power to sink us both into its reality. So his first words did not begin the story where I remembered him ending it in our last session, but picked up midstream the ceaseless play of voices only he heard, always, summoning him, possessing him, enabling him to speak, to be.

Despair was in my heart. The fiction of our immunity had been exposed for the vicious lie it was, a not so subtle device for wresting us from our homes, our loved ones, the afflicted among us, and sending us to aid strangers. First they blamed us, called the sickness Barbados fever, a contagion from those blood-soaked islands, brought to these shores by refugees from the fighting in Santo Domingo. We were not welcome anywhere. A dark skin was seen not only as a badge of shame for its wearer. Now we were evil incarnate, the mask of long agony and violent death. Black servants were discharged. The draymen, carters, barbers, caterers, oyster sellers, street vendors could find no custom. It mattered not that some of us were born here and spoke no language but the English language, second-, even third-generation African Americans who knew no other country, who laughed at the antics of newly landed immigrants, Dutchmen, Welshmen, Scots, Irish, Frenchmen who had turned our marketplaces into Babel, stomping along in their clodhopper shoes, strange costumes, haughty airs, Lowlander gibberish that sounded like men coughing or dogs barking. My fellow countrymen searching everywhere but in their own hearts, the foulness upon which this city is erected, to lay blame on others for the killing fever, pointed their fingers at foreigners and called it Palatine fever, a pestilence imported from those low countries in Europe where, I have been told, war for control of the sea-lanes, the human cargoes transported thereupon, has raged for a hundred years.

But I am losing the thread, the ironical knot I wished to untangle for you. How the knife was plunged in our hearts, then cruelly twisted. We were proclaimed carriers of the fever and treated as pariahs, but when it became expedient to command our services to nurse the sick and bury the dead, the previous allegations were no longer mentioned. Urged on by desperate counselors, the mayor granted us a blessed immunity. We were ordered to save the city.

I swear to you, and the bills of mortality, published by the otherwise unreliable Mr. Carey, support of my contention, that the fever dealt with us severely. Among the city's poor and destitute the fever's ravages were most deadly and we are always the poorest of the poor. If an ordinance forbidding ringing of bells to mourn the dead had not been passed, that awful tolling would have marked our days, the watches of the night in our African American community, as it did in those environs of the city we were forbidden to inhabit. Every morning before I commenced my labors for the sick and dying, I would hear moaning, screams of pain, fearful cries and supplications, a chorus of lamentations scarring daybreak, my people awakenening to a nightmare that was devouring their will to live.

The small strength I was able to muster each morning was sorely tried the moment my eyes and ears opened upon the sufferings of my people, the reality that gave the lie to the fiction of our immunity. When my duties among the whites were concluded, how many nights did I return and struggle till dawn with victims here, my friends, parishioners, wandering sons of Africa whose faces I could not look upon without seeing my own. I was commandeered to rise and go forth to the general task of saving the city, forced to leave this neighborhood where my skills were sorely needed. I nursed those who hated me, deserted the ones I loved, who loved me.

I recite the story many, many times to myself, let many voices speak to me till one begins to sound like the sea or rain or my feet those mornings shuffling through thick dust.

We arrived at Bush Hill early. To spare ourselves a long trek in the oppressive heat of day. Yellow haze hung over the city. Plumes of smoke from blazes in Potter's Field, from fires on street corners curled above the rooftops, lending the dismal aspect of a town sacked and burned. I've listened to the Santo Domingans tell of the burning of Cap François. How the capital city was engulfed by fires set in cane fields by the rebelling slaves. Horizon in flames all night as they huddled offshore in ships, terrified, wondering where next they'd go, if any port would permit them to land, empty-handed slaves, masters whose only wealth now was naked black bodies locked in the hold, wide-eyed witnesses of an empire's downfall, chanting, moaning, uncertain as the sea rocked them, whether or not anything on earth could survive the fearful conflagration consuming the great city of Cap François.

Dawn breaking on a smoldering landscape, writhing columns of smoke, a general cloud of haze the color of a fever victim's eyes. I turn and stare at it a moment, then fall in again with my brother's footsteps trudging through untended fields girding Bush Hill.

From a prisoner-of-war ship in New York harbor where the British had interned him he'd seen that city shed its graveclothes of fog. Morning after morning it would paint itself damp and gray, a flat sketch on the canvas of sky, a tentative, shivering screen of housefronts, sheds, sprawling warehouses floating above the river. Then shadows and hollows darkened. A jumble of masts, spars, sails began to sway, little boats plied lanes between ships, tiny figures inched along wharves and docks, doors opened, windows slid up or down, lending an illusion of depth and animation to the portrait. This city infinitely beyond his reach, this charade other men staged to mock him, to mark the distance he could not travel, the shore he'd never reach, the city, so to speak, came to life and with its birth each morning dropped the palpable weight of his despair. His loneliness and exile. Moored in pewter water, on an island that never stopped moving but never arrived anywhere. The city a mirage of light and air, chimera of paint, brush, and paper, mattered naught except that it was denied him. It shimmered. Tolled. Unsettled the water place where he was sentenced to dwell. Conveyed to him each morning the same doleful tidings: *The dead are legion, the living a froth on dark, layered depths. But you are neither, and less than both.* Each night he dreamed it burning, razed the city till nothing remained but a dry, black crust, crackling, crunching under his boots as he strides, king of the nothing he surveys. We passed holes dug into the earth where the sick are interred. Some died in these shallow pits, awash in their own vomited and voided filth, before a bed in the hospital could be made ready for them. Others believed they were being buried alive, and unable to crawl out, howled till reason or strength deserted them. A few, past caring, slept soundly in these ditches, resisted the attendants sent to rouse them and transport them inside, once they realized they were being resurrected to do battle again with the fever. I'd watched the red-bearded French doctor from Santo Domingo with his charts and assistants inspecting this zone, his *salle d'attente* he called it, greeting and reassuring new arrivals, interrogating them, nodding and bowing, hurrying from pit to pit, peering down at his invisible patients like a gardener tending seeds.

An introduction to the grave, a way into the hospital that prefigured the way most would leave it. That's what this bizarre rite of admission had seemed at first. But through this and other peculiar strategems, Deveze, with his French practice, had transformed Bush Hill from lazarium to a clinic where victims of the fever, if not too weak upon arrival, stood a chance of surviving.

The cartman employed by Bush Hill had suddenly fallen sick. Faithful Wilcox had never missed a day, ferrying back and forth from town to hospital, hospital to Potter's Field. Bush Hill had its own cemetery now. Daily rations of dead could be disposed of less conspicuously in a plot on the grounds of the estate, screened from the horror-struck eyes of the city. No one had trusted the hospital. Tales of bloody chaos reigning there had filtered back to the city. Citizens believed it was a place where the doomed were stored until they died. Fever victims would have to be dragged from their beds into Bush Hill's cart. They'd struggle and scream, pitch themselves from the rolling cart, beg for help when the cart passed a rare pedestrian daring or foolish enough to be abroad in the deadly streets.

I wondered for the thousandth time why some were stricken, some not. Dr. Rush and this Deveze dipped their hands into the entrails of corpses, stirred the black, corrupted blood, breathed infected vapors exhaled from mortified remains. I'd observed both men steeped in noxious fluids expelled by their patients, yet neither had fallen prey to the fever. Stolid, dim Wilcox maintained daily concourse with the sick and buried the dead for two months before he was infected. They say a woman, undiscovered until boiling stench drove her neighbors into the street crying for aid, was the cause of Wilcox's downfall. A large woman, bloated into an even more cumbersome package by gases and liquids seething inside her body, had slipped from his grasp as he and another had hoisted her up into the cart. Catching against a rail, her body had slammed down and burst, spraying Wilcox like a fountain. Wilcox did not pride himself on being the tidiest of men, nor did his job demand one who was overfastidious, but the reeking stench from that accident was too much even for him and he departed in a huff to change his polluted garments. He never returned. So there I was at Bush Hill, where Rush had assigned me with my brother, to bury the flow of dead that did not ebb just because the Charon who was their familiar could no longer attend them.

The doctors believe they can find the secret of the fever in the victims' dead bodies. They cut, saw, extract, weigh, measure. The dead are carved into smaller and smaller bits and the butchered parts studied but they do not speak. What I know of the fever I've learned from the words of those I've treated, from stories of the living that are ignored by the good doctors. When lancet and fleam bleed the victims, they offer up stories like prayers.

It was a jaunty day. We served our white guests and after they'd eaten, they served us at the long, linen-draped tables. A sumptuous feast in the oak grove prepared by many and willing hands. All the world's eyes seemed to be watching us. The city's leading men, black and white, were in attendance to celebrate laying the cornerstone of St. Thomas Episcopal African Church. In spite of the heat and clouds and mettlesome insects, spirits were high. A gathering of whites and blacks in good Christian fellowship to commemorate the fruit of shared labor. Perhaps a new day was dawning. The picnic occurred in July. In less than a month the fever burst upon us.

When you open the dead, black or white, you find: the dura mater covering the brain is white and fibrous in appearance. The leptomeninges covering the brain are clear and without opacifications. The brain weighs 1450 grams and is formed symmetrically. Cut sections of the cerebral hemispheres reveal normal-appearing gray matter throughout.

The white matter of the corpus callosum is intact and bears no lesions. The basal ganglia are in their normal locations and grossly appear to be without lesions. The ventricles are symmetrical and filled with crystal-clear cerebrospinal fluid.

The cerebellum is formed symmetrically. The nuclei of the cerebellum are unremarkable. Multiple sections through the pons, medulla oblongata, and upper brain stem reveal normal gross anatomy. The cranial nerves are in their normal locations and unremarkable.

The muscles of the neck are in their normal locations. The cartilages of the larynx and the hyoid bone are intact. The thyroid and parathyroid glands are normal on their external surface. The mucosa of the larynx is shiny, smooth and without lesions. The vocal cords are unremarkable. A small amount of bloody material is present in the upper trachea.

The heart weighs 380 grams. The epicardial surface is smooth, glistening and without lesions. The myocardium of the left ventricle and septum are of a uniform meaty-red, firm appearance. The endocardial surfaces are smooth, glistening and without lesions. The auricular appendages are free from thrombi. The valve leaflets are thin and delicate, and show no evidence of vegetation.

The right lung weighs 400 grams. The left lung 510 grams. The pleural surfaces of the lungs are smooth and glistening.

The esophageal mucosa is glistening, white and folded. The stomach contains a large amount of black, noxious bile. A vermiform appendix is present. The ascending, transverse, and descending colon reveal hemorrhaging, striations, disturbance of normal mucosa patterns throughout. A small amount of bloody, liquid feces is present in the ano-rectal canal.

The liver weighs 1720 grams. The spleen weighs 150 grams. The right kidney weighs 190 grams. The left kidney weighs 180 grams. The testes show a glistening white tunica albuginea. Sections are unremarkable.

Dr. Rush and his assistants examined as many corpses as possible in spite of the hurry and tumult of never-ending attendance on the sick. Rush hoped to prove his remedy, his analysis of the cause and course of the fever correct. Attacked on all sides by his medical brethren for purging and bleeding patients already in a drastically weakened state, Rush lashed back at his detractors, wrote pamphlets, broadsides, brandished the stinking evidence of his postmortems to demonstrate conclusively how the sick drowned in their own poisoned fluids. The putrefaction, the black excess, he proclaimed, must be drained away, else the victim inevitably succumbs.

Dearest:

I shall not return home again until this business of the fever is terminated. I fear bringing the dread contagion into our home. My life is in the hands of God and as long as He sees fit to spare me I will persist in my labors on behalf of the sick, dying, and dead. We are losing the battle. Eighty-eight were buried this past Thursday. I tremble for your safety. Wish the lie of immunity were true. Please let me know by way of a note sent to the residence of Dr. Rush that you and our dear Martha are well. I pray every hour that God will preserve you both. As difficult as it is to rise each morning and go with Thomas to perform our duties, the task would be unbearable if I did not hold in my heart a vision of these horrors ending, a blessed shining day when I return to you and drop this weary head upon your sweet bosom.

Allen, Allen, he called to me. Observe how even after death, the body rejects this bloody matter from nose and bowel and mouth. Verily, the patient who had expired at least an hour before, continued to stain the cloth I'd wrapped around him. We'd searched the rooms of a regal mansion, discovering six members of a family, patriarch, son, son's wife and three children, either dead or in the last frightful stages of the disease. Upon the advice of one of Dr. Rush's most outspoken critics, they had refused mercury purges and bleeding until now, when it was too late for an earthly remedy to preserve them. In the rich furnishing of this opulent mansion, attended by one remaining servant whom fear had not driven away, three generations had withered simultaneously, this proud family's link to past and future cut off absolutely, the great circle broken. In the first bedroom we'd entered we'd found William Spurgeon, merchant, son and father, present manager of the family fortune, so weak he could not speak, except with pained blinks of his terrible golden eyes. Did he welcome us? Was he apologizing to good Dr. Rush for doubting his cure? Did he fear the dark faces of my brother and myself? Quick, too quickly, he was gone. Answering no questions. Revealing nothing of his state of mind. A savaged face frozen above the blanket. Ancient beyond years. Jaundiced eyes not fooled by our busy ministrations, but staring through us, fixed on the eternal stillness soon to come. And I believe I learned in that yellow cast of his eyes, the exact hue of the sky, if sky it should be called, hanging over the next world where we abide.

Allen, Allen. He lasted only moments and then I wrapped him in a sheet from the chest at the foot of his canopied bed. We lifted him into a humbler litter, crudely nailed together, the lumber still green. Allen, look. Stench from the coffin cut through the oppressive odors permeating this doomed household. See. Like an infant the master of the house had soiled his swaddling clothes. Seepage formed a dark river and dripped between roughly jointed boards. We found his wife where she'd fallen, naked, yellow above the waist, black below. As always the smell presaged what we'd discover behind a closed door. This woman had possessed closets of finery, slaves who dressed, fed, bathed, and painted her, and yet here she lay, no one to cover her modesty, to lift her from the floor. Dr. Rush guessed from the discoloration she'd been dead two days, a guess confirmed by the loyal black maid, sick herself, who'd elected to stay when all others had deserted her masters. The demands of the living too much for her. She'd simply shut the door on her dead mistress. No breath, no heartbeat, Sir. I could not rouse her, Sir. I intended to return, Sir, but I was too weak to move her, too exhausted by my labors, Sir. Tears rolled down her creased black face and I wondered in my heart how this abused and despised old creature in her filthy apron and turban, this frail, worn woman, had survived the general calamity while the strong and pampered toppled around her.

I wanted to demand of her why she did not fly out the door now, finally freed of her burden, her lifelong enslavement to the whims of white people. Yet I asked her nothing. Considered instead myself, a man who'd worked years to purchase his wife's freedom, then his own, a so-called freeman, and here I was following in the train of Rush and his assistants, a functionary, a lackey, insulted daily by those I risked my life to heal.

Why did I not fly? Why was I not dancing in the streets, celebrating God's judgment on this wicked city? Fever made me freer than I'd ever been. Municipal government had collapsed. Anarchy ruled. As long as fever did not strike me I could come and go anywhere I pleased. Fortunes could be amassed in the streets. I could sell myself to the highest bidder, as nurse or undertaker, as surgeon trained by the famous Dr. Rush to apply his lifesaving cure. Anyone who would enter houses where fever was abroad could demand outrageous sums for negligible services. To be spared the fever was a chance for anyone, black or white, to be a king.

So why do you follow him like a puppy, you confounded black fool? He wagged his finger. *You* . . . His finger a gaunt, swollen-jointed, cracked-bone, chewed thing. Like the nose on his face. The nose I'd thought looked more like finger than nose. *Fool. Fool.* Finger wagging, then the cackle. The barnyard braying. Berserk chickens cackling in his skinny, goiter-knobbed throat. You are a fool, you black son of Ham. You slack-witted, Nubian ape. You progeny of Peeping Toms and orang-utans. Who forces you to accompany that madman Rush on his mur-derous tours? He kills a hundred for every one he helps with his lamebrain, nonsensical, unnatural, Sangrado cures. Why do you tuck your monkey tail between your legs and skip after that butcher? Are you his shadow, a mindless, spineless black puddle of slime with no will of its own?

You are a good man, Allen. You worry about the souls of your people in this soulless wilderness. You love your family and your God. You are a beacon and steadfast. Your fatal flaw is narrowness of vision. You cannot see beyond these shores. The river, that stinking gutter into which the city shovels its shit and extracts its drinking water, that long-suffering string of spittle winds to an ocean. A hundred miles downstream the foamy mouth of the land sucks on the Atlantic's teat, trade winds saunter and a whole wide world awaits the voyager. I know, Allen. I've been everywhere. Buying and selling everywhere.

If you would dare be Moses to your people and lead them out of this land, you'd find fair fields for your talent. Not lapdogging or doggy-trotting behind or fetch doggy or lie doggy or doggy open your legs or doggy stay still while I beat you. Follow the wound that is a river back to the sea. Be gone, be gone. While there's still time. If there is time, *mon frère*. If the pestilence has not settled in you already, breathed from my foul guts into yourself, even as we speak.

Here's a master for you. A real master, Allen. The fever that's supping on my innards. I am more slave than you've ever been. I do its bidding absolutely. Cough up my lungs. Shit hunks of my bowel. When I die, they say my skin will turn as black as yours, Allen.

Return to your family. Do not leave them again. Whatever the Rushes promise, whatever they threaten.

Once, ten thousand years ago I had a wife and children. I was like you, Allen, proud, innocent, forward looking, well-spoken, well-mannered, a beacon and steadfast. I began to believe the whispered promise that I could have more. More of what, I didn't ask. Didn't know, but I took my eyes off what I loved in order to obtain this more. Left my wife and children and when I returned they were gone. Forever lost to me. The details are not significant. Suffice to say the circumstances of my leaving were much like yours. Very much like yours, Allen. And I lost every-thing. Became a wanderer among men. Bad news people see coming from miles away. A pariah. A joke. I'm not black like you, Allen. But I will be soon. Sooner than you'll be white. And if you're ever white, you'll be as dead as I'll be when I'm black.

Why do you desert your loved ones? What impels you to do what you find so painful, so unjust? Are you not a man? And free?

Her sleepy eyes, your lips on her warm cheek, each time may be the last meeting on this earth. The circumstances are similar, my brother. My shadow. My dirty face.

The dead are legion, the living a froth on dark, layered depths.

Master Abraham. There's a gentleman to see you, Sir. The golden-haired lad bound to me for seven years was carted across the seas, like you, Allen, in the bowels of a leaky tub. A son to replace my son his fathers had clubbed to death when they razed the ghetto of Antwerp. But I could not tame the inveterate hate, his aversion and contempt for me. From my aerie, at my desk secluded among barrels, bolts, crates, and trunks of the shop's attic, I watched him steal, drink, fornicate. I overheard him denounce me to a delegate sent round to collect a tithe during the emergency. 'Tis well known in the old country that Jews bring the fever. Palatine fever that slays whole cities. They carry it under dirty fingernails, in the wimples of lizardy private parts. Pass it on with the evil eye. That's why we hound them from our towns, exterminate them. Beware of Master Abraham's glare. And the black-coated vulture listened intently. I could see him toting up the account in his small brain. Kill the Jew. Gain a shop and sturdy prentice, too. But I survived till fever laid me low and the cart brought me here to Bush Hill. For years he robbed and betrayed me and all my revenge was to treat him better. Allow him to pilfer, lie, embezzle. Let him grow fat and careless as I knew he would. With a father's boundless kindness I destroyed him. The last sorry laugh coming when I learned he died in agony, fever shriven, following by a day his Water Street French whore my indulgence allowed him to keep.

In Amsterdam I sold diamonds, Allen. In Barcelona they plucked hairs from my beard to fashion charms that brought ill fortune to their enemies. There were nights in dungeons when the mantle of my suffering was all I possessed to wrap round me and keep off mortal cold. I cursed God for choosing me, choosing my people to cuckold and slaughter. Have you heard of the Lamed-Vov, the Thirty Just Men set apart to suffer the reality humankind cannot bear? Saviors. But not Gods like your Christ. Not magicians, not sorcerers with bags of tricks, Allen. No divine immunities. Flesh and blood saviors. Men like we are, Allen. If man you are beneath your sable hide. Men who cough and scratch their sores and bleed and stink. Whose teeth rot. Whose wives and children are torn from them. Who wander the earth unable to die, but men always, men till God plucks them up and returns them to His side where they must thaw ten centuries to melt the crust of earthly grief and misery they've taken upon themselves. Ice men. Snowmen. I thought for many years I might be one of them. In my vanity. My self-pity. My foolishness. But no. One lifetime of sorrows enough for me. I'm just another customer. One more in the crowd lined up at his stall to purchase his wares.

You do know, don't you, Allen, that God is a bookseller? He publishes one book—the text of suffering—over and over again. He disguises it between new boards, in different shapes and sizes, prints on varying papers, in many fonts, adds prefaces and postscripts to deceive the buyer, but it's always the same book.

You say you do not return to your family because you don't want to infect them. Perhaps your fear is well-founded. But perhaps it also masks a greater fear. Can you imagine yourself, Allen, as other than you are? A freeman with no charlatan Rush to blame. The weight of your life in your hands.

You've told me tales of citizens paralyzed by fear, of slaves on shipboard who turn to stone in their chains, their eyes boiled in the sun. Is it not possible that you suffer the converse of this immobility? You, sir, unable to stop an endless round of duty and obligation. Turning pages as if the next one or the next will let you finish the story and return to your life.

Your life, man. Tell me what sacred destiny, what nigger errand keeps you standing here at my filthy pallet? Fly, fly, fly away home. Your house is on fire, your children burning.

I have lived to see the slaves free. My people frolic in the streets. Black and white. The ones who believe they are either or both or neither. I am too old for dancing. Too old for foolishness. But this full moon makes me wish for two good legs. For three. Straddled a broomstick when I was a boy. Giddy-up, Giddy-up. Galloping m'lord, m'lady, around the yard I should be sweeping. Dust in my wake. Chickens squawking. My eyes everywhere at once so I would not be caught out by mistress or master in the sin of idleness. Of dreaming. Of following a child's inclination. My broom steed snatched away. Become a rod across my back. Ever cautious. Dreaming with one eye open. The eye I am now, old and gimpy limbed, watching while my people celebrate the rumor of Old Pharaoh's capitulation.

I've shed this city like a skin, wiggling out of it tenscore and more years, by miles and els, fretting, twisting. Many days I did not know whether I'd wrenched freer or crawled deeper into the sinuous pit. Somewhere a child stood, someplace green, keeping track, waiting for me. Hoping I'd meet him again, hoping my struggle was not in vain. I search that child's face for clues to my blurred features. Flesh drifted and banked, eroded by wind and water, the landscape of this city fitting me like a skin. Pray for me, child. For my unborn parents I carry in this orphan's potbelly. For this ancient face that slips like water through my fingers.

Night now. Bitter cold night. Fires in the hearths of lucky ones. Many of us still abide in dark cellars, caves dug into the earth below poor men's houses. For we are poorer still, burrow there, pull earth like blanket and quilt round us to shut out cold, sleep multitudes to a room, stacked and crosshatched and spoon fashion, ourselves the fuel, heat of one body passed to others and passed back from all to one. No wonder then the celebration does not end as a blazing chill sweeps off the Delaware. Those who leap and roar round the bonfires are better off where they are. They have no place else to go.

Given the derivation of the words, you could call the deadly, winged visitors an *unpleasantness from Egypt*.

Putrid stink rattles in his nostrils. He must stoop to enter the cellar. No answer as he shouts his name, his mission of mercy. Earthen floor, ceiling and walls buttressed by occasional beams, slabs of wood. Faint bobbing glow from his lantern. He sees himself looming and shivering on the walls, a shadowy presence with more substance than he feels he possesses at this late hour. After a long day of visits, this hovel his last stop before returning to his brother's house for a few hours of rest. He has learned that exhaustion is a swamp he can wade through and on the far side another region where a thin trembling version of himself toils while he observes, bemused, slipping in and out of sleep, amazed at the likeness, the skill with which that other mounts and sustains him. Mimicry. Puppetry. Whatever controls this other, he allows the impostor to continue, depends upon it to work when he no longer can. After days in the city proper with Rush, he returns to these twisting streets beside the river that are infected veins and arteries he must bleed.

At the rear of the cave, so deep in shadow he stumbles against it before he sees it, is a mound of rags. When he leans over it, speaking down into the darkness, he knows instantly this is the source of the terrible smell, that something once alive is rotting under the rags. He thinks of autumn leaves blown into mountainous, crisp heaps, the north wind cleansing itself and the city of summer. He thinks of anything, any image that will rescue him momentarily from the nauseating stench, postpone what he must do next. He screams no, no to himself as he blinks away his wife's face, the face of his daughter. His neighbors had promised to check on them, he hears news almost daily. There is no rhyme or reason in whom the fever takes, whom it spares, but he's in the city every day, exposed to its victims, breathing fetid air, touching corrupted flesh. Surely if someone in his family must die, it will be him. His clothes are drenched in vinegar, he sniffs the nostrum of gunpowder, bark and asafetida in a bag pinned to his coat. He's prepared to purge and bleed himself, he's also ready and quite willing to forgo these precautions and cures if he thought surrendering his life might save theirs. He thinks and unthinks a picture of her hair, soft against his cheek, the wet warmth of his daughter's backside in the crook of his arm as he carries her to her mother's side where she'll be changed and fed. No. Like a choking mist, the smell of decaying flesh stifles him, forces him to turn away, once, twice, before he watches himself bend down into the brunt of it and uncover the sleepers.

Two Santo Domingan refugees, slave or free, no one knew for sure, inhabited this cellar. They had moved in less than a week before, the mother huge with child, man and woman both wracked by fever. No one knows how long the couple's been unattended. There was shame in the eyes and voices of the few from whom he'd gleaned bits and pieces of the Santo Domingans' history. Since no one really knew them and few nearby spoke their language, no one was willing to risk, et cetera. Except for screams one night, no one had seen or heard signs of life. If he'd been told nothing about them, his nose would have led him here.

He winces when he sees the dead man and woman, husband and wife, not entwined as in some ballad of love eternal, but turned back to back, distance between them, as if the horror were too visible, too great to bear, doubled in the other's eyes. What had they seen before they flung away from each other? If he could, he would rearrange them, spare the undertakers this vision.

Rat feet and rat squeak in the shadows. He'd stomped his feet, shooed them before he entered, hollered as he threw back the covers, but already they were accustomed to his presence, back at work. They'd bite indiscriminately, dead flesh, his flesh. He curses and flails his staff against the rags, strikes the earthen floor to keep the scavangers at bay. Those sounds are what precipitate the high-pitched cries that first frighten him, then shame him, then propel him to a tall packing crate turned on its end, atop which another crate is balanced. Inside the second wicker container, which had imported some item from some distant place into this land, twin brown babies hoot and wail.

We are passing over the Dismal Swamp. On the right is the Appalachian range, some of the oldest mountains on earth. Once there were steep ridges and valleys all through here but erosion off the mountains created landfill several miles deep in places. This accounts for the rich loamy soil of the region. Over the centuries several southern states were formed from this gradual erosion. The cash crops of cotton and tobacco so vital to southern prosperity were ideally suited to the fertile soil.

Yeah, I nurse these old funky motherfuckers, all right. White people, especially old white people, lemme tell you, boy, them peckerwoods stink. Stone dead fishy wet stink. Talking all the time bout niggers got BO. Well, white folks got the stink and gone, man. Don't be putting my hands on them, neither. Never. Huh uh. If I touch them, be wit gloves. They some nasty people, boy. And they don't be paying me enough to take no chances wit my health. Matter of fact they ain't paying me enough to really be expecting me to work. Yeah. Starvation wages. So I ain't hardly touching them. Or doing much else either. Got to smoke a cigarette to get close to some of them. Piss and shit theyselves like babies. They don't need much taking care anyway. Most of them three-quarters dead already. Ones that ain't is crazy. Nobody don't want them round, that's why they here. Talking to theyselves. Acting like they speaking to a roomful of people and not one soul in the ward paying attention. There's one old black dude, must be a hundred, he be muttering away to hisself nonstop everyday. Pitiful, man. Hope I don't never get that old. Shoot me, bro, if I start to getting old and fucked up in body and mind like them. Don't want no fools like me hanging over me when I can't do nothing no more for my ownself. Shit. They ain't paying me nothing so that's what I do. Nothing. Least I don't punch em or tease em or steal they shit like some the staff. And I don't pretend I'm God like these so-called professionals and doctors flittin round here drawing down that long bread. Naw. I just mind my own business, do my time. Cop a little TV, sneak me a joint when nobody's around. It ain't all that bad, really. Long as I ain't got no ole lady and crumb crushers. Don't know how the married cats make it on the little bit of chump change they pay us. But me, I'm free. It ain't that bad, really.

By the time his brother brought him the news of their deaths . . .

Almost an afterthought. The worst, he believed, had been overcome. Only a handful of deaths the last weeks of November. The city was recovering. Commerce thriving. Philadelphia must be revictualed, refueled, rebuilt, reconnected to the countryside, to markets foreign and domestic, to products, pleasures, and appetites denied during the quarantine months of the fever. A new century would soon be dawning. We must forget the horrors. The Mayor proclaims a new day. Says let's put the past behind us. Of the eleven who died in the fire he said extreme measures were necessary as we cleansed ourselves of disruptive influences. The cost could have been much greater, he said I regret the loss of life, especially the half dozen kids, but I commend all city officials, all volunteers who helped return the city to the arc of glory that is its proper destiny.

When they cut him open, the one who decided to stay, to be a beacon and steadfast, they will find: liver (1720 grams), spleen (150 grams), right kidney (190 grams), left kidney (180 grams), brain (1450 grams), heart (380 grams), and right next to his heart, the miniature hand of a child, frozen in a grasping gesture, fingers like hard tongues of flame, still reaching for the marvel of the beating heart, fascinated still, though the heart is cold, beats not, the hand as curious about this infinite stillness as it was about thump and heat and quickness.

1989

ANNA LEE WALTERS

The Warriors

In our youth, we saw hobos come and go, sliding by our faded white house like wary cats who did not want us too close. Sister and I waved at the strange procession of passing men and women hobos. Just between ourselves, Sister and I talked of that hobo parade. We guessed at and imagined the places and towns we thought the hobos might have come from or had been. Mostly they were white or black people. But there were Indian hobos, too. It never occurred to Sister and me that this would be Uncle Ralph's end.

Sister and I were little, and Uncle Ralph came to visit us. He lifted us over his head and shook us around him like gourd rattles. He was Momma's younger brother, and he could have disciplined us if he so desired. That was part of our custom. But he never did. Instead, he taught us Pawnee words. *"Pari* is Pawnee and *pita* is man," he said. Between the words, he tapped out drumbeats with his fingers on the table top, ghost dance and round dance songs that he suddenly remembered and sang. His melodic voice lilted over us and hung around the corners of the house for days. His stories of life and death were fierce and gentle. Warriors dangled in delicate balance.

He told us his version of the story of Pahukatawa, a Skidi Pawnee warrior. He was killed by the Sioux, but the animals, feeling compassion for him, brought Pahukatawa to life again. "The Evening Star and the Morning Star bore children and some people say that these offspring are who we are," he often said. At times he pointed to those stars and greeted them by their Pawnee names. He liked to pray for Sister and

According to Anna Lee Walters, the first step in creating and promoting contemporary Native American art is to show that the cultural traditions of these communities are vital, thriving, and "by no means [the product] of a vanishing or defeated people." Born in Oklahoma in 1946 of Pawnee and Otoe-Missouria descent, Walters advances this undertaking by working in a variety of media and fields. She is an author and painter, a one-time college curricular consultant, and an editor at the Navajo Community College Press. Her writings include both collections of short stories—*The Sun Is Not Merciful* (1985) and *Ghost Singer* (1988)—and nonfiction works, such as *The Spirit of Native America: Beauty and Mysticism in American Indian Art* (1989). Walters now lives in Arizona on the Navajo Nation.

me, for everyone and every tiny thing in the world, but we never heard him ask for anything for himself from *Atius,* the Father.

"For beauty is why we live," Uncle Ralph said when he talked of precious things only the Pawnees know. "We die for it, too." He called himself an ancient Pawnee warrior when he was quite young. He told us that warriors must brave all storms and odds and stand their ground. He knew intimate details of every battle the Pawnees ever fought since Pawnee time began, and Sister and I knew even then that Uncle Ralph had a great battlefield of his own.

As a child I thought that Uncle Ralph had been born into the wrong time. The Pawnees had been ravaged so often by then. The tribe of several thousand when it was at its peak over a century before were then a few hundred people who had been closely confined for more than a hundred years. The warrior life was gone. Uncle Ralph was trapped in a transparent bubble of a new time. The bubble bound him tight as it blew around us.

Uncle Ralph talked obsessively of warriors, painted proud warriors who shrieked poignant battle cries at the top of their lungs and died with honor. Sister and I were little then, lost from him in the world of children who saw everything with children's eyes. And though we saw with wide eyes the painted warriors that he fantasized and heard their fierce and haunting battle cries, we did not hear his. Now that we are old and Uncle Ralph has been gone for a long time, Sister and I know that when he died, he was tired and alone. But he was a warrior.

The hobos were always around in our youth. Sister and I were curious about them, and this curiosity claimed much of our time. They crept by the house at all hours of the day and night, dressed in rags and odd clothing. They wandered to us from the railroad tracks where they had leaped from slow-moving boxcars onto the flatland. They hid in high clumps of weeds and brush that ran along the fence near the tracks. The hobos usually traveled alone, but Sister and I saw them come together, like poor families, to share a can of beans or a tin of sardines that they ate with sticks or twigs. Uncle Ralph also watched them from a distance.

One early morning, Sister and I crossed the tracks on our way to school and collided with a tall, haggard white man. He wore a very old-fashioned pin-striped black jacket covered with lint and soot. There was fright in his eyes when they met ours. He scurried around us, quickening his pace. The pole over his shoulder where his possessions hung in a bundle at the end bounced as he nearly ran from us.

"Looks just like a scared jackrabbit," Sister said, watching him dart away.

That evening we told Momma about the scared man. She warned us about the dangers of hobos as our father threw us a stern look. Uncle Ralph was visiting but he didn't say anything. He stayed the night and Sister asked him, "Hey, Uncle Ralph, why do you suppose they's hobos?"

Uncle Ralph was a large man. He took Sister and put her on one knee. "You see, Sister," he said, "hobos are a different kind. They see things in a different way. Them hobos are kind of like us. We're not like other people in some ways and yet we are. It has to do with what you see and feel when you look at this old world."

His answer satisfied Sister for a while. He taught us some more Pawnee words that night.

Not long after Uncle Ralph's explanation, Sister and I surprised a black man with white whiskers and fuzzy hair. He was climbing through the barbed-wire fence that marked our property line. He wore faded blue overalls with pockets stuffed full of handkerchiefs. He wiped sweat from his face. When it dried, he looked up and saw us. I remembered what Uncle Ralph had said and wondered what the black man saw when he looked at us standing there.

"We might scare him," Sister said softly to me, remembering the white man who had scampered away.

Sister whispered, "Hi," to the black man. Her voice was barely audible.

"Boy, it's sure hot," he said. His voice was big and he smiled.

"Where are you going?" Sister asked.

"Me? Nowheres, I guess," he muttered.

"Then what you doing here?" Sister went on. She was bold for a seven-year-old kid. I was older but I was also quieter. "This here place is ours," she said.

He looked around and saw our house with its flowering mimosa trees and rich green mowed lawn stretching out before him. Other houses sat around ours.

"I reckon I'm lost," he said.

Sister pointed to the weeds and brush further up the road. "That's where you want to go. That's where they all go, the hobos."

I tried to quiet Sister but she didn't hush. "The hobos stay up there," she said. "You a hobo?"

He ignored her question and asked his own. "Say, what is you all? You not black, you not white. What is you all?"

Sister looked at me. She put one hand on her chest and the other hand on me. "We Indians!" Sister said.

He stared at us and smiled again. "Is that a fact?" he said.

"Know what kind of Indians we are?" Sister asked him.

He shook his fuzzy head. "Indians is Indians, I guess," he said.

Sister wrinkled her forehead and retorted, "Not us! We not like others. We see things different. We're Pawnees. We're warriors!"

I pushed my elbow into Sister's side. She quieted.

The man was looking down the road and he shuffled his feet. "I'd best go," he said.

Sister pointed to the brush and weeds one more time. "That way," she said.

He climbed back through the fence and brush as Sister yelled, "Bye now!" He waved a damp handkerchief.

Sister and I didn't tell Momma and Dad about the black man. But much later Sister told Uncle Ralph every word that had been exchanged with the black man. Uncle Ralph listened and smiled.

Months later when the warm weather had cooled and Uncle Ralph came to stay with us for a couple of weeks, Sister and I went to the hobo place. We had planned it for a long time. That afternoon when we pushed away the weeds, not a hobo was in sight.

The ground was packed down tight in the clearing among the high weeds. We walked around the encircling brush and found folded cardboards stacked together. Burned cans in assorted sizes were stashed under the cardboards, and there were remains of old fires. Rags were tied to the brush, snapping in the hard wind.

Sister said, "Maybe they're all in the boxcars now. It's starting to get cold."

She was right. The November wind had a bite to it and the cold stung our hands and froze our breaths as we spoke.

"You want to go over to them boxcars?" she asked. We looked at the Railroad Crossing sign where the boxcars stood.

I was prepared to answer when a voice roared from somewhere behind us.

"Now, you young ones, you git on home! Go on! Git!"

A man crawled out of the weeds and looked angrily at us. His eyes were red and his face was unshaven. He wore a red plaid shirt with striped gray and black pants too large for him. His face was swollen and bruised. An old woolen pink scarf hid some of the bruise marks around his neck, and his topcoat was splattered with mud.

Sister looked at him. She stood close to me and told him defiantly, "You can't tell us what to do! You don't know us!"

He didn't answer Sister but tried to stand. He couldn't. Sister ran to him and took his arm and pulled on it. "You need help?" she questioned.

He frowned at her but let us help him. He was tall. He seemed to be embarrassed by our help.

"You Indian, ain't you?" I dared to ask him.

He didn't answer me but looked at his feet as if they could talk so he wouldn't have to. His feet were in big brown overshoes.

"Who's your people?" Sister asked. He looked to be about Uncle Ralph's age when he finally lifted his face and met mine. He didn't respond for a minute. Then he sighed. "I ain't got no people," he told us as he tenderly stroked his swollen jaw.

"Sure you got people. Our folks says a man's always got people," I said softly. The wind blew our clothes and covered the words.

But he heard. He exploded like a firecracker. "Well, I don't! I ain't got no people! I ain't got nobody!"

"What you doing out here anyway?" Sister asked. "You hurt? You want to come over to our house?"

"Naw," he said. "Now you little ones, go on home. Don't be walking round out here. Didn't nobody tell you little girls ain't supposed to be going round by themselves? You might git hurt."

"We just wanted to talk to hobos," Sister said.

"Naw, you don't. Just go on home. Your folks is probably looking for you and worrying 'bout you."

I took Sister's arm and told her we were going home. Then we said bye to the man. But Sister couldn't resist a few last words, "You Indian, ain't you?"

He nodded his head like it was a painful thing to do. "Yeah, I'm Indian."

"You ought to go on home yourself," Sister said. "Your folks probably looking for you and worrying 'bout you."

His voice rose again as Sister and I walked away from him. "I told you kids, I don't have no people!" There was exasperation in his voice.

Sister would not be outdone. She turned and yelled, "Oh yeah? You Indian ain't you? Ain't you?" she screamed. "We your people!"

His topcoat and pink scarf flapped in the wind as we turned away from him.

We went home to Momma and Dad and Uncle Ralph then. Uncle Ralph met us at the front door. "Where you all been?" he asked looking toward the railroad tracks. Momma and Dad were talking in the kitchen.

"Just playing, Uncle," Sister and I said simultaneously.

Uncle Ralph grabbed both Sister and me by our hands and yanked us out the door. "*Awkuh!*" he said, using the Pawnee expression to show his dissatisfaction.

Outside, we sat on the cement porch. Uncle Ralph was quiet for a long time, and neither Sister nor I knew what to expect.

"I want to tell you all a story," he finally said. "Once, there were these two rats who ran around everywhere and got into everything all the time. Everything they were told not to do, well they went right out and did. They'd get into one mess and then another. It seems that they never could learn."

At that point Uncle Ralph cleared his throat. He looked at me and said, "Sister, do you understand this story? Is it too hard for you? You're older."

I nodded my head up and down and said, "I understand."

Then Uncle Ralph looked at Sister. He said to her, "Sister, do I need to go on with this story?"

Sister shook her head from side to side. "Naw, Uncle Ralph," she said.

"So you both know how this story ends?" he said gruffly. Sister and I bobbed our heads up and down again.

We followed at his heels the rest of the day. When he tightened the loose hide on top of his drum, we watched him and held it in place as he laced the wet hide down. He got his drumsticks down from the top shelf of the closet and began to pound the drum slowly.

"Where you going, Uncle Ralph?" I asked. Sister and I knew that when he took his drum out, he was always gone shortly after.

"I have to be a drummer at some doings tomorrow," he said.

"You a good singer, Uncle Ralph," Sister said. "You know all them old songs."

"The young people nowadays, it seems they don't care 'bout nothing that's old. They just want to go to the Moon." He was drumming low as he spoke.

"We care, Uncle Ralph," Sister said.

"Why?" Uncle Ralph asked in a hard, challenging tone that he seldom used on us.

Sister thought for a moment and then said, "I guess because you care so much, Uncle Ralph."

His eyes softened as he said, "I'll sing you an *Eruska* song, a song for the warriors."

The song he sang was a war dance song. At first Sister and I listened attentively, but then Sister began to dance the men's dance. She had never danced before and tried to imitate what she had seen. Her chubby body whirled and jumped the way she'd seen the men dance. Her head tilted from side to side the way the men moved theirs. I laughed aloud at her clumsy effort, and Uncle Ralph laughed heartily, too.

Uncle Ralph went in and out of our lives after that. We heard that he sang at one place and then another, and people came to Momma to find him. They said that he was only one of a few who knew the old ways and the songs.

When he came to visit us, he always brought something to eat. The Pawnee custom was that the man, the warrior, should bring food, preferably meat. Then, whatever food was brought to the host was prepared and served to the man, the warrior, along with the host's family. Many times Momma and I, or Sister and I, came home to an empty house to find a sack of food on the table. Momma or I cooked it for the next meal, and Uncle Ralph showed up to eat.

As Sister and I grew older, our fascination with the hobos decreased. Other things took our time, and Uncle Ralph did not appear as frequently as he did before.

Once while I was home alone, I picked up Momma's old photo album. Inside was a gray photo of Uncle Ralph in an army uniform. Behind him were tents on a flat terrain. Other photos showed other poses but only in one picture did he smile. All the photos were written over in black ink in Momma's handwriting. "Ralphie in Korea," the writing said.

Other photos in the album showed our Pawnee relatives. Dad was from another tribe. Momma's momma was in the album, a tiny gray-haired woman who no longer lived. And Momma's momma's dad was in the album; he wore old Pawnee leggings and the long feathers of a dark bird sat upon his head. I closed the album when Momma, Dad, and Sister came home.

Momma went into the kitchen to cook. She called me and Sister to help. As she put on a bibbed apron, she said, "We just came from town, and we saw someone from home there." She meant someone from her tribal community.

"This man told me that Ralphie's been drinking hard," she said sadly. "He used to do that quite a bit a long time ago, but we thought it had stopped. He seemed to be all right for a few years." We cooked and then ate in silence.

Washing the dishes, I asked Momma, "How come Uncle Ralph never did marry?"

Momma looked up at me but was not surprised by my question. She answered, "I don't know, Sister. It would have been better if he had. There was one woman who I thought he really loved. I think he still does. I think it had something to do with Mom. She wanted him to wait."

"Wait for what?" I asked.

"I don't know," Momma said, and sank into a chair.

After that we heard unsettling rumors of Uncle Ralph drinking here and there.

He finally came to the house once when only I happened to be home. He was haggard and tired. His appearance was much like that of the white man that Sister and I met on the railroad tracks years before.

I opened the door when he tapped on it. Uncle Ralph looked years older than his age. He brought food in his arms. "*Nowa,* Sister," he said in greeting. "Where's the other one?" He meant my sister.

"She's gone now, Uncle Ralph. School in Kansas," I answered. "Where you been, Uncle Ralph? We been worrying about you."

He ignored my question and said, "I bring food. The warrior brings home food. To his family, to his people." His face was lined and had not been cleaned for days. He smelled of cheap wine.

I asked again, "Where you been, Uncle Ralph?"

He forced himself to smile. "Pumpkin Flower," he said, using the Pawnee name, "I've been out with my warriors all this time."

He put one arm around me as we went to the kitchen table with the food. "That's what your Pawnee name is. Now don't forget it."

"Did somebody bring you here, Uncle Ralph, or are you on foot?" I asked him.

"I'm on foot," he answered. "Where's your Momma?"

I told him that she and Dad would be back soon. I started to prepare the food he brought.

Then I heard Uncle Ralph say, "Life is sure hard sometimes. Sometimes it seems I just can't go on."

"What's wrong, Uncle Ralph?" I asked.

Uncle Ralph let out a bitter little laugh. "What's wrong?" he repeated. "What's wrong? All my life, I've tried to live what I've been taught, but Pumpkin Flower, some things are all wrong!"

He took a folded pack of Camel cigarettes from his coat pocket. His hand shook as he pulled one from the pack and lit the end. "Too much drink," he said sadly. "That stuff is bad for us."

"What are you trying to do, Uncle Ralph?" I asked him.

"Live," he said.

He puffed on the shaking cigarette a while and said, "The old people said to live beautifully with prayers and song. Some died for beauty, too."

"How do we do that, Uncle Ralph, live for beauty?" I asked.

"It's simple, Pumpkin Flower," he said. "Believe!"

"Believe what?" I asked.

He looked at me hard. "*Awkuh!*" he said. "That's one of the things that is wrong. Everyone questions. Everyone doubts. No one believes in the old ways anymore. They want to believe when it's convenient, when it doesn't cost them anything and they get something in return. There are no more believers. There are no more warriors. They are all gone. Those who are left only want to go to the Moon."

A car drove up outside. It was Momma and Dad. Uncle Ralph heard it too. He slumped in the chair, resigned to whatever Momma would say to him.

Momma came in first. Dad then greeted Uncle Ralph and disappeared into the back of the house. Custom and etiquette required that Dad, who was not a member of Momma's tribe, allow Momma to handle her brother's problems.

She hugged Uncle Ralph. Her eyes filled with tears when she saw how thin he was and how his hands shook.

"Ralphie," she said, "you look awful, but I am glad to see you."

She then spoke to him of everyday things, how the car failed to start and the latest gossip. He was silent, tolerant of the passing of time in this way. His eyes sent me a pleading look while his hands shook and he tried to hold them still.

When supper was ready, Uncle Ralph went to wash himself for the meal. When he returned to the table, he was calm. His hands didn't shake so much.

At first he ate without many words, but in the course of the meal he left the table twice. Each time he came back, he was more talkative than before, answering Momma's questions in Pawnee. He left the table a third time and Dad rose.

Dad said to Momma, "He's drinking again. Can't you tell?" Dad left the table and went outside.

Momma frowned. A determined look grew on her face.

When Uncle Ralph sat down to the table once more, Momma told him, "Ralphie, you're my brother but I want you to leave now. Come back when you're sober."

He held a tarnished spoon in mid-air and put it down slowly. He hadn't finished eating, but he didn't seem to mind leaving. He stood, looked at me with his red eyes, and went to the door. Momma followed him. In a low voice she said, "Ralphie, you've got to stop drinking and wandering—or don't come to see us again."

He pulled himself to his full height then. His frame filled the doorway. He leaned over Momma and yelled, "Who are you? Are you God that you will say what will be or will not be?"

Momma met his angry eyes. She stood firm and did not back down.

His eyes finally dropped from her face to the linoleum floor. A cough came from deep in his throat.

"I'll leave here," he said. "But I'll get all my warriors and come back! I have thousands of warriors and they'll ride with me. We'll get our bows and arrows. Then we'll come back!" He staggered out the door.

In the years that followed, Uncle Ralph saw us only when he was sober. He visited less and less. When he did show up, he did a tapping ritual on our front door. We welcomed the rare visits. Occasionally he stayed at our house for a few days at a time when he was not drinking. He slept on the floor.

He did odd jobs for minimum pay but never complained about the work or money. He'd acquired a vacant look in his eyes. It was the same look that Sister and I had seen in the hobos when we were children. He wore a similar careless array of clothing and carried no property with him at all.

The last time he came to the house, he called me by my English name and asked if I remembered anything of all that he'd taught me. His hair had turned pure white. He looked older than anyone I knew. I marveled at his appearance and said, "I remember everything." That night I pointed out his stars for him and told him how Pahukatawa lived and died and lived again through another's dreams. I'd grown, and Uncle Ralph could not hold me on his knee anymore. His arm circled my waist while we sat on the grass.

He was moved by my recitation and clutched my hand tightly. He said, "It's more than this. It's more than just repeating words. You know that, don't you?"

I nodded my head. "Yes, I know. The recitation is the easiest part but it's more than this, Uncle Ralph."

He was quiet, but after a few minutes his hand touched my shoulder. He said, "I couldn't make it work. I tried to fit the pieces."

"I know," I said.

"Now before I go," he said, "do you know who you are?"

The question took me by surprise. I thought very hard. I cleared my throat and told him, "I know that I am fourteen. I know that it's too young."

"Do you know that you are a Pawnee?" he asked in a choked whisper.

"Yes, Uncle," I said.

"Good," he said with a long sigh that was swallowed by the night.

Then he stood and said, "Well, Sister, I have to go. Have to move on."

"Where are you going?" I asked. "Where all the warriors go?" I teased.

He managed a smile and a soft laugh. "Yeah, wherever the warriors are, I'll find them."

I said to him, "Before you go, I want to ask you . . . Uncle Ralph, can women be warriors too?"

He laughed again and hugged me merrily. "Don't tell me you want to be one of the warriors too?"

"No, Uncle," I said. "Just one of yours." I hated to let him go because I knew I would not see him again.

He pulled away. His last words were, "Don't forget what I've told you all these years. It's the only chance not to become what everyone else is. Do you understand?"

I nodded and he left.

I never saw him again.

The years passed quickly. I moved away from Momma and Dad and married. Sister left before I did.

Years later in another town, hundreds of miles away, I awoke in a terrible gloom, a sense that something was gone from the world the Pawnees knew. The despair filled days, though the reason for the sense of loss went unexplained. Finally, the telephone rang. Momma was on the line. She said, "Sister came home for a few days not too long ago. While she was here and alone, someone tapped on the door, like Ralphie always does. Sister yelled, 'Is that you, Uncle Ralphie? Come on in.' But no one entered."

Then I understood that Uncle Ralph was dead. Momma probably knew too. She wept softly into the phone.

Later Momma received an official call confirming Uncle Ralph's death. He had died from exposure in a hobo shanty, near the railroad tracks outside a tiny Oklahoma town. He'd been dead for several days and nobody knew but Momma, Sister, and me.

Momma reported to me that the funeral was well attended by the Pawnee people. Uncle Ralph and I had said our farewells years earlier. Momma told me that someone there had spoken well of Uncle Ralph before they put him in the ground. It was said that "Ralphie came from a fine family, an old line of warriors."

Ten years later, Sister and I visited briefly at Momma's and Dad's home. We had been separated by hundreds of miles for all that time.

As we sat under Momma's flowering mimosa trees, I made a confession to Sister. I said, "Sometimes I wish that Uncle Ralph were here. I'm a grown woman but I still miss him after all these years."

Sister nodded her head in agreement. I continued. "He knew so many things. He knew why the sun pours its liquid all over us and why it must do just that. He knew why babes and insects crawl. He knew that we must live beautifully or not live at all."

Sister's eyes were thoughtful, but she waited to speak while I went on. "To live beautifully from day to day is a battle all the way. The things that he knew are so beautiful. And to feel and know that kind of beauty is the reason that we should live at all. Uncle Ralph said so. But now, there is no one who knows what that beauty is or any of the other things that he knew."

Sister pushed back smoky gray wisps of her dark hair. "You do," she pronounced. "And I do, too."

"Why do you suppose he left us like that?" I asked.

"It couldn't be helped," Sister said. "There was a battle on."

"I wanted to be one of his warriors," I said with an embarrassed half-smile.

She leaned over and patted my hand. "You are," she said. Then she stood and placed one hand on her bosom and one hand on my arm. "We'll carry on," she said.

I touched her hand resting on my arm. I said, "Sister, tell me again. What is the battle for?"

She looked down toward the fence where a hobo was coming through. We waved at him.

"Beauty," she said to me. "Our battle is for beauty. It's what Uncle Ralph fought for, too. He often said that everyone else just wanted to go to the Moon. But remember, Sister, you and I done been there. Don't forget, after all, we're children of the stars."

1985

SEVEN

Figuring the Body

The stories in this chapter represent the body as a kind of protagonist, give it the same importance as other stories give to a character. Of course, in some ways our bodies *do* endure the realities of life: they sweat, sicken, work out, give birth, make love, dance—and die. All of these stories endow their protagonists with bodies that allow them to speak truths that would otherwise remain unspoken.

The body's ability simultaneously to be mute and give voice is, though paradoxical, widely understood. Body language is something we pay equal attention to as to spoken language, even if we are not consciously aware of doing so; although the body is visible, it can enact the invisible. In George Garrett's "An Evening Performance," the fire-diver's plunge figures a moment of spiritual transcendence, an essentially mysterious celebration of the spirit over the fetters that hold us to the everyday. In "China" (Charles Johnson), an aging man remakes himself through the art of kung fu. The final high kick that marks his new identity is made even more spectacular because it's seen through the untrustworthy eyes of his wife, whose own physical decay stands in counterpoint to his bodily success.

Some of the characters in these stories continue to speak even through the veil of death. Estela Portillo Trambley's "Pay the Criers" witnesses the power of the dead body, for only when Chucho's mother-in-law is dead can he see her true worth, only her dead body can finally persuade him of the value of her life. Edgar Allan Poe's stories chronicle his fascination with death and speech, as does his "The Facts in the Case of M. Valdemar" in which a corpse provides the missing facts, the body testifies to secret knowledge, a voice—from the dead—speaks, coming "from a vast distance, or from some deep cavern within the earth." Triggered by a tray of sugar candies, a memory of childhood and of death speaks to Miranda in "The Grave" (Katherine Anne Porter). She remembers a day in her childhood when she saw into the mysteriousness of life; when, in graveyard amulets and a dead rabbit, she discovered the cycles of the body, subject to birth and death, sweetness and decay.

In some ways the final decade of the twentieth century is a perilous place for a body to be: invariably our essential vulnerability is revealed most vividly through the body. Allen Barnett's "The *Times* As It Knows Us" records the gay community's acute susceptibility to the threat of AIDS, silence, and early death. But these cicatrices, our bodies, are the medium through which we are able to live in this world, not yet being able to exist in the ether of pure spirit, in the realm of pure thought.

GEORGE GARRETT

An Evening Performance

For several weeks, maybe a month or so, there she stood, a plump woman in a sequined one-piece bathing suit, poised on a stylized tower which rose into the very clouds, like Jacob's dreamy ladder, with here and there around it a few birds in tense swift V's, and below, far, far below, there was a tub, flaming and terrible, into which she was surely going to plunge. Beneath in fiery letters was printed: ONE OF THE FABULOUS WONDERS OF MODERN TIMES/STELLA THE HIGH DIVER/SHE DIVES ONE HUNDRED FEET/INTO A FLAMING CAULDRON.

These posters had appeared mysteriously one Monday morning, and they were everywhere, on store windows, on the sides of buildings, on telephone and light poles, tacked to green trees; and you can believe they caused a stir. The children on the way to school (for it was just the beginning of the school year) bunched around them in excited clusters —staring at her buxom magnificence, wondering at her daring—and buzzed about it all day long like a hive of disturbed bees. By midmorning grumbling adults were ripping the posters down from windows and buildings, and a couple of policemen went up and down the main street and some of the side streets, taking them off telephone and light poles. But there were so many! And it was such a mystery. Lurid and unsettling as a blast of trumpets, they had come nevertheless in the night as silently as snow.

It would be later, much later, that the night counterman at the Paradise Diner on the outskirts of town, beyond the last glare of filling stations and the winking motels and the brilliant inanity of used-car lots —where, no matter how carnival-colorful with flags and whirligigs, no matter how brightly lit, the rows of cars stood lonesome like sad wooden

Born in Orlando, Florida, in 1929, George Garrett attended both Columbia and Princeton universities. He published his first collection of poems in 1957, and since then he has held a variety of professorial and writer-in-residence positions across the U.S. A prolific writer of novels and free verse, of critical essays and film scripts, Garrett routinely traverses generic categories. Similarly, his subject matter runs the gamut—from short stories depicting rural life in the South to longer works on Florida politics and evangelical religion. His most famous work, *Death of the Fox* (1971), is a historical novel about Sir Walter Raleigh.

horses from some carousel set out to graze—it would be later when he would remember that the man, the angry little man with the limp, had stopped there for coffee that same night that the posters had appeared.

In spite of all effort, a few of the posters remained, tantalizing in their vague promise of a future marvel, teased by the wind and the weather, faded by the still summer-savage sun and the first needling rains of autumn, the red letters blurring and dribbling away, fuzzy now as if they had been written by a shaking finger in something perishable like blood. Talked about for a while—and there were those who swore they remembered seeing such a thing and certainly those who had heard of it, a subject of some debate and even a little sermonizing in certain of the more fundamentalist churches where amusement is, by definition, nearly equivalent to vice—the promise faded with the posters. There were few who hoped that Stella would ever dive there, fewer still who believed in her coming. It seemed, after all, only another joke of some kind, pointless, mirthless, and in a strange way deeply distressing.

Then one evening in late October with the weather now as cool and gray as wash water the truck came and parked in the field by the old Fairgrounds. At first it was nothing to take much notice of, merely a big, battered truck and pretty soon an Army surplus squad tent, sprouting (sagging in a most unmilitary, careless way) like a khaki mushroom beside it.

And there were people.

There were three of them. There was the man, gimpy (his left leg might have been wooden), his face puckered and fierce and jowly and quizzical like a Boston bulldog, his eyes glazed and almost lightless like the little button eyes of a doll; fierce and tired he seemed, spoke in mutters, showing from time to time a ruined mouth with teeth all awry and at all angles like an old fence; and sometimes around the town, shopping for groceries at the Supermarket, once taking a load of dirty clothes to the Washeteria, buying cigarettes and aspirins and comic books at the drugstore, and busily sorting out bolts and nuts and screws and clamps and brackets at the hardware store (for what?), he talked to himself, a harsh, steady, and indecipherable monotone. There was the little girl, a frail thing made entirely of glazed china with altogether unlikely eyes and hair as bright as new pennies, like a shower of money, richly brushed and shining and worn long to her waist. She wore white always, starched and ironed and fabulously clean; and the women had to wonder how her mother (?)—the woman anyhow—living in a sagging tent and a worn-out truck managed that. The little girl was heard to answer to the name of Angel and did not play with the other children who sometimes, after school, gathered in shrill clots around the tent and the truck to stare until the terrible man came out, limping, waving a pick handle, and chased them away.

The woman was an equal curiosity. She was short, broad-shouldered, wide-hipped, huge-handed, sturdy as a man. Her hair, dyed redder than you'd care to believe, was cut in a short bowl. She appeared to be in early middle age, though she might easily have been old—she wore such savage makeup, wild, accented, slanted eyes, a mouth of flame, and always two perfectly round spots of red like dying roses on her high cheekbones. Still, she had a smile that was a glory and she smiled often. She was not heard to speak to anyone and when she was talked to she smiled and stared, uncomprehending. It was not long before everyone knew she was a mute; it was proved when she was seen to communicate with the man, her hands as swift as wings and not a word.

The truth came out like a jack-in-the-box in a week or so. One fine morning the man had unloaded an enormous pile of boards and pipes beside the truck, and by noon he had erected in the center of the field what seemed to be the beginnings of a good-size drilling derrick.

"For oil?" That was the joke around town before a few prominent men and a policeman went out there in cars, parked at the edge of the field, and walked to where he was working. He paid them no mind at all as they straggled toward him, and, as they drew near, they could see that he was sweat-soaked and working at his task with an unbecoming fury, all in hasty, jerky gestures like a comedian in a silent movie. He did not stop his work until they spoke to him.

"What are you trying to do here?" the policeman said.

The man spat and put his heavy wrench on the ground.

"What the hell does it look like I'm doing?" he said and someone giggled. "I'm putting up the tower."

"What kind of a tower?"

"The tower for Stella," the man said, sighing between his teeth. "How can she dive without a tower? That's logic, ain't it?"

"Oh," the policeman said. "You got to have a license to put on any kind of a exhibition around here."

The lame man lowered his head, seemed to shrink and sag like a slowly deflating balloon, and muttered to himself. Finally he raised his head and looked at them, and they could see the tears glisten in his eyes.

"How much do the license cost?" he said.

"Twenty-five dollars."

"We don't have to do the dive," the man said. "We got a lots of tricks. I can put up just a little bit of a trapeze and Angel can do things that would make your eyes pop out of your head. If worse come to worst we don't have to build nothing at all. If I have to I can stand on the back end of the truck and swallow swords and fire and Angel and Stella can dance."

"Any kind of exhibition costs twenty-five dollars for the license."

The man shrugged and hung his head again.

"Don't you have the money?"

He shook his head, but still would not look at them.

"Well, what the hell?" the policeman said. "You better take that tower down and get on out of town. We got a law—"

"Wait a minute," a merchant said. "You aim to sell tickets, don't you?"

The man nodded.

"If you put on the high dive, I reckon you may get as many as a thousand to see it, counting kids and all. What kind of a price do you charge?"

When the man looked up again, he had his ruined smile for them all. "Two bits a head," he said. "We got a roll of tickets printed up and everything."

The merchant made a hasty calculation. "All right," he said. "I'll tell you what I'll do. I'll get your license for you and you cut me in for half of what you take."

"*Half?*" the man said. "Half is too much. That's a dirty shame. It ain't hardly worth it for half. Besides, the high dive is dangerous."

"Take it or leave it."

"All right," the man said. "I can't do nothing but take it."

"Tell you what else I'll do," the merchant said. "I got a nigger boy helps me down to the store. I'll send him to help you put that tower up. How soon can you put on the show?"

"Tomorrow evening if the weather's good."

While they were standing there talking the woman had come across the field from the tent and stood holding the hand of the little girl, smiling her wonderful smile. She seemed to have not the least notion of what was going on, but as they walked away they saw that she had turned on the man, unsmiling, and as he shook and shook his head, her hands flashed at him like the wings of a wild bird in a cage.

All that day the tower grew and by noon of the next day it was finished. It stood not nearly so tall as the cloud- and bird-troubled structure on the posters, but menacingly high, a rickety skeleton that swayed a little in the light breeze. All the way to the top there was rope ladder and on the top a small platform with an extended plank for a diving board. At the foot of the tower the lame man had created a large wooden and canvas tank into which he and the woman and the Negro who worked for the merchant poured buckets of water, drawn from a public spigot, all afternoon, until it was filled about to the depth of a tall man. There was a large GI can of gasoline nearby. The lame man rigged up a string of colored lights and two large searchlights intended to focus on the diver at the top. He set up a card table at the corner where the main road turned into the Fairgrounds. He put up a few of the posters on the poles and the side of the truck, and by midafternoon everything was ready.

Then the weather turned. The wind came from the north, steady, and with it a thin rain like cold needles. The tower moved with the wind and shone with wet. The woman and the little girl stayed in the tent. The lame man stood at the card table, with a newspaper on his head to keep off the rain, waiting for the first customers to arrive.

Just at dark the merchant arrived. There was a good crowd, equal at least to their expectation, gathered in a ring around the tower, standing in raincoats and underneath umbrellas, silently waiting.

"Well," the merchant said, "it looks like we did all right irregardless of the weather."

"Yeah," the man replied. "Except she don't want to do it."

"What's that?"

"I mean it's too risky at a time like this."

"You should have thought of that before," the merchant said. "If you don't go through with it now, no telling what might happen."

"Oh, we'll give them a show," the man said. "I'll swallow swords if I have to. We'll do something."

"She's got to dive," the merchant said. "Or else you got a case of fraud on your hands."

After that the two of them went into the tent. Inside the woman was sitting on an Army cot, wrapped up in a man's bathrobe, and the little girl was beside her. It was cold and damp and foul in the tent. The merchant winced at the smell of it.

"Tell her she's got to do it."

The lame man waved his hands in deft code to her. She moved her hands slowly in reply and, smiling, shook her head. Outside the people had started to clap their hands in unison.

"She says it's too dangerous. It's dangerous anyhow, but on a night like this—"

"Come on," the merchant said. "It can't be that bad. There must be a trick to it."

The lame man shook his head.

"No, sir," he said. "It ain't no trick to it. It's the most dangerous activity in the world. She don't like to do it one bit."

"That's a fine thing," the merchant said. "Just fine and dandy. If she don't like it, why the hell do you put up posters and build towers and sell tickets, that's what I'd like to know."

"Somebody's got to do it. If it wasn't us, it would just have to be somebody else."

"Oh my God!" the merchant said, throwing up his hands. "Now you listen here. If you don't get the show going in five minutes, I'll have you all slapped right in the jail. Five minutes."

He opened the flap of the tent and went out into the dark and the chill rain. He could hear the little girl crying and the lame man muttering to himself.

Almost at once the lame man followed him. He started up the truck and turned on all the lights. Then the woman appeared in her outsize bathrobe and wearing now a white bathing cap. She walked to the foot of the tower and leaned against it, one hand clutching a rung of the rope ladder, smiling.

"Ladies and gentlemen," the lame man said. "You are about to witness a performance that defies the laws of nature and science. This little lady you see before you is fixing to climb to the top of the tower. There, at that terrible altitude, she's going to stand and dive into a flaming tank of water that's barely six feet deep. You won't believe your eyes. It's a marvel of the modern world. 'How does she do it?' some of you will ask. Now some show people will give you all kinds of fancy reasons for how and why they do their work. They'll tell you they learned it from the wise men of the East. They'll tell you about magicians and dreams and the Secrets of the Ancient World. Not us. The way that Stella does this dive is skill, skill pure and simple. When Stella climbs that tower and dives into the flames she's doing something anyone could do who has the heart and the skill and the nerve for it. That's what's different and special about our show. When Stella sails through the air and falls in the fire and comes up safe and smiling, she is the living and breathing proof of the boundless possibility of all mankind. It should make you happy. It should make you glad to be alive."

"Let's get on with it," someone shouted, and the crowd hollered and whistled.

"All right, we won't give you no special buildup," the lame man continued in an even voice. "We just say, there it is. See for yourself. And without further ado I give you Stella, the high diver."

He touched her. She removed the bathrobe and, opening her arms wide, showed herself, pale and stocky in the tight bathing suit with the winking sequins. Then she turned and began to climb the rope ladder. It was a perilous ascent and the ladder swung with the weight of her. When she reached the top, she rested, kneeling on the platform; then she stood up and unhitched the rope ladder and it fell away in a limp curve like a dead snake.

The crowd gasped.

"Do you see?" the lame man shouted. "Now there's no other way to get down except by diving!"

He hobbled over to the tank and sloshed gasoline on top of the water. He stood back and looked up at her. She stood on the diving plank and looked down. The tower rattled and moved in the wind and she seemed very small and far away. She stood on the end of the plank looking down, then she signaled to the man. He lit the gasoline and jumped back awkwardly as the flames shot up. Just at that instant she dived. Soaring and graceful, her arms wide apart, she seemed for a breathless time to hang at that great height in the wind, caught in the brilliant snare of the searchlights. Then she seemed to fold into herself like a fan and straight and swift as a thrown spear she descended, plummeting into the tank with a great and sparkling flash of fire and water.

There was a hushed moment while the crowd waited to see if she was still alive, but then she emerged, climbed out of the tank smiling, and showed herself to them, damp and unscathed. She put on her bathrobe and hurried back to the tent. Some of the people began to leave, but many stood gazing at the tower and the vacant tank. The lame man switched off the lights and followed after her, disappearing into the tent.

The merchant entered the tent. The three of them, sitting in a row along the edge of the cot, were eating something out of a can. A red lantern glared at their feet.

"Is that all?" the merchant said. "I mean is that all there is to it?"

The man nodded.

"Kind of brief, don't you think, for two bits a head?"

"That's all there is to it," the man said. "She could have killed herself. Ain't that enough for one evening? They ought to be glad."

The merchant looked at her. She was eating from the can and seemed as happy as could be.

"Can't you swallow some swords or something? We want everybody to feel they got their money's worth."

"Goddamnit, they did!" the lame man said. "They got all they're going to."

The merchant tried to persuade him to do something more, but he continued to refuse. So the merchant took his share of the money and left them. Soon the rest of the people left too.

The next morning the three of them were gone. The tower was gone, the truck, the tent, and they might never have been there at all, for all the trace they left. Except for the dark spots on the grass where the flaming water had splashed, except for a few posters remaining (and they were not true to fact or life), there was no trace of them.

But if the evening performance had been brief, it remained with them, haunting, a long time afterwards. Some of the preachers continued to denounce it as the work of the devil himself. The drunkards and tellers of tall tales embroidered on it and exaggerated it and preserved it until the legend of that high dive was like a beautiful tapestry before which they might act out their lives, strangely dwarfed and shamed. The children pestered and fidgeted and wanted to know when the three would come again.

A wise man said it had been a terrible thing.

"It made us all sophisticated," he said. "We can't be pleased by any ordinary marvels anymore—tightrope walkers, fire-eaters, pretty girls being fired out of cannons. It's going to take a regular apocalypse to make us raise our eyebrows again."

He was almost right, as nearly correct as a man could hope to be. How could he even imagine that more than one aging, loveless woman slept better ever after, smiled as she dreamed herself gloriously descending for all the world to see from a topless tower into a lake of flame?

1961

CHARLES JOHNSON

China

If one man conquer in battle a thousand men,
and if another conquers himself, he is the
greatest of conquerors.

The Dhammapada

Evelyn's problems with her husband, Rudolph, began one evening in early March—a dreary winter evening in Seattle—when he complained after a heavy meal of pig's feet and mashed potatoes of shortness of breath, an allergy to something she put in his food perhaps, or brought on by the first signs of wild flowers around them. She suggested they get out of the house for the evening, go to a movie. He was fifty-four, a postman for thirty-three years now, with high blood pressure, emphysema, flat feet, and, as Evelyn told her friend Shelberdine Lewis, the lingering fear that he had cancer. Getting old, he was also getting hard to live with. He told her never to salt his dinners, to keep their Lincoln Continental at a crawl, and never run her fingers along his inner thigh when they sat in Reverend William Merrill's church, because anything, even sex, or laughing too loud—Rudolph was serious—might bring on heart failure.

So she chose for their Saturday night outing a peaceful movie, a mildly funny comedy a *Seattle Times* reviewer said was fit only for titters and nasal snorts, a low-key satire that made Rudolph's eyelids droop as he shoveled down unbuttered popcorn in the darkened, half-empty theater. Sticky fluids cemented Evelyn's feet to the floor. A man in the last row laughed at all the wrong places. She kept the popcorn on her lap, though she hated the unsalted stuff and wouldn't touch it, sighing as Rudolph pawed across her to shove his fingers inside the cup.

Charles Johnson was born in Evanston, Illinois, in 1948, and it was in the Midwest that his career as writer and artist began. In 1969 Johnson started publishing drawings and articles as a cartoonist and reporter for the *Chicago Tribune*. At the same time he attended Southern Illinois University where he studied with author John Gardner, under whose guidance Johnson published his first novel, the critically acclaimed *Faith and the Good Thing* (1974). Since then his artwork has appeared in periodicals nationwide, he has received awards for both his short stories and his television scripts for PBS, and he has composed numerous essays on contemporary African American writing. Currently he is director of the Creative Writing Program at the University of Washington in Seattle.

She followed the film as best she could, but occasionally her eyes frosted over, flashed white. She went blind like this now and then. The fibers of her eyes were failing; her retinas were tearing like soft tissue. At these times the world was a canvas with whiteout spilling from the far left corner toward the center; it was the sudden shock of an empty frame in a series of slides. Someday, she knew, the snow on her eyes would stay. Winter eternally: her eyes split like her walking stick. She groped along the fractured surface, waiting for her sight to thaw, listening to the film she couldn't see. Her only comfort was knowing that, despite her infirmity, her Rudolph was in even worse health.

He slid back and forth from sleep during the film (she elbowed him occasionally, or pinched his leg), then came full awake, sitting up suddenly when the movie ended and a "Coming Attractions" trailer began. It was some sort of gladiator movie, Evelyn thought, blinking, and it was pretty trashy stuff at that. The plot's revenge theme was a poor excuse for Chinese actors or Japanese (she couldn't tell those people apart) to flail the air with their hands and feet, take on fifty costumed extras at once, and leap twenty feet through the air in perfect defiance of gravity. Rudolph's mouth hung open.

"Can people really do that?" He did not take his eyes off the screen, but talked at her from the right side of his mouth. "Leap that high?"

"It's a *movie*," sighed Evelyn. "A *bad* movie."

He nodded, then asked again, "But can they?"

"Oh, Rudolph, for God's sake!" She stood up to leave, her seat slapping back loudly. "They're on *trampolines*! You can see them in the corner—there!—if you open your eyes!"

He did see them, once Evelyn twisted his head to the lower left corner of the screen, and it seemed to her that her husband looked disappointed—looked, in fact, the way he did the afternoon Dr. Guylee told Rudolph he'd developed an extrasystolic reaction, a faint, moaning sound from his heart whenever it relaxed. He said no more and, after the trailer finished, stood—there was chewing gum stuck to his trouser seat—dragged on his heavy coat with her help and followed Evelyn up the long, carpeted aisle, through the exit of the Coronet Theater, and to their car. He said nothing as she chattered on the way home, reminding him that he could not stay up all night puttering in his basement shop because the next evening they were to attend the church's revival meeting.

Rudolph, however, did not attend the revival. He complained after lunch of a light, dancing pain in his chest, which he had conveniently whenever Mount Zion Baptist Church held revivals, and she went alone, sitting with her friend Shelberdine, a beautician. She was forty-one;

Evelyn, fifty-two. That evening Evelyn wore spotless white gloves, tan therapeutic stockings for the swelling in her ankles, and a white dress that brought out nicely the brown color of her skin, the most beautiful cedar brown, Rudolph said when they were courting thirty-five years ago in South Carolina. But then Evelyn had worn a matching checkered skirt and coat to meeting. With her jet black hair pinned behind her neck by a simple wooden comb, she looked as if she might have been Andrew Wyeth's starkly beautiful model for *Day of the Fair.* Rudolph, she remembered, wore black business suits, black ties, black wing tips, but he also wore white gloves because he was a senior usher—this was how she first noticed him. He was one of four young men dressed like deacons (or blackbirds), their left hands tucked into the hollow of their backs, their right carrying silver plates for the offering as they marched in almost military fashion down each aisle: Christian soldiers, she'd thought, the cream of black manhood, and to get his attention she placed not her white envelope or coins in Rudolph's plate but instead a note that said: "You have a beautiful smile." It was, for all her innocence, a daring thing to do, according to Evelyn's mother—flirting with a randy young man like Rudolph Lee Jackson, but he did have nice, tigerish teeth. A killer smile, people called it, like all the boys in the Jackson family: a killer smile and good hair that needed no more than one stroke of his palm to bring out Quo Vadis rows pomaded sweetly with the scent of Murray's.

And, of course, Rudolph was no dummy. Not a total dummy, at least. He pretended nothing extraordinary had happened as the congregation left the little whitewashed church. He stood, the youngest son, between his father and mother, and let old Deacon Adcock remark, "Oh, how strong he's looking now," which was a lie. Rudolph was the weakest of the Jackson boys, the pale, bookish, spiritual child born when his parents were well past forty. His brothers played football, they went into the navy; Rudolph lived in Scripture, was labeled 4-F, and hoped to attend Moody Bible Institute in Chicago, if he could ever find the money. Evelyn could tell Rudolph knew exactly where she was in the crowd, that he could feel her as she and her sister, Debbie, waited for their father to bring his DeSoto—the family prize—closer to the front steps. When the crowd thinned, he shambled over in his slow, ministerial walk, introduced himself, and unfolded her note.

"You write this?" he asked. "It's not right to play with the Lord's money, you know."

"I like to play," she said.

"You do, huh?" He never looked directly at people. Women, she guessed, terrified him. Or, to be exact, the powerful emotions they caused in him terrified Rudolph. He was a pud puller, if she ever saw one. He kept his eyes on a spot left of her face. "You're Joe Montgomery's daughter, aren't you?"

"Maybe," teased Evelyn.

He trousered the note and stood marking the ground with his toe. "And just what you expect to get, Miss Playful, by fooling with people during collection time?"

She waited, let him look away, and, when the back-and-forth swing of his gaze crossed her again, said in her most melic, soft-breathing voice: "*You.*"

Up front, portly Reverend Merrill concluded his sermon. Evelyn tipped her head slightly, smiling into memory; her hand reached left to pat Rudolph's leg gently; then she remembered it was Shelberdine beside her, and lifted her hand to the seat in front of her. She said a prayer for Rudolph's health, but mainly it was for herself, a hedge against her fear that their childless years had slipped by like wind, that she might return home one day and find him—as she had found her father—on the floor, bellied up, one arm twisted behind him where he fell, alone, his fingers locked against his chest. Rudolph had begun to run down, Evelyn decided, the minute he was turned down by Moody Bible Institute. They moved to Seattle in 1956—his brother Eli was stationed nearby and said Boeing was hiring black men. But they didn't hire Rudolph. He had kidney trouble on and off before he landed the job at the Post Office. Whenever he bent forward, he felt dizzy. Liver, heart, and lungs—they'd worn down gradually as his belly grew, but none of this was as bad as what he called "the Problem." His pecker shrank to no bigger than a pencil eraser each time he saw her undress. Or when Evelyn, as was her habit when talking, touched his arm. Was she the cause of this? Well, she knew she wasn't much to look at anymore. She'd seen the bottom of a few too many candy wrappers. Evelyn was nothing to make a man pant and jump her bones, pulling her fully clothed onto the davenport, as Rudolph had done years before, but wasn't sex something else you surrendered with age? It never seemed all that good to her anyway. And besides, he'd wanted oral sex, which Evelyn—if she knew nothing else—thought was a nasty, unsanitary thing to do with your mouth. She glanced up from under her spring hat past the pulpit, past the choir of black and brown faces to the agonized beauty of a bearded white carpenter impaled on a rood, and in this timeless image she felt comforted that suffering was inescapable, the loss of vitality inevitable, even a good thing maybe, and that she had to steel herself—yes—for someday opening her bedroom door and finding her Rudolph face down in his breakfast oatmeal. He would die before her, she knew that in her bones.

And so, after service, Sanka, and a slice of meat pie with Shelberdine downstairs in the brightly lit church basement, Evelyn returned home to tell her husband how lovely the Griffin girls had sung that day, that their neighbor Rod Kenner had been saved, and to listen, if necessary, to Rudolph's fear that the lump on his shoulder was an early-warning sign of something evil. As it turned out, Evelyn found that except for their cat, Mr. Miller, the little A-frame house was empty. She looked in his bedroom. No Rudolph. The unnaturally still house made Evelyn uneasy, and she took the excruciating painful twenty stairs into the basement to peer into a workroom littered with power tools, planks of wood, and the blueprints her husband used to make bookshelves and cabinets. No Rudolph. Frightened, Evelyn called the eight hospitals in Seattle, but no one had a Rudolph Lee Jackson on his books. After her last call the star-burst clock in the living room read twelve-thirty. Putting down the wall phone, she felt a familiar pain in her abdomen. Another attack of Hershey squirts, probably from the meat pie. She hurried into the bathroom, lifted her skirt, and lowered her underwear around her ankles, but kept the door wide open, something impossible to do if Rudolph was home. Actually, it felt good not to have him underfoot, a little like he was dead already. But the last thing Evelyn wanted was that or, as she lay down against her lumpy backrest, to fall asleep, though she did, nodding off and dreaming until something shifted down her weight on the side of her bed away from the wall.

"Evelyn," said Rudolph, "look at this." She blinked back sleep and squinted at the cover of a magazine called *Inside Kung-Fu,* which Rudolph waved under her nose. On the cover a man stood bowlegged, one hand cocked under his armpit, the other corkscrewing straight at Evelyn's nose.

"Rudolph!" She batted the magazine aside, then swung her eyes toward the cluttered nightstand, focusing on the electric clock beside her water glass from McDonald's, Preparation H suppositories, and Harlequin romances. "It's morning!" Now she was mad. At least, working at it. "Where have you been?"

Her husband inhaled, a wheezing, whistlelike breath. He rolled the magazine into a cylinder and, as he spoke, struck his left palm with it. "That movie we saw advertised? You remember—it was called *The Five Fingers of Death.* I just saw that and one called *Deep Thrust.*"

"Wonderful." Evelyn screwed up her lips. "I'm calling hospitals and you're at a Hong Kong double feature."

"Listen," said Rudolph. "You don't understand." He seemed at that moment as if he did not understand either. "It was a Seattle movie premiere. The Northwest is crawling with fighters. It has something to do with all the Asians out here. Before they showed the movie, four students from a kwoon in Chinatown went onstage—"

"A what?" asked Evelyn.

"A kwoon—it's a place to study fighting, a meditation hall." He looked at her but was really watching, Evelyn realized, something exciting she had missed. "They did a demonstration to drum up their membership. They broke boards and bricks, Evelyn. They went through what's called kata and kumite and . . ." He stopped again to breathe. "I've never seen anything so beautiful. The reason I'm late is because I wanted to talk with them after the movie."

Evelyn, suspicious, took a Valium and waited.

"I signed up for lessons," he said.

She gave a glacial look at Rudolph, then at his magazine, and said in the voice she used five years ago when he wanted to take a vacation to Upper Volta or, before that, invest in a British car she knew they couldn't afford:

"You're fifty-*four* years old, Rudolph."

"I know that."

"You're no Muhammad Ali."

"I know that," he said.

"You're no Bruce Lee. Do you want to be Bruce Lee? Do you know where he is now, Rudolph? He'd dead—dead here in a Seattle cemetery and buried up on Capital Hill."

His shoulders slumped a little. Silently, Rudolph began undressing, his beefy backside turned toward her, slipping his pajama bottoms on before taking off his shirt so his scrawny lower body would not be fully exposed. He picked up his magazine, said, "I'm sorry if I worried you," and huffed upstairs to his bedroom. Evelyn clicked off the mushroom-shaped lamp on her nightstand. She lay on her side, listening to his slow footsteps strike the stairs, then heard his mattress creak above her—his bedroom was directly above hers—but she did not hear him click off his own light. From time to time she heard his shifting weight squeak the mattress springs. He was reading that foolish magazine, she guessed; then she grew tired and gave this impossible man up to God. With a copy of *The Thorn Birds* open on her lap, Evelyn fell heavily to sleep again.

At breakfast the next morning any mention of the lessons gave Rudolph lockjaw. He kissed her forehead, as always, before going to work, and simply said he might be home late. Climbing the stairs to his bedroom was painful for Evelyn, but she hauled herself up, pausing at each step to huff, then sat on his bed and looked over his copy of *Inside Kung-Fu*. There were articles on empty-hand combat, soft-focus photos of ferocious-looking men in funny suits, parables about legendary Zen masters, an interview with someone named Bernie Bernheim, who began to study karate at age fifty-seven and became a black belt at age sixty-one, and page after page of advertisements for exotic Asian weapons: nunchaku, shuriken, sai swords, tonfa, bo staffs, training bags of all sorts, a wooden dummy shaped like a man and called a Mook Jong, and weights. Rudolph had circled them all. He had torn the order form from the last page of the magazine. The total cost of the things he'd circled—Evelyn added them furiously, rounding off the figures—was $800.

Two minutes later she was on the telephone to Shelberdine.

"Let him tire of it," said her friend. "Didn't you tell me Rudolph had Lower Lombard Strain?"

Evelyn's nose clogged with tears.

"Why is he doing this? Is it me, do you think?"

"It's the Problem," said Shelberdine. "He wants his manhood back. Before he died, Arthur did the same. Someone at the plant told him he could get it back if he did twenty-yard sprints. He went into convulsions while running around the lake."

Evelyn felt something turn in her chest. "You don't think he'll hurt himself, do you?"

"Of course not."

"Do you think he'll hurt *me*?"

Her friend reassured Evelyn that Mid-Life Crisis brought out these shenanigans in men. Evelyn replied that she thought Mid-Life Crisis started around age forty, to which Shelberdine said, "Honey, I don't mean no harm, but Rudolph always was a little on the slow side," and Evelyn agreed. She would wait until he worked this thing out of his system, until Nature defeated him and he surrendered, as any right-thinking person would, to the breakdown of the body, the brutal fact of decay, which could only be blunted, it seemed to her, by decaying *with* someone, the comfort every Negro couple felt when, aging, they knew enough to let things wind down.

Her patience was rewarded in the beginning. Rudolph crawled home from his first lesson, hunched over, hardly able to stand, afraid he had permanently ruptured something. He collapsed face down on the living room sofa, his feet on the floor. She helped him change into his pajamas and fingered Ben-Gay into his back muscles. Evelyn had never seen her husband so close to tears.

"I can't *do* push-ups," he moaned. "Or sit-ups. I'm so stiff—I don't know my body." He lifted his head, looking up pitifully, his eyes pleading. "Call Dr. Guylee. Make an appointment for Thursday, okay?"

"Yes, dear." Evelyn hid her smile with one hand. "You shouldn't push yourself so hard."

At that, he sat up, bare-chested, his stomach bubbling over his pajama bottoms. "That's what it means. *Gung-fu* means 'hard work' in Chinese. Evelyn"—he lowered his voice—"I don't think I've ever really done hard work in my life. Not like this, something that asks me to give *every*thing, body and soul, spirit and flesh. I've always felt . . ." He looked down, his dark hands dangling between his thighs. "I've never been able to give *every*thing to *any*thing. The world never let me. It won't let me put all of myself into play. Do you know what I'm saying? Every job I've ever had, everything I've ever done, it only demanded part of me. It was like there was so much *more* of me that went unused after the job was over. I get that feeling in church sometimes." He lay back down, talking now into the sofa cushion. "Sometimes I get that feeling with you."

Her hand stopped on his shoulder. She wasn't sure she'd heard him right, his voice was so muffled. "That I've never used all of you?"

Rudolph nodded, rubbing his right knuckle where, at the kwoon, he'd lost a stretch of skin on a speedbag. "There's still part of me left over. You never tried to touch all of me, to take everything. Maybe you can't. Maybe no one can. But sometimes I get the feeling that the unused part—the unlived life—*spoils*, that you get cancer because it sits like fruit on the ground and rots." Rudolph shook his head; he'd said too much and knew it, perhaps had not even put it the way he felt inside. Stiffly, he got to his feet. "Don't ask me to stop training." His eyebrows spread inward. "If I stop, I'll die."

Evelyn twisted the cap back onto the Ben-Gay. She held out her hand, which Rudolph took. Veins on the back of his hand burgeoned abnormally like dough. Once when she was shopping at the Public Market she'd seen monstrous plastic gloves shaped like hands in a magic store window. His hand looked like that. It belonged on Lon Chaney. Her voice shook a little, panicky, "I'll call Dr. Guylee in the morning."

Evelyn knew—or thought she knew—his trouble. He'd never come to terms with the disagreeableness of things. Rudolph had always been too serious for some people, even in South Carolina. It was the thing, strange to say, that drew her to him, this crimped-browed tendency in Rudolph to listen with every atom of his life when their minister in Hodges, quoting Marcus Aurelius to give his sermon flash, said, "Live with the gods," or later in Seattle, the habit of working himself up over

Reverend Merrill's reading from Ecclesiastes 9:10: "Whatsoever thy hand findeth to do, do it with all thy might." Now, he didn't *really* mean that, Evelyn knew. Nothing in the world could be taken that seriously; that's *why* this was the world. And, as all Mount Zion knew, Reverend Merrill had a weakness for high-yellow choirgirls and gin, and was forever complaining that his salary was too small for his family. People made compromises, nodded at spiritual commonplaces—the high seriousness of biblical verses that demanded nearly superhuman duty and self-denial—and laughed off their lapses into sloth, envy, and the other deadly sins. It was what made living so enjoyably *human:* this built-in inability of man to square his performance with perfection. People were naturally soft on themselves. But not her Rudolph.

Of course, he seldom complained. It was not in his nature to complain when, looking for "gods," he found only ruin and wreckage. What did he expect? Evelyn wondered. Man was evil—she'd told him that a thousand times—or, if not evil, hopelessly flawed. Everything failed; it was some sort of law. But at least there was laughter, and lovers clinging to one another against the cliff; there were novels—wonderful tales of how things should be—and perfection promised in the afterworld. He'd sit and listen, her Rudolph, when she put things this way, nodding because he knew that in his persistent hunger for perfection in the here and now he was, at best, in the minority. He kept his dissatisfaction to himself, but occasionally Evelyn would glimpse in his eyes that look, that distant, pained expression that asked: *Is this all?* She saw it after her first miscarriage, then her second; saw it when he stopped searching the want ads and settled on the Post Office as the fulfillment of his potential in the marketplace. It was always there, that look, after he turned forty, and no new, lavishly praised novel from the Book-of-the-Month Club, no feature-length movie, prayer meeting, or meal she fixed for him wiped it from Rudolph's eyes. He was, at least, this sort of man before he saw that martial-arts B movie. It was a dark vision, Evelyn decided, a dangerous vision, and in it she whiffed something that might destroy her. What that was, she couldn't say, but she knew her Rudolph better than he knew himself. He would see the error—the waste of time—in his new hobby, and she was sure he would mend his ways.

In the weeks, then months that followed Evelyn waited, watching her husband for a flag of surrender. There was no such sign. He became worse than before. He cooked his own meals, called her heavy soul food dishes "too acidic," lived on raw vegetables, seaweed, nuts, and fruit to make his body "more alkaline," and fasted on Sundays. He ordered books on something called Shaolin fighting and meditation from a store in California, and when his equipment arrived UPS from Dolan's Sports in New Jersey, he ordered more—in consternation, Evelyn read the list —leg stretchers, makiwara boards, air shields, hand grips, bokken, focus mitts, a full-length mirror (for heaven's sake) so he could correct his form, and protective equipment. For proper use of his headgear and gloves, however, he said he needed a sparring partner—an opponent —he said, to help him instinctively understand "combat strategy," how to "flow" and "close the Gap" between himself and an adversary, how to create by his movements a negative space in which the other would be neutralized.

"Well," crabbed Evelyn, "if you need a punching bag, don't look at *me*."

He sat across the kitchen table from her, doing dynamic-tension exercises as she read a new magazine called *Self*. "Did I ever tell you what a black belt means?" he asked.

"You told me."

"Sifu Chan doesn't use belts for ranking. They were introduced seventy years ago because Westerners were impatient, you know, needed signposts and all that."

"You told me," said Evelyn.

"Originally, all you got was a white belt. It symbolized innocence. Virginity." His face was immensely serious, like a preacher's. "As you worked, it got darker, dirtier, and turned brown. Then black. You were a master then. With even more work, the belt became frayed, the threads came loose, you see, and the belt showed white again."

"Rudolph, I've heard this before!" Evelyn picked up her magazine and took it into her bedroom. From there, with her legs drawn up under the blankets, she shouted: "I *won't* be your punching bag!"

So he brought friends from his kwoon, friends she wanted nothing to do with. There was something unsettling about them. Some were street fighters. Young. They wore tank-top shirts and motorcycle jackets. After drinking racks of Rainier beer on the front porch, they tossed their crumpled empties next door into Rod Kenner's yard. Together, two of Rudolph's new friends—Truck and Tuco—weighed a quarter of a ton. Evelyn kept a rolling pin under her pillow when they came, but she knew they could eat that along with her. But some of his new friends were students at the University of Washington. Truck, a Vietnamese only two years in America, planned to apply to the Police Academy once his training ended; and Tuco, who was Puerto Rican, had been fighting since he could make a fist; but a delicate young man named Andrea, a blue sash, was an actor in the drama department at the university. His kwoon training, he said, was less for self-defense than helping him understand his movements onstage—how, for example, to convincingly explode across a room in anger. Her husband liked them, Evelyn realized in horror. And they liked him. They were separated by money, background, and religion, but something she could not identify made them seem, those nights on the porch after his class, like a single body. They called Rudolph "Older Brother" or, less politely, "Pop."

His sifu, a short, smooth-figured boy named Douglas Chan, who Evelyn figured couldn't be over eighteen, sat like the Dalai Lama in their tiny kitchen as if he owned it, sipping her tea, which Rudolph laced with Korean ginseng. Her husband lit Chan's cigarettes as if he were President Carter come to visit the common man. He recommended that Rudolph study T'ai Chi, "soft" fighting systems, ki, and something called Tao. He told him to study, as well, Newton's three laws of physics and apply them to his own body during kumite. What she remembered most about Chan were his wrist braces, ornamental weapons that had three straps and, along the black leather, highly polished studs like those worn by Steve Reeves in a movie she'd seen about Hercules. In a voice she thought girlish, he spoke of eye gouges and groin-tearing techniques, exercises called the Delayed Touch of Death and Dim Mak, with the casualness she and Shelberdine talked about bargains at Thriftway. And then they suited up, the boyish Sifu, who looked like Maharaj-ji's rougher brother, and her clumsy husband; they went out back, pushed aside the aluminum lawn furniture, and pommeled each other for half an hour. More precisely, her Rudolph was on the receiving end of hook kicks, spinning back fists faster than thought, and foot sweeps that left his body purpled for weeks. A sensible man would have known enough to drive to Swedish Hospital pronto. Rudolph, never known as a profound thinker, pushed on after Sifu Chan left, practicing his flying kicks by leaping to ground level from a four-foot hole he'd dug by their cyclone fence.

Evelyn, nibbling a Van de Kamp's pastry from Safeway—she was always nibbling, these days—watched from the kitchen window until twilight, then brought out the Ben-Gay, a cold beer, and rubbing alcohol on a tray. She figured he needed it. Instead, Rudolph, stretching under the far-reaching cedar in the backyard, politely refused, pushed the tray aside, and rubbed himself with Dit-Da-Jow, "iron-hitting wine," which smelled like the open door of an opium factory on a hot summer day. Yet this ancient potion not only instantly healed his wounds (said Rudolph) but prevented arthritis as well. She was tempted to see if it healed brain damage by pouring it into Rudolph's ears, but apparently he was doing something right. Dr. Guylee's examination had been glowing; he said Rudolph's muscle tone, whatever that was, was better. His cardiovascular system was healthier. His erections were outstanding —or upstanding—though lately he seemed to have no interest in sex.

Evelyn, even she, saw in the crepuscular light changes in Rudolph's upper body as he stretched: Muscles like globes of light rippled along his shoulders; larval currents moved on his belly. The language of his new, developing body eluded her. He was not always like this. After a cold shower and sleep his muscles shrank back a little. It was only after his workouts, his weight lifting, that his body expanded like baking bread, filling out in a way that obliterated the soft Rudolph-body she knew. This new flesh had the contours of the silhouetted figures on medical charts: the body as it must be in the mind of God. Glistening with perspiration, his muscles took on the properties of the free weights he pumped relentlessly. They were profoundly tragic, too, because their beauty was earthbound. It would vanish with the world. You are ugly, his new muscles said to Evelyn; old and ugly. His self-punishment made her feel sick. She was afraid of his hard, cold weights. She hated them. Yet she wanted them, too. They had a certain monastic beauty. She thought: *He's doing this to hurt me.* She wondered: What was it like to be powerful? Was clever cynicism—even comedy—the by-product of bulging bellies, weak nerves, bad posture? Her only defense against the dumbbells that stood between them—she meant both his weights and his friends—was, as always, her acid southern tongue:

"They're all fairies, right?"

Rudolph looked dreamily her way. These post-workout periods made him feel, he said, as if there were no interval between himself and what he saw. His face was vacant, his eyes—like smoke. In this after-glow (he said) he saw without judging. Without judgment, there were no distinctions. Without distinctions, there was no desire. Without desire . . .

He smiled sideways at her. "Who?"

"The people in your kwoon." Evelyn crossed her arms. "I read somewhere that most body builders are homosexual."

He refused to answer her.

"If they're not gay, then maybe I should take lessons. It's been good for you, right?" Her voice grew sharp. "I mean, isn't that what you're saying? That you and your friends are better'n everybody else?"

Rudolph's head dropped; he drew a long breath. Lately, his responses to her took the form of quietly clearing his lungs.

"You should do what you *have* to, Evelyn. You don't have to do what anybody else does." He stood up, touched his toes, then brought his forehead straight down against his unbent knees, which was physically impossible, Evelyn would have said—and faintly obscene.

It was a nightmare to watch him each evening after dinner. He walked around the house in his Everlast leg weights, tried push-ups on his fingertips and wrists, and, as she sat trying to watch "The Jeffersons," stood in a ready stance before the flickering screen, throwing punches each time the scene, or shot, changed to improve his timing. It took the fun out of watching TV, him doing that—she preferred him falling asleep in his chair beside her, as he used to. But what truly frightened Evelyn was his "doing nothing." Sitting in meditation, planted cross-legged in a full lotus on their front porch, with Mr. Miller blissfully curled on his lap, a Bodhisattva in the middle of houseplants she set out for the sun. Looking at him, you'd have thought he was dead. The whole thing smelled like self-hypnosis. He breathed too slowly, in Evelyn's view—only three breaths per minute, he claimed. He wore his gi, splotchy with dried blood and sweat, his calloused hands on his knees, the forefingers on each tipped against his thumbs, his eyes screwed shut.

During his eighth month at the kwoon, she stood watching him as he sat, wondering over the vivid changes in his body, the grim firmness where before there was jolly fat, the disquieting steadiness of his posture, where before Rudolph could not sit still in church for five minutes without fidgeting. Now he sat in zazen for forty-five minutes a day, fifteen when he awoke, fifteen (he said) at work in the mailroom during his lunch break, fifteen before going to bed. He called this withdrawal (how she hated his fancy language) similar to the necessary silences in music, "a stillness that prepared him for busyness and sound." He'd never breathed before, he told her. Not once. Not clear to the floor of himself. Never breathed and emptied himself as he did now, picturing himself sitting on the bottom of Lake Washington: himself, Rudolph Lee Jackson, at the center of the universe; for if the universe was infinite, any point where he stood would be at its center—it would shift and move with him. (That saying, Evelyn knew, was minted in Douglas Chan's mind. No Negro preacher worth the name would speak that way.) He told her that in zazen, at the bottom of the lake, he worked to discipline his mind and maintain one point of concentration; each thought, each feeling that overcame him he saw as a fragile bubble, which he could inspect passionlessly from all sides; then he let it float gently to the surface, and soon—as he slipped deeper into the vortices of himself, into the Void—even the image of himself on the lake floor vanished.

Evelyn stifled a scream.

Was she one of Rudolph's bubbles, something to detach himself from? On the porch, Evelyn watched him narrowly, sitting in a rain-whitened chair, her chin on her left fist. She snapped the fingers on her right hand under his nose. Nothing. She knocked her knuckles lightly on his forehead. Nothing. (Faker, she thought.) For another five minutes he sat and breathed, sat and breathed, then opened his eyes slowly as if he'd slept as long as Rip Van Winkle. "It's dark," he said, stunned. When he began, it was twilight. Evelyn realized something new: He was not living time as she was, not even that anymore. Things, she saw, were slower for him; to him she must seem like a woman stuck in fast-forward. She asked:

"What do you see when you go in there?"

Rudolph rubbed his eyes. "Nothing."

"Then *why* do you do it? The world's out here!"

He seemed unable to say, as if the question were senseless. His eyes angled up, like a child's, toward her face. "Nothing is peaceful sometimes. The emptiness is full. I'm not afraid of it now."

"You empty yourself?" she asked. "Of me, too?"

"Yes."

Evelyn's hand shot up to cover her face. She let fly with a whimper. Rudolph rose instantly—he sent Mr. Miller flying—then fell back hard on his buttocks; the lotus cut off blood to his lower body—which provided more to his brain, he claimed—and it always took him a few seconds before he could stand again. He reached up, pulled her hand down, and stroked it.

"What've I done?"

"That's it," sobbed Evelyn. "I don't know what you're doing." She lifted the end of her bathrobe, blew her nose, then looked at him through streaming, unseeing eyes. "And you don't either. I wish you'd never seen that movie. I'm sick of all your weights and workouts—sick of them, do you hear? Rudolph, I want you back the way you were: *sick*." No sooner than she said this Evelyn was sorry. But she'd done no harm. Rudolph, she saw, didn't want anything; everything, Evelyn included, delighted him, but as far as Rudolph was concerned, it was all shadows in a phantom history. He was humbler now, more patient, but he'd lost touch with everything she knew was normal in people: weakness, fear, guilt, self-doubt, the very things that gave the world thickness and made people do things. She *did* want him to desire her. No, she didn't. Not if it meant oral sex. Evelyn didn't know, really, what she wanted anymore. She felt, suddenly, as if she might dissolve before his eyes. "Rudolph, if you're 'empty,' like you say, you don't know who —or what—is talking to you. If you said you were praying, I'd understand. It would be God talking to you. But this way . . ." She pounded her fist four, five times on her thigh. "It could be *evil* spirits, you know! There *are* evil spirits, Rudolph. It could be the Devil."

Rudolph thought for a second. His chest lowered after another long breath. "Evelyn, this is going to sound funny, but I don't believe in the Devil."

Evelyn swallowed. It had come to that.

"Or God—unless we are gods."

She could tell he was at pains to pick his words carefully, afraid he might offend. Since joining the kwoon and studying ways to kill, he seemed particularly careful to avoid her own most effective weapon: the wry, cutting remark, the put-down, the direct, ego-deflating slash. Oh, he was becoming a real saint. At times, it made her want to hit him.

"Whatever is just *is,*" he said. "That's all I know. Instead of worrying about whether it's good or bad, God or the Devil, I just want to be quiet, work on myself, and interfere with things as little as possible. Evelyn," he asked suddenly, "how can there be *two* things?" His brow wrinkled; he chewed his lip. "You think what I'm saying is evil, don't you?"

"I think it's strange! Rudolph, you didn't grow up in China," she said. "They can't breathe in China! I saw that today on the news. They burn soft coal, which gets into the air and turns into acid rain. They wear face masks over there, like the ones we bought when Mount St. Helens blew up. They all ride bicycles, for Christ's sake! They want what we have." Evelyn heard Rod Kenner step onto his screened porch, perhaps to listen from his rocker. She dropped her voice a little. "You grew up in Hodges, South Carolina, same as me, in a right and proper colored church. If you'd *been* to China, maybe I'd understand."

"I can only be what I've been?" This he asked softly, but his voice trembled. "Only what I was in Hodges?"

"You can't be Chinese."

"I don't want to be Chinese!" The thought made Rudolph smile and shake his head. Because she did not understand, and because he was tired of talking, Rudolph stepped back a few feet from her, stretching again, always stretching. "I only want to be what I *can* be, which isn't the greatest fighter in the world, only the fighter *I* can be. Lord knows, I'll probably get creamed in the tournament this Saturday." He added, before she could reply, "Doug asked me if I'd like to compete this weekend in full-contact matches with some people from the kwoon. I have to." He opened the screen door. "I will."

"You'll be killed—you know that, Rudolph." She dug her finger-nails into her bathrobe, and dug this into him: "You know, you never were very strong. Six months ago you couldn't open a pickle jar for me."

He did not seem to hear her. "I bought a ticket for you." He held the screen door open, waiting for her to come inside. "I'll fight better if you're there."

She spent the better part of that week at Shelberdine's mornings and Reverend Merrill's church evenings, rinsing her mouth with prayer, sitting most often alone in the front row so she would not have to hear Rudolph talking to himself from the musty basement as he pounded out bench presses, skipped rope for thirty minutes in the backyard, or shadowboxed in preparation for a fight made inevitable by his new muscles. She had married a fool, that was clear, and if he expected her to sit on a bench at the Kingdome while some equally stupid brute spilled the rest of his brains—probably not enough left now to fill a teaspoon—then he was wrong. How could he see the world as "perfect"?—That was his claim. There was poverty, unemployment, twenty-one children dying every minute, every day, every year from hunger and malnutrition, over twenty murdered in Atlanta; there were sixty thousand nuclear weapons in the world, which was dreadful, what with Seattle so close to Boeing; there were far-right Republicans in the White House: *good* reasons, Evelyn thought, to be "negative and life-denying," as Rudolph would put it. It was almost sin to see harmony in an earthly hell, and in a fit of spleen she prayed God would dislocate his shoulder, do some minor damage to humble him, bring him home, and remind him that the body was vanity, a violation of every verse in the Bible. But Evelyn could not sustain her thoughts as long as he could. Not for more than a few seconds. Her mind never settled, never rested, and finally on Saturday morning, when she awoke on Shelberdine's sofa, it would not stay away from the image of her Rudolph dead before hundreds of indifferent spectators, paramedics pounding on his chest, bursting his rib cage in an effort to keep him alive.

From Shelberdine's house she called a taxi and, in the steady rain that northwesterners love, arrived at the Kingdome by noon. It's over already, Evelyn thought, walking the circular stairs to her seat, clamping shut her wet umbrella. She heard cheers, booing, an Asian voice with an accent over a microphone. The tournament began at ten, which was enough time for her white belt husband to be in the emergency ward at Harborview Hospital by now, but she had to see. At first, as she stepped down to her seat through the crowd, she could only hear—her mind grappled for the word, then remembered—kiais, or "spirit shouts," from the great floor of the stadium, many shouts, for contests were progressing in three rings simultaneously. It felt like a circus. It smelled like a locker room. Here two children stood toe to toe until one landed a front kick that sent the other child flying fifteen feet. There two lean-muscled female black belts were interlocked in a delicate ballet, like dance or a chess game, of continual motion. They had a kind of sense, these women—she noticed it immediately—a feel for space and their place in it. (Evelyn hated them immediately.) And in the farthest circle she saw, or rather felt, Rudolph, the oldest thing on the deck, who, sparring in the adult division, was squared off with another white belt, not a boy who might hurt him—the other man was middle-aged, graying, maybe only a few years younger than Rudolph —but they were sparring just the same.

Yet it was not truly him that Evelyn, sitting down, saw. Acoustics in the Kingdome whirlpooled the noise of the crowd, a rivering of voices that affected her, suddenly, like the pitch and roll of voices during service. It affected the way she watched Rudolph. She wondered: Who are these people? She caught her breath when, miscalculating his distance from his opponent, her husband stepped sideways into a roundhouse kick with lots of snap—she heard the cloth of his opponent's gi crack like a gunshot when he threw the technique. She leaned forward, gripping the huge purse on her lap when Rudolph recovered and retreated from the killing to the neutral zone, and then, in a wide stance, rethought strategy. This was not the man she'd slept with for twenty years. Not her hypochondriac Rudolph who had to rest and run cold water on his wrists after walking from the front stairs to the fence to pick up the *Seattle Times*. She did not know him, perhaps had never known him, and now she never would, for the man on the floor, the man splashed with sweat, rising on the ball of his rear foot for a flying kick—was he so foolish he still thought he could fly?—would outlive her; he'd stand healthy and strong and think of her in a bubble, one hand on her headstone, and it was all right, she thought, weeping uncontrollably, it was all right that Rudolph would return home after visiting her wet grave, clean out her bedroom, the pillboxes and paperback books, and throw open her windows to let her sour, rotting smell escape, then move a younger woman's things onto the floor space darkened by her color television, her porcelain chamber pot, her antique sewing machine. And then Evelyn was on her feet, unsure why, but the crowd had stood suddenly to clap, and Evelyn clapped, too, though for an instant she pounded her gloved hands together instinctively until her vision cleared, the momentary flash of retinal blindness giving way to a frame of her husband, the postman, twenty feet off the ground in a perfect flying kick that floored his opponent and made a Japanese judge who looked like Oddjob shout "ippon"—one point—and the fighting in the farthest ring, in herself, perhaps in all the world, was over.

1983

ESTELA PORTILLO TRAMBLEY

Pay the Criers

Rain knows the earth and loves it well, for rain is the passion of the earth. It is tears, joy, hope, melted into cool torrents that fall on the longing and the hunger of the earth in rigorous tenderness to give her life. How well it speaks of senses in its cool excitement. The beginning of passion is a burst of flame. Its culmination speaks of an open door unto light, a lucidity of life, more life, forever life.

The giver, rain, comforts, forgives, understands, as it tells of mountains, oceans, skies, and a breathing consciousness of all things. Earth and rain become dark moisture that finds its brightness of a womb. The first beginning was in rain. After copulation . . . there is a silence. It is similar to the silence that follows love. Like love, it confirms the truth of immortality. Like love, it has the vastness of acceptance. This glorious silence is that open door into a clean, free clarity.

Chucho listened to the silence and watched the water on mud puddles circling for an open way. The smell of rain is rich with life. He, too, was full of the same silence. He stood looking out the door leading to the backyard. The desert had welcomed the rain as Juana had welcomed love. He could hear her soft breathing from the bed. He looked up to see the sky, a cloudless blue. The sun had found its throne again. Juana had gotten up from the bed and was now behind him. The silence was part of her too. His glance now fell upon the jarros full of rain water outside the doorway. The water played with light like singing senses. The rain had given.

Chucho felt Juana's small hands caressing his body. The smell of the clay from the jarros increased the pleasure. The aftermath of love

---

In re-creating the experiences of Mexican American culture, Estela Portillo Trambley draws on, in her own words, "the earth-roots, the historical consciousness of the Mejicana." If these roots have a physical component, though, they must be deeply planted in the city of El Paso, where she was born in 1936, received her bachelor's and master's degrees at the University of Texas, and continues to live today. She has served as director of theater arts at El Paso Community College, as well as a high-school English teacher and a radio talk-show host. Her artistic achievements are equally diverse; she has produced and published both dramas and musicals, haiku, and a collection of short stories, *Rain of Scorpions* (1975). Portillo Trambley is also the editor of the 1974 volume, *Chicanas en Literatura y Arte.* In addition, she has published two novels: *Trini* (1983) and *Masihani* (forthcoming).

and set earth became the same affirmation. Juana's cheek felt warm and
soft on his bare back . . . now her half-opened lips pressed hard, tenacious in their love. The lips held a reverence and a claim. Outside the
door there was a newness in the world as if all the ills that fester with
droughts had been swept away.

"Will you stay, Chucho?"

"I have things to do."

"You must keep your promise, Chucho."

He shrugged his shoulders indifferently. Droughts lengthen out into
interminable desperations for Juana. A time and a place had defined
her among the vanquished. This is why inquietude existed within the
well-being of love, why melancholy sought a claim. It was now that
Chucho became aware of his dead mother-in-law, hidden in the darkness of the room. This was the focus now, the presence of a dead woman
who had been a part of them. This was also the reason for Juana's
misery.

His thoughts returned to the early afternoon when he had come
home after a long absence. Chucho had found Juana, grief-stricken,
over the dead body of her mother. The old woman's long drawn-out
battle was over. She had given in to death. Juana was clutching the old
purse stuffed with bills and coins that the mother had entrusted to her
with her last breath. Juana had promised to use the money for a grand
funeral. When life left the body, Juana, lost in her despair, let it fall to
the floor. She clung to the dead mother with a lostness.

A clap of thunder and lightning broke the heaviness of death. It was
at this moment that Chucho had arrived as if he had brought the
welcomed rain. She now turned from the dead mother to the live haven
of his arms. He gave comfort simply and silently. Waiting for Chucho
to come home had been long and frugal for Juana. Now in the realness
of his compassion, Juana felt the body hunger, tormented and bursting
into flame.

As he made love to Juana, his glance fell upon the purse fallen to
the floor. He knew what it contained. For many years, he had fought
with his mother-in-law and with his wife over the use of this money.
The old mother, Refugio, had worked hard for it. She had saved it
religiously for her funeral for a long time. "A waste!" Chucho had
screamed. Refugio was their only means of support. She meted out the
necessary money for frugal survival. The purse had grown fat with time.
"I wonder how much?" Chucho asked himself as he caressed his weeping wife.

"Oh, Chucho, it was a bad time . . . I've been so alone."

"Hush, don't cry; I'm back."

Another clap of thunder brought Juana closer to him. The natural shocks of the body found their end. It was enough. Chucho whispered in Juana's ear, "I will take care of everything. I'll see about the funeral." He felt the sudden tenseness of her body. She held her breath. She knew too well her husband's ways. The fear, however, was secondary to her husband's arms. He was here; he could do as he wished. The gentle rain soon became heavy storm; with it, ascended the heartbeats of the living, a symphony of open doors, the light of life, more life, forever life.

In the shadows of the room, the old cot with the body of the dead woman served as a counterpoint, now lost, as Juana and Chucho swam the colors of the struggle. At one time, the now dead woman had known a struggle too. When youth had passed, the colors of struggle became greys in black descents of tragic things. The colors, the greys, even the black descent had ended for Refugio. Was there some kind of open door in death?

In life, Refugio had been a lusty warrior full of battle cry. The ready passion, the ready appetite, the way out of things, all had been her banner. Her crude grasp had been bloody and her blow heavy. This was her kind of grandeur. In the midst of her poor, monotonous greys, the armed savage had many times touched, harshly and with numbness, the consequence of rainbow spectrums so delicate they had made her fear a shattering of spirit. Perhaps this was why she had scorned impracticality, dream, illusion. But she had walked stoutly across the actuality of things. Her vision had small radius outside the slavish ways in the life struggle. The focus had always been to keep fighting, to keep abreast. If there was rest she reached for greys, for her eyes were now unaccustomed to the colors of the youthful dream or hope. She was earth with its tenacity, its instinctual freedom, and its voracity. The roughness of Refugio gave way only to a simple faith, a childish belief in the ritual wonders of her church. Its pageantry made her one with God, the master in the center of the ring. She had wanted a warrior's funeral when her time came with all its mummery and the jugglers of immortal hope. A fiery skyrocket must streak the heavens with her names for one last time to make up for shackles and for colors lost. A feast in her honor where tears would be wept in ceremonious grace. This had been the wish of the dead woman on the cot.

This was the woman that Chucho and Juana had forgotten when the flame had burst the glory—affirmation of the seed denying death in the dark corner. Now in the silence and the calm, her deadness became real to those well satisfied with love. Juana could not stand the thought of what she had done. Anxiety, too, suffocated her with doubt.

"You must take the money into town and pay the criers, Chucho."
Now Chucho stood looking out the door. His wife's anxiety had made
him rise impatiently from her side to seek a cleaner refuge with the rain.
He reached down and picked up the old worn purse full of money. He
put it in the pocket of the coat lying on a chair and returned to watch
the rain. Suddenly, he turned and began to dress.

Juana sensed herself alone again. She looked towards the cot apprehensively and shivered with guilt. A horror began to grow. She had
proved herself faithless to her mother. The money was now in Chucho's
hands, easily taken. When she had come up behind him at the door,
she was still warm with love, but guilt was taking hold. Chucho sensed
it. Now that the rain had stopped, the jolt of life sounds from the barrio
made his blood race. He must go. He walked away from the door to
finish dressing. Juana's hold on him had been broken without ceremony. Juana felt the consequence of her stupidity. "Oh, God . . . I wish
I could trust him . . . I wish I could erase the fears." But there had been
so many times before when he had used her for his ends. The money
is for the funeral; he must use it for that . . . he must. Her voice was
thick with anxiety.

"You must pay the criers." He dared not look her in the face.

"Yes, yes . . . now leave me alone." He finished dressing hurriedly.
He was alone in his pride and his plans. The shadows grew and made
her cringe against her own weakness. This was the stamp long ago given
to her by her dead mother and a disgusted husband when they had
shared the wine. This creature well accepted condemnation as the
measure of her life. The pain of loss found pulse again. "My mother's
dead . . . my mother's dead . . . what can I do?" The weakness was a
falling . . . a fearful falling. . . .

The dark hysteria grew. There will be no funeral. He will spend the
money. In sudden desperation, she reached for Chucho's coat before he
picked it up and fumbled through the pockets. He was beside her with
a curse. He hit her and the blow erased the world for a second as she
fell backwards against a chair. Again, she had done the wrong thing.
He would leave her now. In desperate defeat, she had tried and failed.

"You must keep your promise, Chucho."

No! He was gone. The money was gone; her mother was gone. Her
sobs came slow at first; soon they were hard and painful. Instinct took
its course. The blind child from the womb went to her mother. She
dragged herself across the floor to the cot where her dead mother lay.
Her arms reached out to touch a stiffness; it was little comfort.
"Mamacita . . . que voy a hacer? What is there without you? Without

him?" She laid her head on the bosom of a dead woman, cradling her non-existing safeness, a nipple of security with no nourishment but touch. . . . Where? How?

Chucho walked out of the two room hut he had helped Refugio build. The old bitch was dead! He touched the pocket of his coat where the money was. He had got the best of her after all.

He quickened his steps when he reached the bottom of the hill. The smell of food for evening meals mixed strangely with the fragrance of wet earth. Yes . . . the first thing he would buy would be a good supper for his best friend Chapo and himself. The best in the house . . . he could afford it. The anticipation made him rather light-headed. He felt joy rising to the throat, escaping into a shout of joy. All the things that would be his in the next few hours! The lighting of lamps in the houses that he passed reminded him of the people of the world! They had all the meaning for the time he touched them, talked to them, shared with them. He would treat everyone tonight. It was a beautiful thought. He would be the giver . . . he, Chucho! Never before could he give so much. He was always broke. Tonight he had much money. The glory of the feeling filled him.

He would tell Chapo about the money and then he would buy a full tank of gas for Chapo's old car. Tonight he would try his luck at the gambling table. Tonight he would visit Adela's girls . . . yes, this would be a night to remember. He reached the bottom of the hill and turned towards Chapo's house. Chapo washed cars all day long with a trance-like vigor. This was the pattern of his day. Soap, mop, hose, car after car. Chapo was a machine, numb to the soul, grateful for the pittance to buy existence for another day. He had to close his eyes against himself as a man to give his life away for a few centavos. He had lost the freedom, poor Chapo! Chucho knew deep down in himself he would never give up the freedom. He was condemned by everyone as shiftless, worthless, no-account, but he would never give up the freedom.

The old dead bitch had been the worst one. He remembered her wild roars and accusations. Why tell him what he already knew? He drank too much and played the fool too often. The old woman's venom had been a fearsome thing. But, then, he curiously remembered times when they had laughed together. There was always relief in the eyes of his simple wife when he was friends with his mother-in-law. It meant peace for a little while. But the old woman had never understood his need for the freedom . . . perhaps because she had never had it herself.

One time he had seen some ice-skaters in the city. He had watched

their graceful, skillful skating with great wonderment. Such a difficult
thing looked so easy, so effortless. That was beauty. Somehow he felt it
had something to do with the freedom he loved so well, but he could
not explain it. The skaters must work hard for that beauty . . . very hard.
The easy, swift, graceful gliding was the work conquered and transformed into a freedom now a part of them. Yes, yes . . . that was it . . .
ease came with becoming a something in action. That is what he wanted
to do in life . . . find an ease of action. Now, he was only a spectator of
a great number of confusions and fears. But he was also a spectator and
he shared the freedom with others.

There were glimpses of many kinds of beauties that went beyond
the traps of every day. Each man must be involved in his destiny, but
first he must recognize the part he plays, and the ease behind the play.
Otherwise, the skill that brought the freedom would never be found.
He remembered watching the skaters and remarking to Chapo:

"I want a skill like that, Chapo."

"You want to be a skater?" Chapo was never too surprised at
Chucho's remarks.

"I want a skill for life, a smooth running to a freedom to make
people see that I can see."

"Oh, you have a skill for life, Chucho. You can drink more, fight
harder . . . you have been in jail more often than anyone I know . . .
why I remember . . ."

"Never mind, Chapo, I mean . . . never mind."

"I know what you mean, Chucho, it doesn't buy you any bread.
What do you care? You have a mother-in-law with a good job."

"Oh, shut up, Chapo!"

"You play with many blows for the freedom, Chucho, but at least
you still have the freedom. Look at me! That bastard without balls pays
me like a slave because I need the money for food for my little ones. I
would like to spit in his face . . . but I don't think about it. I just wash
cars until they shine. Pretty soon, I get my centavos and I go home . . .
we eat one more day."

"I find a skill . . . a good skill . . . then I will skate through life like
a god." Chucho reached Chapo's shack. Next to it stood Chapo's bright
green car like a sentinel against total decay. The oil lamps were lit.
Chapo must be sitting down to supper.

Chucho let out a shrill whistle; then, he called out, "Chapo!" The
door opened and Chapo came out hurriedly, closing the door behind
him. Chucho was not welcomed at Chapo's house. All the neighborhood women considered him a bad influence.

"Hey, Chapo . . . let's fill the car tank with gas . . . and maybe you would like some new tires?"

"You joking?"

"The old woman died today. I got the money."

"May she rest in peace . . . all the money?"

"All the money . . ."

"Ah . . . jaaaaaaaa!" Chapo grabbed Chucho and happily began to wrestle like a bear. They fell to the ground with much laughter and rolled around in happy jest. Finally they lay there looking up at the first stars of evening.

"It's going to be quite a night, eh, Chapo?"

"Hey, let's get going." Chapo jumped to his feet and kicked Chucho, who was still looking at the stars.

"You see something special, you old dog?"

"A bigness . . ."

"Let's go!"

A moment later the old green car was rattling off towards town where city lights spoke of temporary lightning dreams.

"I am waiting for Chucho," Juana's voice was tired. She sat in her neighbor's kitchen. She had waited for Chucho to come back two nights now, waited with the growing stench of death. It did not change the indecisions in her life. She just waited for Chucho until the neighbor found her. It was now two days since the afternoon of life and death. The days had divided themselves in Juana's mind into convulsive terrors, where the chasms with no anchors whirled into a darkness. Memories were a surer stronghold. Then, the neighbor had come to warn her.

"Someone told the authorities about your mother. They're coming today to take her to the crematory if she is not buried right away."

Juana began to cry softly. "I can do nothing until Chucho comes."

"He will not come. He is passed out somewhere. Why wait for the scoundrel?"

"But what can I do? I have no money. No one can help."

"They are going to take her to the crematory today, just wait and see."

"When he feels guilty, he always comes back; he spent all my mother's money, so he will be back."

"Chucho . . . feel guilty? The devil he does!"

"Not guilty . . . it is more of a remorse, after he drinks too much . . . there is always the remorse." Juana remembered well her mother and her husband in the aftermath of drink. The tears for tears' sake, open memories like wet catacombs of sorrows that echoed a burning. Yes, there would be remorse when Chucho came back.

"The crematory will test its new efficiency if your mother is not buried by this afternoon."

"No . . . it is against our religion. My mother's body cannot be burned."

"If there is no money to bury her, she will be burned."

Juana began to weep again. "Mamacita . . . forgive me . . . what did I do to you?" It was a piteous crying of self-accusation. The neighbor stroked the disheveled head of the poor girl in sympathy. Such a soft, helpless thing. That brute of a Chucho should be flogged!

They both heard the car stop at the bottom of the hill. The voices of Chucho and Chapo were heavy with happy memories.

"Oh, Chucho, thank you for the beautiful tires. You are a good friend. Was that a good time or was that a good time?"

There was a short silence as they heard the men go into the house. Suddenly, a long, drawn-out bellow filled the air. Both women ran outside. Chucho was standing at the door looking like a wild man. He shook his head in disbelief and let out another bellow like a wounded animal. He fell to his knees and began to pound the wooden planks of the porch. Chapo stood by helpless and greatly distressed by Chucho's agony.

Chucho moaned, "She's still here. Oh, God . . . the rot! the rot!"

"We'll do something, Chucho." Chapo clumsily reassured, walking nervously around Chucho's kneeling body.

"It's not fair! It's not fair! Life should not rot!" Again he hit his fists against the planked floor.

Juana had run across to him to comfort. He needed her. She went on her knees to take his head in her hands and kiss his forehead as if to stop the suffering. She knew the heights and depths of her husband as she knew the old surface freedoms of his ways. She must tell him right away. "Chucho, the authorities are coming to take her away because there is no money to bury her."

Chucho looked into her face in bewilderment. "I cannot believe the stench . . . but her face, it is the young face of a virgin . . . God forgive me!"

"They will burn her body, Chucho."

He put his arms around her body as if to ask for forgiveness. "I won't let them, Juana."

"You have some money left?" There was a ray of hope in Juana's voice. Chucho shook his head in utter despair, not because of the money, but because he could not imagine the body being burned. It was against God . . . never! never!

He raised himself to his feet and picked up his clinging wife. He turned to Chapo.

"She must not be burned, Chapo."

"What can we do?"

"Get some money somehow."

"Let's take the tires back, Chucho." Juana looked from one to the other, hoping.

Chucho said nothing for he was thinking hard. "The money from the tires will not be enough. We must go to our friends, to our many friends. We can take the body with us, so the authorities will not find it. We can tie it to the trunk of the car." He turned to Juana. "Get some saffron."

The neighbor shook her head in disapproval. Juana stood by helplessly and asked blankly, "Saffron?"

"Yes . . . it will stop the smell. Get as much as you can."

She seemed unable to move. She had no certainties in her experience bank. The neighbor took Juana's arm gently. "Come, I'll go with you." As she led the girl away, she turned to the two men. "You're a couple of fools if you think they are going to let you drive around with a dead body that should have been buried a long time ago."

"They'll have to catch us first . . . go . . . get the stuff."

Half an hour later a mummy-like body was being carried from the house into the trunk of the car. The saffron had been found; sheets had been used to wrap the body carefully. Chucho and Chapo then tied the body to the trunk securely. Juana and the neighbor watched in quiet disbelief. The trunk door remained half-way open when the job was done. It could not be helped. Chapo seemed skeptical.

"You sure it will work, Chucho?"

"Of course I'm not sure, but something has to be done. I'm not going to leave her for the authorities to burn. She was a very brave woman."

"You hated her guts, Chucho."

Chucho did not answer. He got into the car and turned on the ignition. "Get in." Chapo jumped in beside Chucho murmuring, "¡Que Dios nos bendiga!" As the car started off, Chucho called out of the window, "Don't tell the authorities anything. You know nothing." The car rattled down the road in a cloud of dust.

When the car had disappeared, the neighbor turned to Juana, "Stay with me if you want."

"No . . . thank you. I have many things to do before Chucho comes back. He will come back soon."

The neighbor walked away shaking her head. Juana sat down on the porch steps to watch the dying afternoon glorious in color. All traces of the rain were gone. The land had settled down to wait for the long drought. Gravely, her eyes looked out to the familiar desert, waiting too. She imagined an apricot tree fully in bloom. She never had seen one; she looked out into the glare of the sun and her mind's eye saw the apricot tree. There was no mother now, no weekly ritual of expectation, no stories from her mother so full of the outside world. The apricot tree grew in beauty with the mounting loneliness. What was she to do? Tears came to her eyes. She opened the palm of her hand to catch the tears. They glistened in the reflection on the sun. Colors could be found in slight whispers. She looked for a jewel in the wetness. Soon . . . she lost the world around.

Chapo's face was fiercely red. He shook his fists in the air, "Thieves . . . they would not even give me a part of the price we paid for them. We can twist the tires around their necks . . . we have to take the money."

Chucho shrugged his shoulders. "Never mind . . . that small amount won't help . . . and we need the tires to get around."

"Where you wanna go now?"

"Let's try La Sevilla. The sun has set; our night friends will be there." La Sevilla was the favorite bar among the poor, for the owner Mando would many times forget an old bill. Here Chucho had spent money two nights before. Chucho was right; there were many people as Chucho and Chapo went in. Here were the faces of night friends wiped free of fear, this was the place to grapple with the honest fear and the honest hope. Eyes were the full story, here, past the neon lights. The nuances and puppet strings simply did not belong where eyes spoke truth. How well loneliness speaks; it has no cotton mouth or twisted word; tried lies have no place where men go to seek themselves.

Outside, the red neon cast a fierceness on the exposed dead body in the trunk of the car. On and off . . . on and off; the vigil yet was young, a reversion of destiny where one dead woman waited for the living to find life. Inside, the place was filled with tourists and Mando worked feverishly for a "good" night, wiping clean the altar full with communal warmth. The welcomes, too, were warm for Chucho and Chapo. The current carried them towards the usual rectitude that built, slowing to a common human victory.

"Have a drink, Chucho. This is for you, Chapo."

"Listen, the gypsy is still here, Chucho, the one that found the spirit of the mountain in you the other night. Hey, Gitano, look who just came in."

The gypsy saw Chucho and rushed to him with arms outstretched. "You have come back . . . to share the spirit . . . ah! what a night it was! My music and you, the bull, in the arena."

"Not tonight, Gitano . . . I have a mission."

"We all have a mission . . . there will be tears and joy this night." He began a lament on his guitar that extended itself to find the sad waiting in all who heard. Waiting for what? No one really knew. Chucho gulped his drink and slammed his glass upon the bar. "There is something much sadder than your music . . . it is a sadness of the world. If you only knew!"

Chucho put his head down on the bar feeling the weight of Refugio's death. "I did a terrible thing, muchachos . . . a terrible thing."

"What's the matter with him, Chapo?"

"He did a terrible thing."

Chucho raised his head and wiped his eyes with his sleeve unashamedly. "All that money I spent the other night . . . it was the money to pay for a fine funeral for my mother-in-law. Now the authorities will cremate her if we don't find the money to bury her."

"We need the money for the living, Chucho; the dead don't care about their funeral."

Gitano's wailing song rose to torture in sound. Chucho's voice was earnest: "You don't understand. This was no ordinary woman. She was a beautiful fighter. She spat on misfortune and dug her heels for a fight because life was a grand thing to her."

"Is that the mother-in-law that had you thrown in jail so often . . . eh, Chucho . . . here have another drink; you can't think straight."

"The fights . . . it was because we cared as human beings, muchachos. Listen, this is no joke. I will not let the authorities cremate her." Gitano's song began to gather wisps of growing frenzy. It was a happy frenzy that well belonged to the snapping of fingers and the flame tapping of feet.

"Hey, Chucho . . . toro! toro!" The boys began to jostle him. "Dance . . . fight the bull as you did the other night . . . come on, Chucho . . . Olé!"

Chucho was determined to convince them of his plight; Chapo, on the other hand, had been caught up with the music and the mood. Refugio was a far-away thought when someone put another drink in his hand. Chucho screamed "She deserves a burial . . . you understand . . . she deserves it!"

The boys laughed and continued their chant: "Ola . . . toro! Dance for her, Chucho . . . she would like for you to dance for her . . . Dance for her . . . dance for her . . ."

Chucho looked into their faces in half-denial. "But she is . . ." Suddenly he jumped up on the table next to Gitano. "I dance for her!" He exclaimed to the world. "I dance for Refugio! You understand, I dance for Refugio." The frenzy grew as Chucho dared life and pain and fear with his feet and the furious movements of his body. "She felt life like this!" The dance became hard and unrelenting until both Gitano and Chucho were spent. There was no clapping. Only a silence. The toro now sat as clown upon the table to make things tolerable.

"That was a good thing to do for her, Chucho . . . a good thing." Voices rose in agreement. Chucho looked at them like a prince of sadness and confided, "You know what? She liked autumns best because it was a time of realness when the fruits were gathered and the flowers had given of their bloom to all. She used to say dreams were cruel because the waiting sometimes has no end. But autumn . . . ah! It gives men heart, the golden things that are . . . you think I'm crazy . . . eh?"

"You talk as if you loved her . . . who loves his mother-in-law?"

"One who remembers long after . . . long after the things of heart . . . that's who!"

Chucho took another drink from an outstretched hand and gulped it down. Then he took another and another. "Hey, look at Chucho go . . . more! more! more!"

Chucho fell back upon the table like one dead; his eyes were closed. Everybody stared in silence. He spoke slowly and deliberately. "We have the body tied to the back of the car. Just go out the door and see for yourselves; she is waiting . . . how can I go to her without help . . . she is waiting." The crowd mumbled disbelief, but almost all of them hurried out to see. The commotion grew; so did the crowd until Mando went out himself to look. He ran back into the bar and shouted at Chucho, "You crazy fool. You have a dead body outside my place. You know what the authorities will do to me? I'll lose my license. Get her out of here . . . do you hear?" Chucho, still lying on the table, sat up and saw his friends too lost in the circus of things. He knew he could ask no more. He spotted Chapo looking anxiously at the crowd. "Hey, Chapo . . . let's go!"

Outside the neon lights still claimed the body. Chucho and Chapo got into the car without a word. They drove off with the crowd still looking on. They drove down the street drowned in the neon promises of desires, eerie in their brightness. After a while, Chapo asked, "Where to?"

"Adela's place." Chucho leaned back thinking of the woman in the trunk.

"Chucho, she's stinking terrible. Did you see the dogs sniff and run?"

"Shut up. Let's find some money."

"They were right back there. You talk as if you love her."

"I loved her. That is why I hated her so much. But when she bought wine . . . those were very warm times. She used to tell me about her man. He was shot mysteriously. She never found out who did it; she had to bury him by herself. She lost four children in the epidemic. She survived everything. When we drank too much wine we understood things without saying."

"What did you understand, Chucho?"

"Life . . . and each other."

"That's a lot."

"That way we could hold on tight."

"She used to call you a coward."

"She called me everything. She had a big mouth. She was just jealous of my freedom. She worked hard; she had a right to resent me, I suppose."

"Remember when she cracked your skull?"

"What's the matter with you? You bring up all the bad things. Drive and don't talk." The silence was brief for they soon arrived at Adela's. Her place was a dilapidated two story building that seemed almost deserted except for lamp-light and shadows that escaped through drawn shades. Most of the windows were dark. The place did not wear a sign. In earlier days, Adela had catered to the best clientele. The police commissioner had been her confidant and protector. But all good things had come to an end. Both Adela and the establishment had resigned themselves to second-rate flurries.

Chapo parked the car as Chucho hurried to the door of the establishment. Chapo soon caught up with him. One of the girls opened the door, then silently disappeared. They entered a small foyer dimly lighted and filled with artificial palms weighed down with dust. Beyond was the sitting room. Behind an old, flowered, satin sofa was a beaded curtain, covering the stairway leading to the rooms. As usual, Adela came into the room with her greeting for customers. Chucho and Chapo had been there a few nights ago. They had been most splendid and companionable. They seemed to be sober tonight.

She gave Chucho a hug. "Still sporting?" She then kissed him fondly.

"Not tonight, Adela. We have a mission."

The middle-aged madam took his arm and led him to the sofa. "A mission?"

Chapo followed doggedly behind. Chucho asked right out, "Adela, we need some money."

Instinctively, Adela straightened her back and her tone became businesslike. "You came to ask me for money?"

"It is to bury my mother-in-law. It was her money I spent the other night. If I don't raise the money, the authorities will burn her."

"You get your wish then. You were always damning her to hell." She was both amused and cautious.

"You and your girls . . . everybody says you have the biggest hearts."

"No!"

"No," echoed Chapo.

"NO!" repeated the madam. She stood up and looked at them. Then she began to pace the floor up and down as she explained. "You say this is a good cause. Every time an old customer asks for help, they all have good causes. Believe me, we have heard stories of real distress. But, if I am not around, my poor girls are fleeced. They give all . . . foolish, foolish creatures! They cannot afford the luxury of helping everybody who asks. They have next to nothing. Only I stand between them and the world. I sympathize with you. I like you, but they are little sheep . . . little sheep."

"This is one exception, Adela."

"If I make one exception, I will have to make many. That is the way. I cannot do it. However, I shall make a small personal contribution." She lifted her skirt and pulled out some money from the fold of her garter. "Here . . . I know it is not much, but I hope it helps." Chucho took the money, graciously accepting her generosity. He thanked her and kissed her before departing. Adela begged him to come back again. Out in the street, Chucho put up the collar of his old, worn coat. The wind was now raw. Chapo followed behind him. They got into the car without saying a word. They drove around a while and then decided to go to Kiko's. There would be winners there tonight. When they came to Kiko's place, they found it in total darkness. Chucho jumped out of the car and went to inquire next door. In a little while he was back.

"The place was raided. Everybody's in jail." They both stared out into the darkness.

"There will be no criers, Chucho. You cannot pay the criers."

"To hell with the criers, those wailing banshees, fakes!" Laughter spilled from opened doorways. Far off in the distance, the howl of a coyote could be heard. They continued staring into the darkness. "The criers are not good enough, Chapo."

"What are we going to do with the body, Chucho. We are going to land in jail."

"We are going to bury her ourselves, Chapo, out there where the coyote cries."

"You are crazy. We are going to dig a grave in this freezing weather? With what shovel?"

"We shall go to the undertaker and borrow a shovel."

"He's asleep."

"We'll borrow it anyway. It's justice since he refused to bury her just because we had no money."

"Now, Chucho?"

"Yes . . . but first we buy a couple of bottles with Adela's money. It will keep us warm."

It was well past midnight when they got to the outskirts of the city. The climb up the hill and the biting wind had been torturous. The weight of the body and the overpowering stench made the bitter wind welcome. The heat of over-exertion mixed in with the smell of rotting flesh would have been intolerable if it had not been for the cold. Nevertheless, their fingers and faces were half-frozen. Chucho climbed the hill first, carrying the greater part of the weight. Chapo held the lower part of the body. Around his waist he had tied a rope that dragged the shovel after him. Twice they stopped to rest, but not for long, for too many stops meant wasted effort.

When they finally reached the top, they did not know how much time had passed, but the lights of the city still blinked back in reassurance. Distant and much smaller, they had lost their glaring vulgarity. They were now clear lights in sympathy with the night. The men began to feel the cold.

"Let us build a fire, Chapo."

They began to gather sagebrush and dead pieces of wood. It was hard to start the fire without protection from the wind. In time, they managed to start one behind a huge boulder that broke the wind. Soon it was blazing bright.

"I think I am freezing to death, Chucho."

Chucho began to scan the area for the proper burial ground. He finally pointed to a high spot next to a dead clump of trees. The spot was close to the edge of the hill with a full view of the town . . . her town, thought Chucho. He walked over to the spot and dug his foot on the soft earth. "We'll dig the grave here." They took turns with the shovel. Every so often, Chucho would take out a bottle and drink, then he would hand it to Chapo, who did the same. In the midst of the warm glow, they looked down into the town that spoke of lifetimes. Then, one would resume the digging while the other scooped the earth out of the shallow grave. They had laid the body next to the boulder where they had built the fire. It was hardly discernible from where they were digging. Finally, the grave was ready. Chucho went back to where Refugio's body lay. "Come, help me carry it to the grave. Careful! Be gentle!" Chapo did as he was told. When they reached the grave Chucho laid it down close to the edge of the grave almost reverently. "Now we wait."

"Wait?"

"For the sunrise. I want her to see it one more time." Chapo did not answer. He took out the bottle in his pocket and offered it to Chucho. They drank in silence. Chucho asked Chapo for his knife.

"What are you going to do, Chucho?" It was something crazy; Chapo was sure. Chucho took the knife that Chapo offered him and sat down on the ground next to the body. He picked up its head and held it on his lap. Then, he carefully cut into the cloth that covered the face of the dead woman. He stopped when the face was fully exposed. "There, she will be able to see."

They watched the lights from the town gradually disappear as they waited for the sunrise. The fire, too, was dying. Chapo decided to look for more firewood. Chucho sat watching with the head of the dead woman still on his lap. From time to time, he would look down at the face as if trying to understand something on the other side of life . . . past death.

"Do you suppose, Chucho, that where she is now there are city lights?" Chapo was now warming himself in the replenished fire. The town was now in almost total darkness. The friends of night had given up the quest.

The first light rose in the East. It took the darkness gently like a lover. The city did not have long to sleep. The mingling of lives with chance would have another day to try. Chucho was holding the head of the dead woman high as they faced the East. "Look at the sunrise, Refugio. It is like the sunrise already in your face. Chapo, look . . . what beautiful peace, look! All the strength of life is in her face. Are all faces beautiful in death?"

Chapo left the fire and looked at the face. "She was a fine looking woman." Chucho felt the stiff, dead weight in his arms. As he watched the coming of the morning, tears filled his eyes. "Refugio, I didn't give you fancy criers. I, the poor fool, found my own way. I hope it is good enough. You deserved a grand funeral."

"She cannot hear you, Chucho."

"But I am listening now, Chapo, to all the sounds she left, good and bad. You are clear to me now, Refugio." He bent his head and kissed her fully on the lips.

"I love you, Refugio, for having lived." With care, he laid the body down on the ground. Then he jumped into the shallow grave. He took off his coat and made a pillow for Refugio's head.

"That is your only coat, Chucho."

"Here, help me lower the body." With great effort they lowered it until Refugio's head rested on Chucho's coat. Chucho scuttled out of the grave. Both men, dirty, tired, and half-frozen, looked down at the body, and suddenly became very conscious of death. The silence of the two men expected something more than finality. There was the morning and the sunrise unexplained, like the life of days; then, there was the still, white form deep in the earth. Both spoke of something more . . . but what?

Chucho found his way out of the mystery. The grave had to be covered. Then there were the coyotes.

"Let's fill the grave . . . then, we must find the rocks to cover it." They took different paths to find the rocks. Each one would come back with some and he would put them beside the grave. It was a long, tedious job, but the rocks were gathered. The sun was high when they finally filled the grave and then sat down to fit the rocks into the mound.

In the atmosphere that diffuses light, there is celestial song of currents and a higher mathematics. There is the push and flux of life that finds its way to man. Man tastes it as a freedom, a way of depths, a way of new life. If the skill lies in the freedom, thought Chucho, then it belongs to death as well as life. The sunrise became part of the "not enough." Refugio has sufficed. Clowns must be because the world sometimes does not see. The task was done; the moment of somber thought passed. They were filled with a great relief and a great joy. They began to laugh. Then, they clapped each other on the back. There was an intensity in their horseplay; there was a realness in their jest. Chucho took out his bottle and peered into it. "Look . . . there is still some left." He took two gulps and handed the bottle to Chapo. A thought came to Chucho, "A plain cross with two good pieces of wood and her name on it. It would please her."

They found the wood. They sat down near the grave again to make a cross, sharing the rest of the drink.

1975

EDGAR ALLAN POE

The Facts in the Case of M. Valdemar

Of course I shall not pretend to consider it any matter for wonder, that the extraordinary case of M. Valdemar has excited discussion. It would have been a miracle had it not—especially under the circumstances. Through the desire of all parties concerned, to keep the affair from the public, at least for the present, or until we had further opportunities for investigation—through our endeavors to effect this—a garbled or exaggerated account made its way into society, and became the source of many unpleasant misrepresentations; and, very naturally, of a great deal of disbelief.

It is now rendered necessary that I give the *facts*—as far as I comprehend them myself. They are, succinctly, these:

My attention, for the last three years, had been repeatedly drawn to the subject of Mesmerism; and, about nine months ago, it occurred to me, quite suddenly, that in the series of experiments made hitherto, there had been a very remarkable and most unaccountable omission: —no person had as yet been mesmerized *in articulo mortis*. It remained to be seen, first, whether, in such condition, there existed in the patient any susceptibility to the magnetic influence; secondly, whether, if any existed, it was impaired or increased by the condition; thirdly, to what extent, or for how long a period, the encroachments of Death might be arrested by the process. There were other points to be ascertained, but these most excited my curiosity—the last in especial, from the immensely important character of its consequences.

In looking around me for some subject by whose means I might test these particulars, I was brought to think of my friend, M. Ernest Valdemar, the well-known compiler of the "Bibliotheca Forensica," and

Born in 1809 into a Boston theater family, Edgar Allan Poe led a rather unsettled life. After his mother died in 1811, Poe was placed under the guardianship of his godfather, John Allan. He spent a number of years in Scotland and England with this family, was forced to leave the University of Virginia due to his profligate tendencies, and later engineered his own expulsion from West Point. Poe considered himself primarily a poet, but today his status rests mostly on his prose works: macabre psychological studies, such as "Ligeia" and "The Tell-Tale Heart"; excursions into early forms of science fiction; and what is considered the first detective story, "The Murders in the Rue Morgue." Poe died in 1849 in Baltimore.

author (under the *nom de plume* of Issachar Marx) of the Polish versions of "Wallenstein" and "Gargantua." M. Valdemar, who has resided principally at Harlem, N.Y., since the year of 1839, is (or was) particularly noticeable for the extreme spareness of his person—his lower limbs much resembling those of John Randolph; and, also, for the whiteness of his whiskers, in violent contrast to the blackness of his hair—the latter, in consequence, being very generally mistaken for a wig. His temperament was markedly nervous, and rendered him a good subject for mesmeric experiment. On two or three occasions I had put him to sleep with little difficulty, but was disappointed in other results which his peculiar constitution had naturally led me to anticipate. His will was at no period positively, or thoroughly, under my control, and in regard to *clairvoyance*, I could accomplish with him nothing to be relied upon. I always attributed my failure at these points to the disordered state of his health. For some months previous to my becoming acquainted with him, his physicians had declared him in a confirmed phthisis. It was his custom, indeed, to speak calmly of his approaching dissolution, as of a matter neither to be avoided nor regretted.

When the ideas to which I have alluded first occurred to me, it was of course very natural that I should think of M. Valdemar. I knew the steady philosophy of the man too well to apprehend any scruples from *him;* and he had no relatives in America who would be likely to interfere. I spoke to him frankly upon the subject; and, to my surprise, his interest seemed vividly excited. I say to my surprise; for, although he had always yielded his person freely to my experiments, he had never before given me any tokens of sympathy with what I did. His disease was of that character which would admit of exact calculation in respect to the epoch of its termination in death; and it was finally arranged between us that he would send for me about twenty-four hours before the period announced by his physicians as that of his decease.

It is now rather more than seven months since I received, from M. Valdemar himself, the subjoined note:

"MY DEAR P——

You may as well come *now.* D—— and F—— are agreed that I cannot hold out beyond to-morrow midnight; and I think they have hit the time very nearly.

VALDEMAR"

I received this note within half an hour after it was written, and in fifteen minutes more I was in the dying man's chamber. I had not seen him for ten days, and was appalled by the fearful alteration which the brief interval had wrought in him. His face wore a leaden hue; the eyes were utterly lustreless; and the emaciation was so extreme, that the skin had been broken through by the cheek-bones. His expectoration was excessive. The pulse was barely perceptible. He retained, nevertheless, in a very remarkable manner, both his mental power and a certain degree of physical strength. He spoke with distinctness—took some palliative medicines without aid—and, when I entered the room, was occupied in penciling memoranda in a pocket-book. He was propped up in the bed by pillows. Doctors D—— and F—— were in attendance.

After pressing Valdemar's hand, I took these gentlemen aside, and obtained from them a minute account of the patient's condition. The left lung had been for eighteen months in a semi-osseous or cartilaginous state, and was, of course, entirely useless for all purposes of vitality. The right, in its upper portion, was also partially, if not thoroughly, ossified, while the lower region was merely a mass of purulent tubercles, running one into another. Several extensive perforations existed; and, at one point, permanent adhesion to the ribs had taken place. These appearances in the right lobe were of comparatively recent date. The ossification had proceeded with very unusual rapidity; no sign of it had been discovered a month before, and the adhesion had only been observed during the three previous days. Independently of the phthisis, the patient was suspected of aneurism of the aorta; but on this point the osseous symptoms rendered an exact diagnosis impossible. It was the opinion of both physicians that M. Valdemar would die about midnight on the morrow (Sunday). It was then seven o'clock on Saturday evening.

On quitting the invalid's bedside to hold conversation with myself, Doctors D—— and F—— had bidden him a final farewell. It had not been their intention to return; but, at my request, they agreed to look in upon the patient about ten the next night.

When they had gone, I spoke freely with M. Valdemar on the subject of his approaching dissolution, as well as, more particularly, of the experiment proposed. He still professed himself quite willing and even anxious to have it made, and urged me to commence it at once. A male and a female nurse were in attendance; but I did not feel myself altogether at liberty to engage in a task of this character with no more reliable witnesses than these people, in case of sudden accident, might prove. I therefore postponed operations until about eight the next night, when the arrival of a medical student, with whom I had some acquaintance (Mr. Theodore L——l), relieved me from further embarrassment.

It had been my design, originally, to wait for the physicians; but I was induced to proceed, first, by the urgent entreaties of M. Valdemar, and secondly, by my conviction that I had not a moment to lose, as he was evidently sinking fast.

Mr. L——l was so kind as to accede to my desire that he would take notes of all that occurred; and it is from his memoranda that what I now have to relate is, for the most part, either condensed or copied *verbatim*.

It wanted about five minutes of eight when, taking the patient's hand, I begged him to state, as distinctly as he could, to Mr. L——l, whether he (M. Valdemar) was entirely willing that I should make the experiment of mesmerizing him in his then condition.

He replied feebly, yet quite audibly: "Yes, I wish to be mesmerized"—adding immediately afterward: "I fear you have deferred it too long."

While he spoke thus, I commenced the passes which I had already found most effectual in subduing him. He was evidently influenced with the first lateral stroke of my hand across his forehead; but, although I exerted all my powers, no further perceptible effect was induced until some minutes after ten o'clock, when Doctors D—— and F—— called, according to appointment. I explained to them, in a few words, what I designed, and as they opposed no objection, saying that the patient was already in the death agony, I proceeded without hesitation—exchanging, however, the lateral passes for downward ones, and directing my gaze entirely into the right eye of the sufferer.

By this time his pulse was imperceptible and his breathing was stertorious, and at invervals of half a minute.

This condition was nearly unaltered for a quarter of an hour. At the expiration of this period, however, a natural although a very deep sigh escaped from the bosom of the dying man, and the stertorious breathing ceased—that is to say, its stertoriousness was no longer apparent; the intervals were undiminished. The patient's extremities were of an icy coldness.

At five minutes before eleven, I perceived unequivocal signs of the mesmeric influence. The glassy roll of the eye was changed for that expression of uneasy *inward* examination which is never seen except in cases of sleep-waking, and which it is quite impossible to mistake. With a few rapid lateral passes I made the lids quiver, as in incipient sleep, and with a few more I closed them altogether. I was not satisfied, however, with this, but continued the manipulations vigorously, and with the fullest exertion of the will, until I had completely stiffened the limbs of the slumberer, after placing them in a seemingly easy position.

The legs were at full length; the arms were nearly so, and reposed on the bed at a moderate distance from the loins. The head was very slightly elevated.

When I had accomplished this, it was fully midnight, and I requested the gentlemen present to examine M. Valdemar's condition. After a few experiments, they admitted him to be in an unusually perfect state of mesmeric trance. The curiosity of both the physicians was greatly excited. Dr. D—— resolved at once to remain with the patient all night, while Dr. F—— took leave with a promise to return at daybreak. Mr. L——l and the nurses remained.

We left M. Valdemar entirely undisturbed until about three o'clock in the morning, when I approached him and found him in precisely the same condition as when Dr. F—— went away—that is to say, he lay in the same position; the pulse was imperceptible; the breathing was gentle (scarcely noticeable, unless through the application of a mirror to the lips); the eyes were closed naturally; and the limbs were as rigid and as cold as marble. Still, the general appearance was certainly not that of death.

As I approached M. Valdemar I made a kind of half effort to influence his right arm into pursuit of my own, as I passed the latter gently to and fro above his person. In such experiments with this patient, I had never perfectly succeeded before, and assuredly I had little thought of succeeding now; but to my astonishment, his arm very readily, although feebly, followed every direction I assigned it with mine. I determined to hazard a few words of conversation.

"M. Valdemar," I said, "are you asleep?" He made no answer, but I perceived a tremor about the lips, and was thus induced to repeat the question, again and again. At its third repetition, his whole frame was agitated by a very slight shivering; the eyelids unclosed themselves so far as to display a white line of a ball; the lips moved sluggishly, and from between them, in a barely audible whisper, issued the words:

"Yes;—asleep now. Do not wake me!—let me die so!"

I here felt the limbs, and found them as rigid as ever. The right arm, as before, obeyed the direction of my hand. I questioned the sleep-waker again:

"Do you still feel pain in the breast, M. Valdemar?"

The answer now was immediate, but even less audible than before:

"No pain—I am dying!"

I did not think it advisable to disturb him further just then, and nothing more was said or done until the arrival of Dr. F——, who came a little before sunrise, and expressed unbounded astonishment at finding the patient still alive. After feeling the pulse and applying a mirror to the lips, he requested me to speak to the sleep-waker again. I did so, saying:

"M. Valdemar, do you still sleep?"

As before, some minutes elapsed ere a reply was made; and during the interval the dying man seemed to be collecting his energies to speak. At my fourth repetition of the question, he said very faintly, almost inaudibly:

"Yes; still asleep—dying."

It was now the opinion, or rather the wish, of the physicians, that M. Valdemar should be suffered to remain undisturbed in his present apparently tranquil condition, until death should supervene—and this, it was generally agreed, must now take place within a few minutes. I concluded, however, to speak to him once more, and merely repeated my previous question.

While I spoke, there came a marked change over the countenance of the sleep-waker. The eyes rolled themselves slowly open, the pupils disappearing upwardly; the skin generally assumed a cadaverous hue, resembling not so much parchment as white paper; and the circular hectic spots which, hitherto, had been strongly defined in the centre of each cheek, *went out* at once. I use this expression, because the suddenness of their departure put me in mind of nothing so much as the extinguishment of a candle by a puff of the breath. The upper lip, at the same time, writhed itself away from the teeth, which it had previously covered completely; while the lower jaw fell with an audible jerk, leaving the mouth widely extended, and disclosing in full view the swollen and blackened tongue. I presume that no member of the party then present had been unaccustomed to death-bed horrors; but so hideous beyond conception was the appearance of M. Valdemar at this moment, that there was a general shrinking back from the region of the bed.

I now feel that I have reached a point of this narrative at which every reader will be startled into positive disbelief. It is my business, however, simply to proceed.

There was no longer the faintest sign of vitality in M. Valdemar; and concluding him to be dead, we were consigning him to the charge of the nurses, when a strong vibratory motion was observable in the tongue. This continued for perhaps a minute. At the expiration of this period, there issued from the distended and motionless jaws a voice—such as it would be madness in me to attempt describing. There are, indeed, two or three epithets which might be considered as applicable to it in part; I might say, for example, that the sound was harsh, and broken and hollow; but the hideous whole is indescribable, for the simple reason that no similar sounds have ever jarred upon the ear of humanity. There were two particulars, nevertheless, which I thought then, and still think, might fairly be stated as characteristic of the intonation—as well adapted to convey some idea of its unearthly peculiarity. In the first place, the voice seemed to reach our ears—at least mine—from a vast distance, or from some deep cavern within the earth. In the second place, it impressed me (I fear, indeed, that it will be impossible to make myself comprehended) as gelatinous or glutinous matters impress the sense of touch.

I have spoken both of "sound" and of "voice." I mean to say that the sound was one of distinct—of even wonderfully, thrillingly distinct—syllabification. M. Valdemar *spoke*—obviously in reply to the question I had propounded to him a few minutes before. I had asked him, it will be remembered, if he still slept. He now said:

"Yes;—no;—I *have been* sleeping — and now —now—*I am dead.*"

No person present even affected to deny, or attempted to repress, the unutterable, shuddering horror which these few words, thus uttered, were so well calculated to convey. Mr. L——l (the student) swooned. The nurses immediately left the chamber, and could not be induced to return. My own impressions I would not pretend to render intelligible to the reader. For nearly an hour, we busied ourselves, silently—without the utterance of a word—in endeavors to revive Mr. L——l. When he came to himself, we addressed ourselves again to an investigation of M. Valdemar's condition.

It remained in all respects as I have last described it, with the exception that the mirror no longer afforded evidence of respiration. An attempt to draw blood from the arm failed. I should mention, too, that this limb was no further subject to my will. I endeavored in vain to make it follow the direction of my hand. The only real indication, indeed, of the mesmeric influence, was now found in the vibratory movement of the tongue, whenever I addressed M. Valdemar a question. He seemed to be making an effort to reply, but had no longer sufficient volition. To queries put to him by any other person than myself he seemed utterly insensible—although I endeavored to place each member of the company in mesmeric *rapport* with him. I believe that I have now related all that is necessary to an understanding of the sleep-waker's state at this epoch. Other nurses were procured; and at ten o'clock I left the house in company with the two physicians and Mr. L——l.

In the afternoon we all called again to see the patient. His condition remained precisely the same. We had now some discussion as to the propriety and feasibility of awakening him; but we had little difficulty in agreeing that no good purpose would be served by so doing. It was evident that, so far, death (or what is usually termed death) had been arrested by the mesmeric process. It seemed clear to us all that to awaken M. Valdemar would be merely to insure his instant, or at least his speedy, dissolution.

From this period until the close of last week—*an interval of nearly seven months*—we continued to make daily calls at M. Valdemar's house, accompanied, now and then, by medical and other friends. All this time the sleep-waker remained *exactly* as I have last described him. The nurses' attentions were continual.

It was on Friday last that we finally resolved to make the experiment of awakening, or attempting to awaken him; and it is the (perhaps) unfortunate result of this latter experiment which has given rise to so much discussion in private circles—to so much of what I cannot help thinking unwarranted popular feeling.

For the purpose of relieving M. Valdemar from the mesmeric trance, I made use of the customary passes. These for a time were unsuccessful. The first indication of revival was afforded by a partial descent of the iris. It was observed, as especially remarkable, that this lowering of the pupil was accompanied by the profuse out-flowing of a yellowish ichor (from beneath the lids) of a pungent and highly offensive odor.

It was now suggested that I should attempt to influence the patient's arm as heretofore. I made the attempt and failed. Dr. F—— then intimated a desire to have me put a question. I did so, as follows:

"M. Valdemar, can you explain to us what are your feelings or wishes now?"

There was an instant return of the hectic circles on the cheeks: the tongue quivered, or rather rolled violently in the mouth (although the jaws and lips remained rigid as before), and at length the same hideous voice which I have already described, broke forth:

"For God's sake!—quick!—quick!—put me to sleep—or, quick!—waken me!—quick!—*I say to you that I am dead!*"

I was thoroughly unnerved, and for an instant remained undecided what to do. At first I made an endeavor to recompose the patient; but, failing in this through total abeyance of the will, I retraced my steps and as earnestly struggled to awaken him. In this attempt I soon saw that I should be successful—or at least I soon fancied that my success would be complete—and I am sure that all in the room were prepared to see the patient awaken.

be complete—and I am sure that all in the room were prepared to see the patient awaken.

For what really occurred, however, it is quite impossible that any human being could have been prepared.

As I rapidly made the mesmeric passes, amid ejaculations of "dead! dead!" absolutely *bursting* from the tongue and not from the lips of the sufferer, his whole frame at once—within the space of a single minute, or less, shrunk—crumbled—absolutely *rotted* away beneath my hands. Upon the bed, before that whole company, there lay a nearly liquid mass of loathsome—of detestable putrescence.

1845

KATHERINE ANNE PORTER

The Grave

The grandfather, dead for more than thirty years, had been twice disturbed in his long repose by the constancy and possessiveness of his widow. She removed his bones first to Louisiana and then to Texas as if she had set out to find her own burial place, knowing well she would never return to the places she had left. In Texas she set up a small cemetery in a corner of her first farm, and as the family connection grew, and oddments of relations came over from Kentucky to settle, it contained at last about twenty graves. After the grandmother's death, part

Katherine Anne Porter was born in 1890 in Indian Creek, Texas. After working periodically as a newspaper writer in Chicago and Denver, she moved at the age of thirty to Mexico, the setting for a number of her short stories and novellas. Her intricate and symbol-laden *Collected Stories* (1965) was awarded both the National Book Award and the Pulitzer Prize for fiction. Porter's sojourn in Germany was cut short by the rise of Nazism, which yielded her a wealth of material for her future writing, including the novel *Ship of Fools* (1962). After Porter returned to America, she went on to work as a teacher and free-lance essayist. She died in Silver Spring, Maryland, in 1980.

necessary to take up the bodies and bury them again in the family plot in the big new public cemetery, where the grandmother had been buried. At last her husband was to lie beside her for eternity, as she had planned.

The family cemetery had been a pleasant small neglected garden of tangled rose bushes and ragged cedar trees and cypress, the simple flat stones rising out of uncropped sweet-smelling wild grass. The graves were lying open and empty one burning day when Miranda and her brother Paul, who often went together to hunt rabbits and doves, propped their twenty-two Winchester rifles carefully against the rail fence, climbed over, and explored among the graves. She was nine years old and he was twelve.

They peered into the pits all shaped alike with such purposeful accuracy, and looking at each other with pleased adventurous eyes, they said in solemn tones: "These were graves!" trying by words to shape a special, suitable emotion in their minds, but they felt nothing except an agreeable thrill of wonder: they were seeing a new sight, doing something they had not done before. In them both there was also a small disappointment at the entire commonplaceness of the actual spectacle. Even if it had once contained a coffin for years upon years, when the coffin was gone a grave was just a hole in the ground. Miranda leaped into the pit that had held her grandfather's bones. Scratching around aimlessly and pleasurably as any young animal, she scooped up a lump of earth and weighted it in her palm. It had a pleasantly sweet, corrupt smell, being mixed with cedar needles and small leaves, and as the crumbs fell apart, she saw a silver dove no larger than a hazel nut, with spread wings and a neat fan-shaped tail. The breast had a deep round hollow in it. Turning it up to the fierce sunlight, she saw that the inside of the hollow was cut in little whorls. She scrambled out, over the pile of loose earth that had fallen back into one end of the grave, calling to Paul that she had found something, he must guess what . . . His head appeared smiling over the rim of another grave. He waved a closed hand at her. "I've got something too!" They ran to compare treasures, making a game of it, so many guesses each, all wrong, and a final showdown with opened palms. Paul had found a thin wide gold ring carved with intricate flowers and leaves. Miranda was smitten at sight of the ring and wished to have it. Paul seemed more impressed by the dove. They made a trade, with some little bickering. After he had got the dove in his hand, Paul said, "Don't you know what this is? This is a screw head for a *coffin!* . . . I'll bet nobody else in the world has one like this!"

Miranda glanced at it without covetousness. She had the gold ring on her thumb; it fitted perfectly. "Maybe we ought to go now," she said, "maybe one of the niggers'll see us and tell somebody." They knew the land had been sold, the cemetery was no longer theirs, and they felt like trespassers. They climbed back over the fence, slung their rifles loosely under their arms—they had been shooting at targets with various kinds of firearms since they were seven years old—and set out to look for the rabbits and doves or whatever small game might happen along. On these expeditions Miranda always followed at Paul's heels along the path, obeying instructions about handling her gun when going through fences; learning how to stand it up properly so it would not slip and fire unexpectedly; how to wait her time for a shot and not just bang away in the air without looking, spoiling shots for Paul, who really could hit things if given a chance. Now and then, in her excitement at seeing birds whizz up suddenly before her face, or a rabbit leap across her very toes, she lost her head, and almost without sighting she flung her rifle up and pulled the trigger. She hardly ever hit any sort of mark. She had no proper sense of hunting at all. Her brother would be often completely disgusted with her. "You don't care whether you get your bird or not," he said. "That's no way to hunt." Miranda could not understand his indignation. She had seen him smash his hat and yell with fury when he had missed his aim. "What I like about shooting," said Miranda, with exasperating inconsequence, "is pulling the trigger and hearing the noise."

"Then, by golly," said Paul, "whyn't you go back to the range and shoot at bullseyes?"

"I'd just as soon," said Miranda, "only like this, we walk around more."

"Well, you just stay behind and stop spoiling my shots," said Paul, who, when he made a kill, wanted to be certain he had made it. Miranda, who alone brought down a bird once in twenty rounds, always claimed as her own any game they got when they fired at the same moment. It was tiresome and unfair and her brother was sick of it.

"Now, the first dove we see, or the first rabbit, is mine," he told her. "And the next will be yours. Remember that and don't get smarty."

"What about snakes?" asked Miranda idly. "Can I have the first snake?"

Waving her thumb gently and watching her gold ring glitter, Miranda lost interest in shooting. She was wearing her summer roughing outfit: dark blue overalls, a light blue shirt, a hired-man's straw hat, and thick brown sandals. Her brother had the same outfit except his was a sober hickory-nut color. Ordinarily Miranda preferred her overalls to any other dress, though it was making rather a scandal in the countryside, for the year was 1903, and in the back country the law of female decorum had teeth in it. Her father had been criticized for letting his girls dress like boys and go careering around astride barebacked horses. Big sister Maria, the really independent and fearless one, in spite of her rather affected ways, rode at a dead run with only a rope knotted around her horse's nose. It was said the motherless family was running down, with the Grandmother no longer there to hold it together. It was known that she had discriminated against her son Harry in her will, and that he was in straits about money. Some of his old neighbors reflected with vicious satisfaction that now he would probably not be so stiff-necked, nor have any more high-stepping horses either. Miranda knew this, though she could not say how. She had met along the road old women of the kind who smoked corn-cob pipes, who had treated her grand-mother with most sincere respect. They slanted their gummy old eyes side-ways at the granddaughter and said, "Ain't you ashamed of yoself, Missy? It's aginst the Scriptures to dress like that. Whut yo Pappy thinkin about?" Miranda, with her powerful social sense, which was like a fine set of antennae radiating from every pore of her skin, would feel ashamed because she knew well it was rude and ill-bred to shock anybody, even bad-tempered old crones, though she had faith in her father's judgment and was perfectly comfortable in the clothes. Her father had said, "They're just what you need, and they'll save your dresses for school. . . ." This sounded quite simple and natural to her. She had been brought up in rigorous economy. Wastefulness was vulgar. It was also a sin. These were truths; she had heard them repeated many times and never once disputed.

Now the ring, shining with the serene purity of fine gold on her rather grubby thumb, turned her feelings against her overalls and sock-less feet, toes sticking through the thick brown leather straps. She wanted to go back to the farmhouse, take a good cold bath, dust herself with plenty of Maria's violet talcum powder—provided Maria was not present to object, of course—put on the thinnest, most becoming dress she owned, with a big sash, and sit in a wicker chair under the trees . . . These things were not all she wanted, of course; she had vague stirrings of desire for luxury and a grand way of living which could not take precise form in her imagination but were founded on family legend of past wealth and leisure. These immediate comforts were what she could have, and she wanted them at once. She lagged rather far behind Paul, and once she thought of just turning back without a word and going home. She stopped, thinking that Paul would never do that to her, and so she would have to tell him. When a rabbit leaped, she let Paul have it without dispute. He killed it with one shot.

When she came up with him, he was already kneeling, examining the wound, the rabbit trailing from his hands. "Right through the head," he said complacently, as if he had aimed for it. He took out his sharp, competent bowie knife and started to skin the body. He did it very cleanly and quickly. Uncle Jimbilly knew how to prepare the skins so that Miranda always had fur coats for her dolls, for though she never cared much for her dolls she liked seeing them in fur coats. The children knelt facing each other over the dead animal. Miranda watched admiringly while her brother stripped the skin away as if he were taking off a glove. The flayed flesh emerged dark scarlet, sleek, firm; Miranda with thumb and finger felt the long fine muscles with the silvery flat strips binding them to the joints. Brother lifted the oddly bloated belly. "Look," he said, in a low amazed voice. "It was going to have young ones."

Very carefully he slit the thin flesh from the center ribs to the flanks, and a scarlet bag appeared. He slit again and pulled the bag open, and there lay a bundle of tiny rabbits, each wrapped in a thin scarlet veil. The brother pulled these off and there they were, dark gray, their sleek wet down lying in minute even ripples, like a baby's head just washed, their unbelievably small delicate ears folded close, their little blind faces almost featureless.

Miranda said, "Oh, I want to *see*," under her breath. She looked and looked—excited but not frightened, for she was accustomed to the sight of animals killed in hunting—filled with pity and astonishment and a kind of shocked delight in the wonderful little creatures for their own sakes, they were so pretty. She touched one of them ever so carefully. "Ah, there's blood running over them," she said and began to tremble without knowing why. Yet she wanted most deeply to see and to know. Having seen, she felt at once as if she had known all along. The very memory of her former ignorance faded, she had always known just this. No one had ever told her anything outright, she had been rather unobservant of the animal life around her because she was so accustomed to animals. They seemed simply disorderly and unaccountably rude in their habits, but altogether natural and not very interesting. Her brother had spoken as if he had known about everything all along. He may have seen all this before. He had never said a word to her, but she knew now a part at least of what he knew. She understood a little of the secret, formless intuitions in her own mind and body, which had been clearing up, taking form, so gradually and so steadily she had not realized that she was learning what she had to know. Paul said cautiously, as if he were talking about something forbidden: "They were just about ready to be born." His voice dropped on the last word. "I know," said Miranda, "like kittens. I know, like babies." She was quietly and terribly agitated, standing again with her rifle under her arm, looking down at the bloody heap. "I don't want the skin," she said. "I won't have it." Paul buried the young rabbits again in their mother's body, wrapped the skin around her, carried her to a clump of sage bushes, and hid her away. He came out again at once and said to Miranda, with an eager friendliness, a confidential tone quite unusual in him, as if he were taking her into an important secret on equal terms: "Listen now. Now you listen to me, and don't ever forget. Don't you ever tell a living soul that you saw this. Don't tell a soul. Don't tell Dad because I'll get into trouble. He'll say I'm leading you into things you ought not to do. He's always saying that. So now don't you go and forget and blab out sometime the way you're always doing . . . Now, that's a secret. Don't you tell."

Miranda never told, she did not even wish to tell anybody. She thought about the whole worrisome affair with confused unhappiness for a few days. Then it sank quietly into her mind and was heaped over by accumulated thousands of impressions, for nearly twenty years. One day she was picking her path among the puddles and crushed refuse of a market street in a strange city of a strange country, when without warning, plain and clear in its true colors as if she looked through a frame upon a scene that had not stirred nor changed since the moment it happened, the episode of that far-off day leaped from its burial place before her mind's eye. She was so reasonlessly horrified she halted suddenly staring, the scene before her eyes dimmed by the vision back of them. An Indian vendor had held up before her a tray of dyed sugar sweets, in the shapes of all kinds of small creatures: birds, baby chicks, baby rabbits, lambs, baby pigs. They were in gay colors and smelled of vanilla, maybe. . . . It was a very hot day and the smell in the market, with its piles of raw flesh and wilting flowers, was like the mingled sweetness and corruption she had smelled that other day in the empty cemetery at home: the day she had remembered always until now vaguely as the time she and her brother had found treasure in the opened graves. Instantly upon this thought the dreadful vision faded, and she saw clearly her brother, whose childhood face she had forgotten, standing again in the blazing sunshine, again twelve years old, a pleased sober smile in his eyes, turning the silver dove over and over in his hands.

1944

ALLEN BARNETT

The *Times* As It Knows Us

Time will say nothing but I told you so,
Time only knows the price we have to pay.

W. H. Auden

"With regard to human affairs," Spinoza said, "not to laugh, not to cry, not to become indignant, but to understand." It's what my lover, Samuel, used to repeat to me when I was raging at the inexplicable behavior of friends or at something I had read in the newspaper. I often intend to look the quote up myself, but that would entail leafing through Samuel's books, deciphering the margin notes, following underlined passages back to where his thoughts were formed, a past closed off to me.

"Not to laugh, not to cry, not to become indignant, but to understand," he would say. But I can't understand, I'd cry, like a child at the end of a diving board afraid to jump into the deep end of the pool.

"Then let go of it," he would say. "I can't," I'd say about whatever had my heart and mind in an insensible knot. And he would come up behind me and put his arms around me. "Close your eyes," he'd say. "Close them tight. Real tight. Tighter."

Samuel would tell me to reach out my arms and clench my fists. "Squeeze as hard as you can," he would say, and I would, knowing that he believed in the physical containment of emotions in a body's gesture. "Now, let go," he would say, and I did. If I felt better, though, it was because his mustache was against the back of my neck, and I knew full well that when I turned my head, his mouth would be there to meet mine.

The fiction and the social commitments of Allen Barnett were rarely separate. His award-winning short stories share, with other equally educational activities, the burden of increasing public awareness of the AIDS epidemic, which has emotionally and physically ravaged America's gay communities. "The *Times* As It Knows Us," for example, which addresses the mainstream press's trivialization and distortion of gay subcultures' involvement in the AIDS crisis, is of a piece with Barnett's participation in establishing the Gay and Lesbian Alliance Against Defamation. More generally, the stories that constitute his 1990 collection, *The Body and Its Dangers*, explore the struggle between spiritual fulfillment and physical limitation, between emotional need and family ties. AIDS cut these literary explorations short in 1991; Barnett was thirty-six years old when he died.

The day that Samuel went into the emergency room, he took a pile of college catalogues with him, not suspecting this hospital was the only thing he would ever be admitted to again. I got to him just as a nurse was hanging a garnet-colored sack above his bed. Soon a chorus of red angels would be singing in his veins. He told me he wanted to go back to school to get a degree in Biomedical Ethics, the battlefront he believed least guarded by those most affected by Acquired Immune Deficiency Syndrome. "Do you think you'll need an advanced degree?" I asked. His eyes opened, and his head jerked, as if the fresh blood had given him new insight, anagnorisis from a needle.

"That's not what I meant to say," I said. He said, "Not to worry." He died before they knew what to treat him for, what an autopsy alone would tell them, before he could even be diagnosed.

Vergil said, "Perhaps someday even this stress will be a joy to recall." I'm still waiting.

PART I

Noah called Perry a "fat, manipulative sow who doesn't hear anything he doesn't want to hear."

The endearments "fat" and "sow" meant that the argument we were having over brunch was still on friendly terms, but "manipulative" cued us all to get our weapons out and to take aim. Perry was an easy target, and we had been stockpiling ammunition since Tuesday, when an article on how AIDS had affected life in the Pines featured the seven members of our summer house. Perry had been the reporter's source. It was Saturday.

"What I resent," Joe said, newspaper in hand, "is when she writes, 'They arrive at the house on Friday night to escape the city. When everyone is gathered, the bad news is shared: A friend died that morning. They are silent while a weekend guest, a man with AIDS, weeps for a few moments. But grief does not stop the party. Dinner that night is fettucine in a pesto and cream-cheese sauce, grilled salmon, and a salad created at one of New York's finest restaurants.'"

Perry said, "That's exactly what happened that night."

"You made it sound as if we were hanging streamers and getting into party dresses," said Enzo, who had cooked that meal. "It was dinner, not the Dance of the Red Masque." He put a plate of buttered English muffins in front of us, and four jars of jam from the gourmet shop he owned in Chelsea.

Joe said, "I don't like the way she implies that death has become so mundane for us, we don't feel it anymore: Paul died today. Oh, that's

too bad; what's for dinner? Why couldn't you tell her that we're learning to accommodate grief. By the way, Enzo, what's the black stuff on
the pasta?"

"Domestic truffles. They're from Texas," he answered from the
kitchen counter, where he was mixing blueberries, nectarines, apricots,
and melon into a salad.

Stark entered the fight wearing nothing but the Saks Fifth Avenue
boxer shorts in which he had slept. "Just because our lives overlap on
the weekend, Perry, doesn't give you rights to the intimate details of
our health." His large thumb flicked a glob of butter and marmalade off
the front of his shorts and into his mouth. Our eyes met. He smiled, and
I looked away.

"What intimate details?"

Stark took the paper from Joe and read aloud, "'The house is well
accustomed to the epidemic. Last year, one member died, another's
lover died over the winter. This year, one has AIDS, one has ARC, and
three others have tested positive for antibodies to the AIDS virus.'"

"She doesn't identify anybody," Perry protested.

"The article is about us, even if our names are not used," Enzo said.
He placed a cake ring on the coffee table. Noah, who had just had
liposuction surgery done on his abdomen, looked at it nostalgically.

Perry, on the other hand, was eating defensively, the way some
people drive a car. "I was told this was going to be a human-interest
piece," he said. "They wanted to know how AIDS is impacting on our
lives—"

"Please don't use *impact* as a verb."

"—and I thought we were the best house on the Island to illustrate
how the crisis had turned into a lifestyle. But none of you wanted your
name in the paper."

I said, "How we represent ourselves is never the way the *Times*
does."

"They officially started using the word *gay* in that article," Perry
said, pointing to the paper like a tour guide to the sight of a famous
battle.

"It didn't cost them anything," I said. Indeed, the *Times* had just
started using the word *gay* instead of the more clinical *homosexual*, a
semantic leap that coincided with the adoption of Ms. instead of Miss,
and of publishing photographs of both the bride and the groom in
Sunday's wedding announcements. And in the obituaries, they had
finally agreed to mention a gay man's lover as one of his survivors.

"You're mad at me because she didn't write what you wouldn't tell
her," Perry said to me.

Noah said, "We are mad at you because we didn't want to be in the piece and we are. And you made us look like a bunch of shallow faggots."

"Me?" Perry screamed. "I didn't write it."

Noah slapped the coffee table. "Yes, you, the media queen. You set up the interview because you wanted your name in the paper. If it weren't for AIDS, you'd still be doing recreation therapy at Bellevue."

"And you'd still be stealing Percodan and Demerol from the nurses' station."

"Yeah," Noah shouted, "you may have left the theater but you turned AIDS into a one-man show. The more people die, the brighter your spotlight gets."

"I have done nothing I am ashamed of," Perry said. "And you are going to be hard pressed to find a way to apologize for that remark." The house shook on its old pilings as Perry stamped out. Noah glared into space. The rest of us sat there wondering whether the weekend was ruined.

"I don't think that the article is so awful." Horst said. He was Perry's lover. "She doesn't really say anything bad about anybody."

Horst was also the one in the article with AIDS. Every day at 4 A.M., he woke to blend a mixture of orange juice and AL721—a lecithin-based drug developed in Israel from egg yolks and used for AIDS treatment—because it has to be taken when there is no fat in the stomach. For a while, he would muffle the blender in a blanket but stopped, figuring that if he woke us, we would just go back to sleep. He laughed doubtfully when I told him that the blender had been invented by a man named Fred who had died recently. It was also the way he laughed when Perry phoned to say their cat had died.

Stark asked Noah, "Don't you think you were a little hard on Perry?"

Noah said, "The next thing you know, he'll be getting an agent."

I said, "We're all doing what we can, Noah. There's even a role for personalities like his."

He would look at none of us, however, so we let it go. We spoke of Noah among ourselves as not having sufficiently mourned Miguel, as if grief were a process of public concern or social responsibility, as if loss was something one just *did,* like jury duty, or going to high school. His late friend had been a leader at the beginning of the epidemic; he devised a training program for volunteers who would work with the dying; he devised systems to help others intervene for the sick in times of bureaucratic crisis. He was the first to recognize that AIDS would be a problem in prisons. A liberal priest in one of the city prisons once asked him, "Do you believe your sexuality is genetic or environmentally determined?" Miguel said, "I think of it as a calling, Father." Dead, however, Miguel could not lead; dead men don't leave footsteps in which to follow. Noah floundered.

And we all made excuses for Noah's sarcasm and inappropriate humor. He once said to someone who had put on forty pounds after starting AZT, "If you get any heavier, I won't be your pallbearer." He had known scores of others who had died before and after Miguel, helped arrange their funerals and wakes. But each death was beginning to brick him into a silo of grief, like the stones in the walls of old churches that mark the dead within.

"Let's go for a walk," his lover, Joe, said.

Noah didn't budge but their dog, Jules, came out from under a couch, a little black scottie that they had had for seventeen years. Jules began to cough, as if choking on the splintered bones of chicken carcass.

"Go for it, Bijou," Noah said. (Even the dog in our house had a drag name.) One of his bronchial tubes was collapsed, and several times a day he gagged on his own breath. He looked up at us through button eyes grown so rheumy with cataracts that he bumped into things and fell off the deck, which was actually kind of cute. Taking one of the condoms that were tossed into the shopping bag like S & H green stamps at the island grocery store, Joe rolled it down the length of Jules's tail.

"Have you ever thought of having Jules put to sleep?" Stark asked.

"Yes, but Joe won't let me," Noah said. But we knew it was Noah keeping Jules alive, or half-alive, stalling one more death.

Stark said, "I noticed that his back is sagging so much that his stomach and cock drag along the boardwalk."

"Yeah," Joe said, "but so do Noah's."

I took The Living Section containing the offending article and threw it on the stack of papers I had been accumulating all summer. My role as a volunteer was speaking to community groups about AIDS and I collected articles to keep up with all facets of the epidemic. But I had actually been saving them since they first appeared in the *Times* on a Saturday morning in July several years ago. RARE CANCER SEEN IN 41 HOMOSEXUALS the headline of the single-column piece announced, way in the back of the paper. I read it and lowered the paper to my lap. "Uh, oh," I said.

I remember how my lover, Samuel, had asked from our bedroom, "What is it?" He was wearing a peach-colored towel around his waist, from which he would change into a raspberry-colored polo shirt and jeans. There was a swollen bruise in the crook of his arm, where he had donated plasma the day before for research on the hepatitis vaccine. As he read the article, I put the lid on the ginger jar, straightened the cushions of the sofa we had bought together, and scraped some dried substance from its plush with my thumbnail. I looked at him leaning against the door arch. He was always comfortable with his body, whether he stood or sat. Over the years, we had slipped without thinking into a monogamous relationship, and space alone competed with me for his attention. No matter where he was, space seemed to yearn for Samuel, as if he gave it definition. He once stood me in the middle of an empty stage and told me to imagine myself being projected into the entire theater. From way in the back of the house, he said, "You have a blind spot you're not filling above your right shoulder." I concentrated on that space, and he shouted, "Yes, yes, do you feel it? That's stage presence." But I could not sustain it the way he did.

Samuel looked up from the article. "It says here that there is evidence to point away from contagion. None of these men knew one another."

"But they all had other infections," I said. Hepatitis, herpes, amebiasis—all of which I had had. Samuel used to compare me to the Messenger in Greek tragedies, bearing news of some plague before it hit the rest of the populace.

"It also says cytomegalovirus," he said. "What's that?"

"*Cyto* means cell; *megalo* is large," I said. "That doesn't tell you much."

"Well, if you haven't had it," he said, "there's probably nothing to worry about."

Perry's guest for the week came in with the day's paper, a generous gesture, I thought, since our house's argument had embarrassed him into leaving through the back door. His name was Nils but we called him Mr. Norway, for that was where he was from, and where he was a crowned and titled bodybuilder. By profession, he was an anthropologist, but he preferred being observed over observing, even if the mirror was his only audience. I didn't like him much. When he sat down and began to read the paper I assumed he had bought for us, I tried to admire him, since it was unlikely that I would read the Oslo *Herald* were I in Norway. I couldn't help thinking, however, that the steroids Nils took to achieve his award-winning mass had made him look like a Neanderthal man. On the other hand, I thought, perhaps that was appropriate for an anthropologist.

I picked up the last section of the paper and turned to the obituaries. "Gosh, there are a lot of dead people today," I said.

"You are reading the death notices every day," Nils said. "I thought so."

"We all do," said Stark, "then we do the crossword puzzle."

We deduced the AIDS casualties by finding the death notices of

men, their age and marital status, and then their occupation. Fortunately, this information usually began the notice, or we would have
been at it for hours. If the deceased was female, old, married, or worked
where no one we knew would, we skipped to the next departed.
A "beloved son" gave us pause, for we were all that; a funeral home
was a clue, because at the time, few of them would take an AIDS
casualty—those that did usually resembled our parents' refinished base-
ments.

Stark looked over my shoulder and began at the end of the columns.
"Here's a birthday message in the In Memoriams for someone who died
thirty-six years ago. 'Till memory fades and life departs, you live forever
in my heart.'"

"Who do people think read these things?" Enzo asked.

"I sometimes wonder if the dead have the *Times* delivered," I said.

We also looked for the neighborhood of the church where a service
would be held, for we knew the gay clergy. We looked at who had
bought the notice, and what was said in it. When an AIDS-related
condition was not given as the cause of death, we looked for coded
half-truths: cancer, pneumonia, meningitis, after a long struggle, after a
short illness. The dead giveaway, so to speak, was to whom contributions could be made in lieu of flowers. Or the lyrics of Stephen
Sondheim.

It was good we had this system for finding the AIDS deaths, otherwise we might have had to deal with the fact that other people were
dying, too, and tragically, and young, and leaving people behind wondering what it was all about. Of course, the difference here was that
AIDS was an infectious disease and many of the dead were people with
whom we had had sex. We also read the death notices for anything that
might connect us to someone from the past.

"Listen to this." I read, "'Reyes, Peter. Artist and invaluable friend.
Left our sides after a courageous battle. His triumphs on the stage are
only footnotes to the starring role he played in our hearts. We will
deeply miss you, darling, but will carry the extra richness you gave us
until we build that wall again together. Contributions in his name can
be made to The Three Dollar Bill Theater. Signed, The people who loved
you.'"

Stark said, "You learn who your friends are, don't you?"

Horst looked thoughtfully into the near distance; his eyes watered.
He said, "That is touching."

"You know what I want my death notice to read?" Enzo asked.
"'Dead GWM, loved 1950s rock and roll, Arts & Crafts ceramics, back
issues of *Gourmet* magazine. Seeking similar who lived in past for quiet
nights leading to long-term relationship.'"

"There's another one," Stark said, his head resting on my shoulder, his face next to mine. "Mazzochi, Robert."

"Oh, God," I said into the open wings of the newspaper.

The newsprint began to spread in runnels of ink. I handed the paper over to Stark, who read out loud, "'Mazzochi, Robert, forty-four on July ———, 1987. Son of Victor and Natalia Mazzochi of Stonington, Connecticut. Brother of Linda Mazzochi of Washington, D.C. Served as lieutenant in the United States Army. Came back from two terms of duty in Vietnam, unscarred and unblaming. With the Department of Health and Human Services NYC since 1977. A warm, radiant, much-loved man.'"

"What a nice thing to say," Horst said. "Did you know him well?"

"He was that exactly," I said.

There was another one for him, which Stark read. "'Robert, you etched an indelible impression and left. Yes, your spirit will continue to enrich us forever, but your flesh was very particular flesh. Not a day will go by, Milton.'"

The others sat looking at me as I stood there and wept. There was Stark, an investment banker from Scotland; Horst, a mountain peasant from a farm village in Switzerland; and Enzo, who grew up in Little Italy and studied cooking in Bologna (he dressed like a street punk and spoke like a Borghese); and there was Mr. Norway on his biennial tour of gay America. They were waiting for a cue from me, some hint as to what I needed from them. I felt as if I had been spun out of time, like a kite that remains aloft over the ocean even after its string breaks. I felt awkward, out of time and out of place, like not being able to find the beat to music, which Samuel used to say that even the deaf could feel surging through the dance floor. Robert's funeral service was being held at that very moment.

The last time I had seen him was a Thursday afternoon in early October, a day of two funerals. Two friends had died within hours of one another that week. I went to the funeral of the one who had been an only child, and whose father had died before him. I went, I guess, for his mother's sake. Watching her weep was the saddest thing I had ever seen.

Afterward, I made a bargain with myself. If Robert Mazzochi was still alive, I would go to work. If he was dead, I would take the day off. When he did not answer his home phone, I called the hospital with which his doctor was associated, and the switchboard gave me his room number. I visited him on my way to work, a compromise of sorts.

"How did you know I was here?" he asked.

"Deduction."

Eggplant-colored lesions plastered his legs. Intravenous tubes left in too long had bloated his arms. Only strands were left to his mane of salt and pepper hair. He was in the hospital because thrush had coated his esophagus. The thrush irritated his diaphragm and made him hiccough so violently he could not catch his breath. Robert believed that he would have suffocated had his lover Milton not been there to perform the Heimlich maneuver. He was waiting for the nurse to bring him Demerol, which relaxed him and made it easier to breathe.

I finally said, "I can't watch you go through this."

He looked at me for a long moment. "If I've learned anything through all this, it's about hope," he said. "Hope needs firmer ground to stand on than I've got. I'm just dangling here."

"'Nothing is hopeless. We must hope for everything,'" I said. "That's Euripides. It's a commandment to hope. It would be a sin not to."

"Then why are you leaving me?" he asked, and I couldn't answer him. He said, "Don't worry. I am surrounded by hopeful people. Milton's hope is the most painful. But I could be honest with you."

"The truth hurts, too," I said.

"Yes, but you could take it."

"For a while."

We used to meet after work for an early supper before he went to his KS support group. One night he said to me, "I never knew that I was handsome until I lost my looks." He was still handsome as far as I was concerned, but when he pulled his wallet out to pay the check, his driver's license fell to the table. He snatched it back again, but I had seen the old picture on it, seen what must have told him that he had been a beautiful man.

The nurse came in and attached a bag of Demerol to the intravenous line feeding his arm. "We might have been lovers," Robert said to me, "if it hadn't been for Milton."

"And Samuel," I said.

The Demerol went right to his head. He closed his eyes and splayed his fingers and smiled. "My feet may never touch ground again," he said, and floated there briefly. "This is as good as it will ever get."

The rest of the day passed slowly, like a book that doesn't give one much reason to turn the page, leaving the effort all in your hands. Perry was sulking somewhere. Stark and Nils had gone to Cherry Grove. A book of Rilke's poetry, which he was not reading, lay opened on Horst's lap.

"Genius without instinct," he said during the second movement of Mozart's *Jeunehomme* piano concerto. "He knew exactly what he was doing."

"Are you all right?" I asked Enzo, who was lying in the sun, in and out of a doze.

"It's just a cold," he said. "Maybe I'll lie down for a while."

"You didn't eat breakfast today. I was watching you," I said.

"I couldn't."

"You should have something. Would you like some pasta al'burro?"

Enzo smiled. "My mother used to make that for me when I was sick."

"I could mix it with Horst's AL721. It might taste like spaghetti alla carbonara."

Horst said, "You should have some of that elixir my brother sent me from Austria. It has lots of minerals and vitamins."

"Elixir?" Enzo asked.

"That potion that's in the refrigerator."

Enzo and I worried about what Horst meant by potion, for Horst went to faith healers, he had friends who were witches, he ate Chinese herbs by the fistful, and kept crystals on his bedside. These he washed in the ocean and soaked in the sun to reinvigorate them when he figured they'd been overworked. He said things like "Oh, I am glad you wore yellow today. Yellow is a healing color." Around his neck, he wore an amulet allegedly transformed from a wax-paper yogurt lid into metal by a hermit who lived in Peru, and which had been acquired by a woman who had sought him out to discuss Horst's illness. "You don't have to say anything," the hermit told her at the mouth of his cave, "I know why you're here." Fabulous line, I said to myself, that should come in handy.

Enzo and I found a silver-colored canister in the refrigerator. Its instructions were written in German, which neither of us could read. I wet a finger and stuck it in the powder. "It tastes safe," I said.

"Athletes drink it after a workout," Horst said.

"I'll have some after my nap," Enzo said.

"If you have a fever, you sweat out a lot of minerals."

"I'll mix it with cranberry juice," Enzo assured him.

"You lose a lot of minerals when you sweat," Horst said. He had been repeating himself a lot lately, as if by changing the order of the words in a sentence, he could make himself better understood.

"If you want me to cook tonight, I will," I said.

Enzo said, "The shopping's done already," and handed me a large manila envelope from the city's health department in which he kept his recipes. They were all cut from the *Times*, including the evening's menu: tuna steaks marinated in oil and herbs (herbs that Horst had growing in pots on the deck) and opma.

"What is opma?"

"It's an Indian breakfast dish made with Cream of Wheat."

"We're having a breakfast dish for dinner?" I asked.

"If this gets out, we'll be ruined socially," he said, and went to bed, leaving Horst and me alone.

Horst and I had been alone together most of the summer, except for a visit by his sister and brother, both of whom were too shy to speak whatever English they knew. Gunther cooked Horst's favorite meals. Katja dragged our mattresses, pillows, and blankets out on the deck to air. When she turned to me and said in perfect, unaccented English, "I have my doubts about Horst," I wondered how long it had taken her to put that sentence together. Gunther and I walked the beach early in the morning before Horst was up. He wanted to know all he could about Horst's prognosis, but I was afraid to tell him what I knew because I did not know what Horst wanted him to think. But fear translates, and hesitant truth translates instantly. I did not enjoy seeing them return to Switzerland, for when they thanked me for looking after their brother, I knew I had done nothing to give them hope.

"Remember my friend you met in co-op care?" I asked Horst. "He has lymphoma. The fast-growing kind."

"He should see my healer. Lymphoma is her specialty," he said. "Oh, I just remembered. Your office called yesterday. They said it was very important. Something about not getting rights for photographs. They need to put something else in your movie."

"What time did they call?"

"In the morning."

"Did you write it down?"

"No, but I remember the message. I'm sorry I forgot to tell you. I figured if it was important that they would have called back."

"They are respecting my belated mourning period," I said.

"What does this mean?"

"I'll have to go into town on Monday."

"That's too bad. How long will you stay?"

"Three or four days."

I began to look over the recipes that Enzo had handed me, angry at Horst for not telling me sooner but far more angry that I would have to leave the Island and go back to editing films I had thought were finished. Samuel had died when we were behind schedule and several hundred thousand dollars over budget on a documentary series titled *Auden in America*. Working seven-day weeks and twelve-hour days, it took a case of shingles to remind me of how much I was suffering the loss of what he had most fulfilled in me.

Perry came in while I was banging drawers and pans about the kitchen. "What's with her?" he asked Horst.

"Oh, she's got a craw up her ass," Horst said.

"I beg your pardon," I said.

"He is mad at me for not taking a message, but I say to hell with him." He raised a long, thin arm, flicked his wrist, and said, "Hoopla."

"I am not mad at you," I said, although I was. I believed that he had been using his illness to establish a system of priorities that were his alone. No one else's terrors or phone messages carried weight in his scheme of things. If he said something wasn't important, like the way he woke us up with the blender, knowing we would eventually go back to sleep, we had to take his word for it because he was dying.

And that was something we could not deny; the skeleton was rising in his face. Every two steps Death danced him backward, Horst took one forward. Death was the better dancer, and who could tell when our once-around-the-floor was next, when the terrible angel might extend a raven wing and say, "Shall we?"

And then I was angry at myself for thinking that, for elevating this thing with a metaphor. What was I doing personifying Death as a man with a nice face, a way with the girls? This wasn't a sock hop, I thought, but a Depression-era marathon with a man in a black suit who probably resembled Perry calling, "Yowsa, yowsa, yowsa, your lover's dead, your friends are dying."

As I cleared aside the kitchen counter, I came across another note in Horst's spindly handwriting. I read it out loud, "'Sugar, your mother called. We had a nice chat. Love, Heidi.'"

"Oh, I forgot again," Horst said.

"It's all right," I said, and paused. "I'm more concerned with what you talked about."

"We talked female talk for ten minutes."

"Does that mean you talked about condoms or bathroom tiles?"

"We talked about you, too."

"What did you say?" I asked.

"I said that you were fabulous."

"Oh, good. Did you talk about . . . yourself?"

"Yes, I told her about the herb garden," he said. "I'm going to bed now for a little nap. I want to preserve my energy for tonight's supper that you are cooking." Then he went into his room and closed the door.

I looked at Perry, who registered nothing—neither about the exchange nor about the fact that his lover, who had been a bundle of energy for three days, was taking a nap.

"Aren't you out to your mother?" he asked.

"She probably knows. We just never talk about it."

"I'm surprised you don't share this part of your life with her."

"What part?" I asked.

"You shouldn't close yourself off to her, especially now."

"It wouldn't be any different if AIDS hadn't happened," I said.

"You'd have less to talk about."

"I almost called her when Samuel died."

Perry said, "I think we should get stoned and drunk together."

Horst came back out of his room. "I forgot to show you these pictures of us my sister took when I was home for harvest last time."

He showed me pictures of him and Perry carrying baskets and sitting on a tractor together. In my favorite, they were both wearing overalls, holding pitchforks, and smoking cigars.

"You two were never more handsome," I said. I looked at Perry, who pulled the joint out of his pocket. He had recently taken up smoking marijuana again after three years of health-conscious abstinence.

"Look how big my arms were then," Horst said. Then suddenly, he pounded the counter with both his fists. Everything rattled. "I hate this thing!" he said. And then he laughed at his own understatement.

"What time is dinner?" he asked.

"At nine, *liebchen*."

Horst nodded and went to bed, closing the door behind him.

Perry looked at me. I poured the vodka that was kept in the freezer while he lit the joint. I knew what was coming. It was the first time we had been alone together since Sam's death. Perry had known Sam from their days together working with a theater company for the deaf. Samuel loved sign language, which he attempted to teach me but which I would not learn, for it seemed a part of his life before we met, and I was jealous of the years I did not know him, jealous of the people as well, even the actors in their deafness, rumored to be sensuous lovers. When Samuel danced, he translated the lyrics of songs with his arms and fingers, the movement coming from his strong, masculine back and shoulders the way a tenor sings from his diaphragm. Sometimes I would leave the dance floor just to watch him.

"It was easier for you," Perry said, referring to Sam's sudden death. "It was all over for you fast."

"You make it sound as if I went to Canada to avoid the draft."

"You didn't have to force yourself to live in hope. It's hard to sustain all this denial."

"Maybe you shouldn't make such an effort," I said.

He looked at me. "Do you want to hear some bad news?" Perry

asked, knowing what the effect would be but unable to resist it. The Messenger in Greek tragedies, after all, gets the best speeches. "Bruce was diagnosed this week. PCP."

I heard a bullet intended for me pass through a younger man's lungs. I backed away from the kitchen counter for a few minutes, wiping my hands on a dish towel in a gesture that reminded me of my mother.

"Are you all right?" Perry asked.

"Actually, I'm not sure how much longer I can take this."

"You're just a volunteer," he said. "I work with this on a daily basis."

"I see," I said. "How does that make you feel when you pay your rent?"

There are people who are good at denying their feelings; there are those who are good at denying the feelings of others. Perry was good at both. "Touché," he said.

"Have you ever thought about leaving the AIDS industry for a while?" I asked him.

"I couldn't," Perry said, as if asked to perform a sexual act he had never even imagined. "AIDS is my mission."

I finished my drink and poured myself another. "Someone quoted Dylan Thomas in the paper the other day: 'After the first death there is no other.'"

"What does it mean?"

"I don't know, except that I believed it once."

"We need more occasions to mourn our losses," he said.

"What do you want, Grieve-a-Thons?"

The *Times* had already done the article: "New Rituals Ease Grief as AIDS Toll Increases"; white balloons set off from courtyards; midnight cruises around Manhattan; catered affairs and delivered pizzas. It was the "bereavement group" marching down Fifth Avenue on Gay Pride Day bearing placards with the names of the dead that made me say, No, no, this has gone too far.

"I'm very distrustful of this sentimentality, this tendency toward willful pathos," I said. "A kid I met on the train was going to a bereavement counselor."

"You've become a cynic since this all began."

"That's not cynicism, that's despair."

"I haven't been of much help to you," Perry said. "I never even called to see how you were doing when you had shingles."

"I didn't need help," I said, although I had mentioned this very fact in my journal: "March 30. I am blistered from navel to spine. My guts rise and fall in waves. Noah paused a long time when I told him what

I had and then asked about my health in general. Dr. Dubreuil said that shingles are not predictive of AIDS, but I know that the herpes zoster virus can activate HIV in vitro. So should that frighten me? We pin our hopes on antivirals that work in vitro. What should we fear? What should we draw hope from? What is reasonable? I worry: How much fear is choice of fear in my case? Horst has them now, as well. When I called Perry to ask him what shingles looked like, he said, 'Don't worry, if you had them, you would know it.' He hasn't called back, though the word is out."

"I have a confession to make," Perry said. "I read your journal, I mean, the Reluctant Journal."

That is what I called my diary about daily life during the epidemic: who had been diagnosed, their progress, sometimes their death. I wrote what I knew about someone who had died: what he liked in bed, his smile, his skin, the slope of his spine.

I asked Perry: "Did you read the whole thing or just the parts where your name was mentioned?"

"I read the whole thing. Out loud. To the rest of the house when you weren't here," he said. "You just went white under your tan, Blanche."

I laid the Saran Wrap over the tuna steaks that I had been preparing. The oil made the cellophane adhere to the fish in the shape of continents; the herbs were like mountain ridges on a map.

"I was just joking," Perry said.

"Right."

"You had that coming to you."

"I suppose I did."

"I don't know what to say to you about Samuel that you haven't already said to yourself," he said. "I think of him every time you enter the room. I don't know how that makes me feel about you."

"Sometimes I miss him so much I think that I am him."

I took things to the sink in order to turn my back on Perry for a moment, squaring my shoulders as I washed the double blade of the food processor's knife. What connected the two of us, I asked myself, but Samuel, who was dead? What did we have in common but illness, sexuality, death? Perry had told himself that asking me to share the house this summer was a way of getting back in touch with me after Samuel died. The truth was that he could no longer bear the sole burden of taking care of Horst. He wanted Horst to stay on the Island all summer and me to stay with him. "It would be good for you to take some time off between films, and Horst loves you," he had said, knowing all along that I knew what he was asking me to do.

Perry was silent while I washed dishes. Finally, he said, "I saw Raymond Dubreuil in co-op care last Friday night. He was still doing his rounds at midnight."

"There aren't enough doctors like him," I said, still unable to turn around.

"He works eighteen-hour days sometimes. What would happen to us if something should happen to him?"

"I asked him what he thought about that *Times* article that said an infected person had a greater chance of developing AIDS the longer they were infected. Ray said the reporter made years of perfect health sound worse than dying within eighteen months of infection."

Perry had brought up a larger issue and placed it between us like a branch of laurel. I turned around. His hand was on the counter, middle two fingers folded under and tucked to the palm, his thumb, index, and little finger extended in the deaf's sign for "I love you." But he did not raise his hand. I thought of Auden's lines from *The Rake's Progress*, "How strange! Although the heart dare everything / The hand draws back and finds no spring of courage." For a passing moment, I loathed Perry, and I think the feeling was probably mutual. He had what I was certain was a damaged capacity to love.

Joe came in followed by Stark and Nils. Joe kissed me and put his arm around my shoulder. "Nils told me a friend of yours died. I'm sorry. Are you okay?"

Perry slapped the counter.

"Don't get me started," I said. "Where's Noah?"

"We've been visiting a friend with a pool," Joe said. "Here's something for your diary. This guy just flew all the way to California and back to find a psychic who would assure him that he won't die of AIDS."

"Why didn't he just get the antibody test?" I asked.

"Because if it came out positive, he'd commit suicide. Anyway, Noah's coming to take you to tea. Where's Enzo?"

Stark came out of the room he shared with Enzo. "His body's there, but I can't attest to anything else. Does this mean you're cooking dinner?"

Nils came out of my room, which had the guest bed in it. He had changed into a pastel-colored muscle shirt bought in the Grove. I stiffened as he put an arm around me. "Come to tea and I will buy you a drink," Nils said.

"We'll be there soon," Perry said in a tone that implied wounds from the morning were being healed. Nils left to save us a place before the crowd got there. While the others were getting ready, Perry began to scour the kitchen counter. Someone was always cleaning the sink or dish rack for fear of bacteria or salmonella, mainly because of Horst, but you never know. Perry asked, "You don't like Nils, do you?"

"No. He has ingrown virginity."

"Meaning he wouldn't put out for you?"

"And another thing . . . all I've heard this week is that the Pines is going to tea later, that we're eating earlier, that there's more drag, fewer drugs, more lesbians, and less sexual tension. For an anthropologist, he sounds like the *New York Times.*"

Noah's long, slow steps could be heard coming around the house. When he saw Perry in the kitchen, he stopped in the center of the deck. Noah looked at Perry, raised his eyebrows, then turned and entered the house through the sliding door of his and Joe's room. Perry turned to the mirror and ran a comb through his mustache. From a tall vase filled with strings of pearls bought on Forty-second Street for a dollar, he selected one to wrap around his wrist. The pearls were left over from the previous summer, when the statistics predicting the toll on our lives were just beginning to come true; there were dozens of strands, in white, off-white, the colors of after-dinner mints. This will be over soon, my friend Anna says, they will find a cure, they have to. I know what she is saying. When it began, we all thought it would be over in a couple of years; perhaps the *Times* did as well, and did not report on it much, as if the new disease would blow over like a politician's sex scandal. AIDS to them was what hunger is to the fed, something we think we can imagine because we've been on a diet.

From behind the closed door of their bedroom, I heard Joe whisper loudly to Noah, "You're not going to change anything by being angry at him." Perry stared at the door for a moment as if he should prepare to bolt. Instead, he asked, "Are you still mad at me about the article?"

"I never was."

"But you were angry."

I looked over at the stack of papers accumulating near the couch, only then beginning to wonder what I achieved by saving them, what comfort was to be gained. "I always expect insight and consequence from their articles, and I'm disappointed when they write on our issues and don't report more than what we already know," I said. "And sometimes I assume that there is a language to describe what we're going through, and that they would use it if there was."

"You should have told me about your friend," Perry said.

"This is one I can't talk about," I said. "As for your suggestion . . . I don't know how I would begin to tell my mother about my life as I know it now."

"You could say, 'I've got some good news and some bad news.'"

"What's the good news?"

"You don't have AIDS."

Noah was still taking a shower when the others left for tea. He came out of the bathroom with an oversized towel wrapped around his waist and lotion rubbed into his face and hands. I could see the tiny scar on his back where the liposuction surgery had vacuumed a few pounds of fat. Tall and mostly bald, older than he would confess to, he was certainly as old as he looked. For a moment, he regarded me as if I were a dusty sock found under the bed. Then his face ripened.

"Dish alert," he said. "Guess who's having an affair with a twenty-two year-old and I'm not supposed to tell anyone?"

"Perry," I said almost instantly. "The bastard."

"They were together in Washington for the international AIDS conference, supposedly in secret, but word has gotten back that they were making out in public like a couple of Puerto Rican teenagers on the subway."

"Does Horst know?"

"Of course. Perry thinks that talking about dishonest behavior makes it honest. As far as I'm concerned, it's another distraction from Horst's illness. Perry distanced himself from everyone when it became obvious that they were dying. Last year it was Miguel, this year it's Horst. When I confronted him, he said, 'Don't deny me my denial.'"

"Oh, that's brilliant. As long as he claims to be in denial, he doesn't even have to appear to suffer," I said. "One of these days, all this grief he's avoiding is going to knock him on his ass."

"But then he'll wear it around town like an old cloth coat so that everyone will feel sorry for him. He won't be happy until people in restaurants whisper 'Brava' as he squeezes past them to his table."

"What's the boyfriend like?"

"What kind of person has an affair with a man whose lover is dying of AIDS?" Noah asked.

I said, "The kind that probably splits after the funeral."

"He's what my Aunt Gloria would call a mayonnaise Jew, someone trying to pass for a WASP."

"I don't know if I should be offended by that or not," I said.

"But get this: He's had three lovers since he graduated from Harvard. The first one's lover died of AIDS. The second one had AIDS. Now there's Perry. So this kid gets the antibody test. It came back negative, and now he's got survivor's guilt." Noah gave me one of his bland, expressionless looks. "Perry acts as if this were the most misunderstood love affair since Abélard and Héloïse. He told me it was one of those things in life you just have no control over."

"For someone so emotionally adolescent, he's gotten a lot of mileage out of this epidemic," I said.

"Where else would he be center stage with a degree in drama therapy?" Noah asked. "He even quoted your journal at the last AIDS conference."

"What?"

"In Washington. He quoted you in a paper he presented. I knew he hadn't told you yet," Noah said. "He was certain you'd be honored. He would have been."

"Do you know what he used?"

"Something about an air of pain, the cindered chill of loss. It was very moving. You wondered if there wasn't a hidden cost to constant bereavement. You know Perry, he probably presented your diary as the work of a recent widower whose confidentiality had to be protected. That way he didn't have to give you credit."

I once went to an AIDS conference. Perry treated them like summer camp—Oh, Mary, love your hat, let's have lunch. I had seen him deliver papers that were barely literate and unprepared, and what was prepared was plagiarized. Claiming he was overwhelmed with work, he feigned modesty and said he could only speak from his heart. When social scientists provided remote statistics on our lives, Perry emoted and confessed. "My personal experience is all I can offer as the essence of this presentation." And it worked. It gave everyone the opportunity to cry and feel historic.

Noah asked, "Are you coming to tea? There's someone I want you to meet."

"Another widower?" I asked. "More damaged goods?"

"I'll put it to you this way," Noah said, "you have a lot in common."

With regard to human affairs, Noah was efficient. "Let me count the ways," I said, "a recent death, the ache of memory, reduced T-cell functions, positive sero status . . ."

"Yes, well, there's that."

"And maybe foreshortened futures, both of us wary of commitment should one or the other get sick, the dread of taking care of someone else weighed against the fear of being sick and alone."

"I doubt that Samuel would like your attitude."

"Samuel will get over it," I said. "And I'm not interested in a relationship right now. I'm only interested in sex."

"Safer sex, of course."

"I want to wake up alone, if that's what you mean."

Noah raised his eyebrows and lowered them again, as if to say that he would never understand me. I said, "Let me tell you a story. I hired a Swedish masseur recently because I wanted to be touched by someone, and no one in particular, if you get my innuendo. At one point, he worked a cramped muscle so hard that I cried out. And he said, 'That's it, go ahead, let it out'—as if I was holding something back, you know, intellectualizing a massage. I asked him if he felt anything, and he said, 'I feel'—long pause—'sorrow.' I told him that I had been a little blue lately but it wasn't as bad as all that."

Noah nodded. He said, "The real reason I didn't want to be interviewed for the piece in the *Times* was because Perry invited the reporter for dinner and told her we'd all get into drag if she brought a photographer."

Before I went down to the beach, I looked in on Enzo. Stark was right. The only time I'd ever seen anyone like this before was when Horst was first diagnosed. Perry had scheduled people just to sit with him, when none of us thought he would even survive. Enzo's skin was moist, his lips dry, his breath light. He was warm, but not enough for alarm.

These summer evenings I sat on the beach in a sling-back chair, listening to my cassette player and writing things about Samuel. I recalled our life together backward. The day he went into the hospital, he had cooked himself something to eat and left the dishes in the sink. Then he was dead, and washing his dishes was my last link to him as a living being. This evening, the pages of my journal felt like the rooms of my apartment when I came home and found it burglarized. Like my apartment, I knew I had to either forsake it or reclaim it as my own. Though in this case something had been taken, nothing was missing. I was angry with Perry, but it was not the worst thing he could have done. The worst is not when we can say it is the worst.

I started to write about Robert. The words of his obituary, "warm, radiant, much-loved man," somewhat assuaged my remorse at having abandoned him to the attention of the more hopeful. The beach was nearly empty at this time of the day—as it was in the morning—except for those like me who were drawn by the light of the early evening, the color of the water, the sand, the houses seen without the protection of sunglasses. Others passed and I nodded from my beach chair. We smiled. Everyone agreed that the Island was friendlier this year, as if nothing were at stake when we recognized one another's existence. Verdi's Requiem was on my Walkman, a boat was halfway between the shore and the horizon. One full sail pulled the boat across the halcyon surface of the water. Near me a man stood with his feet just in the waves. He turned and held his binoculars as if he were offering me a drink. "They're strong," he said. I found the sailboat in the glasses. I found a handsome and popular Episcopal priest who I knew from experience to be a fine lover in bed. He was in collar and was praying. There was another handsome man. He was indistinct but I recognized his expression. He reached into a box and released his fist over the boat's rail. Another man and a woman repeated the gesture. *Libera me.* The surviving lover shook the entire contents of the cloth-wrapped box overboard. The winds that spin the earth took the ashes and grains of bones and spilled them on the loden-green sea. He was entirely gone now but for the flecks that stuck to their clothes and under their nails, but for the memory of him, and for the pleasure of having known him. The boaters embraced with that pleasure so intense they wept at it. *Dies magna et amara valde.* I returned the binoculars to the man. It was a beautiful day and it was wonderful to be alive.

PART II

Two old couches, one ersatz wicker, the other what my mother used to call colonial, sat at a right angle to one another in the middle of our living room. Enzo and Horst were lying on them with their heads close together, like conspiring convalescents. Horst's cheeks were scarlet.

"You aren't feeling well, are you?" I asked.

Horst said, "No, but I didn't want to tell Perry and spoil his weekend."

"How is Enzo doing?"

"He thinks he has a cold, but I don't think so."

From where I stood, I could lay my hand on both their foreheads. I felt like a television evangelist. Enzo's forehead was the warmer of the two.

"I hear there's a flu going around," Horst said.

"Where did you hear that? You haven't been in town in a week."

"I had a flu shot," he said. "I think I'm not worried."

Without opening his eyes, Enzo said, "You had better get started if you are going to cook supper before everyone gets back. I put all the ingredients out for you."

I heated oil as the recipe instructed. "When the oil is very hot add mustard seeds," it read. "Keep the lid of the pan handy should the seeds sputter and fly all over." In the first grade, I recalled giving a girl named Karen Tsakos a mustard-seed bracelet in a Christmas exchange, selecting it myself from the dollar rack at a store called Gaylord's. "Aren't mustard seeds supposed to be a symbol of something?" I asked as they began to explode between me and the cabinet where the lids were kept.

"Hope, I think," Enzo said.

"Perhaps I should put more in."

"No, faith," Horst said, lying down in his bedroom.

"Faith is a fine invention, as far as I can see, but microscopes are prudent, in case of emergency," I said, approximating a poem by Emily Dickinson. Horst laughed, but Enzo showed no sign whatsoever that he knew what I was talking about. I wasn't so sure myself what Dickinson meant by an emergency: Could a microscope confirm one's belief in a crisis of faith, or, in a crisis of nature, such as an epidemic illness, was man best left to his own devices?

"How's dinner coming?" Stark asked, returning five minutes before it was to have been on the table.

"It's not ready," I said.

"Why not?"

"I didn't start it in time," I said.

"Why not?"

"Because I was at a funeral."

He picked up one of Miguel's old porno magazines and disappeared into the bathroom with it. He emerged ten minutes later and asked, "Is there anything I could be doing?" ·

"You can light the coals, and grill the tuna steaks. I've got to watch the opma," I said. "Enzo, what are gram beans?"

"The little ones."

Perry returned next and kissed me. "I forgot to tell you that Luis is in the hospital again," he said loudly. "His pancreas collapsed but he seems to be getting better."

"Enzo, I think I burned the gram beans."

"Luis's lover, Dennis, just took the antibody test," Perry said. "He was sero-negative."

"Oh, that's good."

"Yeah. Luis said, 'Thank God for hemorrhoids.'"

"Enzo, which of these is the cumin?"

"Don't cumin my mouth," Perry said, going into his room to check on Horst. I watched him brush the hair off Horst's forehead and take the thermometer out of Horst's mouth to kiss him. Perry's face darkened when he read the thermometer, as if he didn't know what to think. I added the Cream of Wheat to the gram beans.

Nils came up to me and wrapped a huge arm around my shoulder. "They told me down at tea that if dinner was scheduled for nine, that meant ten in Fire Island time."

"Dinner would have been ready at nine o'clock if I hadn't been given this god-awful recipe to make," I said, sounding more angry than

I intended, and Nils hastened away. Noah came to the stove. "You are bitter, aren't you?"

"He's like Margaret Mead on steroids," I said.

"He's writing a book," Noah said.

"Yeah, sure, *Coming of Age in Cherry Grove.*"

"What's this here?" Noah asked.

"Opma."

"Where did you get the recipe?"

"From the *New York Times.*"

"I hate that paper."

Stark came running into the kitchen with the tuna steaks and put them in the electric broiler. The recipe said to grill them four minutes on each side.

"The grill will never get hot enough," he said. "Is that opma?"

"In the flesh."

"It looks like Cream of Wheat with peas in it."

Noah found the radio station we always listened to during dinner on Saturday nights. "Clark, what's the name of this song?" he asked, a game we played as part of the ritual. Enzo usually played along as he did the cooking.

"'The Nearness of You,'" I answered.

"Who's singing?"

"Julie London."

"Who wrote it?"

"Johnny Mercer." Enzo didn't say anything, though the correct answer was Hoagy Carmichael. Perry sang as he helped Joe set the table, making up his own lyrics as he went along, the way a child does, with more rhyme than reason. We were all aware that he and Noah were behaving as if the other were not in the room, but their orbits were getting closer. As the song closed, Perry and I turned to one another and imitated the deep voice of the singer: "It's just the queerness of you." Then I made everyone laugh by stirring the thickening opma with both hands on the spoon. Jules, the dog, began hacking in the center of the room.

"Did you have a productive cough, dear?" Joe asked. Horst laughed from his bedroom.

"Enzo, come tell me if the opma is done," I said. He kind of floated up off the couch as if he was pleasantly drunk. I knew then that he was seriously ill. He took the wooden spoon from me and poked the opma twice. "It's done," he said.

We went to the table. I sat in the center, with Enzo on my right,

Nils across from me, Joe on my left. Perry and Noah faced each other from the opposite ends, like parents. This was how we sat, each and every week. The guest was always in the same chair, whether he knew it or not. For the first several minutes of dinner, the table was a tangle of large arms passing the salad and popping open beer cans.

"Eat something, darling," I said to Enzo, who was only staring at the fish on his plate. "You haven't eaten anything all day."

Perry said, "This is the best opma I ever had."

Horst looked up as if he had something to announce, his fork posed in the air. We all turned to him. His fork fell to his plate with a clatter, and he said, "I think I have to lie down."

Perry said, "This opma will taste good reheated."

"So Fred told me this story at tea about the last of the police raids on the Meat Rack in the early seventies," Noah said.

"You're going to love this, Clark," Perry said.

"The cops came in one night with huge flashlights and handcuffs. There were helicopters and strobe lights; they had billy clubs and German shepherds. And they started dragging away dozens of men. The queens were crying and screaming and pleading with the cops because they would get their names in the paper and lose their jobs, you know, this was when it was still illegal for two men to dance with one another. The guys that got away hid under the bushes until everything was clear. Finally, after everything was perfectly quiet, some queen whispered, 'Mary, Mary!' And someone whispered back, 'Shhh, no names!'"

"Nils, would you like this?" Enzo asked. I looked up at Nils, whose forearms circled his plate. Everyone looked at me looking at him. I picked up Enzo's tuna steak with my fork and dropped it on Nils's plate. Enzo got up and stumbled to the couch.

Stark and Joe cleared the table. Perry went outside and smoked a cigar. With his back turned toward the house, he was calling attention to himself. I sat on the arm of the couch, looking down at Enzo and looking out at Perry, wondering who needed me most. But Noah was also looking at Perry. I could see him in his room, a finger on his lip, looking through the doors that opened out onto the deck. He stepped back from my sight and called, "Perry, this doesn't fit me. Would you like to try it on?"

The next thing I knew, Perry was wearing a black velvet Empress gown, like the one Madame X wears in the Sargent painting. In one hand, he held its long train, in the other, a cigar. Between the cleavage of the dress was Perry's chest hair, the deepest part of which was gray.

"Where'd you get that dress?" Stark asked.

"Noah inherited Miguel's hope chest. It was in the will."

Enzo was smiling, but I knew he was faking it. I whispered, "Do you need help to your bed?"

He clutched my hand and I helped him into his room. His forehead was scalding. "I'll be right back," I told him. I ran into the kitchen and pulled a dish towel from the refrigerator handle and soaked it under cold water. By this time, Noah was wearing the silver-lined cape that went with Perry's gown, a Frederick's of Hollywood merry widow, and silver lamé high heels. On his bald head was a tiny silver cap. I smiled as I passed through them, but they didn't see me.

Horst was sitting on Enzo's bed when I got back to him. This was the room in which Miguel had died the year before, and which Horst did not want this summer, though it was bigger and cooler than his own room and its glass doors opened onto the deck. "I could hear his breathing over all the commotion," Horst said. "Have you taken any aspirin?"

"I've been taking aspirin, Tylenol, and Advil every two hours," Enzo said, his voice strengthened by fear's adrenaline.

Horst asked, "Did you take your temperature?"

"I don't have a thermometer."

Horst got his own. "I cleaned it with peroxide," he said. "I hope that is good enough." Before I could ask him how to use it, he was on his way back to bed.

I pulled the thermometer from its case, pressed a little button, and placed it in Enzo's mouth. Black numbers pulsed against a tiny gray screen. I watched its numbers climb like a scoreboard from hell. Outside, Nils's arms were flailing because the high heels he was wearing were stuck between the boards of the deck. The thermometer beeped. Perry and Noah, in full drag, walked off with Nils between them.

"You have a temperature of a hundred and three point two," I said. This was the first time in my life I had ever been able to read a thermometer. "Do you want me to get the Island doctor?"

"Let's see if it goes down. Can you get me some cranberry juice?"

I went into the kitchen. Stark and Joe were reading. "How's he doing?" Joe asked.

"I think we should get him to a doctor."

"The number's on the ferry schedule," Joe said, and went back to his book.

A machine at the doctor's office said in the event of an emergency, to leave a number at the sound of the beep. I could not imagine the doctor picking up messages that late at night. But what I really feared was the underlying cause of Enzo's fever. I put the phone in its cradle.

"Don't we know any doctors?" I asked.

Stark and Joe shook their heads. Joe said that Noah or Perry might. I suddenly realized how isolated the Island was at night. At this point, there was no way of getting Enzo off the Island short of a police helicopter.

He was asleep when I took him his juice. He was not the handsomest of men, but at this moment he was downright homely. He cooked all our meals for us, meals to which even Horst's fickle appetite responded. He overstocked the refrigerator with more kinds of foodstuff than we could identify. We wondered why he did it, even as we stored away a few extra pounds, telling ourselves we were delaying the sudden weight loss associated with the first signs of AIDS. Perry had put on so much weight, his posture changed. He tilted forward as he walked. If he should develop the AIDS-associated wasting-away syndrome, Noah told him, months might go by before anyone would notice. I took the towel off Enzo's head and soaked it in cold water again.

"You'll be sure to clean Horst's thermometer before you give it back to him," he said, holding my hand, which held the towel to his face.

"Yes, of course."

"I mean it."

"Let me take your temperature again. This thermometer is really groovy." His temperature had risen to just shy of 104. With all I knew about AIDS, I suddenly realized I did not even know what this meant. "When was the last time you took some aspirin?"

"An hour ago. I'll give it another one."

The house shook as Perry, Noah, and Nils returned, all aglow with the success of their outing. Perspiration hung off Perry's chest hair like little Italian lights strung about the Tavern on the Green. Nils got into a clean tank top and went dancing.

Noah snapped open a Japanese fan and waved it at his face. "Dish alert," he said. He could be charming. For a moment, I forgot Enzo, the thermometer in my hand.

Joe said, "Clark thinks Enzo needs a doctor."

Noah asked, "What's his temperature?"

I stood in the doorway. "It's one hundred and four," I said, exaggerating a little.

"That's not too bad."

"It isn't?"

"Is he delirious?" Noah asked.

"What if he's too sick to be delirious?"

Perry said, "Miguel's temperature used to get much higher than that. He'd be ranting and raving in there sometimes."

"Yes, but Miguel is dead," I said.

When we opened the house this summer, I threw away his sheets, the polyester bathrobes, the towels from Beth Israel, St. Vincent's, Sloan-Kettering, and Mt. Sinai that filled our closets and dresser drawers from all of Miguel's hospital visits. Noah had watched me, neither protesting nor liking what I was doing. But I could not conceive of any nostalgia that would want to save such souvenirs. The hospital linen was part and parcel of the plastic pearls, the battery-operated hula doll, the Frederick's of Hollywood merry widow, five years' worth of porno magazine subscriptions, the measure of extremes they went to for a laugh last year, the last summer of Miguel's life. Why did we need them when we were still getting postdated birthday presents from Miguel: sweaters on our birthday, Smithfield hams at Christmas, magazine subscriptions in his name care of our address—anything he could put on his Visa card once he realized that he would expire before it did.

"If Enzo's temperature gets too high, we can give him an alcohol bath, or a shower, to bring it down," Noah said.

"So can I go to bed now?" Stark asked.

"Sure," I said. "Just don't sleep too soundly."

I went into my own room, which smelled of Nils's clothes, his sweat and the long trip, of coconut suntan lotion and the salty beach. I missed Samuel at moments like this, missed his balance of feelings, of moderated emotions as if he proportioned them out, the pacifying control he had over me. I fell asleep, woke and listened for Enzo's breath, and fell asleep again. I halfway woke again and sensed my longing even before Nils's presence woke me completely. In the next bed, a sheet pulled up to his nipples, Nils's chest filled the width of the bed.

Drunk one night on the beach, he had said to me, "Perry doesn't think there's hope for anyone who is diagnosed in the next few years."

"We've pinned our hopes on so many," I said, aware that Nils was delving for useful information, "that I don't know what role hope plays anymore. They're predicting as many deaths in 1991 alone as there were Americans killed in Vietnam. Some of those are bound to be people one knows."

"Hope is the capacity to live with the uncertain," he said.

I had read that line myself somewhere. "Bullshit," I said. Nils stepped back and looked at me as if I had desecrated the theology of some deified psychotherapist.

"You don't need hope to persevere," I said.

"What do you need, then?" Nils asked.

"Perseverance," I answered, and laughed at myself. And then told him a story I had heard at a funeral service. It was the story of an Hassidic rabbi and a heckler. The rabbi had told his congregation that we must try to put everything into the service of God, even that which was negative and we didn't like. The heckler called out, "Rabbi, how do we put a disbelief in God into His service?" The rabbi's answer made me think that God and hope are interchangeable. He told the heckler, "If a man comes to you in a crisis, do not tell him to have faith, that God will take care of everything. Act instead as if God does not exist. Do what you can do to help the man."

Nils put his arm around me and pulled me up close to him as we walked. There was a strong wind that night, and the waves were high. The moon was low across the water and illuminated the waves as they reached for it. I felt massive muscles working in Nils's thighs and loins, a deep and deeper mechanism than I had ever felt in a human body, and which seemed to have as its source of energy that which lifted the waves and kept the moon suspended. He was that strong, and I would feel that secure. A bulwark against the insentient night, his body: if I did not need hope to persevere, I needed that. He stopped and held me, kissed my head politely, and pushed me out at arms' length. He made me feel like the canary sent down the mine to warn him of dangerous wells of feeling, wells that he could draw upon but needn't descend himself.

When I woke again, the oily surface of his back was glowing. The sky held more prophecy than promise of light. I got up to check on Enzo. He was not in bed. Stark was sitting up waiting for him to come out of the bathroom. He patted the bed next to him. I sat down and he put his arm around me.

"Has he been sleeping?" I asked.

"Like the dead."

"Do you think we should have gotten a helicopter off the Island?"

"No, but I wish we had."

Enzo could be heard breathing through the thin door. Stark said, "It's been like that all night."

The toilet flushed, we heard Enzo moan, then the thud of his body falling against the bathroom door.

Stark carefully pushed it opened and looked in. "All hell broke loose," he said.

Enzo was lying in a puddle of excrement. In his delirium, he had forgotten to pull his pajamas down before sitting on the toilet. When he tried to step out of them, his bowels let go a spray of watery stool. His legs were covered, as were the rugs and the wall against which he fainted.

"You're burning up, darling," Stark whispered to him.

"I'm afraid he'll dehydrate," I said.

I pulled off Enzo's soiled pajamas, turned the shower on, and took off the old gym shorts I slept in. "Hand him over," I said from within the lukewarm spray.

Enzo wrapped his arms around my back and laid his hot head on my shoulder. Our visions of eternal hell must come from endless febrile nights like this, I thought. I gradually made the water cooler and sort of two-stepped with him so that it would run down his back, and sides, and front. The shower spray seemed to clothe our nakedness. If I closed my eyes, we were lovers on a train platform. We could have been almost anywhere, dancing in the sad but safe aftermath of some other tragedy, say the Kennedy assassinations, the airlift from Saigon, the bombing of a Belfast funeral. Stark used the pump bottle of soap— bought to protect Horst from whatever bacteria, fungus, or yeast might accumulate on a shared bar—to lather Enzo's legs. I slowly turned the water cooler.

"Can we get your head underwater a little bit?" I asked, though Enzo was barely conscious. "Let's see if we can get your fever down."

"I think we're raising it," Stark murmured. He was washing Enzo's buttocks and his hand would reach through Enzo's legs and wash his genitals almost religiously. He reached through Enzo's legs and lathered my genitals as well. He pulled on my testicles and loosened them in their sack. He pulled and squeezed them just to the pleasure point of pain. He winked at me but he didn't smile. I noticed there were interesting shampoos on the shelf that I had never tried.

"I can't stand much longer, you guys," Enzo whispered in my ear. "I'm sorry."

I maneuvered him around to rinse the soap off. Stark waited with huge towels. While I dried us both, Stark changed Enzo's bedclothes, tucking the fresh sheets in English style. Then he helped me carry him back to bed.

"Let's take his temperature before he falls asleep," I said. Stark stared in my face as we waited. The thermometer took so long, I was afraid it was broken. It finally went off with a tremulous beep. "Dear God," I said.

"What is it?"

Despite the shower, his fever was over 105. "Do we have any rubbing alcohol?" I asked.

Stark couldn't find any after checking both bathrooms. I said, "Get the vodka, then."

He returned with the ice-covered bottle from the freezer; the liquor within it was gelatinous. "Do you think this wise?" he asked.

"Not the imported. Get the stuff we give the guests. Wait," I said. "Leave that one here and bring me a glass."

Stark brought the domestic vodka and a sponge. "Do you know what you're doing?" he asked.

"Alcohol brings a temperature down by rapidly evaporating off the body," I said. "Vodka happens to evaporate faster than rubbing alcohol. Other than that, no, I don't have the faintest idea."

Stark watched me for a while, then took Enzo's temperature himself. It had fallen to 104.8. "I think we should get some aspirin in him," he said, which we woke Enzo to do. He drank a little juice. Fifteen minutes later, I took his temperature again. Enzo's temperature had gone down to 104.6. While waiting for this reading, Stark had fallen back to sleep. I wondered whether he didn't want me in bed with him. That would have been pleasant, temporary; he was a solid man, like a park bench.

But instead, I went out to the living room. My stack of newspapers was near the couch. I could look in on Enzo if I clipped the articles I intended to save. Just the night before, Noah had shaken his head at all the papers and said, "It looks like poor white trash lives here."

"My roots must be showing," I said.

I clipped my articles and put them in an accordion file that I kept closed with an old army-issue belt. Sometimes margin notes reminded me why I was saving something, such as the obituary of an interior designer, in which, for the first time, the lover was mentioned as a survivor. Or the piece in which being sero-positive for HIV antibodies became tantamount to HIV infection, indicating that our language for talking about AIDS was changing. "With the passage of time, scientists are beginning to believe that all those infected will develop symptoms and die," the article said. It really doesn't sit well to read about one's mortality in such general terms.

In the magazine section, a popular science writer wrote that there was no moral message in AIDS. Over the illustration, I scrawled, "When late is worse than never." Scientists had been remiss, he said, for "viewing it as a contained and peculiar affliction of homosexual men." In the margin I wrote, "How much did they pay you to say this?"

Then there were those living-out-loud columns written by a woman who had given up on actual journalism to raise her children. Some of them were actually quite perceptive, but I had never forgiven her for the one in which the writer confessed that she had been berated by a gay man in a restaurant for saying, "They were so promiscuous—no wonder they're dying."

Horst emerged from his bedroom to blend his AL721, which was kept in the freezer in ice-cube trays. He did not see me and I did not say anything for fear of frightening him because he concentrated so severely on his task. If you did not know him, you would not think he was ill, but very, very old. He had always been a vulnerable and tender man, but now he was fragile. He hoped that the elixir in his blender could keep the brush of death's wings from crushing him entirely.

When Samuel called to tell me two years ago that Horst had been diagnosed, I began to weep mean, fat tears. My assistant editor sent me out for a walk. I wandered aimlessly around SoHo for a while, once trying to get into the old St. Patrick's, its small walled-in cemetery covered with the last of autumn's spongy brown leaves. I fingered cowhide and pony pelts hanging in a window; I bought a cheap stop-watch from a street vendor, some blank tapes, and spare batteries for my tape cassette. Eventually, hunger made me find a place to rest, a diner with high ceilings and windows looking onto a busy street. After I ordered, I thought of Horst again, and something odd happened: the room—no, not the room, but my vision went, like after you've looked at the sun too long. All I could see was a glowing whiteness, like a dentist's lamp, or the inside of a Nautilus shell. For a brilliant moment, I saw nothing, and knew nothing, but this whiteness that had anesthe-tized and cauterized the faculties by which one savors the solid world. Like a film dissolving from one scene to another, the room came back, but the leftover whiteness limned the pattern of one man's baldness, glittered off the earring of his companion, turned the white shirt my waitress wore to porcelain, fresh and rigid, as it was from the Chinese laundry. She stood over me with a neon-bright plate in one hand and the beer's foam glowing in the other, waiting for me to lift my elbows and give her room to put down my lunch.

"Oh, shit," Horst said, knocking the orange-juice carton over and spilling some into the silverware drawer.

"I'll clean it up," I said softly.

"I knew you were there," he said. "I heard you in here. How is Enzolina?"

"His temperature was very high. We got it down a little bit."

"You must sleep, too." He leaned over me and kissed my cheek. "It's okay about Perry and his boyfriend," he said, obviously having heard Noah speaking that afternoon. "Perry is still affectionate and he takes care of me. And I don't feel so sexual anymore. But Noah shouldn't have told you, because it would only make you angry."

Whether it was the lateness of the hour or the sensitive logic of pain, I thought I heard resignation in Horst's voice, as if he were putting one foot in the grave just to test the idea of it.

"Have you met the boyfriend?"

"Oh, yes. He's very bland. I don't know what Perry sees in him," Horst said. "Perry thinks the three of us should go into therapy together, but I'm not doing it. I don't have to assuage their guilt."

"Where will Perry be when you get really sick?"

"Probably at a symposium in Central Africa." He laughed and waved his hand like an old woman at an off-color joke. Horst used to be hardy, real peasant stock. He was the kind of man who could wear a ponytail and make it look masculine. Here was a man gang-banged for four days by a bunch of Turks on the Orient Express who lived to turn the memory into a kind of mantra. He said, "Perry needs so many buffers from reality."

"Most of us do."

"Not you."

"You're wrong," I said. Then I showed him the article on the death of an iconoclastic theater director that had started on the front page of the *Times*. "Look, there's a typo. It says he died of AIDS-related nymphoma."

He laughed and laid his head in my lap. "I am homesick for Switzerland," he said. "I'd like to go home, but I don't know if I could handle the trip. And I don't want to be a burden on my family."

"You wouldn't be."

"I've been thinking lately I don't want to be cremated. I want to be buried in the mountains. But it's so expensive."

"Horst, don't worry about expenses," I said.

"How is Samuel?" he asked.

"He's dead, honey. He died this winter."

"Oh, I'm sorry," he said, and covered his face with his hands. Memory lapses are sometimes part of the deterioration. I wondered whether Perry had noticed or ignored them. "I forget these things," he added.

"It's late, you're tired." He started up. I said, "Horst, I think you should go home if you want to. Just make sure you come back."

My fingertips were pungent with the smell of newsprint, like cilantro, or the semen smell of ailanthus seeds in July. "Did you see that piece in today's paper?" we asked one another over the phone when a point we held dear was taken up on the editorial page. "Yes, haven't they come far and in such a short time," we responded. I filed it all away, with little science and what was beginning to feel like resignation: *C* for condoms, *S* for Heterosexuals, *P* for Prevention and Safer Sex, *R* for Race and Minorities, *O* for Obits.

"I can't tell you how bored I am with this," a man said to me on the beach one evening when he learned that another friend had gone down for the count. He said, "Sometimes I wish there was something else to talk about," which is what my mother used to say as she put her makeup on for a night out with my father. "I just wish we could go out and talk about anything but you kids and the house," she'd say with the vague longing I recall with numbing resonance. "I just wish there was something else to talk about."

They would eat at a place called D'Amico's Steak House, where the menus were as large as parking spaces. She would have frogs' legs, which she told me tasted like chicken, but were still a leap toward the exotic, no matter how familiar the landing. Her desire had no specific object; she was not an educated woman; she did not even encourage fantasy in her children; but it still arouses whatever Oedipal thing there is left unresolved in me, and I often wish to be able to satisfy it—to give her nights and days of conversation so rooted in the present that no reference to when we were not happy could ever be made, and no dread of what to come could be imagined. But we both know that there's no forgetting that we were once unhappy. Our conversation is about my sisters' lives and their children. She ends our infrequent telephone conversations with "Please take care of yourself," emphasizing, without naming, her fear of losing me to an illness we haven't talked about, or to the ebbs of time and its hostilities that have carried me further and further away from perfect honesty with her.

But language also takes you far afield. Metaphors adumbrate; facts mitigate. For example, "Nothing is hopeless; we must hope for everything." I had believed this until I realized the lie of its intrinsic metaphor, that being without hope is not being, plunged into the abyss that nothingness fills. We have not come far since the world had one language and few words. Babel fell before we had a decent word for death, and then we were numb, shocked at the thought of it, and this lisping dumb word—*death, death, death*—was the best we could come up with.

And simply speak, disinterested and dryly, the words that fill your daily life: "Lewis has KS of the lungs," or "Raymond has endocarditis but the surgeons won't operate," or "Howard's podiatrist will not remove a bunion until he takes the test," or "Cytomegalovirus has inflamed his stomach and we can't get him to eat," or "The DHPG might restore the sight in his eye," or "The clinical trial for ampligen has filled up," or "They've added dementia to the list of AIDS-related illnesses," or "The AZT was making him anemic," or "His psoriasis flaked so badly, the maid wouldn't clean his room," or "They found tuberculosis in his glands," or "It's a form of meningitis carried in pigeon shit; his mother told him he should never have gone to Venice," or "The drug's available on a compassionate basis," or "The drug killed him," or "His lung collapsed and stopped his heart," or "This is the beginning of his decline," or "He was *so* young." What have you said and who wants to hear it?

"Oh, your life is not so awful," a woman at my office told me. She once lived in India and knew whereof she spoke. At Samuel's funeral, a priest told me, "I don't envy you boys. This is your enterprise now, your vocation." He kissed me, as if sex between us was an option he held, then rode to the altar on a billow of white to a solitary place setting meant to serve us all.

Enzo's temperature remained the same through the night. I poured myself a drink—though I did not need it—to push myself over the edge of feeling. I took it down to the beach. There were still a few bright stars in the sky. Everything was shaded in rose, including the waves and the footprints in the sand, deceiving me and the men coming home from dancing into anticipating a beautiful day.

Since the deaths began, the certified social workers have quoted Shakespeare at us: "Give sorrow words." But the words we used now reek of old air in churches, taste of the dust that has gathered in the crevices of the Nativity and the Passion. Our condolences are arid as leaves. We are actors who have over-rehearsed our lines. When I left the Island one beautiful weekend, Noah asked, "Were you so close to this man you have to go to his funeral?" I told myself all the way to Philadelphia that I did not have to justify my mourning. One is responsible for feeling something and being done with it.

Give sorrow occasion and let it go, or your heart will imprison you in constant February, a chain-link fence around frozen soil, where your dead will stack in towers past the point of grieving. *Let your tears fall for the dead, and as one who is suffering begin the lament . . . do not neglect his burial.* Think of him, the one you loved, on his knees, on his elbows, his face turned up to look back in yours, his mouth dark in his dark beard. He was smiling because of you. You tied a silky rope around his wrists, then down around the base of his cock and balls, his anus raised for you. When you put your mouth against it, you ceased to exist. All else fell away. You had brought him, and he you, to that point where you are most your mind and most your body. His prostate pulsed against your fingers like a heart in a cave, *mind, body, body, mind,* over and over. Looking down at him, he who is dead and gone, then lying across the broken bridge of his spine, the beachhead of his back, you would gladly

change places with him. *Let your weeping be bitter and your wailing fervent;
then be comforted for your sorrow.* Find in grief the abandon you used to
find in love; grieve the way you used to fuck.

Perry was out on the deck when I got back. He was naked and had
covered himself with one hand when he heard steps on our boardwalk.
With the other hand, he was hosing down the bathroom rugs on which
Enzo had been sick. I could tell by the way he smiled at me that my
eyes must have been red and swollen.

"There's been an accident," he said.

"I was a witness. Do you need help?"

"I've got it," he said, and waddled back inside for a bucket and
disinfectant to do the bathroom floors.

Enzo opened the curtains on his room. I asked him how he was
feeling.

"My fever's down a little. And my back hurts."

Stark asked him, "Do you think you can stay out here a couple of
days and rest? Or do you want to go into the hospital?"

"You can fly in and be there in a half an hour," I said.

"One of us will go in with you," Stark said.

"I'm not sure. I think so," Enzo said, incapable of making a decision.

"What if I call your doctor and see what he says?" I asked.

The doctor's service answered and I left as urgent a message as I
could. I began breaking eggs into a bowl, adding cinnamon and almond
concentrate. The doctor's assistant called me back before the yolks and
egg whites were beaten together. "What are the symptoms?" he asked.

"Fever, diarrhea."

"Back pain?"

"Yes."

"Is his breathing irregular?" the assistant asked.

"His breathing is irregular, his temperature is irregular, his pulse is
irregular, and his bowel movement is irregular. My bet is he's dehydrated. What else do you need to know?"

"Has he been diagnosed with AIDS yet?"

"No," I said, "but he had his spleen removed two years ago. And
Dr. Williams knows his medical history."

"I'll call you back," he said.

"How is he?" asked Noah. It was early for him to be out of bed. I
began to suspect that no one had slept well.

"He's weak and now his back hurts. I think he'd like to go to the
hospital."

"It's Sunday. They aren't going to do anything for him. All they'll do is admit him. He might as well stay here and I'll drive him in tomorrow."

Horst came out of Enzo's room. "That's not true. They can test oxygen levels in his blood for PCP and start treatment right away. And the sooner they catch these things, the easier they are to treat."

Horst had said what none of us would say—PCP—for if it was *Pneumocystis carinii* pneumonia, then Enzo did have AIDS. One more person in the house would have it, one more to make it impossible to escape for a weekend, one more to remind us of how short our lives were becoming.

The phone rang. Dr. Williams's assistant told me to get Enzo in right away. "Get yourself ready," I said. "Your doctor will be coming in just to see you. I'll call the airline to get you a seat on the seaplane."

"Okay," Enzo said, relieved to have the decision made for him. He put his feet on the floor and got his bearings. Stark helped him fill a bag. Then I looked outside and saw what appeared to be a sheet unfurling over the trees. Fog was coming through the brambles the way smoke unwraps from a cigarette and lingers in the heat of a lamp.

"Oh, my God, will you look at that," Joe said. "Another lousy beach day. This has been the worst summer."

Perry called the Island airline. All flights were canceled for the rest of the morning. Visibility of three miles was needed for flight to the Island, and we couldn't even see beyond our deck. Even voices from the neighboring houses sounded muffled and far away for the first time all summer.

"We're going to have to find someone who will drive him in," Perry said. "Unless he thinks he can handle the train."

"He's too sick for the train," I said.

"Who do we know with a car?" Perry asked. Joe took Jules out for a walk. Noah went behind the counter, where the batter for French toast was waiting. He began slicing challah and dipping it into batter, though no one was ready to eat.

Perry said, "I wonder if Frank is driving back today."

"Call him," I said.

But Perry didn't get the response he expected. We heard him say, "Frank, he's very sick. His doctor said to get him in right away." He turned to us. "Frank says he'll drive Enzo in if the fog doesn't clear up."

"Well, I can understand why he would feel put upon," Noah said. "I wouldn't want to give up my weekend, either."

At that point, I said, "I'm going in with Enzo."

Noah said, "He can go into the emergency room by himself. He doesn't need anyone with him." I said nothing but I did not turn away from him either. Perry looked at me and then to Noah. His lower lip dropped from under his mustache. Noah said, "Well, doesn't he have someone who could meet him there?"

"Enzo," I called, "is there anyone who could meet you in the city?"

"I guess I could call my friend Jim," he said.

"See," Noah said.

"Jim's straight," I said, not that I thought it really made any difference, but it sounded as if it did. We did, supposedly, know the ropes of this disease. "Enzo, who would you rather have with you, me or Jim?"

"You."

Noah raised his eyebrows and shrugged one shoulder. "I don't know why you feel you have to go into the emergency room."

"Because I am beginning to see what it will be like to be sick with this thing and not have anyone bring me milk or medication because it isn't convenient or amusing any longer."

Noah said, "I have been working at the Gay Men's Health Crisis for the past six years. I was one of the first volunteers."

"Oh, good, the institutional response. That reassures me," I said. Starting into my room to pack a bag, I bumped into Nils, who was coming out of the shower and didn't have any clothes on, not even a towel. Although Nils walked the beach in a bikini brief that left nothing to—nor satisfied—the imagination, he quickly covered himself and pressed his body against the wall to let me pass.

"I'm sorry if I kept you up last night," he said to me.

"It wasn't you. I was worried about Enzo," I said.

By eleven-thirty the fog was packed in as tight as cotton in a new jar of aspirin. Our friend with the car decided that since it was not a beach day, he could be doing things in the city. We were to meet him at the dock for the twelve o'clock ferry. He could not, however, take me as well, for he had promised two guests a ride and only had room for four in his jaunty little car.

Enzo and Perry seemed embarrassed by this. "I don't mind taking the train," I said. "I'll be able to read the Sunday *Times*."

Nils put his arm around me and walked me to the door. "I'll be gone when you come back. I'd like to leave you my address." I wanted to say a house gift would be more appropriate, something for the kitchen or a flowering plant. "It's unlikely that I'll ever get that far north," I said, "but thanks all the same. Maybe I'll drop you a line." The last thing I saw as I was leaving was his large head down over his plate, his arms on the table, a fork in a fist. He was a huge and odd-looking man. Stark said he had a face like the back of a bus, but it was actually worse than that. Nils was also the author of two books, working on a third about the Nazi occupation of Oslo. I saw the others join him around the table. He was probably ten times smarter than anyone there. Sharp words and arguments often defined the boundaries of personalities in this house, but Nils did not touch any of our borders. He simply did not fit in. And though tourists are insufferable after a point, I knew I should ask his forgiveness for my sin of inhospitality, but I couldn't make the overture to deserve it.

On the ferry, Enzo said, "I'm glad you're coming."

"I wanted out of that house," I said.

"I know."

We listened to our tape players so as not to speak about what was on our minds. People wore white sweaters and yellow mackintoshes. They held dogs in their laps, or the Sports section, or a beach towel in a straw purse; a man had his arm around his lover's shoulder, his fingertips alighted on the other's collarbone. No one spoke. It didn't seem to matter that the weekend was spoiled. We were safe in this thoughtless fog. The bay we crossed was shallow; it could hide neither monsters from the deep nor German submarines. It seemed all we needed to worry about was worrying too much; what we had to fear was often small and could be ignored. But as we entered the harbor on the other side, a dockworker in a small motorboat passed our ferry and shouted, "AIDS!" And in case we hadn't heard him, shouted again, "AIDS, AIDS!"

A man slid back the window and shouted back, "Crib death!" Then he slunk in his seat, ashamed of himself.

I read the paper on the train. I listened to Elgar, Bach, Barber, and Fauré. An adagio rose to its most poignant bar; the soprano sang the Pie Jesù with a note of anger, impatient that we should have to wait so long for everlasting peace, or that the price was so high, or that we should have to ask at all. I filled the empty time between one place and another with a moderate and circumspect sorrow delineated by the beginning, middle, and end of these adagios. Catharsis is not a release of emotion, it is a feast. Feel this. Take that. And you say, Yes, sir, thank you, sir. Something hardens above the eyes and your throat knots and you feel your self back into being. Friends die and I think, Good, that's over, let go of these intolerable emotions, life goes on. The train ride passed; I finished mourning another one. The train ride was not as bad as people say it is.

And Enzo had only arrived at the hospital ten minutes before me. The nurses at the emergency desk said I couldn't see him.

"I'm his care partner from the Gay Men's Health Crisis," I said, telling them more than they were prepared to hear. "Can I just let him know I'm here?" The lie worked as I was told it would.

Dr. Williams was there as well, standing over Enzo's gurney, which was in the middle of the corridor. "Was there any diarrhea?" he asked. Enzo said no, I said yes. "Fever?" "Over a hundred and five." "Did you have a productive cough?" he asked, and Enzo smiled. He pounded on the small of Enzo's back. "Does that hurt?" It did. The doctor was certain that Enzo's infection was one to which people who have had their spleens removed are vulnerable. We were moved to a little curtained room in the emergency ward.

"I'm not convinced it isn't PCP," Enzo said to me.

"Neither am I," said the attending physician, who had been outside the curtain with Enzo's chart. "Dr. Williams's diagnosis seems too logical. I want to take some tests just to make sure."

He asked for Enzo's health history: chronic hepatitis; idiopathic thrombocytopenia purpura; the splenectomy; herpes. Enzo sounded as if he were singing a tenor aria from *L'Elisir d'Amore*. The attending physician leaned over him, listened for the high notes, and touched him more like a lover than a doctor.

"You don't have to stay," Enzo said to me.

"I want to see if he comes back," I said.

"He reminds you of Samuel."

"A little bit."

"Do you think he's gay?"

"I don't think he'd be interested in me even if he was. Maybe you, though," I said.

Enzo smiled at that and fell asleep. The afternoon passed with nurses coming in to take more blood. He was wheeled out twice for X rays. A thermos of juice had broken in his overnight bag. I rinsed his sodden clothes and wrapped them in newspaper to take back to the house to wash. But his book about eating in Paris was ruined. He had been studying all summer for his trip to France the coming fall. Restaurants were highlighted in yellow, like passages in an undergraduate's philosophy book; particular dishes were starred.

He woke and saw me with it. "My shrink told me that we couldn't live our lives as if we were going to die of AIDS. I've been putting off this vacation for years," he said. "If there's anything you want to do, Clark, do it now."

"Do you want me to call anyone?" I asked.

"Have you called the house yet?"

"I thought I'd wait until we had something to tell them."

"Okay," he said, and went back to sleep. I read what I hadn't thrown away of the *Times*. In the magazine was an article titled "She Took the Test." I began to read it but skipped past the yeasty self-examination to get to the results. Her test had come back negative. I wondered whether she would have written the piece had it come back positive.

Enzo woke and asked again, "Have you called the house yet?"

"No, I was waiting until we knew something certain."

"If I had PCP, you would tell them right away," he said.

"Yes, Enzo, but we don't know that yet," I said, but he had already fallen back to sleep. He hadn't had anything to eat all day, and hadn't been given anything to reduce the fever. Because he was dehydrated, they had him on intravenous, but he seemed to be sweating as quickly as the fluid could go into his body. I felt the accusation anyway, and it was just. I had not called the house precisely because they were waiting for me to call and because I was angry at them.

It was eight o'clock that evening before the handsome doctor returned again. "There is too much oxygen in your blood for it to be PCP," he told us. "But we found traces of a bacterial pneumonia, the kind of infection Dr. Williams was referring to. Losing your spleen will open you up to these kinds of things, and there's no prevention. We'll put you on intravenous penicillin for a week and you'll be fine."

Enzo grinned. He would not have to cancel his trip to Paris. His life and all the things he had promised himself were still available to him. An orderly wheeled him to his room, and I followed behind with his bag. It was not AIDS, but it would be someday, a year from now, maybe, two, unless science or the mind found prophylaxis. He knew this as well as I did. Not this year, he said, but surely within five. No one knows how this virus will affect us over the years, what its impact will be on us when we are older, ten years after infection, fifteen—fifteen years from now? When I was eleven years old, I never thought I would live to be twenty-six, which I thought to be the charmed and perfect age. I think fifteen years from now, and I come to fifty. How utterly impossible that seems to me, how unattainable. I have not believed that I would live to the age of forty for two years now.

"You'll call the house now," he said as I was leaving.

"Yes."

"I appreciate your being here."

I turned in the doorway. Several responses came to mind—that I hadn't really done so much, that anybody would have done what I had done. Enzo saw me thinking, however, and smiled to see me paused in thought. "I wanted to say that reality compels us to do the right thing if we live in the real world," I said. "But that's not necessarily true, is it?"

"It can put up a compelling argument," Enzo said. "Don't be mad at Noah. I didn't expect him to drive me in."

With Enzo in his room, the penicillin going into his veins, feeling better simply at the idea of being treated, I submitted to my own exhaustion and hunger. I went home and collected a week's worth of mail from a neighbor. There was nothing to eat in the refrigerator, but on the door was a review from the *Times* of a restaurant that had just opened in the neighborhood and that I had yet to try. The light was flashing on my answering machine, but I could not turn it on, knowing the messages would be from my housemates. I called the man who drove Enzo in to tell him how much suffering he had saved Enzo from, exaggerating for the answering machine, which I was glad had answered for him. I turned my own off so that I couldn't receive any more messages and left my apartment with the mail I wanted to read.

Walking down a dark street of parking garages to the restaurant that had been reviewed, I saw a gold coin-shaped wrapper—the kind that chocolate dollars and condoms come in—embedded in the hot asphalt. Pop caps glittered in the street like an uncorked galaxy stuck in the tar.

Horst's prediction came true. While Horst was dying two years later, Perry was at an AIDS conference with his new little boyfriend. When confronted, he'd say, "Horst wanted me to go." Perry would include Horst's death notice with fund-raising appeals for the gay youth organization he volunteered for. Everyone who knows him learns to expect the worst from him. And Enzo would be right, also. A year or so later, he was diagnosed with KS, then with lymphoma.

The *Times* would eventually report more on the subject and still get things wrong. Not journalism as the first draft of history, but a rough draft, awkward and splintered and rude and premeditated. They will do a cover story on the decimation of talent in the fashion industry and never once mention that the designers, stylists, illustrators, show room assistants, makeup artists, or hairdressers were gay. How does one write about a battle and not give name to the dead, even if they are your enemy?

The dead were marching into our lives like an occupying army. Noah's defenses were weakening, but the illness did not threaten him personally. He was sero-negative and would stay that way. Even so, he had found himself in a standstill of pain, a silo of grief, which I myself had not entered, though I knew its door well. Perry thought of Samuel every time he saw me, and, in turn, probably thought of Horst. I suspected he saw his new boyfriend as a vaccine against loneliness and not as an indication that he had given up hope. We had found ourselves in an unacceptable world. And an unacceptable world can compel unacceptable behavior.

But that night, I turned around without my supper and went back home to listen to my messages. The first was from Horst, who would have been put up to call because he was the closest to me and the closest to death. "Clark, are you there? It's Horst," he said, as if I wouldn't have recognized his accent. "We want to know how Enzolina is. Please call. We love you."

For a long stretch of tape, there was only the sound of breathing, the click of the phone, over and over again. Perry's voice came next.

"I was very touched by your going into the hospital today and how you took care of Enzo last night. I want to tell you that now," he said, in a low voice. "I hope you understand that there was nothing to be done last night, and you were doing it. Sometimes I don't think Horst understands that the nights he is almost comatose that I am suffering beside him, fully conscious. I saw your face when Noah did not offer to drive Enzo in. I thought perhaps it was because they can't take the dog on the train, or because he had taken tomorrow off to spend with Joe. But I can't make any excuses for him. You are so morally strict sometimes, like an unforgiving mirror. Oh, let's see . . . Horst is feeling much better. Call us please."

Then Stark called to find out whether either Enzo or I needed anything, and told me when he would be home if I wanted to call. And then Joe. "Where are you, Clark? Oh, God, you should have seen Noah go berserk today when he took the garbage out and found maggots in the trash cans. He screamed, 'I can't live like this the rest of the summer.' He's been cleaning windows and rolling up rugs. She's been a real mess all day. Oh, God, now he's sweeping under the bed. I can't decide if I should calm him down or stay out of his way. The house should look nice when you get back."

Finally Noah called. "Clark, where are you, Superman? I have to tell you something. You know the novel you lent me to read? I accidentally threw it in the washing machine with my bedclothes. Please call."

My lover, Samuel, used to tell a story about himself. It was when he was first working with the Theater of the Deaf. The company had been improvising a new piece from an outline that Samuel had devised, when he said something that provoked a headstrong and violent young actor, deaf since birth. "I understand you," Samuel said in sign, attempting to silence him, if that's the word. The young actor's eyes became as wild as a horse caught in a burning barn; his arms flew this way and that, as if furious at his own imprecision. Samuel needed an interpreter. "You do not understand this," the actor was saying, pointing to his ears. "You will never understand."

You let go of people, the living and the dead, and return to your self, to your own resources, like a widower, a tourist alone in a foreign country. Your own senses become important, and other people's sensibilities a kind of Novocaine, blocking out your own perceptions, your ability to discriminate, your taste. There is something beyond understanding, and I do not know what it is, but as I carried the phone with me to the couch, a feeling of generosity came over me, of creature comforts having been satisfied well and in abundance, like more than enough to eat and an extra hour of sleep in the morning. Though I hadn't had either, I was in a position to anticipate them both. The time being seeps in through the senses: the plush of a green sofa; the music we listen to when we attempt to forgive ourselves our excesses; the crazing pattern on the ginger jar that reminds us of why we bought it in the first place, not to mention the shape it holds, the blessing of smells it releases. The stretch of time and the vortex that it spins around, thinning and thickening like taffy, holds these pleasures, these grace notes, these connections to others, to what it is humanly possible to do.

1990

EIGHT

The Fabulous

The stories in this chapter belong to an ancient lineage that includes religious myths, fairy tales, gothic narratives, and ghost stories. They all contain elements of myth or magic, differing only in degree, from slightly eerie to out-and-out surreal. These stories allow us to cross the chasm that separates us from those realms that our prosaic, quotidian, everyday world denies.

In Bernard Malamud's "Angel Levine," the reader, just like the protagonist, has to confront the problem of belief. Although the suffering that Manischevitz undergoes imposes the desire to believe, he is unable to have faith that a black man—who looks like "a case worker from the Welfare Department"—could be a Jewish angel, come in answer to his prayers. His eyes can see only what they are used to seeing: "he had been expecting something, but not this."

Edith Wharton also includes an otherworldly visitor in her classic ghost story, "Afterward," and Sarah Orne Jewett derives "The Landscape Chamber" from the gothic tradition, tailoring the form to suit her own ends. These two stories are outriders from the unconscious badlands, able to give us access to that which is usually suppressed. In fact, the gothic and the ghost story, which enact the same repressed desires and conflicts that wreak havoc in our unconscious, are fertile ground for psychoanalytic criticism.

The stories in this chapter also reveal to us the irrational, so often restrained by the cause-effect logic that characterizes Western thought. Franz Kafka felt compelled to write tales of transformation in which animals become human, humans become insects, nightmares become real. In "A Report to an Academy," an ape has changed himself into a man through education and training, but he is still able to recall the chasm he has bridged: "Of course what I felt then as an ape I can represent now only in human terms, and therefore I misrepresent it, but although I cannot reach back to the truth of the old ape life, there is no doubt that it lies somewhere in the direction I have indicated." Nathaniel Hawthorne also takes on the subject of transformations in "Drowne's Wooden Image," a creation story in which a carver infuses life (or does he?) into one of his wooden subjects.

The final two stories present characters who are best described as mysterious presences, but one is benign, the other deadly. Herman Melville's Bartleby in "Bartleby, the Scrivener" is bafflingly opaque, withdrawing from life and refusing each task, each meal, each overture with the response "I prefer not to." In John Cheever's "Torch Song," however, Joan, who seems at first "innocently and incorrigibly convivial," is eventually seen as a "lewd and searching shape," a seeker after death; when she finally turns her solicitous attention to the narrator, he knows he is doomed.

Our waking world is very different from our sleeping world in which we sometimes dream and sometimes suffer nightmares, in which we encounter devils or angels, the quick, the dead, the not-quite-human—at least as far as we remember—only infrequently. But this chapter, "The Fabulous," rescues stories from the dreamscapes that lie somewhere across the chasm, somewhere in the far distance, somewhere these writers return us to.

BERNARD MALAMUD

Angel Levine

Manischevitz, a tailor, in his fifty-first year suffered many reverses and indignities. Previously a man of comfortable means, he overnight lost all he had, when his establishment caught fire, after a metal container of cleaning fluid exploded, and burned to the ground. Although Manischevitz was insured against fire, damage suits by two customers who had been hurt in the flames deprived him of every penny he had saved. At almost the same time, his son, of much promise, was killed in the war, and his daughter, without so much as a word of warning, married a lout and disappeared with him as off the face of the earth. Thereafter Manischevitz was victimized by excruciating backaches and found himself unable to work even as a presser—the only kind of work available to him—for more than an hour or two daily, because beyond that the pain from standing was maddening. His Fanny, a good wife and mother, who had taken in washing and sewing, began before his eyes to waste away. Suffering shortness of breath, she at last became seriously ill and took to her bed. The doctor, a former customer of

Bernard Malamud was born in 1914 in Brooklyn, New York, where he spent his childhood. The son of Russian Jews, Malamud granted a compassionate voice to the experiences of European oppression and immigrant life in his well-wrought parables and novels. The author of such different fiction as *The Natural* (1952) and *The Fixer* (1966) and the recipient of both a Pulitzer Prize and two National Book Awards, Malamud is frequently ranked as one of the top American writers. From 1961 he taught English and writing at Bennington College, Vermont. Malamud died in New York in 1986, just short of his seventy-second birthday.

Manischevitz, who out of pity treated them, at first had difficulty diagnosing her ailment, but later put it down as hardening of the arteries at an advanced age. He took Manischevitz aside, prescribed complete rest for her, and in whispers gave him to know there was little hope.

Throughout his trials Manischevitz had remained somewhat stoic, almost unbelieving that all this had descended on his head, as if it were happening, let us say, to an acquaintance or some distant relative; it was in sheer quantity of woe, incomprehensible. It was also ridiculous, unjust, and because he had always been a religious man, an affront to God. Manischevitz believed this in all his suffering. When his burden had grown too crushingly heavy to be borne he prayed in his chair with shut hollow eyes: "My dear God, sweetheart, did I deserve that this should happen to me?" Then recognizing the worthlessness of it, he set aside the complaint and prayed humbly for assistance: "Give Fanny back her health, and to me for myself that I shouldn't feel pain in every step. Help now or tomorrow is too late." And Manischevitz wept.

Manischevitz's flat, which he had moved into after the disastrous fire, was a meager one, furnished with a few sticks of chairs, a table, and bed, in one of the poorer sections of the city. There were three rooms: a small, poorly papered living room; an apology for a kitchen with a wooden icebox; and the comparatively large bedroom where Fanny lay in a sagging secondhand bed, gasping for breath. The bedroom was the warmest room in the house and it was here, after his outburst to God, that Manischevitz, by the light of two small bulbs overhead, sat reading his Jewish newspaper. He was not truly reading because his thoughts were everywhere; however the print offered a convenient resting place for his eyes, and a word or two, when he permitted himself to comprehend them, had the momentary effect of helping him forget his troubles. After a short while he discovered, to his surprise, that he was actively scanning the news, searching for an item of great interest to him. Exactly what he thought he would read he couldn't say—until he realized, with some astonishment, that he was expecting to discover something about himself. Manischevitz put his paper down and looked up with the distinct impression that someone had come into the apartment, though he could not remember having heard the sound of the door opening. He looked around: the room was very still, Fanny sleeping, for once, quietly. Half frightened, he watched her until he was satisfied she wasn't dead; then, still disturbed by the thought of an unannounced visitor, he stumbled into the living room and there had the shock of his life, for at the table sat a black man reading a newspaper he had folded up to fit into one hand.

"What do you want here?" Manischevitz asked in fright.

The Negro put down the paper and glanced up with a gentle expression. "Good evening." He seemed not to be sure of himself, as if he had got into the wrong house. He was a large man, bonily built, with a heavy head covered by a hard derby, which he made no attempt to remove. His eyes seemed sad, but his lips, above which he wore a slight mustache, sought to smile; he was not otherwise prepossessing. The cuffs of his sleeves, Manischevitz noted, were frayed to the lining, and the dark suit was badly fitted. He had very large feet. Recovering from his fright, Manischevitz guessed he had left the door open and was being visited by a case worker from the Welfare Department—some came at night—for he had recently applied for welfare. Therefore he lowered himself into a chair opposite the Negro, trying, before the man's uncertain smile, to feel comfortable. The former tailor sat stiffly but patiently at the table, waiting for the investigator to take out his pad and pencil and begin asking questions; but before long he became convinced the man intended to do nothing of the sort.

"Who are you?" Manischevitz at last asked uneasily.

"If I may, insofar as one is able to, identify myself, I bear the name of Alexander Levine."

In spite of his troubles, Manischevitz felt a smile growing on his lips. "You said Levine?" he politely inquired.

The Negro nodded. "That is exactly right."

Carrying the jest further, Manischevitz asked, "You are maybe Jewish?"

"All my life I was, willingly."

The tailor hesitated. He had heard of black Jews but had never met one. It gave an unusual sensation.

Recognizing in afterthought something odd about the tense of Levine's remark, he said doubtfully, "You ain't Jewish any more?"

Levine at this point removed his hat, revealing a white part in his black hair, but quickly replaced it. He replied, "I have recently been disincarnated into an angel. As such, I offer you my humble assistance, if to offer is within my province and power—in the best sense." He lowered his eyes in apology. "Which calls for added explanation: I am what I am granted to be, and at present the completion is in the future."

"What kind of angel is this?" Manischevitz gravely asked.

"A bona fide angel of God, within prescribed limitations," answered Levine, "not to be confused with the members of any particular sect, order, or organization here on earth operating under a similar name."

Manischevitz was thoroughly disturbed. He had been expecting something, but not this. What sort of mockery was it—provided that Levine was an angel—of a faithful servant who had from childhood lived in the synagogues, concerned with the word of God?

To test Levine he asked, "Then where are your wings?"

The Negro blushed as well as he could. Manischevitz understood this from his altered expression. "Under certain circumstances we lose privileges and prerogatives upon returning to earth, no matter for what purpose or endeavoring to assist whomsoever."

"So tell me," Manischevitz said triumphantly, "how did you get here?"

"I was translated."

Still troubled, the tailor said, "If you are a Jew, say the blessing for bread."

Levine recited it in sonorous Hebrew.

Although moved by the familiar words Manischevitz still felt doubt he was dealing with an angel.

"If you are an angel," he demanded somewhat angrily, "give me the proof."

Levine wet his lips. "Frankly, I cannot perform either miracles or near-miracles, due to the fact that I am in a condition of probation. How long that will persist or even consist depends on the outcome."

Manischevitz racked his brains for some means of causing Levine positively to reveal his true identity, when the Negro spoke again:

"It was given me to understand that both your wife and you require assistance of a salubrious nature?"

The tailor could not rid himself of the feeling that he was the butt of a jokester. Is this what a Jewish angel looks like? he asked himself. This I am not convinced.

He asked a last question. "So if God sends to me an angel, why a black? Why not a white that there are so many of them?"

"It was my turn to go next," Levine explained.

Manischevitz could not be persuaded. "I think you are a faker."

Levine slowly rose. His eyes indicated disappointment and worry. "Mr. Manischevitz," he said tonelessly, "if you should desire me to be of assistance to you any time in the near future, or possibly before, I can be found"—he glanced at his fingernails—"in Harlem."

He was by then gone.

The next day Manischevitz felt some relief from his backache and was able to work four hours at pressing. The day after, he put in six hours; and the third day four again. Fanny sat up a little and asked for some halvah to suck. But after the fourth day the stabbing, breaking ache afflicted his back, and Fanny again lay supine, breathing with blue-lipped difficulty.

Manischevitz was profoundly disappointed at the return of his active pain and suffering. He had hoped for a longer interval of easement, long enough to have a thought other than of himself and his troubles. Day by day, minute after minute, he lived in pain, pain his only memory, questioning the necessity of it, inveighing, though with affection, against God. Why *so much*, Gottenyu? If He wanted to teach His servant a lesson for some reason, some cause—the nature of His nature—to teach him, say, for reasons of his weakness, his pride, perhaps, during his years of prosperity, his frequent neglect of God—to give him a little lesson, why then any of the tragedies that had happened to him, any *one* would have sufficed to chasten him. But *all together*—the loss of both his children, his means of livelihood, Fanny's health and his—that was too much to ask one frail-boned man to endure. Who, after all, was Manischevitz that he had been given so much to suffer? A tailor. Certainly not a man of talent. Upon him suffering was largely wasted. It went nowhere, into nothing: into more suffering. His pain did not earn him bread, nor fill the cracks in the wall, nor lift, in the middle of the night, the kitchen table; only lay upon him, sleepless, so sharply oppressive that he could many times have cried out yet not heard himself this misery.

In this mood he gave no thought to Mr. Alexander Levine, but at moments when the pain wavered, slightly diminishing, he sometimes wondered if he had been mistaken to dismiss him. A black Jew and angel to boot—very hard to believe, but suppose he had been sent to succor him, and he, Manischevitz, was in his blindness too blind to understand? It was this thought that put him on the knife-point of agony.

Therefore the tailor, after much self-questioning and continuing doubt, decided he would seek the self-styled angel in Harlem. Of course he had great difficulty because he had not asked for specific directions, and movement was tedious to him. The subway took him to 116th Street, and from there he wandered in the open dark world. It was vast and its lights lit nothing. Everywhere were shadows, often moving. Manischevitz hobbled along with the aid of a cane, and not knowing where to seek in the blackened tenement buildings, would look fruitlessly through store windows. In the stores he saw people and everybody was black. It was an amazing thing to observe. When he was too tired, too unhappy to go farther, Manischevitz stopped in front of a tailor's shop. Out of familiarity with the appearance of it, with some sadness he entered. The tailor, an old skinny man with a mop of woolly gray hair, was sitting cross-legged on his workbench, sewing a pair of tuxedo pants that had a razor slit all the way down the seat.

"You'll excuse me, please, gentleman," said Manischevitz, admiring the tailor's deft thimbled fingerwork, "but you know maybe somebody by the name Alexander Levine?"

The tailor, who, Manischevitz thought, seemed a little antagonistic to him, scratched his scalp.

"Cain't say I ever heared dat name."

"Alex-ander Lev-ine," Manischevitz repeated it.

The man shook his head. "Cain't say I heared."

Manischevitz remembered to say: "He is an angel, maybe."

"Oh *him*," said the tailor, clucking. "He hang out in dat honky-tonk down here a ways." He pointed with his skinny finger and returned to sewing the pants.

Manischevitz crossed the street against a red light and was almost run down by a taxi. On the block after the next, the sixth store from the corner was a cabaret, and the name in sparkling lights was Bella's. Ashamed to go in, Manischevitz gazed through the neon-lit window, and when the dancing couples had parted and drifted away, he discovered at a table on the side, toward the rear, Alexander Levine.

He was sitting alone, a cigarette butt hanging from the corner of his mouth, playing solitaire with a dirty pack of cards, and Manischevitz felt a touch of pity for him, because Levine had deteriorated in appearance. His derby hat was dented and had a gray smudge. His ill-fitting suit was shabbier, as if he had been sleeping in it. His shoes and trouser cuffs were muddy, and his face covered with an impenetrable stubble the color of licorice. Manischevitz, though deeply disappointed, was about to enter, when a big-breasted Negress in a purple evening gown appeared before Levine's table, and with much laughter through many white teeth, broke into a vigorous shimmy. Levine looked at Manischevitz with a haunted expression, but the tailor was too paralyzed to move or acknowledge it. As Bella's gyrations continued Levine rose, his eyes lit in excitement. She embraced him with vigor, both his hands clasped around her restless buttocks, and they tangoed together across the floor, loudly applauded by the customers. She seemed to have lifted Levine off his feet and his large shoes hung limp as they danced. They slid past the windows where Manischevitz, white-faced, stood staring in. Levine winked slyly and the tailor left for home.

Fanny lay at death's door. Through shrunken lips she muttered concerning her childhood, the sorrows of the marriage bed, the loss of her children; yet wept to live. Manischevitz tried not to listen, but even without ears he would have heard. It was not a gift. The doctor panted up the stairs, a broad but bland, unshaven man (it was Sunday), and soon shook his head. A day at most, or two. He left at once to spare himself Manischevitz's multiplied sorrow; the man who never stopped hurting. He would someday get him into a public home.

Manischevitz visited a synagogue and there spoke to God, but God had absented himself. The tailor searched his heart and found no hope. When she died, he would live dead. He considered taking his life although he knew he wouldn't. Yet it was something to consider. Considering, you existed. He railed against God—Can you love a rock, a broom, an emptiness? Baring his chest, he smote the naked bones, cursing himself for having, beyond belief, believed.

Asleep in a chair that afternoon, he dreamed of Levine. He was standing before a faded mirror, preening small decaying opalescent wings. "This means," mumbled Manischevitz, as he broke out of sleep, "that it is possible he could be an angel." Begging a neighbor lady to look in on Fanny and occasionally wet her lips with water, he drew on his thin coat, gripped his walking stick, exchanged some pennies for a subway token, and rode to Harlem. He knew this act was the last desperate one of his woe: to go seeking a black magician to restore his wife to invalidism. Yet if there was no choice, he did at least what was chosen.

He hobbled to Bella's, but the place seemed to have changed hands. It was now, as he breathed, a synagogue in a store. In the front, toward him, were several rows of empty wooden benches. In the rear stood the Ark, its portals of rough wood covered with rainbows of sequins; under it a long table on which lay the sacred scroll unrolled, illuminated by the dim light from a bulb on a chain overhead. Around the table, as if frozen to it and the scroll, which they all touched with their fingers, sat four Negroes wearing skullcaps. Now as they read the Holy Word, Manischevitz could, through the plate-glass window, hear the singsong chant of their voices. One of them was old, with a gray beard. One was bubble-eyed. One was humpbacked. The fourth was a boy, no older than thirteen. Their heads moved in rhythmic swaying. Touched by this sight from his childhood and youth, Manischevitz entered and stood silent in the rear.

"Neshoma," said bubble eyes, pointing to the word with a stubby finger. "Now what dat mean?"

"That's the word that means soul," said the boy. He wore eyeglasses.

"Let's git on wid de commentary," said the old man.

"Ain't necessary," said the humpback. "Souls is immaterial

substance. That's all. The soul is derived in that manner. The immateriality is derived from the substance, and they both, causally an' otherwise, derived from the soul. There can be no higher."

"That's the highest."

"Over de top."

"Wait a minute," said bubble eyes. "I don't see what is dat immaterial substance. How come de one gits hitched up to de odder?" He addressed the humpback.

"Ask me somethin' hard. Because it is substanceless immateriality. It couldn't be closer together, like all the parts of the body under one skin—closer."

"Hear now," said the old man.

"All you done is switched de words."

"It's the premium mobile, the substanceless substance from which comes all things that were incepted in the idea—you, me, and everything and -body else."

"Now how did all dat happen? Make it sound simple."

"It de speerit," said the old man. "On de face of de water moved de speerit. An' dat was good. It say so in de Book. From de speerit ariz de man."

"But now listen here. How come it become substance if it all de time a spirit?"

"God alone done dat."

"Holy! Holy! Praise His Name."

"But has dis spirit got some kind of a shade or color?" asked bubble eyes, deadpan.

"Man, of course not. A spirit is a spirit."

"Then how come we is colored?" he said with a triumphant glare.

"Ain't got nothing to do wid dat."

"I still like to know."

"God put the spirit in all things," answered the boy. "He put it in the green leaves and the yellow flowers. He put it with the gold in the fishes and the blue in the sky. That's how come it came to us."

"Amen."

"Praise Lawd and utter loud His speechless Name."

"Blow de bugle till it bust the sky."

They fell silent, intent upon the next word. Manischevitz, with doubt, approached them.

"You'll excuse me," he said. "I am looking for Alexander Levine. You know him maybe?"

"That's the angel," said the boy.

"Oh *him*," snuffed bubble eyes.

"You'll find him at Bella's. It's the establishment right down the street," the humpback said.

Manischevitz said he was sorry that he could not stay, thanked them, and limped across the street. It was already night. The city was dark and he could barely find his way.

But Bella's was bursting with jazz and the blues. Through the window Manischevitz recognized the dancing crowd and among them sought Levine. He was sitting loose-lipped at Bella's side table. They were tippling from an almost empty whiskey fifth. Levine had shed his old clothes, wore a shiny new checkered suit, pearl-gray derby hat, cigar, and big, two-tone, button shoes. To the tailor's dismay, a drunken look had settled upon his formerly dignified face. He leaned toward Bella, tickled her earlobe with his pinky while whispering words that sent her into gales of raucous laughter. She fondled his knee.

Manischevitz, girding himself, pushed open the door and was not welcomed.

"This place reserved."

"Beat it, pale puss."

"Exit, Yankel, semitic trash."

But he moved toward the table where Levine sat, the crowd breaking before him as he hobbled forward.

"Mr. Levine," he spoke in a trembly voice. "Is here Manischevitz."

Levine glared blearily. "Speak yo' piece, son."

Manischevitz shivered. His back plagued him. Tremors tormented his legs. He looked around, everybody was all ears.

"You'll excuse me. I would like to talk to you in a private place."

"Speak, Ah is a private pusson."

Bella laughed piercingly. "Stop it, boy, you killin' me."

Manischevitz, no end disturbed, considered fleeing but Levine addressed him:

"Kindly state the pu'pose of yo' communication with yo's truly."

The tailor wet cracked lips. "You are Jewish. This I am sure."

Levine rose, nostrils flaring. "Anythin' else yo' got to say?"

Manischevitz's tongue lay like a slab of stone.

"Speak now or fo'ever hold off."

Tears blinded the tailor's eyes. Was ever man so tried? Should he say he believed a half-drunk Negro was an angel?

The silence slowly petrified.

Manischevitz was recalling scenes of his youth as a wheel in his mind whirred: believe, do not, yes, no, yes, no. The pointer pointed to yes, to between yes and no, to no, no it was yes. He sighed. It moved but one still had to make a choice.

"I think you are an angel from God." He said it in a broken voice, thinking, If you said it it was said. If you believed it you must say it. If you believed, you believed.

The hush broke. Everybody talked but the music began and they went on dancing. Bella, grown bored, picked up the cards and dealt herself a hand.

Levine burst into tears. "How you have humiliated me."

Manischevitz apologized.

"Wait'll I freshen up." Levine went to the men's room and returned in his old suit.

No one said goodbye as they left.

They rode to the flat via subway. As they walked up the stairs Manischevitz pointed with his cane at his door.

"That's all been taken care of," Levine said. "You go in while I take off."

Disappointed that it was so soon over, but torn by curiosity, Manischevitz followed the angel up three flights to the roof. When he got there the door was already padlocked.

Luckily he could see through a small broken window. He heard an odd noise, as though of a whirring of wings, and when he strained for a wider view, could have sworn he saw a dark figure borne aloft on a pair of strong black wings.

A feather drifted down. Manischevitz gasped as it turned white, but it was only snowing.

He rushed downstairs. In the flat Fanny wielded a dust mop under the bed, and then upon the cobwebs on the wall.

"A wonderful thing, Fanny," Manischevitz said. "Believe me, there are Jews everywhere."

1955

EDITH WHARTON

Afterward

"Oh, there *is* one, of course, but you'll never know it."

The assertion, laughingly flung out six months earlier in a bright June garden, came back to Mary Boyne with a new perception of its significance as she stood, in the December dusk, waiting for the lamps to be brought into the library.

The words had been spoken by their friend Alida Stair, as they sat at tea on her lawn at Pangbourne, in reference to the very house of which the library in question was the central, the pivotal "feature." Mary Boyne and her husband, in quest of a country place in one of the southern or southwestern counties, had, on their arrival in England, carried their problem straight to Alida Stair, who had successfully solved it in her own case; but it was not until they had rejected, almost capriciously, several practical and judicious suggestions that she threw out: "Well, there's Lyng, in Dorsetshire. It belongs to Hugo's cousins, and you can get it for a song."

The reason she gave for its being obtainable on these terms—its remoteness from a station, its lack of electric light, hot water pipes, and other vulgar necessities—were exactly those pleading in its favor with two romantic Americans perversely in search of the economic drawbacks which were associated, in their tradition, with unusual architectural felicities.

"I should never believe I was living in an old house unless I was thoroughly uncomfortable," Ned Boyne, the more extravagant of the two, had jocosely insisted; "the least hint of convenience would make me think it had been bought out of an exhibition, with the pieces numbered, and set up again." And they had proceeded to enumerate, with humorous precision, their various doubts and demands, refusing

Edith Wharton was born in 1862 in New York City. Like her major literary model, Henry James, Wharton was raised in a prominent upper-class family. It is this socioeconomic environment and its inhabitants that would eventually populate her stories and novels, among them *The House of Mirth* (1905) and the Pulitzer Prize–winning *The Age of Innocence* (1920). After 1907 Wharton lived almost exclusively in France, where she crafted novels comparing the American and European cultures. Wharton's adopted homeland awarded her the Legion of Honor for her relief work during the First World War. She died in St.-Brice-sous-Forêt, France, in 1937.

to believe that the house their cousin recommended was *really* Tudor
till they learned it had no heating system, or that the village church was
literally in the grounds till she assured them of the deplorable uncertainty of the water supply.

"It's too uncomfortable to be true!" Edward Boyne had continued
to exult as the avowal of each disadvantage was successively wrung
from her; but he had cut short his rhapsody to ask, with a relapse to
distrust: "And the ghost? You've been concealing from us the fact that
there is no ghost!"

Mary, at the moment, had laughed with him, yet almost with her
laugh, being possessed of several sets of independent perceptions, had
been struck by a note of flatness in Alida's answering hilarity.

"Oh, Dorsetshire's full of ghosts, you know."

"Yes, yes; but that won't do. I don't want to have to drive ten miles
to see somebody else's ghost. I want one of my own on the premises.
Is there a ghost at Lyng?"

His rejoinder had made Alida laugh again, and it was then that she
had flung back tantalizingly: "Oh, there *is* one, of course, but you'll
never know it."

"Never know it?" Boyne pulled her up. "But what in the world
constitutes a ghost except the fact of it being known for one?"

"I can't say. But that's the story."

"That there's a ghost, but that nobody knows it's a ghost?"

"Well—not till afterward, at any rate."

"Till afterward?"

"Not till long long afterward."

"But if it's once been identified as an unearthly visitant, why hasn't
it *signalement* been handed down in the family? How has it managed to
preserve its incognito?"

Alida could only shake her head. "Don't ask me. But it has."

"And then suddenly"—Mary spoke up as if from cavernous depths
of divination—"suddenly, long afterward, one says to one's self '*That
was it?*'"

She was startled at the sepulchral sound with which her question
fell on the banter of the other two, and she saw the shadow of the same
surprise flit across Alida's pupils. "I suppose so. One just has to wait."

"Oh, hang waiting!" Ned broke in. "Life's too short for a ghost who
can only be enjoyed in retrospect. Can't we do better than that, Mary?"

But it turned out that in the event they were not destined to, for
within three months of their conversation with Mrs. Stair they were
settled at Lyng, and the life they had yearned for, to the point of planning
it in advance in all its daily details, had actually begun for them.

It was to sit, in the thick December dusk, by just such a wide-hooded fireplace, under just such black oak rafters, with the sense that beyond the mullioned panes the downs were darkened to a deeper solitude: it was for the ultimate indulgence of such sensations that Mary Boyne, abruptly exiled from New York by her husband's business, had endured for nearly fourteen years the soul-deadening ugliness of a Middle Western town, and that Boyne had ground on doggedly at his engineering till, with a suddenness that still made her blink, the prodigious windfall of the Blue Star Mine had put them at a stroke in possession of life and the leisure to taste it. They had never for a moment meant their new state to be one of idleness; but they meant to give themselves only to harmonious activities. She had her vision of painting and gardening (against a background of grey walls), he dreamed of the production of his long-planned book on the "Economic Basis of Culture"; and with such absorbing work ahead no existence could be too sequestered: they could not get far enough from the world, or plunge deep enough into the past.

Dorsetshire had attracted them from the first by an air of remoteness out of all proportion to its geographical position. But to the Boynes it was one of the ever-recurring wonders of the whole incredibly compressed island—a nest of counties, as they put it—that for the production of its effects so little of a given quality went so far: that so few miles made a distance, and so short a distance a difference.

"It's that," Ned had once enthusiastically explained, "that gives such depth to their effects, such relief to their contrasts. They've been able to lay the butter so thick on every delicious mouthful."

The butter had certainly been laid on thick at Lyng: the old house hidden under a shoulder of the downs had almost all the finer marks of commerce with a protracted past. The mere fact that it was neither large nor exceptional made it, to the Boynes, abound the more completely in its special charm—the charm of having been for centuries a deep dim reservoir of life. The life had probably not been of the most vivid order: for long periods, no doubt, it had fallen as noiselessly into the past as the quiet drizzle of autumn fell, hour after hour, into the fish pond between the yews; but these backwaters of existence sometimes breed, in their sluggish depths, strange acuities of emotion, and Mary Boyne had felt from the first the mysterious stir of intenser memories.

The feeling had never been stronger than on this particular afternoon when, waiting in the library for the lamps to come, she rose from her seat and stood among the shadows of the hearth. Her husband had gone off, after luncheon, for one of his long tramps on the downs. She had noticed of late that he preferred to go alone; and, in the tried security of their personal relations, had been driven to conclude that his book was bothering him, and that he needed the afternoons to turn over in solitude the problems left from the morning's work. Certainly the book was not going as smoothly as she had thought it would, and there were lines of perplexity between his eyes such as had never been there in his engineering days. He had often, then, looked fagged to the verge of illness, but the native demon of worry had never branded his brow. Yet the few pages he had so far read to her—the introduction, and a summary of the opening chapter—showed a firm hold on his subject, and an increasing confidence in his powers.

The fact threw her into deeper perplexity, since, now that he had done with business and its disturbing contingencies, the one other possible source of anxiety was eliminated. Unless it were his health, then? But physically he had gained since they had come to Dorsetshire, grown robuster, ruddier, and fresher eyed. It was only within the last week that she had felt in him the undefinable change which made her restless in his absence, and as tongue-tied in his presence as though it were *she* who had a secret to keep from him!

The thought that there *was* a secret somewhere between them struck her with a sudden rap of wonder, and she looked about her down the long room.

"Can it be the house?" she mused.

The room itself might have been full of secrets. They seemed to be piling themselves up, as evening fell, like the layers and layers of velvet shadow dropping from the low ceiling, the rows of books, the smoke-blurred sculpture of the hearth.

"Why, of course—the house is haunted!" she reflected.

The ghost—Alida's imperceptible ghost—after figuring largely in the banter of their first month or two at Lyng, had been gradually left aside as too ineffectual for imaginative use. Mary had, indeed, as became the tenant of a haunted house, made the customary inquiries among her rural neighbors, but, beyond a vague "They do say so, Ma'am," the villagers had nothing to impart. The elusive specter had apparently never had sufficient identity for a legend to crystallize about it, and after a time the Boynes had set the matter down to their profit-and-loss account, agreeing that Lyng was one of the few houses good enough in itself to dispense with supernatural enhancements.

"And I suppose, poor ineffectual demon, that's why it beats its beautiful wings in vain in the void," Mary had laughingly concluded.

"Or, rather," Ned answered in the same strain, "why, amid so much that's ghostly, it can never affirm its separate existence as *the* ghost." And thereupon their invisible housemate had finally dropped out of their references, which were numerous enough to make them soon unaware of the loss.

Now, as she stood on the hearth, the subject of their earlier curiosity revived in her with a new sense of its meaning—a sense gradually acquired through daily contact with the scene of the lurking mystery. It was the house itself, of course, that possessed the ghost-seeing faculty, that communed visually but secretly with its own past; if one could only get into close enough communion with the house, one might surprise its secret, and acquire the ghost sight on one's own account. Perhaps, in his long hours in this very room, where she never trespassed till the afternoon, her husband *had* acquired it already, and was silently carrying about the weight of whatever it had revealed to him. Mary was too well versed in the code of the spectral world not to know that one could not talk about the ghosts one saw: to do so was almost as great a breach of taste as to name a lady in a club. But this explanation did not really satisfy her. "What, after all, except for the fun of the shudder," she reflected, "would he really care for any of their old ghosts?" And thence she was thrown back once more on the fundamental dilemma: the fact that one's greater or less susceptibility to spectral influences had no particular bearing on the case, since, when one *did* see a ghost at Lyng, one did not know it.

"Not till long afterward," Alida Stair had said. Well, supposing Ned *had* seen one when they first came, and had known only within the last week what had happened to him? More and more under the spell of the hour, she threw back her thoughts to the early days of their tenancy, but at first only to recall a lively confusion of unpacking, settling, arranging of books, and calling to each other from remote corners of the house as, treasure after treasure, it revealed itself to them. It was in this particular connection that she presently recalled a certain soft afternoon of the previous October, when, passing from the first rapturous flurry of exploration to a detailed inspection of the old house, she had pressed (like a novel heroine) a panel that opened on a flight of corkscrew stairs leading to a flat ledge of the roof—the roof which, from below, seemed to slope away on all sides too abruptly for any but practiced feet to scale.

The view from this hidden coign was enchanting, and she had flown down to snatch Ned from his papers and give him the freedom of her discovery. She remembered still how, standing at her side, he had passed his arm about her while their gaze flew to the long tossed horizon line of the downs, and then dropped contentedly back to trace the arabesque of yew hedges about the fish pond, and the shadow of the cedar on the lawn.

"And now the other way," he had said, turning her about within his arm; and closely pressed to him, she had absorbed, like some satisfying draught, the picture of the grey-walled court, the squat lions on the gates, and the lime avenue reaching up to the highroad under the downs.

It was just then, while they gazed and held each other, that she had felt his arm relax, and heard a sharp "Hullo!" that made her turn to glance at him.

Distinctly, yes, she now recalled that she had seen, as she glanced, a shadow of anxiety, of perplexity, rather, fall across his face; and, following his eyes, had beheld the figure of a man—a man in loose greyish clothes, as it appeared to her—who was sauntering down the lime avenue to the court with the doubtful gait of a stranger who seeks his way. Her shortsighted eyes had given her but a blurred impression of slightness and greyishness, with something foreign, or at least unlocal, in the cut of the figure or its dress; but her husband had apparently seen more—seen enough to make him push past her with a hasty "Wait!" and dash down the stairs without pausing to give her a hand.

A slight tendency to dizziness obliged her, after a provisional clutch at the chimney against which they had been leaning, to follow him first more cautiously; and when she had reached the landing she paused again, for a less definite reason, leaning over the banister to strain her eyes through the silence of the brown sun-flecked depths. She lingered there till, somewhere in those depths, she heard the closing of a door; then, mechanically impelled, she went down the shallow flights of steps till she reached the lower hall.

The front door stood open on the sunlight of the court, and hall and court were empty. The library door was open, too, and after listening in vain for any sound of voices within, she crossed the threshold, and found her husband alone, vaguely fingering the papers on his desk.

He looked up, as if surprised at her entrance, but the shadow of anxiety had passed from his face, leaving it even, as she fancied, a little brighter and clearer than usual.

"What was it? Who was it?" she asked.

"Who?" he repeated, with the surprise still all on his side.

"The man we saw coming toward the house."

He seemed to reflect. "The man? Why, I thought I saw Peters; I dashed after him to say a word about the stable drains, but he had disappeared before I could get down."

"Disappeared? But he seemed to be walking so slowly when we saw him."

Boyne shrugged his shoulders. "So I thought; but he must have got up steam in the interval. What do you say to our trying a scramble up Meldon Steep before sunset?"

That was all. At the time the occurrence had been less than nothing, had, indeed, been immediately obliterated by the magic of their first vision from Meldon Steep, a height which they had dreamed of climbing ever since they had first seen its bare spine rising above the roof of Lyng. Doubtless it was the mere fact of the other incident's having occurred on the very day of their ascent to Meldon that had kept it stored away in the fold of memory from which it now emerged; for in itself it had no mark of the portentous. At the moment there could have been nothing more natural than that Ned should dash himself from the roof in the pursuit of dilatory tradesmen. It was the period when they were always on the watch for one or the other of the specialists employed about the place; always lying in wait for them, and rushing out at them with questions, reproaches, or reminders. And certainly in the distance the grey figure had looked like Peters.

Yet now, as she reviewed the scene, she felt her husband's explanation of it to have been invalidated by the look of anxiety on his face. Why had the familiar appearance of Peters made him anxious? Why, above all, if it was of such prime necessity to confer with him on the subject of the stable drains, had the failure to find him produced such a look of relief? Mary could not say that any one of these questions had occurred to her at the time, yet, from the promptness with which they now marshalled themselves at her summons, she had a sense that they must all along have been there, waiting their hour.

II

Weary with her thoughts, she moved to the window. The library was now quite dark, and she was surprised to see how much faint light the outer world still held.

As she peered out into it across the court, a figure shaped itself far down the perspective of bare limes: it looked a mere blot of deeper grey in the greyness, and for an instant, as it moved toward her, her heart thumped to the thought "It's the ghost!"

She had time, in that long instant, to feel suddenly that the man of whom, two months earlier, she had had a distant vision from the roof, was now, at his predestined hour, about to reveal himself as *not* having been Peters; and her spirit sank under the impending fear of the disclosure. But almost with the next tick of the clock the figure, gaining substance and character, showed itself even to her weak sight as her husband's; and she turned to meet him, as he entered, with the confession of her folly.

"It's really too absurd," she laughed out, "but I never *can* remember!"

"Remember what?" Boyne questioned as they drew together.

"That when one sees the Lyng ghost one never knows it."

Her hand was on his sleeve, and he kept it there, but with no response in his gesture or in the lines of his preoccupied face.

"Did you think you'd seen it?" he asked, after an appreciable interval.

"Why, I actually took *you* for it, my dear, in my mad determination to spot it!"

"Me—just now?" His arm dropped away, and he turned from her with a faint echo of her laugh. "Really, dearest, you'd better give it up, if that's the best you can do."

"Oh, yes, I give it up. Have *you?* she asked, turning round on him abruptly.

The parlormaid had entered with letters and a lamp, and the light struck up into Boyne's face as he bent above the tray she presented.

"Have *you?*" Mary perversely insisted, when the servant had disappeared on her errand of illumination.

"Have I what?" he rejoined absently, the light bringing out the sharp stamp of worry between his brows as he turned over the letters.

"Given up trying to see the ghost." Her heart beat a little at the experiment she was making.

Her husband, laying his letters aside, moved away into the shadow of the hearth.

"I never tried," he said, tearing open the wrapper of a newspaper.

"Well, of course," Mary persisted, "the exasperating thing is that there's no use trying, since one can't be sure till so long afterward."

He was unfolding the paper as if he had hardly heard her; but after a pause, during which the sheets rustled spasmodically between his hands, he looked up to ask, "Have you any idea *how long?*"

Mary had sunk into a low chair beside the fireplace. From her seat she glanced over, startled, at her husband's profile, which was projected against the circle of lamplight.

"No; none. Have *you?*" she retorted, repeating her former phrase with an added stress of intention.

Boyne crumpled the paper into a bunch, and then, inconsequently, turned back with it toward the lamp.

"Lord, no! I only meant," he exclaimed, with a faint tinge of impatience, "is there any legend, any tradition, as to that?"

"Not that I know of," she answered; but the impulse to add "What makes you ask?" was checked by the reappearance of the parlormaid, with tea and a second lamp.

With the dispersal of shadows, and the repetition of the daily domestic office, Mary Boyne felt herself less oppressed by that sense of something mutely imminent which had darkened her afternoon. For a few moments she gave herself to the details of her task, and when she looked up from it she was struck to the point of bewilderment by the change in her husband's face. He had seated himself near the farther lamp, and was absorbed in the perusal of his letters; but was it something he had found in them, or merely the shifting of her own point of view, that had restored his features to their normal aspect? The longer she looked the more definitely the change affirmed itself. The lines of tension had vanished, and such traces of fatigue as lingered were of the kind easily attributable to steady mental effort. He glanced up, as if drawn by her gaze, and met her eyes with a smile.

"I'm dying for my tea, you know; and here's a letter for you," he said.

She took the letter he held out in exchange for the cup she proffered him, and, returning to her seat, broke the seal with the languid gesture of the reader whose interests are all enclosed in the circle of one cherished presence.

Her next conscious motion was that of starting to her feet, the letter falling to them as she rose, while she held out to her husband a newspaper clipping.

"Ned! What's this? What does it mean?"

He had risen at the same instant, almost as if hearing her cry before she uttered it; and for a perceptible space of time he and she studied each other, like adversaries watching for an advantage, across the space between her chair and his desk.

"What's what? You fairly made me jump!" Boyne said at length, moving toward her with a sudden half-exasperated laugh. The shadow of apprehension was on his face again, not now a look of fixed foreboding, but a shifting vigilance of lips and eyes that gave her the sense of his feeling himself invisibly surrounded.

Her hand shook so that she could hardly give him the clipping.

"This article—from the *Waukesha Sentinel*—that a man named Elwell has brought suit against you—that there was something wrong about the Blue Star Mine. I can't understand more than half."

They continued to face each other as she spoke, and to her astonishment she saw that her words had the almost immediate effect of dissipating the strained watchfulness of his look.

"Oh, *that!*" He glanced down the printed slip, and then folded it with the gesture of one who handles something harmless and familiar. "What's the matter with you this afternoon, Mary? I thought you'd got bad news."

She stood before him with her undefinable terror subsiding slowly under the reassurance of his tone.

"You knew about this, then—it's all right?"

"Certainly I knew about it; and it's all right."

"But what *is* it? I don't understand. What does this man accuse you of?"

"Pretty nearly every crime in the calendar." Boyne had tossed the clipping down, and thrown himself into an armchair near the fire. "Do you want to hear the story? It's not particularly interesting—just a squabble over interests in the Blue Star."

"But who is this Elwell? I don't know the name."

"Oh, he's a fellow I put into it—gave him a hand up. I told you all about him at the time."

"I dare say. I must have forgotten." Vainly she strained back among her memories. "But if you helped him, why does he make this return?"

"Probably some shyster lawyer got hold of him and talked him over. It's all rather technical and complicated. I thought that kind of thing bored you."

His wife felt a sting of compunction. Theoretically, she deprecated the American wife's detachment from her husband's professional interests, but in practice she had always found it difficult to fix her attention on Boyne's report of the transactions in which his varied interests involved him. Besides, she had felt during their years of exile, that, in a community where the amenities of living could be obtained only at the cost of efforts as arduous as her husband's professional labors, such brief leisure as he and she could command should be used as an escape from immediate preoccupations, a flight to the life they always dreamed of living. Once or twice, now that this new life had actually drawn its magic circle about them, she had asked herself if she had done right; but hitherto such conjectures had been no more than the retrospective excursions of an active fancy. Now, for the first time, it startled her a little to find how little she knew of the material foundation on which her happiness was built.

She glanced at her husband, and was again reassured by the composure of his face; yet she felt the need of more definite grounds for her reassurance.

"But doesn't this suit worry you? Why have you never spoken to me about it?"

He answered both questions at once. "I didn't speak of it at first because it *did* worry me—annoyed me, rather. But it's all ancient history now. Your correspondent must have got hold of a back number of the *Sentinel*."

She felt a quick thrill of relief. "You mean it's over? He's lost his case?"

There was a just perceptible delay in Boyne's reply. "The suit's been withdrawn—that's all."

But she persisted, as if to exonerate herself from the inward charge of being too easily put off. "Withdrawn it because he saw he had no chance?"

"Oh, he had no chance," Boyne answered.

She was still struggling with a dimly felt perplexity at the back of her thoughts.

"How long ago was it withdrawn?"

He paused, as if with a slight return to his former uncertainty. "I've just had the news now; but I've been expecting it."

"Just now—in one of your letters?"

"Yes; in one of my letters."

She made no answer, and was aware only, after a short interval of waiting, that he had risen, and, strolling across the room, had placed himself on the sofa at her side. She felt him, as he did so, pass an arm about her, she felt his hand seek hers and clasp it, and turning slowly, drawn by the warmth of his cheek, she met his smiling eyes.

"It's all right—it's all right?" she questioned, through the flood of her dissolving doubts; and "I give you my word it was never righter!" he laughed back at her, holding her close.

III

One of the strangest things she was afterward to recall out of all the next day's strangeness was the sudden and complete recovery of her sense of security.

It was in the air when she woke in her low-ceiled, dusky room; it went with her downstairs to the breakfast table, flashed out at her from the fire, and reduplicated itself from the flanks of the urn and the sturdy flutings of the Georgian teapot. It was as if in some roundabout way, all her diffused fears of the previous day, with their moment of sharp concentration about the newspaper article—as if this dim questioning of the future, and startled return upon the past, had between them liquidated the arrears of some haunting moral obligation. If she had indeed been careless of her husband's affairs, it was, her new state seemed to prove, because her faith in him instinctively justified such carelessness; and his right to her faith had now affirmed itself in the very face of menace and suspicion. She had never seen him more untroubled, more naturally and unconsciously himself, than after the cross-examination to which she had subjected him: it was almost as if he had been aware of her doubts, and had wanted the air cleared as much as she did.

It was as clear, thank heaven, as the bright outer light that surprised her almost with a touch of summer when she issued from the house for her daily round of the gardens. She had left Boyne at his desk, indulging herself, as she passed the library door, by a last peep at his quiet face, where he bent, pipe in mouth, above his papers; and now she had her own morning's task to perform. The task involved, on such charmed winter days, almost as much happy loitering about the different quarters of her domain as if spring were already at work there. There were such endless possibilities still before her, such opportunities to bring out the latent graces of the old place, without a single irreverent touch of alteration, that the winter was all too short to plan what spring and autumn executed. And her recovered sense of safety gave, on this particular morning, a peculiar zest to her progress through the sweet still place. She went first to the kitchen garden, where the espaliered pear trees drew complicated patterns on the walls, and pigeons were fluttering and preening about the silvery-slated roof of their cot. There was something wrong about the piping of the hothouse, and she was expecting an authority from Dorchester, who was to drive out between trains and make a diagnosis of the boiler. But when she dipped into the damp heat of the greenhouses, among the spiced scents and waxy pinks and reds of old-fashioned exotics—even the flora of Lyng was in the note!—she learned that the great man had not arrived, and, the day being too rare to waste in an artificial atmosphere, she came out again and paced along the springy turf of the bowling green to the gardens behind the house. At their farther end rose a grass terrace, looking across the fish pond and yew hedges to the long house front with its twisted chimney stacks and blue roof angles all drenched in the pale gold moisture of the air.

Seen thus, across the level tracery of the gardens, it sent her, from open windows and hospitably smoking chimneys, the look of some warm human presence, of a mind slowly ripened on a sunny wall of experience. She had never before had such a sense of her intimacy with it, such a conviction that its secrets were all beneficent, kept, as they said to children, "for one's good," such a trust in its power to gather up her life and Ned's into the harmonious pattern of the long long story it sat there weaving in the sun.

She heard steps behind her, and turned, expecting to see the gardener accompanied by the engineer from Dorchester. But only one figure was in sight, that of a youngish slightly built man, who, for reasons she could not on the spot have given, did not remotely resemble her notion of an authority on hothouse boilers. The newcomer, on seeing her, lifted his hat, and paused with the air of a gentleman— perhaps a traveler—who wishes to make it known that his intrusion is involuntary. Lyng occasionally attracted the more cultivated traveler, and Mary half expected to see the stranger dissemble a camera, or justify his presence by producing it. But he made no gesture of any sort, and after a moment she asked, in a tone responding to the courteous hesitation of his attitude: "Is there anyone you wish to see?"

"I came to see Mr. Boyne," he answered. His intonation, rather than his accent, was faintly American, and Mary, at the note, looked at him more closely. The brim of his soft felt hat cast a shade on his face, which, thus obscured, wore to her shortsighted gaze a look of seriousness, as of a person arriving on business, and civilly but firmly aware of his rights.

Past experience had made her equally sensible to such claims; but she was jealous of her husband's morning hours, and doubtful of his having given anyone the right to intrude on them.

"Have you an appointment with my husband?" she asked.

The visitor hesitated, as if unprepared for the question.

"I think he expects me," he replied.

It was Mary's turn to hesitate. "You see this is his time for work: he never sees anyone in the morning."

He looked at her a moment without answering; then, as if accepting her decision, he began to move away. As he turned, Mary saw him pause and glance up at the peaceful house front. Something in his air suggested weariness and disappointment, the dejection of a traveler who has come from far off and whose hours are limited by the timetable. It occurred to her that if this were the case her refusal might have made his errand vain, and a sense of compunction caused her to hasten after him.

"May I ask if you have come a long way?"

He gave her the same grave look. "Yes—I have come a long way."

"Then, if you'll go to the house, no doubt my husband will see you now. You'll find him in the library."

She did not know why she had added the last phrase, except from a vague impulse to atone for her previous inhospitability. The visitor seemed about to express his thanks, but her attention was distracted by the approach of the gardener with a companion who bore all the marks of being the expert from Dorchester.

"This way," she said, waving the stranger to the house; and an instant later she had forgotten him in the absorption of her meeting with the boiler maker.

The encounter led to such far-reaching results that the engineer ended by finding it expedient to ignore his train, and Mary was beguiled into spending the remainder of the morning in absorbed confabulation among the flower pots. When the colloquy ended, she was surprised to find that it was nearly luncheon time, and she half expected, as she hurried back to the house, to see her husband coming out to meet her. But she found no one in the court but an undergardener raking the gravel, and the hall, when she entered it, was so silent that she guessed Boyne to be still at work.

Not wishing to disturb him, she turned into the drawing room, and there, at her writing table, lost herself in renewed calculations of the outlay to which the morning's conference had pledged her. The fact that she could permit herself such follies had not yet lost its novelty; and somehow, in contrast to the vague fears of the previous days, it now seemed an element of her recovered security, of the sense that, as Ned had said, things in general had never been "righter."

She was still luxuriating in a lavish play of figures when the parlormaid, from the threshold, roused her with an inquiry as to the expediency of serving luncheon. It was one of their jokes that Trimmle announced luncheon as if she were divulging a state secret, and Mary, intent upon her papers, merely murmured an absent-minded assent.

She felt Trimmle wavering doubtfully on the threshold, as if in rebuke of such unconsidered assent; then her retreating steps sounded down the passage, and Mary, pushing away her papers, crossed the hall and went to the library door. It was still closed, and she wavered in her turn, disliking to disturb her husband, yet anxious that he should not exceed his usual measure of work. As she stood there, balancing her impulses, Trimmle returned with the announcement of luncheon, and Mary, thus impelled, opened the library door.

Boyne was not at his desk, and she peered about her, expecting to discover him before the bookshelves, somewhere down the length of the room; but her call brought no response, and gradually it became clear to her that he was not there.

She turned back to the parlormaid.

"Mr. Boyne must be upstairs. Please tell him that luncheon is ready."

Trimmle appeared to hesitate between the obvious duty of obedience and an equally obvious conviction of the foolishness of the injunction laid on her. The struggle resulted in her saying: "If you please, Madam, Mr. Boyne's not upstairs."

"Not in his room? Are you sure?"

"I'm sure, Madam."

Mary consulted the clock. "Where is he, then?"

"He's gone out," Trimmle announced, with the superior air of one who has respectfully waited for the question that a well-ordered mind would have put first.

Mary's conjecture had been right, then. Boyne must have gone to the gardens to meet her, and since she had missed him, it was clear that he had taken the shorter way by the south door, instead of going round to the court. She crossed the hall to the French window opening directly on the yew garden, but the parlormaid, after another moment of inner conflict, decided to bring out: "Please, Madam, Mr. Boyne didn't go that way."

Mary turned back. "Where *did* he go? And when?"

"He went out of the front door, up the drive, Madam." It was a matter of principle with Trimmle never to answer more than one question at a time.

"Up the drive? At this hour?" Mary went to the door herself, and glanced across the court through the tunnel of bare lines. But its perspective was as empty as when she had scanned it on entering.

"Did Mr. Boyne leave no message?"

Trimmle seemed to surrender herself to a last struggle with the forces of chaos.

"No, Madam. He just went out with the gentleman."

"The gentleman? What gentleman?" Mary wheeled about, as if to front this new factor.

"The gentleman who called, Madam," said Trimmle resignedly.

"When did a gentleman call? Do explain yourself, Trimmle!"

Only the fact that Mary was very hungry, and that she wanted to consult her husband about the greenhouses, would have caused her to lay so unusual an injunction on her attendant; and even now she was detached enough to note in Trimmle's eye the dawning defiance of the respectful subordinate who has been pressed too hard.

"I couldn't exactly say the hour, Madam, because I didn't let the gentleman in," she replied, with an air of discreetly ignoring the irregularity of her mistress's course.

"You didn't let him in?"

"No, Madam. When the bell rang I was dressing, and Agnes—"

"Go and ask Agnes, then," said Mary.

Trimmle still wore her look of patient magnanimity. "Agnes would not know, Madam, for she had unfortunately burnt her hand in trimming the wick of the new lamp from town"—Trimmle, as Mary was aware, had always been opposed to the new lamp—"and so Mrs. Dockett sent the kitchenmaid instead."

Mary looked again at the clock. "It's after two! Go and ask the kitchenmaid if Mr. Boyne left any word."

She went into luncheon without waiting, and Trimmle presently brought her there the kitchenmaid's statement that the gentleman had called about eleven o'clock, and that Mr. Boyne had gone out with him without leaving any message. The kitchenmaid did not even know the caller's name, for he had written it on a slip of paper, which he had folded and handed to her, with the injunction to deliver it at once to Mr. Boyne.

Mary finished her luncheon, still wondering, and when it was over, and Trimmle had brought the coffee to the drawing room, her wonder had deepened to a first faint tinge of disquietude. It was unlike Boyne to absent himself without explanation at so unwonted an hour, and the difficulty of identifying the visitor whose summons he had apparently obeyed made his disappearance the more unaccountable. Mary Boyne's experience as the wife of a busy engineer, subject to sudden calls and compelled to keep irregular hours, had trained her to the philosophic acceptance of surprises; but since Boyne's withdrawal from business he had adopted a Benedictine regularity of life. As if to make up for the dispersed and agitated years, with their "stand-up" lunches, and dinners rattled down to the joltings of the dining cars, he cultivated the last refinements of punctuality and monotony, discouraging his wife's fancy for the unexpected, and declaring that to a delicate taste there were infinite gradations of pleasure in the recurrences of habit.

Still, since no life can completely defend itself from the unforeseen, it was evident that all Boyne's precautions would sooner or later prove unavailable, and Mary concluded that he had cut short a tiresome visit by walking with his caller to the station, or at least accompanying him for part of the way.

This conclusion relieved her from further preoccupation, and she went out herself to take up her conference with the gardener. Thence she walked to the village post office, a mile or so away; and when she turned toward home the early twilight was setting in.

She had taken a footpath across the downs, and as Boyne, meanwhile, had probably returned from the station by the highroad, there was little likelihood of their meeting. She felt sure, however, of his having reached the house before her; so sure that, when she entered it herself, without even pausing to inquire of Trimmle, she made directly for the library. But the library was still empty, and with an unwonted exactness of visual memory she observed that the papers on her husband's desk lay precisely as they had lain when she had gone in to call him to luncheon.

Then of a sudden she was seized by a vague dread of the unknown. She had closed the door behind her on entering, and as she stood alone in the long silent room, her dread seemed to take shape and sound, to be there breathing and lurking among the shadows. Her shortsighted eyes strained through them, half-discerning an actual presence, something aloof, that watched and knew; and in the recoil from that intangible presence she threw herself on the bell rope and gave it a sharp pull.

The sharp summons brought Trimmle in precipitately with a lamp, and Mary breathed again at this sobering reappearance of the usual.

"You may bring tea if Mr. Boyne is in," she said, to justify her ring.

"Very well, Madam. But Mr. Boyne is not in," said Trimmle, putting down the lamp.

"Not in? You mean he's come back and gone out again?"

"No, Madam. He's never been back."

The dread stirred again, and Mary knew that now it had her fast.

"Not since he went out with—the gentleman?"

"Not since he went out with the gentleman."

"But who *was* the gentleman?" Mary insisted, with the shrill note of someone trying to be heard through a confusion of noises.

"That I couldn't say, Madam." Trimmle, standing there by the lamp, seemed suddenly to grow less round and rosy, as though eclipsed by the same creeping shade of apprehension.

"But the kitchenmaid knows—wasn't it the kitchenmaid who let him in?"

"She doesn't know either, Madam, for he wrote his name on a folded paper."

Mary, through her agitation, was aware that they were both designating the unknown visitor by a vague pronoun, instead of the conventional formula which, till then, had kept their allusions within the bounds of conformity. And at the same moment her mind caught at the suggestion of the folded paper.

"But he must have a name! Where's the paper?"

She moved to the desk, and began to turn over the documents that littered it. The first that caught her eye was an unfinished letter in her husband's hand, with his pen lying across it, as though dropped there at a sudden summons.

"My dear Parvis"—who was Parvis?—"I have just received your letter announcing Elwell's death, and while I suppose there is now no further risk of trouble, it might be safer—"

She tossed the sheet aside, and continued her search; but no folded paper was discoverable among the letters and pages of manuscript which had been swept together in a heap, as if by a hurried or a startled gesture.

"But the kitchenmaid *saw* him. Send her here," she commanded, wondering at her dullness in not thinking sooner of so simple a solution.

Trimmle vanished in a flash, as if thankful to be out of the room, and when she reappeared, conducting the agitated underling, Mary had regained her self-possession, and had her questions ready.

The gentleman was a stranger, yes—that she understood. But what had he said? And, above all, what had he looked like? The first question was easily enough answered, for the disconcerting reason that he had said so little—had merely asked for Mr. Boyne, and, scribbling something on a bit of paper, had requested that it should at once be carried in to him.

"Then you don't know what he wrote? You're not sure it *was* his name?"

The kitchenmaid was not sure, but supposed it was, since he had written it in answer to her inquiry as to whom she should announce.

"And when you carried the paper in to Mr. Boyne, what did he say?"

The kitchenmaid did not think that Mr. Boyne had said anything, but she could not be sure, for just as she had handed him the paper and he was opening it, she had become aware that the visitor had followed her into the library, and she had slipped out, leaving the two gentlemen together.

"But then, if you left them in the library, how do you know that they went out of the house?"

This question plunged the witness into a momentary inarticulateness, from which she was rescued by Trimmle, who, by means of ingenious circumlocutions, elicited the statement that before she could cross the hall to the back passage she had heard the two gentlemen behind her, and had seen them go out of the front door together.

"Then, if you saw the strange gentleman twice, you must be able to tell me what he looked like."

But with this final challenge to her powers of expression it became clear that the limit of the kitchenmaid's endurance had been reached. The obligation of going to the front door to "show in" a visitor was in itself so subversive of the fundamental order of things that it had thrown her faculties into hopeless disarray, and she could only stammer out, after various panting efforts: "His hat, mum, was different-like, as you might say—"

"Different? How different?" Mary flashed out, her own mind, in the same instant, leaping back to an image left on it that morning, and then lost under layers of subsequent impressions.

"His hat had a wide brim, you mean, and his face was pale—a youngish face?" Mary pressed her, with a white-lipped intensity of interrogation. But if the kitchenmaid found any adequate answer to this challenge, it was swept away for her listener down the rushing current of her own convictions. The stranger—the stranger in the garden! Why had Mary not thought of him before? She needed no one now to tell her that it was he who had called for her husband and gone away with him. But who was he, and why had Boyne obeyed him?

IV

It leaped out at her suddenly, like a grin out of the dark, that they had often called England so little—"such a confoundedly hard place to get lost in."

A confoundedly hard place to get lost in! That had been her husband's phrase. And now, with the whole machinery of official investigation sweeping its flashlights from shore to shore, and across the dividing straits; now, with Boyne's name blazing from the walls of every town and village, his portrait (how that wrung her!) hawked up and down the country like the image of a hunted criminal; now the little compact populous island, so policed, surveyed, and administered, revealed itself as a Sphinxlike guardian of abysmal mysteries, staring back into his wife's anguished eyes as if with the wicked joy of knowing something they would never know!

In the fortnight since Boyne's disappearance there had been no word of him, no trace of his movements. Even the usual misleading reports that raise expectancy in tortured bosoms had been few and fleeting. No one but the kitchenmaid had seen Boyne leave the house, and no one else had seen "the gentleman" who accompanied him. All inquiries in the neighborhood failed to elicit the memory of a stranger's presence that day in the neighborhood of Lyng. And no one had met Edward Boyne, either alone or in company, in any of the neighboring villages, or on the road across the downs, or at either of the local railway stations. The sunny English noon had swallowed him as completely as if he had gone out into Cimmerian night.

Mary, while every official means of investigation was working at its highest pressure, had ransacked her husband's papers for any trace of antecedent complications, of entanglements or obligations unknown to her, that might throw a ray into the darkness. But if any such had existed in the background of Boyne's life, they had vanished like the slip of paper on which the visitor had written his name. There remained no possible thread of guidance except—if it were indeed an exception— the letter which Boyne had apparently been in the act of writing when he received his mysterious summons. That letter, read and reread by his wife, and submitted by her to the police, yielded little enough to feed conjecture.

"I have just heard of Elwell's death, and while I suppose there is now no further risk of trouble, it might be safer—" That was all. The "risk of trouble" was easily explained by the newspaper clipping which had apprised Mary of the suit brought against her husband by one of his associates in the Blue Star enterprise. The only new information conveyed by the letter was the fact of its showing Boyne, when he wrote it, to be still apprehensive of the results of the suit, though he had told his wife that it had been withdrawn, and though the letter itself proved that the plaintiff was dead. It took several days of cabling to fix the identity of the "Parvis" to whom the fragment was addressed, but even after these inquiries had shown him to be a Waukesha lawyer, no new facts concerning the Elwell suit were elicited. He appeared to have had no direct concern in it, but to have been conversant with the facts merely as an acquaintance, and possible intermediary; and he declared himself unable to guess with what object Boyne intended to seek his assistance.

This negative information, sole fruit of the first fortnight's search, was not increased by a jot during the slow weeks that followed. Mary knew that the investigations were still being carried on, but she had a vague sense of their gradually slackening, as the actual march of time seemed to slacken. It was as though the days, flying horror-struck from the shrouded image of the one inscrutable day, gained assurance as the distance lengthened, till at last they fell back into their normal gait. And so with the human imaginations at work on the dark event. No doubt it occupied them still, but week by week and hour by hour it grew less absorbing, took up less space, was slowly but inevitably crowded out of the foreground of consciousness by the new problems perpetually bubbling up from the cloudy caldron of human experience.

Even Mary Boyne's consciousness gradually felt the same lowering of velocity. It still swayed with the incessant oscillations of conjecture; but they were slower, more rhythmical in their beat. There were even moments of weariness when, like the victim of some poison which leaves the brain clear, but holds the body motionless, she saw herself domesticated with the Horror, accepting its perpetual presence as one of the fixed conditions of life.

These moments lengthened into hours and days, till she passed into a phase of stolid acquiescence. She watched the routine of daily life with the incurious eye of a savage on whom the meaningless processes of civilization make but the faintest impression. She had come to regard herself as part of the routine, a spoke of the wheel, revolving with its motion; she felt almost like the furniture of the room in which she sat, an insensate object to be dusted and pushed about with the chairs and tables. And this deepening apathy held her fast at Lyng, in spite of the entreaties of friends and the usual medical recommendation of "change." Her friends supposed that her refusal to move was inspired by the belief that her husband would one day return to the spot from which he had vanished, and a beautiful legend grew up about this imaginary state of waiting. But in reality she had no such belief: the depths of anguish enclosing her were no longer lighted by flashes of hope. She was sure that Boyne would never come back, that he had gone out of her sight as completely as if Death itself had waited that day on the threshold. She had even renounced, one by one, the various theories as to his disappearance which had been advanced by the press, the police, and her own agonized imagination. In sheer lassitude her mind turned from these alternatives of horror, and sank back into the blank fact that he was gone.

No, she would never know what had become of him—no one would ever know. But the house *knew;* the library in which she spent her long lonely evenings knew. For it was here that the last scene had been enacted, here that the stranger had come, and spoken the word which had caused Boyne to rise and follow him. The floor she trod had felt his tread; the books on the shelves had seen his face; and there were moments when the intense consciousness of the old dusky walls seemed about to break out into some audible revelation of their secret. But the revelation never came, and she knew it would never come. Lyng was not one of the garrulous old houses that betray the secrets entrusted to them. Its very legend proved that it had always been the mute accomplice, the incorruptible custodian, of the mysteries it had surprised. And Mary Boyne, sitting face to face with its silence, felt the futility of seeking to break it by any human means.

V

"I don't say it *wasn't* straight, and yet I don't say it *was* straight. It was business."

Mary, at the words, lifted her head with a start, and looked intently at the speaker.

When, half an hour before, a card with "Mr. Parvis" on it had been brought up to her, she had been immediately aware that the name had been a part of her consciousness ever since she had read it at the head of Boyne's unfinished letter. In the library she had found awaiting her a small sallow man with a bald head and gold eyeglasses, and it sent a tremor through her to know that this was the person to whom her husband's last known thought had been directed.

Parvis, civilly, but without vain preamble—in the manner of a man who has his watch in his hand—had set forth the object of his visit. He had "run over" to England on business, and finding himself in the neighborhood of Dorchester, had not wished to leave it without paying his respects to Mrs. Boyne; and without asking her, if the occasion offered, what she meant to do about Bob Elwell's family.

The words touched the spring of some obscure dread in Mary's bosom. Did her visitor, after all, know what Boyne had meant by his unfinished phrase? She asked for an elucidation of his question, and noticed at once that he seemed surprised at her continued ignorance of the subject. Was it possible that she really knew as little as she said?

"I know nothing—you must tell me," she faltered out; and her visitor thereupon proceeded to unfold his story. It threw, even to her confused perceptions, and imperfectly initiated vision, a lurid glare on the whole hazy episode of the Blue Star Mine. Her husband had made his money in that brilliant speculation at the cost of "getting ahead" of someone less alert to seize the chance; and the victim of his ingenuity was young Robert Elwell, who had "put him on" to the Blue Star scheme.

Parvis, at Mary's first cry, had thrown her a sobering glance through his impartial glasses.

"Bob Elwell wasn't smart enough, that's all; if he had been, he might have turned round and served Boyne the same way. It's the kind of thing that happens every day in business. I guess it's what the scientists call the survival of the fittest—see?" said Mr. Parvis, evidently pleased with the aptness of his analogy.

Mary felt a physical shrinking from the next question she tried to frame: it was as though the words on her lips had a taste that nauseated her.

"But then—you accuse my husband of doing something dishonorable?"

Mr. Parvis surveyed the question dispassionately. "Oh, no, I don't. I don't even say it wasn't straight." He glanced up and down the long lines of books, as if one of them might have supplied him with the definition he sought. "I don't say it *wasn't* straight, and yet I don't say it *was* straight. It was business." After all, no definition in his category could be more comprehensive than that.

Mary sat staring at him with a look of terror. He seemed to her like the indifferent emissary of some evil power.

"But Mr. Elwell's lawyers apparently did not take your view, since I suppose the suit was withdrawn by their advice."

"Oh, yes; they knew he hadn't a leg to stand on, technically. It was when they advised him to withdraw the suit that he got desperate. You see, he'd borrowed most of the money he lost in the Blue Star, and he was up a tree. That's why he shot himself when they told him he had no show."

The horror was sweeping over Mary in great deafening waves.

"He shot himself? He killed himself because of *that?*"

"Well, he didn't kill himself, exactly. He dragged on two months before he died." Parvis emitted the statement as unemotionally as a gramophone grinding out its record.

"You mean that he tried to kill himself, and failed? And tried again?"

"Oh, he didn't have to *try* again," said Parvis grimly.

They sat opposite each other in silence, he swinging his eyeglasses thoughtfully about his finger, she, motionless, her arms stretched along her knees in an attitude of rigid tension.

"But if you knew all this," she began at length, hardly able to force her voice above a whisper, "how is it that when I wrote you at the time of my husband's disappearance you said you didn't understand the letter?"

Parvis received this without perceptible embarrassment: "Why, I didn't understand it—strictly speaking. And it wasn't the time to talk about it, if I had. The Elwell business was settled when the suit was withdrawn. Nothing I could have told you would have helped you to find your husband."

Mary continued to scrutinize him. "Then why are you telling me now?"

Still Parvis did not hesitate. "Well, to begin with, I supposed you knew more than you appear to—I mean about the circumstances of Elwell's death. And then people are talking of it now; the whole matter's been raked up again. And I thought if you didn't know you ought to."

She remained silent, and he continued: "You see, it's only come out lately what a bad state Elwell's affairs were in. His wife's a proud woman, and she fought on as long as she could, going out to work, and taking sewing at home when she got too sick—something with the heart, I believe. But she had his mother to look after, and the children, and she broke down under it, and finally had to ask for help. That called attention to the case, and the papers took it up, and a subscription was started. Everybody out there liked Bob Elwell, and most of the prominent names in the place are down on the list, and people began to wonder why—"

Parvis broke off to fumble in an inner pocket. "Here," he continued, "here's an account of the whole thing from the *Sentinel*—a little sensational, of course. But I guess you'd better look it over."

He held out a newspaper to Mary, who unfolded it slowly, remembering, as she did so, the evening when, in that same room, the perusal of a clipping from the Sentinel had first shaken the depths of her security.

As she opened the paper, her eyes, shrinking from the glaring headlines, "Widow of Boyne's Victim Forced to Appeal for Aid," ran down the column of text to two portraits inserted in it. The first was her husband's, taken from a photograph made the year they had come to England. It was the picture of him that she liked best, the one that stood on the writing table upstairs in her bedroom. As the eyes in the photograph met hers, she felt it would be impossible to read what was said of him, and closed her lids with the sharpness of the pain.

"I thought if you felt disposed to put your name down—" she heard Parvis continue.

She opened her eyes with an effort, and they fell on the other portrait. It was that of a youngish man, slightly built, with features somewhat blurred by the shadow of a projecting hat brim. Where had she seen that outline before? She stared at it confusedly, her heart hammering in her ears. Then she gave a cry.

"This is the man—the man who came for my husband!"

She heard Parvis start to his feet, and was dimly aware that she had slipped backward into the corner of the sofa, and that he was bending above her in alarm. She straightened herself, and reached out for the paper, which she had dropped.

"It's the man! I should know him anywhere!" she persisted in a voice that sounded to her own ears like a scream.

Parvis's answer seemed to come to her from far off, down endless fog-muffled windings.

"Mrs. Boyne, you're not very well. Shall I call somebody? Shall I get a glass of water?"

"No, no, no!" She threw herself toward him, her hand frantically clutching the newspaper. "I tell you, it's the man! I *know* him! He spoke to me in the garden!"

Parvis took the journal from her, directing his glasses to the portrait. "It can't be, Mrs. Boyne. It's Robert Elwell!"

"Robert Elwell?" Her white stare seemed to travel into space. "Then it was Robert Elwell who came for him."

"Came for Boyne? The day he went away from here?" Parvis's voice dropped as hers rose. He bent over, laying a fraternal hand on her, as if to coax her gently back into her seat. "Why, Elwell was dead! Don't you remember?"

Mary sat with hers eyes fixed on the picture, unconscious of what he was saying.

"Don't you remember Boyne's unfinished letter to me—the one you found on his desk that day? It was written just after he'd heard of Elwell's death." She noticed an odd shake in Parvis's unemotional voice. "Surely you remember!" he urged her.

Yes, she remembered: that was the profoundest horror of it. Elwell had died the day before her husband's disappearance; and this was Elwell's portrait; and it was the portrait of the man who had spoken to her in the garden. She lifted her head and looked slowly about the library. The library could have borne witness that it was also the portrait of the man who had come in that day to call Boyne from his unfinished letter. Through the misty surgings of her brain she heard the faint boom of half-forgotten words—words spoken by Alida Stair on the lawn at Pangbourne before Boyne and his wife had ever seen the house at Lyng, or had imagined that they might one day live there.

"This was the man who spoke to me," she repeated.

She looked again at Parvis. He was trying to conceal his disturbance under what he probably imagined to be an expression of indulgent commiseration; but the edges of his lips were blue. "He thinks me mad; but I'm not mad," she reflected; and suddenly there flashed upon her a way of justifying her strange affirmation.

She sat quiet, controlling the quiver of her lips, and waiting till she could trust her voice; then she said, looking straight at Parvis: "Will you answer me one question, please? When was it that Robert Elwell tried to kill himself?"

"When—when?" Parvis stammered.

"Yes; the date. Please try to remember."

She saw that he was growing still more afraid of her. "I have a reason," she insisted.

"Yes, yes. Only I can't remember. About two months before, I should say."

"I want the date," she repeated.

Parvis picked up the newspaper. "We might see here," he said, still humoring her. He ran his eyes down the page. "Here it is. Last October —the—"

She caught the words from him. "The 20th, wasn't it?" With a sharp look at her, he verified. "Yes, the 20th. Then you *did* know?"

"I know now." Her gaze continued to travel past him. "Sunday, the 20th—that was the day he came first."

Parvis's voice was almost inaudible. "Came *here* first?"

"Yes."

"You saw him twice, then?"

"Yes, twice." She just breathed it at him. "He came first on the 20th of October. I remember the date because it was the day we went up Meldon Steep for the first time." She felt a faint gasp of inward laughter at the thought that but for that she might have forgotten.

Parvis continued to scrutinize her, as if trying to intercept her gaze.

"We saw him from the roof," she went on. "He came down the lime avenue toward the house. He was dressed just as he is in that picture. My husband saw him first. He was frightened, and ran down ahead of me; but there was no one there. He had vanished."

"Elwell had vanished?" Parvis faltered.

"Yes." Their two whispers seemed to grope for each other. "I couldn't think what had happened. I see now. He *tried* to come then; but he wasn't dead enough—he couldn't reach us. He had to wait for two months to die; and then he came back again—and Ned went with him."

She nodded at Parvis with the look of triumph of a child who has worked out a difficult puzzle. But suddenly she lifted her hands with a desperate gesture, pressing them to her temples.

"Oh, my God! I sent him to Ned—I told him where to go! I sent him to this room!" she screamed.

She felt the walls of books rush toward her, like inward falling ruins; and she heard Parvis, a long way off, through the ruins, crying to her, and struggling to get at her. But she was numb to his touch, she did not know what he was saying. Through the tumult she heard but one clear note, the voice of Alida Stair, speaking on the lawn at Pangbourne.

"You won't know till afterward," it said. "You won't know till long, long afterward."

1909

SARAH ORNE JEWETT

The Landscape Chamber

I

I was tired of ordinary journeys, which involved either the loneliness and discomfort of fashionable hotels, or the responsibilities of a guest in busy houses. One is always doing the same things over and over; I now promised myself that I would go in search of new people and new scenes, until I was again ready to turn with delight to my familiar occupations. So I mounted my horse one morning, without any definite plan of my journey, and rode eastward, with a business-like haversack strapped behind the saddle. I only wished that the first day's well-known length of road had been already put behind me. One drawback to a woman's enjoyment of an excursion of this sort is the fact that when she is out of the saddle she is uncomfortably dressed. But I compromised matters as nearly as possible by wearing a short corduroy habit, light both in color and weight, and putting a linen blouse and belt into my pack, to replace the stiff habit-waist. The wallet on the saddle held a flat drinking-cup, a bit of chocolate, and a few hard biscuits, for provision against improbable famine. Autumn would be the best time for such a journey, if the evenings need not be so often spent in stuffy rooms, with kerosene lamps for company. This was early summer, and I had long days in which to amuse myself. For a book I took a much-beloved small copy of "The Sentimental Journey."

After I left my own neighborhood I was looked at with curious eyes. I was now and then recognized with surprise, but oftener viewed with suspicion, as if I were a criminal escaping from justice. The keepers of the two country taverns at which I rested questioned me outright, until I gave a reassuring account of myself. Through the middle of the day I

Born in 1849 in South Berwick, Maine, Sarah Orne Jewett often accompanied her father, a country doctor, on his rounds, which sharpened her powers of observation and deepened her appreciation of this region and its people. From the age of eighteen, she was publishing short stories and sketches, many of which documented the language, customs, and sentiments of the small-town neighborhoods in southern Maine. Jewett's reputation grew among the major publishing centers of late nineteenth-century America, culminating in her 1896 collection of tales, The Country of the Pointed Firs. A serious accident in 1901 cut her writing life drastically short; Jewett remained in South Berwick, the town that she helped in part to create, until her death in 1909.

let the horse stand unsaddled in the shade, by the roadside, while I sat near, leaning against the broad trunk of a tree, and ate a bit of luncheon, or slept, or read my book, or strolled away up the shore of a brook or to the top of a hill. On the third or fourth day I left my faithful companion so long that he grew restless, and at last fearful, as petted horses will. The silence and strangeness of the place and my disappearance frightened him. When I returned, I found that the poor creature had twisted a forward shoe so badly that I could neither pull it off altogether, nor mount again. There was nothing to do but to lead him slowly to some farm-house, where I could get assistance; so on went the saddle, and away we plodded together sadly along the dusty road. The horse looked at me with anxious eyes, and was made fretful by the difficulty of the projecting shoe. I should have provided myself with some pincers, he seemed to tell me; the foot was aching from the blows I had given it with a rough-edged stone in trying to draw the tenacious nails. It was all my fault, having left him in such a desolate place, fastened to a tree that grew against a creviced ledge of rock. We were both a little sulky at this mischance so early in the careless expedition.

The sea was near, and the salt-marshes penetrated deep into the country, like abandoned beds of rivers winding inland among the pine woods and upland pastures. The higher land separated these marshes, like a succession of low promontories trending seaward, and the road climbed and crossed over from one low valley to another. There had been no houses for some distance behind us. I knew that there was a village with a good tavern a few miles ahead; so far, indeed, that I had planned to reach it at sundown. I began to feel very tired, and the horse tossed his head more and more impatiently, resenting my anxious, dragging hold upon the rein close at his mouth. There was nobody to be seen; the hills became steeper, the unshaded strips of marshland seemed hotter, and I determined at last to wait until some traveler appeared who could give us assistance. Perhaps the blacksmith himself might be out adventuring that afternoon.

We halted by some pasture bars in the shade of an old cider-apple tree, and I threw the bridle over a leaning post in the unsteady fence; and there the horse and I waited, and looked at each other reproachfully. It was some time before I discovered a large rusty nail lying in the short grass, within reach of my hand. My pocket-knife was already broken, because I had tried to use it for a lever, and this was just what I needed. I quickly caught up the disabled hoof again, and with careful prying the tough nails loosed their hold at last, and the bent shoe dropped with a clink. The horse gave a whinny of evident relief, and seemed to respect me again, and I was ready to mount at once; in an

instant life lost its depressing aspect. "Keep your feet out of clefts now!"
I said joyfully, with a friendly stroke of the good creature's neck and
tangled mane, and a moment afterward we were back in the stony road.
Alas, the foot had been strained, and our long halt had only stiffened
it. I was mounted on three feet, not four. Nothing was to be done but
to go forward, step by step, to the far-away village, or to any friendly
shelter this side of it.

The afternoon was waning: sometimes I rode, sometimes I walked;
those three miles of marsh and hill seemed interminable. At last I saw
the chimneys of a house; the horse raised his head high, and whinnied
loud and long.

These chimneys were most reassuring; being high and square, they
evidently belonged to a comfortable house of the last century, and my
spirits rose again. The country was still abandoned by human beings. I
had seen no one since noon, but the road was little used, and was
undoubtedly no longer the main highway of that region. I wondered
what impression I should make in such a migratory guise. The saddle
and its well-stuffed haversack and my own dustiness amused me unexpectedly, and I understood for the first time that the rest and change of
this solitary excursion had done me much good. I was no longer listless
and uninterested, but ready for adventure of any sort. It had been a
most sensible thing to go wandering alone through the country. But
now the horse's ankle was swollen. I grew anxious again, and looked
at the chimneys with relief. Presently I came in sight of the house.

It was disappointing, for the first view gave an impression of dreariness and neglect. The barn and straggling row of out-buildings were
leaning this way and that, mossy and warped; the blinds of the once
handsome house were broken; and everything gave evidence of unhin-
dered decline from thrift and competence to poverty and ruin. A good
colonial mansion, I thought, abandoned by its former owners, and
tenanted now by some shiftless outcasts of society, who ask but meagre
comfort, and are indifferent to the decencies of life. Full of uncertainty,
I went along the approach to the barn, noticing, however, with surprise
that the front yard had been carefully tended; there were some dark
crimson roses in bloom, and broken lines of box which had been
carefully clipped at no remote period. Nobody was in sight. I went to
the side door, and gave a knock with my whip at arm's length, for the
horse was eager to reach the uninviting, hungry-looking stable. Some
time elapsed before my repeated summons were answered; then the
door slowly opened, and a woman just this side of middle age stood
before me, waiting to hear my errand. She had a pathetic look, as if she
were forced by circumstances to deny all requests, however her own

impulses might lead her toward generosity. I was instantly drawn toward her, in warm sympathy: the blooming garden was hers; she was very poor. I would plead my real fatigue, and ask for a night's lodging, and perhaps my holiday might also give her pleasure. But a curious hardness drew her face into forbidding angles, even as her sweet and womanly eyes watched me with surprised curiosity.

"I should be very sorry to take the horse any farther to-day," said I, after stating my appealing case. "I will give you as little trouble as possible." At this moment the haggard face of an elderly man peered at me over her shoulder.

"We don't keep tavern, young lady," he announced, in an unexpectedly musical, low voice, "but since your horse is—"

"I am ready to pay any price you ask," I interrupted, impatiently; and he gave me an eager look and then came to the outer step, ignoring both his daughter and me, as he touched the horse with real kindliness. "'Tis a pretty creature!" he said, admiringly, and at once stooped stiffly down to examine the lifted foot. I explained the accident in detail, grateful for such intelligent sympathy, while he stroked the lamed ankle.

"There's no damage done," he assured me presently, looking up with transient self-forgetfulness. "A common liniment will do; there's a bottle in the house, but 't will cost you something," and his face clouded again.

I turned to the daughter, who gave me a strange, appealing look. Her eyes begged me entreatingly, "Give him his own way"; her firm-set mouth signified her assent to the idea that I had no right to demand favors.

"Do what you think best," I said, "at your own price. I shall be very grateful to you"; and having come to this understanding, the father and I unbuckled the saddle-girths, while the daughter stood watching us. The old man led the limping horse across the green dooryard to a weather-beaten stable, talking to him in a low tone. The creature responded by unusual docility. I even saw him, though usually so suspicious and fretful with strangers, put his head close to his leader's shoulder with most affectionate impulse. I gathered up my belongings,—my needments, as somebody had called them, after Spenser's fashion, in the morning,—and entered the door.

II

Along the by-ways and in the elder villages of New England stand many houses like this, from which life and vigor have long been ebbing, until all instincts of self-preservation seem to have departed. The commonplace, thrifty fears of increasing damage from cracks, or leaks, or falling plaster no longer give alarm; as age creeps through the human frame, pilfering the pleasures of enthusiasm and activity one by one, so it is with a decaying house. The old man's shrewd eyes alone seemed unrelated to his surroundings. What sorrow or misfortune had made him accept them? I wondered, as I stared about the once elegant room. Nothing new had been brought to it for years; the leather-bound books in the carved secretary might have belonged to his grandfather. The floor was carpetless and deeply worn; the faded paper on the walls and the very paint looked as old as he. The pinch of poverty could nowhere be much sharper than here, but the exquisite cleanness and order of the place made one ignore the thought of poverty in its common aspect, for all its offensive and repulsive qualities were absent. I sat down in a straight-backed mahogany chair, feeling much relieved, and not without gratitude for this unexpected episode. The hostess left me alone. I was glad enough to have the long day shortened a little, and to find myself in this lonely, mysterious house. I was pleased by the thought that the price of my food and lodging would be very welcome, and I grew more and more eager to know the history of my new friends. I have never been conscious of a more intense desire to make myself harmonious, or to win some degree of confidence. And when the silence of the old sitting-room grew tiresome I went out to the stable, whence my host had not returned, and was quite reconciled at finding that I was looked upon by him, at least, merely as an appendage to my four-footed companion.

The old man regarded me with indifference, and went on patiently rubbing the horse's foot. I was silent after having offered to take his place and being contemptuously refused. His clothes were curiously old and worn, patched bravely, and an embroidery of careful darns. The color of them was not unlike the dusty gray of long-neglected cobwebs. There was unusual delicacy and refinement in his hands and feet, and I was sure, from the first glance at my new friends and the first sound of their voices, that they had inherited gentle blood, though such an inheritance had evidently come through more than one generation to whom had been sternly denied any approach to luxury or social advantage. I have often noticed in country villages the descendants of those clergymen who once ruled New England sternly and well, and while they may be men and women of undeveloped minds, without authority and even of humble circumstances, they yet bear the mark of authority and dignified behavior, like silver and copper coins with a guinea stamp.

I was more and more oppressed by the haunting sense of poverty, for I saw proofs everywhere that the inhabitants of the old house made no practical protest against its slow decay. The woman's share of work was performed best, as one might see by their mended clothes; but the master's domain was hopelessly untended, not only as to the rickety buildings, but in the land itself, which was growing wild bushes at its own sweet will, except for a rough patch near the house, which had been dug and planted that year. Was this brooding, sad old man discouraged by life? Did he say to himself, "Let things be; they will last my time"? I found myself watching his face with intense interest, but I did not dare to ask questions, and only stood and watched him. The sad mouth of the man might have been a den from which stinging wild words could assail a curious stranger. I was afraid of what he might say to me, yet I longed to hear him speak.

The summer day was at its close. I moved a step forward to get away from the level sunbeams which dazzled my eyes, and ventured to give some news about myself and the lonely journey that had hitherto brought me such pleasure. The listener looked up with sincere attention, which made me grow enthusiastic at once, and I described my various experiences, and especially the amusing comments which I had heard upon my mode of traveling about the country. It amazed me to think that I was within sixty miles of home and yet a foreigner. At last I asked a trivial question about some portion of the scenery, which was pleasantly answered. The old man's voice was singularly sweet and varied in tone, the exact reverse of a New Englander's voice of the usual rural quality. I was half startled at seeing my horse quickly turn his head to look at the speaker, as if with human curiosity equal to my own. I felt a thrill of vague apprehension. I was unwise enough for a moment to dread taking up my residence in this dilapidated mansion; a creeping horror, such as one feels at hearing footsteps behind one in a dark, strange place, made me foolishly uneasy, and I stood looking off across the level country through the golden light of closing day, beyond the marshes and beyond the sand dunes to the sea. What had happened to this uncanny father and daughter, that they were contented to let the chances of life slip by untouched, while their ancestral dwelling gradually made itself ready to tumble about their ears?

I could see that the horse's foot was much better already, and I watched with great sympathy the way that the compassionate, patient fingers touched and soothed the bruised joint. But I saw no sign of any other horse in the stable, save a few stiffened, dusty bits of harness hung on a high peg in the wall; and as I looked at these, and renewed my wonder that such a person should have no horse of his own, especially at such a distance from any town, the old man spoke again.

"Look up at that bit of dry skin over the harnesses," said he. "That was the pretty ear of the best mare that ever trod these roads. She leaped the stable-yard gate one day, caught her foot in a rope, and broke her neck. She was like those swallows one minute, and the next she was a heap of worthless flesh, a heavy thing to be dragged away and hidden in the earth." His voice failed him suddenly, poor old fellow; it told me that he had suffered cruel sorrows that made this loss of a pleasure almost unbearable. So far life had often brought me successes, and I had gained a habit of expecting my own enterprises to be lucky. I stood appalled before this glimpse of a defeated life and its long procession of griefs.

Presently the master of the place went into the house, and returned with a worn wooden trencher of bits of hard bread and some meal. The hungry creature in the stall whinnied eagerly, and nestled about, while our host ascended the broken stairway to the stable loft; and after waiting for some time, I heard the rustle of an armful of hay which came down into the crib. I looked that way, and was not surprised, when I noticed the faded, dusty dryness of it, to see my dainty beast sniff at it with disappointment, and look round at me inquiringly. The old man joined me, and I protested hastily against such treatment of my favorite.

"Cannot we get somebody to bring some better hay, and oats enough for a day or two, if you are unprovided?" I asked.

"The creature must not be overfed," he said, grudgingly, with a new harsh tone. "You will heat the foot, and we must keep the beast quiet. Anything will serve to-night; to-morrow he can graze all day, and keep the foot moving gently; next day, he can be shod."

"But there is danger in giving him green grass," I suggested. "This is too rich pasturage about the house; surely you know enough of horses to have learned that. He will not be fit to ride, either. If I meant to give him a month of pasture, it would be another thing. No; send somebody for at least an armful of decent hay. I will go myself. Are there houses near?"

The old man had gone into the stall, and was feeding the hungry horse from the trencher. I was startled to see him snatch back two or three bits of the bread and put them into his pocket, as if, with all his fondness for the horse and a sincere desire to make him comfortable, he nevertheless grudged the food. I became convinced that the poor soul was a miser. He certainly played the character exactly, and yet there was an appealing look in his eyes, which, joined with the tones of his voice, made me sure that he fought against his tyrannous inclinations. I wondered irreverently if I should be killed that night, after the fashion of traditional tavern robberies, for the sake of what might be found in my pocket, and sauntered toward the house. It remained to be proved whether the daughter was the victim or the upholder of her father's traits.

I had the satisfaction of finding that the daughter was just arranging a table for supper. As I passed the wide-open door of a closet, I was tempted to look in by the faint ancient odor of plum cakes and Madeira wine which escaped; but I never saw a barer closet than that, or one that looked hungrier in spite of the lingering fragrance of hospitality. It gave me a strange feeling as if there were a still subtler link with the past, and some invisible presence would have me contrast the house's former opulence with its present meagreness. When we sat at table I was not surprised to find, on a cloth that was half covered with darns and patches, some pieces of superb old English silver and delicate china. The fare was less than frugal, but was nobly eked out with a dish of field strawberries, as if kind Nature had come to the rescue. Cream there was none, nor sugar, nor even tea or butter. I had an aching sense of the poverty of the family, and curiously questioned in my own mind how far they found it possible to live without money. There was some thin, crisp corn bread, which had been baked in the morning, or whenever there had last been a fire. It was very good. Perhaps my entertainers even gathered their own salt from the tide-pools to flavor the native corn. Look where I would, I could see nothing for which money had been lately spent; here was a thing to be wondered at in this lavish America, and I pushed back my chair at last, while I was still half hungry, from a dread that there would be nothing for breakfast unless I saved it then.

The father and daughter were very agreeable, I must confess; they talked with me about my journey now, and my plans, as if they were my personal friends, and the strange meal was full of pleasure, after all. What had brought a lady and gentleman to such a pass?

After supper the daughter disappeared for a time, busy with her household cares; a little later the father went out of the stable and across the fields, before I could call to him or offer my company. He walked with a light, quick step, like an Indian, as if he were used to taking journeys on foot. I found myself uncommonly tired; the half illness which had fettered me seemed to have returned, after the unusual anxiety and weariness of the afternoon, and I longed to go to bed and to sleep. I had been interested in much that my entertainers had said of the early history of that part of the country, and while we sat at the table I had begun to look forward to a later evening talk, but almost before daylight faded I was forced to go to bed.

My hostess led me through a handsome empty hall, of the wide and stately colonial type, to a comfortable upper room, furnished with a gloomy-looking curtained bedstead and heavy mahogany furniture of the best old fashion. It seemed as if the room had been long unused,

and also as if the lower part of the house were in a much worse state
of disrepair and threadbareness than this. But the two large windows
stood open to the fading sky and sweet country air, and I bade my
hostess good-night cheerfully. She lingered to see if I were comfortable;
it was the first time I had been alone with her. "You can see that we
are not used to entertaining company," she whispered, reddening with
sensitiveness, and smiling apologetically. "Father has kept everybody
away for so many years that I rarely have any one to speak to, or
anything to do but to keep the poor old house clean. Father means to
be kind, but he"—and she turned away, much embarrassed by my
questioning look—"he has a monomania; he inherits it from my grandfather. He fears want, yet seems to have no power to provide against it.
We are poor, God knows, yet we have resources; or had them once,"
she added, sorrowfully. "It was the horse that made him willing to let
you in. He loves horses, yet he has long denied himself even that useful
pleasure."

"But surely he ought to be controlled," I urged. "You must have
suffered."

"I know all that you are eager to say," she replied; "but I promised
my dear mother to be patient with him. It will not be long now; he is
very feeble. I have a horror that this habit of parsimony has rooted itself
too deeply in my own life to be shaken off. You will hear mockery
enough of us among the farmers."

"You surely have friends?"

"Only at a distance," she said, sadly. "I fear that they are no longer
friends. I have *you*," she added, turning to me quickly, in a pathetic way
that made me wish to put my arms about her. "I have been longing for
a friendly face. Yes, it is very hard," and she drearily went out of the
door, and left me alone with the dim light of the sky outside, the gloomy
shadows of the room within. I tried to fancy some clew to the weird
misery of this poverty-stricken household, as I lay down; but I fell asleep
very soon, and slept all night, without even a dream.

III

Daylight brought a new eagerness and a less anxious curiosity about my
strange entertainers. I opened my eyes in broad sunlight. I was puzzled
by the unfamiliar India-cotton hangings of the great bedstead; then I
caught sight of my dusty habit and my riding-cap and whip, near by.
I instantly resolved that even if I found my horse in the restored condition there was every reason to expect, I would make this house my

headquarters for as long time as its owners would keep me, or I could content myself. I would try to show some sisterly affection to the fast-aging woman who was so enslaved by her father's delusions. I had come out in search of adventure; it would be a difficult task to match my present surroundings.

I listened for the sound of footsteps or voices from below, but it was still very early, and I looked about the long-untenanted room with deliberate interest and scrutiny. As I changed my position a little, I caught sight of a curious old painting on the large oval panel above the empty fireplace. The colors were dull, the drawing was quaintly conventional, and I recognized the subject, though not immediately. The artist had pleased himself by making a study of the old house itself, and later, as I dressed, I examined it in detail.

From the costume of the figures I saw that it must have been painted more than a hundred years before. In astonishing contrast to the present condition, it appeared like a satirical show of the house's possibilities. Servants held capering steeds for gay gentlemen to mount, and ladies walked together in fine attire down the garden alleys of the picture. Once a hospitable family had kept open house behind the row of elms, and once the follies of the world and the fashions of brilliant, luxurious life had belonged to this decayed and withering household. I wondered if the miserly old man, to whose strangely sweet and compelling voice I had listened the evening before, could bear to look at this picture, and acknowledge his unlikeness to his prosperous ancestors.

It was well for me that the keeping of hens is comparatively inexpensive, for I breakfasted comfortably, and was never so heartily rejoiced at the vicinity of a chicken-coop. My proposal to stay with my new friends for a few days met with no opposition from either host or hostess; and again, as I looked in their pinched and hopeless faces, I planned some secret excuses for making a feast of my own, or a happy holiday. The fields and hills of the old picture were still unchanged, but what ebb and flow of purpose, of comfort, of social condition, had enriched and impoverished the household!

"Where did she sleep?" asked the master of the house, suddenly, with a strange, suspicious glare at his daughter.

"In the landscape chamber," the pale woman said, without lifting her eyes to his, though she grew whiter and thinner as she spoke.

I looked at him instinctively to see his eyes blaze with anger, and expected a torrent of abuse, because he was manifestly so much displeased. Nothing was said, but with a feeling of uneasiness we left the table, and I went out to the kitchen with my new friend.

"There is no reason why I should not have put you into the landscape chamber," she told me instantly. "It is a fancy of my father's. I had aired that room thoroughly in the morning, but the front guest-chambers have been closed for some time."

"Who painted the strange old picture?" I asked. "Some member of the family?" But I was answered that it was the work of a Frenchman, who was captured in war-time, and paroled under the charge of her great-grandfather.

"He must have had a gay visit," I suggested, "if he has left a faithful picture of the house as he saw it."

"The house used to be like that always," was the faint response, and the speaker hesitated, as if she considered whether we did right in discussing her family history; then she turned quickly away. "I believe we are under some miserable doom. Father will be sure to tell you so, at any rate," she added, with an effort at gayety. "He believes that he fights against it, but I always say that he was cowardly, and accepted it," and she sighed wearily.

I looked at her with fresh surprise and conjecture. I forgot for the time this great, busy, prosaic world of which we were both a part, and I felt as if I had lost a score of years for each day's journey, and had gone backward into the past. New England holds many strange households within its borders, but there could not be another which approached this. The very air of the house oppressed me, and I strayed out into the beautiful wide fields, and found my spirits rising again at once. I turned at last to look back at the group of gray buildings in the great level and landscape. They were such a small excrescence upon the fruitful earth, those roofs which covered awful stagnation and hindrance of the processes of spiritual life and growth. What power could burst the bonds, and liberate the man and woman I had left, from a mysterious tyranny?

I was bareheaded and the morning grew very hot. I went toward a group of oaks, to shelter myself in the shade, and found the ancient burying-place of the family. There were numerous graves, but none were marked except the oldest. There was a group of rude but stately stones, with fine inscriptions, yet curiously enough the latest of them bore a date soon after the beginning of the century; all the more recent graves were low and unmarked in any way. The family fortunes had waned long ago, perhaps; I might be wronging the present master of the house, though I remembered what had been said to me of some mysterious doom. I could not help thinking of my new acquaintances most intently, and was startled at the sound of footsteps. I saw the old man, muttering and bending his head until he could see nothing but the ground at his feet. He only picked up some dead branches that had fallen from the oaks, and went away toward the house again; always looking at the ground, as if he expected to find something. It came to my mind with greater distinctness that he was a miser, poor only by his own choice; and I indignantly resolved to urge the daughter to break her allegiance to him for a time, to claim her own and set herself free. But the miser had no cheerful sense of his hoards, no certainty of a munificence which was more to him than any use of it; there was a look upon his face as of a preying conscience within, a gnawing reptile of shame and guilt and evil memory. Had he sacrificed all sweet family life and natural ties to his craving for wealth? I watched the bent and hungry figure out of sight.

When I reached the house again, I went through the open door of the wide hall, and gained my landscape chamber without being seen by any one. I was tired and dizzy with the unusual heat, and, quickly drawing the close shutters, I threw myself on the bed to rest. All the light in the room came from the shaded hall; there was absolute silence, except some far-off country sounds of birds high in the air or lowing cattle. The house itself was still as a tomb.

I went to sleep, but it was not sound sleep. I grew heavy and tired with my own weight. I heard soft footsteps coming up the stairs; some one stopped as if to listen outside the wide-open door; then the gray, shadowy figure of the old man stood just within, and his eyes peered about the room. I was behind the curtains; one had been unfastened, and hid me from his sight at first, but as he took one step forward he saw me, lying asleep. He bent over me, until I felt my hair stir with his breath, but I did not move. His presence was not frightful, strange to say; I felt as if I were only dreaming. I opened my eyes a little as he went away, apparently satisfied, to the closet door, and unlocked it, starting and looking at me anxiously as the key turned in the lock. Then he disappeared. I had a childish desire to shut him in and keep him prisoner, for reasons that were not clear to myself. Whether he only wished to satisfy himself that a concealed treasure was untouched I do not know, but presently he came out, and carefully locked the door again, and went away on tiptoe. I fancied that he lingered before the picture above the chimney-place, and wondered if his conscience pricked him as he acknowledged the contrast between past and present. Then he groaned softly, and went out. My heart began to beat very fast. I sprang up and tried to lock the door into the hall. My enthusiasm about spending a few days in this dismal place suddenly faded out, for I could not bear the thought that the weird old man was free to prowl about at his own sad will. But as I stood undecided in my doorway, a song sparrow perched on the sill of the wide hall window, and sang his heart away in a most cheerful strain. There was something so touching

and appealing in the contrast that I felt a wistful clutch at my throat
while I smiled, as one does when tears are coming like April showers
to one's eyes. Without thinking what I did, I went back into the room,
threw open the shutters again, and stood before the dingy landscape.
How the horses pranced up to the door, and how fine the ladies were
in their hoop-petticoats and high feathers! I imagined that the picture
had been a constant rebuke to the dwellers in the house through their
wasting lives and failing fortunes. In every human heart, said I, there is
such a picture of the ideal life,—the high possibilities and successes, the
semblance of duties done and of spiritual achievements. It forever measures our incompleteness by its exact likeness to that completeness
which we would not fight hard enough to win. But as I looked up at
the panel, the old landscape became dim, and I knew what it was only
because a cloud was hiding the sun; yet I was glad to leave the shadows
of the room, and to hurry down the wide stairway.

I saw nothing of the daughter, though I searched for her, and even
called her, through the house. When I reached the side door I found
her father crossing the yard, and wondered if he would show any
consciousness of our having so lately met. He stood still and waited for
me, and my first impulse made me ask, "What did you want just now?
I was not asleep when you were in my room; you frightened me."

"Do not be afraid," he answered with unexpected patience. "You
must take us as you find us. It is a sad old house, but you need not be
afraid; we are much more afraid of you!" and we both smiled amiably.

"But your daughter," said I; "I have been asking her to come away
for a time, to visit me or take a journey. It would be much better for
you both; and she needs a change and a little pleasuring. God does not
mean that we shall make our lives utterly dismal." I was afraid, and did
not dare to meet the old man's eyes after I had spoken so plainly.

He laughed coldly, and glanced at his mended coat-sleeve.

"What do you know about happiness? You are too young," said he.
"At your age I thought I knew the world. What difference would it
make if the old place here were like the gay ghost of it in our landscape
chamber? The farmers would be jealous of our luxury; reverence and
respect would be turned into idle curiosity. This quiet countryside would
be disgraced by such a flaunting folly. No, we are very comfortable, my
child and I; you must not try to disturb us," and he looked at me with
a kind of piteous suspicion.

There was a large block of stone under one of the old elms, which
had been placed there long ago for a mounting-block, and here we
seated ourselves. As I looked at my companion, he seemed like a man
unused to the broad light of day. I fancied that a prisoner, who had just

ended many years of dungeon life, would wear exactly such a face. And yet it was such a lovely summer day of a joyful world, if he would only take or make it so. Alas, he matched the winter weather better. I could not bear to think of the old house in winter!

"Who is to blame?" said the old man suddenly, in a strange eager tone which startled me, and made me shrink away from him. "We are in bondage. I am a generous-hearted man, yet I can never follow my own impulses. I longed to give what I had with a lavish hand, when I was younger, but some power restrained me. I have grown old while I tried to fight it down. We are all in prison while we are left in this world, —that is the truth; in prison for another man's sin." For the first time I understood that he was not altogether sane. "If there were an ancestor of mine, as I have been taught, who sold his soul for wealth, the awful price was this, and he lost the power of using it. He was greedy for gain, and now we cannot part with what we have, even for common comfort. His children and his children's children have suffered for his fault. He has lived in the hell of watching us from generation to generation; seeing our happiness spoiled, our power of usefulness wither away. Wherever he is, he knows that we are all misers because he was miserly, and stamped us with the mark of his own base spirit. He has watched his descendants shrivel up and disappear one by one, poor and ungenerous in God's world. We fight against the doom of it, but it wins at last. Thank God, there are only two of us left."

I had sprung to my feet, frightened by the old man's vehemence. I could not help saying that God meant us to be free and unconquered by any evil power; the gray, strange face looked blindly at me, and I could not speak again. This was the secret of the doom, then. I left the old man crying, while I hurried away to find the mistress of the desolate house, and appeal to her to let me send a companion for her father, who could properly care for him here, or persuade him to go away to some place where he would forget his misery among new interests and scenes. She herself must not be worn out by his malady of unreason.

But I only dashed my sympathy against the rock of her hopelessness. "I think we shall all disappear some night in a winter storm, and the world will be rid of us,—father and the house and I, all three," she said, with bitter dreariness, and turned to her work again.

Early that evening, I said good-by to my new friends, for the horse was sound, and not to be satisfied by such meagre stabling. Our host seemed sorry to let the creature go, and stood stroking him affectionately after I had mounted. "How the famous old breed holds its own!" he said wistfully. "I should like to have seen the ancestor who has stamped his likeness so unmistakably on all his descendants."

"But among human beings," I could not resist saying, "there is freedom, thank God! We can climb to our best possibilities, and outgrow our worst inheritance."

"No, no!" cried the old man bitterly. "You are young and fortunate. Forget us, if you can; we are of those who have no hope in a world of fate."

I looked back again and again, as I rode away. It was a house of shadows and strange moods, and I was glad when I had fairly left it behind me; yet I looked forward to seeing it again. I well remember the old man's clutch at the money I offered him, and the kiss and the bunch of roses that the daughter gave me. But late that evening I was not sorry to shut myself into my prosaic room at a village hotel, rather than try to sleep again behind the faded figured curtains of the landscape chamber.

1888

FRANZ KAFKA

A Report to an Academy

Honored members of the Academy!

You have done me the honor of inviting me to give your Academy an account of the life I formerly led as an ape.

I regret that I cannot comply with your request to the extent you

The novels and short stories of Franz Kafka encapsulate the absurdity and alienation of modern life. Born in Prague, July 3, 1883, into a middle-class Jewish family, Kafka experienced firsthand the repercussions from nationalism and anti-Semitism. Yet he felt similarly isolated within the religious community and the University of Prague as well as within the bureaucracy where he worked for his entire life. In his writing, however, he was encouraged by select groups of Jewish intellectuals, who persuaded him to publish some of his most unnerving tales, including "The Metamorphosis" (1915) and "The Penal Colony" (1919). Before his death on June 3, 1924, the despondent writer asked that all of his unpublished manuscripts be destroyed. His friend Max Brod disregarded the instruction, thus saving The Trial (1925), The Castle (1926), and Amerika (1927)—all of Kafka's novels.

desire. It is now nearly five years since I was an ape, a short space of time, perhaps, according to the calendar, but an infinitely long time to gallop through at full speed, as I have done, more or less accompanied by excellent mentors, good advice, applause, and orchestral music, and yet essentially alone, since all my escorters, to keep the image, kept well off the course. I could never have achieved what I have done had I been stubbornly set on clinging to my origins, to the remembrances of my youth. In fact, to give up being stubborn was the supreme command-ment I laid upon myself; free ape as I was, I submitted myself to that yoke. In revenge, however, my memory of the past has closed the door against me more and more. I could have returned at first, had human beings allowed it, through an archway as wide as the span of heaven over the earth, but as I spurred myself on in my forced career, the opening narrowed and shrank behind me; I felt more comfortable in the world of men and fitted it better; the strong wind that blew after me out of my past began to slacken; today it is only a gentle puff of air that plays around my heels; and the opening in the distance, through which it comes and through which I once came myself, has grown so small that, even if my strength and my will power sufficed to get me back to it, I should have to scrape the very skin from my body to crawl through. To put it plainly, much as I like expressing myself in images, to put it plainly: your life as apes, gentlemen, insofar as something of that kind lies behind you, cannot be farther removed from you than mine is from me. Yet everyone on earth feels a tickling at the heels; the small chimpanzee and the great Achilles alike.

But to a lesser extent I can perhaps meet your demand, and indeed I do so with the greatest pleasure. The first thing I learned was to give a handshake; a handshake betokens frankness; well, today, now that I stand at the very peak of my career, I hope to add frankness in words to the frankness of that first handshake. What I have to tell the Academy will contribute nothing essentially new, and will fall far behind what you have asked of me and what with the best will in the world I cannot communicate—nonetheless, it should indicate the line an erstwhile ape has had to follow in entering and establishing himself in the world of men. Yet I could not risk putting into words even such insignificant information as I am going to give you if I were not quite sure of myself and if my position on all the great variety stages of the civilized world had not become quite unassailable.

I belong to the Gold Coast. For the story of my capture I must depend on the evidence of others. A hunting expedition sent out by the firm of Hagenbeck—by the way, I have drunk many a bottle of good red wine since then with the leader of that expedition—had taken up its position in the bushes by the shore when I came down for a drink at evening among a troop of apes. They shot at us; I was the only one that was hit; I was hit in two places.

Once in the cheek; a slight wound; but it left a large, naked, red scar which earned me the name of Red Peter, a horrible name, utterly inappropriate, which only some ape could have thought of, as if the only difference between me and the performing ape Peter, who died not so long ago and had some small local reputation, were the red mark on my cheek. This by the way.

The second shot hit me below the hip. It was a severe wound, it is the cause of my limping a little to this day. I read an article recently by one of the ten thousand windbags who vent themselves concerning me in the newspapers, saying: my ape nature is not yet quite under control; the proof being that when visitors come to see me, I have a predilection for taking down my trousers to show them where the shot went in. The hand which wrote that should have its fingers shot away one by one. As for me, I can take my trousers down before anyone if I like; you would find nothing but a well-groomed fur and the scar made—let me be particular in the choice of a word for this particular purpose, to avoid misunderstanding—the scar made by a wanton shot. Everything is open and aboveboard; there is nothing to conceal; when the plain truth is in question, great minds discard the niceties of refinement. But if the writer of the article were to take down his trousers before a visitor, that would be quite another story, and I will let it stand to his credit that he does not do it. In return, let him leave me alone with his delicacy!

After these two shots I came to myself—and this is where my own memories gradually begin—between decks in the Hagenbeck steamer, inside a cage. It was not a four-sided barred cage; it was only a three-sided cage nailed to a locker; the locker made the fourth side of it. The whole construction was too low for me to stand up in and too narrow to sit down in. So I had to squat with my knees bent and trembling all the time, and also, since probably for a time I wished to see no one, and to stay in the dark, my face was turned toward the locker while the bars of the cage cut into my flesh behind. Such a method of confining wild beasts is supposed to have its advantages during the first days of captivity, and out of my own experiences I cannot deny that from the human point of view this is really the case.

But that did not occur to me then. For the first time in my life I could see no way out; at least no direct way out; directly in front of me was the locker, board fitted close to board. True, there was a gap running right through the boards which I greeted with the blissful howl of ignorance when I first discovered it, but the hole was not even wide enough to stick one's tail through and not all the strength of an ape could enlarge it.

I am supposed to have made uncommonly little noise, as I was later informed, from which the conclusion was drawn that I would either soon die or if I managed to survive the first critical period would be very amenable to training. I did survive this period. Hopelessly sobbing, painfully hunting for fleas, apathetically licking a cocoanut, beating my skull against the locker, sticking out my tongue at anyone who came near me—that was how I filled in time at first in my new life. But over and above it all only the one feeling: no way out. Of course what I felt then as an ape I can represent now only in human terms, and therefore I misrepresent it, but although I cannot reach back to the truth of the old ape life, there is no doubt that it lies somewhere in the direction I have indicated.

Until then I had had so many ways out of everything, and now I had none. I was pinned down. Had I been nailed down, my right to free movement would not have been lessened. Why so? Scratch your flesh raw between your toes, but you won't find the answer. Press yourself against the bar behind you till it nearly cuts you in two, you won't find the answer. I had no way out but I had to devise one, for without it I could not live. All the time facing that locker—I should certainly have perished. Yet as far as Hagenbeck was concerned, the place for apes was in front of a locker—well then, I had to stop being an ape. A fine, clear train of thought, which I must have constructed somehow with my belly, since apes think with their bellies.

I fear that perhaps you do not quite understand what I mean by "way out." I use the expression in its fullest and most popular sense. I deliberately do not use the word "freedom." I do not mean the spacious feeling of freedom on all sides. As an ape, perhaps, I knew that, and I have met men who yearn for it. But for my part I desired such freedom neither then nor now. In passing: may I say that all too often men are betrayed by the word freedom. And as freedom is counted among the most sublime feelings, so the corresponding disillusionment can be also sublime. In variety theaters I have often watched, before my turn came on, a couple of acrobats performing on trapezes high in the roof. They swung themselves, they rocked to and fro, they sprang into the air, they floated into each other's arms, one hung by the hair from the teeth of the other. "And that too is human freedom," I thought, "self-controlled movement." What a mockery of holy Mother Nature! Were the apes to see such a spectacle, no theater walls could stand the shock of their laughter.

No, freedom was not what I wanted. Only a way out; right or left, or in any direction; I made no other demand; even should the way out prove to be an illusion; the demand was a small one, the disappointment could be no bigger. To get out somewhere, to get out! Only not to stay motionless with raised arms, crushed against a wooden wall.

Today I can see it clearly; without the most profound inward calm I could never have found my way out. And indeed perhaps I owe all that I have become to the calm that settled within me after my first few days in the ship. And again for that calmness it was the ship's crew I had to thank.

They were good creatures, in spite of everything. I find it still pleasant to remember the sound of their heavy footfalls which used to echo through my half-dreaming head. They had a habit of doing everything as slowly as possible. If one of them wanted to rub his eyes, he lifted a hand as if it were a drooping weight. Their jests were coarse, but hearty. Their laughter had always a gruff bark in it that sounded dangerous but meant nothing. They always had something in their mouths to spit out and did not care where they spat it. They always grumbled that they got fleas from me; yet they were not seriously angry about it; they knew that my fur fostered fleas, and that fleas jump; it was a simple matter of fact to them. When they were off duty some of them often used to sit down in a semicircle around me; they hardly spoke but only grunted to each other; smoked their pipes, stretched out on lockers; smacked their knees as soon as I made the slightest movement; and now and then one of them would take a stick and tickle me where I liked being tickled. If I were to be invited today to take a cruise on that ship I should certainly refuse the invitation, but just as certainly the memories I could recall between its decks would not all be hateful.

The calmness I acquired among these people kept me above all from trying to escape. As I look back now, it seems to me I must have had at least an inkling that I had to find a way out or die, but that my way out could not be reached through flight. I cannot tell now whether escape was possible, but I believe it must have been; for an ape it must always be possible. With my teeth as they are today I have to be careful even in simply cracking nuts, but at that time I could certainly have managed by degrees to bite through the lock of my cage. I did not do it. What good would it have done me? As soon as I had poked out my head I should have been caught again and put in a worse cage; or I might have slipped among the other animals without being noticed, among the pythons, say, who were opposite me, and so breathed out my life in their embrace; or supposing I had actually succeeded in sneaking out as far as the deck and leaping overboard, I should have rocked for a little on the deep sea and then been drowned. Desperate remedies. I did not think it out in this human way, but under the influence of my surroundings I acted as if I had thought it out.

I did not think things out; but I observed everything quietly. I watched these men go to and fro, always the same faces, the same movements, often it seemed to me there was only the same man. So this man or these men walked about unimpeded. A lofty goal faintly dawned before me. No one promised me that if I became like them the bars of my cage would be taken away. Such promises for apparently impossible contingencies are not given. But if one achieves the impossible, the promises appear later retrospectively precisely where one had looked in vain for them before. Now, these men in themselves had no great attraction for me. Had I been devoted to the aforementioned idea of freedom, I should certainly have preferred the deep sea to the way out that suggested itself in the heavy faces of these men. At any rate, I watched them for a long time before I even thought of such things, indeed, it was only the mass weight of my observations that impelled me in the right direction.

It was so easy to imitate these people. I learned to spit in the very first days. We used to spit in each other's faces; the only difference was that I licked my face clean afterwards and they did not. I could soon smoke a pipe like an old hand; and if I also pressed my thumb into the bowl of the pipe, a roar of appreciation went up between-decks; only it took me a very long time to understand the difference between a full pipe and an empty one.

My worst trouble came from the schnapps bottle. The smell of it revolted me; I forced myself to it as best I could; but it took weeks for me to master my repulsion. This inward conflict, strangely enough, was taken more seriously by the crew than anything else about me. I cannot distinguish the men from each other in my recollection, but there was one of them who came again and again, alone or with friends, by day, by night, at all kinds of hours; he would post himself before me with the bottle and give me instructions. He could not understand me, he wanted to solve the enigma of my being. He would slowly uncork the bottle and then look at me to see if I had followed him; I admit that I always watched him with wildly eager, too eager attention; such a student of humankind no human teacher ever found on earth. After the bottle was uncorked he lifted it to his mouth; I followed it with my eyes right up to his jaws; he would nod, pleased with me, and set the bottle to his lips; I, enchanted with my gradual enlightenment, squealed and scratched myself comprehensively wherever scratching was called for; he rejoiced, tilted the bottle, and took a drink; I, impatient and desperate to emulate him, befouled myself in my cage, which again gave him great satisfaction; and then, holding the bottle at arm's length and bringing it up with a swing, he would empty it at one draught, leaning back at an exaggerated angle for my better instruction. I, exhausted by too much effort, could follow him no farther and hung limply to the bars, while he ended his theoretical exposition by rubbing his belly and grinning.

After theory came practice. Was I not already quite exhausted by my theoretical instruction? Indeed I was; utterly exhausted. That was part of my destiny. And yet I would take hold of the proffered bottle as well as I was able; uncork it, trembling; this successful action would gradually inspire me with new energy; I would lift the bottle, already following my original model almost exactly; put it to my lips and—and then throw it down in disgust, utter disgust, although it was empty and filled only with the smell of the spirit, throw it down on the floor in disgust. To the sorrow of my teacher, to the greater sorrow of myself; neither of us being really comforted by the fact that I did not forget, even though I had thrown away the bottle, to rub my belly most admirably and to grin.

Far too often my lesson ended in that way. And to the credit of my teacher, he was not angry; sometimes indeed he would hold his burning pipe against my fur, until it began to smolder in some place I could not easily reach, but then he would himself extinguish it with his own kind, enormous hand; he was not angry with me, he perceived that we were both fighting on the same side against the nature of apes and that I had the more difficult task.

What a triumph it was then both for him and for me, when one evening before a large circle of spectators—perhaps there was a celebration of some kind, a gramophone was playing, an officer was circulating among the crew—when on this evening, just as no one was looking, I took hold of a schnapps bottle that had been carelessly left standing before my cage, uncorked it in the best style, while the company began to watch me with mounting attention, set it to my lips without hesitation, with no grimace, like a professional drinker, with rolling eyes and full throat, actually and truly drank it empty; then threw the bottle away, not this time in despair but as an artistic performer; forgot, indeed, to rub my belly; but instead of that, because I could not help it, because my senses were reeling, called a brief and unmistakable "Hallo!" breaking into human speech, and with this outburst broke into the human community, and felt its echo: "Listen, he's talking!" like a caress over the whole of my sweat-drenched body.

I repeat: there was no attraction for me in imitating human beings;

I imitated them because I needed a way out, and for no other reason. And even that triumph of mine did not achieve much. I lost my human voice again at once; it did not come back for months; my aversion for the schnapps bottle returned again with even greater force. But the line I was to follow had in any case been decided, once for all.

When I was handed over to my first trainer in Hamburg I soon realized that there were two alternatives before me: the Zoological Gardens or the variety stage. I did not hesitate. I said to myself: do your utmost to get onto the variety stage; the Zoological Gardens means only a new cage; once there, you are done for.

And so I learned things, gentlemen. Ah, one learns when one has to; one learns when one needs a way out; one learns at all costs. One stands over oneself with a whip; one flays oneself at the slightest opposition. My ape nature fled out of me, head over heels and away, so that my first teacher was almost himself turned into an ape by it, had soon to give up teaching and was taken away to a mental hospital. Fortunately he was soon let out again.

But I used up many teachers, indeed, several teachers at once. As I became more confident of my abilities, as the public took an interest in my progress and my future began to look bright, I engaged teachers for myself, established them in five communicating rooms, and took lessons from them all at once by dint of leaping from one room to the other.

That progress of mine! How the rays of knowledge penetrated from all sides into my awakening brain! I do not deny it: I found it exhilarating. But I must also confess: I did not overestimate it, not even then, much less now. With an effort which up till now has never been repeated I managed to reach the cultural level of an average European. In itself that might be nothing to speak of, but it is something insofar as it has helped me out of my cage and opened a special way out for me, the way of humanity. There is an excellent idiom: to fight one's way through the thick of things; that is what I have done, I have fought through the thick of things. There was nothing else for me to do, provided always that freedom was not to be my choice.

As I look back over my development and survey what I have achieved so far, I do not complain, but I am not complacent either. With my hands in my trouser pockets, my bottle of wine on the table, I half lie and half sit in my rocking chair and gaze out of the window: if a visitor arrives, I receive him with propriety. My manager sits in the anteroom; when I ring, he comes and listens to what I have to say. Nearly every evening I give a performance, and I have a success that could hardly be increased. When I come home late at night from banquets, from scientific receptions, from social gatherings, there sits waiting for me a half-trained little chimpanzee and I take comfort from her as apes do. By day I cannot bear to see her; for she has the insane look of the bewildered half-broken animal in her eye; no one else sees it, but I do, and I cannot bear it. On the whole, at any rate, I have achieved what I set out to achieve. But do not tell me that it was not worth the trouble. In any case, I am not appealing for any man's verdict, I am only imparting knowledge, I am only making a report. To you also, honored Members of the Academy, I have only made a report.

Translated by Willa and Edwin Muir
1917

NATHANIEL HAWTHORNE

Drowne's Wooden Image

One sunshiny morning, in the good old times of the town of Boston, a young carver in wood, well known by the name of Drowne, stood contemplating a large oaken log, which it was his purpose to convert into the figure-head of a vessel. And while he discussed within his own mind that sort of shape or similitude it were well to bestow upon this excellent piece of timber, there came into Drowne's workshop a certain

---

Although Nathaniel Hawthorne was born in Salem, Massachusetts, in 1804, one could easily claim that his artistic memory reached back to the founding years of the Massachusetts Bay Colony. His Puritan ancestors held important positions in the Salem area, one of whom even presided over the town's infamous witch trials. Such history found its way, transformed into allegories of great psychological complexity, into many of Hawthorne's most famous short stories, such as "Young Goodman Brown" (1835), as well as *The Scarlet Letter* (1850), the novel that ensured him a widespread and lasting readership. With his wife, Sophia Peabody, Hawthorne was acquainted with many of the writers and thinkers of the transcendentalist movement, but he preferred the friendship of former college classmate and U.S. president, Franklin Pierce, in whose company he died in 1864.

Captain Hunnewell, owner and commander of the good brig called the Cynosure, which had just returned from her first voyage to Fayal.

"Ah! that will do, Drowne, that will do!" cried the jolly captain, tapping the log with his rattan. "I bespeak this very piece of oak for the figure-head of the Cynosure. She has shown herself the sweetest craft that ever floated, and I mean to decorate her prow with the handsomest image that the skill of man can cut out of timber. And, Drowne, you are the fellow to execute it."

"You give me more credit than I deserve, Captain Hunnewell," said the carver, modestly, yet as one conscious of eminence in his art. "But, for the sake of the good brig, I stand ready to do my best. And which of these designs would you prefer? Here—" pointing to a staring, half length figure, in a white wig and scarlet coat—"here is an excellent model, the likeness of our gracious king. Here is the valiant Admiral Vernon. Or, if you prefer a female figure, what say you to Britannia with the trident?"

"All very fine, Drowne; all very fine," answered the mariner. "But as nothing like the brig ever swam the ocean, so I am determined she shall have such a figure-head as old Neptune never saw in his life. And what is more, as there is a secret in the matter, you must pledge your credit not to betray it."

"Certainly," said Drowne, marvelling, however, what possible mystery there could be in reference to an affair so open, of necessity, to the inspection of all the world, as the figure-head of a vessel. "You may depend, captain, on my being as secret as the nature of the case will permit."

Captain Hunnewell then took Drowne by the button, and communicated his wishes in so low a tone, that it would be unmannerly to repeat what was evidently intended for the carver's private ear. We shall, therefore, take the opportunity to give the reader a few desirable particulars about Drowne himself.

He was the first American who is known to have attempted,—in a very humble line, it is true,—that art in which we can now reckon so many names already distinguished, or rising to distinction. From his earliest boyhood, he had exhibited a knack—for it would be too proud a word to call it genius—a knack, therefore, for the imitation of the human figure, in whatever material came most readily to hand. The snows of a New England winter had often supplied him with a species of marble as dazzling white, at least, as the Parian or the Carrara, and if less durable, yet sufficiently so to correspond with any claims to permanent existence possessed by the boy's frozen statues. Yet they won admiration from maturer judges than his schoolfellows, and were, indeed, remarkably clever, though destitute of the native warmth that might have made the snow melt beneath his hand. As he advanced in life, the young man adopted pine and oak as eligible materials for the display of his skill, which now began to bring him a return of solid silver, as well as the empty praise that had been an apt reward enough for his productions of evanescent snow. He became noted for carving ornamental pump-heads, and wooden urns for gate-posts, and decorations, more grotesque than fanciful, for mantel-pieces. No apothecary would have deemed himself in the way of obtaining custom, without setting up a gilded mortar, if not a head of Galen or Hippocrates, from the skilful hand of Drowne. But the great scope of his business lay in the manufacture of figure-heads for vessels. Whether it were the monarch himself, or some famous British admiral or general, or the governor of the province, or perchance the favourite daughter of the ship-owner, there the image stood above the prow, decked out in gorgeous colours, magnificently gilded, and staring the whole world out of countenance, as if from an innate consciousness of its own superiority. These specimens of native sculpture had crossed the sea in all directions, and been not ignobly noticed among the crowded shipping of the Thames, and wherever else the hardy mariners of New England had pushed their adventures. It must be confessed, that a family likeness pervaded these respectable progeny of Drowne's skill—that the benign countenance of the king resembled those of his subjects, and that Miss Peggy Hobart, the merchant's daughter, bore a remarkable similitude to Britannia, Victory, and other ladies of the allegoric sisterhood; and, finally, that they had all had a kind of wooden aspect, which proved an intimate relationship with the unshaped blocks of timber in the carver's workshop. But, at least, there was no inconsiderable skill of hand, nor a deficiency of any attribute to render them really works of art, except that deep quality, be it of soul or intellect, which bestows life upon the lifeless, and warmth upon the cold, and which, had it been present, would have made Drowne's wooden image instinct with spirit.

The captain of the Cynosure had now finished his instructions.

"And Drowne," said he, impressively, "you must lay aside all other business, and set about this forthwith. And as to the price, only do the job in first rate style, and you shall settle that point yourself."

"Very well, captain," answered the carver, who looked grave and somewhat perplexed, yet had a sort of smile upon his visage. "Depend upon it, I'll do my utmost to satisfy you."

From that morning, the men of taste about Long Wharf and the Town Dock, who were wont to show their love for the arts by frequent visits to Drowne's workshop, and admiration of his wooden images, began to be sensible of a mystery in the carver's conduct. Often he was absent in the daytime. Sometimes, as might be judged by gleams of light from the shop windows, he was at work until a late hour of the evening; although neither knock nor voice, on such occasions, could gain admittance for a visitor, or elicit any word of response. Nothing remarkable, however, was observed in the shop at those hours when it was thrown open. A fine piece of timber, indeed, which Drowne was known to have reserved for some work of especial dignity, was seen to be gradually assuming shape. What shape it was destined ultimately to take, was a problem to his friends, and a point on which the carver preserved a rigid silence. But day after day, though Drowne was seldom noticed in the act of working upon it, this rude form began to be developed, until it became evident to all observers, that a female figure was growing into mimic life. At each new visit they beheld a larger pile of wooden chips, and a nearer approximation to something beautiful. It seemed as if the hamadryad of the oak had sheltered herself from the unimaginative world within the heart of her native tree, and that it was only necessary to remove the strange shapelessness that had incrusted her, and reveal the grace and loveliness of a divinity. Imperfect as the design, the attitude, the costume, and especially the face of the image, still remained, there was already an effect that drew the eye from the wooden cleverness of Drowne's earlier productions, and fixed it upon the tantalizing mystery of this new project.

Copley, the celebrated painter, then a young man, and a resident of Boston, came one day to visit Drowne; for he had recognized so much of moderate ability in the carver, as to induce him, in the dearth of any professional sympathy, to cultivate his acquaintance. On entering the shop, the artist glanced at the inflexible images of king, commander, dame, and allegory, that stood around; on the best of which might have been bestowed the questionable praise, that it looked as if a living man had here been changed to wood, and that not only the physical, but the intellectual and spiritual part, partook of the stolid transformation. But in not a single instance did it seem as if the wood were imbibing the ethereal essence of humanity. What a wide distinction is here, and how far would the slightest portion of the latter merit have outvalued the utmost degree of the former!

"My friend Drowne," said Copley, smiling to himself, but alluding to the mechanical and wooden cleverness that so invariably distinguished the images, "you are really a remarkable person! I have seldom met with a man, in your line of business, that could do so much; for one other touch might make this figure of General Wolfe, for instance, a breathing and intelligent human creature."

"You would have me think that you are praising me highly, Mr. Copley," answered Drowne, turning his back upon Wolfe's image in apparent disgust. "But there has come a light into my mind. I know, what you know as well, that the one touch, which you speak of as deficient, is the only one that would be truly valuable, and that, without it, these works of mine are no better than worthless abortions. There is the same difference between them and the works of an inspired artist, as between a sign post daub and one of your best pictures."

"This is strange!" cried Copley, looking him in the face, which now, as the painter fancied, had a singular depth of intelligence, though, hitherto, it had not given him greatly the advantage over his own family of wooden images. "What has come over you? How is it that, possessing the idea which you have now uttered, you should produce only such works as these?"

The carver smiled, but made no reply. Copley turned again to the images, conceiving that the sense of deficiency which Drowne had just expressed, and which is so rare in a merely mechanical character, must surely imply a genius, the tokens of which had heretofore been overlooked. But no; there was not a trace of it. He was about to withdraw, when his eyes chanced to fall upon a half-developed figure which lay in a corner of the workshop, surrounded by scattered chips of oak. It arrested him at once.

"What is here? Who has done this?" he broke out, after contemplating it in speechless astonishment for an instant. "Here is the divine, the life-giving touch! What inspired hand is beckoning this wood to arise and live? Whose work is this?"

"No man's work," replied Drowne. "The figure lies within that block of oak, and it is my business to find it."

"Drowne," said the true artist, grasping the carver fervently by the hand, "you are a man of genius!"

As Copley departed, happening to glance backward from the threshold, he beheld Drowne bending over the half created shape, and stretching forth his arms as if he would have embraced and drawn it to his heart; while, had such a miracle been possible, his countenance expressed passion enough to communicate warmth and sensibility to the lifeless oak.

"Strange enough!" said the artist to himself. "Who would have looked for a modern Pygmalion in the person of a Yankee mechanic!"

As yet, the image was but vague in its outward presentment; so that, as in the cloud-shapes around the western sun, the observer rather felt, or was led to imagine, than really saw what was intended by it. Day by day, however, the work assumed greater precision, and settled its irregular and misty outline into distincter grace and beauty. The general design was now obvious to the common eye. It was a female figure, in what appeared to be a foreign dress; the gown being laced over the bosom, and opening in front, so as to disclose a skirt or petticoat, the folds and inequalities of which were admirably represented in the oaken substance. She wore a hat of singular gracefulness, and abundantly laden with flowers, such as never grew in the rude soil of New England, but which, with all their fanciful luxuriance, had a natural truth that it seemed impossible for the most fertile imagination to have attained without copying from real prototypes. There were several little appendages to this dress, such as a fan, a pair of ear-rings, a chain about the neck, a watch in the bosom, and a ring upon the finger, all of which would have been deemed beneath the dignity of a sculpture. They were put on, however, with as much taste as a lovely woman might have shown in her attire, and could therefore have shocked none but a judgment spoiled by artistic rules.

The face was still imperfect; but, gradually, by a magic touch, intelligence and sensibility brightened through the features, with all the effect of light gleaming forth from within the solid oak. The face became alive. It was a beautiful, though not precisely regular, and somewhat haughty aspect, but with a certain piquancy about the eyes and mouth which, of all expressions, would have seemed the most impossible to throw over a wooden countenance. And now, so far as carving went, this wonderful production was complete.

"Drowne," said Copley, who had hardly missed a single day in his visits to the carver's workshop, "if this work were in marble, it would make you famous at once; nay, I would almost affirm that it would make an era in the art. It is as ideal as an antique statue, and yet as real as any lovely woman whom one meets at a fireside or in the street. But I trust you do not mean to desecrate this exquisite creature with paint, like those staring kings and admirals yonder?"

"Not paint her?" exclaimed Captain Hunnewell, who stood by; — "not paint the figure-head of the Cynosure! And what sort of a figure should I cut in a foreign port, with such an unpainted oaken stick as this over my prow? She must, and she shall, be painted to the life, from the topmost flower in her hat down to the silver spangles on her slippers."

"Mr. Copley," said Drowne, quietly, "I know nothing of marble statuary, and nothing of a sculptor's rules of art. But of this wooden image—this work of my hands—this creature of my heart—" and here his voice faltered and choked, in a very singular manner—"of this—of her—I may say that I know something. A well-spring of inward wisdom gushed within me, as I wrought upon the oak with my whole strength, and soul, and faith! Let others do what they may with marble, and adopt what rules they choose. If I can produce my desired effect by painted wood, those rules are not for me, and I have a right to disregard them."

"The very spirit of genius!" muttered Copley to himself. "How otherwise should this carver feel himself entitled to transcend all rules, and make me ashamed of quoting them."

He looked earnestly at Drowne, and again saw that expression of human love which, in a spiritual sense, as the artist could not help imagining, was the secret of the life that had been breathed into this block of wood.

The carver, still in the same secrecy that marked all his operations upon this mysterious image, proceeded to paint the habiliments in their proper colours, and the countenance with nature's red and white. When all was finished, he threw open his workshop, and admitted the towns-people to behold what he had done. Most persons, at their first entrance, felt impelled to remove their hats, and pay such reverence as was due to the richly dressed and beautiful young lady, who seemed to stand in a corner of the room, with oaken chips and shavings scattered at her feet. Then came a sensation of fear; as if, not being actually human, yet so like humanity, she must therefore be something preternatural. There was, in truth, an indefinable air and expression that might reasonably induce the query—who and from what sphere this daughter of the oak should be. The strange rich flowers of Eden on her head; the complexion, so much deeper and more brilliant than those of our native beauties; the foreign, as it seemed, and fantastic garb, yet not too fantastic to be worn decorously in the street; the delicately wrought embroidery of the skirt; the broad gold chain about her neck; the curious ring upon her finger; the fan, so exquisitely sculptured in open work, and painted to resemble pearl and ebony;—where could Drowne, in his sober walk of life, have beheld the vision here so matchlessly embodied! And then her face! In the dark eyes, and around the voluptuous mouth, there played a look made up of pride, coquetry, and a gleam of mirthfulness, which impressed Copley with the idea that the image was secretly enjoying the perplexed admiration of himself and all other beholders.

"And will you," said he to the carver, "permit this masterpiece to become the figure-head of a vessel? Give the honest captain yonder figure of Britannia—it will answer his purpose far better,—and send this fair queen to England, where, for aught I know, it may bring you a thousand pounds."

"I have not wrought it for money," said Drowne.

"What sort of a fellow is this!" thought Copley. "A Yankee, and throw away the chance of making his fortune! He has gone mad; and thence has come this gleam of genius."

There was still further proof of Drowne's lunacy, if credit were due to the rumour that he had been seen kneeling at the feet of the oaken lady, and gazing with a lover's passionate ardour into the face that his own hands had created. The bigots of the day hinted that it would be no matter of surprise if an evil spirit were allowed to enter this beautiful form, and seduce the carver to destruction.

The fame of the image spread far and wide. The inhabitants visited it so universally, that, after a few days of exhibition, there was hardly an old man or a child who had not become minutely familiar with its aspect. Even had the story of Drowne's wooden image ended here, its celebrity might have been prolonged for many years, by the reminiscences of those who looked upon it in their childhood, and saw nothing else so beautiful in after life. But the town was now astounded by an event, the narrative of which has formed itself into one of the most singular legends that are yet to be met with in the traditionary chimney-corners of the New England metropolis, where old men and women sit dreaming of the past, and wag their heads at the dreamers of the present and the future.

One fine morning, just before the departure of the Cynosure on her second voyage to Fayal, the commander of that gallant vessel was seen to issue from his residence in Hanover street. He was stylishly dressed in a blue broadcloth coat, with gold lace at the seams and button-holes, an embroidered scarlet waistcoat, a triangular hat, with a loop and broad binding of gold, and wore a silver-hilted hanger at his side. But the good captain might have been arrayed in the robes of a prince or the rags of a beggar, without in either case attracting notice, while obscured by such. a companion as now leaned on his arm. The people in the street started, rubbed their eyes, and either leaped aside from their path, or stood as if transfixed to wood or marble in astonishment.

"Do you see it?—do you see it?" cried one, with tremulous eagerness. "It is the very same!"

"The same?" answered another, who had arrived in town only the night before. "What do you mean? I see only a sea-captain in his shore-going clothes, and a young lady in a foreign habit, with a bunch of beautiful flowers in her hat. On my word, she is as fair and bright a damsel as my eyes have looked on this many a day!"

"Yes; the same!—the very same!" repeated the other. "Drowne's wooden image has come to life!"

Here was a miracle indeed! Yet, illuminated by the sunshine, or darkened by the alternate shade of the houses, and with its garments fluttering lightly in the morning breeze, there passed the image along the street. It was exactly and minutely the shape, the garb, and the face, which the townspeople had so recently thronged to see and admire. Not a rich flower upon her head, not a single leaf, but had had its prototype in Drowne's wooden workmanship, although now their fragile grace had become flexible, and was shaken by every footstep that the wearer made. The broad gold chain upon the neck was identical with the one represented on the image, and glistened with the motion imparted by the rise and fall of the bosom which it decorated. A real diamond sparkled on her finger. In her right hand she bore a pearl and ebony fan, which she flourished with a fantastic and bewitching coquetry, that was likewise expressed in all her movements, as well as in the style of her beauty and the attire that so well harmonized with it. The face, with its brilliant depth of complexion, had the same piquancy of mirthful mischief that was fixed upon the countenance of the image, but which was here varied and continually shifting, yet always essentially the same, like the sunny gleam upon a bubbling fountain. On the whole, there was something so airy and yet so real in the figure, and withal so perfectly did it represent Drowne's image, that people knew not whether to suppose the magic wood etherealized into a spirit, or warmed and softened into an actual woman.

"One thing is certain," muttered a Puritan of the old stamp. "Drowne has sold himself to the devil; and doubtless this gay Captain Hunnewell is a party to the bargain."

"And I," said a young man who overheard him, "would almost consent to be the third victim, for the liberty of saluting those lovely lips."

"And so would I," said Copley, the painter, "for the privilege of taking her picture."

The image, or apparition, whichever it might be, still escorted by the bold captain, proceeded from Hanover street through some of the cross-lanes that make this portion of the town so intricate, to Ann street, thence into Dock-square, and so downward to Drowne's shop, which stood just on the water's edge. The crowd still followed, gathering volume as it rolled along. Never had a modern miracle occurred in such broad daylight, nor in the presence of such a multitude of witnesses. The airy image, as if conscious that she was the object of the murmurs and disturbance that swelled behind her, appeared slightly vexed and flustered, yet still in a manner consistent with the light vivacity and sportive mischief that were written in her countenance. She was observed to flutter her fan with such vehement rapidity, that the elaborate delicacy of its workmanship gave way, and it remained broken in her hand.

Arriving at Drowne's door, while the captain threw it open, the marvellous apparition paused an instant on the threshold, assuming the very attitude of the image, and casting over the crowd that glance of sunny coquetry which all remembered on the face of the oaken lady. She and her cavalier then disappeared.

"Ah!" murmured the crowd, drawing a deep breath, as with one vast pair of lungs.

"The world looks darker, now that she has vanished," said some of the young men.

But the aged, whose recollections dated as far back as witch-times, shook their heads, and hinted that our forefathers would have thought it a pious deed to burn the daughter of the oak with fire.

"If she be other than a bubble of the elements," exclaimed Copley, "I must look upon her face again!"

He accordingly entered the shop; and there, in her usual corner, stood the image, gazing at him, as it might seem, with the very same expression of mirthful mischief that had been the farewell look of the apparition when, but a moment before, she turned her face towards the crowd. The carver stood beside his creation, mending the beautiful fan, which by some accident was broken in her hand. But there was no longer any motion in the life-like image, nor any real woman in the workshop, nor even the witchcraft of a sunny shadow, that might have deluded people's eyes as it flitted along the street. Captain Hunnewell, too, had vanished. His hoarse, sea-breezy tones, however, were audible on the other side of a door that opened upon the water.

"Sit down in the stern sheets, my lady," said the gallant captain. "Come, bear a hand, you lubbers, and set us on board in the turning of a minute-glass."

And then was heard the stroke of oars.

"Drowne," said Copley, with a smile of intelligence, "you have been a truly fortunate man. What painter or statuary ever had such a subject! No wonder that she inspired a genius into you, and first created the artist who afterwards created her image."

Drowne looked at him with a visage that bore the traces of tears, but from which the light of imagination and sensibility, so recently illuminating it, had departed. He was again the mechanical carver that he had been known to be all his lifetime.

"I hardly understand what you mean, Mr. Copley," said he, putting his hand to his brow. "This image! Can it have been my work? Well—

I have wrought it in a kind of dream; and now that I am broad awake, I must set about finishing yonder figure of Admiral Vernon."

And forthwith he employed himself on the stolid countenance of one of his wooden progeny, and completed it in his own mechanical style, from which he was never known afterwards to deviate. He followed his business industriously for many years, acquired a competence, and, in the latter part of his life, attained to a dignified station in the church, being remembered in records and traditions as Deacon Drowne, the carver. One of his productions, an Indian chief, gilded all over, stood during the better part of a century on the cupola of the Province House, bedazzling the eyes of those who looked upward, like an angel of the sun. Another work of the good deacon's hand—a reduced likeness of his friend Captain Hunnewell, holding a telescope and quadrant—may be seen, to this day, at the corner of Broad and State streets, serving in the useful capacity of sign to the shop of a nautical instrument maker. We know not how to account for the inferiority of this quaint old figure, as compared with the recorded excellence of the Oaken Lady, unless on the supposition, that in every human spirit there is imagination, sensibility, creative power, genius, which, according to circumstances, may either be developed in this world, or shrouded in a mask of dulness until another state of being. To our friend Drowne, there came a brief season for that one occasion, but, quenched in disappointment, left him again the mechanical carver in wood, without the power even of appreciating the work that his own hands had wrought. Yet who can doubt, that the very highest state to which a human spirit can attain, in its loftiest aspirations, is its truest and most natural state, and that Drowne was more consistent with himself when he wrought the admirable figure of the mysterious lady, than when he prepared a whole progeny of blockheads?

There was a rumor in Boston, about this period, that a young Portuguese lady of rank, on some occasion of political or domestic disquietude, had fled from her home in Fayal, and put herself under the protection of Captain Hunnewell, on board of whose vessel, and at whose residence, she was sheltered until a change of affairs. This fair stranger must have been the original of Drowne's Wooden Image.

1837

HERMAN MELVILLE

Bartleby, the Scrivener
A Story of Wall Street

I am a rather elderly man. The nature of my avocations, for the last thirty years, has brought me into more than ordinary contact with what would seem an interesting and somewhat singular set of men, of whom, as yet, nothing, that I know of, has ever been written—I mean, the law-copyists, or scriveners. I have known very many of them, professionally and privately, and, if I pleased, could relate divers histories, at which good-natured gentlemen might smile, and sentimental souls might weep. But I waive the biographies of all other scriveners, for a few passages in the life of Bartleby, who was a scrivener, the strangest I ever saw, or heard of. While, of other law-copyists, I might write the complete life, of Bartleby nothing of that sort can be done. I believe that no materials exist, for a full and satisfactory biography of this man. It is an irreparable loss to literature. Bartleby was one of those beings of whom nothing is ascertainable, except from the original sources, and, in his case, those are very small. What my own astonished eyes saw of Bartleby, *that* is all I know of him, except, indeed, one vague report, which will appear in the sequel.

Ere introducing the scrivener, as he first appeared to me, it is fit I make some mention of myself, my *employés*, my business, my chambers, and general surroundings, because some such description is indispensable to an adequate understanding of the chief character about to be presented. Imprimis: I am a man who, from his youth upwards, has been filled with a profound conviction that the easiest way of life is the best. Hence, though I belong to a profession proverbially energetic and nervous, even to turbulence, at times, yet nothing of that sort have I

Born in New York City in 1819, Herman Melville was brought up in the genteel atmosphere of a once prominent family. Shortly after his father's death in 1832, Melville sought financial security and adventure at sea. He converted his experiences about a voyage he made to French Polynesia aboard a whaling vessel into such works as the immensely popular *Typee* (1846) and the financial failure, *Moby-Dick; or, The Whale* (1851). Although his popularity was generally precarious during his lifetime, Melville greatly impressed his sometime neighbor Nathaniel Hawthorne with his intricate symbolism and metaphysical excursions. Late in his life Melville withdrew from society and turned his attention to poetry, publishing four collections before his death in 1891 in New York.

ever suffered to invade my peace. I am one of those unambitious lawyers who never address a jury, or in any way draw down public applause; but, in the cool tranquillity of a snug retreat, do a snug business among rich men's bonds, and mortgages, and title-deeds. All who know me, consider me an eminently *safe* man. The late John Jacob Astor, a personage little given to poetic enthusiasm, had no hesitation in pronouncing my first grand point to be prudence; my next, method. I do not speak it in vanity, but simply record the fact, that I was not unemployed in my profession by the late John Jacob Astor; a name which, I admit, I love to repeat; for it hath a rounded and orbicular sound to it, and rings like unto bullion. I will freely add, that I was not insensible to the late John Jacob Astor's good opinion.

Some time prior to the period at which this little history begins, my avocations had been largely increased. The good old office, now extinct in the State of New York, of a Master in Chancery, had been conferred upon me. It was not a very arduous office, but very pleasantly remunerative. I seldom lose my temper; much more seldom indulge in dangerous indignation at wrongs and outrages; but I must be permitted to be rash here and declare, that I consider the sudden and violent abrogation of the office of Master in Chancery, by the new Constitution, as a——premature act; inasmuch as I had counted upon a life-lease of the profits, whereas I only received those of a few short years. But this is by the way.

My chambers were up stairs, at No.——Wall Street. At one end, they looked upon the white wall of the interior of a spacious skylight shaft, penetrating the building from top to bottom.

This view might have been considered rather tame than otherwise, deficient in what landscape painters call "life." But, if so, the view from the other end of my chambers offered, at least, a contrast, if nothing more. In that direction, my windows commanded an unobstructed view of a lofty brick wall, black by age and everlasting shade; which wall required no spy-glass to bring out its lurking beauties, but, for the benefit of all near-sighted spectators, was pushed up to within ten feet of my window-panes. Owing to the great height of the surrounding buildings, and my chambers being on the second floor, the interval between this wall and mine not a little resembled a huge square cistern.

At the period just preceding the advent of Bartleby, I had two persons as copyists in my employment, and a promising lad as an office-boy. First, Turkey; second, Nippers; third, Ginger Nut. These may seem names, the like of which are not usually found in the Directory. In truth, they were nicknames, mutually conferred upon each other by my three clerks, and were deemed expressive of their respective persons or characters. Turkey was a short, pursy Englishman, of about my own age—that is, somewhere not far from sixty. In the morning, one might say, his face was of a fine florid hue, but after twelve o'clock, meridian —his dinner hour—it blazed like a grate full of Christmas coals; and continued blazing—but, as it were, with a gradual wane—till six o'clock P.M., or thereabouts; after which, I saw no more of the proprietor of the face, which, gaining its meridian with the sun, seemed to set with it, to rise, culminate, and decline the following day, with the like regularity and undiminished glory. There are many singular coincidences I have known in the course of my life, not the least among which was the fact, that, exactly when Turkey displayed his fullest beams from his red and radiant countenance, just then, too, at that critical moment, began the daily period when I considered his business capacities as seriously disturbed for the remainder of the twenty-four hours. Not that he was absolutely idle, or averse to business then; far from it. The difficulty was, he was apt to be altogether too energetic. There was a strange, inflamed, flurried, flighty recklessness of activity about him. He would be incautious in dipping his pen into his inkstand. All his blots upon my documents were dropped there after twelve o'clock, meridian. Indeed, not only would he be reckless, and sadly given to making blots in the afternoon, but, some days, he went further, and was rather noisy. At such times, too, his face flamed with augmented blazonry, as if cannel coal had been heaped on anthracite. He made an unpleasant racket with his chair; spilled his sand-box; in mending his pens, impatiently split them all to pieces, and threw them on the floor in a sudden passion; stood up, and leaned over his table, boxing his papers about in a most indecorous manner, very sad to behold in an elderly man like him. Nevertheless, as he was in many ways a most valuable person to me, and all the time before twelve o'clock, meridian, was the quickest, steadiest creature, too, accomplishing a great deal of work in a style not easily to be matched—for these reasons, I was willing to overlook his eccentricities, though, indeed, occasionally, I remonstrated with him. I did this very gently, however, because, though the civilest, nay, the blandest and most reverential of men in the morning, yet, in the afternoon, he was disposed, upon provocation, to be slightly rash with his tongue—in fact, insolent. Now, valuing his morning services as I did, and resolved not to lose them—yet, at the same time, made uncomfortable by his inflamed ways after twelve o'clock—and being a man of peace, unwilling by my admonitions to call forth unseemly retorts from him, I took upon me, one Saturday noon (he was always worse on Saturdays) to hint to him, very kindly, that, perhaps, now that he was growing old, it might be well to abridge his labors; in short, he need not come to my chambers after twelve o'clock, but, dinner over, had best go home to his lodgings, and rest himself till tea-time. But no; he insisted upon his afternoon devotions. His countenance became intolerably fervid, as he oratorically assured me—gesticulating with a long ruler at the other end of the room—that if his services in the morning were useful, how indispensable, then, in the afternoon?

"With submission, sir," said Turkey, on this occasion, "I consider myself your right-hand man. In the morning I but marshal and deploy my columns; but in the afternoon I put myself at their head, and gallantly charge the foe, thus"—and he made a violent thrust with the ruler.

"But the blots, Turkey," intimated I.

"True; but, with submission, sir, behold these hairs! I am getting old. Surely, sir, a blot or two of a warm afternoon is not to be severely urged against gray hairs. Old age—even if it blot the page—is honorable. With submission, sir, we *both* are getting old."

This appeal to my fellow-feeling was hardly to be resisted. At all events, I saw that go he would not. So, I made up my mind to let him stay, resolving, nevertheless, to see to it that, during the afternoon, he had to do with my less important papers.

Nippers, the second on my list, was a whiskered, sallow, and, upon the whole, rather piratical-looking young man, of about five-and-twenty. I always deemed him the victim of two evil powers—ambition and indigestion. The ambition was evinced by a certain impatience of the duties of a mere copyist, an unwarrantable usurpation of strictly professional affairs such as the original drawing up of legal documents. The indigestion seemed betokened in an occasional nervous testiness and grinning irritability, causing the teeth to audibly grind together over mistakes committed in copying; unnecessary maledictions, hissed, rather than spoken, in the heat of business; and especially by a continual discontent with the height of the table where he worked. Though of a very ingenious mechanical turn, Nippers could never get this table to suit him. He put chips under it, blocks of various sorts, bits of pasteboard, and at last went so far as to attempt an exquisite adjustment, by final pieces of folded blotting paper. But no invention would answer. If, for the sake of easing his back, he brought the table-lid at a sharp angle well up towards his chin, and wrote there like a man using the steep roof of a Dutch house for his desk, then he declared that it stopped the circulation in his arms. If now he lowered the table to his waistbands, and stooped over it in writing, then there was a sore aching in his back. In short, the truth of the matter was, Nippers knew not what he wanted. Or, if he wanted anything, it was to be rid of a scrivener's table altogether. Among the manifestations of his diseased ambition was a fondness he had for receiving visits from certain ambiguous-looking fellows in seedy coats, whom he called his clients. Indeed, I was aware that not only was he, at times, considerable of a ward-politician, but he occasionally did a little business at the justices' courts, and was not unknown on the steps of the Tombs. I have good reason to believe, however, that one individual who called upon him at my chambers, and who, with a grand air, he insisted was his client, was no other than a dun, and the alleged title-deed, a bill. But, with all his failings, and the annoyances he caused me, Nippers, like his compatriot Turkey, was a very useful man to me; wrote a neat, swift hand; and, when he chose, was not deficient in a gentlemanly sort of deportment. Added to this, he always dressed in a gentlemanly sort of way; and so, incidentally, reflected credit upon my chambers. Whereas, with respect to Turkey, I had much ado to keep him from being a reproach to me. His clothes were apt to look oily, and smell of eating-houses. He wore his pantaloons very loose and baggy in summer. His coats were execrable, his hat not to be handled. But while the hat was a thing of indifference to me, inasmuch as his natural civility and deference, as a dependent Englishman, always led him to doff it the moment he entered the room, yet his coat was another matter. Concerning his coats, I reasoned with him; but with no effect. The truth was, I suppose, that a man with so small an income could not afford to sport such a lustrous face and a lustrous coat at one and the same time. As Nippers once observed, Turkey's money went chiefly for red ink. One winter day, I presented Turkey with a highly respectable-looking coat of my own—a padded gray coat, of a most comfortable warmth, and which buttoned straight up from the knee to the neck. I thought Turkey would appreciate the favor, and abate his rashness and obstreperousness of afternoons. But no; I verily believe that buttoning himself up in so downy and blanket-like a coat had a pernicious effect upon him—upon the same principle that too much oats are bad for horses. In fact, precisely as a rash, restive horse is said to feel his oats, so Turkey felt his coat. It made him insolent. He was a man whom prosperity harmed.

Though, concerning the self-indulgent habits of Turkey, I had my own private surmises, yet, touching Nippers, I was well persuaded that, whatever might be his faults in other respects, he was, at least, a temperate young man. But, indeed, nature herself seemed to have been his vintner, and, at his birth, charged him so thoroughly with an irritable, brandy-like disposition, that all subsequent potations were needless. When I consider how, amid the stillness of my chambers, Nippers would sometimes impatiently rise from his seat, and stooping over his table, spread his arms wide apart, seize the whole desk, and move it, and jerk it, with a grim, grinding motion on the floor, as if the table were a perverse voluntary agent, intent on thwarting and vexing him, I plainly perceive that, for Nippers, brandy-and-water were altogether superfluous.

It was fortunate for me that, owing to its peculiar cause—indigestion—the irritability and consequent nervousness of Nippers were mainly observable in the morning, while in the afternoon he was comparatively mild. So that, Turkey's paroxysms only coming on about twelve o'clock, I never had to do with their eccentricities at one time. Their fits relieved each other, like guards. When Nippers' was on, Turkey's was off; and *vice versa*. This was a good natural arrangement, under the circumstances.

Ginger Nut, the third on my list, was a lad, some twelve years old. His father was a carman, ambitious of seeing his son on the bench instead of a cart, before he died. So he sent him to my office, as student at law, errand-boy, cleaner, and sweeper, at the rate of one dollar a week. He had a little desk to himself, but he did not use it much. Upon inspection, the drawer exhibited a great array of the shells of various sorts of nuts. Indeed, to this quick-witted youth, the whole noble science of the law was contained in a nutshell. Not the least among the employments of Ginger Nut, as well as one which he discharged with the most alacrity, was his duty as cake and apple purveyor for Turkey and Nippers. Copying lawpapers being proverbially a dry, husky sort of business, my two scriveners were fain to moisten their mouths very often with Spitzenbergs, to be had at the numerous stalls nigh the Custom House and Post Office. Also, they sent Ginger Nut very frequently for that peculiar cake—small, flat, round, and very spicy—after which he had been named by them. Of a cold morning, when business was but dull, Turkey would gobble up scores of these cakes, as if they were mere wafers—indeed, they sell them at the rate of six or eight for a penny—the scrape of his pen blending with the crunching of the crisp particles in his mouth. Of all the fiery afternoon blunders and flurried rashness of Turkey, was his once moistening a ginger-cake between his lips, and clapping it on to a mortgage, for a seal. I came within an ace of dismissing him then. But he mollified me by making an oriental bow, and saying—

"With submission, sir, it was generous of me to find you in stationery on my own account."

Now my original business—that of a conveyancer and title hunter, and drawer-up of recondite documents of all sorts—was considerably increased by receiving the Master's office. There was now great work for scriveners. Not only must I push the clerks already with me, but I must have additional help.

In answer to my advertisement, a motionless young man one morning stood upon my office threshold, the door being open, for it was summer. I can see that figure now—pallidly neat, pitiably respectable, incurably forlorn! It was Bartleby.

After a few words touching his qualifications, I engaged him, glad to have among my corps of copyists a man of so singularly sedate an aspect, which I thought might operate beneficially upon the flighty temper of Turkey, and the fiery one of Nippers.

I should have stated before that ground-glass folding-doors divided my premises into two parts, one of which was occupied by my scriveners, the other by myself. According to my humor, I threw open these doors, or closed them. I resolved to assign Bartleby a corner by the folding-doors, but on my side of them, so as to have this quiet man within easy call, in case any trifling thing was to be done. I placed his desk close up to a small side-window in that part of the room, a window which originally had afforded a lateral view of certain grimy brickyards and bricks, but which, owing to subsequent erections, commanded at present no view at all, though it gave some light. Within three feet of the panes was a wall, and the light came down from far above, between two lofty buildings, as from a very small opening in a dome. Still further to a satisfactory arrangement, I procured a high green folding screen, which might entirely isolate Bartleby from my sight, though not remove him from my voice. And thus, in a manner, privacy and society were conjoined.

At first, Bartleby did an extraordinary quantity of writing. As if long famishing for something to copy, he seemed to gorge himself on my documents. There was no pause for digestion. He ran a day and night line, copying by sunlight and by candle-light. I should have been quite delighted with his application, had he been cheerfully industrious. But he wrote on silently, palely, mechanically.

It is, of course, an indispensable part of a scrivener's business to verify the accuracy of his copy, word by word. Where there are two or more scriveners in an office, they assist each other in this examination, one reading from the copy, the other holding the original. It is a very dull, wearisome, and lethargic affair. I can readily imagine that, to some sanguine temperaments, it would be altogether intolerable. For example, I cannot credit that the mettlesome poet, Byron, would have contentedly sat down with Bartleby to examine a law document of, say five hundred pages, closely written in a crimpy hand.

Now and then, in the haste of business, it had been my habit to assist in comparing some brief document myself, calling Turkey or

Nippers for this purpose. One object I had, in placing Bartleby so handy to me behind the screen, was, to avail myself of his services on such trivial occasions. It was on the third day, I think, of his being with me, and before any necessity had arisen for having his own writing examined, that, being much hurried to complete a small affair I had in hand, I abruptly called to Bartleby. In my haste and natural expectancy of instant compliance, I sat with my head bent over the original on my desk, and my right hand sideways, and somewhat nervously extended with the copy, so that, immediately upon emerging from his retreat, Bartleby might snatch it and proceed to business without the least delay.

In this very attitude did I sit when I called to him, rapidly stating what it was I wanted him to do—namely, to examine a small paper with me. Imagine my surprise, nay, my consternation, when, without moving from his privacy, Bartleby, in a singularly mild, firm voice, replied, "I would prefer not to."

I sat awhile in perfect silence, rallying my stunned faculties. Immediately it occurred to me that my ears had deceived me, or Bartleby had entirely misunderstood my meaning. I repeated my request in the clearest tone I could assume; but in quite as clear a one came the previous reply, "I would prefer not to."

"Prefer not to," echoed I, rising in high excitement, and crossing the room with a stride. "What do you mean? Are you moonstruck? I want you to help me compare this sheet here—take it," and I thrust it towards him.

"I would prefer not to," said he.

I looked at him steadfastly. His face was leanly composed; his gray eyes dimly calm. Not a wrinkle of agitation rippled him. Had there been the least uneasiness, anger, impatience, or impertinence in his manner; in other words, had there been anything ordinarily human about him, doubtless I should have violently dismissed him from the premises. But as it was, I should have as soon thought of turning my pale plaster-of-paris bust of Cicero out of doors. I stood gazing at him awhile, as he went on with his own writing, and then reseated myself at my desk. This is very strange, thought I. What had one best do? But my business hurried me. I concluded to forget the matter for the present, reserving it for my future leisure. So, calling Nippers from the other room, the paper was speedily examined.

A few days after this, Bartleby concluded four lengthy documents, being quadruplicates of a week's testimony taken before me in my High Court of Chancery. It became necessary to examine them. It was an important suit, and great accuracy was imperative. Having all things arranged, I called Turkey, Nippers, and Ginger Nut, from the next room, meaning to place the four copies in the hands of my four clerks, while

I should read from the original. Accordingly, Turkey, Nippers, and Ginger Nut had taken their seats in a row, each with his document in his hand, when I called to Bartleby to join this interesting group.

"Bartleby! quick, I am waiting."

I heard a slow scrape of his chair legs on the uncarpeted floor, and soon he appeared standing at the entrance of his hermitage.

"What is wanted?" said he, mildly.

"The copies, the copies," said I, hurriedly. "We are going to examine them. There"—and I held towards him the fourth quadruplicate.

"I would prefer not to," he said, and gently disappeared behind the screen.

For a few moments I was turned into a pillar of salt, standing at the head of my seated column of clerks. Recovering myself, I advanced towards the screen, and demanded the reason for such extraordinary conduct.

"*Why* do you refuse?"

"I would prefer not to."

With any other man I should have flown outright into a dreadful passion, scorned all further words, and thrust him ignominiously from my presence. But there was something about Bartleby that not only strangely disarmed me, but, in a wonderful manner, touched and disconcerted me. I began to reason with him.

"These are your own copies we are about to examine. It is labor saving to you, because one examination will answer for your four papers. It is common usage. Every copyist is bound to help examine his copy. Is it not so? Will you not speak? Answer!"

"I prefer not to," he replied in a flute-like tone. It seemed to me that, while I had been addressing him, he carefully revolved every statement that I made; fully comprehended the meaning; could not gainsay the irresistible conclusion; but, at the same time, some paramount consideration prevailed with him to reply as he did.

"You are decided, then, not to comply with my request—a request made according to common usage and common sense?"

He briefly gave me to understand, that on that point my judgment was sound. Yes: his decision was irreversible.

It is not seldom the case that, when a man is browbeaten in some unprecedented and violently unreasonable way, he begins to stagger in his own plainest faith. He begins, as it were, vaguely to surmise that, wonderful as it may be, all the justice and all the reason is on the other side. Accordingly, if any disinterested persons are present, he turns to them for some reinforcement for his own faltering mind.

"Turkey," said I, "what do you think of this? Am I not right?"

"With submission, sir," said Turkey, in his blandest tone, "I think that you are."

"Nippers," said I, "what do *you* think of it?"

"I think I should kick him out of the office."

(The reader of nice perceptions will have perceived that, it being morning, Turkey's answer is couched in polite and tranquil terms, but Nippers replies in ill-tempered ones. Or, to repeat a previous sentence, Nippers' ugly mood was on duty, and Turkey's off.)

"Ginger Nut," said I, willing to enlist the smallest suffrage in my behalf, "what do *you* think of it?"

"I think, sir, he's a little *luny*," replied Ginger Nut, with a grin.

"You hear what they say," said I, turning towards the screen, "come forth and do your duty."

But he vouchsafed no reply. I pondered a moment in sore perplexity. But once more business hurried me. I determined again to postpone the consideration of this dilemma to my future leisure. With a little trouble we made out to examine the papers without Bartleby, though at every page or two Turkey deferentially dropped his opinion, that this proceeding was quite out of the common; while Nippers, twitching in his chair with a dyspeptic nervousness, ground out, between his set teeth, occasional hissing maledictions against the stubborn oaf behind the screen. And for his (Nippers') part, this was the first and the last time he would do another man's business without pay.

Meanwhile Bartleby sat in his hermitage, oblivious to everything but his own peculiar business there.

Some days passed, the scrivener being employed upon another lengthy work. His late remarkable conduct led me to regard his ways narrowly. I observed that he never went to dinner; indeed, that he never went anywhere. As yet I had never, of my personal knowledge, known him to be outside of my office. He was a perpetual sentry in the corner. At about eleven o'clock though, in the morning, I noticed that Ginger Nut would advance towards the opening in Bartleby's screen, as if silently beckoned thither by a gesture invisible to me where I sat. The boy would then leave the office, jingling a few pence, and reappear with a handful of ginger-nuts, which he delivered in the hermitage, receiving two of the cakes for his trouble.

He lives, then, on ginger-nuts, thought I; never eats a dinner, properly speaking; he must be a vegetarian, then, but no; he never eats even vegetables, he eats nothing but ginger-nuts. My mind then ran on in reveries concerning the probable effects upon the human constitution of living entirely on ginger-nuts. Ginger-nuts are so called, because they contain ginger as one of their peculiar constituents, and the final flavoring one. Now, what was ginger? A hot, spicy thing. Was Bartleby hot and spicy? Not at all. Ginger, then, had no effect upon Bartleby. Probably he preferred it should have none.

Nothing so aggravates an earnest person as a passive resistance. If the individual so resisted be of a not inhuman temper, and the resisting one perfectly harmless in his passivity, then, in the better moods of the former, he will endeavor charitably to construe to his imagination what proves impossible to be solved by his judgment. Even so, for the most part, I regarded Bartleby and his ways. Poor fellow! thought I, he means no mischief; it is plain he intends no insolence; his aspect sufficiently evinces that his eccentricities are involuntary. He is useful to me. I can get along with him. If I turn him away, the chances are he will fall in with some less indulgent employer, and then he will be rudely treated, and perhaps driven forth miserably to starve. Yes. Here I can cheaply purchase a delicious self-approval. To befriend Bartleby; to humor him in his strange wilfulness, will cost me little or nothing, while I lay up in my soul what will eventually prove a sweet morsel for my conscience. But this mood was not invariable with me. The passiveness of Bartleby sometimes irritated me. I felt strangely goaded on to encounter him in new opposition—to elicit some angry spark from him answerable to my own. But, indeed, I might as well have essayed to strike fire with my knuckles against a bit of Windsor soap. But one afternoon the evil impulse in me mastered me, and the following little scene ensued:

"Bartleby," said I, "when those papers are all copied, I will compare them with you."

"I would prefer not to."

"How? Surely you do not mean to persist in that mulish vagary?" No answer.

I threw open the folding-doors nearby, and turning upon Turkey and Nippers, exclaimed:

"Bartleby a second time says, he won't examine his papers. What do you think of it, Turkey?"

It was afternoon, be it remembered. Turkey sat glowing like a brass boiler; his bald head steaming; his hands reeling among his blotted papers.

"Think of it?" roared Turkey. "I think I'll just step behind his screen, and black his eyes for him!"

So saying, Turkey rose to his feet and threw his arms into a pugilistic position. He was hurrying away to make good his promise, when I detained him, alarmed at the effect of incautiously rousing Turkey's combativeness after dinner.

"Sit down, Turkey," said I, "and hear what Nippers has to say. What do you think of it, Nippers? Would I not be justified in immediately dismissing Bartleby?"

"Excuse me, that is for you to decide, sir. I think his conduct quite unusual, and, indeed, unjust, as regards Turkey and myself. But it may only be a passing whim."

"Ah," exclaimed I, "you have strangely changed your mind, then —you speak very gently of him now."

"All beer," cried Turkey; "gentleness is effects of beer—Nippers and I dined together to-day. You see how gentle *I* am, sir. Shall I go and black his eyes?"

"You refer to Bartleby, I suppose. No, not to-day, Turkey," I replied; "pray, put up your fists."

I closed the doors, and again advanced towards Bartleby. I felt additional incentives tempting me to my fate. I burned to be rebelled against again. I remembered that Bartleby never left the office.

"Bartleby," said I, "Ginger Nut is away; just step around to the Post Office, won't you?" (it was but a three minutes' walk) "and see if there is anything for me."

"I would prefer not to."

"You *will* not?"

"I *prefer* not."

I staggered to my desk, and sat there in a deep study. My blind inveteracy returned. Was there any other thing in which I could procure myself to be ignominiously repulsed by this lean, penniless wight?— my hired clerk? What added thing is there, perfectly reasonable, that he will be sure to refuse to do?

"Bartleby!"

No answer.

"Bartleby," in a louder tone.

No answer.

"Bartleby," I roared.

Like a very ghost, agreeably to the laws of magical invocation, at the third summons, he appeared at the entrance of his hermitage.

"Go to the next room, and tell Nippers to come to me."

"I would prefer not to," he respectfully and slowly said, and mildly disappeared.

"Very good, Bartleby," said I, in a quiet sort of serenely-severe self-possessed tone, intimating the unalterable purpose of some terrible retribution very close at hand. At the moment I half intended something of the kind. But upon the whole, as it was drawing towards my dinner-hour, I thought it best to put on my hat and walk home for the day, suffering much from perplexity and distress of mind.

Shall I acknowledge it? The conclusion of this whole business was, that it soon became a fixed fact of my chambers, that a pale young scrivener, by the name of Bartleby, had a desk there; that he copied for me at the usual rate of four cents a folio (one hundred words); but he was permanently exempt from examining the work done by him, that duty being transferred to Turkey and Nippers, out of compliment, doubtless, to their superior acuteness; moreover, said Bartleby was never, on any account, to be dispatched on the most trivial errand of any sort; and that even if entreated to take upon him such a matter, it was generally understood that he would "prefer not to"—in other words, that he would refuse point blank.

As days passed on, I became considerably reconciled to Bartleby. His steadiness, his freedom from all dissipation, his incessant industry (except when he chose to throw himself into a standing revery behind his screen), his great stillness, his unalterableness of demeanor under all circumstances, made him a valuable acquisition. One prime thing was this—*he was always there*—first in the morning, continually through the day, and the last at night. I had a singular confidence in his honesty. I felt my most precious papers perfectly safe in his hands. Sometimes, to be sure, I could not, for the very soul of me, avoid falling into sudden spasmodic passions with him. For it was exceeding difficult to bear in mind all the time those strange peculiarities, privileges, and unheard-of exemptions, forming the tacit stipulations on Bartleby's part under which he remained in my office. Now and then, in the eagerness of dispatching pressing business, I would inadvertently summon Bartleby, in a short, rapid tone, to put his finger, say, on the incipient tie of a bit of red tape with which I was about compressing some papers. Of course, from behind the screen the usual answer, "I prefer not to," was sure to come; and then, how could a human creature, with the common infirmities of our nature, refrain from bitterly exclaiming upon such perverseness—such unreasonableness? However, every added repulse of this sort which I received only tended to lessen the probability of my repeating the inadvertence.

Here it must be said, that, according to the custom of most legal gentlemen occupying chambers in densely populated law buildings, there were several keys to my door. One was kept by a woman residing in the attic, which person weekly scrubbed and daily swept and dusted my apartments. Another was kept by Turkey for convenience sake. The third I sometimes carried in my own pocket. The fourth I knew not who had.

Now, one Sunday morning I happened to go to Trinity Church, to hear a celebrated preacher, and finding myself rather early on the ground I thought I would walk round to my chambers for a while. Luckily I had my key with me; but upon applying it to the lock, I found it resisted by something inserted from the inside. Quite surprised, I called out; when to my consternation a key was turned from within; and thrusting his lean visage at me, and holding the door ajar, the apparition of Bartleby appeared, in his shirt-sleeves, and otherwise in a strangely tattered *deshabille*, saying quietly that he was sorry, but he was deeply engaged just then, and—preferred not admitting me at present. In a brief word or two, he moreover added, that perhaps I had better walk round the block two or three times, and by that time he would probably have concluded his affairs.

Now, the utterly unsurmised appearance of Bartleby, tenanting my law-chambers of a Sunday morning, with his cadaverously gentlemanly *nonchalance*, yet withal firm and self-possessed, had such a strange effect upon me, that incontinently I slunk away from my own door, and did as desired. But not without sundry twinges of impotent rebellion against the mild effrontery of this unaccountable scrivener. Indeed, it was his wonderful mildness chiefly, which not only disarmed me, but un-manned me, as it were. For I consider that one, for the time, is sort of unmanned when he tranquilly permits his hired clerk to dictate to him, and order him away from his own premises. Furthermore, I was full of uneasiness as to what Bartleby could possibly be doing in my office in his shirt-sleeves, and in an otherwise dismantled condition on a Sunday morning. Was anything amiss going on? Nay, that was out of the question. It was not to be thought of for a moment that Bartleby was an immoral person. But what could he be doing there?—copying? Nay again, whatever might be his eccentricities, Bartleby was an eminently decorous person. He would be the last man to sit down to his desk in any state approaching to nudity. Besides, it was Sunday; and there was something about Bartleby that forbade the supposition that he would by any secular occupation violate the proprieties of the day.

Nevertheless, my mind was not pacified; and full of a restless curi-osity, at last I returned to the door. Without hindrance I inserted my key, opened it, and entered. Bartleby was not to be seen. I looked round anxiously, peeped behind his screen; but it was very plain that he was gone. Upon more closely examining the place, I surmised that for an indefinite period Bartleby must have ate, dressed, and slept in my office, and that too without plate, mirror, or bed. The cushioned seat of a rickety old sofa in one corner bore the faint impress of a lean, reclining form. Rolled away under his desk, I found a blanket; under the empty grate, a blacking box and brush; on a chair, a tin basin, with soap and a ragged towel; in a newspaper a few crumbs of ginger-nuts and a morsel of cheese. Yes, thought I, it is evident enough that Bartleby has been making his home here, keeping bachelor's hall all by himself. Immediately then the thought came sweeping across me, what miserable friendlessness and loneliness are here revealed! His poverty is great; but his solitude, how horrible! Think of it. Of a Sunday, Wall Street is deserted as Petra; and every night of every day it is an emptiness. This building, too, which of week-days hums with industry and life, at nightfall echoes with sheer vacancy, and all through Sunday is forlorn. And here Bartleby makes his home; sole spectator of a solitude which he has seen all populous—a sort of innocent and transformed Marius brooding among the ruins of Carthage!

For the first time in my life a feeling of overpowering stinging melancholy seized me. Before, I had never experienced aught but a not unpleasing sadness. The bond of a common humanity now drew me irresistibly to gloom. A fraternal melancholy! For both I and Bartleby were sons of Adam. I remembered the bright silks and sparkling faces I had seen that day, in gala trim, swan-like sailing down the Mississippi of Broadway; and I contrasted them with the pallid copyist, and thought to myself, Ah, happiness courts the light, so we deem the world is gay; but misery hides aloof, so we deem that misery there is none. These sad fancyings—chimeras, doubtless, of a sick and silly brain—led on to other and more special thoughts, concerning the eccentricities of Bartleby. Presentiments of strange discoveries hovered round me. The scrivener's pale form appeared to me laid out, among uncaring strangers, in its shivering winding-sheet.

Suddenly I was attracted by Bartleby's closed desk, the key in open sight left in the lock.

I mean no mischief, seek the gratification of no heartless curiosity, thought I; besides, the desk is mine, and its contents, too, so I will make bold to look within. Everything was methodically arranged, the papers smoothly placed. The pigeon-holes were deep, and removing the files of documents, I groped into their recesses. Presently I felt something there, and dragged it out. It was an old bandanna handkerchief, heavy and knotted. I opened it, and saw it was a saving's bank.

I now recalled all the quiet mysteries which I had noted in the man. I remembered that he never spoke but to answer; that, though at intervals he had considerable time to himself, yet I had never seen him reading—no, not even a newspaper; that for long periods he would stand looking out, at his pale window behind the screen, upon the dead brick wall; I was quite sure he never visited any refectory or eating-house; while his pale face clearly indicated that he never drank beer like Turkey; or tea and coffee even, like other men; that he never went anywhere in particular that I could learn; never went out for a walk, unless, indeed, that was the case at present; that he had declined telling who he was, or whence he came, or whether he had any relatives in the world; that though so thin and pale, he never complained of ill-health. And more than all, I remembered a certain unconscious air of pallid—how shall I call it—of pallid haughtiness, say, or rather an austere reserve about him, which has positively awed me into my tame compliance with his eccentricities, when I had feared to ask him to do the slightest incidental thing for me, even though I might know, from his long-continued motionlessness, that behind his screen he must be standing in one of those dead-wall reveries of his.

Revolving all these things, and coupling them with the recently discovered fact, that he made my office his constant abiding place and home, and not forgetful of his morbid moodiness; revolving all these things, a prudential feeling began to steal over me. My first emotions had been those of pure melancholy and sincerest pity; but just in proportion as the forlornness of Bartleby grew and grew to my imagination, did that same melancholy merge into fear, that pity into repulsion. So true it is, and so terrible, too, that up to a certain point the thought or sight of misery enlists our best affections; but, in certain special cases, beyond that point it does not. They err who would assert that invariably this is owing to the inherent selfishness of the human heart. It rather proceeds from a certain hopelessness of remedying excessive and organic ill. To a sensitive being, pity is not seldom pain. And when at last it is perceived that such pity cannot lead to effectual succor, common sense bids the soul be rid of it. What I saw that morning persuaded me that the scrivener was the victim of innate and incurable disorder. I might give alms to his body; but his body did not pain him; it was his soul that suffered, and his soul I could not reach.

I did not accomplish the purpose of going to Trinity Church that morning. Somehow, the things I had seen disqualified me for the time from church-going. I walked homeward, thinking what I would do with Bartleby. Finally, I resolved upon this—I would put certain calm questions to him the next morning, touching his history, etc., and if he declined to answer them openly and unreservedly (and I supposed he would prefer not), then to give him a twenty dollar bill over and above whatever I might owe him, and tell him his services were no longer required; but that if in any other way I could assist him, I would be happy to do so, especially if he desired to return to his native place, wherever that might be, I would willingly help to defray the expenses. Moreover, if, after reaching home, he found himself at any time in want of aid, a letter from him would be sure of a reply.

The next morning came.

"Bartleby," said I, gently calling to him behind his screen.

No reply.

"Bartleby," said I, in a still gentler tone, "come here; I am not going to ask you to do anything you would prefer not to do—I simply wish to speak to you."

Upon this he noiselessly slid into view.

"Will you tell me, Bartleby, where you were born?"

"I would prefer not to."

"Will you tell me *anything* about yourself?"

"I would prefer not to."

"But what reasonable objection can you have to speak to me? I feel friendly towards you."

He did not look at me while I spoke, but kept his glance fixed upon my bust of Cicero, which, as I then sat, was directly behind me, some six inches above my head.

"What is your answer, Bartleby?" said I, after waiting a considerable time for a reply, during which his countenance remained immovable, only there was the faintest conceivable tremor of the white attenuated mouth.

"At present I prefer to give no answer," he said, and retired into his hermitage.

It was rather weak in me I confess, but his manner, on this occasion, nettled me. Not only did there seem to lurk in it a certain calm disdain, but his perverseness seemed ungrateful, considering the undeniable good usage and indulgence he had received from me.

Again I sat ruminating what I should do. Mortified as I was at his behavior, and resolved as I had been to dismiss him when I entered my office, nevertheless I strangely felt something superstitious knocking at my heart, and forbidding me to carry out my purpose, and denouncing me for a villain if I dared to breathe one bitter word against this forlornest of mankind. At last, familiarly drawing my chair behind his screen, I sat down and said: "Bartleby, never mind, then, about revealing your history; but let me entreat you, as a friend, to comply as far as may be with the usages of this office. Say now, you will help to examine papers tomorrow or next day: in short, say now, that in a day or two you will begin to be a little reasonable:—say so, Bartleby."

"At present I would prefer not to be a little reasonable," was his mildly cadaverous reply.

Just then the folding-doors opened, and Nippers approached. He seemed suffering from an unusually bad night's rest, induced by severer indigestion than common. He overheard those final words of Bartleby.

"*Prefer not*, eh?" gritted Nippers—"I'd *prefer* him, if I were you, sir," addressing me—"I'd *prefer* him; I'd give him preferences, the stubborn mule! What is it, sir, pray, that he *prefers* not to do now?"

Bartleby moved not a limb.

"Mr. Nippers," said I, "I'd prefer that you would withdraw for the present."

Somehow, of late, I had got into the way of involuntarily using this word "prefer" upon all sorts of not exactly suitable occasions. And I trembled to think that my contact with the scrivener had already and seriously affected me in a mental way. And what further and deeper aberration might it not yet produce? This apprehension had not been without efficacy in determining me to summary measures.

As Nippers, looking very sour and sulky, was departing, Turkey blandly and deferentially approached.

"With submission, sir," said he, "yesterday I was thinking about Bartleby here, and I think that if he would but prefer to take a quart of good ale every day, it would do much towards mending him, and enabling him to assist in examining his papers."

"So you have got the word, too," said I, slightly excited.

"With submission, what word, sir?" asked Turkey, respectfully crowding himself into the contracted space behind the screen, and by so doing, making me jostle the scrivener. "What word, sir?"

"I would prefer to be left alone here," said Bartleby, as if offended at being mobbed in his privacy.

"*That's* the word, Turkey," said I—"*that's* it."

"Oh, *prefer?* oh yes—queer word. I never use it myself. But, sir, as I was saying, if he would but prefer—"

"Turkey," interrupted I, "you will please withdraw."

"Oh certainly, sir, if you prefer that I should."

As he opened the folding-door to retire, Nippers at his desk caught a glimpse of me, and asked whether I would prefer to have a certain paper copied on blue paper or white. He did not in the least roguishly accent the word "prefer." It was plain that it involuntarily rolled from his tongue. I thought to myself, surely I must get rid of a demented man, who already has in some degree turned the tongues, if not the heads of myself and clerks. But I thought it prudent not to break the dismission at once.

The next day I noticed that Bartleby did nothing but stand at his window in his dead-wall revery. Upon asking him why he did not write, he said that he had decided upon doing no more writing.

"Why, how now? what next?" exclaimed I, "do no more writing?"

"No more."

"And what is the reason?"

"Do you not see the reason for yourself?" he indifferently replied.

I looked steadfastly at him, and perceived that his eyes looked dull and glazed. Instantly it occurred to me, that his unexampled diligence in copying by his dim window for the first few weeks of his stay with me might have temporarily impaired his vision.

I was touched. I said something in condolence with him. I hinted that of course he did wisely in abstaining from writing for a while; and urged him to embrace that opportunity of taking wholesome exercise in the open air. This, however, he did not do. A few days after this, my other clerks being absent, and being in a great hurry to dispatch certain letters by the mail, I thought that, having nothing else earthly to do, Bartleby would surely be less inflexible than usual, and carry these letters to the Post Office. But he blankly declined. So, much to my inconvenience, I went myself.

Still added days went by. Whether Bartleby's eyes improved or not, I could not say. To all appearance, I thought they did. But when I asked him if they did he vouchsafed no answer. At all events, he would do no copying. At last, in replying to my urgings, he informed me that he had permanently given up copying.

"What!" exclaimed I; "suppose your eyes should get entirely well —better than ever before—would you not copy then?"

"I have given up copying," he answered, and slid aside.

He remained as ever, a fixture in my chamber. Nay—if that were possible—he became still more of a fixture than before. What was to be done? He would do nothing in the office; why should he stay there? In plain fact, he had now become a millstone to me, not only useless as a necklace, but afflictive to bear. Yet I was sorry for him. I speak less than truth when I say that, on his own account, he occasioned me uneasiness. If he would but have named a single relative or friend, I would instantly have written, and urged their taking the poor fellow away to some convenient retreat. But he seemed alone, absolutely alone in the universe. A bit of wreck in the mid-Atlantic. At length, necessities connected with my business tyrannized over all other considerations. Decently as I could, I told Bartleby that in six days' time he must unconditionally leave the office. I warned him to take measures, in the interval, for procuring some other abode. I offered to assist him in this endeavor, if he himself would but take the first step towards a removal. "And when you finally quit me, Bartleby," added I, "I shall see that you go not away entirely unprovided. Six days from this hour, remember."

At the expiration of that period, I peeped behind the screen, and lo! Bartleby was there.

I buttoned up my coat, balanced myself; advanced slowly towards him, touched his shoulder, and said, "The time has come; you must quit this place; I am sorry for you; here is money; but you must go."

"I would prefer not," he replied, with his back still towards me.

"You *must*."

He remained silent.

Now I had an unbounded confidence in this man's common honesty. He had frequently restored to me sixpences and shillings carelessly dropped upon the floor, for I am apt to be very reckless in such shirt-button affairs. The proceeding, then, which followed will not be deemed extraordinary.

"Bartleby," said I, "I owe you twelve dollars on account; here are thirty-two; the odd twenty are yours—Will you take it?" and I handed the bills towards him.

But he made no motion.

"I will leave them here, then," putting them under a weight on the table. Then taking my hat and cane and going to the door, I tranquilly turned and added—"After you have removed your things from these offices, Bartleby, you will of course lock the door—since every one is now gone for the day but you—and if you please, slip your key underneath the mat, so that I may have it in the morning. I shall not see you again; so good-bye to you. If, hereafter, in your new place of abode, I can be of any service to you, do not fail to advise me by letter. Good-bye, Bartleby, and fare you well."

But he answered not a word; like the last column of some ruined temple, he remained standing mute and solitary in the middle of the otherwise deserted room.

As I walked home in a pensive mood, my vanity got the better of my pity. I could not but highly plume myself on my masterly management in getting rid of Bartleby. Masterly I call it, and such it must appear to any dispassionate thinker. The beauty of my procedure seemed to consist in its perfect quietness. There was no vulgar bullying, no bravado of any sort, no choleric hectoring, and striding to and fro across the apartment, jerking out vehement commands for Bartleby to bundle himself off with his beggarly traps. Nothing of the kind. Without loudly bidding Bartleby depart—as an inferior genius might have done—I *assumed* the ground that depart he must; and upon that assumption built all I had to say. The more I thought over my procedure, the more I was charmed with it. Nevertheless, next morning, upon awakening, I had my doubts—I had somehow slept off the fumes of vanity. One of the coolest and wisest hours a man has, is just after he awakes in the morning. My procedure seemed as sagacious as ever—but only in theory. How it would prove in practice—there was the rub. It was truly a beautiful thought to have assumed Bartleby's departure; but, after all, that assumption was simply my own, and none of Bartleby's. The great point was, not whether I had assumed that he would quit me, but whether he would prefer to do so. He was more a man of preferences than assumptions.

After breakfast, I walked down town, arguing the probabilities *pro* and *con*. One moment I thought it would prove a miserable failure, and Bartleby would be found all alive at my office as usual; the next moment it seemed certain that I should find his chair empty. And so I kept veering about. At the corner of Broadway and Canal Street, I saw quite an excited group of people standing in earnest conversation.

"I'll take odds he doesn't," said a voice as I passed.

"Doesn't go?—done!" said I, "put up your money."

I was instinctively putting my hand in my pocket to produce my own, when I remembered that this was an election day. The words I had overheard bore no reference to Bartleby, but to the success or non-success of some candidate for the mayoralty. In my intent frame of mind, I had, as it were, imagined that all Broadway shared in my excitement, and were debating the same question with me. I passed on, very thankful that the uproar of the street screened my momentary absent-mindedness.

As I had intended, I was earlier than usual at my office door. I stood listening for a moment. All was still. He must be gone. I tried the knob. The door was locked. Yes, my procedure had worked to a charm; he indeed must be vanished. Yet a certain melancholy mixed with this: I was almost sorry for my brilliant success. I was fumbling under the door mat for the key, which Bartleby was to have left there for me, when accidentally my knee knocked against a panel, producing a summoning sound, and in response a voice came to me from within—"Not yet; I am occupied."

It was Bartleby.

I was thunderstruck. For an instant I stood like the man who, pipe in mouth, was killed one cloudless afternoon long ago in Virginia, by summer lightning; at his own warm open window he was killed, and remained leaning out there upon the dreamy afternoon, till someone touched him, when he fell.

"Not gone!" I murmured at last. But again obeying that wondrous ascendancy which the inscrutable scrivener had over me, and from which ascendancy, for all my chafing, I could not completely escape, I slowly went down stairs and out into the street, and while walking round the block, considered what I should next do in this unheard-of perplexity. Turn the man out by an actual thrusting I could not; to drive him away by calling him hard names would not do; calling in the police was an unpleasant idea; and yet, permit him to enjoy his cadaverous triumph over me—this, too, I could not think of. What was to be done? or, if nothing could be done, was there anything further that I could *assume* in the matter? Yes, as before I had prospectively assumed that Bartleby would depart, so now I might retrospectively assume that departed he was. In the legitimate carrying out of this assumption, I might enter my office in a great hurry, and pretending not to see Bartleby at all, walk straight against him as if he were air. Such a proceeding would in a singular degree have the appearance of a home-thrust. It was hardly possible that Bartleby could withstand such an application of the doctrine of assumption. But upon second thoughts the success of the plan seemed rather dubious. I resolved to argue the matter over with him again.

"Bartleby," said I, entering the office, with a quietly severe expression, "I am seriously displeased. I am pained, Bartleby. I had thought better of you. I had imagined you of such a gentlemanly organization, that in any delicate dilemma a slight hint would suffice—in short, an assumption. But it appears I am deceived. Why," I added, unaffectedly starting, "You have not even touched that money yet," pointing to it, just where I had left it the evening previous.

He answered nothing.

"Will you, or will you not, quit me?" I now demanded in a sudden passion, advancing close to him.

"I would prefer *not* to quit you," he replied, gently emphasizing the *not*.

"What earthly right have you to stay here? Do you pay any rent? Do you pay my taxes? Or is this property yours?"

He answered nothing.

"Are you ready to go on and write now? Are your eyes recovered? Could you copy a small paper for me this morning? or help examine a few lines? or step round to the Post Office? In a word, will you do anything at all, to give a coloring to your refusal to depart the premises?"

He silently retired into his hermitage.

I was now in such a state of nervous resentment that I thought it but prudent to check myself at present from further demonstrations. Bartleby and I were alone. I remembered the tragedy of the unfortunate Adams and the still more unfortunate Colt in the solitary office of the latter; and how poor Colt, being dreadfully incensed by Adams, and imprudently permitting himself to get wildly excited, was at unawares hurried into his fatal act—an act which certainly no man could possibly deplore more than the actor himself. Often it had occurred to me in my ponderings upon the subject that had that altercation taken place in the public street, or at a private residence, it would not have terminated as it did. It was the circumstance of being alone in a solitary office, up stairs, of a building entirely unhallowed by humanizing domestic associations—an uncarpeted office, doubtless, of a dusty, haggard sort of appearance—this it must have been, which greatly helped to enhance the irritable desperation of the hapless Colt.

But when this old Adam of resentment rose in me and tempted me concerning Bartleby, I grappled him and threw him. How? Why, simply by recalling the divine injunction: "A new commandment give I unto you, that ye love one another." Yes, this it was that saved me. Aside from higher considerations, charity often operates as a vastly wise and prudent principle—a great safeguard to its possessor. Men have committed murder for jealousy's sake, and anger's sake, and hatred's sake, and selfishness' sake, and spiritual pride's sake; but no man, that ever I heard of, ever committed a diabolical murder for sweet charity's sake. Mere self-interest, then, if no better motive can be enlisted, should, especially with high-tempered men, prompt all beings to charity and philanthropy. At any rate, upon the occasion in question, I strove to drown my exasperated feelings towards the scrivener by benevolently construing his conduct. Poor fellow, poor fellow! thought I, he don't mean anything; and besides, he has seen hard times, and ought to be indulged.

I endeavored, also, immediately to occupy myself, and at the same time to comfort my despondency. I tried to fancy, that in the course of the morning, at such time as might prove agreeable to him, Bartleby, of his own free accord, would emerge from his hermitage and take up some decided line of march in the direction of the door. But no. Half-past twelve o'clock came; Turkey began to glow in the face, overturn his inkstand, and become generally obstreperous; Nippers abated down into quietude and courtesy; Ginger Nut munched his noon apple; and Bartleby remained standing at his window in one of his profoundest dead-wall reveries. Will it be credited? Ought I to acknowledge it? That afternoon I left the office without saying one further word to him.

Some days now passed, during which, at leisure intervals I looked a little into "Edwards on the Will," and "Priestley on Necessity." Under the circumstances, those books induced a salutary feeling. Gradually I slid into the persuasion that these troubles of mine, touching the scrivener, had been all predestined from eternity, and Bartleby was billeted upon me for some mysterious purpose of an all-wise Providence, which it was not for a mere mortal like me to fathom. Yes, Bartleby, stay there behind your screen, thought I; I shall persecute you no more; you are harmless and noiseless as any of these old chairs; in short, I never feel so private as when I know you are here. At last I see it, I feel it; I penetrate to the predestined purpose of my life. I am content. Others may have loftier parts to enact; but my mission in this world, Bartleby, is to furnish you with office-room for such period as you may see fit to remain.

I believe that this wise and blessed frame of mind would have continued with me, had it not been for the unsolicited and uncharitable remarks obtruded upon me by my professional friends who visited the rooms. But thus it often is, that the constant friction of illiberal minds wears out at last the best resolves of the more generous. Though to be sure, when I reflected upon it, it was not strange that people entering my office should be struck by the peculiar aspect of the unaccountable Bartleby, and so be tempted to throw out some sinister observations concerning him. Sometimes an attorney, having business with me, and calling at my office, and finding no one but the scrivener there, would undertake to obtain some sort of precise information from him touching my whereabouts; but without heeding his idle talk, Bartleby would remain standing immovable in the middle of the room. So after contemplating him in that position for a time, the attorney would depart, no wiser than he came.

Also, when a reference was going on, and the room full of lawyers and witnesses, and business driving fast, some deeply-occupied legal gentleman present, seeing Bartleby wholly unemployed, would request him to run round to his (the legal gentleman's) office and fetch some papers for him. Thereupon, Bartleby would tranquilly decline, and yet remain idle as before. Then the lawyer would give a great stare, and turn to me. And what could I say? At last I was made aware that all through the circle of my professional acquaintance, a whisper of wonder was running round, having reference to the strange creature I kept at my office. This worried me very much. And as the idea came upon me of his possibly turning out a long-lived man, and keeping occupying my chambers, and denying my authority; and perplexing my visitors; and scandalizing my professional reputation; and casting a general gloom over the premises; keeping soul and body together to the last upon his savings (for doubtless he spent but half a dime a day), and in the end perhaps outlive me, and claim possession of my office by right of his perpetual occupancy: as all these dark anticipations crowded upon me more and more, and my friends continually intruded their relentless remarks upon the apparition in my room; a great change was wrought in me. I resolved to gather all my faculties together, and forever rid me of this intolerable incubus.

Ere revolving any complicated project, however, adapted to this end, I first simply suggested to Bartleby the propriety of his permanent departure. In a calm and serious tone, I commended the idea to his careful and mature consideration. But, having taken three days to meditate upon it, he apprised me, that his original determination remained the same; in short, that he still preferred to abide with me.

What shall I do? I now said to myself, buttoning up my coat to the last button. What shall I do? what ought I to do? what does conscience say I *should* do with this man, or, rather, ghost. Rid myself of him, I must; go, he shall. But how? You will not thrust him, the poor, pale, passive mortal—you will not thrust such a helpless creature out of your door? you will not dishonor yourself by such cruelty? No, I will not, I cannot do that. Rather would I let him live and die here, and then mason up his remains in the wall. What, then, will you do? For all your coaxing, he will not budge. Bribes he leaves under your own paperweight on your table; in short, it is quite plain that he prefers to cling to you.

Then something severe, something unusual must be done. What! surely you will not have him collared by a constable, and commit his innocent pallor to the common jail? And upon what ground could you procure such a thing to be done?—a vagrant, is he? What! he a vagrant, a wanderer, who refuses to budge? It is because he will not be a vagrant, then, that you seek to count him *as* a vagrant. That is too absurd. No visible means of support: there I have him. Wrong again: for indubitably he *does* support himself, and that is the only unanswerable proof that any man can show of his possessing the means so to do. No more, then. Since he will not quit me, I must quit him. I will change my offices; I will move elsewhere, and give him fair notice, that if I find him on my new premises I will then proceed against him as a common trespasser.

Acting accordingly, next day I thus addressed him: "I find these chambers too far from the City Hall; the air is unwholesome. In a word, I propose to remove my offices next week, and shall no longer require your services. I tell you this now, in order that you may seek another place."

He made no reply, and nothing more was said.

On the appointed day I engaged carts and men, proceeded to my chambers, and, having but little furniture, everything was removed in a few hours. Throughout, the scrivener remained standing behind the screen, which I directed to be removed the last thing. It was withdrawn;

and, being folded up like a huge folio, left him the motionless occupant of a naked room. I stood in the entry watching him a moment, while something from within me upbraided me.

I re-entered, with my hand in my pocket—and—and my heart in my mouth.

"Good-bye, Bartleby; I am going—good-bye, and God some way bless you; and take that," slipping something in his hand. But it dropped upon the floor, and then—strange to say—I tore myself from him whom I had so longed to be rid of.

Established in my new quarters, for a day or two I kept the door locked, started at every footfall in the passages. When I returned to my rooms, after any little absence, I would pause at the threshold for an instant, and attentively listen, ere applying my key. But these fears were needless. Bartleby never came nigh me.

I thought all was going well, when a perturbed-looking stranger visited me, inquiring whether I was the person who had recently occupied rooms at No.—Wall Street.

Full of forebodings, I replied that I was.

"Then, sir," said the stranger, who proved a lawyer, "you are responsible for the man you left there. He refuses to do any copying; he refuses to do anything; he says he prefers not to; and he refuses to quit the premises."

"I am very sorry, sir," said I, with assumed tranquillity, but an inward tremor, "but, really, the man you allude to is nothing to me—he is no relation or apprentice of mine, that you should hold me responsible for him."

"In mercy's name, who is he?"

"I certainly cannot inform you. I know nothing about him. Formerly I employed him as a copyist; but he has done nothing for me now for some time past."

"I shall settle him, then—good morning, sir."

Several days passed, and I heard nothing more; and, though I often felt a charitable prompting to call at the place and see poor Bartleby, yet a certain squeamishness, of I know not what, withheld me.

All is over with him, by this time, thought I, at last, when, through another week, no further intelligence reached me. But, coming to my room the day after, I found several persons waiting at my door in a high state of nervous excitement.

"That's the man—here he comes," cried the foremost one, whom I recognized as the lawyer who had previously called upon me alone.

"You must take him away, sir, at once," cried a portly person among them, advancing upon me, and whom I knew to be the landlord of

No. —Wall Street. "These gentlemen, my tenants, cannot stand it any longer; Mr. B——," pointing to the lawyer, "has turned him out of his room, and he now persists in haunting the building generally, sitting upon the banisters of the stairs by day, and sleeping in the entry by night. Everybody is concerned; clients are leaving the offices; some fears are entertained of a mob; something you must do, and that without delay."

Aghast at this torrent, I fell back before it, and would fain have locked myself in my new quarters. In vain I persisted that Bartleby was nothing to me—no more than to any one else. In vain—I was the last person known to have anything to do with him, and they held me to the terrible account. Fearful, then, of being exposed in the papers (as one person present obscurely threatened), I considered the matter, and, at length, said, that if the lawyer would give me a confidential interview with the scrivener, in his (the lawyer's) own room, I would, that afternoon, strive my best to rid them of the nuisance they complained of.

Going up stairs to my old haunt, there was Bartleby silently sitting upon the banister at the landing.

"What are you doing here, Bartleby?" said I.

"Sitting upon the banister," he mildly replied.

I motioned him into the lawyer's room, who then left us.

"Bartleby," said I, "are you aware that you are the cause of great tribulation to me, by persisting in occupying the entry after being dismissed from the office?"

No answer.

"Now one of two things must take place. Either you must do something, or something must be done to you. Now what sort of business would you like to engage in? Would you like to re-engage in copying for some one?"

"No; I would prefer not to make any change."

"Would you like a clerkship in a dry-goods store?"

"There is too much confinement about that. No, I would not like a clerkship; but I am not particular."

"Too much confinement," I cried, "why, you keep yourself confined all the time!"

"I would prefer not to take a clerkship," he rejoined, as if to settle that little item at once.

"How would a bar-tender's business suit you? There is no trying of the eye-sight in that."

"I would not like it at all; though, as I said before, I am not particular."

His unwonted wordiness inspirited me. I returned to the charge.

"Well, then, would you like to travel through the country collecting bills for the merchants? That would improve your health."

"No, I would prefer to be doing something else."

"How, then, would going as a companion to Europe, to entertain some young gentleman with your conversation—how would that suit you?"

"Not at all. It does not strike me that there is anything definite about that. I like to be stationary. But I am not particular."

"Stationary you shall be, then," I cried, now losing all patience, and, for the first time in all my exasperating connections with him, fairly flying into a passion. "If you do not go away from these premises before night, I shall feel bound—indeed, I *am* bound--to—to—to quit the premises myself!" I rather absurdly concluded, knowing not with what possible threat to try to frighten his immobility into compliance. Despairing of all further efforts, I was precipitately leaving him, when a final thought occurred to me—one which had not been wholly unindulged before.

"Bartleby," said I, in the kindest tone I could assume under such exciting circumstances, "will you go home with me now—not to my office, but my dwelling—and remain there till we can conclude upon some convenient arrangement for you at our leisure? Come, let us start now, right away."

"No: at present I would prefer not to make any change at all."

I answered nothing; but, effectually dodging every one by the suddenness and rapidity of my flight, rushed from the building, ran up Wall Street towards Broadway, and, jumping into the first omnibus, was soon removed from pursuit. As soon as tranquillity returned, I distinctly perceived that I had now done all that I possibly could, both in respect to the demands of the landlord and his tenants, and with regard to my own desire and sense of duty, to benefit Bartleby, and shield him from rude persecution. I now strove to be entirely care-free and quiescent; and my conscience justified me in the attempt; though, indeed, it was not so successful as I could have wished. So fearful was I of being again hunted out by the incensed landlord and his exasperated tenants, that, surrendering my business to Nippers, for a few days, I drove about the upper part of the town and through the suburbs, in my rockaway; crossed over to Jersey City and Hoboken, and paid fugitive visits to Manhattanville and Astoria. In fact, I almost lived in my rockaway for the time.

When again I entered my office, lo, a note from the landlord lay upon the desk. I opened it with trembling hands. It informed me that the writer had sent to the police, and had Bartleby removed to the

Tombs as a vagrant. Moreover, since I knew more about him than any one else, he wished me to appear at that place, and make a suitable statement of the facts. These tidings had a conflicting effect upon me. At first I was indignant; but, at last, almost approved. The landlord's energetic, summary disposition, had led him to adopt a procedure which I do not think I would have decided upon myself; and yet, as a last resort, under such peculiar circumstances, it seemed the only plan.

As I afterwards learned, the poor scrivener, when told that he must be conducted to the Tombs, offered not the slightest obstacle, but, in his pale, unmoving way, silently acquiesced.

Some of the compassionate and curious by-standers joined the party; and headed by one of the constables arm-in-arm with Bartleby, the silent procession filed its way through all the noise, and heat, and joy of the roaring thoroughfares at noon.

The same day I received the note, I went to the Tombs, or, to speak more properly, the Halls of Justice. Seeking the right officer, I stated the purpose of my call, and was informed that the individual I described was, indeed, within. I then assured the functionary that Bartleby was a perfectly honest man, and greatly to be compassionated, however unaccountably eccentric. I narrated all I knew, and closed by suggesting the idea of letting him remain in as indulgent confinement as possible, till something less harsh might be done—though, indeed, I hardly knew what. At all events, if nothing else could be decided upon, the almshouse must receive him. I then begged to have an interview.

Being under no disgraceful charge, and quite serene and harmless in all his ways, they had permitted him freely to wander about the prison, and, especially, in the inclosed grass-platted yards thereof. And so I found him there, standing all alone in the quietest of the yards, his face towards a high wall, while all around, from the narrow slits of the jail windows, I thought I saw peering out upon him the eyes of murderers and thieves.

"Bartleby!"

"I know you," he said, without looking round—"and I want nothing to say to you."

"It was not I that brought you here, Bartleby," said I, keenly pained at his implied suspicion. "And to you, this should not be so vile a place. Nothing reproachful attaches to you by being here. And see, it is not so sad a place as one might think. Look, there is the sky, and here is the grass."

"I know where I am," he replied, but would say nothing more, and so I left him.

As I entered the corridor again, a broad meat-like man, in an apron, accosted me, and, jerking his thumb over my shoulder, said—"Is that your friend?"

"Yes."

"Does he want to starve? If he does, let him live on the prison fare, that's all."

"Who are you?" asked I, not knowing what to make of such an unofficially speaking person in such a place.

"I am the grub-man. Such gentlemen as have friends here, hire me to provide them with something good to eat."

"Is this so?" said I, turning to the turnkey.

He said it was.

"Well, then," said I, slipping some silver into the grub-man's hands (for so they called him), "I want you to give particular attention to my friend there; let him have the best dinner you can get. And you must be as polite to him as possible."

"Introduce me, will you?" said the grub-man, looking at me with an expression which seemed to say he was all impatience for an opportunity to give a specimen of his breeding.

Thinking it would prove of benefit to the scrivener, I acquiesced; and, asking the grub-man his name, went up with him to Bartleby.

"Bartleby, this is a friend; you will find him very useful to you."

"Your sarvant, sir, your sarvant," said the grub-man, making a low salutation behind his apron. "Hope you find it pleasant here, sir; nice grounds—cool apartments—hope you'll stay with us some time—try to make it agreeable. What will you have for dinner to-day?"

"I prefer not to dine to-day," said Bartleby, turning away. "It would disagree with me; I am unused to dinners." So saying, he slowly moved to the other side of the inclosure, and took up a position fronting the dead-wall.

"How's this?" said the grub-man, addressing me with a stare of astonishment. "He's odd, ain't he?"

"I think he is a little deranged," said I, sadly.

"Deranged? deranged is it? Well, now, upon my word, I thought that friend of yourn was a gentleman forger; they are always pale and genteel-like, them forgers. I can't help pity 'em—can't help it, sir. Did you know Monroe Edwards?" he added, touchingly, and paused. Then, laying his hand piteously on my shoulder, sighed, "he died of consumption at Sing-Sing. So you weren't acquainted with Monroe?"

"No, I was never socially acquainted with any forgers. But I cannot stop longer. Look to my friend yonder. You will not lose by it. I will see you again."

Some few days after this, I again obtained admission to the Tombs, and went through the corridors in quest of Bartleby; but without finding him.

"I saw him coming from his cell not long ago," said a turnkey, "may be he's gone to loiter in the yards."

So I went in that direction.

"Are you looking for the silent man?" said another turnkey, passing me. "Yonder he lies—sleeping in the yard there. 'Tis not twenty minutes since I saw him lie down."

The yard was entirely quiet. It was not accessible to the common prisoners. The surrounding walls, of amazing thickness, kept off all sounds behind them. The Egyptian character of the masonry weighed upon me with its gloom. But a soft imprisoned turf grew under foot. The heart of the eternal pyramids, it seemed, wherein, by some strange magic, through the clefts, grass-seed, dropped by birds, had sprung.

Strangely huddled at the base of the wall, his knees drawn up, and lying on his side, his head touching the cold stones, I saw the wasted Bartleby. But nothing stirred. I paused; then went close up to him; stooped over, and saw that his dim eyes were open; otherwise he seemed profoundly sleeping. Something prompted me to touch him. I felt his hand, when a tingling shiver ran up my arm and down my spine to my feet.

The round face of the grub-man peered upon me now. "His dinner is ready. Won't he dine to-day, either? Or does he live without dining?"

"Lives without dining," said I, and closed the eyes.

"Eh!—He's asleep, ain't he?"

"With kings and counselors," murmured I.

There would seem little need for proceeding further in this history. Imagination will readily supply the meagre recital of poor Bartleby's interment. But, ere parting with the reader, let me say, that if this little narrative has sufficiently interested him, to awaken curiosity as to who Bartleby was, and what manner of life he led prior to the present narrator's making his acquaintance, I can only reply, that in such curiosity I fully share, but am wholly unable to gratify it. Yet here I hardly know whether I should divulge one little item of rumor, which came to my ear a few months after the scrivener's decease. Upon what basis it rested, I could never ascertain; and hence, how true it is I cannot now tell. But, inasmuch as this vague report has not been without a certain suggestive interest to me, however sad, it may prove the same with some others; and so I will briefly mention it. The report was this: that Bartleby had been a subordinate clerk in the Dead Letter Office at Washington, from which he had been suddenly removed by a change in the administration. When I think over this rumor, hardly can I express the emotions which seize me. Dead letters! does it not sound like dead men?

Conceive a man by nature and misfortune prone to a pallid hopeless-ness, can any business seem more fitted to heighten it than that of continually handling these dead letters, and assorting them for the flames? For by the cart-load they are annually burned. Sometimes from out the folded paper the pale clerk takes a ring—the finger it was meant for, perhaps, moulders in the grave; a bank-note sent in swiftest charity —he whom it would relieve, nor eats nor hungers any more; pardon for those who died despairing; hope for those who died unhoping; good tidings for those who died stifled by unrelieved calamities. On errands of life, these letters speed to death.

Ah, Bartleby! Ah, humanity!

1853

JOHN CHEEVER

Torch Song

After Jack Lorey had known Joan Harris in New York for a few years, he began to think of her as the Widow. She always wore black, and he was always given the feeling, by a curious disorder in her apartment, that the undertakers had just left. This impression did not stem from malice on his part, for he was fond of Joan. They came from the same city in Ohio and had reached New York at about the same time in the middle thirties. They were the same age, and during their first summer in the city they used to meet after work and drink Martinis in places

John Cheever, who would come to be called "the Chekhov of the suburbs," was born in 1912 in Quincy, Massachusetts. At the age of seventeen, he was expelled from the Thayer Academy. This experience provided the aspiring writer with material for his first published story, which appeared in the New Republic in 1930 and which initiated the frequent appearance of his work in the nation's top periodicals, especially the New Yorker. Cheever's short stories and novels—The Wapshot Chronicle (1957), The Enormous Radio and Other Stories (1954), Falconer (1977)—are best known for their subtle and ironic explorations of the moral condition of middle-class, suburban America. The Stories of John Cheever (1978) received that year's Pulitzer Prize for fiction. Cheever died in Ossining, New York, in 1982, the same year in which he was awarded the National Medal for Literature.

like the Brevoort and Charles', and have dinner and play checkers at the Lafayette.

Joan went to a school for models when she settled in the city, but it turned out that she photographed badly, so after spending six weeks learning how to walk with a book on her head she got a job as a hostess in a Longchamps. For the rest of the summer she stood by the hatrack, bathed in an intense pink light and the string music of heartbreak, swinging her mane of dark hair and her black skirt as she moved forward to greet the customers. She was then a big, handsome girl with a wonderful voice, and her face, her whole presence, always seemed infused with a gentle and healthy pleasure at her surroundings, whatever they were. She was innocently and incorrigibly convivial, and would get out of bed and dress at three in the morning if someone called her and asked her to come out for a drink, as Jack often did. In the fall, she got some kind of freshman executive job in a department store. They saw less and less of each other and then for quite a while stopped seeing each other altogether. Jack was living with a girl he had met at a party, and it never occurred to him to wonder what had become of Joan.

Jack's girl had some friends in Pennsylvania, and in the spring and summer of his second year in town he often went there with her for weekends. All of this—the shared apartment in the Village, the illicit relationship, the Friday-night train to a country house—was what he had imagined life in New York to be, and he was intensely happy. He was returning to New York with his girl one Sunday night on the Lehigh line. It was one of those trains that move slowly across the face of New Jersey, bringing back to the city hundreds of people, like the victims of an immense and strenuous picnic, whose faces are blazing and whose muscles are lame. Jack and his girl, like most of the other passengers, were overburdened with vegetables and flowers. When the train stopped in Pennsylvania Station, they moved with the crowd along the platform, toward the escalator. As they were passing the wide, lighted windows of the diner, Jack turned his head and saw Joan. It was the first time he had seen her since Thanksgiving, or since Christmas. He couldn't remember.

Joan was with a man who had obviously passed out. His head was in his arms on the table, and an overturned highball glass was near one of his elbows. Joan was shaking his shoulders gently and speaking to him. She seemed to be vaguely troubled, vaguely amused. The waiters had cleared off all the other tables and were standing around Joan, waiting for her to resurrect her escort. It troubled Jack to see in these straits a girl who reminded him of the trees and the lawns of his home town, but there was nothing he could do to help. Joan continued to shake the man's shoulders, and the crowd pressed Jack past one after another of the diner's windows, past the malodorous kitchen, and up the escalator.

He saw Joan again, later that summer, when he was having dinner in a Village restaurant. He was with a new girl, a Southerner. There were many Southern girls in the city that year. Jack and his belle had wandered into the restaurant because it was convenient, but the food was terrible and the place was lighted with candles. Halfway through dinner, Jack noticed Joan on the other side of the room, and when he had finished eating, he crossed the room and spoke to her. She was with a tall man who was wearing a monocle. He stood, bowed stiffly from the waist, and said to Jack, "We are very pleased to meet you." Then he excused himself and headed for the toilet. "He's a count, he's a Swedish count," Joan said. "He's on the radio, Friday afternoons at four-fifteen. Isn't it exciting?" She seemed to be delighted with the count and the terrible restaurant.

Sometime the next winter, Jack moved from the Village to an apartment in the East Thirties. He was crossing Park Avenue one cold morning on his way to the office when he noticed, in the crowd, a woman he had met a few times at Joan's apartment. He spoke to her and asked about his friend. "Haven't you heard?" she said. She pulled a long face. "Perhaps I'd better tell you. Perhaps you can help." She and Jack had breakfast in a drugstore on Madison Avenue and she unburdened herself of the story.

The count had a program called "The Song of the Fiords," or something like that, and he sang Swedish folk songs. Everyone suspected him of being a fake, but that didn't bother Joan. He had met her at a party and, sensing a soft touch, had moved in with her the following night. About a week later, he complained of pains in his back and said he must have some morphine. Then he needed morphine all the time. If he didn't get morphine, he was abusive and violent. Joan began to deal with those doctors and druggists who peddle dope, and when they wouldn't supply her, she went down to the bottom of the city. Her friends were afraid she would be found some morning stuffed in a drain. She got pregnant. She had an abortion. The count left her and moved to a flea bag near Times Square, but she was so impressed by then with his helplessness, so afraid that he would die without her, that she followed him there and shared his room and continued to buy his narcotics. He abandoned her again, and Joan waited a week for him to return before she went back to her place and her friends in the Village.

It shocked Jack to think of the innocent girl from Ohio having lived with a brutal dope addict and traded with criminals, and when he got to his office that morning, he telephoned her and made a date for dinner that night. He met her at Charles'. When she came into the bar, she seemed as wholesome and calm as ever. Her voice was sweet, and reminded him of elms, of lawns, of those glass arrangements that used to be hung from porch ceilings to tinkle in the summer wind. She told him about the count. She spoke of him charitably and with no trace of bitterness, as if her voice, her disposition, were incapable of registering anything beyond simple affection and pleasure. Her walk, when she moved ahead of him toward their table, was light and graceful. She ate a large dinner and talked enthusiastically about her job. They went to a movie and said goodbye in front of her apartment house.

That winter, Jack met a girl he decided to marry. Their engagement was announced in January and they planned to marry in July. In the spring, he received, in his office mail, an invitation to cocktails at Joan's. It was for a Saturday when his fiancée was going to Massachusetts to visit her parents, and when the time came and he had nothing better to do, he took a bus to the Village. Joan had the same apartment. It was a walk-up. You rang the bell above the mailbox in the vestibule and were answered with a death rattle in the lock. Joan lived on the third floor. Her calling card was in a slot in the mailbox, and above her name was written the name Hugh Bascomb.

Jack climbed the two flights of carpeted stairs, and when he reached Joan's apartment, she was standing by the open door in a black dress. After she greeted Jack, she took his arm and guided him across the room. "I want you to meet Hugh, Jack," she said.

Hugh was a big man with a red face and pale-blue eyes. His manner was courtly and his eyes were inflamed with drink. Jack talked with him for a little while and then went over to speak to someone he knew, who was standing by the mantlepiece. He noticed then, for the first time, the indescribable disorder of Joan's apartment. The books were in their shelves and the furniture was reasonably good, but the place was all wrong, somehow. It was as if things had been put in place without thought or real interest, and for the first time, too, he had the impression that there had been a death there recently.

As Jack moved around the room, he felt that he had met the ten or twelve guests at other parties. There was a woman executive with a fancy hat, a man who could imitate Roosevelt, a grim couple whose play was in rehearsal, and a newspaperman who kept turning on the radio for news of the Spanish Civil War. Jack drank Martinis and talked with the woman in the fancy hat. He looked out of the window at the back yards and the ailanthus trees and heard, in the distance, thunder exploding off the cliffs of the Hudson.

Hugh Bascomb got very drunk. He began to spill liquor, as if drinking, for him, were a kind of jolly slaughter and he enjoyed the bloodshed and the mess. He spilled whiskey from a bottle. He spilled a drink on his shirt and then tipped over someone else's drink. The party was not quiet, but Hugh's hoarse voice began to dominate the others. He attacked a photographer who was sitting in a corner explaining camera techniques to a homely woman. "What did you come to the party for if all you wanted to do was to sit there and stare at your shoes?" Hugh shouted. "What did you come for? Why don't you stay at home?"

The photographer didn't know what to say. He was not staring at his shoes. Joan moved lightly to Hugh's side. "Please don't get into a fight now, darling," she said. "Not this afternoon."

"Shut up," he said. "Let me alone. Mind your own business." He lost his balance, and in struggling to steady himself he tipped over a lamp.

"Oh, your lovely lamp, Joan," a woman sighed.

"Lamps!" Hugh roared. He threw his arms into the air and worked them around his head as if he were bludgeoning himself. "Lamps. Glasses. Cigarette boxes. Dishes. They're killing me. They're killing me, for Christ's sake. Let's all go up to the mountains and hunt and fish and live like men, for Christ's sake."

People were scattering as if a rain had begun to fall in the room. It had, as a matter of fact, begun to rain outside. Someone offered Jack a ride uptown, and he jumped at the chance. Joan stood at the door, saying goodbye to her routed friends. Her voice remained soft, and her manner, unlike that of those Christian women who in the face of disaster can summon new and formidable sources of composure, seemed genuinely simple. She appeared to be oblivious of the raging drunk at her back, who was pacing up and down, grinding glass into the rug, and haranguing one of the survivors of the party with a story of how he, Hugh, had once gone without food for three weeks.

In July, Jack was married in an orchard in Duxbury, and he and his wife went to West Chop for a few weeks. When they returned to town, their apartment was cluttered with presents, including a dozen after-dinner coffee cups from Joan. His wife sent her the required note, but they did nothing else.

Late in the summer, Joan telephoned Jack at his office and asked if he wouldn't bring his wife to see her; she named an evening the following week. He felt guilty about not having called her, and accepted the invitation. This made his wife angry. She was an ambitious girl who liked a social life that offered rewards, and she went unwillingly to Joan's Village apartment with him.

Written above Joan's name on the mailbox was the name Franz Denzel. Jack and his wife climbed the stairs and were met by Joan at the open door. They went into her apartment and found themselves among a group of people for whom Jack, at least, was unable to find any bearings.

Franz Denzel was a middle-aged German. His face was pinched with bitterness or illness. He greeted Jack and his wife with that elaborate and clever politeness that is intended to make guests feel that they have come too early or too late. He insisted sharply upon Jack's sitting in the chair in which he himself had been sitting, and then went and sat on a radiator. There were five other Germans sitting around the room, drinking coffee. In a corner was another American couple, who looked uncomfortable. Joan passed Jack and his wife small cups of coffee with whipped cream. "These cups belonged to Franz's mother," she said. "Aren't they lovely? They were the only things he took from Germany when he escaped from the Nazis."

Franz turned to Jack and said, "Perhaps you will give us your opinion on the American educational system. That is what we were discussing when you arrived."

Before Jack could speak, one of the German guests opened an attack on the American educational system. The other Germans joined in, and went on from there to describe every vulgarity that had impressed them in American life and to contrast German and American culture generally. Where, they asked one another passionately, could you find in America anything like the Mitropa dining cars, the Black Forest, the pictures in Munich, the music in Bayreuth? Franz and his friends began speaking in German. Neither Jack nor his wife nor Joan could understand German, and the other American couple had not opened their mouths since they were introduced. Joan went happily around the room, filling everyone's cup with coffee, as if the music of a foreign language were enough to make an evening for her.

Jack drank five cups of coffee. He was desperately uncomfortable. Joan went into the kitchen while the Germans were laughing at their German jokes, and he hoped she would return with some drinks, but when she came back, it was with a tray of ice cream and mulberries.

"Isn't this pleasant?" Franz asked, speaking in English again.

Joan collected the coffee cups, and as she was about to take them back to the kitchen, Franz stopped her.

"Isn't one of those cups chipped?"

"No, darling," Joan said. "I never let the maid touch them. I wash them myself."

"What's that?" he asked, pointing at the rim of one of the cups.

"That's the cup that's always been chipped, darling. It was chipped when you unpacked it. You noticed it then."

"These things were perfect when they arrived in this country," he said.

Joan went into the kitchen and he followed her.

Jack tried to make conversation with the Germans. From the kitchen there was the sound of a blow and a cry. Franz returned and began to eat his mulberries greedily. Joan came back with her dish of ice cream. Her voice was gentle. Her tears, if she had been crying, had dried as quickly as the tears of a child. Jack and his wife finished their ice cream and made their escape. The wasted and unnerving evening enraged Jack's wife, and he supposed that he would never see Joan again.

Jack's wife got pregnant early in the fall, and she seized on all the prerogatives of an expectant mother. She took long naps, ate canned peaches in the middle of the night, and talked about the rudimentary kidney. She chose to see only other couples who were expecting children, and the parties that she and Jack gave were temperate. The baby, a boy, was born in May, and Jack was very proud and happy. The first party he and his wife went to after her convalescence was the wedding of a girl whose family Jack had known in Ohio.

The wedding was at St. James's, and afterward there was a big reception at the River Club. There was an orchestra dressed like Hungarians, and a lot of champagne and Scotch. Toward the end of the afternoon, Jack was walking down a dim corridor when he heard Joan's voice. "Please don't, darling," she was saying. "You'll break my arm. *Please* don't, darling." She was being pressed against the wall by a man who seemed to be twisting her arm. As soon as they saw Jack, the struggle stopped. All three of them were intensely embarrassed. Joan's face was wet and she made an effort to smile through her tears at Jack. He said hello and went on without stopping. When he returned, she and the man had disappeared.

When Jack's son was less than two years old, his wife flew with the baby to Nevada to get a divorce. Jack gave her the apartment and all its furnishings and took a room in a hotel near Grand Central. His wife got her decree in due course, and the story was in the newspapers. Jack had a telephone call from Joan a few days later.

"I'm awfully sorry to hear about your divorce, Jack," she said. "She seemed like *such* a nice girl. But that wasn't what I called you about. I want your help, and I wondered if you could come down to my place tonight around six. It's something I don't want to talk about over the phone."

He went obediently to the Village that night and climbed the stairs. Her apartment was a mess. The pictures and the curtains were down and the books were in boxes. "You moving, Joan?" he asked.

"That's what I wanted to see you about, Jack. First, I'll give you a drink." She made two Old-Fashioneds. "I'm being evicted, Jack," she said. "I'm being evicted because I'm an immoral woman. The couple who have the apartment downstairs—they're charming people, I've always thought—have told the real-estate agent that I'm a drunk and a prostitute and all kinds of things. Isn't that fantastic? This real-estate agent has always been so nice to me that I didn't think he'd believe them, but he's canceled my lease, and if I make any trouble, he's threatened to take the matter up with the store, and I don't want to lose my job. This nice real-estate agent won't even talk with me any more. When I go over to the office, the receptionist leers at me as if I were some kind of dreadful woman. Of course, there have been a lot of men here and we sometimes are noisy, but I can't be expected to go to bed at ten every night. Can I? Well, the agent who manages this building has apparently told all the other agents in the neighborhood that I'm an immoral and drunken woman, and none of them will give me an apartment. I went in to talk with one man—he seemed to be such a nice old gentleman—and he made me an indecent proposal. Isn't it fantastic? I have to be out of here on Thursday and I'm literally being turned out into the street."

Joan seemed as serene and innocent as ever while she described this scourge of agents and neighbors. Jack listened carefully for some sign of indignation or bitterness or even urgency in her recital, but there was none. He was reminded of a torch song, of one of those forlorn and touching ballads that had been sung neither for him nor for her but for their older brothers and sisters by Marion Harris. Joan seemed to be singing her wrongs.

"They've made my life miserable," she went on quietly. "If I keep the radio on after ten o'clock, they telephone the agent in the morning and tell him I had some kind of orgy here. One night when Philip—I don't think you've met Philip; he's in the Royal Air Force; he's gone back to England—one night when Philip and some other people were here, they called the police. The police came bursting in the door and talked to me as if I were I don't know what and then looked in the bedroom. If they think there's a man up here after midnight, they call me on the telephone and say all kinds of disgusting things. Of course, I can put my furniture into storage and go to a hotel, I guess. I guess a hotel will take a woman with my kind of reputation, but I thought perhaps you might know of an apartment. I thought—"

It angered Jack to think of this big, splendid girl's being persecuted by her neighbors, and he said he would do what he could. He asked her to have dinner with him, but she said she was busy.

Having nothing better to do, Jack decided to walk uptown to his hotel. It was a hot night. The sky was overcast. On his way, he saw a parade in a dark side street off Broadway near Madison Square. All the buildings in the neighborhood were dark. It was so dark that he could not see the placards the marchers carried until he came to a street light. Their signs urged the entry of the United States into the war, and each platoon represented a nation that had been subjugated by the Axis powers. They marched up Broadway, as he watched, to no music, to no sound but their own steps on the rough cobbles. It was for the most part an army of elderly men and women—Poles, Norwegians, Danes, Jews, Chinese. A few idle people like himself lined the sidewalks, and the marchers passed between them with all the self-consciousness of enemy prisoners. There were children among them dressed in the costumes in which they had, for the newsreels, presented the Mayor with a package of tea, a petition, a protest, a constitution, a check, or a pair of tickets. They hobbled through the darkness of the loft neighborhood like a mortified and destroyed people, toward Greeley Square.

In the morning, Jack put the problem of finding an apartment for Joan up to his secretary. She started phoning real-estate agents, and by afternoon she had found a couple of available apartments in the West Twenties. Joan called Jack the next day to say that she had taken one of the apartments and to thank him.

Jack didn't see Joan again until the following summer. It was a Sunday evening; he had left a cocktail party in a Washington Square apartment and had decided to walk a few blocks up Fifth Avenue before he took a bus. As he was passing the Brevoort, Joan called to him. She was with a man at one of the tables on the sidewalk. She looked cool and fresh, and the man appeared to be respectable. His name, it turned out, was Pete Bristol. He invited Jack to sit down and join in a celebration. Germany had invaded Russia that weekend, and Joan and Pete were drinking champagne to celebrate Russia's changed position in the war. The three of them drank champagne until it got dark. They had dinner and drank champagne with their dinner. They drank more champagne afterward and then went over to the Lafayette and then to two or three other places. Joan had always been tireless in her gentle way. She hated to see the night end, and it was after three o'clock when Jack stumbled into his apartment. The following morning he woke up haggard and sick, and with no recollection of the last hour or so of the previous evening. His suit was soiled and he had lost his hat. He didn't get to his office until eleven. Joan had already called him twice, and she called him again soon after he got in. There was no hoarseness at all in her voice. She said that she had to see him, and he agreed to meet her for lunch in a seafood restaurant in the Fifties.

He was standing at the bar when she breezed in, looking as though she had taken no part in that calamitous night. The advice she wanted concerned selling her jewelry. Her grandmother had left her some jewelry, and she wanted to raise money on it but didn't know where to go. She took some rings and bracelets out of her purse and showed them to Jack. He said that he didn't know anything about jewelry but that he could lend her some money. "Oh, I couldn't borrow money from you, Jack," she said. "You see, I want to get the money for Pete. I want to help him. He wants to open an advertising agency, and he needs quite a lot to begin with." Jack didn't press her to accept his offer of a loan after that, and the project wasn't mentioned again during lunch.

He next heard about Joan from a young doctor who was a friend of theirs. "Have you seen Joan recently?" the doctor asked Jack one evening when they were having dinner together. He said no. "I gave her a checkup last week," the doctor said, "and while she's been through enough to kill the average mortal—and you'll never know what she's been through—she still has the constitution of a virtuous and healthy woman. Did you hear about the last one? She sold her jewelry to put him into some kind of business, and as soon as he got the money, he left her for another girl, who had a car—a convertible."

Jack was drafted into the Army in the spring of 1942. He was kept at Fort Dix for nearly a month, and during this time he came to New York in the evening whenever he could get permission. Those nights had for him the intense keenness of a reprieve, a sensation that was heightened by the fact that on the train in from Trenton women would often press upon him dog-eared copies of *Life* and half-eaten boxes of candy, as though the brown clothes he wore were surely cerements. He telephoned Joan from Pennsylvania Station one night. "Come right over, Jack," she said. "Come right over. I want you to meet Ralph."

She was living in that place in the West Twenties that Jack had found for her. The neighborhood was a slum. Ash cans stood in front of her house, and an old woman was there picking out bits of refuse and garbage and stuffing them into a perambulator. The house in which Joan's apartment was located was shabby, but the apartment itself seemed familiar. The furniture was the same. Joan was the same big, easygoing girl. "I'm so glad you called me," she said. "It's so good to see you. I'll make you a drink. I was having one myself. Ralph ought to be here by now. He promised to take me to dinner." Jack offered to take her to Cavanagh's, but she said that Ralph might come while she was out. "If he doesn't come by nine, I'm going to make myself a sandwich. I'm not really hungry."

Jack talked about the Army. She talked about the store. She had been working in the same place for—how long was it? He didn't know. He had never seen her at her desk and he couldn't imagine what she did. "I'm terribly sorry Ralph isn't here," she said. "I'm sure you'd like him. He's not a young man. He's a heart specialist who loves to play the viola." She turned on some lights, for the summer sky had got dark. "He has this dreadful wife on Riverside Drive and four ungrateful children. He—"

The noise of an air-raid siren, lugubrious and seeming to spring from pain, as if all the misery and indecision in the city had been given a voice, cut her off. Other sirens, in distant neighborhoods, sounded, until the dark air was full of their noise. "Let me fix you another drink before I have to turn out the lights," Joan said, and took his glass. She brought the drink back to him and snapped off the lights. They went to the windows, and, as children watch a thunderstorm, they watched the city darken. All the lights nearby went out but one. Air-raid wardens had begun to sound their whistles in the street. From a distant yard came a hoarse shriek of anger. "Put out your lights, you Fascists!" a woman screamed. "Put out your lights, you Nazi Fascist Germans. Turn out your lights. Turn out your lights." The last light went off. They went away from the window and sat in the lightless room.

In the darkness, Joan began to talk about her departed lovers, and from what she said Jack gathered that they had all had a hard time. Nils, the suspect count, was dead. Hugh Bascomb, the drunk, had joined the Merchant Marine and was missing in the North Atlantic. Franz, the German, had taken poison the night the Nazis bombed Warsaw. "We listened to the news on the radio," Joan said, "and then he went back to his hotel and took poison. The maid found him dead in the bathroom the next morning." When Jack asked her about the one who was going to open an advertising agency, she seemed at first to have forgotten him. "Oh, Pete," she said after a pause. "Well, he was always very sick, you know. He was supposed to go to Saranac, but he kept putting it off and putting it off and—" She stopped talking when she heard steps on the stairs, hoping, he supposed, that it was Ralph, but whoever it was turned at the landing and continued to the top of the house. "I wish Ralph would come," she said, with a sigh. "I want you to meet him." Jack asked her again to go out, but she refused, and when the all-clear sounded, he said goodbye.

Jack was shipped from Dix to an infantry training camp in the Carolinas and from there to an infantry division stationed in Georgia. He had been in Georgia three months when he married a girl from the Augusta boarding-house aristocracy. A year or so later, he crossed the continent in a day coach and thought sententiously that the last he might see of the country he loved was the desert towns like Barstow, that the last he might hear of it was the ringing of the trolleys on the Bay Bridge. He was sent into the Pacific and returned to the United States twenty months later, uninjured and apparently unchanged. As soon as he received his furlough, he went to Augusta. He presented his wife with the souvenirs he had brought from the islands, quarreled violently with her and all her family, and, after making arrangements for her to get an Arkansas divorce, left for New York.

Jack was discharged from the Army at a camp in the East a few months later. He took a vacation and then went back to the job he had left in 1942. He seemed to have picked up his life at approximately the moment when it had been interrupted by the war. In time, everything came to look and feel the same. He saw most of his old friends. Only two of the men he knew had been killed in the war. He didn't call Joan, but he met her one winter afternoon on a crosstown bus.

Her fresh face, her black clothes, and her soft voice instantly destroyed the sense—if he had ever had such a sense—that anything had changed or intervened since their last meeting, three or four years ago. She asked him up for cocktails and he went to her apartment the next Saturday afternoon. Her room and her guests reminded him of the parties she had given when she had first come to New York. There was a woman with a fancy hat, an elderly doctor, and a man who stayed close to the radio, listening for news from the Balkans. Jack wondered which of the men belonged to Joan and decided on an Englishman who kept coughing into a handkerchief that he pulled out of his sleeve. Jack was right. "Isn't Stephen brilliant?" Joan asked him a little later, when they were alone in a corner. "He knows more about the Polynesians than anyone else in the world."

Jack had returned not only to his old job but to his old salary. Since living costs had doubled and since he was paying alimony to two wives, he had to draw on his savings. He took another job, which promised more money, but it didn't last long and he found himself out of work. This didn't bother him at all. He still had money in the bank, and anyhow it was easy to borrow from friends. His indifference was the consequence not of lassitude or despair but rather of an excess of hope. He had the feeling that he had only recently come to New York from Ohio. The sense that he was very young and that the best years of his life still lay before him was an illusion that he could not seem to escape. There was all the time in the world. He was living in hotels then, moving from one to another every five days.

In the spring, Jack moved to a furnished room in the badlands west of Central Park. He was running out of money. Then, when he began to feel that a job was a desperate necessity, he got sick. At first, he seemed to have only a bad cold, but he was unable to shake it and he began to run a fever and to cough blood. The fever kept him drowsy most of the time, but he roused himself occasionally and went out to a cafeteria for a meal. He felt sure that none of his friends knew where he was, and he was glad of this. He hadn't counted on Joan.

Late one morning, he heard her speaking in the hall with his landlady. A few moments later, she knocked on his door. He was lying on the bed in a pair of pants and a soiled pajama top, and he didn't answer. She knocked again and walked in. "I've been looking everywhere for you, Jack," she said. She spoke softly. "When I found out that you were in a place like this I thought you must be broke or sick. I stopped at the bank and got some money, in case you're broke. I've brought you some Scotch. I thought a little drink wouldn't do you any harm. Want a little drink?"

Joan's dress was black. Her voice was low and serene. She sat in a chair beside his bed as if she had been coming there every day to nurse him. Her features had coarsened, he thought, but there were still very few lines in her face. She was heavier. She was nearly fat. She was wearing black cotton gloves. She got two glasses and poured Scotch into them. He drank his whiskey greedily. "I didn't get to bed until three last night," she said. Her voice had once before reminded him of a gentle and despairing song, but now, perhaps because he was sick, her mildness, the mourning she wore, her stealthy grace, made him uneasy. "It was one of those nights," she said. "We went to the theatre. Afterward, someone asked us up to his place. I don't know who he was. It was one of those places. They're so strange. There were some meat-eating plants and a collection of Chinese snuff bottles. Why do people collect Chinese snuff bottles? We all autographed a lampshade, as I remember, but I can't remember much."

Jack tried to sit up in bed, as if there were some need to defend himself, and then fell back again, against the pillows. "How did you find me, Joan?" he asked.

"It was simple," she said. "I called that hotel. The one you were staying in. They gave me this address. My secretary got the telephone number. Have another little drink."

"You know, you've never come to a place of mine before—never," he said. "Why did you come now?"

"Why did I come, darling?" she asked. "What a question! I've known you for thirty years. You're the oldest friend I have in New York.

Remember that night in the Village when it snowed and we stayed up until morning and drank whiskey sours for breakfast? That doesn't seem like twelve years ago. And that night—"

"I don't like to have you see me in a place like this," he said earnestly. He touched his face and felt his beard.

"And all the people who used to imitate Roosevelt," she said, as if she had not heard him, as if she were deaf. "And that place on Staten Island where we all used to go for dinner when Henry had a car. Poor Henry. He bought a place in Connecticut and went out there by himself one weekend. He fell asleep with a lighted cigarette and the house, the barn, everything burned. Ethel took the children out to California." She poured more Scotch into his glass and handed it to him. She lighted a cigarette and put it between his lips. The intimacy of this gesture, which made it seem not only as if he were deathly ill but as if he were her lover, troubled him.

"As soon as I'm better," he said, "I'll take a room at a good hotel. I'll call you then. It was nice of you to come."

"Oh, don't be ashamed of this room, Jack," she said. "Rooms never bother me. It doesn't seem to matter to me where I am. Stanley had a filthy room in Chelsea. At least, other people told me it was filthy. I never noticed it. Rats used to eat the food I brought him. He used to have to hang the food from the ceiling, from the light chain."

"I'll call you as soon as I'm better," Jack said. "I think I can sleep now if I'm left alone. I seem to need a lot of sleep."

"You really *are* sick, darling," she said. "You must have a fever." She sat on the edge of his bed and put a hand on his forehead.

"How is that Englishman, Joan?" he asked. "Do you still see him?"

"What Englishman?" she said.

"You know. I met him at your house. He kept a handkerchief up his sleeve. He coughed all the time. You know the one I mean."

"You must be thinking of someone else," she said. "I haven't had an Englishman at my place since the war. Of course, I can't remember everyone." She turned and, taking one of hands, linked her fingers in his.

"He's dead, isn't he?" Jack said. "That Englishman's dead." He pushed her off the bed, and got up himself. "Get out," he said.

"You're sick, darling," she said. "I can't leave you alone here."

"Get out," he said again, and when she didn't move, he shouted, "What kind of an obscenity are you that you can smell sickness and death the way you do?"

"You poor darling."

"Does it make you feel young to watch the dying?" he shouted. "Is that the lewdness that keeps you young? Is that why you dress like a crow? Oh, I know there's nothing I can say that will hurt you. I know there's nothing filthy or corrupt or depraved or brutish or base that the others haven't tried, but this time you're wrong. I'm not ready. My life isn't ending. My life's beginning. There are wonderful years ahead of me. There are, there are wonderful, wonderful, wonderful years ahead of me, and when they're over, when it's time, then I'll call you. Then, as an old friend, I'll call you and give you whatever dirty pleasure you take in watching the dying, but until then, you and your ugly and misshapen forms will leave me alone."

She finished her drink and looked at her watch. "I guess I'd better show up at the office," she said. "I'll see you later. I'll come back tonight. You'll feel better then, you poor darling." She closed the door after her, and he heard her light step on the stairs.

Jack emptied the whiskey bottle into the sink. He began to dress. He stuffed his dirty clothes into a bag. He was trembling and crying with sickness and fear. He could see the blue sky from his window, and in his fear it seemed miraculous that the sky should be blue, that the white clouds should remind him of snow, that from the sidewalk he could hear the shrill voices of children shrieking, "I'm the king of the mountain, I'm the king of the mountain, I'm the king of the mountain." He emptied the ashtray containing his nail parings and cigarette butts into the toilet, and swept the floor with a shirt, so that there would be no trace of his life, of his body, when that lewd and searching shape of death came there to find him in the evening.

1947

Acknowledgments (continued from p. ii)

Truman Capote, "Children on Their Birthdays." From *Selected Writings of Truman Capote* by Truman Capote. Copyright 1948 by Truman Capote. Reprinted by permission of Random House, Inc.

Raymond Carver, "Boxes." From *Where I'm Calling From* by Raymond Carver, copyright © 1986, 1987, 1988. Reprinted with permission of Atlantic Monthly Press.

John Cheever, "Torch Song." From *The Stories of John Cheever* by John Cheever. Copyright 1947 by John Cheever. Reprinted by permission of Alfred A. Knopf, Inc.

Anton Chekhov, "The Darling." From *The Darling and Other Stories* by Anton Chekhov, translated by Constance Garnett. Copyright © 1916 by Macmillan Company. Reprinted by permission of the estate of Constance Garnett and Chatto & Windus.

Louise Erdrich, "Love Medicine." From *Love Medicine* by Louise Erdrich. Copyright © 1984 by Louise Erdrich. Reprinted by permission of Henry Holt and Company, Inc.

William Faulkner, "Barn Burning." From *Collected Stories of William Faulkner* by William Faulkner. Copyright © 1950 by Random House, Inc. and renewed 1977 by Jill Faulkner Summers. Reprinted by permission of Random House, Inc.

George Garrett, "An Evening Performance." From *An Evening Performance* by George Garrett. Copyright © 1985 by George Garrett. Used by permission of Doubleday, a division of Bantam Doubleday Dell Publishing Group, Inc.

William Goyen, "Tapioca Surprise." From *The Collected Stories of William Goyen.* Copyright © 1975 by William Goyen. Used with permission from International Creative Management, Inc.

Ernest Hemingway, "A Day's Wait." From *Winner Take Nothing* by Ernest Hemingway. Reprinted with permission of Charles Scribner's Sons, an imprint of Macmillan Publishing Company. Copyright © 1933 by Charles Scribner's Sons; renewal copyright © 1961 by Mary Hemingway.

Zora Neale Hurston, "The Gilded Six-Bits." From *Spunk* by Zora Neale Hurston. Copyright 1933. Reprinted by permission from the heirs of Zora Neale Hurston: Winifred Hurston Clark, Clifford J. Hurston, Edgar Hurston, Sr., Lucy Ann Hurston, Zora Mack Goins, and Barbara Hurston Lewis.

Shirley Jackson, "Flower Garden." From *The Lottery* by Shirley Jackson. Copyright © 1948, 1949 by Shirley Jackson. Renewal copyright © 1976, 1977 by Laurence Hyman, Barry Hyman, Mrs. Sarah Webster, and Mrs. Joanne Schnurer. Reprinted by permission of Farrar, Straus & Giroux, Inc.

Henry James, "Paste." From *The Complete Tales of Henry James* by Henry James, published by HarperCollins Publishers. Copyright © 1964 by Leon Edel.

Sarah Orne Jewett, "The Landscape Chamber." From *The King of Folly Island and Other People* by Sarah Orne Jewett, published by Houghton Mifflin Company. Copyright © 1888 by Sarah Orne Jewett.

Charles Johnson, "China." From *The Sorcerer's Apprentice* by Charles Johnson. Reprinted with the permission of Atheneum Publishers, an imprint of Macmillan Publishing Company. Copyright © 1983 by Charles Johnson. First appeared in MSS, 1983.

James Joyce, "The Dead." From *Dubliners* by James Joyce. Copyright 1916 by B. W. Heubsch. Definitive text Copyright © 1967 by the Estate of James Joyce. Used by permission of Viking Penguin, a division of Penguin Books USA Inc.

Franz Kafka, "A Report to an Academy." From *Franz Kafka: The Complete Stories* by Franz Kafka, edited by Nahum N. Glatzer. Copyright © 1946, 1947, 1948, 1949, 1954, 1958, 1971 by Schocken Books Inc. Reprinted by permission of Schocken Books, published by Pantheon Books, a division of Random House, Inc.

D. H. Lawrence, "The Lovely Lady." From *Complete Short Stories of D. H. Lawrence* by D. H. Lawrence. Copyright 1933 by The Estate of D. H. Lawrence. Renewed © 1961 by Angelo Ravagliand C. Montague Weekley, Executors to the Estate of Frieda Lawrence. Used by permission of Viking Penguin, a division of Penguin Books USA Inc.

Doris Lessing, "To Room Nineteen." From *A Man and Two Women.* Copyright 1958, 1962, 1963 by Doris Lessing. Reprinted by permission of Simon & Schuster and Jonathan Clowes Ltd., London, on behalf of Doris Lessing.